Christopher Kaczor,
editor

PROPORTIONALISM

FOR AND AGAINST

MARQUETTE UNIVERSITY PRESS

Marquette Studies in Philosophy
No. 19
Andrew Tallon, Series Editor

Library of Congress Cataloging-in-Publication Data

Proportionalism : for and against / Christopher Kaczor, editor.
    p. cm. — (Marquette studies in philosophy ; no. 19)
Includes bibliographical references and index.
    ISBN 0-87462-618-8 (pbk. : alk. paper)
    1. Christian ethics—Catholic authors. I. Kaczor, Christopher Robert, 1969– II. Marquette studies in philosophy ; #19.
    BJ1249 .P78 2000
    241'.042--dc21
                                                            00-010315

Cover design by Andrew J. Tallon

©Marquette UniversityPress
Milwaukee, Wisconsin USA
Printed by Thomson-Shore

All rights reserved.

Marquette University Press
MILWAUKEE

The Association of Jesuit University Presses

Contents

Acknowledgements 6
Contributors 8
Introduction 9
Historical Roots? 20
    Thomas Aquinas, *Summa theologiae*, II-II, 64, 7 (Latin/English)

Arguments for Proportionalism

1) Peter Knauer, S.J. The Hermeneutical Function of the Principle of Double Effect 25
2) Josef Fuchs, S.J. The Absoluteness of Moral Terms 60
3) Louis Janssens. Ontic Evil and Moral Evil 100
4) Bruno Schüller, S.J. Direct Killing/Indirect Killing 148
5) Richard McCormick, S.J. Ambiguity in Moral Choice 166

Challenges to Proportionalism

6) Paul Quay, S.J. Morality by Calculation of Values 215
7) Germain Grisez. Against Consequentialism 239
8) John Connery, S.J. Catholic Ethics: Has the Norm for Rule-Making Changed? 295
9) Germain Grisez. Moral Absolutes: A Critique of the View of Josef Fuchs, S.J. 317
10) John Finnis. Christian Witness 371

Overviews and Evaluations

11) James J. Walter. Proportionate Reason and its Three Levels of Inquiry: Structuring the Ongoing Debate 393
12) Edward V. Vacek, S.J. Proportionalism: One View of the Debate 406
13) Bartholomew M. Kiely, S.J. The Impracticality of Proportionalism 436
14) Christopher Kaczor. Proportionalism and the Pill 466

Bibliography 477
Index 488

For Ralph McInerny
whose virtues inspire

Acknowledgements

The following articles are reprinted with permission.

Peter Knauer. "The Hermeneutical Function of the Principle of Double Effect." *Natural Law Forum* [more recently, *American Journal of Jurisprudence*] 12 (1967): 132-162.

Josef Fuchs. "The Absoluteness of Moral Terms." *Gregorianum* 52 (1971): 415-485.

Louis Janssens. "Ontic Evil and Moral Evil." *Louvain Studies* 4.2 (Fall 1972): 115-56.

Bruno Schüller. "Direct Killing/Indirect Killing." In *Readings in Moral Theology* No. 1: Moral Norms and Catholic Tradition, ed. Charles E. Curran and Richard A. McCormick, S.J. New York: Paulist Press, 1979, 138-157. Originally printed as, "Direckte Tötung—Indirekte Tötung" *Theologie und Philosophie* 47 (1972).

Richard McCormick. "Ambiguity in Moral Choice." In *Doing Evil to Achieve Good; Moral Choice in Conflict Situations*, ed. by Richard McCormick and Paul Ramsey. Chicago: Loyola University Press, 1978, 7-53.

Paul Quay. "Morality by Calculation of Values." *Theology Digest* 25 (1975): 347-364.

Germain Grisez. "Against Consequentialism." *American Journal of Jurisprudence* (1978): 21-72.

John Connery. "Catholic Ethics: Has the Norm for Rule-Making Changed?" *Theological Studies* 42 (1981): 232-50.

James J. Walter. "Proportionate Reason and its Three Levels of Inquiry: Structuring the Ongoing Debate." *Louvain Studies* 10 (1984): 30-40.

Germain Grisez. "Moral Absolutes: A Critique of the View of Josef Fuchs, S.J." *Anthropotes* 2 (1985): 155-201.

Bartholomew M. Kiely. "The Impracticality of Proportionalism." *Gregorianum* 66 (1985): 655-86.

Edward V. Vacek. "Proportionalism: One View of the Debate." *Theological Studies* 46 (1985): 287-314.

John Finnis. "Christian Witness." In *Moral Absolutes: Tradition, Revision, and Truth.* Washington, DC: Catholic University Press: 1991.

Christopher Kaczor. "Proportionalism and the Pill: How Developments in Theory Lead to Contradictions to Practice." *The Thomist* 63 (April 1999): 269-281.

I would like to give special thanks to my Rains Research Assistants Jill Frazee, Stacy Bautista, and Kirstin Pesola who helped invaluably in the proofreading and editing of this volume.

Contributors

Peter Knauer, S.J., is Professor of Fundamental Theology at Sank Gregor am Main, Philosophisches-Theologisches Fakultate, Frankfurt am Main, Germany.

Louis Janssens is Professor Emeritus in moral theology at the Catholic University Louvain, Belgium.

Bruno Schüller, S.J., is Professor Emeritus in moral theology at the University of Münster, Germany.

Richard McCormick, S.J., was John A. O'Brien Professor Emeritus of Christian Ethics at the University of Notre Dame.

Josef Fuchs, S.J., is Professor Emeritus of Moral Theology at the Pontifical Gregorian University, Rome.

Paul Quay, S.J., was Professor of Physics and Spiritual Theology at St. Louis University.

Germain Grisez is Flynn Professor of Christian Ethics at Mount Saint Mary's College, Emmitsburg Maryland.

John Connery, S.J., was Professor of Theology Loyola University Chicago.

Bartholomew M. Kiely, S.J., is Professor of Psychology at the Pontifical Gregorian University, Rome.

James J. Walter is Austin and Ann O'Malley Professor of Bioethics, Department of Theological Studies, Loyola Marymount University, Los Angeles.

Edward V. Vacek, S.J., is McKeever Professor of Moral Theology at St. John's University.

John Finnis is Professor of Law and Legal Philosophy at Oxford University and Biolchini Professor of Law at the University of Notre Dame.

Christopher Kaczor is assistant professor of philosophy, Loyola Marymount University, Los Angeles.

INTRODUCTION

A revolution has taken place among those teaching and writing about ethics in the Catholic tradition. As Richard McCormick notes, a generation ago moralists debated about the morality of: "knitting as servile work, of organ-playing at non-Catholic services, of calling non-Catholic ministers for dying non-Catholics, of steady dating among adolescents, of the gravity of using 'rhythm' without a proportionate reason" (McCormick 1989a, 4). He continues in the article to describe another debate about whether chewing gum broke the Eucharistic fast and Roman theologians who warned of the dangers of "masked balls" and certain dances such as the fox-trot, charleston, rumba, and boogie-woogie (McCormick 1989a, 5).

Times have changed. Today a majority of ethicists in this same tradition question, if not deny, the existence of any moral absolute whatsoever. Unanimous agreement on Catholic teaching about abortion, euthanasia, just war, and sexuality dissolved in just a few years into a cantankerous battle among theologians and philosophers fighting not only about the resolution to this or that particularly difficult case, but also about what constitutes the very fundamentals of morality, in most cases a battle over the moral theory called "proportionalism."

What is proportionalism? This book offers an introductory answer to this question through a number of the "foundational articles" of those who first advocated this new approach to resolving conflict situations in the moral life and through some of the fundamental critiques of this revision. Among ethicists in the contemporary Catholic tradition, proportionalism is arguably the most influential and prevalent theory of making moral decisions. No less an authority on the subject than Richard McCormick has noted: "So-called proportionalists include some of the best known names in moral theology throughout the world. ... My acquaintance with the literature leads me to believe that most theologians share similar perspectives" (McCormick 1989a, 10, 19). The sociological influence of proportionalism should not be underestimated.

Although proportionalism is perhaps the most influential moral theory in Catholic circles, it might also lay claim to being among the most controversial. Though often accused by its critics of being a form of classical utilitarianism, proportionalism is more accurately described as a type of moral analysis that determines the rightness or wrongness of an act by reference to the proportion of non-moral goods and evils caused by the act. If the non-moral good is in due proportion or relationship with the non-moral evil, then the act is justified, even if the non-moral evil is the causal means for achieving the non-moral good. According to advocates of proportionalism, traditional understandings of "intrinsically evil acts," such as intentionally killing innocent human persons, should give way to an analysis in terms of proportionate reason and choosing the lesser of two evils. Critics of proportionalism in general defend the existence of intrinsically evil acts and charge that proportionalism itself is an unworkable solution to moral conflict.

The ongoing debate over "proportionalism" has five principal points of contention.[1] These include the nature, function, and purpose of the "principle of double effect," i.e., the criteria for forming judgments about actions with more than one morally significant effect; the possibility of exceptionless moral norms; the distinction between moral evil and non-moral evil; the moral importance of the distinction between intended and foreseen consequences; and finally the existence of "intrinsically evil acts."

By way of approaching these topics, this book is divided into five parts. The first section presents Thomas Aquinas' treatment of self-defense, *Summa theologiae*, II-II, 64, 7. Much of the historical dispute about the origins and genealogy of proportionalism hinges on the interpretation of this article. Advocates of proportionalism often argue that Thomas here implicitly, if not explicitly, endorses proportionalism. Critics argue precisely the opposite and characteristically trace the real roots of proportionalism to the scholasticism of the moral manuals preceding the Second Vatican Council (Pinckaers 1982; Cesserio 1988; Rhonheimer 1993, 1994; Johnstone 1994; Keenan 1993; Kaczor 1998). Thomas's article is presented here in both its Latin and English versions to allow the reader a chance to evaluate the rival interpretations offered later.

An awareness of history should also lead to an awareness of the issue that may have given rise to proportionalism, namely, the debate over contraception. Although proportionalists do not agree on all fundamental matters, nor even about how to apply the theory to given cases, one thing that all revisionists do agree about, and of this one can be confident, is that the use of contraception is in certain circumstances morally permissable, if not obligatory. However, even though proportionalism arose contemporaneously with and in response to the Catholic Church's teaching on contraception, and although sociologically the topics seem to go hand in hand, the two issues are

Introduction

logically quite distinct. Although every proportionalist agrees that contraception may, in certain circumstances, be morally licit, a number of prominent scholars, for example Paul Ramsey, Stanley Hauerwas, William Frankena, Jean Porter, and Alan Donagan, believe that proportionalism is deeply mistaken and nevertheless agree with proportionalists that use of contraception is not always intrinsically evil. To question or reject proportionalism is not thereby to accept the Catholic Church's teaching on birth regulation. It is a confusion, though an understandable confusion, to conflate the two issues. In fact, the universally held conviction that proportionalist reasoning justifies contraception is called into question in the final article in this volume. In any case, this book seeks to help the reader come to a judgment about proportionalism which may or may not lead to conclusions about other contingently related issues.

The second section, "Arguments in Favor of Proportionalism," presents a number of early significant arguments in favor of what came later to be called proportionalism. Each of these contributions laid the groundwork for the contemporary analysis of these issues. The next section entitled "Challenges to Proportionalism" offers a number of significant contributions from critics of this revision. These contributions represent the most commonly voiced objections to proportionalism. The fourth section "Overviews and Evaluations" seeks to aid the reader in coming to a general understanding of the issues involved and the many distinctions drawn. These overviews themselves offer perspectives "pro" and "con" but have the advantage of participating in the debate at a later stage of development. Finally, a bibliography of further readings in proportionalism and related themes in contemporary moral philosophy notes developments of issues treated in this volume in the United States and on the Continent. A word may now be in order about the persons and issues that have shaped the contemporary debate.

THE ADVOCATES OF PROPORTIONALISM

Unlike many philosophical or theological movements whose beginnings are obscure and disputed, most scholars agree that proportionalism began with an article by a young German Jesuit named Peter Knauer in 1965. Although other writers held similar views in an undeveloped way, it was Knauer's article "The Hermeneutic Function of the Principle of Double Effect" that first crystallized the view that later came to be known as proportionalism (Odozor 1995, 15-24; McCormick 1989a, 9-10). In this article, the first appearing in this book, Knauer reinterpreted the "principle of double effect." This method of reasoning, traditional in the moral manuals that were the textbooks for seminarians before the Second Vatican Council, held that an agent may licitly perform an act with two effects, one good but the other evil, if the following conditions are realized: (a) the act itself is good or at least indifferent, (b) the end of the agent is good, (c) the evil brought about is not a means to the good, and (d) there is a proportionately serious reason for allowing the evil effect. Knauer reinterpreted the first three conditions in terms of the fourth, proportionate reason. Thus, for Knauer, the evil brought about by an act was justified if and only if one had a proportionate reason. The other conditions became superfluous. The term "proportionalism" was coined, perhaps first by William May, as a way of capturing the emphasis that Knauer and others placed on the condition of proportionate reason. The explosive response to this article, both for and against, gave rise to the ongoing contemporary debate.[2]

Knauer, however, was not alone in advocating a revision of traditional formulations. Josef Fuchs, S.J., though not the originator of "proportionalism," must surely be among the most influential of proportionalists through his numerous books and articles, and also through his many years of teaching and directing dissertations at Rome's Pontifical Gregorian University.[3]

More theoretical than many fellow ethicists, Fuchs's work and his contribution here is marked by a special concern for the nature and status of moral norms. On this view, proportionalism is, in part, a way of determining whether or not a norm applies in a given case. For instance, generally one should not kill but this norm may not apply in those cases in which the killing itself is in the greater service of life. There can be then, on this view, no exceptionless moral norms governing concrete moral conduct. Fuchs' views on these matters have given rise to critical studies (Grisez 1985; see below 317-70; Finnis 1993).

Like Knauer and Fuchs, Louis Janssens of the Catholic University in Leuven sought to ground a version of proportionalism in the tradition, especially in the thought of Thomas Aquinas.[4]

Janssens read proportionalism in Thomas's account of human action, particularly in his emphasis on how the moral act receives its species from the end. Hence, proportionalism places an emphasis on the end that is sought by the agent and not merely the means used to achieve the end. The means must be proportioned to the end, and therefore no judgment about means can be definitive unless it takes this end into account. Janssens also suggested in a series of articles that Thomas held a distinction between the moral and non-moral evil, sometimes also called the "ontic" or "premoral" evil.[5]

Moral evil is an absolute disvalue, like sin, and may not be intended. On the other hand, premoral or ontic evils such as sickness, sterility, ignorance, or death may be, as a last resort, intended to avoid bringing about even greater non-moral evils.[6]

According to Janssens's reading of Thomas, an agent may at times intend a premorally evil means so that good may come. Janssens's work has occasioned comment and critique from a number of authors (May 1984; Mullady 1986; Johnson 1992).

Approaching the topic from a less historical point of view than Janssens, Fuchs's former student Bruno Schüller, S.J., contributed to the development of proportionalism by introducing to the debate distinctions commonly present in analytic philosophy during the late 1960s and early 1970s, namely the distinction between the "deontological" and "teleological" approach to morality and the distinction between goodness and rightness. A deontological approach is marked by an appeal to duty as the benchmark of right decision making. A teleological approach is characterized by a concern to preserve or maximize non-moral goods or values in coming to a decision about the rightness or wrongness of an act. These distinctions became standard in the proportionalist literature.

Schüller made another important contribution to the debate by arguing that the distinction between "directly" intended effects and merely foreseen or "indirect" effects of human action lacked moral importance in cases in which the effect was a non-moral good or evil. In other words, there is no difference in moral posture between merely foreseeing that a premoral evil will come about as a result of an act and intending that evil as a means to achieving a good end. On the other hand, one may not licitly intend a moral evil on Schüller's view, even for the sake of a great good. Intending a moral evil, for example, intending the sin of another, cannot be justified by a proportionate reason. As one might expect, not all agreed with Schüller's account of the importance of the intention/foresight distinction (Anscombe 1982; Finnis 1987; Paulisio 1996).

Building upon the work of these scholars and stimulated by his own reflections on the subject through his long authorship of the annual "Notes on Moral Theology" appearing in *Theological Studies*, Richard A. McCormick, S.J., made a substantial contribution to the debate by his Marquette lecture entitled, "Ambiguity in Moral Choice." McCormick treats the many topics handled by previous authors, summarizing and reviewing their works. His own contributions and additions here and elsewhere have specialized in problems in medical ethics and other casuistic applications of proportionalism to various contemporary problems. Like the other authors thus far mentioned, McCormick holds that traditional understandings of intrinsically evil acts, such as intentionally killing, should be understood in terms of proportionate reason. The basic rule in conflict situations, and every situation is in some sense a conflict situation, is that one is to choose the lesser of two evils.[7]

The Critics of Proportionalism

A former student of McCormick, Paul Quay, S.J., a theologian and professor of physics, argues against proportionalism in a number of articles (Quay see below 215-38; Quay 1983; Quay 1985). He finds especially problematic the distinction between moral disvalue and premoral or ontic disvalue. According to Quay, the shift from speaking from goods and evils to values and disvalues marks a departure from an objective view of the moral life and an embrace of a subjective understanding of right and wrong. Good and evil are objective terms without reference to the private preferences or desires of the one using the terms. Values and disvalues are not objective but rather depend upon what one "values" or "disvalues." Good and evil are objective and person independent. Values and disvalues on the other hand rest on mere personal preference. If right and wrong are to be determined by the proportion of values and disvalues, then right and wrong are determined by mere individual preference. For Quay, proportionalism at root is an unhealthy subjectivism creeping into moral decision making. McCormick and others strongly disagreed with Quay's characterization of proportionalism.[8]

Among the critics of proportionalism, the foremost is perhaps Germain Grisez. Grisez has developed a moral theory along with other colleagues, especially John Finnis, William May, and Joseph Boyle, that excludes any version of proportionalism that would involve the comparing or commensuration of basic goods. This theory is developed in several articles and expressed completely and systematically in Grisez's multi-volume summa of moral theology, *The Way of the Lord Jesus*. On Grisez's view, one cannot commensurate basic goods such as life, knowledge, and integrity against one another for they have no common denominator prior to choice, just as there is no common denominator prior to choice to commensurate color, weight, and size. In so far as proportionalism presupposes that one can find a proportion between various different basic goods, proportionalism is no more than a rationalization of any choice the agent wishes. As such, Grisez considers proportionalism not only nonsense but "dangerous nonsense" (Grisez see below 246). A number of proportionalists (and non-proportionalists) have in turn criticized Grisez's theory of incommensurable basic human goods.[9]

John Connery, S.J., suggests that proportionalism misappropriates Thomas and the tradition. According to Connery, Knauer, and other proportionalists have misunderstood Thomas's teaching on self-defense, in part by misunderstanding the meaning of "proportion" in ST II-II, 64, 7. Further, proportionalism, in rejecting the importance of the distinction between intended and foreseen effects, represents an unhealthy shift in the moral life, making more decision making difficult, if not impossible. Connery's article received attention from a number of proportionalist critics, among them his former student McCormick.[10]

Bartholomew M. Kiely, S.J., takes up a similar line of argumentation to Connery's but approaches the question from the psychological point of view. In this article, the moral clarity of moral judgments in traditional ethical analysis is contrasted with an opaque proportionalism. Proportionalism fails in so far as it does not sufficiently account for the differences between systematic and non-systematic processes, the importance of reflexive or imminent activity on the part of the agent, and the danger of rationalization. Although proportionalism's norm of choosing the lesser evil at first glance seems quite practical, the author argues for the "impracticality of proportionalism."

Finally, John Finnis, a key collaborator with Grisez, offers a critique of the proportionalist claim that the tradition holds that evil is to be done so that good may come. Finnis argues first that the Catholic tradition coming from the teaching of Paul in Romans 3:8 explicitly and without exception forbids doing "evil that good may come." This teaching presupposes and is reaffirmed by the distinction between *intending* some effect (a choice) and merely *foreseeing* that some effect will take place as the result of a choice. Here, Finnis offers a critique of Schüller. The centrality of choice as self-determinative of the agent gives rise to the possibility of exceptionless moral norms governing human conduct, for instance a norm forbidding evildoing for the sake of bringing about some good. Intending harm is never acceptable, although one may be forced into accepting foreseen bad side-effects of human action. Finnis also seeks to demonstrate that traditionally no one has claimed that it was licit to do "evil to achieve good," despite the counter claims offered by proportionalists.

Another contribution to the discussion critical of developments advocated by proportionalists came from John Paul II. Following more than 25 years of debate on the matter, John Paul II in 1993 issued the encyclical *Veritatis splendor* on "certain fundamentals of the moral teaching of the Church" that addressed the topic of proportionalism explicitly in its second chapter. He writes, "Such theories however are not faithful to the Church's teaching, when they believe they can justify, as morally good, deliberate choices of kinds of behavior contrary to the commandments of the divine and natural law. These theories cannot claim to be grounded in the Catholic moral tradition" (*VS* 76). The voluminous reaction to the encyclical was mixed and, at times, heated.[11] Proportionalists claimed to be misrepresented by the encyclical; critics claimed a decisive and authoritative victory. The encyclical *Veritatis splendor* was nearly as controversial as the movements which gave rise to it.

Both before and after the encyclical, a few scholars have tried to downplay the innovation and controversial character of proportionalism. For instance, one writes: "To discuss concrete moral norms is not to discuss a 'conception of morality.' It is much more modest. [Proportionalists] are but dialoguing with their own tradition on a relatively narrow issue" (McCormick 1984, 114). This observation, however, surely does not take into account the attention these issues have attracted. Richard McCormick more accurately writes elsewhere: "I do not believe 'revolution' is too strong a word for the developments that have occurred in moral theology in the last 30 years" (McCormick 1989a, 6-7).[12]

He continues: "In 1970 Germain Grisez wrote of Knauer that he 'is carrying through a revolution in principle while pretending only a clarification of traditional ideas.' Grisez was, I believe, right. That 'revolution in principle' gradually led to a vast literature that huddles under the umbrella-term 'proportionalism'" (McCormick 1989a, 9).

Vast is exactly the right word. The explosion of literature that this subject has generated suggests not a small or insignificant adjustment of the resolution to a marginal question, but something very important indeed. The importance of this subject is reflected in part by the inflated, indeed abrasive, rhetoric used in the debate. For instance, one proportionalist author describes those in sympathy with him as sensible, revered, remarkable, insightful, and interesting (McCormick

1994). On the other hand, those who disagree with his point of view are confused and guilty of elementary philosophical mistakes (McCormick 1994). He describes one critic of proportionalism as delivering an "analytic howler," and another is said to be volunteering to be an "Inquisitor" (McCormick 1994). Opponents of proportionalism have been depicted as the "*immobilisiti*" (McCormick 1989a, 21) who crush the faithful under unchanging principles (Talvacchia and Walsh 1995, 308) in the course of waging ongoing war with police action (Stevens 1995, 77).

Of course, there has also been not a little inflammatory rhetoric from those holding the opposite perspective. Proportionalists, we learn from one author, are "superficial utilitarians whose Christian principles are for sale." According to others, they promote: "deviant moral theology," [14] and "utilitarian laxism."[15]

Some would seem to liken proportionalists to the probabilists of the sixteenth and seventeenth centuries, who Pascal scalded with his *Provincial Letters*. Indeed, "it was not without reason that one moralist became known as the lamb of God because he took away so many of the sins of the world" (Mahoney 1990, 138). Clearly the hyperbolic language used reflects that it is issues of great importance and not mere quibbles and slight adjustments at the margins that are at stake.

Proportionalism poses and answers questions of signal importance about the fundamentals of ethics, faith's relationship to reason, the nature of the human person and this person's relationship to God. When proportionalism is considered sociologically, philosophically, and theologically, it is clear that we are certainly not dealing with a marginal, insignificant movement, but rather a revolutionary one. The question at hand is, as McCormick pointed out: "Is the revolution justified?" The essays contained here offer various answers to that question in order to help the reader come to a conclusion about proportionalism, whether for or against it.

Notes

1. In addition to numerous articles, books continue to be published on the theme. For instance, A. M. Weiß, *Sittlicher Wert und nichtsittliche Werte. Zur Relevanz der Unterscheidung in der moraltheologischen Diskussion um deontologische Normen*, (Universitätsverlag Freiburg Schweiz, 1996); Eberhard Schockenhoff, *Naturrecht und Menschenwürde*, (Matthias-Grünewald-Verlag, 1996); Todd Salzman, *Deontology and Teleology*, (Leuven University Press, 1995); and Garth Hallet, *Greater Good: The Case for Proportionalism*. (Georgetown University Press, 1995); and my own *Proportionalism and the Natural Law Tradition* (Catholic University Press).

2. Knauer himself offers an extensive sample of the reactions to his work in his article "Fundamentalethik: teleologische als deontologische Normenbegründung," *Theologie und Philosophie* 55 (1980) 321-60.
3. The most up to date and complete bibliography of Fuchs' work available in print at the moment with more than 400 entries is to be found as an appendix in Fuch's book *Für eine menschliche Moral: Grundfragen der theologischen Ethik.* (Freiburg, Schweiz: Univ.-Verl, 1997).
4. A complete bibliography of Janssens's distinguished career may be found as an appendix in *Personalist Morals: Essays in Honor of Professor Louis Janssens* (ed. Joseph Selling) (Leuven: Leuven University Press, 1988).
5. Many articles could be cited but see in particular Janssens's articles "Norms and Priorities in a Love Ethics" *Louvain Studies* 6 (1976-77) 207-238; "A Moral Understanding of Some Arguments of Saint Thomas," *Ephemerides Theologicae Lovanienses* 63 (1987) 354-360; "St. Thomas Aquinas and the Question of Proportionality." *Louvain Studies* 6.3 (Spring 1982) 26-46; "Ontic Good and Evil-Premoral Values and Disvalues" *Louvain Studies* 12.1 (Spring 1987) 62-82; "Teleology and Proportionality: Thoughts about the Encyclical *Veritatis Splendor*" in *The Splendor of Accuracy: An Examination of the Assertions Made by Veritatis Splendor.* ed. Joseph A. Selling and Jan Jans (Grand Rapids, Michigan: William B. Eerdmans Publishing Co, 1994) 99-113. Janssens's work has been criticized, not only by a number of essays found in this volume, but also by Servais Pinckaers "La question des actes intrinséquement mauvais et le 'proportionalisme.'" *Revue Thomiste* 82 (1982): 181-212 and Mark Johnson's "Proportionalism and a Text of the Young Aquinas: Quodlibetum IX, Q. 7, A. 2." *Theological Studies* 53 (1992): 683-699.
6. The most lengthy treatment available of the moral/premoral distinction in Janssens, Knauer, Schüller, and McCormick as well as in critics is authored by A. M. Weiß, *Sittlicher Wert und nichtsittliche Werte. Zur Relevanz der Unterscheidung in der moraltheologischen Diskussion um deontologiche Normen,* (Universitätsverlag Freiburg Schweiz, 1996).
7. Several responses to this essay as well as McCormick's rejoinder to these responses can be found in *Doing Evil to Achieve Good; Moral Choice in Conflict Situations.* edited by Richard McCormick and Paul Ramsey, (Chicago: Loyola University Press) 1978.
8. Richard McCormick offers a critique of Quay's article, "Reflections on the Literature" *Readings in Moral Theology 1,* pgs. 309-315.
9. Among proportionalists, Garth Hallet has offered extensive criticism of Grisez's theory of incommensurable basic goods, most recently in his book, *Greater Good: The Case for Proportionalism* (Washington, D.C.: Georgetown University Press, 1995). From a non-proportionalist perspective, see Russell Hittenger's *A Critique of the New Natural Law Theory* (Notre Dame, University of Notre Dame Press, 1987).
10. McCormick, "Notes on Moral Theology: 1981" *Theological Studies* 43 (1982): 82-91. Connery then offered a critique of the critique in "The Teleology of Proportionate Reason" *Theological Studies* 44 (1983) 489-496. McCormick had the last word in "Notes on Moral Theology: 1983" *Theological Studies* 45 (1984) 88-94. See also, McCormick, "Reflections on the Literature" *Readings in Moral Theology* 1, pgs. 301-309.
11. A sample of several reactions to the encyclical include *The Splendor of Accuracy: An Examination of the Assertions Made by Veritatis Splendor.* ed. Joseph A. Selling

Introduction

and Jan Jans (Grand Rapids, Michigan: William B. Eerdmans Publishing Co, 1994); *Moraltheologie im Abseits?* ed. Dietmar Mieth, (Freiburg, Basel, Wien: Herder, 1994); Richard McCormick, "Some Early Reactions to *Veritatis splendor*." *Theological Studies* 55 (1994) 481-506; *Veritatis splendor: American Responses,* Michael E. Allsopp & John J. O'Keefe, editors, (Kansas City, MO: Sheed and Ward, 1995); and *Veritatis Splendor and the Renewal of Moral Theology,* ed. Romanus Cessario, O.P. and Augustine DiNoia, O.P. (Chicago, Midwest Theological Forum, 1999).

12. For remarks seemingly minimizing the importance or the significance of the changes, see McCormick, *Notes on Moral Theology 1981 through 1984,* p. 69.
13. Such rhetoric is not unusual. This epithet is from Ermecke as cited by McCormick, *Notes on Moral Theology.* Vol. 1 809.
14. This revision is often called dissenting. For the charge that it is also "deviant", see Richard R. Roach, "Medicine and Killing: The Catholic View," *Journal of Medicine and Philosophy* 4 (1979) 383-97, as cited by McCormick, *Notes on Moral Theology 1981 through 1984,* p.2.
15. One could cite others for this charge but specifically see Diaro Composta, "Il consequenzialismo: Uno nuova corrente della 'Nuova Morale'" *Divinitas* 25 (1981) 127-56, as cited by McCormick, *Notes on Moral Theology 1981 through 1984,* p.57.

Thomas Aquinas
Summa of theology,
Second part of the Second part,
question 64, article 7

To the seventh article, thus we begin. It seems that it is licit to no one to kill another in defending himself.

1. For Augustine writes to Publicola: "As far as killing human beings is concerned, I do not agree with the opinion that someone can kill lest he be killed by others, save perhaps a soldier, someone with a public duty, doing it not for his own sake but for others, having accepted the legitimate power to do so, if this is fitting to his office." But he who in defending himself kills another kills him for this reason lest he be killed by him. Therefore, this seems to be illicit.

2. Furthermore, in the first book *On Free Choice* it is said: "How are they free from sin before divine providence who for the sake of these things which it is fitting to condemn are polluted by killing someone? However, these things are said to be worthy of condemnation which men are able to lose unwillingly, as is clear from what was previously said." The life of the body however is one of these. Therefore, it is licit to no one to kill a man for the sake of preserving the life of the body.

Summa theologiae II^a II^ae q. 64, a. 7

3. Praeterea, Nicolaus I Papa dicit, ut habetur in Decretis, tit. de: De clericis pro quibus consuluisti, scilicet qui se defendo paganum occiderunt, si postea per poenitentiam emendati possent ad pristinum statum redire, aut ad altiorem ascendere, scito nos nullam occasionem dare, nec ullam tribuere licentiam eis quemlibet hominem quolibet modo occidendi. Sed ad praecepta moralia servanda tenentur communiter clerici, et laici. Ergo etiam laicis non est licitum occidere aliquem, se defendo.

4. Praeterea, homicidium est gravius peccatum, quam simplex fornicatio, vel adulterium. Sed nulli licet committere simplicem fornicationem, vel adulterium, vel quodcumque aliud peccatum mortale, pro conservatione propriae vitae; quia vita spiritualis praeferenda est corporali. Ergo nulli licet, defendendo seipsum, alium occidere, ut propriam vitam conservet.

5. Praeterea, si arbor est mala, et fructus, ut habetur Matth. 7 [17-18]. Sed ipsa defensio sui videtur esse illicita: secundum illud Rom. 12, [19]: Non vos defendentes, carissimi. Ergo et occisio hominis exinde procedens est illicita.

Sed contra est quod Exod. 22, [2] dicitur: Si effringens fur domum sive suffodiens inventus

3. Furthermore, Pope Nicholas I says and it is held in the Decretals, dist. 50: Concerning the clerics, on whose behalf you ask, namely who kill a pagan in self-defense, if later they are able through penance to return to a pristine condition, or to ascend to higher state, I know that we give no possibility nor grant any permission to those for any kind of killing of any man. But clerics and laymen are together bound to observe the moral precepts. Therefore, also for laymen it is not licit to kill another in defending oneself.

4. Furthermore, homicide is a more grave sin than simple fornication or adultery. But to no one is it licit to commit simple fornication, or adultery, or any other mortal sin for the sake of conserving one's own life; since the life of the spirit is to be preferred to the life of the body. Therefore, it is licit to no one in defending himself to kill another so that his own life might be saved.

5. Furthermore, if the tree is bad, so also is the fruit, as is said in Matt. 7 [17-18]. But the very defense of oneself seems to be illicit, according to Romans 12 [19]: Do not defend yourselves, dearest ones. Therefore, also the killing of the man which follows is illicit.

But on the contrary is what is said in Exod. 22 [2]: If a thief will have been found piercing through

fuerit, et accepto vulnere, mortuus fuerit, percussor non erit reus sanguinis. Sed multo magis licitum est defendere propriam vitam, quam proriam domum. Ergo etiam si aliquis occidat aliquem pro defensione vitae suae, non erit reus homicidii.

Respondeo dicendum, quod nihil prohibet unius actus esse duos effectus: quorum *alter* solum sit in intentione, *alius* vero sit praeter intentionem: morales autem actus recipiunt speciem secundum id, quod intenditur; non autem ab eo, quod est praeter intentionem, cum sit per accidens, ut ex supra dictis patet; ex actu ergo alicuius seipsum defendentis *duplex* effectus sequi potest: *unus* quidem conservatio propriae vitae: *alius* autem occisio invadentis: *actus* ergo hujusmodi, ex hoc quod intenditur conservatio propriae vitae, non habet rationem illiciti: cum hoc sit cuilibet naturale, quod se conservet in esse, quantum potest: potest tamen aliquis actus ex bona intentione proveniens, illicitus reddi, si non sit proportionatus fini; et ideo si aliquis ad defendendum propriam vitam utatur majori violentia, quam oportet, erit illicitum: si vero moderate violentiam repellat, erit licita defensio: nam secundum jura vim vi repellere licet cum moderamine inculpatae tutelae [*Decretal.* Gregory IX, lib. V,

or breaking into to a home, and having received a wound, will have died, the killer will not be guilty for his blood. But how much more is it licit to defend one's own life than one's property. Therefore, also if someone kills another for the sake of defense of his own life, he will not have the guilt of homicide.

Nothing prevents that there be two effects of one act: of which the *one* is in the intention, but the *other* is outside the intention. However moral acts take their species from that which is intended, not however from that which is outside the intention, since it is accidental, as is clear from things said before. Therefore, from the act of one defending himself, a *two-fold* effect is able to follow: *one* the preservation of his own life, the *other* however the death of the aggressor. Therefore, an *act* of this type, from the fact that the preservation of one's own life is intended, does not have the character of the illicit, since it is natural to anyone to preserve himself in his being insofar as he is able. Nevertheless, it can happen that some act proceeding from a good intention, be rendered illicit, if it is not proportioned to the end. Therefore, if someone for the sake of defending his life uses more force than is necessary, it will be illicit. If however he repels the violence moderately, it will be a licit defense. For according to rights, it

Summa theologiae II^a II^{ae} q. 64, a. 7

tit. xii, cap. 18 *Significati*]: nec est necessarium ad salutem, ut homo actum moderatae tutelae praetermittat ad evitandum occisionem alterius; quia plus tenetur homo vitae suae providere, quam vitae alienae: sed quia occidere hominem non licet, nisi publica auctoritate propter bonum commune, ut ex supra dictis patet, illicitum est, quod homo intendat occidere hominem, ut seipsum defendat, nisi ei qui habet publicam auctoritatem, qui intendens hominem occidere ad sui defensionem, refert hoc ad publicum bonum, ut patet in milite pugnante contra hostes, et in ministro judicis pugnante contra latrones; quamvis etiam et isti peccent, si privata libidine moveantur.

Ad primum ergo dicendum, quod auctoritas Augustini intelligenda est in eo casu quo quis intendit occidere hominem ut seipsum a morte liberet. In quo etiam casu intelligitur auctoritas indicta ex libro de Libro Arbitrio. Unde signanter dicitur, pro his rebus: in quo designatur intentio. Et per hoc patet responsio ad secundum.

Ad tertium dicendum, quod irregularitas consequitur actum homicidii etiamsi sit absque peccato: ut patet in iudice qui iuste aliquem condemnat ad mortem. Et propter hoc Clericus etiamsi se defendendo interficiat

is licit to repel force with force with the moderation of a blameless defense. Nor is it necessary for salvation that a man forgo an act of moderate defense so that he might avoid the death of another, since man is held to provide more for his own life than for the life of another. But since it is not licit to kill a man, except for the public authority acting for the common good, as is clear from what was said above, it is illicit that a man intend to kill a man, so that he might defend himself, save for him who has public authority, who intends to kill a man for his own defense referring this to the public good, as is clear in the case of a soldier fighting against the enemy, and an officer of the law fighting against thieves. Although even these too would sin, if they were moved by private animosity.

To the first objection it should be said that the authority of Augustine is to be understood to apply to the case in which someone intends to kill a human being, *in order that* he might free himself from death. In that way also is the adduced authority from the book *On Free Choice of the Will*. Hence, it is said pointedly 'for these things' by which intention is designated. This solves the second objection.

To the third objection it should be said that irregularity follows an act of homicide even if there is no sin: as is clear in the case of a judge who justly condemns another to

aliquem, irregularis est, quamvis non intendat interficere, sed seipsum defendere.

Ad quartum dicendum quod actus fornicationis, vel adulterii non ordinatur ad conservationem propriae vitae ex necessitate, sicut actus, ex quo quandoque sequitur homicidium.

Ad quintum dicendum quod ibi prohibetur defensio, quae est cum livore vindicatae. Unde Glossa dicit: Non vos defendentes: idest, non sitis referientes adverarios.

death. And on this account, a cleric even if he kills another in defending himself, is irregular, although he did not intend to kill but to defend himself.

To the fourth objection it should be said that the act of fornication or adultery is not ordained to the preservation of one's life from necessity, just as the act from which sometimes death follows.

To the fifth objection it should be said that a defense is prohibited which is with the spite of vindication. Hence, the Gloss says: Not defending yourselves: that is, do not thirst for paying back enemies.

The Hermeneutic Function of the Principle of Double Effect

Peter Knauer, S.J.

The principle of double effect leads a marginal existence in the handbooks of moral theology and appears useful only in making possible a species of hairsplitting. It is, in reality, the fundamental principle of all morality. It responds to the question whether the causing or permitting of an injury is morally evil. I speak of its hermeneutic function because the principle of double effect enables one to grasp—much more effectively than usually happens in traditional ethics—the meaning of the fundamental concepts of traditional morality in their interrelation in the tradition itself.

I. Presupposition

How does man recognize whether an act is morally good? Traditionally, the morally good has been determined in three distinct ways: Either it is that which "orders man to his last end, that is, God." Or it is that which "corresponds to human nature." Or it is "the simply good."

The first definition is pious but it remains, in the final analysis, abstract. It does not say what concrete acts are ordered to God. In reality an ordering to God is recognized when an act is seen as morally good in itself. This logical order is not convertible. Moreover, it may be asked whether man acts directly in relation to God.

The second definition, requiring "correspondence to human nature," is more concrete. But this formula gives a reasonable meaning only if human nature is defined as "openness to reality in general." Taken rigorously, the correspondence required is not to particular human nature but to the whole of reality.[1] But the formula remains still ambiguous. It does not yet reflect the distinction between physical and moral evil. In fact, a physical evil, such as a sickness or an error or any injury, is not yet in contradiction to nature in a moral sense; such an evil is not a moral evil, even if moral evil is definable only in relation to it.

The most exact is the third definition, according to which the morally good is "the simply good." By "good" is here meant nothing other than the physical goodness of any reality whatsoever, that goodness by which something becomes desirable in any sense, according to the axiom *ens et bonum convertuntur*. What is "simply" good, and therefore morally good, is such a value, if it is willed in such a way that the physical evil possibly associated with it remains objectively beyond the intention of the person willing. Then the good alone, that is, "the simply good," determines the intention.

What is physical evil is known by everyone from experience. Sickness or error or other destruction is never willed for itself but only on account of some other associated good. The question is whether, by reason of this good, the permission or causing of the evil is justified or not. The unjustified permission or causing of evil signifies simply that the evil itself is also intended; then, by intention, the act becomes morally evil.

The principle of double effect, rightly understood, responds to the question whether in a given case the permission or causing of evil is justified or not. In answering this question it reveals itself as a principle which provides the criterion for every moral judgment.

Moral evil, I contend, consists in the last analysis in the permission or causing of a physical evil which is not justified by a commensurate reason. Not every permission or causing of physical evil is a moral evil, but every moral evil depends on the permission or causing of physical evil. This relation, of course, as far as cooperation in the sins of others is concerned, is indirect.

It is essential now to come to a more exact understanding of the proper meaning in ethics of "commensurate reason."

II. An Old Formulation and a Modern One

1. The principle of double effect appears to have been first formulated by Thomas Aquinas.[2] He argues for the permissibility of self-defense by force in the following way:

> I reply that it must be said that nothing prevents there being two effects of one act, of which one effect alone would be in the intention and the other would be beyond intention. But moral acts receive their species according to what is intended, not from what is beyond intention, since the latter is accidental as appears from what has been said above.
>
> Therefore, from the act of someone defending himself a double effect can follow: one is the preservation of his own life, the other is the killing of the attacker. An act of this kind in which the preservation of one's own life is intended does not have the character of the unlawful, since it is natural for everyone to preserve himself in his being as far as he can.
>
> But some act arising from a good intention can be made unlawful if it is not proportionate to the end. And so, if someone in defending his own life uses greater violence than is necessary, it will be unlawful. But if he moderately repels violence, it will be a lawful defense.[3]

It must first be noted that the concept of "effect" is not used here as a correlative to "cause," but in a more general sense; "aspect" might be a more exact term. It is evident that the good effect here is not different from this object as elsewhere the effect from its cause.

In the interpretation of the text it is also important to pay attention to the third paragraph, where in reality only one possibility of a moral offense is noted. Thomas does not use the criterion of "correspondence to nature." The approach taken is this: In sinning, man seeks a real good, but his act in its total existential entirety is not proportioned to this good. Then the evil arising thereby, whether it is desired or not, belongs objectively to the act and is objectively what is "intended."

In the text of Thomas the expression "what is intended" provides the most matter for consideration. The concept of intention in ethics evidently means something different from what it means in psychology. In ethics an injury can be "intended" even if the person acting would have preferred its absence or was not thinking much about it. Conversely, as in the killing of an aggressor, an effect can be beyond moral intention, although the person acting was psychologically concentrated on it.

Several other relevant points should be observed in reference to the traditional teaching on "the sources of morality" (*fontes moralitatis*). According to what St. Thomas says elsewhere, moral acts are "determined" by the end of the act, by the *finis operis*.[4] In the present text he says that moral acts are determined by "what is intended." At first glance it seems surprising to say that what must be meant here is not the "end of the person acting" (*finis operantis*) but the "end of the work" (*finis operis*). Yet in order to avoid contradiction with the passages elsewhere, the "end of the act" must mean "what is intended." What results from taking this approach?

By *finis operis* there should not be understood—as unfortunately often happens—only the external effect, the effect that could be photographed. In ethics, *finis operis* means the act which is willed and intended as such. The classic example in the manuals runs as follows: Someone giving alms has as *finis operis* the relief of the needs of a poor man.[5] But almsgiving is not merely a physical act. It becomes a moral act through the intention of the donor. The external action consists in money going from one hand to another. Is this action payment for a purchase or the giving of a present? Is it money lent to the other? Is it the repayment of a debt? Is it a bribe? Whatever in fact the action is depends on what the person transferring the money wills the action objectively to be. That is not a matter of his arbitrary declaration but of his actual intent. All physical evils which are not justified, and which arise in the pursuit of a value, are in the moral sense *eo ipso* morally intended and belong to the *finis operis* itself.

The *finis operantis*, which is regarded as a second "source of morality" is not to be identified merely with the moral intention of the person acting. By *finis operantis*, the external end, there is meant the act towards which the person acting relates his first action. Thus someone may give alms in order to obtain a tax advantage. The *finis operantis* of the first act is related to, and is indeed identical with, the *finis operis* of this second act. If someone performs a single act without relating it to another act, he has only a *finis operis* of his act, and, to speak exactly, there is no *finis operantis*.[6]

In addition to the *finis operis* and the *finis operantis*, another traditional source of morality is the circumstances of an act. Their only function is to determine the act quantitatively. A theft is a theft according to the *finis operis* whether the amount stolen is large or small; but the gravity of the offense depends on the amount. If the theft is connected with breaking and entering, then this fact is not the addition of another circumstance but a change in the *finis operis* itself.[7]

The division of *finis operis* and *finis operantis* into an external physical act and an internal intention cannot be maintained in one and the same act; this is an arbitrary distinction arising on Cartesian foundations. Neither the pure external happening nor the psychological intention is morally understandable alone; only the objective relation, in which both have a part, is understandable. This conclusion means that the moral species of the *finis operis* depends on whether this relation is one of correspondence or one of final contradiction, while the *finis operantis* relates to the *finis operis* of another act.

For the time being I will rest with this formal definition of *finis* in ethics; at a later point I shall return to the topic to give a more exact definition.

2. Today the principle of double effect is most briefly formulated as follows:

> One may permit the evil effect of his act only if this is not intended in itself but is indirect and justified by a commensurate reason.

The modern formula seems to be different in more than one respect from that of St. Thomas. He required the act to correspond to its end (*actus sit proportionatus fini*). The present formula speaks of a "commensurate reason" (*ratio proportionata*). The principle of double effect is, I believe, rightly understood if it is recognized that in fact both requirements mean the same thing.

Thomas also held that the evil might not be effected directly. According to him, the intention must be accidental (*per accidens*); it must be beyond intention (*praeter intentionem*). The usual explanation of this terminology understands the pair of concepts, "direct-indirect," in the sense of direct or indirect physical causality; but this explanation is questionable. *I say that an evil effect is not "directly intended" only if there is a "commensurate ground" for its permission or causation.* There are not two distinct requirements when I speak of the "indirect causing" of evil and of "a commensurate reason" for the act. The principle may be adequately formulated as follows: One may permit the evil effect of his act only if he has a commensurate reason for it.

The objectivity of all ethics depends on the determination of commensurate. A "commensurate reason" is not an arbitrary X, equivalent to "serious reason in the circumstances." The customary deformed understanding of this concept identifies "commensurate" with "serious." From this deformation, an unhealthy confusion in ethics has resulted. These observations must suffice for now; I shall return later to attempt further clarification.

III. The Same Priniciple in a Variety of Expressions

The key concept in the modern formulation of the principle of double effect is the requirement of a "commensurate reason." This concept can be found in various other chapters of traditional ethics: "Cooperation in the Sin of Another," "Intrinsic Malice and Extrinsic Malice," "Affirmative and Negative Laws of Nature." In scholastic ethics all of these articles were put in different drawers. But in each there is rediscovered the structure of the principle of double effect: the causing or permitting of a physical evil is morally permitted because of a commensurate reason; without a commensurate reason the act is morally evil.

1. "Formal" cooperation in the sin of another is absolutely forbidden in every case. "Material" cooperation is permitted if there is a commensurate reason.[8] If a commensurate reason is lacking, material cooperation in the sin of another becomes formal and therefore forbidden. The absence of a commensurate reason is decisive.

It is evident that the permission or causing of evil on behalf of another becomes moral evil only through the application of the principle of double effect. If I have a commensurate reason for permitting or cooperating with the evil, the evil remains indirect for me. I only participate materially therein, while the formal content of my act is distinct from the evil, so that my act in reality is good. But if my act lacks a commensurate reason, I directly and formally cause or permit evil on behalf of another and become guilty myself. In short, the pair of concepts, the formal and the material, as they are used in the teaching on cooperation in the sin of another, are fundamentally the same as "direct" and "indirect" in the modern formulation of the principle of double effect.

2. There is a way of acting, which, according to the common teaching, is "intrinsically" evil and therefore universally forbidden. Other

ways of acting are only "extrinsically" evil and therefore permitted in the presence of commensurate reasons. But if there is no commensurate reason, then they also are absolutely forbidden in every case. This teaching means, I maintain, that then they are "intrinsically" evil. What is intrinsically an evil act is brought about when no commensurate reason can justify the permission or causing of the extrinsic evil, that is, any given premoral physical evil or injury. This is a thesis which has special significance for contemporary ethics. It says that "morally evil" and "intrinsically evil" are synonymous expressions.

Yet, are there not acts which universally are intrinsically evil so that the question of whether there is a commensurate reason or not is simply superfluous? For example, is not murder under all circumstances forbidden? Such a judgment of universal condemnation is only reached by an implicit application of the principle of double effect. As long an act is judged according to its external appearance and independently of the character of its reason, it is not understandable as a human act; it is not something that can yet be judged morally. Once it is determined whether or not the reason for an act is commensurate, the moral species of the act may be determined. Murder, for example, consists by definition in causing the death of a man without a commensurate ground. If the same external act, such as causing of the death of a man, has a commensurate ground, then it is from the beginning an act morally different from murder—either self-defense or a lawful act of justice in order to protect the community.

Again, the same conclusion is reached: The terms examined are contained in the principle of double effect. The pair of concepts, intrinsic—extrinsic, signify the same thing as "direct" and "indirect" in the formulation of the principle.

There are further pairs of concepts which also stand in the same relation to the requirement of a commensurate reason. There are, for example, *per se—per accidens* and "in intention"— "beyond intention" in the text cited from St. Thomas. The use of these different concepts for one and the same reality reveals that the scholastics had not reflected thoroughly enough on their meanings.

3. Especially instructive is a comparison of the principle of double effect with the traditional teaching's distinction between affirmative and negative laws of nature.

Negative laws (for example, "You shall not murder," "You shall not lie") oblige, as the manuals say, "always and everywhere." They permit no exceptions but are universally valid.

There are, however, affirmative laws corresponding to the negative laws. For example, corresponding to the instances given above, these are, "You shall revere and protect human life," "You shall speak the truth." In contrast to the negative obligations these affirmative laws only oblige "*semper, sed non pro semper.*" A commensurate reason justifies the nonobservance of such laws. If a commensurate reason is lacking, however, no justification is possible. In such a case the affirmative laws become absolute, "*semper et pro semper*," exactly like the negative law.

The negative law, in fact, is already contained in the affirmative. The negative law is only the application of the affirmative in cases in which there is no commensurate reason excusing from nonobservance. The pure nonobservance of the affirmative law is already identical with active infraction of its negative form. A permission of evil which is not justified by a commensurate reason amounts morally to positively causing it. The physical distinction between these cases is very secondary for moral judgment. It is only the more exact specification of the behavior which depends on this ground, for example, when we want to distinguish between homicide and murder.

But the affirmative laws go further than the negative laws in their power of obligation. The sphere where their application is unconditioned is identical with that of the negative laws, which must always be observed if there is a lack of commensurate reason. The "semper" of the affirmative laws is to be observed without restriction. But attention is to be given them even when a commensurate reason permits their present nonobservance.

What do I mean by this? I will give a medical decision as an example. There is a therapy against cancer based on present knowledge of the cells, a therapy which produces disturbances in the blood. To cause such disturbance without commensurate reason would be an injury to the health of the patient and so an intrinsically evil violation of negative law. But if such therapy holds the promise of improvement in the total health of the patient, the physician permissibly accepts in exchange the unavoidable evils which accompany it. He has a commensurate reason which makes "indirect" his action of causing an evil. His act is a justified nonobservance of the affirmative law which demands that he have care for the healthy state of blood in his patient. This value in his work evidently manifests an affirmative law corresponding to the negative law, but going beyond it.[9] If the physician is dispensed from the direct observance of the affirmative law, it remains valid, and he may not content himself forever with the necessity which forced it not to be observed. He is obliged to seek better solutions. In this obligation the meaning of the affirmative law controls the negative. If a better therapy is developed, what has been permitted can no longer be applied.

This example also shows explicitly what in ethics is unchangeable natural law. In ethics, only the obligation to seek the best possible solutions in their total existential entirety is unchangeable. The best solutions cannot be determined in advance as in a catalogue; they must be developed within the dynamic of the affirmative obligation that there be development. In this development only the prohibition of direct permission or causing of evil is unchangeable.

Negative and affirmative precepts thus constitute still another area ruled by the principle of double effect. To the negative law there corresponds the absolute prohibition of directly causing or permitting evil in any way. To cause or permit evil indirectly is like the nonobservance of an affirmative law where this nonobservance is justified by a commensurate reason. A commensurate reason would evidently be the observance of another, more compelling affirmative law which in existing conditions could not be observed at the same time as the first law. The obligation would remain to seek the possibility of being able to observe both laws. In the principle of double effect there is a commitment to advance in all the interrelated areas of reality (Janssens 1947, 621-33).

IV. What is a Commensurate Reason?

I have indicated that the expression "commensurate reason" determines the meaning of all the other concepts. Through lack of a commensurate reason, material cooperation in sin becomes formal; extrinsic malice becomes intrinsic malice; and affirmative law takes the shape of an unconditional negative. The principle of double effect means that to cause or permit an evil without commensurate reason is a morally bad act. The evil is no longer accidental in the intention of the person acting, but it becomes constitutive of the moral content of the act, the *finis operis*, or internal object. If a commensurate reason is present, the permission or causing of the evil becomes indirect and is *objectively no longer the object of moral intention*. The commensurate reason occupies the same area as what is directly willed and alone determines the entire moral content of the act. *If the reason of an act is commensurate, it alone determines the* finis operis, *so that the act is morally good*. The permission or causing of a physical evil is indirect or direct when there is or is not present a commensurate reason. Self-defense is a good example. The external operations are the same as those of a murder, for there is a use of deadly weapons. The moral distinction is recognized only when the unavoidable death of the attacker has a commensurate reason in self-defense. The object of the act is then the commensurate reason which consists in the preservation of one's own life against attack.

But when is the reason for an act a commensurate reason? There is a reason for every act even if it is morally evil. One can only will something on the condition that he is able to see a value in it in some aspect. The freedom of the will is grounded in this fact. Because the will by its nature is directed to the good as such, it can either will a good positively insofar as it is good or reject it insofar as it is only one good and not simply the good. The possibility of both decisions is based on the same judgment according to which the object is really a (but not the) good.[10]

Thus the reason for each act is an actual good. A thief steals only because he hopes for a use from the money. Even the one who acts from pure hate against the moral law seeks an actual value, although in a mistaken way. In his existential decision he wills to determine himself. But does he reach in this way what makes the freedom worth striving for?

For an act to be morally good it is not enough that it always seeks a value and so always has a reason. What is required is that this reason be commensurate. What does this mean? "Commensurate" to what?

This question is commonly answered in this way: The good achieved must correspond to the evil accepted in exchange, and indeed the good must outweigh the evil. But this answer is no advance. Such a quantitative comparison is not possible, as it is a matter of qualitatively different values which cannot be compared with one another. When some years ago in Germany the speed limit in city traffic was experimentally abolished, the death toll in traffic accidents rose threefold, and therefore the fifty-kilometer limit was very soon restored; but the death toll was still quite high. Could the loss in human life be compared with the advantages which a speedier traffic system brings? The different values which are measurable by themselves are incommensurable with each other. There is no common measure for them.

A comparison becomes possible if it is established what function one value has for another. Faster traffic causes a loss of more human lives. But if there were no traffic, the preservation of life as a whole surely would not be greater. The preservation of life in great part depends on a sound economy, which, in turn, today depends on the fastest possible traffic. Thus the complete throttling of traffic would not serve the preservation of human life as a whole. By this standard, this end would not be a commensurate reason. At the same time, faster traffic is a greater good the more it is accompanied by safety. This valuation rests on the foundation that the value sought is commensurate when it is achieved in the highest possible measure for the whole.

The example of traffic is instructive in another aspect. Speed limits, regulation of automobiles, and other limits on the freedom of individuals serve in fact to produce faster traffic and greater safety in relation to the whole. The limitations of freedom directly serve to achieve the greatest possible freedom for the whole. The violator of traffic rules contradicts the value as a whole which he wishes to realize for himself. There is a contradiction between his deed and its foundation.

A student may desire to learn the most possible. He can be successful in this pursuit only if he interrupts his work from time to time. If he is so bent on his objective of learning that he injures his own health, perhaps for a short time he may achieve something above average, but the result on the whole will be less. In an extreme case he becomes sick from overwork and cannot accomplish anything. Then in the last analysis he contradicts his own purpose. Something similar happens in any immoral act. An objective is sought which has an appropriate price (*tantum—quantum*), but it is sought at any price. In unmeasured desire there is sacrificed what alone would assure the greatest possible achievement of the end.

The government of a developing country has a plan to better the living standard of its people. This objective may be reached only through an ongoing industrialization which requires an extensive renunciation of immediate accomplishments. If instead of such a program the administration forces immediate sharing of goods by use of the police, it may indeed achieve an elevation of the living standard. But this approach quickly leads to a destruction of the economy, and the need becomes greater than before. In seeking an immediate achievement of the objective, there has been a neglect of the total conditions of possibility and thereby a contradiction of the objective itself. In this example there is especially clear what could be called the feedback effect or the reciprocal function of two values. On one hand, a rise in the living standard requires industrialization. Industrialization is not a higher value than a better living standard—the possibility of such a comparison has already been denied—but industrialization is of the greatest urgency if a higher living standard is to be achieved. On the other hand, industrialization cannot be achieved if at the same time there is not at least some beginning of a rise in the living standard, because no industry can be developed with hungry workers.

All of these examples may illustrate that unintelligent and therefore immoral acts are in the last analysis self-contradictions and consist in unmeasured desire taking the fruit from the tree before it is ripe. There is an isolation of the objective from its proper conditions. A good is sought while the conditions for the highest possible realization of the good are abandoned. This state of affairs is described by the language of the old moral theology when it singles out an immoral act as an act against nature, *contra naturam*. There is a destruction of reality itself when part of reality is isolated from its interrelations. If someone pays a price for a good which is not commensurate with the good but, rather, contradicts it and makes the highest possible achievement of the good as a whole impossible, he irresponsibly causes injury. When the expression *contra naturam* is used in ethics, there is not meant physical evil which is against nature only in a premoral, physical sense. What is meant is a physical evil caused or permitted without commensurate reason—that is, in this act there is a long-run contradiction in reality between the value sought and the way of achieving it.

Immediately in the short run there may often be a remarkable achievement. Irrationality first emerges when consideration is given to all the interrelationships and when it is asked if the objective existentially achieved, seen in terms of the whole, best corresponds not only to a particular person but to the totality. What this distinction between individual and totality means may be clarified by the example given above of freedom in traffic. The moral consciousness poses this universalizing question. The distinction between the two approaches is rigorously objective. Whether a reason for an act is commensurate or not is beyond all subjective arbitrariness.[11] The reason for an act is not a commensurate reason if there is a contradiction in the last analysis between the act and the reason.

A similar result is reached if the modern formulation of the principle of double effect is compared with the formulation of St. Thomas. As I noted earlier, Thomas instead of requiring a commensurate reason (*ratio proportionata*) says that the entire act must correspond to its end (*actus sit proportionatus fini*); but end means nothing other than reason for the act. It is simply a matter of a correspondence between the act and its proper reason. Both requirements, that the reason for an act be commensurate (that is, that it be one commensurate to the act itself) or that the act must correspond to its reason, mean the same. An act becomes immoral when it is contradictory to the fullest achievement of its own end in relation to the whole of reality. A short-run "more" of the value is paid by a "lesser" achievement of the same value in the long run.

V. Three Different Meanings of "End"

So far I have used the expression "end" (for which "intention" could be substituted) in an entirely specific sense as identical with reason. It is important to note this in order to avoid an easy misunderstanding. "End" can also have another meaning and simply signify a determinate concrete fact. Thus a band of bank robbers has the end of entering the treasury of a bank. It would be absurd to measure the morality of this act by asking if the band is using the most appropriate means of achieving its end. Such a determination is not meant when I speak of the correspondence required between the act and its proper end. In this requirement what is meant by end is not a concrete fact, but what in a particular fact makes it worth acting for, its *ratio boni*. In the sense I use it, in which the end of an act is identical with its reason, it must be said that the value the robber band is seeking is to become rich. At this level the question is posed whether breaking and entering leads in the long run to the greatest realization of riches as a whole or whether it is in contradiction to such realization.

If end is used as identical with reason, it is still not a concept of ethics. As I have already shown, both good and bad acts have a reason in this sense, as reason means a value. The reason of the worst act is never an evil but always a good, that is, something in fact worth striving for. Therefore, a source of morality is not reached when reason or end in this sense is reached.

In a moral sense the end of an act is what is "intended"—the *finis operis* and, eventually more broadly, the *finis operantis*, the ordering of the act to the *finis operis* of a more comprehensive act. These expressions signify the reason of the act insofar as it is in correspondence with the totality of the act or not. In this moral sense, the reason is no longer considered alone but in its relation to the act itself. If the reason of an act is a commensurate reason, it is in a moral sense the end of the act and intended. It is then completely identical with the *finis operis*, so that the eventual concomitant evil, even if it is considered necessarily part of the exchange, falls outside the *finis operis*. The *finis operis* of the act is, then, simply good.

When the reason of an act is not a commensurate reason so that between it and the act in terms of the horizon of the whole reality there is a contradiction. The reason in itself may be as good and as important as possible, yet the *finis operis* of the act is no longer constituted by this reason. The reason is in contradiction to the act, and the *finis operis* is constituted by the evil effect which accompanies it. In the example of bank robbery, the chief evil effect is the harming of other people in the taking of their property. This harm is intended in the moral sense in a bank robbery, although the gangsters have only their own enrichment in view.

In Part VIII I shall return to the threefold meaning of the concept of end in a discussion of the distinction between mutilation and medically necessary amputation.

VI. The Moral Good as the Best Possible

Every human act brings evil effects with it. The choice of a value always means concretely that there is denial of another value which must be given as a price in exchange. If the chosen value is sought in its entirety in a commensurate way, the evil falls outside what is directly willed. In other cases when the reason of the act is not commensurate, the evils which arise are themselves directly willed even if they are not in the least desired in themselves.

I shall seek to make the matter still clearer through the development of a statement of an Aristotelian ethic. I refer to an easily understood alternative to the scholastic procedure. According to Aristotle, morally right behavior is a mean between two extremes which can be recognized as too much or too little. It is observed that in consideration of the good, the mean itself is an extreme.[12] Thus, for example, bravery is a mean between foolhardiness and cowardice. Aristotle declared that bravery appears more closely related to one of the two extremes, foolhardiness. This observation, which is made by Aristotle himself with some surprise, provides an opportunity for asking whether there is not also a name for right behavior which appears to lie closer to cowardice, the other false extreme. There is, in fact, prudence. It belongs inseparably with bravery. It is clear to everyone that bravery without prudence is in reality only cowardice. If foolhardiness consists in too great a risk so that in the end too little is achieved, bravery consists in achieving the most possible of that for which the entire risk is undertaken. Again, there is the criterion of commensurate reason; that is, of a proportionality of the act to its proper objective. Bravery is readiness for any risk which is justified by the end in its existential entirety. Bravery is thus accompanied by prudence, which holds the risk to the smallest degree possible so that the greatest possible gain may be achieved. Cowardice lacks this measure. It wagers the least, but thereby loses too much of the whole.

The formal structure of winning and losing which is implied in this example is founded on the principle of double effect. Evil may be accepted in exchange if, in relation to the whole, the smallest possible evil is exchanged for the highest possible gain. The whole is the determinative point of view for morality; it distinguishes ethics from a technique based on experience in a particular area. When an act neither sacrifices too much nor gains too little, there is conduct which is commensurate to the end sought. Immoral acts consist in preferring the success of the moment to true gain and thereby spoiling the achievement of true gain in the act which is carried out. A coward naturally always says that he is prudent, and a fool often holds himself to be brave. They both refer to their good intentions, but they are both unmasked when consideration is given to the complementary virtue. Where is the bravery in the pretended prudence of a coward? Where is the prudence in the asserted bravery of the fool? In the presence of the complementary virtue there is recognized that the act has a commensurate reason; that is, it is recognized that the act is in proportion to its end. Liberality accompanied by economy is distinguished from extravagance; economy is only avarice unless it is liberal. Progress is not a pure seeking of what is new, but a preservation of what is good in the old. There is in fidelity to tradition only a spiritless severity unless it fosters the creation of the new. Zeal and discretion go together; otherwise zeal in reality becomes fanaticism, and instead of discretion there is mediocrity. "Be wise as the serpent and simple as the dove" (Matthew 10:16). Such a demand is not paradoxical but excludes slyness and stupidity together. Christian hope works out its salvation "in fear and trembling" (Philip. 2:12); one without the other is either presumption or despair. There are many other examples. This square is of universal applicability.

Moral good consists in the best possible realization of any particular value envisaged in its entirety. This assertion is fundamentally different from the rigorist thesis which says that among different goods the highest must be always chosen. Here, rather, there is freedom as long as the particular value chosen is not itself subverted.

A particularly good example is the problem of the vocation where the choice has to be made between several morally good possibilities. A false model of this choice is provided if vocation is understood as "a specific call which God himself has implanted in me in advance." The will of God which is knowable objectively consists in being able to decide for oneself among different good possibilities. A so-called vocation should not be understood objectively as an advance determination to one possibility. Vocation consists rather in the possibility of having appropriate motives for the way to be chosen. This is the grace of a calling. It is completely possible that someone be called in this sense to different vocations so that he himself must make the actual choice. Only in an unusual case where there is an extraordinary need can there be an obligation which is binding in one direction from the beginning. In such a case any other choice would be self-contradictory because the other possibilities depend for their realization on a condition which must be realized at any cost.

VII. Bad Means

The explanation I have given to this point of the principle of double effect is very different from the usual explanation given in the teaching on what is *voluntarium in causa*. This is usually explained in the following sense: If an evil is the further physical consequence of the good which is willed, or at least does not precede the good which is willed, then the permissibility of the act depends on what is intended by the act. If the evil permitted or caused accompanies the good to be achieved only as a consequence or a concomitant, the act is permitted; otherwise not. But if the evil physically precedes the willed good and so is "the means" to its achievement, then it is directly willed and makes the entire act evil, just as if the evil was intended by the act. In this case, the principle of double effect is replaced by another principle: A good end does not justify bad means.

Such a contrast between these two principles involves a logical error. In the principle that the good end does not justify the bad means, it is already assumed that the means are morally bad.[13] The principle is only applicable if the moral judgment has already been formed; in the moral evil of the means something new is not discovered; the evil was already established. In the principle of double effect, in contrast, a moral judgment of this kind is in the process of being determined. The two principles are not parallel in their applicability. That a means is morally bad signifies in our sense that the reason for the application of the means is not commensurate. The pure determination that the means entails physical evil is not enough to qualify it as morally evil. It may well be that the permission or causing of this evil is only indirect because of a commensurate reason. Provided that an end is sought in its existential entirety in a truly commensurate way, the means determined by this end which can contribute to the best possible realization of the end may justify accepting physical evil in exchange. Of course, one must be satisfied that this price is the smallest possible. In this sense the axiom is valid: *Finis determinat media*.

The principle that the good end does not justify the bad means may rightly be understood in either of the two following senses. On the one hand, it may be a matter of a single act whose reason is a good end. The principle asserts that this end, however serious and good in itself, cannot justify the permission or causing of physical evil in the course of its achievement if it is not a commensurate reason in the sense I have indicated. The act must correspond to the value sought not only in the short run but in its existential entirety. On the other hand, the means may itself consist in a proper act which can be recognized without reference to a further objective as having a reason in itself which suffices for the positing of the act. If this reason is not a commensurate one, then the act may not be morally saved, even if it can be related to another act which is an achievement of an end that in itself is good. The means in the last analysis would contradict the act.

In the second sense, St. Thomas says at the conclusion of his analysis of self-defense that it is not permitted to will the death of the aggressor as an act in itself.[14] Self-defense then would be the *finis operantis* and no longer the *finis operis*. The death of the attacker would be willed even if it were not determined to be necessary in fact for self-defense. Such an act would obviously not be permissible.

But clearly there are cases in which the causing or permitting of an evil precedes the achievement of the end without the act thereby becoming morally bad. The evil is justified by a commensurate reason; although the cause is physically direct, it is not direct in a moral sense. The following example is classic. A dangerous fortress may be made harmless only by being stormed by force, but in the outer bastion of the fortress there are innocent hostages who will lose their lives before the proper end of the action, the storming of the fortress, can be achieved. In traditional ethics this action is permissible as long as there is no other way to avoid the evil. The decisive question is not whether the evil, the deaths of the prisoners during the storming, follows the good which is sought or precedes it; the decisive question is in what way the evil is willed. The act is morally bad if the evil is direct or formal, that is, if the act is willed in such a way that there is no commensurate reason for it and therefore is irresponsible. The purely physical series of events is irrelevant to the moral qualification of good or bad. One and the same means can in one aspect be a value or lead to the realization of a value and simultaneously be a physical evil in another aspect. If there is a commensurate reason for the permitting or causing of the evil, the means is effectively willed only in its good aspect. The effect or, more exactly, the aspect which is physically evil remains morally outside of what is intended.

When the categories direct and indirect are confused with purely physical categories, a blind hairsplitting is introduced into ethics.

Removal of a cancerous uterus is permitted even though as a consequence the fetus within the uterus loses its life. But to remove only the fetus, because the uterus may still be healed, is said by some theologians to be murder; they think the death of the fetus is used as a means and so is directly willed. In other words, a solution which includes both the death of the fetus and the removal of the entire uterus with consequent sterility is said to be better than that the fetus alone lose its life. Who can understand this?

In the case of an ectopic pregnancy, it is almost certain that the woman together with an unborn child will die if the fetus is not removed as early as possible. The "insight" that this is immoral is scarcely demonstrable to any doctor. It is agreed that direct killing is forbidden. But in my opinion, some scholastic moralists have assumed incorrectly that the saving of the mother, which in the normal case is probable if there is immediate removal of the ectopic fetus, is a direct killing. Negative laws (You shall not kill, You shall not speak an untruth, You shall not take the property of another) are understandable only as the prohibition of direct and therefore formal permission or causing of these physical evils (death, error, loss of property, etc.), in cases where by definition there is no commensurate reason. Whether there is a violation of a commandment (that is, whether an act is murder, lying, theft) can be ascertained only if it is established that the reason for the act in its existential entirety is not commensurate. Without a commensurate reason an evil is always willed directly, even if attention is not expressly directed to the evil but it is desired that there be no such evil.

VIII. Exceptions in Ethics

In the recent literature of moral theology there has been evoked from time to time what is called the principle of totality, a principle contrasted with the principle of double effect. The latter is said to relate only to the justification of the "barely permissible," while the principle of totality relates to the "justification of an effect willed for itself by reason of its connection with the whole order of purposes and goods" (Liebhart 1963, 192). The principle of totality justifies an act such as the removal of a sick organ in order to save the whole organism.

In my opinion the principle of totality is in reality not distinguishable from the principle of double effect. The latter bears not merely on the passive permission of an evil but relates to the most active kind of permission; concretely the act itself may cause or effect the evil; the evil is not direct unless it is willed without commensurate reason. In fact, it is not true, for example, that a medically necessary amputation is willed in the moral sense as a removal of an organ. What is willed is only the removal of what is an obstacle to health in its entirety. That this obstacle is identical with the hitherto useful member of the body is accidental for moral judgment (*existimatio moralis*),[15] because a commensurate reason justifies the acceptance of the loss. For the eventual preservation of the organs the existence of the person itself must certainly first be assured. There is not a quantitative relation between a part to the whole, but a priority of dependence of one upon the other. If there is a commensurate reason, the removal of an organ is justified, and the operation is not the mutilation of the organism, which is always impermissible.

The example may also serve to clarify the distinction I have already made between the three meanings of "end." In the operation the surgeon does not think of anything except the skillful removal of the limb of the patient. This removal is the concrete thing which is willed by him, and one can say that this act is "the effect willed in itself." But the morality of the act is not determined on this level. Whether the removal of a limb is a health measure or a mutilation of the patient cannot be recognized in the concrete actuality which might be photographed. The reason why the surgeon removes the limb must be looked at. What value does the act seek to serve? It is done because of the health of the patient. But this by itself does not determine the morality of the act. A purely good intention in the psychological sense does not determine the moral goodness of an act. It must be established that this reason is a commensurate one. If, in the given circumstances, the act is the best possible solution of the problem in terms of the horizon given by the whole of reality, it may be said that the act is morally good. In a moral sense, what is then intended is not the taking of the limb, but the health of the patient. That the obstacle to be removed was once a useful limb falls in a moral sense outside of what is intended and is not directly willed. It is another case if the reason for the removal is not commensurate—for example, if it would be possible to achieve the objective of health in a way which would cause less loss. The removal of the limb would then contradict the best possible achievement of the end. In such a case, in a moral sense the removal of the limb in its function as member of the body would be directly willed, even if the surgeon did not direct his attention to this aspect.

In another respect the example is instructive. In the usual thoughtless dichotomy between physical act and intention any act whatsoever might be labeled by any intention whatsoever. But this is in reality not even possible on the psychological, premoral level. Suppose that blood poisoning could be healed by the injection of a new serum so that the objective of health would not require removal of the poisoned limb; it would be logically impossible to prefer the limb's removal for the same reason as before the discovery of the serum. If a physician desired to carry out such an amputation, he would in fact do it for some other reason, e.g., the avoidance of unusually high expenses. But as to this new reason the question would again have to be asked: Is it a commensurate reason or not? In this example it is seen that the permissibility of a medically necessary amputation is not an exception to the prohibition of mutilation, but in a moral sense is an act which is not a removal of the limb but a healing of the sick.

In a similar way a series of other apparent exceptions to the moral law may be clarified. To return to the example of self defense, the death of an aggressor may be caused if there is no other way to save oneself. Similarly, the lawfulness of the death penalty in traditional morality has been upheld under certain circumstances. In this case Thomas himself thinks that the death of the criminal is directly intended.[16] I do not agree with his formulation. But many moralists have followed him in thinking that the commandment, You shall not kill, is to be understood in a restrictive sense admitting certain exceptions: The guilty may be killed, and an unjust aggressor has already given up his right to life. This analysis is not persuasive. First, one may repel the aggression of an insane man although he is incapable of a moral act and therefore completely incapable of a guilty deed. Conversely, one may not kill an aggressor, however unjust, if in other ways one can save oneself and other possible victims. It is false that a criminal condemned to death has no right to life. How else explain that it is murder if one on his own authority shoots a man on his way to execution?[17] The execution of the judgment of death is not direct killing, and so not murder, because there is no other reasonable possibility of self defense for the human community. Then the *finis operis* of the execution is only the self-defense of the community. I do not thereby contend that one can be satisfied for all time with this solution. The obligation remains to seek better solutions within the realm of the reasonably possible. That in a certain historical situation the death penalty was rightly judged permissible does not indicate that it remains fundamentally and absolutely permissible.

If someone in extreme necessity takes the property of another because it is necessary for him to preserve his life, he does externally what a thief would do. But a theft is only the taking of the property of another without commensurate reason. A thief wills to enrich himself, but the value of possession assumes a legal order. Through the violation of this order the thief contradicts his own end in its existential entirety. The reason for his act is therefore no longer commensurate. A thief is thus guilty morally of the evil he has caused. It is different as to the poor man in extreme need for whom there is no other possibility of saving his life than the taking of the property of another. In order to be reasonable the legal order which protects property rests on the assumption that everyone has a right to life. The poor man in extreme need does not contradict his end, which is the preservation of his life; and he does not contradict it even in terms of a universal observation (and this point of view is the decisive one). Therefore he does not will directly that the former possessor lose his property and suffer injury. It seems to me false to explain this case by asserting that the possessor had no property right in these circumstances to his property, so that he allegedly has suffered no injury.

A lie consists in telling what is false without commensurate reason and therefore directly or formally causes the error of another; trust is expected and at the same time subverted. If such behavior were permitted, then trust in its existential entirety would be impossible; truth could not be shared. But it is something entirely different if, in order to preserve a secret, a false answer is given to an indiscreet question. Then the case is parallel with self-defense; the error of the other is not directly willed. Morally, the answer has the meaning that I will not give away my secret. That the questioner is deceived is an evil which is rightly accepted in exchange for preservation of the secret. I assume, of course, that the question of the other is illegitimate, so that he has no right to the knowledge of the fact, and I assume that in no other way can the secret be preserved. In many cases a clearly evasive answer or the attempt to use ambiguous language, assuming that one has the presence of mind to think so quickly, is entirely inadequate to protect the secret. In these circumstances a false answer instead of such language is not the same as a lie.

A concrete example will make my meaning clearer: A family in East Berlin before the building of the Wall wishes to flee to West Berlin. While it is gathering some small household effects to take to West Berlin, a neighbor remarks on its activity and asks, "Is it true that you are going to West Berlin?" The detection of such preparation for flight carries with it a serious punishment in prison in East Berlin. How can such a question be answered? If answer is evaded ("What does this matter to you?"), all is betrayed. To avoid an answer without betraying the secret, the only course is to repel with scorn the suspicion of desiring to flee. Such a response in my opinion has as little to do with lying as the death of an aggressor in the case of necessary self-defense has to do with murder. On the contrary, it would be objectively immoral to betray a secret which should rightfully be preserved.

Usually an attempt is made to solve this kind of problem of speech with a theory as to ambiguous language. But it must be clear that any answer to an unjustified question, however the answer is phrased, is ambiguous in its nature in that it may in reality merely refuse to give what the inquirer has asked. To an illegitimate question any possible answer, contrary to the tenor of the words used in the answer, may be nothing but a refusal of the correct answer.

IX. Situation Ethics

Scientific ethics has scarcely coped with the preoccupations of so-called situation ethics. Situation ethics asserts that the moral judgment of an act can be given only in the concrete, particular situation; and that a moral judgment in terms of a general, abstract law, which is valid forever, is impossible. According to this doctrine, ethics ceases to be universally reasonable or capable of being objectified.

The basis for this approach is the following misunderstanding. It is thought that the principles of traditional ethics entail substantive statements and moral qualifications which are then universally applied to particular cases. In fact, this appearance is given as long as the negative laws (You shall not kill, You shall not speak an untruth) are not formally understood as prohibitions of what is the direct causation or permission of any given physical evil not justified by a commensurate reason. In this approach the distinction between physical and moral evil is obscured. Situation ethics then develops, not unmasking this error, although refusing to accept its consequences.

A moral judgment is naturally possible only when in a concrete act it is established whether the reason for the act is commensurate or not. On that depends whether the cause or permission of the associated physical evil is indirect, or direct and thus morally bad. With this determination the core of truth in situation ethics is taken into account without destroying the foundation for an objective morality. The answer to the question whether the reason for an act is commensurate or not depends on rigorous objective criteria and not on merely subjective or even imaginary good intention.

But another endeavor of saving the core of truth in situation ethics is erroneous. This is the distinction made between the specific and the individual lawfulness of an act. For example, according to this distinction, an act of marital intercourse without love is lawful according to its *finis operis* and so is in its species unobjectionable, although it lacks individual lawfulness which is determined by the *finis operantis*. Here there recurs in more subtle form the false distinction between the mere externals of an act as the *finis operis* and the inner intention as the *finis operantis* which I have already criticized. The *finis operis* of any act is definable only in relation to an individual intention. An act is only morally good if its reason is commensurate; conversely it is only bad if the reason of the act is not commensurate. A marital act completed with external correctness, but not intended as the expression of personal love, is already bad in its *finis operis*. A special individual ethics is superfluous, because all true ethics is individual.

In response to what I published earlier on the principle of double effect, several critics raised the objection that my thesis served the cause of ethical relativism. This objection is unjust. In what I have asserted up to this point, I have attempted to demonstrate that the fundamental insights of traditional ethics show that an act is morally bad if it implies in the last analysis a self-contradiction, and thus becomes unreasonable. This criterion for *malum intrinsecum* amounts to a universal, unconditional, objective and nonrelative rule. An immoral act is the seeking of any value in the short run while in its total existential reality the act destroys the value. The justness of this criterion cannot be denied by anyone who defends an objective ethics. I believe that this criterion is precise and not manipulable in any way, and that in using it I am a clear opponent of situation ethics. But how could my reflections have given the impression of ethical relativism? The chief reason seems to be that my critics did not sufficiently observe that the concept of a commensurate reason must be understood differently than it is commonly and inexactly understood. It is not my meaning that any act at all is permissible as long as there is a "serious reason" for it. Such a conclusion would indeed be the most evil form of ethical relativism. But a commensurate reason in my thesis is not the same as a serious reason.

A second cause for misunderstanding has been that it is assumed that certain acts like murder, unchastity, hatred of God, etc., are morally evil in advance, so that there is nothing more to prove. This is indeed just and true. If it is once established that the act is murder, then it is established that the act is morally evil. I put the question at an essentially earlier point: How can it be recognized that an act is murder? To do this, the physical fact which could be observed in a photograph does not suffice. As Thomas puts it, "Moral acts are defined by what is intended in them," or by what is directly willed in them.[18] I have sought to establish that the concept "direct" correlates with the concept "commensurate reason." If the concept "direct" is understood in the sense of direct causality or direct attention of the person who is acting, then my thesis is understood in a false sense. It would be the worst relativism if it were seriously asserted that the moral qualification of an act depends on whether or not the person acting concentrates his attention on the good intention.

In one sense, however, I plead for a kind of objective relativism in ethics. I think that there are no prefabricated judgments which can be made, but that the judgment of conscience depends on what a particular event is in reality. Whether, for example, a particular behavior is hatred of God cannot be known in advance; it requires examination. It may be that the hatred is directed to a false image of God which the person refuses to serve. Similarly, a fool observing the killing of an aggressor could say, "You shall not kill," and be filled with the prideful consciousness that he spoke his verdict on behalf of the unchangeable and absolute moral law. He would still have to be told that the killing was not a direct killing in the sense of the commandment.

X. Probabilism

In our discussion of the distinction between affirmative and negative laws of nature, we already saw that what is fundamental is the affirmative obligation to realize in the best possible way all the values of creation. At the second level and only as it contradicts its own end is the direct permission or causing of an evil forbidden. The negative laws are applications of the affirmative laws in particular cases. Based on an understanding of this relationship, probabilism asserts that one may not prevent an act which is possibly good, for the simple reason that one is not sure whether in fact it is good. As long as one is not sure that an act is morally bad, it is established that it is perhaps morally good and the fulfillment of the affirmative obligation to realize the good may be found in it. Because of the priority of the affirmative obligation to the good, it would be in the last analysis a lack of responsibility if such an act were impeded. The tutiorism which is opposed to probabilism is like the conduct of the servant entrusted with the talent who, for fear of losing it, buried it and so made no profit.

The moral system of probabilism already contains the principle of double effect as I have explained it. The simplest example is the one I have already often cited of a medical decision to be made. The doctor is obliged to determine as far as possible whether the therapy he plans is in fact the best possible; but a decision can be so pressing that he cannot wait long. The patient would be dead before the doctor reached the theoretically best medication in the books. If he could know in advance what would be the best possible measure, he would be obliged to apply it to the exclusion of all other methods. But in the actual situation because of the time pressure, the doctor is bound to put aside the achievement of ideal knowledge and is permitted to use the solution for the problem which has apparently the least risk and offers a probability of success. Concretely, he then acts in what is the best possible way considering the matter in its entirety. Care for the health of his patient would not be a commensurate reason which would justify him in letting time elapse while he pursued a long investigation. Such behavior would not be responsible. True responsibility is always a function of the best possible choice in terms of the interrelated whole.

A more general statement is necessary in this connection. In most manuals the principle of double effect is explained in such a way that it concerns only the eventual permissibility of permitting or causing a physical evil in the sense that the act is not expressly forbidden. Exceptions which are justified by commensurate reasons are not, in fact, something indifferent (a human act is never indifferent), but are positively good. They are the observance of an affirmative law which requires the seeking of a determinate value in the best possible way. Every act in which any value is sought in a way corresponding to its existential entirety is *eo ipso* morally good.

My interpretation of commensurate reason shows that someone can be so obliged in given circumstances to the causing or permitting of an evil that there is scarcely any other choice for him. This is the case where any other act would involve the violation of a negative law. For example, in the case of catastrophe the rescue of human lives is to be preferred to the salvaging of valuable goods, unless these on the whole will contribute to the saving of a greater number of human lives.

XI. Contraception

My interpretation of the principle of double effect may also contribute to the solution of the question, so controverted today, as to whether any form of contraception is permissible. The contribution will consist above all in a correct formulation of the question itself. In this section I will assume the results reached above, especially the definition of the concepts "direct" and "commensurate reason." Whoever reads what follows without reference to these conclusions and therefore with an inexact understanding of these concepts, runs the danger of misunderstanding the meaning of my assertions.

The teaching of the Church has been expressed as follows by Pius XI: any form of contraception in any way is immoral, just as lying, theft, and murder are immoral. It is asked today if this principle is truly general without exceptions. The more severe moralists hold that a modification of the prohibition is excluded because the Church would have to admit that it had erred on a fundamental question.

Their opponents believe that this is not a question of infallible teaching and that new arguments that have developed require reconsideration of the doctrine. These opponents would admit that in certain cases contraception is permissible. The two approaches stand in irreconcilable opposition.

The insolubility produced by the problematic seems to me a sign that the question has been put in a false way. The parties to the discussion seem to take for granted a single concept of contraception derived from the encyclical *Casti connubii* of Pius XI: Contraception is said to be present when the conjugal act, which by its nature is directed to the procreation of offspring, is deprived of this natural meaning and power by intention (*de industria*). It is evident that not even the most weighty ground (*nulla profecto ratio ne gravissima quidem*) can effect that such an act against nature, which is evil in itself, be permitted.[19] This apparently clear and precise determination of the concept is not inadequate or false on more exact examination, but is ambiguous.

That a marital act lose its procreative power is a purely physical evil which does not constitute a human act without further content. Thus Pius XI's definition of the concept in reference to immoral contraception notes that this act is done intentionally, *de industria*. In this concept lies the whole ambiguity. Is *de industria* meant as intentional in a psychological or in a moral sense? Let us recall again the example of the medically necessary amputation of a limb. Psychologically the doctor has the removal of the limb in mind. One can say in a psychological sense that he in fact *de industria* removes the limb from the body. But in a moral sense it is his intention to carry out a justified operation. Morally the act is not the removal of the limb but a healing intervention. In a moral sense the act can be justified by a commensurate reason, and the premoral, psychological action is beyond intention; the doctor's moral intention is to remove a once useful member of the body only insofar as it is an obstacle to health. If an act has a commensurate reason the latter prevents evil from being willed directly or *de industria* in the moral sense, so that what psychological attention may be concentrated on is in the moral sense beyond intention, *praeter intentionem*. In other words, if the expression *de industria* used by Pius XI is understood in a moral sense, it is demonstrated according to the logic of its use that it is completely the same as the fundamental moral concepts "direct" or "formal" or "in intention" which we have already shown must be conjugated with the concept of commensurate reason.

Like all the negative laws, the prohibition of contraception means the direct permission or causing of something which must be considered in some respect a physical evil even if it appears worth being sought in some other respect. By direct is meant a causing or permission without a commensurate reason. In a case where there is a commensurate reason for the prevention of pregnancy, the moral content of the act is not the fact of contraception but the nature of the commensurate reason. Naturally in making this determination, an absolute distinction must be observed between "commensurate" and "serious." Pius XI says with complete correctness that, however serious the reason, it cannot make an act right if it is against nature in the moral sense; the same conclusion is reached in terms of my analysis where a commensurate reason is lacking.

In ethics, care must be taken not to identify the physical or psychological order directly with the moral order. A physical evil may be caused or permitted and willed in a psychological sense, and yet the act is not necessarily a moral evil. It is a moral evil if the act has no commensurate reason but in its existential entirety contradicts the value sought. It then becomes in a moral sense contrary to nature. It can be objected that for an act contrary to nature there is never a reason which can be considered commensurate. But a conclusion as to commensurate reason logically precedes the determination that the act is contrary to nature. The objection runs counter to my assertion that the contrariness to the nature of an act is only recognized when its reason is not commensurate, that is, when between the act and its proper reason in terms of the horizon of the entire reality there is a contradiction which shows that the act is in the last analysis counterproductive.

In ethical discussions a distinction must be made between contraception in its moral sense as a prevention of pregnancy not justified by a commensurate reason and the premoral concept of actual prevention of a pregnancy. The second meaning does not yet in a moral sense belong to the *finis operis* of the act. If the concept of contraception in the statement of Pius XI is understood in its moral sense, his judgment is correct and by definition permits no modification. An act which is not founded on a commensurate reason is evil and remains evil because it is a self-contradiction and in the last analysis unreasonable, and it is then to be designated according to the evil physically caused by it—in this case according to the prevention of pregnancy as contraception.

If *de industria* is understood not in a moral, but in a psychological sense, then the judgment of Pius XI is incomprehensible and meaningless as it gives a moral meaning to a fact understood in a premoral sense. This would be roughly like determining the color of an object from its weight. On this level the discussion naturally reaches no conclusion. As long as the distinct meanings of *de industria* are not separated from each other, every statement must remain ambiguous even if it is believed to be clear and even if it is solemnly asserted by ecclesiastical authority.

What I have said up to now on contraception has been of an entirely formal character. I have not asserted what would be a commensurate reason because of which the prevention of a pregnancy willed in a psychological sense would remain beyond moral intention. But, fundamentally, to give such a reason would be to yield to another false framing of the question which has been seriously harmful to the discussion. A catalog of commensurate reasons is expected in terms of which the act for all time could be regarded as permissible, and it is assumed that there would be no need to consider further such permissible behavior. These expectations are deceptive. A list of reasons which might be composed, whether they are commensurate or not, cannot be definitively established in advance. What is at issue is a concept which depends on a relation.

The permissibility of an act, moreover, does not mean that it is permissible for all time. If a doctor uses a medicine with concomitant evil results, he remains obliged to use it as long as there is no better means, but he is also obliged to seek better solutions. Our case is similar. If what is in fact contraceptive conduct in the premoral sense is justified by a commensurate reason so that it is not an act of contraception in the moral sense, this does not mean that this reason will remain commensurate forever. There is a fundamental obligation to seek a solution for the problem which in the achieving of the values sought accepts in exchange the respectively least evil possible within the entire range of possibilities.

Many moralists content themselves in their argument with a pure proof of physical evil. They confuse the physical and the moral sense of contrariness to nature. This is as though the killing of an aggressor in a case of necessity were identified with killing in a moral sense. It is, to be sure, true that contrariness to nature in a moral sense has a relation to a physical evil which can be defined in a physical sense as contrary to nature; but moral evil comes about only through permission or causing of physical evil without commensurate reason. But this physical evil is not as such a moral evil. The same moralists found the permission of periodic continence on the logically insufficient claim that periodic continence is not an active attack on procreation although in fact a choice of times for intercourse is a pure activity. In fact if periodic continence were practiced without commensurate reason, it would not be other than impermissible contraception. This is plain from the text of Pius XII.[20]

The criterion of commensurate reason means that the value whose achievement is realizable only by contraceptive measures in a premoral sense may not in the last analysis be contradicted by these measures by preventing in the long run the highest possible realization of this very value with the smallest possible evil. To prove that a particular act is contraceptive in the moral sense it must be shown that the act in the last analysis does not serve the end of preservation and deepening marital love, but in the long run subverts it.

If it is argued in accordance with scholastic ethics that the foundation of the prohibition of contraception is that the marital act is directed by its nature to the procreation of offspring, this argument is correct only if it is understood in a moral sense. The objective of the procreation of offspring is to be sought in a way commensurate to the objective and not actually subversive of it. It is conceivable that a marital act may lead to irresponsible procreation. Such an act would be a sin both against the expected child and against the children in existence whose appropriate education might not be further provided for. In this moral sense the act would be one hostile to children, an act which could be recognized as a misuse of marriage although physiologically everything appeared to be in order. It would appear that this act was in reality deprived of its natural direction to the procreation of offspring because there would be no correspondence between the act and its end in the final analysis for the moral judgment which must be made in terms of the whole reality.

In this article directed to principles it is not possible for me to enter into further detail. But the following consequences seem valid. If someone may not reasonably be responsible for another pregnancy, the use of periodic continence, where it is not impossible because of external circumstances, seems in the usual case to best correspond to the social and human character of the marital encounter. With adequate motivation it may serve to increase mutual love (Rendu 1965, 606-31). Where periodic continence is objectively impossible, the question is posed whether other ways may be used. These means are to be judged as to whether or not they contradict the highest possible realization of the desired value on the whole. If, for example, a man without conscience compelled his wife against her will to have marital intercourse, the wife would have an evident right to use the necessary means to prevent a pregnancy for which she cannot take the responsibility. As a wife she would not have to use force against her husband. Her conduct would have nothing in common with forbidden contraception in a moral sense. It would be a scandalous mistake if I should be accused because of this position of having abandoned the "hard but healthy Catholic teaching."

XII. Conclusion

The principle of double effect brings into usage a criterion which is implied in every decision of conscience. That an act is good means that a commensurate reason is recognized as present. Conversely, in an immoral act a lack of a commensurate reason is recognized—that is, in terms of the whole reality the act in its existential character directly contradicts the very value which is intended to be sought. A short-term, particular realization of a value is sought at the price of a greater loss for the same value as a whole. This fact is not always clear in advance because a looking back towards the horizon of reality is necessary. The task of scientific moral theology is to prove in behavior which is condemned as immoral that it contradicts the very value which is expressly sought.[21] It must be cautioned that the reason for an act can prove to be commensurate only if the whole horizon is considered and not some particular aspect. Conscience has to do with the whole.

Notes

[1] The concept of nature in ethics does not mean a discoverable and unchangeable particular nature—for example, the nature of man in contrast to that of horses; but according to its origin in Greek philosophy, the concept is a counter concept

to positive human determination (thus *physis* is opposition to *thesis*). It is a human determination that traffic should not move on the left but on the right. This arbitrary determination stems from a necessity arising from nature that for the safety of participants in traffic some fixed order be determined. Cf. for the concept of the law of nature the very perceptive article of P. Antoine, *Conscience et loi naturelle*, 317 Etudes (1963): 162-83.

[2]Cf. J.T. Mangan "An Historical Analysis of the Principle of Double Effect." *Theological Studies* 10 (1949): 41-61. There is no substantial foundation for criticism of Mangan's conclusions by J. Ghoos, "L'acte a double effet—Etude de theologie positive" *Ephemerides Theologicae Lovanienses* 27 (1951): 30-52, esp. 31f.

[3]See above, pp. 20-24. ST II-II, q. 64, a. 7 in corpore: "Respondeo dicendum quod nihil prohibet unius actus esse duos effectus, quorum alter solum sit in intentione, alius vero sit praeter intentionem. Morales autem actus recipiunt speciem secundum id quod intenditur, non autem ab eo quod est praeter intentionem, cum sit per accidens, ut ex supra dictis pates. Ex actu igitur alicuius seipsum defendentis duplex effectus sequi potest: unus quidem conservatio propriae vitae; alius autem occisio invadentis. Actus igitur huiusmodi ex hoc quod intenditur conservatio propriae vitae, non habet rationem illicit: cum hoc sit cuilibet naturale quod se conservet in esse quantum potest. Potest tamen aliquis actus ex bona intentione proveniens illicitus reddi si non sit proportionatus fini. Et ideo si aliquis ad defendendum propriam vitam utatur maiori violentia quam oporteat, erit illicitum. Si vero moderate violentiam repellat, erit licita defensio."

[4] ST I-II, 1, a. 3; 18, 2-7. The *finis operis* is identical with the moral object of an act.

[5]M. Zalba, *Theologiae Moralis Compendium I* (Madrid, 1958) n. 10: "Finis . . . dividitur in: a) OPERIS (intrinsecum), ad quem res vel actio objective ex nature sue ordinatur (obiectum morale actionis) in morali hominum existimatione; . . Sic eleemosyna ordinatur ex se ad subveniendum pauperi." See also A. Vermeersch, *Theologiae Moralis Principia -Responsa -Consilia I* (Rome, 1926) n. 115: "*Finis est id propter quod aliquid fit*. Rationem autem agendi habere, proprium est entis rationalis. Quare finis dicitur primus in intentione; nihil magis voluntarium est, ac proin nihil magis morale. Finis operis seu internus, intrinsecus dicitur, ad quem opus per se, seu nature sue in morali existimatione tendit, ut v.g. internus finis eleemosynae est levamen indigentiae." The *moralis existimatio* commonly spoken of by moralists in their definition of *finis operis* does not mean a kind of vague judgment according to common sense, but a moral-judgment of the act—a judgment which includes a reference to the intention and thereby an implicit application of the principle of double effect as it has been above interpreted.

[6]Cf. A. van Rijen, "Daden met meerdere gevolgen en de leer over de bronnen der zedelijkheid:' in *Jaarboek 1960 van het Werkgenootschap van Kath. Theol. in Nederland* (Hilversum, 1961), 48-82, esp. 70; similarly, F. D'Hoogh "Over de afzonderlijke zedelijke handeling" *Collectanea Mechliniensia* 50 (1965): 356-53; 476-96 (especially 486).

[7]Cf. Thomas, op. cit. supra note 3, at ST I-II, 18, 10; 88, 5.

[8]Here it must be observed that the pair of concepts, "formal"— "material" in the teaching on cooperation with evil is used in a different sense than in the distinction made between "formal" and "material" sin. In a material sin the person acting is in good faith as to the objective permissibility of what he does. For example, he gives his friend candy when in reality it is poison. In formal sin there is complete consciousness of the actual character of transgression in the act,

and therefore the person acting is guilty. In the sense in which the terms are used in reference to cooperation, there can be complete consciousness of what one is doing and nonetheless the act may be material cooperation and not formal cooperation.

[9] If the principle of double effect appears purely formal in its nature and requires for the morality of an act only the presence of a commensurate reason which then makes indirect the evil accepted in exchange, yet the principle contains a content determined by ontology. Any reason whatsoever may be the reason for an act, and yet one may not conclude that any reason is in fact commensurate to the act. Conversely, the question what is evil may also be answered from ontology: it is the lack of completeness which could be present.

[10] The postulation of a necessary *judicium ultimo-practicum*, as it is commonly assumed by the scholastics, would contradict freedom and in the last analysis makes its rational explanation impossible. It is a false assumption that the fundamental form of free choice is the possibility of decision between several goods, among which one chooses that good which reason, working reciprocally with the will, declares to be the greatest. This explanation contains a logical circle which is disguised with difficulty. In reality there is a *libertas specificationis* not only when one compares several objects with one another, but also when one accepts or rejects a single good in itself. The first form, that is, *libertas specificationis inter plura*, is then only a conclusory application of the second *libertas specificationis quoad idem*. A No is naturally more than the pure preservation of an act of the will on the basis of a so-called *libertas exercitii* which under no circumstances can be designated as the fundamental form of the freedom of the will. I make this observation only because I know of no other satisfactory explanation of the freedom of the will in scholasticism.

[11] R. A. McCormick, "Notes on Moral Theology," *Theological Studies* 26 (1965): 603-608, has raised as an objection to my French article mentioned at the beginning of the notes that my explanation of the principle of double effect transgresses the boundaries of an objective ethics. Unfortunately in his account of my work he first confuses "commensurate reason" with any reason ("The formality under which the act is willed is determined by the proportionate reason for acting," (604) and then confuses it with a "reason proportionate to the original goal" (604); and he appears to conclude, contrary to my express statement, that any direct quantitative comparison of one value with another value may create a commensurate reason (606). Above all McCormick objects that I failed to distinguish in my article between "inner" and "outer" commensurate reasons. In reality I had set out this distinction on pages 360-61 as the distinction between *finis operis* and *finis operantis*. I return to it in Part VII of the present paper. His chief objection is that "this reasoning would destroy the concept of that which is intrinsically evil *ex obiecto*" (605). What I have said in Part III.2 above is a response to this objection. What was lacking in my French article was a failure to make explicit the identity of the morally evil and the intrinsically evil, that is, the evil *ex obiecto*. On this account I am grateful to McCormick for his criticism.

[12] Aristotle, *Nicomachean Ethics*, 2.6.15-17.

[13] Cf. F. D'Hoogh, op. cit. supra note 6, at 487.

[14] "... illicitum est, quod homo intendat occidere hominem, ut seipsum defendat. ..."

[15] See supra note 5.

[16]Thomas, *op. cit. supra* note 3, ST II-II, 64, 3 and 7.
[17]See the observations of L. Bender, "Ius in vita," *Angelicum* 30 (1953): 50-62.
[18]See supra note 3.
[19]Pius XI, *Casti connubii*, in *Acta Apostolicae Sedis* (hereafter *AAS*) (1930), 22:559: "At nulla profecto ratio, ne gravissima quidem, efficere potest, ut, quod intrinsece est contra naturam, id cum nature congruens et honestum fiat. Cum autem actus coniugu suapte nature proli generandae sit destinatus, qui, in eo exercendo, naturali hac eum vi atque virtute de industria destituunt, contra naturam agunt et turpe quid atque intrinsece inhonestum operantur."
[20]Cf. Pius XII, "Allocution to the Catholic Society of Italian Midwives" October 29, 1951, *AAS* (1951), 43:846: " . . . sottrarsi sempre e deliberatamente, senza un grave motivo, al suo primario dovere, sarebbe un peccare contro il senso stesso della vita coniugale. Da quella prestazione positive obbligatoria possono esimere, anche per lungo tempo, anzi per l'intera durata del matrimonio, seri motivi, come quelli che si hanno non di redo nella cosiddetta "indicazione" medica, eugenica, economica e sociale. Da ciò consegue che l'osservanza dei tempi infecondi può essere *lecita* sotto l'aspetto morale; e nelle condizioni menzionate è realmente tale. Se però non vi sono, secondo un giudizio ragionevole ed equo, simili gravi ragioni personal) o derivanti dalle circostanze esteriori, la volontà di evitare abitualmente la fecondità della loro undone, pur continuando a soddisfare pienamente la loro sensualità, non può derivare che da un falso apprezzamento della vita e da motivi estranei alle rette norme etiche.

The expression "serious motive" is somewhat inexact. The real meaning is that of a commensurate reason as in the passage of Pius XII in the "Allocution to the International Society of Hematologists," Sept. 12 1958, *AAS 50* (1958): 736.
[21]Richard McCormick, whom I thank for the translation of my article, has asked me to answer this question: Does the principle work also in the sexual area? Take the hypothetical case often used of a woman who is asked to commit adultery in order that her children may be rescued from a concentration camp. If her objective is the saving of the children, is her act contradictory to this objective? Or if a woman for whom prostitution is the only way to keep from starving, is she not like the man in extreme necessity who steals? Why is her act any more adultery than his act is theft? I would reply first that the difficulty is by no means special to the sexual area. We have the same problem in every kind of extortion or blackmail. For example, someone may be threatened with death if he refuses to take part in the falsification of a document. The question must be answered in relation to the whole context. Does life or freedom have any value if in the end one is forced to give up all human rights and in principle be exposed to every extortion? This would be in contradiction to the very values of life and freedom. For extortion always works after the pattern of the salami, one slice of which is taken after the other: it is a menace not only for a part but also for the whole. As for the woman who believes that prostitution is the only way to keep from starving, she is in reality also the victim of extortion. By acceding to an unjust extortion one can never really save anything in the long run.

The Absoluteness of Moral Terms
Joseph Fuchs, S.J.

Christ's mission was not to establish a new moral order, new moral laws. Nor was it His primary intent to teach a moral doctrine corresponding to creation. The significance of His coming was rather to redeem sinful mankind, to transform him interiorly by grace, to make him one who believes and loves. Loving faith must and will bear fruit; it must express and verify itself in morally correct conduct, i.e., by doing what is right, thus giving witness to the truth by "doing the truth"—*testimonium veritati*. Under the dynamic of faith and love, the Christian is concerned not only with living in faith and love, but also with carrying them out by a way of life proper to "man as Christian." Indeed, faith, love, and salvation do not depend upon the rectitude of the norms of living that are basic to one's life practice. Yet faith and love are not genuine, if there is no effort to manifest through one's life practice the "right" mode of life, i.e., corresponding to the reality of human-christian existence. Thus, under the dynamic of faith and love, the problem of the absoluteness of moral norms arises in this present age of "uncertainty" and "revolution." Have we perhaps overstressed the absoluteness of our system of moral norms, and precisely for this reason failed to achieve the "right" life practice as an expression of our faith and love? Or are we perhaps to the point of renouncing the absoluteness of an inherited system of moral norms, and so running the risk of faith and love no longer manifesting themselves in the "right" day-to-day manner?

No small number of convinced Christians are allergic to "absolute" norms; not indeed to the possibility of "right," "objective" and therefore "absolutely" binding judgment in concrete instances, and consequently of moral imperatives, but to "universally binding" and in *this* sense absolute norms of moral action. They make their judgment on experiential grounds, so that what was yesterday an absolute, i.e., presented as always and without exception right, must today yield to other insights. They fear that the so-called absolutes, or universally valid norms characteristic of a static world-view, cannot be absolute for men of a dynamic world-view. They hold that the cultural fact of the discovery of moral norms in the past cannot be taken as a final conclusion, rather, that man must ever address himself anew to this fact, to examine the conclusions reached, to deepen and enlarge and adduce new experiences and evaluations. Their great concern is that abstract and therefore timeless and in *this* sense "absolute" norms do not perhaps take due account of the times; i.e. are not sufficiently realistic and responsive to the concrete mode of reality represented by (redeemed) creation; and that consequently they can obscure rather than illuminate the "objective" and in *this* sense "absolute" task of the present day. That this concern for relevant behavior on the part of the believing and loving Christian and for absolute fidelity to the order of (redeemed) creation in its concrete manifestations is genuinely "Catholic" is unquestionable.

Other convinced Catholics incline toward a view just as typically "Catholic." They fear that with the "dissolution" of so-called absolute ordinances and norms, in the sense of "universally valid" and "timeless" truths, truth itself would be lost. They think that if "absoluteness" understood as "immutability" and "universal validity," yields to the principle of change and historical conditioning, faithfulness to reality, i.e., to (redeemed) creation, will no longer determine concrete action, as the expression of faith and love, but will be replaced by a relativistic subjectivism. They presume that deviation from absoluteness (i.e., timelessness and immutability) might imply also a swerving from absoluteness understood as objectivity oriented to the reality of the (redeemed) created order.

Basically, both tendencies share the same interest: the believing-loving Christian must concern himself with recognizing the *absolutely* valid, or that which always corresponds *objectively* to the concrete human (Christian) reality in a moral matter. For this is the Will of God based on creation and redemption—so that what is objectively right partake somehow in the absoluteness of God. The problem is whether and in what degree the absolute in the sense of the objective as applied to universal or universally valid norms is conceivable or in any sense guaranteed. When we address ourselves to this question, we do so in the conviction that global solutions of the problem are not solutions; nuanced consideration is required. Neither the opinion that love should be the sole moral absolute, nor the conception of natural moral law as an all-embracing set of invariable norms is satisfactory, although there is some truth in both these points of view. It will not escape the informed reader that the problematic thus presented is of importance not only for (Catholic) circles within the Church—particularly in the present climate of "uncertainty"— but also for dialogue with those non-Catholic Christians who are experiencing and dealing with the same problematic on a broad scale, and with all men concerned with genuine morality. For God will judge Christians, Jews and pagans alike according to their works (cf. Rom. 2, 9-11) the righteousness of which they can know fundamentally in their "hearts" (cf. Rom. 2, 15). Accordingly, the following considerations are limited to the shaping of life within the world, i.e., innerworldly, to actions relating man and his world.[1]

I. Absolute: Universally Valid or Objective

"Absoluteness" in moral imperatives is directly opposed, obviously, to all arbitrary judgment and to all relativism, and thereby positively affirms the objectivity, grounded in human reality itself. The real problem, we repeat, lies in determining to what degree the absolute, in the sense of the non-arbitrary but objective, is comprehensible and guaranteed in the case of universally valid norms. We are accustomed to having moral ordinances placed before us in the guise of norms purporting to be universally valid: in *Revelation* (Holy Scripture), in the teaching of the Church, in the formulated tenets of the *natural moral law, conscience* finds itself confronted with moral imperatives in the form of moral norms. In what follows we shall consider what (degree) of the absolute character of norms is implied in the individual instances respectively.

Norms in Holy Scripture

Moral imperatives in Holy Scripture are of the greatest interest, for God's word has absolute value, since He is The Absolute. And since He speaks, therefore, via human concepts and so in terms of universals, Christianity with good reason has been inclined to understand the moral precepts found in Holy Scripture as "universal," ever valid and unchangeable norms, and in this sense, as "absolute." On the other hand, God's speaking in human mode signifies that the moral imperatives appearing in Holy Scripture should not be interpreted as direct divine "dictates." Thus we are inevitably faced not only with the question as to which moral imperatives are actually to be found in Holy Scripture, but also with the question by which hermeneutic rules they are to be understood and evaluated.[2] There is no doubt that here moral theology will have to go to school to contemporary exegesis, to avoid lapsing into unauthorized good-will reading.

Holy Scripture was never meant to be a handbook on morality: consequently it may not be so used. Inasmuch as it speaks of God's ways with mankind, it must speak also of man's behavior—his religio-moral behavior—toward God. Indeed, since Scripture is concerned with the conversion and salvation of the sinner, and therefore with his personal transformation, statements regarding the religio-moral situation of man are central to the Bible. Nevertheless, it is not the particular moral imperatives which have this central position, but the fundamental imperative of fidelity and obedience to God, of the following of Christ, of life according to faith and baptism or, as with John, according to faith and love. But these moral-religious imperatives are transcendental, that is, they refer to the personal human being as a whole and not to specific moral conduct. And even though Holy Scripture speaks also of particular attitudes and values—goodness, mildness, mercy, justice, modesty—these are still not "operative" norms of behavior, since it has yet to be determined which actions are to be regarded as just, modest and kind. Certainly, Scripture knows "operative" norms of conduct as well—a few at least. The question is precisely with reference to these, insofar as the absoluteness of moral norms is the point at issue.

We shall limit ourselves to the New Testament. References there to concrete moral behavior, norms of activity, are relatively few; but these few are important. The critical question is: In what sense are they absolute—in the sense of objective—in the sense of objective, non-arbitrarily grounded imperatives, or more than that, universal norms admitting of no exception? The answer to this question is not altogether easy.

The Christian centuries have tried earnestly to understand the demands of the Sermon on the Mount (Mt. 5-7). No Christian doubts their absolute validity, absolute to be understood in the sense of objective. The question is: absolute validity, as what—as universal norms, or as models for the behavior of the believing and loving citizens of God's kingdom who will be ready for such modes of conduct, perhaps, under determined conditions not individually specified by the

Lord? The latter interpretation seems probable from the context and manner of expression. In recent years there has been renewed and heated discussion of the Lord's word about the *indissolubility of marriage* (Mt. 19, 3-10). Regarding the scope of this word, it is asked: Is it a question of a moral imperative or of something more? Is the moral imperative to be understood as a norm to be followed as universal practice or as an ideal? The discussion makes at least this much clear: The acceptance of an absolute in the sense of an objectively valid moral affirmation in Scripture does not necessarily involve recognizing it as an absolute in the sense of a universal norm.

It should be noted first of all that while Paul ascribes to the Lord definite sayings regarding moral behavior (indissolubility of marriage: I Cor. 7, 10f.) and attributes others to his own personal understanding in the Holy Spirit (virginity: 1 Cor. 7, 12.25), he *presupposes* that most of the behavioral norms of which he speaks are valid. This is particularly to be inferred from the many ordinances in which he accepts the moral wisdom of the "good" men of his time, both Jew and Gentile; one thinks, among other things, of the tables of domestic rules and the catalogue of vices. On the one hand, this means that Paul does not present himself as a teacher of moral living, still less as a teacher of specifically Christian norms of conduct; what he does have to transmit is something quite different from a moral code. On the other hand, his having assumed a given morality can lead us to consider whether such a morality, at least in many of its regulations, is not historically and culturally conditioned. It could scarcely be supposed that the Stoic, Judaic and Diaspora-Judaic ethos which Paul represents was in all respects a timeless ethos. If it is self-evident to us today that the Pauline directives concerning woman's position in marriage, society and the Church (I Cor. 11, 2-16; 14, 34-36; Eph. 5, 22-24; Col. 3, 18; 1 Tim. 2, 11-15) are to be regarded as conditioned by his times, reflecting Jewish tradition and the position of woman in the culture in which Paul and his contemporaries lived, we must indeed ask ourselves with what criterion we decide that those directives which Paul seeks to validate, even theologically, are historically conditioned and thus not absolute (i.e. universal), that they hold as absolute in the objective sense rather for the age whose ideas on the position of women they reflect. Consequently, such directives cannot be normative for a period in which the social position of women is essentially different. Holy Scripture itself gives us no criteria for such a judgment, but it comes from our knowledge of the difference in the social position of women in various ages together with our own insight into moral imperatives which arises out of the various social situations. This same power of discernment will permit us perhaps to make a judgment—at least in principle—as to which suits the nature of women in society better, and hence the moral ideal, the social position of women in Paul's cultural milieu or that of women in our cultural milieu—along with corresponding moral demands.

By analogy with the instance of woman's position in marriage, society and the Church, a further question inevitably arises, whether the possibility of similar considerations regarding other behavioral norms to be found in the Pauline corpus are to be absolutely excluded—on the theoretical level at least, especially since the criteria for such reflections are not provided us by Holy Scripture itself. For the affirmation that certain explicitly mentioned modes of conduct ban one from the kingdom of God, from companionship with Christ and from the life given by the Spirit remains true if these modes were to be judged negatively, in accordance with the moral evaluation proper to the age and accepted by Paul. Paul therefore did not teach such evaluation as thesis, but admitted it as hypothesis in his doctrinal statement on the Christian mystery of salvation. Thus, it remains to be established whether in Paul's cultural milieu, because of the actual conviction of the morally high-ranking segment of society, every "honorable" Christian had to share exactly this conviction, or whether this conviction was the only objectively justified one and was not based on definite options.

(In Paul we have actually a model for "Christian" discovery of moral norms. With him such discovery derives neither from Christ alone nor from the Old Testament alone. It occurs within an existing culture and as a consequence of its established moral values. It draws from Jewish tradition and from Greek popular philosophy, just as it carries along the culture in which Christianity took root. This does not exclude the fact that Paul himself also reflects upon the values he found already present, as, for example, the social position of women, and that, in particular cases, he himself independently—in the Holy Spirit—recommends practices like virginity or that he appeals to the word of the Lord).

The foregoing considerations obviously do not permit us to conclude that the norms of behavior found in the New Testament are no longer valid today. Only, we must reflect whether the criterion of their possible absolute (i.e., universal) validity is Holy Scripture itself, whether it can be and is intended to be.[3] The moral behavioral norms in Scripture are directed to actual persons of a definite era and culture. Hence their character of absoluteness would not signify primarily universality, but objectivity; and the latter can denote either the objectively right evaluation in a particular culturally conditioned human situation or necessary conformity to the moral views of the morally elite in a given society.

Norms of the Ecclesial Community

Neither from Christ nor from Paul or John has the Church inherited a system of moral norms. On the other hand, the ecclesial community—how could it be otherwise?—always maintained definite moral norms and passed them on to later generations. But in this connection it may by no means be said that there was ever in the Church a definitive or in all respects universal code of precepts. Nevertheless, the Church community had "their" morality which, even if it did not derive purely from Revelation, was regarded as being connected with or compatible with Christian belief. This morality—as being the morality of the Christian community—was "Christian" morality. Insofar as it had been handed down, it was a more or less codified morality, which just for this reason was lived in the *one* Church in *different* cultures and epochs. Naturally, this brief exposition is a simplification. But it enables us to understand how the Church, unlike Paul, begins not only to set forth dogmatically particular moral concepts—indissolubility of marriage (word of the Lord) and virginity (Paul's opinion, in the Holy Spirit)—but *in principle* the whole compass of the morality practiced by the Christian community which Paul had not taught but rather "presupposed," as also did the Church *after* Paul with regard to many questions. While Paul, earlier, expressed himself "in obliquo" and hypothetically on moral questions, the Church slowly began to do this "in recto" and dogmatically. The Church teaches in rebus fidei *et morum* and indeed, as she repeatedly declared during Vatican Council II, also in regard to moral questions on which she had no explicit revelation. Now the question: If the

Church addresses herself thematically and dogmatically to moral questions, have we then pronouncements that are true universals? Is the claim of absoluteness for the norms transmitted by the Church a claim of universal norms? Does the Church give us thereby a system of universal morally valid norms which God has not given us in Holy Scripture?

In general, then, unlike Paul, the Church "teaches" norms of moral conduct. Why, really? The answer often given runs: Because the Church has to teach the way to salvation and true morality is the way to salvation. This answer might be considered valid if taken *cum grano salis*. For ultimately there is the question whether marriage, for example, is to be understood and lived according to Congolese or Western European style; surely not an unimportant cultural and ethical question, but not in itself determinative of salvation. Still the matter admits of a different interpretation. The manner in which faith and love—which do determine salvation!—are expressed in daily life, by premarital abstinence or premarital intercourse, for example, is not a matter of totally free choice. And since man must strive to incarnate his faith and love in the "true" way of human beings, the Church assists him by her "teaching." Clearly, this answer also does not entirely satisfy. In any case, it remains true that the materiality of culturally and ethically right mastery of the concrete reality of life—education, economy, technology, sexuality, etc.—are not directly concerned with salvation, or union with God; only faith and love, *together with the effort* to incarnate this materiality in the "true" way in the reality of life are thus concerned. That the material mode of this Incarnation can represent only a *secundarium*, already makes it reasonable that within certain limits moral pluralism might well be possible. If, for example, faith and love have to be expressed in the maintenance of the "right" social position of woman, then the concrete expression in the Pauline conception and in the twentieth century Western European conceptions must (!) be regarded as necessarily differing from each other. Yet the Christian community is obliged to see to it, that moral behavior as an expression of faith and love does not come down to fulfilling one's own wishes, as also it must not fail to manifest the unconditional character of faith and love by unconditionality in stating moral precepts. However, it could follow from what has been said that this quality of absoluteness does not represent primarily the universality of a norm, but an anti-thesis to arbitrary judgment; or, positively stated, orientation toward concrete human (total) reality, and in this sense, "objectivity," "truth." This objectivity-truth is achieved, on the one hand, through right understanding of the revealed word of God, insofar as it contains morally significant affirmations; on the other hand, through the right moral understanding of man's concrete reality, in which connection, obviously, the light of revelation and the moral understanding of man are not to be viewed as two completely unrelated possibilities.

With respect to norms of moral behavior, the light of the Gospel does not manifest itself in formally expressed statements alone. Rather there is also the possibility suggested by Vatican II in the Constitution on the Church in the Modern World, when reference is made to the necessity of judging contingent realities in the world of men in light of the Gospel.[4] Edward Schillebeeckx alludes to this statement;[5] nevertheless, he is of the opinion that the Christian, on the basis of his faith, can more easily assert negatively the incompatibility of a given social situation with his faith than discover positively how the situation might be changed. Karl Rahner has spoken, in the sense of Vatican II of a moral faith-instinct.[6] Maurizio Flick and Zoltán Alszeghy have pursued in greater detail the question of the significance of the Gospel— which itself gives no directives—for moral judgment of contingent human realities.[7] They maintain that it is possible, especially for a believer, to draw "an objective *picture* of revealed reality" on the basis of the content of revelation. Inasmuch as the development of dogma has not rarely been indebted to such an "objective picture," a great deal might be gained also for the proper mastering of concrete human reality via such an "objective picture." However, they are also of the opinion that actual problems, those, for example, pertaining to development and progress, can find direct solutions neither in the Gospel and faith, nor in theology, but only in a Christian ideology, which, of course, must be approached in terms of the eventual possibility of a critique by the Gospel and theology (and their "objective picture of revealed reality"). Only on this condition can a "political theology" venture an attempt to make the Gospel and faith effective for the reality of the world.[8] The "imperatives,"[9] known or determined corresponding to a "political theology," do not follow directly from faith and the Gospel, therefore, but only from an ethical interpretation ("political ethics"). And this ethics is "human" ethics; theological only to the extent that it has been projected by the believer as an imperative of a Christian theology which, in turn, depends in any case on an "objective picture of revealed reality."[10] It need scarcely be said that the imperatives of a Christian theology so projected are not absolutes in the sense of universalia. They represent the attempt to be as objectively relevant as possible to given realities through man's reflection in light of the Gospel, as described above; they are not to be arbitrary precepts, therefore, but the most objective possible, and in this reduced sense, absolutes.

The assistance of the Holy Spirit has been promised to the endeavors of the Church. Inasmuch as the Church, to a far greater extent than Holy Scripture, has begun to address herself directly and dogmatically to moral questions, she becomes, in a much higher degree than the Scripture, concretely important because of the assistance of the Spirit of Christ. Some concepts of moral theology create the impression that the Holy Spirit slowly began to impart via the Church what He had not conveyed through Scripture—a vast collection of moral behavioral norms proclaimed for the whole world and for all time; absolute, in the sense of universally valid norms. However, under this aspect, the Church is seen often in an all too spiritualized way; how very much the Spirit is merely "incarnated" in the Church is overlooked; in other words, how very human the Church is and remains despite the assistance of the Spirit. She arrives at norms of moral conduct only by way of a long process of learning to understand and to evaluate. And this comprehension and evaluation are accomplished not only by the hierarchy of the ecclesial community who, it may be, ultimately provide a decisive orientation, but by the Church as a whole, within the community of believers— where, not rarely, a special role falls to the theologians. It is far from true that a moral question is submitted to the pastors of the Church, so that in solitary reflection they can reach an authoritative decision. Before there is question of "decision" the "teaching" Church is in all instances a "learning" Church. The Spirit assists the *whole process* of teaching and leading in the Church; i.e., comprehending, discovering, evaluating, mutual listening, deciding.[11] He guarantees that error, which in human comprehension-discovery-evaluation-listening-deciding, can never be absolutely excluded, will not become in the end an essential component of the Church. Will not, perhaps, the same ecclesial community or a particular cultural group within it—

pluralistic, therefore—occasionally begin to experience and evaluate in a new and different way, regarding specific points? In this connection it is noteworthy that in the two thousand years of the Church seemingly no definitive doctrinal decision on moral questions has been made, at least insofar as these would be related to natural law, without being at the same time revealed. On the other hand, this is not to say that the non-definitive authoritative orientations of the Church are meaningless, as if one might ignore them, oblivious to the fact that they also come under the assistance of the Spirit of Christ abiding with the Church. Hence a certain "presumption" of truth must be granted them. Yet one may not see in such instances any conclusive legislation or doctrinal laying down of an ethical norm, the validity of which would be guaranteed by the Holy Spirit. Declarations by the Church *in rebus morum* can be understood in all cases as an attempt to formulate "absolute," i.e. non-arbitrary, but objective imperatives, properly conformed to a concrete human reality and expressed in terms of a *presumptively* valid ecclesial orientation. If, on the contrary, such pronouncements had the assurance of infallibility, they could be set forth as universally valid norms, guaranteed to hold true always, everywhere and without exception. But even in such a case there would have to be a reservation; for it can be imagined and probably demonstrated if need be, that a strict behavioral norm stated as a universal, contains *unexpressed* conditions and qualifications which as such limit its universality.

The Church arrives at moral pronouncements—in the sphere of natural law morality, at least—via man's reflection on himself. But man is not a static being, whose nature is incapable of development. Furthermore, man is not by nature a Christian and a member of the Church. Thus, new questions will come up again, because of new experiences, insights and evaluations, therefore, in a new light and a changed culture. Even Christian man is obliged to question in retrospect, to go back to the past in order to find out what was once believed in the Church—even authoritatively, perhaps—about the right way to embody faith and love concretely. And more than this, without losing contact with the Christian wisdom of the past, he must always be thinking out once again various questions that affect his life, one time this way, one time that way.[12] It cannot be that the Christian and ecclesial past (from which year to which year?) enjoyed the prerogative of finding the (non-revealed) "truth" about moral behavior, while future Christians would have only the task of recording, confirming, applying the "truth" of the past—conclusive, absolute and universal in the strict sense—without advertence to really new problems never before reflected upon or resolved. Furthermore, it happens not infrequently, that old problems presenting themselves in a new guise are, at bottom, new problems. Also, it is scarcely conceivable that all Church traditions or decisions concerning moral behavioral norms would be in the full sense timeless and unconditioned, i.e., absolute, in the sense that they would be completely explicit and not in some respect conditioned either by fixed ideas or value judgments or by man's limited understanding of himself.[13] For example the opposition of the Church in the past to religious freedom is understandable if religious freedom and indifferentism are equated conceptually. Moreover, it is today an historical fact that the sexual morality handed down in the Church came under the influence of certain non-Christian (Jewish and pagan) evaluations in the first Christian centuries and is conditioned by them. The Church is not a "spiritualized" reality, thinking, speaking and existing in a vacuum, unrelated to any actual culture, and under such conditions devising norms of moral conduct that are in the purest sense "universal." But if norms of conduct can include culturally and historically conditioned elements, only then is there a possibility that they can be expressed in a manner that will respond to concrete human reality; i.e., be objective, and in this sense, absolute. ("Can" means that even in the moral judgment of a real situation, the Church could err.)

The Natural Moral Law

If Holy Scripture and the Church do not provide a system of universal moral norms, one expects this at least from the moral law of nature (natural moral law, natural moral order, order of creation, natural law). A well-defined concept of natural law underlies this expectation. Natural law is understood to be the summary of precepts which are based on the given and unvarying nature of man as such and which can be deduced from it. In his critical study, "The Natural Law Yesterday and Today,"[14] E. Chiavacci terms this concept "preceptive." According to this view, "immutable" nature points out to the man who "reads" and "understands" her what right behavior can and must be once and for all in the different areas of reality. A concept of this sort ends in a codifiable summation of the numerous precepts of natural law, which, because rooted in an unchangeable nature, is unvarying and universal. Thus it is maintained that all these precepts (norms) are to be applied in actual life situations appropriately, to be sure, but unequivocally.

This notion of a static-universal system of norms is valid to the extent that it believes man is and always will be man (tautology!) and that he must always conduct himself rightly—that is, as man. But this quite accurate perception does not entail as a necessary consequence a static-universal system of moral norms. The state of being man does not, *in the first place*, exclude that the human state may differ in different epochs and cultures, just as it is actualized in different individuals and life situations without placing man's nature in question. Against this assertion of the unchangeableness of human nature stands Aquinas' affirmation of its mutability.[15] The two positions are not in conflict if man along with his component structures and his ways even of being human, together with their structures, are differentiated rather than divided. Only there must be no attempt to distinguish what precisely is changeable from what is unchangeable. For even that which essentially constitutes man, that which therefore belongs to his nature unalterably, as also his permanent structures, is basically mutable. Mutability belongs to man's immutable essence; irrevocably, man is man (tautology!). To be sure, a priori, some essential elements of man's nature can be identified: body-soul unity, personality, accountability, interpersonality; while one cannot say with equal a priori validity, respecting other components of existential man, whether they belong necessarily and unchangeably to human nature. But even these a priori and inalienable elements of man's nature subsist in it in variable modes, a fact which can be correspondingly significant for moral behavior.

The question of mutability-immutability, secondly, is connected with the historicity of man.[16] History is possible only in virtue of the mutability of that which remains ever the same. Now man is an historical being; not only in terms of the successive variations of past, present and future, but above all in the sense that man himself designs and brings to realization the plot-lines of his given existence and its progress on into the future. He has to actualize what is sketched out for himself as possibility. In the process of his self-realization, he continually modifies his existence. In his spiritual and bodily aspects and his external relationships (environmental change), he becomes to an ever increasing degree a different person. Morality would have him live rightly the actual man, i.e., the man (humanity) of each actual moment, the present with the past enfolded within it and the projective future: that is, starting from each present reality he should "humanize" himself and his world. Whatever leads to our unfolding, in the fullest and best sense of the word, is good.[17]

Mutability and historicity, thirdly, are connected with the fact that man is person and nature in one. Person and nature can be placed counter to each other, so that nature expresses the intrapersonal given of man and his world, while person represents the I, possessing and shaping itself in terms of the given nature. However, one's personhood also is *given* and in *this* sense it is nature, indeed the determining element of one's humanness, and in this sense of human nature. The nature of man consists above all in his being a person (i.e., possessing *ratio*). Nature is not understood as human, unless it is thought of as a *personal* nature. Thus, it is not enough to say nature (for example, sexuality) "belongs to" the human person.[18] For then it would be possible to understand nature (sexuality) as non-personal;[19] hence one could speak of the meaning of sexuality, rather than of the meaning of *human* sexuality and make the consideration of this meaning (i.e., sexuality) a moral problem for the person reflecting upon his sexuality. The term "law of nature" is not merely open to misunderstanding; it frequently is responsible for it. It would be possible and perhaps more meaningful to speak of "person" as moral norm instead of "nature."[20] But then there would be danger that "personhood" would be viewed too one-sidedly; that is, with practically no consideration of nature, provided person and nature are to be thus differentiated. In any case, nature, considered intrapersonally, cannot be the norm of moral behavior. Rather man is essentially person and has to understand himself therefore as person—"in a human nature"—and achieve self-realization according to this self-understanding. Self-realization entails that he himself must discover the available possibilities for his action and his development and determine on the basis of his present understanding of himself which of these possibilities are "right," "reasonable," "human" (in the full and positive sense of these words), and so contributive to "human progress." In this way he arrives simultaneously at the moral judgment of a concrete situation and the affirmation of moral norms.

In reality, this is tantamount to the traditional statement that the *lex naturalis* is a *lex interna* (or *indita*), not a *lex externa* (or *scripta*). The preceptive understanding of natural law as a summary of precepts conformable to nature is not quite in keeping with this traditional concept; for, thus, a *lex interna* becomes furtively a *lex externa* resembling general positive or positively formulated laws. The *lex interna* signified the possibility and duty of man (humanity) to discern, as he himself evaluates himself, what in concrete "human" action is capable of being—inasmuch as man is essentially person-reason—and what can be affirmed propositionally in the problem area of "behavioral norms." Here we are obviously dealing with moral perceptions of an absolute nature. But it is equally obvious that absolute means at least primarily correspondence of behavior to personal human reality; objectivity, therefore, and not, or at least not primarily, universal validity.

Conscience

As explained according to traditional manuals, the function of conscience was the application of the moral law, or its norms, to the concrete case, a formulation founded on a "preceptive" understanding of the moral law, oriented to the specificity of positive law. The traditional statement has, naturally, some validity; in forming the dictates of conscience, we never begin at pure zero. We always bring to our actions existing orientations and norms. Yet conscience—as judgment of concrete action—is not only and not on the deepest level, the application of general norms. Knowledge of the essential function of conscience casts light also on the essence and meaning of behavioral norms.[21]

The function of conscience is to help man, as agent, make his action authentic (i.e., self-realizing). Hence conscience ought to assist action toward objectivity, toward truth, in conformity with the concrete human reality. It is necessary *above all* that action be conformable to the evaluating judgment (of conscience) with respect to the given concrete moment and its options. For this judgment itself belongs at the moment of action to the concrete human reality; it is, so to speak, its final form, so that the agent is enabled to realize himself only by fidelity to this judgment (mediating truth to him, yet erring occasionally). Clearly, *for this very reason*, the agent must strive for objectivity in forming this judgment regarding the concrete reality; i.e., that ratio which makes the judgment may be *recta ratio* (The terms ratio-recta ratio derive from scholastic tradition. Here they signify, rather than specifically discursive thinking, an evaluative observing-understanding-judging, which can also occur "intuitively.") Now the behavioral norms of the moral law should also be recta ratio; only insofar as they are recta ratio, are they behavioral norms and can they, as such, objectively have a meaning for the function of conscience as recta ratio in action. The difference between judgment of conscience and norm of action consists basically in the fact that man with his evaluating ratio forms a moral judgment of his conduct *either* at the moment of action and in reference to it *or* in advance and not with reference to the actuality of the particular event as such. In terms of the concrete situation, then, it is clear that the norm of action cannot represent an exhaustive judgment of the actual reality, and that the actor must judge in light of his conscience to what degree a norm of conduct corresponds morally to a given situation.

Insofar as only the ratio (recta ratio) of conscience judges the reality ultimately and comprehensively in terms of the concrete element in it that is to be actualized, it exercises merely an auxiliary function, as compared to the ratio (recta ratio) of behavioral norms. As a consequence, the *decisive* aspect of such norms, is that they are *recta* ratio, thus their objectivity; to the extent that they are objective, they are absolute. Of course, they can be behavioral *norms* only insofar as they are discernible *in advance*; therefore they are necessarily abstract and in some way generalized. On this point further consideration is called for.

II. The Absoluteness of Human Behavioral Norms

The title of this section requires clarification. Our previous reflection on behavioral norms in Holy Scripture, Church teaching and natural law, should have made it evident that the affirmations in Scripture and in the teaching of the Church on absolute norms of behavior are not as definitive as might be supposed, particularly if the absoluteness denoted is to be primarily synonymous with universality. In addition to this, Christian behavioral norms, in their material content, are not *distinctively* Christian norms, that would hold only for Christians, but "human" norms, i.e. corresponding to the (authentic) humanness of man, which we have traditionally called norms of the natural moral law, or moral law of nature.[22] These observations suggest the need for further reflection on the absoluteness of moral norms of behavior considered as *human* (related to natural law), hence, insofar as they can be discerned by man himself as *recta ratio*.

The Human as *Recta Ratio*

We shall continue to employ the traditional term *recta ratio*. The human is in it, that which is humanly right. Whatever is not recta ratio is necessarily non-human, not worthy of man, antithetic to a steadily advancing "humanization." Recta ratio does not mean innate discernment or moral truth, "inscribed" somehow, somewhere. Hence it does not denote a norm of conduct "inscribed in our nature," at least not in the sense that one "could read off" a moral regulation from a natural reality. The "nature" upon which the moral law is inscribed is preeminently and formally nature as ratio, but only, of course, as recta ratio. From this viewpoint, the preferred expression would probably be that of Paul in Romans: the moral law is "engraved on the heart" (Rom. 2,15).[23] Apart from this, realities of the natural order, ratio excepted, can neither provide a basis for, nor affirm, any "moral" laws. Considered positively, then, the task of homo-ratio in "discovering" or "projecting" behavioral norms consists in understanding man himself, his own total reality, together with his world, in order to assess the significance of the alternatives for action available to him and so arrive at a moral affirmation. There will be some a priori and hence self-evident affirmations: for example, that man has to act responsibly and in an inter-personal and social context. Others will presuppose experience; for instance, conduct as related to the life of another or sexual behavior. In this regard some things will be immediately evident, e.g., that there should be respect for life (it may not be destroyed at will), that sexuality has to be viewed in relation to a particular culture, etc. Still other affirmations call for long and perhaps varied experience, until man understands the value of different possibilities for the realization of genuine humanness. How mankind and the Christian centuries as well have striven in the most diverse ways to come to an evaluative understanding of sexuality and marriage and their actualization!

Criteria of Evaluation

Do criteria for the evaluating ratio exist? A prime criterion is obviously correspondence of behavior, hence also of the behavioral norms to be discovered to the "meaning," in general, of being man and to the significance of particular givens; i.e., sexuality and marriage as *human* givens.[24] It is probable that penetration of meaning occurs far less frequently on a priori or metaphysical ground than has often been supposed. It implies varied experience on the part of man (humanity) and a long apprenticeship in unprejudiced weighing of these manifold experiences. And it is not only the "meaning" itself of experienced realities that constitutes a criterion for the evaluating ratio, but also practical knowledge of the outcomes and consequences which determined modes of conduct can have—and this under all kinds of presuppositions,[25] for example, in the economic sphere, in social life or in the area of sexuality and marriage. Of itself experience yields no norms of conduct; assessment of its outcome is required to enable us to perceive in which direction to seek or not to seek—genuine human self-realization. A basic criterion for true penetration of human reality, as well as for a just appraisal of experience, is to be found in the interpersonality of the human person.[26] The conduct of individual persons in the different areas of life has to be scrutinized in terms of its interpersonal significance and implications. No one is a self-enclosed individual; each one lives as a person in relation to persons. Humanness essentially involves inter-human relations. Technological and economic progress, for instance, cannot be assessed in the concrete as "human values," unless interpersonal and social aspects are fundamentally involved in the judgment.

To arrive at a behavioral norm regarding, for example, premarital intercourse or birth control, a whole *complex* of factors obviously has to be considered. (It should not be necessary to add that this takes place in an *explicit* manner only in scientific reflection.) What must be determined is the significance of the action as value or non-value for the individual, for interpersonal relations and for human society, in connection, of course, with the total reality of man and his society and in view of his whole culture. Furthermore, the *priority* and *urgency* of the different values implied must be weighed.[27] By this procedure, man as assessor (the evaluating human society) arrives at a judgment, tentatively or with some measure of certitude, as to which mode of behavior might further man's self-realization and self-development. As soon as this judgment has been made, it is recognized as a moral norm by the ever-present conviction reflected in it, that this human action is bound absolutely to recta ratio. Simultaneously asserted is the fact that the many values to be considered according to their priority and urgency, or non-values, do not, strictly speaking, belong as yet to the moral sphere; that is, they are not as yet moral precepts, but are, in this connection, pre-moral. Only the all-embracing view and total appraisal which, as such, determine the mode of action that is good for men, lead to a *moral* statement. This implies that one or other aspect of an action cannot of itself and without regard for the remaining factors determine the morality of an action.

Relativism?

Facts—social, cultural, technological, economic, etc.— change. Man's experiences, i.e., those of human societies, likewise change, on the basis of changing data. Evaluations also, the mind's grasp of human realities, and self-understanding can be altered. One thinks, for example, of the efforts toward an expanded conception of marriage and sex in the milieu of the Catholic Church in the recent past. And in the process, man (that is, human society), oriented toward development and progress, also changes himself. All these manifold possible—and actual—alterations have to be brought into the moral judgment of human conduct. Such "new" aspects could call for action, which, independent of such aspects would be out of the question; or they might exclude a course of action which would be commanded under other circumstances. If the minimum family income set decades ago is linked to certain social and economic factors, if the institution of private property in our present economic, social and political situation must be viewed as differing in its concrete signification from previous decades or the Middle Ages, if conceptual grasp and interpersonal and social experience in the realm of family and marriage necessarily codetermine behavior in this area, then on principle corresponding "changes" regarding the "right" human behavior in *other* spheres of life cannot be ruled out. Under this aspect, behavior norms have, at least theoretically, a provisory character.

Changes in the data, differences in concepts and experiences—or even interpretations—occur not only in successive cultures, if not, in cases of actual pluralism,[28] within the same culture. This is readily understandable if heterogeneous economic, social or political situations admit, respectively, of different modes of behavior. But what if varying experiences and concepts and varying self-images of men in different societies or groups lead to different options and so to a diversity of statements on behavior norms in relation to similar bodies of facts? One might point out, perhaps, that in many cases a given self-concept and a given viewpoint and form of a reality, e.g., marriage in, let us say, a certain African tribe, may not "in themselves" correspond in all respects to recta ratio. Then, of course, the question arises, whether another form of marriage, presupposing another culture, may legitimately be imposed upon men belonging to an endemic culture—by missionaries, for instance[29]—provided the indigenous culture itself has not changed by a rather gradual process, and provided it admits of a "human" form of marriage. But might it not be assumed also that on the basis of dissimilar experiences, a *heterogeneous* self-concept and *varying* options and evaluations on the part of man (humanity) "projecting" himself into his future in human fashion—secundum rectam rationem—are entirely possible, and that these options and evaluations within the chosen system postulate varied forms of behavior? Who would expect human individuals, groups or societies to arrive at self-understanding and values exempt from all one-sidedness or merely from incompleteness? There recta ratio which is to guide our conduct has to allow for such conditionality, essentially connected with humanness; without it man de facto does not exist. Moreover, must it not be supposed that the behavioral norms encountered in a particular civilization or cultural area were formulated partly in consideration of just this civilization and culture, hence for them alone? And this despite the fact that definitive or generally valid norms of conduct were actually intended, simply because one does not advert to the possibility of other civilizations and cultures.

Is this relativism? Some time ago, when H. J. Wallraff called Christian social doctrine a "structure of indeterminate propositions"[30] and in connection with the institution of private property accepted only a few general statements on social ethics, the realization of which depended heavily upon economic, social and political factors, he found himself vulnerable to the charge of relativism. The title of his work was "Vom Naturrecht zum Relativismus: ein Beispiel des Eigentums."[31] Exception was taken to the subsequent statement: "Principles for a normative science would have to be drawn from the social reality."[32] Here the decisive truth was overlooked, that if behavioral norms are to be operative, the entire pertinent reality (including the social factor) has to be taken into account and enter into the judgment. The a priori, hence universal, non-historical social ethics that stands opposed to this, that provides norms in advance for every social reality, sacrifices the indispensable objectivity and therefore validity of duly concrete solutions to an a priori universalism. The critical question, then, is not one of relativism but of objectivity, or the "truth" of the action which must be in conformity with the whole concrete reality of man (of society). Now Wallraff had spoken earlier of indeterminate propositions that must be concretized through *political decisions* (thus involving some compromise), but still in relation to the given social reality. Our own previous consideration, however, had to do with *moral behavior norms* which men (humanity) "discover" as being appropriate to their actual civilization, experience, etc. We asked: Is this relativism? And now the correlative question: Is it not rather the necessary connection with concrete human reality to which human behavior must be adapted if it is to be "objective" and "true" and so "right," *secundum rectam rationem*? The demand to be this is absolute! Rightly does Chiavacci point out[33] that the objectivity of morality is not necessarily based on an unchangeable being (in other words, on a "preceptive" understanding of natural law), but on the indispensable correspondence of act to being.

III. The "Applicability" of Moral Norms

If the absoluteness of moral norms is constituted primarily by their objective effectiveness vis-a-vis the given reality and thus not preeminently by their universality or their universal validity, the question inevitably arises concerning the applicability of moral norms to reality in the concrete.

The So-Called Exceptions to the Norm

A very small step in the direction of universal validity in applying moral norms brings home the realization that possibly they cannot be stated, as we once believed they had to be, so as to apply, to all epochs or in all cultures, or social groups or in all conceivable individual cases. And so we have the problem of the *exception* to the moral norm, a matter discussed chiefly in Anglo-Saxon circles in past years. The title of an Irish article is symptomatic: "Toward a Theory of Exceptions."[34] The author, N. D. O'Donoghue, starts with the possibility and the fact of exceptions to behavioral norms, understood, actually, in the same way as by Fletcher and Robinson, for instance, when they concede absoluteness in the sense of admitting no exceptions to only *one* norm— that of love.[35] An ethical system, according to O'Donoghue, is possible only because, despite change and diversity, man and his structures abide, yet since the same man and his structures also exhibit changes and differences, exceptions must occur, in such a way, however, that they remain exceptions. The conclusion is then: Moral norms necessarily admit of exceptions. Princeton University's renowned theologian, Paul Ramsey, the "most influential and most prominent advocate of a 'Principles Ethics'" among his Protestant colleagues, holds the contrary opinion. His title is significant: "The Case of the Curious Exception."[36] Ramsey reasons as follows. If there is an exception, it must be based objectively on the actual situation, so that when the same situation is repeated, the same exception must hold. This means, however, that the norm to be applied in general is not meant for the case at hand, or that it must give way to a "better" norm. The "exceptional case" obliges us, therefore, to a "refining" of the previous norm, since it did not take into account certain elements of the particular situation or perhaps considered them only implicitly. Accordingly, Ramsey's solution is: Fundamentally, there are no exceptions—provided the formulation of the norm becomes ever more refined and precise. This solution is the correct one. Frequently our statements of norms are inexact, inasmuch as they do not—perhaps cannot—take into consideration all the possibilities of the human reality. When, as he must, Ramsey finally confronts the question whether *all* norms can be "refined," the question will really be asking, at least logically, whether all the already "refined" norms are to be refined still further. In this connection one thinks of the changeableness and historicity of man (of humanity), of his culture, his value systems, etc. Ramsey appears to incline rather to a static concept of man. Thus the "refining" entails not only the ever improved and more precise comprehension and articulation, but also a "re-formulation" for modes of reality which hitherto could not be taken into consideration.

Dennis E. Hurley, Archbishop of Durban,[37] has published another attempt to advocate the simultaneous validity of the norm and the justification of the exception. In his view, where a case of conflict occurs, duties and rights stand in opposition to each other. An overriding right can cancel the obligations of certain absolute norms of morality and so make permissible some (not all) *"intrinsece mala"* (killing, stealing, lying, etc.). Charles Curran[38] appeals to a "theory of compromise," in terms of which—particularly in virtue of man's situation in consequence of original sin—what really ought not happen, may and must happen on occasion. The often invoked theory of the lesser evil (or the greater good), like the two attempts just mentioned, also seeks to maintain simultaneously the validity of the norms and the vindication of the exceptions.[39] Yet would Ramsey not rightfully reply, that the justification of the exception in view of the overriding right, of the necessary compromises and of the lesser evil, must be objectively based on (human) reality itself; i.e., the norm sustaining the exception is not stated with sufficient precision, and, given this formulation, does not at all represent the true norm governing the concrete reality? The justification of the apparent exception lies in the fact that the supposed norm simply does not possess the range of validity it appears to have, judging by its inexact formulation. This does not militate against the validity of the (true) norm; rather it permits the objectively-based, so-called exception to call attention more pointedly to the objective range and true validity of the norm.[40]

Further consideration leads to a like result. Hurley maintains that killing, stealing, lying, etc. are intrinsically evil; yet they might be warranted in view of important opposing obligations. According to press reports, a French bishop is supposed to have said in a presentation at a Conference of French bishops on *Humanae Vitae* that, according to *Humanae Vitae* the use of contraceptives is an *evil*, like killing; but killing in a morally justified war of defense and the use of contraceptives in certain cases of conflict would not be morally culpable (in no sense wicked). Have we not overlooked the distinction—crucial in this case—between *evil* and *wickedness;* that is, between evil in the *pre*moral (physical, ontic) sense and evil in the *moral* sense (wickedness). Objectively, there is no conflict of moral precepts, only a conflict of value judgments (bona "physica") in the *pre*moral sense.[41] Only the right—"secundum rectam rationem"—solution of this conflict makes the "absence of conflict" evident in the *moral* situation. Killing is a realization of an evil, but it is not always a moral evil. In this regard, there is also no moral norm applying to *killing*, but only such as designates *unjust* killing as immoral. If someone (with *Humanae vitae*) regards the use of contraceptives as a *malum*, but considers certain exceptions morally justifiable, he must understand that the *malum* of contraceptive use affirmed by him in this form lies in the *pre*moral sphere ("it is evil") while only the objective *unjustified* realization of the evil belongs in the area of the moral ("it is wicked"). In general: Whoever sets up negative norms, but regards exceptions as justified, by reason of overriding right, or warranted compromise, or for the sake of the lesser evil (or the greater good), shows by this that the malum repudiated by the norm is *not* (yet) to be understood as *moral* evil. Hence its realization to avoid another malum (or for the sake of a relatively higher bonum) can be justified *morally* on the ground mentioned previously. If, on the contrary, it is preferred to give this norm moral validity, its formulation in universal terms has to be restricted, and the "exception" is no longer an exception. The norm is *objective* only within the limits of the restriction.

Moral and Premoral Evil

The basic distinction between moral and premoral evil[42] should be carried still further in the interest of clarifying the significance of moral norms for concrete behavior. Morality, in the true (not transferred or analogous) sense is expressible only by a human action, by an action which originates in the deliberate and free decision of a human person. An action of this kind can be performed only with the intention of the agent. One may not say, therefore, that killing as a realization of a human evil may be morally good or morally bad; for killing as such, since it implies nothing about the intention of the agent, cannot, purely as such, constitute a human act. On the other hand, "killing because of avarice" and "killing in self-defense" do imply something regarding the intention of the agent; the former cannot be morally good, the latter may be.

Here we take up the question: When is human action, or when is man in his action (morally) good? Must not the answer be: When he *intends and effects* a human good (value)—in the premoral sense, for example, life, health, joy, culture, etc. (for only this is recta ratio); but not when he *has in view and effects* a human *non-good,* an evil (non-value)—in the premoral sense, for example, death, wounding, wrong, etc. What if he intends and effects good, but this necessarily involves effecting evil also? We answer: If the realization of the evil through the intended realization of good is justified as a proportionally related cause,[43] then in this case only good was intended. Man has almost always judged in this manner. A surgical operation is a health measure, its purpose is to cure, but it is at the same time the cause of an evil, namely, wounding. This, however, appears to be justified in view of the desired cure and is capable of being incorporated in the *one human* act—a curative measure. The surgical operation is *morally* right, because the person acting desires and effects only a good—in the *pre*moral sense—namely, restoration of health. If the surgeon were to do more than was required in performing this operation, that "more" would not be justified by the treatment indicated; that is, it would be taken up *as an evil*—in the *pre*moral sense—into the surgeon's intention; it would be *morally* bad. The conclusion in definitive terms is: 1) An action cannot be judged morally in its materiality (killing, wounding, going to the moon), without reference to the intention of the agent; without this, we are not dealing with a human action, and only with respect to a human action may one say in a true sense whether it is morally good or bad.[44] 2) The evil (in a premoral sense) effected by a human agent must not be intended as such, and must be justified in terms of the totality of the action by appropriate reasons.

These considerations are not without significance for the question of the application of norms to the concrete case. We have already seen this in connection with the so-called exceptions to the norm. The problem presents itself also in the form of the traditional doctrine of the three sources of practical morality (*tres fontes moralitatis*). According to this doctrine, morality in a comprehensive sense, as applied to a concrete action is determined not only by the morality of the act as such, but also by the morality of the circumstances and purpose of the action, with the reservation, however, that neither the purpose nor special circumstances can rescind the negative morality of an action.

This point has the value only of a "rule of thumb" (although it has also the theoretical force that something *morally* bad cannot become morally good in view of a good purpose). In theoretically precise reflection, one must, of course, establish some additional points. For 1) a moral judgment of an action may not be made in anticipation of the agent's intention, since it would not be the judgment of a "human" act. 2) A moral judgment is legitimately formed only under a *simultaneous* consideration of the three elements (action, circumstance, purpose), premoral in themselves; for the actualization of the three elements (taking money from another, who is very poor, to be able to give pleasure to a friend) is not a combination of three human actions that are morally judged on an individual basis, but a single human action. A surgical operation is not made up of several human actions (wounding, healing, for the purpose of restoring health), but it is only one healing action, the moral quality of which is based on a synchronous view of the three—premoral— elements in conformity with an evaluating recta ratio. The same thing could be said about the transplant of an organ from a living human organism, about underground coal-mining with its threat to health, about the moon-landing and the incalculable dangers involved, etc. But now the critical question: What value do our norms have with respect to the morality of the action as such, prior, that is, to the consideration of the circumstances and intention? We answer: They cannot be moral norms, unless circumstances and intention are taken into account. They can be considered as moral norms only because we tacitly assume to judge the action in the light of possible circumstances and intention. But since, *theoretically*, this is impossible, and since *in practice* these elements of an action are necessarily incomplete, we cannot rule out the possibility that in the practical application an objectively based instance of conflict—the exceptional case—can show that the norm does not have, objectively, the range of validity previously supposed. The absoluteness of a norm depends more upon the objectivity of its relationship to reality than upon its universality.

"The end does not justify the means," that is, the morally bad means. This tenet is, of course, correct. When and to the extent that it has been established that an action is morally bad, it may not be performed as a means toward attaining a good end. On the other hand if there is question only of evil in the *pre*moral sense, such as death, wounding, dishonor, etc., the intention and the realization of a good can possibly justify the doing of an evil, e.g., the evil of a surgical operation in the interest of health, or a transplant. Needless to say: 1) the performing of the evil is not judged independently of the intention as *morally* bad; 2) in the *one* human action (health care, transplant) the performing of the evil is not an isolated (human) action, but only an element of the one action. Therefore, a morally bad (human-) action, is not being used as means to a good end. This point was often overlooked in the traditional statement of the principle of an act with a double effect. Thus, in cases in which, during the course of the action, the bad effect preceded the good, temporally or physically, opinion was always inclined toward prohibition, on the grounds that otherwise the good effect would be achieved *through* the realization of the bad effect (as means). Actually, many good Christians cannot understand why, in a situation where life is endangered, as, for instance, ectopic pregnancy or uterine diseases, the removal of the fetus was prohibited, while the removal of an organ from the mother, whose serious illness was anticipated because of the pregnancy, *together with* the fetus was permitted; although in both cases, there was liability involved with respect to the life of the fetus—a (premoral) value.[45] The theory failed to take into account that the evil involved is such, not on moral but on premoral grounds (like wounding, loss of honor, death, etc.) and that consequently its actualization occurs, not as a separate human act with its own morality and not, in this context, as an immoral means to a good end, but as a component of one action which is specified through the intention of the agent. Once more: moral norms are not likely to be fully expressed so long as intentions and circumstances are not taken into consideration, at least implicitly. They are objective, therefore, only when this qualification can be presupposed.

"Ethical" Norms and "Abstract" Norms

Under this title Edward Schillebeeckx has treated the problem of the applicability of norms to real cases in the third volume of his collected works[46] and in 1968 in *Concilium*.[47] He points out that some Catholic theologians—G. de Brie, Karl Rahner, Josef Fuchs are named—in view of the all-too-simple solutions of the problematic of situation ethics, have attempted to compensate by having the moral requirement of the situation from abstract norms drawn from the concept "man" as well as from strictly situation-conditioned elements. Against this solution Schillebeeckx cites the epistemological difficulty that *two* norms are posited by it. In reality, however, there would be solely the concrete reality of the particular individual's ethical norm. The *abstract* norm would not be an *ethical* norm at all, that is, a demand of reality. Rather, it would only repeat the ethical norm in the abstract and inadequately and would have moral significance only in virtue of its existential connection with the concrete reality. This significance would lie in the fact that it is "the inadequate indeed, but still real referent to the single operative concrete ethical norm";[48] i.e., in the direction indicated by it, the ethical norm is to be sought, without its being itself capable of providing this ethical norm satisfactorily. Apart from the question of terminology, the authors cited above legitimately suppose, precisely as Schillebeeckx, only a single ethical norm (as required by the actual case) and admissibly understood the relationship of the "abstract" to the concrete reality as "ethical" norm epistemologically in precisely the same way as he; they have said this explicitly.

But the question of interest to us here, is rather that of the significance of the abstract norm for the concrete reality as ethical norm. Schillebeeckx probably does not mean to say merely that an abstract norm cannot form the basis of an exhaustive judgment of a concrete reality. He would doubtless also wish to say that only in the confrontation with an actual situation will the moral value and the moral exigency, toward which the abstract norm merely pointed in a partial manner, be fully revealed and understood. Or he has in mind that the abstract norm can only be arrived at via the concrete reality through abstraction and conceptualization. But this would imply that the concrete reality to which it is to be applied later on, is *conceivable* of a different *kind* than the concrete reality that represented the point of departure. Thus, it can no longer serve as the ethical norm; i.e. as meeting the concrete requirements of the new reality. If he indeed meant to say this, he perceived the problem treated above and sought to solve it in his own way: the norm for concrete action is constituted by the *one* moral judgment of the whole complex (the action in abstracto, circumstances, intention) and not by the moral judgment of an action in abstracto *and* the added judament of circumstances and intention.

"*Intrinsece Malum?*"

The question of the applicability of moral norms may arise in still another form known from tradition. If the absoluteness of the moral norm signifies objectivity more than universal validity, can moral norms be universal at all, in the sense of being applicable always, everywhere and without exception, so that the action encompassed by them could never be objectively justified? Traditionally we are accustomed to speak of an "*intrinsece malum.*"

Viewed theoretically, there seems to be no possibility of norms of this kind for human action in the inner-wordly realm. The reason is that an action cannot be judged morally at all, considered purely in itself, but only together with all the "circumstances" and the "intention." Consequently, a behavioral norm, universally valid in the full sense, would presuppose that those who arrive at it could know or foresee adequately *all the possible combinations* of the action concerned with circumstances and intentions, with (pre-moral) values and non-values (*bona* and *mala* "*physica*").[49] A priori, such knowledge is not attainable. An a priori affirmation would not come to be a moral judgment by way of the premoral. Add to this that the conception opposed to this does not take into consideration the significance for an objective understanding of morality attached to, first, practical experience and induction, second, civilization and cultural differences, third, man's historicity and "creative" perceptions.

Despite all this, we often make statements connoting "universal validity." But "Thou shalt not *kill*" is obviously too broadly stated; it would be better to say, "Thou shalt not *commit murder*"; that is, "Thou shalt not kill unjustly." This last formulation is universal and exact. Nevertheless, a high price has been paid for this advantage over the formulation "Thou shalt not kill." For while "killing" expresses an unequivocal fact, "murder" does not, since it leaves undetermined when killing is lawful and when it is not. Accordingly the inference is self-evident: A precise description of an action as a statement of fact would, theoretically, scarcely admit of a universal moral judgment in the strict sense. An operative universal moral norm contains a *formal element* not yet defined materially, "lawful," "in an authorized manner." Hence the attempt on the part of moral theology to discover which values, realizable in this world can justify "killing" and which cannot. If it is believed that, in moral theology, the line between "lawful" and "unlawful" has to be precisely drawn, we have once again a definitive statement of fact and, within its limits, a universal moral judgment. But here we must pause for further reflection. How could one make a judgment that would take in *all* the human possibilities— even granting that one had succeeded in understanding rightly and judging rightly those possibilities that were foreseen? Today, actually, such reflection begins thus: Might there not be at the present time and in the future a society in which—as distinguished from earlier societies—by reason of its social and cultural structures, capital punishment would not be an appropriate and therefore warranted means of administering justice? Further, is there meanwhile no life situation that might justify suicide, as for example, the only means of preserving a state secret, a possibility which presumably is open to consideration, inasmuch as it was excluded indeed in the norm as stated in the past, without however having been reflected upon at any time. "Killing" vs. "murder" was mentioned as only one example that might shed more light on the problem of the applicability of behavior norms stated as universals.

Theoretically, no other answer seems possible: Probably there can be no universal norms of *behavior* in the strict sense of *"intrinsece malum."* *Practically,* however, norms properly formulated as universals have their worth, and indeed on several counts. 1) Such norms, insofar as they are based on true perception, indicate a value or a non-value in the premoral sense. But negative values are to be avoided; in particular, as evil they may never serve as intentions for human action, and only for adequate reasons may they be actualized concurrently with relatively higher or more urgent values. 2) There can be norms stated as universals, including, that is, a precise delineation of the action, to which we cannot conceive of any kind of exception; e.g., cruel treatment of a child which is of no benefit to the child.[50] Despite misgivings on the level of theory, we get along very well with norms of this kind. 3) Norms can be stated as universals (in the case of specific culture or society, particularly), corresponding to human and social situations that have been actually experienced. In these instances, Aquinas' opinion concerning so-called secondary principles of the natural law, including, therefore, "operative" behavioral norms, holds true by analogy: They can be applied in *ordinary cases* ("valent ut in pluribus").[51] And this for the reason that they are stated so as to suit conditions wont to occur in practice (and only for such); they suffice for ordinary use in practical living. 4) The extent of the inapplicability of a norm to a concrete case (for which it was actually not intended), the degree to which specific norms of our society are stated with precise relevance to present-day conditions in our society, or to those of yesterday's society (from which our present one derives) and so are not relevant to ours; or are generalized and so apply to other societies and cultures as well—such difficulties can neither be presumed as free of doubt, nor may they be completely ignored. Where the first suspicion of one or other of the conditions mentioned above exists, a point of reference is at hand for a thorough examination, to determine the factor upon which the delimit process should be objectively based.

The absence of a distinction—made only later—between *theoretical* and *practical* possibility characterized not only the moral-theological discussion of the past on "intrinsece malum" and the universality of behavioral norms, but also, by way of consequence, the official ecclesiastical use of these expressions. Apart from this, the terms would have a better meaning if they could be aligned with the term "absolute" in the sense we have given it above. Every action that is *objectively—secundum rectam rationem*—not justified in the concrete human situation (according to Schillebeeckx, the sole norm and only adequate norm of conduct) is "*intrinsece malum*" and therefore absolutely to be avoided.[52]

IV. Norms as Authentic Orientation

To summarize: Moral theology is concerned primarily with objectivity—its true *absolutum*—which consists in the recta ratio of a human-Christian actualization of the concrete reality. Recta ratio can be satisfactorily present only in a conscience situation. But human society requires and "discovers"—"creates"—norms stated as universals; the same is true of scientific moral theology. Nevertheless, universality in norms has certain limits, at least theoretically, because of the objectivity required of a true *absolutum*. What are the practical implications?

Formal Principles and Material Norms of Action

Undoubtedly there are universal ethical statements in the strict sense. Nevertheless they always remain *formal* in a certain sense, at least insofar as they are not *material* norms of action, i.e. norms which indicate whether actions exactly described materially are ethically permissible or not. That our actions must be authentic self-realization, or what is the same, that we have to do the good and not the evil, is nothing other than the formal formulation of man's ethical self-understanding. This formal and hence absolutely universal formulation can be applied to *different spheres of life* without losing its formal character: the imperative to be just, chaste, and merciful thus materially states nothing about the materially determined actions which can express justice, chastity, and mercy. Likewise the formal formulation of the ethical self-understanding can express itself in *transcendental norms*, which thus do not describe the material content of actions, for example, that the Christian man has to realize himself as Christian, that he should live faith and love, baptism and the following of Christ in every action. They are universal. *Categorical evaluations* on the other hand may be influenced to a certain degree by determined experiences, by factual options in a given society, and by a specific self-understanding. Above all this applies to the *hierarchy* of values, for example, in the area of marriage and family. This applies in the same way and even more to *"operative" norms of action*, which were treated above. In this case to defend as a theoretical possibility the complete universality of ethical statements—perhaps on the basis of an *a priori* metaphysical understanding of determined actions—is to succumb to the utopia of rationalism.

Moral-Theological Reflection

Ethical, or moral-theological, reflection is always associated with moral experience. This however, can never be a solipsistic experience. Its substance is always related to the moral consciousness of the community.[53] But this moral consciousness is shaped by manifold experiences and diverse influences. In the Christian community led by the Spirit, the human-Christian self-concept is always the matrix and potential corrective of the moral understanding, even when the Christian message as such transmits behavioral norms that are scarcely "operative," definitive and universal. On the other hand, it cannot be denied that in the course of the centuries, Old Testament-Jewish concepts and the ethical opinions of non-Christian ideologies of various kinds exercised their influence. It is likewise undeniable that in the Christian communities of those centuries *"errare humanum est"* and that error in the moral sphere cannot therefore be excluded *a limine*.

If today in Christian as well as non-Christian sectors, the universality of norms is being questioned on theoretical and on practical levels as well, with very manifest consequences, the fact still remains that *men of today* also and the Christian community of today are susceptible to *error*. There is equal a priori probability, however, that, in their reflections, they can achieve *true* insight. In this connection, where might the basis be found that would validate the right or necessity of questioning or "rethinking," for without penetrating and common reflection in relation to this basis, will not a community run the risk of deviating from "its own" *clear sighted* moral sense, which has developed within it and in virtue of its own particular reality? Theoretically speaking, three possibilities that could warrant doubt or re-thinking come to mind. *First*, it can be shown that in the Christian past, faulty evaluations were made and false norms set. If such could be and were identified hitherto, similar identifications could *in principle* be made also today. Those erroneous evaluations and norms could have been objectively "false" for men of earlier times as well, although today we could probably show why the errors were scarcely avoidable or even not avoidable at all because of the state of knowledge—or awareness—at that time. *Second*, inasmuch as we ourselves formulate moral norms, such norms may well be imprecise or the most likely eventuality, stated in too generalized a manner, either because there was only an implicit awareness of limits, or because limits were not adverted to at all. This helps to explain why, *third*, particular inherited moral statements can be related very accurately to a social situation, a culturally conditioned evaluation, a partially developed self-concept, and the like, rather than to a designated era of the past, whereas for us today those situations and evaluations are "past." In cases where we can prove this and where it is clear that a moral statement has its basis in precisely those givens that have since changed their bases, a moral reformulation is not only conceivable; it is called for.

The Individual and His Conscience

Undoubtedly, the question of the absoluteness of moral norms has considerable significance for the individual and the forming of his situation-conscience, in light of which (not, then,—directly—in light of the norms!) he acts. For since we never begin at zero to form our situation-conscience, but always include norms in our starting point, the question of absoluteness, i.e., universality, regarding the norms of the individual and his concrete behavior, becomes important. To repeat, we are not solipsists either in forming a situation-conscience or in developing a moral sensibility or in appropriating moral norms. Rather, despite the uniqueness of the individual, there is a human orientation to moral questions only in terms of a group, a community, a society, conceived of as a whole. In his moral convictions and in forming his situation-conscience, the individual cannot simply detach himself from his roots in the moral convictions of the community; nor may he forget that he will find the (i.e. "his") right solution of many an individual moral problem only by relating to the moral perceptions and the self-concept of his community. Specific problems usually occur in an integrated context and cannot easily find their distinctively appropriate solutions in another context. In the *ecclesial* community, it is to be noted further, moral traditions can also be co-determined, in that a Christian member's self-concept and ideal of morality, springing from faith (even though the inferences may be partially undeveloped), can contribute to the ratifying of a moral evaluation. On the other hand, doubts and reversed judgments occurring justifiably in a community can also, naturally, influence the mental attitude and the formation of conscience taken by the individual according to his capacity and responsibility, when he decides to participate in the reflective evaluations of his community and follow the judgment of his adviser. Doubtless, much depends on a responsible discernment of spirits, perceptible through[54] and dependent upon a moral faith-instinct (K. Rahner), which, however, must not be equated with mere susceptibility to what has been traditionally handed down.

There is, of course, the theoretical possibility that the "curious exception" (Ramsey) may present itself, not only as a public phenomenon in the life of the community, but also independently in a justified individual case. For the actuality of this possibility, one should not only deal with the uniqueness of the individual and of the particular case—this would be very superficial—but with the basis which in itself is objective and demonstrable—perhaps along the lines of one of the possibilities mentioned in the previous section, "Moral-Theological Reflection." Nevertheless the individual case, granting the demonstrability of the objective basis, probably will be presented as a rule within the community in a similar and analogous manner and be carried through to a competent (not necessarily authoritative) judgment.

The "Pedagogical" Value of Norms

The moral task of the Christian is not to fulfill "norms" but to "humanize" (Christianize) each of man's concrete realities, understood as a divine call. Norms of moral behavior should "help" to bring this about rightly, "objectively." The true significance of these norms consists in this "pedagogical" service—not in a universal validity that could compromise objectivity. Accordingly, the function of the norms is then "only" pedagogical.[55] They are guides to right actualization, that is, they are not intended, being abstract, to be the concrete solution, nor can they even, at least theoretically, designate with precision their own range of validity.[56] Yet, practically speaking, they are indispensably important, because no one who is incorporated in a community is without norms. The "pedagogical" service of norms reaches its highest intensity in cases where the individual (as a member of his community) is not entirely capable of finding his way.[57] To be sure, precisely in such instances norms are liable to be understood and lived as law or taboo because they do not clearly manifest their proper limits.

Once again: the moral task proper to man is not to fulfill norms, so that in the final analysis life's reality would serve merely as material, so to speak, for actualizing moral values; that is, of obeying norms. Inversely, the concrete reality of life itself—that is its actualization—is the real task; hence the mandate to take up a given reality and to form it, "creatively" and in a spirit of self commitment, into something "worthy of man" (and therefore of his Creator and Redeemer).[58] The understanding of concrete reality itself could by itself enable the evaluating individual (Christian) to judge which "designs" of his shaping action are really "human" (Christian). By forming this judgment he would simultaneously and, at least, implicitly recognize the norms, which he has probably carried over; just as the full meaning of the norms "carried over" reveals itself totally only in a comprehending evaluation of the concrete human reality. Nevertheless, in the foreseeable future man will carry over, presumably, less numerous, less detailed and fewer behavioral norms known in advance to fulfill the work of performing responsibly the many tasks involved in shaping man's world. Rather, there will be, probably, fundamental principles, a deepened insight into human and Christian values and a heightened sense of responsibility.[59]

If moral behavioral norms have their "relative" significance for the human and Christian realization of man's world, a reflection on their absoluteness belongs to the task of a theoretical consideration of questions regarding Christian morality. Only theoretically neat attempts at solution, not apologetical efforts, can assist praxis effectively. Indeed, not only should these attempts at solution include a designation of limits, but also the indication of the limits of the designated limits. In other words, abstract discussion is not enough. There should be further reflection on how the theological analysis and its outcomes affect the daily life, not only of the "experts" but also of the "ordinary Christian." This latter provision is of very great importance, because moral judgments—concerning really contingent realities—do not require metaphysical proof, only a so-called moral certitude; *with this we may be and should be content.*

NOTES

[1] Blasphemy is not infrequently referred to as an "intrinsically" bad act. It should be noted, however, that blasphemy, if it is really such, means *expressly* a contradiction addressed to God, i.e. the real essence of immorality, therefore—different from any other innerworldly acts. An analogy would be an act directed against the salvation of one's nearest and dearest.

[2] Cf. J. Blank, "New Testament Morality and Modern Moral Theology," *Concilium* 5, 3, pp. 6-12. Cf. also A. Grabner-Haider, "Zur Geschichtlichkeit der Moral (Biblische Bemerkungen)," *Catholica* 22 (1968): 262-70; W. Kerber, "Hermeneutik in der Moraltheologie," *Theol.u. Phil.* 44 (1969): 42-66, esp. 52-60.

[3] So also H. Rotter, "Zum Erkenntnisprobleme in der Moraltheologie," in J. B. Lotz (ed.), *Neue Erkenntnisprobleme in Philosophie und Theologie,* (Freiburg, 1968) 226-48, on 238ff.

[4] *Gaudium et spes,* n. 46.

[5] E. Schillebeeckx, "The Magisterium and the World of Politics," *Concilium* 6 (1968) 12-21, esp. p. 16.

[6] K. Rahner, "Zum Problem der genetischen Manipulation," in *Schriften Zur Theologie* VIII, pp. 303ff.

[7] M. Flick-Z. Alszeghy, *Metodologia per una teologia dello sviluppo,* (Brescia, 1970), pp. 47-68, 91-99.

[8] *Loc, cit,; cf. Diskussion zur "politischen Theologie,"* ed. by H. Peukert, (Mainz and Munich, 1969.)

[9] K. Rahner distinguishes between norms and imperatives, *The Dynamic Element in the Church,* (London, 1964), pp. 13-41.

[10] In his article " 'Politische Theologie' in der Diskussion'" *St. d. Zt.* 184 (1969) 289-308, J. B. Metz rightly saw that political theology can lead to action only by way of political ethics (pp. 293-96). Yet it is not made clear why "political ethics" precisely as an "ethics of change" (in distinction from an "ethics of order") is assigned specially to political *theology* as a "specifically Christian hermeneutics."

[11] Cf. R. A. McCormick, "The Teaching Role of the Magisterium and of Theologians," in *Proceedings of the Catholic Theological Society of America* 24 (1969), summarized by the author in *Theological Studies* 30 (1969): 647f. On the action of the Spirit in the Church, cf. also K. Demmer, "Kirchliches Lehraüt und Naturrecht" *Theol. u. Gl.* 59 (1969): 191-213; B. Schüller, "Bemerkungen zur authentischen Verkündigung des kirchlichen Lehramtes," *Theol. u. Phil.* 42 (l967): 534-51.

[12] Cf. for the conditioned, not a-historical, character of the moral pronouncements of the Church, Alf. Auer, "Die Erfahrung der Geschichtlichkeit und die Krise der Moral," *Theol. Qu* 149 (1969): 4-22; C. E. Curran, "Natural Law and the Teaching Authority of the Church," in *Christian Morality Today,* (Notre Dame, Indiana, 1966), 79-91; "Absolute Norms and Medical Ethics," in *Absolutes in Moral Theology?,* (Washington, D.C., 1968), 108-53; esp. 127ff; L. Sartori, "La legge naturale e il magistero cristiano," in L. Rossi (ed.), *La Legge Naturale,*

Bologna, 1970, pp. 219-244. According to Curran, changes in the moral teaching of the Church are to be understood as development, not as contradictions of the past: "Natural Law . . . " p. 87.

[13] Cf. E. Chiavacci, "La legge naturale ieri e oggi," in F. Festorazzi *et al.*, *Nuove prospettive di morale coniugale*, (Brescia, 1969), pp. 61-91 on p. 75.

[14] See the foregoing note.

[15] Chiavacci, *loc. cit.*, pp. 65 ff., is of the opinion that Thomas, although he cites many "auctoritates" for other formulations also, basically does not consider detailed norms as natural law; and that this conception derives from other sources. Cf. also D. Mongillo, "L'elemento primario della legge naturale in s. Tommaso," in *La Legge Naturale* (see note 12), 101-23; D. Capone, "Ritorno a s. Tommaso per una visione personalistica in teologia morale," Riv. di teol. mor. 1 (1969), 85ff.

On the whole problem of change with regard to moral questions, cf. J. Grundel, *Wandelbares und Unwandelbares in der Moraltileologie*, (Düsseldorf, 1967), esp. 46-73.

[16] Cf. Alf. Auer, (see note 12); I. Lobo, "Geschichtlichkeit und Erneuerung der Moral," *Concilium* 3 (1967): pp. 363-375; A. Grabner-Haider (see note 2); M. Sheehan, "History: The Context of Morality," in W. Dunphy (ed.), *The New Morality, Continuity and Discontirluity*, (New York, 1967), 37-54.

[17] Cf. Alf. Auer, *loc. cit* (see note 12), p. 12: "Gut ist immer nur, was der Wachstumsbewegung der menschlichen Person und der menschlichen Gemeinschaft dienlich ist. Aber das lässt sich eben nicht nur aus der Vergangenbeit bestimmen; es bedarf auch der Hinwendung zur Zukunft." J. Fuchs, "On the Theology of Human Progress," in *Human Values and Christian Morality*, (Dublin, 1970): 178-203, esp. 185-90. From the moral psychologist's point of view cf. I. Lepp, *La morale nouvelle*, Ital. ed.: *La morale nuova*, (Milano, 1967), 78.

[18] This terminology occurs in the encyclical *Humanae vitae* n. 10.

[19] Cf. C. E. Curran, "Absolute Norms . . ." (see note 12), 118f.

[20] B. Quelquejeu's phrasing tends in this direction, "Brèves notes a propos de 'Nature et Morale' "Supplement de *La vie spirituelle*, n. 81 (1967), 278-81; also L. Janssens, *Personne et Société*. (Gembloux, 1939): 199-243; *Personalisme en Democratisering*, (Brussels, 1957), pp. 93f, H. Mertens, "De persona humana ut norma moralitatis," *Coll. Mechl.* 44 (1969): 526-31.

[21] This is not the place for an analysis of the phenomenon of conscience; only *one* aspect—a fundamental one-conscience as judgment, is being considered.

[22] Cf. J. Fuchs, "Gibt es eine spezifisch christliche Moral?" *St. d. Zt.* 185 (l970): 99-112; "Human, Humanist and Christian Morality," in *Human Values and Christian Morality*, (Dublin, 1970): 112-47; B. Schüller, "Zur theologischen Diskussion über die lex naturalis," *Theol. u. Phil.* 41 (1966): 481-503; "Inwieweit kann die Moraltheologie das Naturrecht entbehren," *Leb. Zeugnis* (Mar. 1965): 41-65; Alf. Auer, "Nach dem Erscheinen der Enzyklika 'Humanae vitae.' Zehn Thesen über die Findung sittlicher Weisungen" *Theol. Qu.* 149 (1969): 75-85, esp. 75-78; F. Böckle, "Was ist das Proprium einer christlichen Ethik?" *Z.f. ev. Ethik* 11 (1967): 148-59; K. Demmer, "Kirchliches Lehramt und Naturrecht" (see note 11), 200; R. A. McCormick, "Human Significance and Christian Significance" in G. H. Outka-P. Ramsey (ed.), *Norm and Context in Christian Ethics*, (New York, 1968): 233-61; J. McMahon, "What does Christianity Add

to Atheistic Humanism?" *Cross Currents* 18 (Spring, 1968): 129-50; J. M. Gustafson, *Christ and the Moral Life*, (New York, 1968), esp. Chap VII.

[23] J. Fuchs, *Human Values . . . loc. cit.* (see foregoing note), pp. 140-147. In the encyclical *Humanae vitae*, n. 12 states: "leges in ipsaviriet mulieris natura inscriptae."

[24] R. A. McCormick insists, probably against J. G. Milhaven (see following note), upon far-reaching effects and consequences of actions whose significance is known without experience: "Human Significance . . . ," *loc. cit.* (see note 22), esp. 25f.

[25] So, especially J. G. Milhaven, "Toward an Epistemology of Ethics," in *Norm and Context* (see note 22): 219-31; published also in *Theol. Studies* 27 (1966): 228-41.

[26] W. Van Der Marck, *Toward a Christian Ethic. Renewal in Moral Theology*, (Shannon, Ireland, 1969), advances the thesis (perhaps somewhat onesidedly) that the moral value of actions consists exclusively in their significance for the creation of positive interpersonal relations. With this can be compared the thesis of J. Fletcher and J. A. T. Robinson regarding love as the sole absolutum; also J. M. Gustafson, "Love Monism, How Does Love Reign?" in J. C. Bennett el al., *Storm over Ethics*, (United Church Press, 1967):26-37.

[27] Cf. B. Schüller, "Zur Problematik allgemein verbindlicher ethischer Grundsätze," *Theol. u. Phil.* 45 (1970): 1-23 esp. 3f.

[28] On the problem of a morality in a pluralistic society, cf. R. Hoffmann, "Das sittliche Minimum in der pluralen Gesellschaft," *Theol. Qu.* 149 (1969): 23-38; also A. Hertz, "Sitte, Sittlichkeit und Moral in der pluralistischen Gesellschaft," *Neue Ordn.* 18 (1964): 187-96; W. Schöllgen, *Moral-fragwürdig? Uber gesellschaftlichen Pluralismus und Moral*, (Hückeswagen, 1967.)

[29] On the problem "norms of morality and the Christianization of the nations" cf. E. Hillman, "The Development of Christian Marriage Structures," *Concilium* 5, 6, 25-38; "Polygamy Reconsidered," *Concilium* 3, 4, 80-89.

[30] H. J. Wallraff, "Die katholische Soziallehre—ein Gefüge von offenen Sätzen," in *Eigentumspolitik, Arbeit und Mitbestimmung*, (Cologne, 1968): 9-34.

[31] H. Schwandorf, "Zum Standort der katholischen Soziallehre heute," *Gesellschaftspolitische Kommentare* (1970): 130-132; continued in no. 12, 144-46.

[32] *Loc. cit.*, 132.

[33] *Loc cit.*, (see note 13), 81.

[34] N. D. O'Donoghue, "Towards a Theory of Exceptions," *The Irish Theol. Qu.* 35 (1951): 217-32.

[35] J. M. Gustafson, "Context Versus Principles: A Misplaced Debate in Christian Ethics," in *New Theology No. 3*, ed. by M. E. Marty and D. G. Peerman, (London, 1966), on p. 86.

[36] P. Ramsey, "The Case of the Curious Exception," in *Norm and Context* (see note 22): 67-135. Cf. also the excellent contribution by D. Evans, "Love, Situation and Rules," *ibid.,* 367-414.

[37] D. Hurley, "A New Moral Principle: When Right and Duty Clash," *The Furrow* 17 (1966): 619-22.

[38] C. E. Curran "Dialogue with Joseph Fletcher," in *A New Look at Christian Morality*, (Notre Dame, Ind., 1968).

[39] Thus, e.g., the commentary on *Humanae vitae* presented at the meeting of French Bishops, n. 16: *Docum. Cath.* 65 (1968): 2055-2066.

[40] To the cited attempts at solution one might compare N. J. Rigali's critique "The Unity of the Moral Order," *Chicago Studies* 8 (1969): 125-43.

[41] Cf. J. De Broglie, "Conflict de devoirs et contraception," *Doctor communis* 22 (1969): 154-75.

[42] For this distinction, cf. W. Van der Marck, *Toward a Christian Ethic*... (see note 26); P. Knauer, "The Hermeneutic Function of the Principle of Double Effect," *Natural Law Forum*, Vol. 12 (1967): 132-62; B. Schüller, "Zur Problematik..." (see note 27).

[43] Cf. P. Knauer, *loc. cit.*; the decisive question treated by Knauer is: What is a "proportionate" reason? C. J. Van der Poel, "The Principle of Double Effect," in *Absolutes in Moral Theology?* (see note 12): 186-210. V.d.P. obviously depends on W. van der Marck, *Toward*... (see note 26), 65-74, and *Love and Fertility*, (London, 1965): 35-63. Cf. also C. E. Curran, in "Absolute Norms in Med. Eth." (see note 12): 12-114.

[44] Reference is made to this especially by W. van der Marck, C. van der Poel and P. Knauer (see foregoing note).

[45] Cf., e.g., P. Knauer, *loc. cit.*, p. 149: "In other words, a solution which includes both the death of the fetus and the removal of the uterus with consequent sterility is said to be better than that the fetus alone lose its life. Who can understand this?" Similarly, C. E. Curran, "Absolute Norms...," *loc. cit.*, p. 112; W. van der Marck, *Love*..., *loc. cit.* 49-52.

[46] E. Schillebeeckx, *God and Man*, Sheed and Ward, (New York, 1969.)

[47] E. Schillebeeckx, "The Magisterium..." (see note 5), 15f.

[48] *Loc. cit.*, p. 16.

[49] P. Knauer, has a similar statement in "The Hermeneutic Function..." (see note 42), p. 138: "What is intrinsically an evil act is brought about when no commensurate reason can justify the permission or causing of the extrinsic evil, that is, any given premoral physical evil or injury." Cf. B. Schüller, "Zur Problematik..." (see note 27), p. 4 and 7.

[50] Cf. J. A. T. Robinson, *Christian Moral Today*, (London, 1964), p. 16.

[51] Thomas Aquinas, ST I-II, 94, 4.

[52] So also J. Coventry, "Christian Conscience," *The Heythrop Journal* 7 (1966): pp. 152f; also C.E. Curran, "Absolute Norms in Moral Theology?" *Norm and Context* (see note 22), p. 169.

[53] Rightly does J. M. Gustafson insist strongly on this in "Moral Discernment in Christian Life" in *Norm and Context* (see note 22), 17-36.

[54] Cf. Gustafson's significant title: "Moral Discernment in Christian Life" (see foregoing note).

[55] By analogy with the Pauline conception of law as a "pedagogue" leading to Christ, R. Marlé in his work, "Casuistique et morales modernes de situation," in E. Castelli (ed.). *Tecnica e casuistica*, (Rome, 1964): 111-20, speaks of a pedagogical function of moral law with respect to the concrete situation.

[56] With Thomas Aquinas, J. de Finance, *Ethica generalis*, 2d ed., (Rome, 1963), p. 186, points out that even an aggregation of norms—being abstract—can never produce a concretum.

[57] In opposition to many psychoanalysts, I. Lepp, from the standpoint of a moral psychologist, also maintains that the "closed morality" with its norms and also the "superego" are extremely important for the individual as well as for society, so long as there has not yet occurred a breakthrough to an "open morality" as he calls it: *loc. cit.* (see note 17), 91ff. In his article "Maßstäbe sittlichen Verhaltens. Zur

Frage der Normenfindung in der Moraltheologie," *Die Neue Ordnung* 23 (1969): 161-74, on p. 164. A. K. Ruff speaks of norms as having an irreplaceable "exoneration function."

[58] Cf. the dynamic contribution of P. Antoine, "Situation présente de la morale," *Le Supplément, no. 92*, 23 (1970): 8-27; also A. Jonsen, "Responsibility..." (see note 12); J. M. Gustafson-J. Laney (eds.), "On Being Responsible," *Issues in Personal Ethics*, Harper Forum Books; J. Rief "Moralverkündigung angesichts der Krise der Moral," *Theol. pr. Qu.* 117 (1969): 124-38.

[59] For this reason as extreme opponents to this theme, P. Ramsey was obliged to write "The Case of the Curious Exception," in *Norms and Context* (see note 22) and J. Fletcher "What's in a Rule. A Situationist's View," in *Norm and Context* (see note 22), 325-349.

ONTIC EVIL AND MORAL EVIL
Louis Janssens

In the first and by far the longest section of his treatise *De actibus humanis*, St. Thomas presents a very painstaking examination of the structure of human action (ST I-II qq. 6-17). Next, he limits his teaching on the moral evaluation of human action to three questions (ST I-II qq. 18-20). The sequence and the interrelationship of those two parts is immediately obvious when it is seen that the way in which the morality of the human action is interpreted definitely rests on one's approach to the structure of the action. This is apparent in the history of the discussion about human action. In the medieval tradition, two distinct currents of thought about the structure and the morality of the human action can be found. The first, which influenced the following centuries by the prestige of Petrus Lombardus, accents the importance of the object (*finis operis*) within the framework of the action, and it assumes the position that the object can be morally evaluated by itself (*in se*) without reference to the agent. The second, which had already been advocated by Anselm of Canterbury and had been elaborated by Abaelardus and his followers, was adopted by St. Thomas who thoroughly systematized it. It ties the definition of the structure and the morality of the human action to the agent.[1]

We start from the Thomistic view because it is, in our opinion, a solid basis for the examination of the fundamental problem we will broach in this study. But let us understand St. Thomas correctly, because it is a fact that he is often interpreted in the light of concepts and presuppositions of the views he actually disputes (Van der Marck 1964, 151-76). From this misinterpretation has originated many difficulties and inconsistencies we find in our textbooks of morality, e.g., the lack of consistency in the moral evaluation of the acts with several effects. The principles which govern this evaluation were formulated in the sixteenth century (Ghoos 1951, 30-53) and are not conformable to the thought of St. Thomas.

I. The Structure and Morality of Human Action According to St. Thomas

Thomas approaches the topic of the structure of the human action in the light of his view of the acting subject, the inner act of the will. This appears already in the introduction to his *De actibus humanis*, in which he gives us the division of his exposition. First he will deal with the *voluntarium*. He calls this an essential condition (*conditio*) of any explanation of strictly human actions because the will, as *appetitus rationalis*, is specifically characteristic of the human being and consequently, only the acts which emanate from the will (*actus voluntarii*) are properly speaking human acts. Next he will go into the study of the acts themselves. In the first place, he will consider the inner act of the will (*actus ab ipsa voluntate eliciti*). Then he will turn his attention to the external actions which are also acts of the will itself (*ipsius voluntatis*) although they depend on other faculties for their realization (ST I-II, q. 6, introduction). The agent, consequently, is so essentially related to the structure of the activity that his activity can only be called *human* to the extent that it originates within a thinking and willing subject who is therefore capable of a free act of the will. "Only those acts of which man is thoroughly in control are properly called human acts. But man is thoroughly in control of his actions by the power of his reason and his will. Therefore only the acts which emanate from the free will, enlightened by the faculty of deliberation (reason), are called human in the proper sense" (ST I-II, 1, 1).

Why is it essentially important (*conditio*) to start from the acting subject in order to arrive at an analysis of the structure of the activity? Thomas replies with most convincing reasoning. "It is self-evident that all the actions which emanate from a certain faculty are shaped by this faculty according to the particular nature of its own object (*secundum rationem sui objecti*)" (ST I-II, 1, 1). Subsequently, St. Thomas adds, the formal object of the will is that which is good or more precisely that which is "apprehended as good (*bonum apprehensum*)" (ST I-II, 1, and 8, 1). Insofar as the action is elicited by the will itself, it is directed toward the attainment of a good. This principle can be applied to each human act, even a sinful act, since in any sinful act, man still intends to reach for something which is apprehended as something good, at least for some particular tendencies, although it is "not in accord with the true good of the whole person (*contra naturam rationalem secundum rei veritatem*)" (ST I-II, 6, 4 ad 3). That we, in each action, seek and endeavor to realize that which is good, the proper object of the will, means that we aim at this good as the end of our action. In this sense St. Thomas writes: "The object of the will is the end and the good. Consequently, it is necessary that all human actions be done for an end (*propter finem*) (ST I-II, 1, 1). Or still more precisely, the good we strive for through an action functions in the act of the will and therefore in us, who are the acting subject, as an end (*bonum habet rationem finis*)" (ST I-II, 1, 4 *sed contra* and *in corp*). It is clear now that the end is the primordial element of the structure of an action, because it is the proper object of the act of the will. But it is equally clear that the subject or the inner act of the will is involved in the definition of the end. St. Thomas considers this thought again and again. "*Voluntas* proprie *est ipsius finis*" (ST I-II, 8, 2). "*Finis* proprie *est objectum interioris actus voluntatis*" (ST I-II, 18, 6). Every end of an action, therefore, is to be taken as an end of the subject, of the inner act of the will, viz., a *finis operantis*. Further on it will be shown that Thomas does not give this principle the sense of a subjectivistic interpretation of human activity. He will emphasize that a definite good, as object and end of an inner act of the will, cannot be pursued by the subject by any kind of action. Nevertheless, he will not abandon the position that the subject or the inner act of the will must be considered as the starting point; on the contrary, he will always stress that the end of the inner act of the will (or the *finis operantis*) determines the concrete structure of the action which fits this end (*finis dat speciem actui humano*).

Our textbooks distinguish between *finis operis* and *finis operantis*. The intention of the authors is evident; it is an attempt to secure a moral evaluation of the action by itself (*in se*) as related to the object or the built-in end of the action, without any reference to the acting subject. Now it is to be noticed that Thomas never uses this distinction in his *De actibus humanis* although he knows it. He mentions it in his commentary on Petrus Lombardus (II *Sent*, dist. I, q. 2, art. 1). But he accentuates immediately that the *finis operis* is always converted into a *finis operantis*: *finis operis semper reducitur in finem operantis*. His reason for this teaching is clear: he draws it from the very definition of end. To the mind of Thomas there is no end without the inner act of the will of the subject and vice-versa. The end is in the strictest sense of the word the peculiar object of the inner act of the will (ST I-II, 18, 6). In other words, the good, which is the appropriate object of the will, can only be termed an end insofar as it is aimed at by the subject in and through his action; it is always a *finis operantis*. According to Thomas, this can be said about both the *finis operis* and the *finis operantis*, as it appears from the definitions he offers in his commentary on Petrus Lombardus: "The *finis operis* is that to which the action is directed by the *acting subject* (*ab agente*); for this reason it is called the cause of the action (*ratio operis*). The *finis operantis* is the goal at which the agent in the end (*principaliter*) aims." Thomas illustrates his definitions with an example. A bricklayer "programs" the operations performed on the construction materials in such a manner that the work becomes a house. The realized house is the *finis operis*; but the profit he derives from this construction, e.g., his wages, is the *finis operantis*. The *finis operis* is a *finis operantis*. The bricklayer must of course, really want the construction of the house (*finis operis*) in order to satisfy his yearning for wages (*finis operantis*). It is true that one end is not operating on the same level as the other. The *finis operis* is the immediate end of the bricklayer (*finis medius*); the *finis operantis* is his main end (*principaliter*).

Consequently, each end is by its very definition the proper object of an inner act of the will, a *finis operantis*. The subject is the center. This view of Thomas is of far-reaching importance because the determining situation of the subject in the activity makes it possible to consider our actions not as a succession of separate and disjointed actions but as the integrated moments of a life history in which unity and wholeness can be realized by virtue of the ends of the agent. In this sense Thomas does not speak of *finis operis* or *finis operantis* in his *De actibus humanis*, but he stresses the varied rank and the interplay of the ends the subject strives to achieve: *finis medius, proximus, remotus, ultimus*, etc. (ST I-II, 1, 3 ad 3; 12, 2 and 3; 13, 3 ad 2; 14, 2).

We have seen that Thomas' view centers on the agent and that *ipso facto* the end of the agent is the fundamental element of the structure of the human act. To have a clear idea of this structure, we must take a closer look at the question: "How does the will of the agent aim at the end itself?" Thomas answers that the will aims at the end in two ways (*voluntas in ipsum finem dupliciter fertur*), either in an absolute way when it wills the end in itself and by itself (*absolute secundum se*), or when it wills the end as the reason that it wills the means to the end (*in ratione volendi ea quae sunt ad finem*) (ST I-II, 8, 3).

Voluntas

When the will strives for the end itself in an absolute way, St. Thomas uses the term *voluntas* (ST, I-II, 12, 1 ad 4) or *simplex actus voluntatis* (ST I-II, 8, 2 *in corp.* and as 1). Some are of the opinion that a mere *velleitas* was meant by *simplex actus voluntatis*. This interpretation runs counter to the terms Thomas uses in the context: *absolute secundum se*. Evidently Thomas wants to accentuate that the good, as the proper object of the will, can be striven for in itself and for its own sake as an end (*voluntas proprie est ipsius finis*) (ST I-II, 8, 2), even if it is not connected with an action. The example Thomas keeps repeating is that we can want health as an absolute end for its own sake, even when we do nothing to stay healthy or to regain our health (ST I-II, 8, 3; q. 12, 1 ad 4). It will appear below that this view is of the utmost importance when we handle the problem of morality.

Intentio and *Electio*

In the second case, the end is also wanted for its own sake, but at the same time it is striven for as the reason of the *election* of the *means* that make it possible to realize the end: *voluntas fertur in finem ut est ratio volendi ea quae sunt ad finem* (ST I-II, 8, 3, ad 1). It is therefore not a matter of a *simplex actus voluntatis* but of an *actus compositus*, made up of the end and the means. For the proper understanding of this view it must be remembered that the end of the subject determines the means. Or, in other words, the sense of means can be attributed only to something from the point of view of the end: *ex fine enim oportet accipere rationes eorum quae sunt ad finem* (ST I-II, 1, introduction).

Traditional terminology had compiled many terms that were more or less technically suited to describe the diverse elements of the human act. Thomas reduces them to the terms *intentio* and *electio*,[2] of which he left us a precise definition. "The *intentio* is the striving toward the end to the extent that it is within the range of the means." "The *electio* is the concentration of the will on the *means* to the extent that they bear upon the attainment of the end" (ST I-II, 12, 4 ad 3; q. 12, 1 ad 4). The material sense of both concepts is the same since they contain the idea of the whole act, end and means. But they are formally quite distinct. The *intentio* is directly aimed at the absolute element of the structure of the action, that is, the end itself which is the reason that the means are willed and consequently is the principle of the act (*finis* as *principium actionis humanae*), the formal element which specifies the act (ST I-II, 1, 3). On the other hand, the *electio* signifies the relative element of the act, viz., the means (by its own definition means indicates a relation to the end) which is only useful until the end has been attained (*finis* as *terminus actionis humanae*) (ST I-II, 1, 3). As we have already said, an end can be striven for in itself and for its own sake. A means *as such* cannot be willed unless the end is willed simultaneously, because it is by nature relative to the end and because the exigencies of the goal specify that which will lead to its realization (*ex fine enim oportet accipere rationes eorum quae sunt ad finem*). For this reason, Thomas writes: "Whenever someone wants a means, he wants the end in the same act (*eodem actu*), but the reverse of this phrase is not always true" (ST I-II, 8, 3 ad 2 and ad 3; 12, 4).

The expression *eodem actu* clearly suggests that the will of the end and the choice of the means constitute only one act of the will: "It is evident that the same act of the will is embedded in the striving for the end as the reason for the choice of the means as well as in the striving for the means" (ST I-II, 8, 3). Thomas illustrates this proposition as follows: "When I say that I want a remedy (means) to recover from an illness (end), I indicate only one act of the will, since the end is the reason that I want the means. Subsequently, one and the same act of the will combines the object (the use of the remedy) and the reason for this object (the end, viz., the recovery from the illness)" (ST I-II, 12, 4).

But this one act of the will is a composite act. Thomas uses the terms *intentio* and *electio* to show the structural elements of this complex whole. Because of both elements the act of the will is a single dynamic event of which the end is the formal and primary element (*finis* as *principium*) which so extensively directs and determines the motion of the will toward the means that the act comes to a stop when the end has been attained (*finis* as *terminus*).

Actus Experior

Since the end is *terminus*, viz., that which must be realized by the act, the dynamic event cannot be confined to the inner act of the will. The action must be *done* in order to effect the end. To act is to be actively in touch with reality (with things, with ourselves, with our fellow men, with a social group, with God). The inner act of the will falls short of this active contact. Our will must rely on the medium of other faculties and our bodiliness as agencies which enable it to effect a real contact with reality. For this reason our action is not only an inner act of the will (*interior actus voluntatis*) but also an exterior event (*actus exterior*).

This brings us again to the question about the unity of the human act. Are the interior act of the will and the exterior event two acts or one? Thomas himself poses this question and writes an entire article in response (ST I-II, 17, 4). He elucidates his answer in a comparison. A reality which is composed of *forma* and *materia*, e.g., the soul and the body of the human being, is only one being (*unum simpliciter*) although it has different parts (*multa secundum quid*). In this way the human act is only one act but at the same time a composite unity of which, on the one hand, the interior act of the will is the formal element and, on the other hand, the exterior act is the material element. In other words, the end which is the proper object of the inner act of the will (ST I-II, 8, 2) is the formal element; the exterior act, as means to this end, is the material element of the very same human act: "*Finis autem comparatur ad id quod ordinatur ad finem, sicut forma ad materiam*" (ST I-II, 1, 4). And as the forma determines the specific being of a reality, so the end of the interior act of the will specifies the concrete totality of the human act (*finis dat speciem actui humano*) (ST I-II, 1, 3 ad 2).

Now it is clear that Thomas begins with the subject when describing the structure of human action. The end of the interior act of the will is the determining and decisive factor. 1) It can be willed absolutely and for its own sake even without any reference to an action in a *simplex actus voluntatis*. 2) It is also the decisive and determining factor of the action: only from the vantage point of the end can it be seen what are the means properly so called and furthermore, that the means are related to the end in such a manner that the action ceases when the end has been attained.[3]

Having taken the subject or the interior act of the will as the basis of his description of the structure of the human act, Thomas also uses the same basis for the moral evaluation of the will and the act. He states in his treatises *De lege aeterna* (ST I-II, q 93) and *De lege naturali* (ST I-II, q 94) that reason is the measure of morality to the extent that it is a participation in the eternal law (*secundum rationem esse*) In *De actibus humanis*, he summarizes this view in one article whose main thrust is: "*Quod ratio humana sit regula voluntatis humanae, ex qua eius bonitas mensuratur, habet ex lege aeterna, quae est ratio divina*" (ST I-II, 19, 4). It appears from this idea that the moral goodness of the human act depends on its accordance with reason. This is true both for the *simplex actus voluntatis* in which the end is aimed at in itself and for its own sake and for the *actus compositus* in which the will is directed towards the end in and through the means.

The Morality of the *Voluntas*

We said that it is Thomas' view that the good which is the proper object of the will is also its end. It is a moral good (*vere bonum*) when it corresponds to reason: "*ipse appetitus finis debiti praesupponit rectam apprehensionem de fine, quae est per rationem*" (ST I-II, 19, 3 ad 2). If it is not within the realm of reason, it is still a good (*apparens bonum*), as far as it is consonant with a particular appetite, in spite of the fact that it is morally vitiated (*contra naturam rationalem secundum rei veritatem*) (ST I-II, 6, 4 ad 3; q. 8, 1; q. 18, 4 ad 1). Whether or not the subject is taking the moral good as the end of his action depends on his inner disposition. In this context Thomas accentuates the meaning of the virtues. The moral virtues (below we will speak about the special place of *prudentia*) are acquired dispositions (habits) which direct us toward the moral good as the end, even when we do not act. Having acquired the virtue of justice, we would, by virtue of an inner *habitus*, love and will the social relations and conditions that fit the dignity of man, even when we do not act or when we find it impossible to overcome certain abuses in our own actions. A virtuous person is directed toward the moral good because he loves and wills it as an end by virtue of an inner disposition *absolute et secundum se*.

Even in his *De actibus humanis* which *per se* concerns human acts, Thomas cannot keep from already mentioning the virtues. He does this particularly in reference to texts of Aristotle.[4] He quotes especially this text of the philosopher: "*Virtus est quae bonum facit habentem et opus ejus bonum reddit.*"

Above all, virtue makes the subject who possesses it a good subject. It is the source of the morally good *simplex actus voluntatis* which enables us to set our will on the moral good in an absolute sense and for its own sake. So the first moral qualification does not concern the particular acts but the subject himself who by virtue of his virtuous dispositions is turned towards the moral good as his end.[5]

But virtue also makes good acts out of the acts of man. Here Thomas quotes the sentence of Aristotle: "*Similes habitus similes actus reddunt*" (ST I-II, 18, art. 5 *sed contra*). In his own doctrine on the virtues, he stresses the point that the virtues endow us with a connaturality or an affinity with the moral good and that they help us to discern the concrete actions which can embody the love of the moral good. He who is just, for instance, is tuned to just actions by the virtue of justice (ST I-II, 19, art. 1 *sed contra*).

II. THE MORALITY OF HUMAN ACTION

We said that according to Thomas the inner act of the will (end) and the exterior act (means) are one and the same concrete act (ST I-II, 17, 4). No wonder that Thomas concludes that they must also be treated as one from the moral viewpoint: "*Actus interior et exterior sunt diversi secundum genus naturae. Sed tamen, ex eis sic diversis constituitur unum in genere moris*" (ST I-II, 20, 3 ad 1). For this reason he reacts sharply against those who are of the opinion that the material event of an act can be evaluated morally without consideration of the subject, of the inner act of the will or of the end. As he sees it, an exterior action considered as nothing but the material event (*secundum speciem naturae*) is an abstraction to which a moral evaluation cannot be applied. This object-event becomes a concrete *human* act only insofar as it is directed towards an end within the inner act of the will. Only this concrete totality has a moral meaning. It is the end of the inner act of the will which specifies the malice or the goodness of the act: "*Finis secundum quod est prior in intentione, secundum hoc pertinet ad voluntatem. Et hoc modo dat speciem actui humano sive morali*" (ST I-II, 1, 3 ad 2). Thomas himself illustrates this as follows. The act of killing a human being (*hoc ipsum quod est*

3 - Ontic Evil and Moral Evil

occidere hominem) as the matter-event (*actus secundem speciem naturae*) can be done for several reasons, e.g., the exercise of justice (undoubtedly Thomas is thinking here of the execution of the death penalty which according to his theories can be justified on certain conditions) or of the gratification of vengeful feelings. Both cases have the same material act in common (*idem actus secundum speciem naturae*), but if we examine them from a moral point of view we will discover very diverse actions (*diversi actus secundum speciem moris*), since in the first case we will find a virtuous act while we will find a vitiated act in the second. It is then possible that acts which have the same features insofar as they are object-events (*actus qui sunt iidem secundum speciem naturae*) fall into very distinct types of morality (*esse diversos secundum speciem moris*) determined by the kind of end of the will towards which the matter-event has been directed (*ordinetur ad diversos fines voluntatis*) (ST I-II, 1, 3 ad 3). The end which the subject intends to work out by his inner act of the will specifies the morality of the act (ST I-II, 1, 3; 18, 6).

Thus in order to determine the morality of a human act, Thomas chooses as his starting point the acting subject, the end which is the proper object of the inner act of the will and which impresses the qualities of good or evil on the action: *finis enim dat speciem in moralibus*.[6]

At first sight it may seem that Thomas contradicts himself.[7] For one thing, he says that the *species moris*—the goodness or the malice of the act—is determined by the end, the object of the inner act of the will. For another, he writes that the *species moris* of the exterior act depends on the fact whether or not its object is in keeping with reason (*secundum rationem* or *praeter rationem*) (ST I-II, 18, 5 and 6). Does he thereby not suggest that the morality of the exterior action can be evaluated by itself and as an element which is disconnected from the subject or the end of the inner act of the will? We must not forget that Thomas immediately proceeds to answer this question as follows: "Nevertheless, the inner act of the will is the *formal* element of the exterior action, because the will itself acts through the medium of the body and because the exterior actions concern morality only insofar as they emanate from the will (*nisi in quantum sunt voluntarii*). From this follows that the *species moris* is formally dependent on the end (of the inner act of the will) and materially dependent on the object of the exterior action" (ST I-II,

18, 6). He adds this terse statement: *actus interior voluntatis comparatur ad exteriorem sicut formale ad materiale* (ST I-II, 18, 6 ad 2).

Let us always keep in mind the primacy of the end, the formal element. This element must be the starting point of the search for insight into the morality of the action. Now Thomas leads us into the alternative: the end itself can be good or bad.

1) First there are the actions with a morally bad end which is not the *finis debitus* sanctioned by reason (ST I-II, 19, 3 ad 2). The bad end vitiates the entire action because the end is the formal element of the entire event of the action. In Thomistic terms we can say: the bad intention vitiates the entire action. Indeed, as we have said above, in the view of Thomas the intention is to will the end as a *reason* that the action is willed (ST I-II, 12, 4 ad 3). When the end is bad, the whole action is the fruit of a *mala voluntas* and because the action is only human as far as it emanates from the will (*voluntarius*) it is entirely bad. It is in this sense that Thomas says that giving alms is a bad action if vanity motivates the giver, at least if the love of vain praise is a real intention, that is, the cause and the reason (*ratio et causa*) of the action: "*Voluntas non potest dici bona, si sit* intentio mala *causa volendi. Qui enim vult dare eleemosynam propter inanem gloriam consequendam, vult id quo de se est bonum*[8] *sub ratione mali, et ideo, prout est volitum ab ipso, est malum. Unde* voluntas *eius est* mala" (ST I-II, 19, 7 ad 2). Thomas is very well aware of the fact that a donation may help the person in need who receives it, that the *finis operis* of the action (to provide relief) is morally good if *it is intended by the acting subject as an end* (in this sense he says "*quod de se est bonum*"), but in the case under examination, the *mala voluntas* or the bad *intentio* of the agent is the reason (*causa*) of the entire event, and because there is the most intimate connection between the agent and the morality of the act, we have here an action which is truly bad since the formal element is bad in itself. The situation is still worse when the subject aims at several bad ends with his action. To illustrate this case. Thomas copied an example of Aristotle. Someone who steals to get the money he intends to use to lead someone into adultery is, strictly speaking, more of an adulterer than a thief (ST I-II, 18, 6). He is both, of course; he is primarily an adulterer because the main end of his inner act of the will is to commit adultery (*finis principalis*), but he is also a thief because he wills the unjust acquisition of money as an immediate end (*finis medius*) which *enables* him to realize his

main goal. The end of the agent—the object of the inner act of the will—consequently, is so determining and cogent that it *communicates its moral malice to the entire action*.

2) Now suppose that the good at which the agent aims as the end of his inner act of the will is a good which is sanctioned by reason (*ipse appetitus finis debiti praesupponit rectam apprehensionem de fine, quae est per rationem*) (ST I-II, 19, 3 ad 2). In this case the entire action is necessarily good if it is not a mere *velleitas* but rather the very will to bring about an end, or in other words, if it concerns a real *intentio finis* which involves the effective will to realize an end for its own sake and also as reason and cause of the action (*ratio et causa volendi*). This thesis does not favor subjectivism. On the contrary, it takes without any reservations the objective aspect of the exterior event into consideration and assigns it its rightful place in the light of the agent or of the inner act of the will. Thomas explains this in two convergent ways.

(a) He uses in most cases his views on the distinction and the intrinsic cohesion between the formal and the material elements.[9] In one and the same human act the formal element is the object of the inner act of the will, viz., the end, while the object event of the exterior action is the material element. That is true about the structure of the human act. It is also true about its morality. The moral goodness of the act of the will is the formal element of the exterior act: *bonitas actus voluntatis est forma exterioris actus* (ST I-II, 20, 1 ad 3). For this reason the end formally specifies the goodness or the malice (*species moris*) of the human act while the material element of the goodness or the badness of this same act receives its material specification from the object of the exterior action (ST I-II, 18, 6). Not any kind of exterior action, however, can become the material element of a morally good end. Thomas emphasizes this: "The end is to the means (exterior action) as *forma* is to the *materia*. According to the way things are, the *materia* cannot receive the *forma*, unless it is properly disposed to it (*nisi sit debito modo disposita ad ipsam*). Consequently nothing can realize its end unless it has been properly directed and ordered toward this goal (*nisi sit debito modo ordinatunt ad ipsum*)" (ST I-II, 4, 4). So writes Thomas when he deals with the matter of our ultimate end and demonstrates that this can be reached only if the will is correctly directed according to its proper relation to that end (*rectitudo voluntatis est per debitum ordinem ad finem ultimum*).

But he evidently intends to give us a principle which is true of the actualization of any morally good end. But how do we ascertain that an exterior action is *materia apta* and in a fitting way is adequate as a medium of the realization of a morally good end? When is the exterior action fittingly directed toward a good end? This cannot be known by viewing the exterior action only as a material event (*secundum speciem naturae*) (ST I-II, 1, 3 ad 3); rather, the object of the exterior action must be left within the whole framework of the act before it can be evaluated according to the measure of morality, viz., the reason (*objectum est ei (= rationi) conveniens vel non conveniens*) (ST I-II, 18, 5). As far as it is a material event, sexual intercourse can conceive life both in the act of adultery and in the marital act (*habent unum effectum secundum speciem naturae*), but when sexual intercourse is taken as the material element *of the whole of the action* of which the end is the formal element, the marriage act and adultery are entirely divergent on the level of the *species moris (secundum quod comparantur ad rationem, differunt specie*) (ST I-II, 18, 5 ad 3).

(b) Thomas endeavors to explain this in another way by the use of the notions "means" (exterior action) and "end" (inner act of the will). He points out that on account of its very definition, the means is related to the end and therefore must be adequately proprotionate (*debita proportio*) to this end. To be a real human act he says, the act must emanate from the will (*voluntarius*). This does entail that the acting subject has a rational knowledge of the end (*non solum apprehenditur res quae est finis, sed etiam cognoscitur ratio finis*) and the means. In other words, he must grasp that the means is by its own definition relative and proportionate to the end (*cognoscitur proportio ejus quod ordinatur in finem ipsum*). Only then can the subject in the mental process of deliberation create the distance which brings about the freedom to act or not to act (ST I-II, 6, 2). The exterior act can only be means insofar as it is in proportion to the end (*proportio actus ad finem*), i.e., insofar as it is suited to effect the end (ST I-II, 6, 2). Insofar as it is a means, the exterior act is not willed for its own sake, but for its going out towards the end (*ex ordinatione ad finem*): the will wills the means only to the extent that it wills the end, so that it wills the end in the means (*unde hoc ipsum quod in eis vult est finis*) (ST I-II, 8, 2). Consequently the end is the reason (*ratio*) and the cause (*causa*) of the will to will the means.[10] So it is the beginning and the principle of the act (*finis ut principium*) (ST I-II,

1 art. 3). The means is relative to the end. Its characteristic is to serve the purpose of effecting the end. For this reason the action ceases when the end has been effected (*Finis* as *terminus*) (ST I-II, 1 art. 3): *id quod est ad finem se habet ad finem ut medium ad terminum* (ST I-II, 12, 4 *sed contra*).

Consequently, the exterior action is a means and as a means, it is relative to, going out towards, and in proportion to the end which is to be effected. This fits the structure of the human act. It also fits the morality of the human act. The end is morally good when it is in keeping with the *exigencies of the reason (conveniens rationi)*. The means of the exterior acts participate in this moral goodness when they not only serve the purpose of effecting the end but moreover, when they are in the correct proportion to the end according to reason. This balanced proportion is an intrinsic element of the exterior action (*debita proportio ad finem et relatio in ipsum inhaeret actioni*); from this results the fact that the exterior action participates in the moral goodness of the end which is the cause of the moral goodness (*secundum habitudinem ad [finem] causam bonitatis*) (ST I-II, 18, 4 *in corp.* and as 2). Thomas describes very clearly this *debita proportio* in a summary of his own view:

> Sin really consists of an action which is not in proportion to an end to which it is directed. It must be noted that the correct proportion to the end is measured with a rule.... The reason is the immediate rule of the actions which emanate from the will. The eternal law is the highest rule. Consequently, the human act is good when it is directed toward the end in keeping with the order determined by the reason and the eternal law; it is sinful when it deviates from this rule (ST I-II, 21, 1, q. 18, 4 ad 2; q. 19, 8).

Just as in the structure of the action, the end is the reason and the cause of the choice of the means, so is the goodness of the end in the morally good action only the total reason and cause of the exterior action if it leads the subject into doing an exterior action of which the object is properly proportioned according to reason to the required end (*debita proportio*). Someone steals, for example, in order to give the stolen goods to a needy person. Judging by the material element of this action, we see that it serves the purposes of the end: *de facto*, the needy person gets relief. But when we judge this action in the light of morality—*secundum ordinem rationis*—we say that there is no *debita proportio* of the action (means) to the end. On the contrary, there is a contradiction between the material and formal elements of the act. The end which is willed by the subject is an affirmation of the right to own property: the thief wants the needy person to own the things he gives him. But, by his exterior action, he disregards the ownership of the victim of the theft.

Now let us put the same material element into a case of a morally good deed. Suppose, for instance, that there is no other means to save a needy man from death by starvation except by giving him things that are taken from another. In this case there is no contradiction between means and end since, under these circumstances, the right to ownership must give way to the right of use. Therefore, this case is not a case of theft.[11] To give an act the character of moral goodness, it is therefore not enough that the end of the subject is morally good: the act is good only when the exterior action (material element, means) is proportioned to the end (formal element) *according to reason*, when there is no contradiction of the means and the end in the whole of the act on the level of reason (*secundum rei veritatem*). Only then is the undivided and composite action morally good, because the means share in the moral goodness of the end within the totality of the act. In other words, by virtue of the *debita proportio* the formal element of the act, the end, communicates its moral goodness to the material element of the act, viz., the exterior action or the means: *secundum habitudinem ad finem, causam bonitatis*.

It is clear that Thomas does not fall into subjectivism because he always uses the subject or the end of the inner act of the will as his starting point. It is always his view that both constituent parts of the act, end and means or material and formal element, must be judged morally in the light of the objective measure of morality. The intention must aim at an end which is morally good according to reason: *ipse appetitus* finis debiti *praesupponit rectam apprehensionem finis, quae est per rationem* (ST I-II, 19, 3 ad 2). The exterior action too (material element, means) must also be *materia debito modo disposita* to be open to the form of the good end. In other words, the means can only share in the moral goodness of the end if it is correctly proportioned (*debita proportio*) to that end according to our understanding of objective truth and if there is no contradiction between end and means.

We said that the moral virtues direct us toward morally good *ends*. *Prudentia* holds a special place among them. The means (*ea quae sunt ad finem*) are its object. Its function is to safeguard the *debita proportio* of the means to morally good ends.[12]

Let us go more into detail about Thomas's view of *debita proportio* by examining a concrete illustration of his special ethics (ST II-II, 64, 7). We choose this example because it refers to an action whose means obviously imply an ontic evil. This will put us on the way to the main point of our problem: Thomas asks: "Is it permissible to kill someone in self-defense?"

First, he establishes the fact that one and the same act can have two effects, of which one has been intended (*in intentione*) as the intended end (*id quod intenditur*) and the other has not been intended as end (*praeter intentionem*).

Then he mentions the principle which governs the moral qualification of the activity: the acts share in the moral species (their being good or bad) of the intended end, while that which has no bearing on the intention of the end (*praeter intentionem*) only happens *per accidens* and therefore has no moral meaning. Thomas already explained this tersely at the beginning of his treatise *De fine ultimo* (ST I-II, 1, 3) and also in his examination of scandal (ST II-II, 43, 3) where he always takes the fundamental principle "*Finis enim dat speciem in moralibus*" as *his starting point*. Thomas now applies this principle when he examines an act of self-defense.

This act can have two effects: self-conservation and the death of the assailant. When the end of the act of my will is only the safeguarding of my own life (*id quod intenditur*) my act is morally right on that level. St. Thomas says that this end is morally good because it is consistent with an urge of human nature: It is natural for each being to protect its existence as much as possible. "*Actus ergo hujusmodi ex hoc quod intenditur conservatio propriae vitae non habet rationem illiciti cum hoc sit cuilibet naturale quod se conservet in esse quantum potest*" (ST II-II, 64, 7; ST, I-II, 94, 2).

But it is not sufficient that an end of an acting subject is morally justifiable. One is not free to do what he pleases to effect a good end. This would be subjectivism. In order to prevent subjectivism, Thomas introduces the matter of the exigencies of the *debita proportio*. The exterior action—material element or means—must be correctly proportioned to the end within the totality of the act: "*Potest tamen aliquis actus* ex bona intentione *proveniens illicitus reddi* si non sit proportionatus fini" (ST II-II, 64, 7 *in corp.*).

What does Thomas think this *debita proportio* is in the case of self-defense?

In the case of self-defense violence (means) is used against the assailant. This use of violence naturally causes ontic evil: it is harmful and hurtful to the assailant to the extent that it scares him, wounds him or perhaps even kills him. That is why it must be restrained as much as possible. In other words the use of violence must be kept within the limits of the measures which are the *means* to the conservation of one's own life (*end*). Or, in Thomas' words: it is right to use violence to protect one's self against violence if the defensive violence stays within the limits indicated by the right to safeguard one's own life (*vim vi repellere licet cum moderamine inculpatae tutelae*), (ST II-II, 64, 7 *in corp.*) for the end of the agent is the reason and the cause of the exterior action which is the means to the end. If it should be necessary to use a kind of violence which causes the death of the assailant, this defensive violence is justifiable as a necessary means. It is still an ontic evil but it is morally justifiable.

When excessive violence is used (*si aliquis ad defendendam propriam vitam utatur majori violentia quam oporteat*) (ST II-II, 64, 7 *in corp.*) the excess exceeds the bounds prescribed by the end of self-defense. The excess is not a means anymore. The end does not sanction it as a reason or a cause. Consequently, the excessive use of violence is not disconnected from *praeter intentionem* but it is implied in the intention as something that is willed for its own sake. When an assailant can be kept under control by menacing him with a weapon, killing him is not morally justifiable.

The only goal of self-defense must be the safeguarding of one's own life. Thomas distinguishes very clearly between the case in which the death of the assailant has actually been intended as the end (*quis intendit occidere hominem ut seipsum a morte liberet*) (ST II-II, 64, 7 ad 1) and the case in which the death has not been actually intended although the assailant has been effectively killed. In this case the death of the assailant stays within the confines of the use of violence as a means to the safeguarding of one's own life, which is the exclusive end of the act of self-defense (*quamvis* non intendat *interficere sed seipsum defendere*) (ST II-II 64, 7 ad 3). Thomas says that this is a case of killing an assailant *per accidens* and *praeter intentionem*. What

3 ~ Ontic Evil and Moral Evil

does he mean by that? He makes it clear in another context where he is dealing with the moral problem of scandal.

Scandal (*scandalum activum*) comes about by improper acts or words which can give the impression to others that they are sinful. There are two types of active scandal. In the first case, there is the intention to lead someone into sin by improper acts or words (ST II-II, 43, 1 ad 4), when he is seduced into sin by inciting, encouraging or showing him how to sin (ST II-II, 43, 1 *in corp.*). In the second case, one performs an action (for instance, he commits a public sin) that by its very nature leads others into temptation (ST II-II, 43, 1 ad 4). Is his sin also a special sin of scandal (*speciale peccatum*)? Scandal can be given *per accidens*, viz., when the agent does not intend it (*praeter intentionem agentis*), e.g., when someone freely resolves to sin by word or deed but does not want (*non intendit*) to be an occasion of sin to someone else. In this case giving scandal is not a special sin because that which happens *per accidens* does not make it a special sin (*quia quod est per accidens, non constituit speciem*). But scandal is scandal *per se* when the purpose of the bad words or bad deeds is to turn someone else into a sinner. This particular purpose brings about a special sin (*ex intentione specialis finis sortitur rationem specialis peccati*). It is always for the same reason: "*finis enim dat speciem in moralibus*" (ST II-II, 43, 3 *in corp.*). Consequently, any sin could be the material element of the special sin of scandal, but this special sin has the special malice of scandal only by virtue of the *formal element*, when the subject has seduction in mind as an end (*ex intentione finis*).[13]

Now we understand why it is the thesis of Thomas that in the act of self-defense the death of the assailant must be something that comes about *per accidens* and *praeter intentionem*. When one specifically intends to kill the assailant, self-conservation loses its status of sole intention. Another specifically intended goal then enters the act (*ex intentione specialis finis*), and thus the action *per se* gets the meaning of murder because *finis dat speciem in moralibus*. If, on the other hand, the safety of one's own life is the sole end (*id quod intenditur*) of the agent, the sense of the action is self-defense and nothing but self-defense. If it happens that the assailant gets killed as a result of a violent act of self-defense, his death happens only *praeter intentionem* and *per accidens*. Consequently, the end of one's inner act of the will should never be the death of another person because this would make his act *per se* an act of murder.

Now Thomas raises an objection. It does not seem necessary that somebody whose life is threatened does everything possible to spare the life of his assailant because we must love our own life more than the life of others. Why should not the death of the assailant be the purpose and the end of the act of self-defense (*id quod intenditur*)? In his answer Thomas takes up another principle: only the public authorities or their delegates have the right to intend the death of someone (*intendens hominem occidere*) for the safeguarding of the common good (*refert hoc ad publicum bonum*). In this case the killing is an intermediate end (*finis medius*) which serves a higher goal, viz., the safeguarding of the common good (*finis principalis*) (ST II-II, 64, 7 *in corp.*). This act does not negate the right to life. What matters here above all is the protection of the right to life and to security of those who respect and serve the common good, since this right and this security are essential elements of the common good, which must be defended against those who endanger it even when it means killing them. The *debita proportio* is unquestionable.

But even in this case the act becomes immoral, says Thomas, if he who is responsible for the common good acts with a bad intention e.g., to take revenge (*privata libidine*).[14] *Finis enim dat speciem in moralibus*!

This example evidently concerns exterior actions in which ontic evil is involved. Thomas formulates some rules of the evaluation of their morality. 1) What has been generally said about human acts is also true here. If the exterior action (material element) is a means to a bad end, the act is bad. The bad end of the subject is the formal element that vitiates the act. 2) To bring about ontic evil can be justifiable if the act which brings it about remains within the bounds of the measure of *means* to the good end. I have the right to use violence within an act of self-defense to keep myself alive: and if need be, killing my assailant does not exceed the bounds of that which I must use as *means* to my end. 3) According to Thomas, it is permissible to will in itself an act which causes ontic evil, provided that certain conditions are present and if this act itself serves a higher end, e.g., the right of the public authorities to kill someone who by grievous offenses endangers the common good. These points show, in any case, that there is a *difference* between ontic evil and moral evil, while there is also a connection between them. This leads us finally to the heart of our problem.

III. Ontic Evil in Our Acts

Of old, a distinction between *malum physicum* and *malum morale* was made. Nowadays, we prefer the term "ontic evil" to the term "physical evil," because the contemporary meaning of "physical" corresponds more to the meaning of "material." It is true, of course, that there is evil in the material world. We say that an earthquake which destroys human lives and entire regions is an evil. A devastating flood is evil: generally speaking, all natural disasters are evil. There are evils which disrupt the corporal life of man, e.g., death (which radically defeats our will to live), pain, sickness. It is true that pain is like a signal which is good because it warns us that something is wrong with our health. But it is also true that it is a signal which is sent forth by something that displeases us and that in itself is ontic evil. Wear and tear of the body, fatigue etc. are evils. There is spiritual and mental evil. Every human being suffers the handicaps and the shortcomings of his own individual psyche—not to mention psychoses and neuroses—which make life difficult for him. And are we not always crippled by our ignorance, which makes us aware of a frustration of our urge to know? Because we are human beings we want to govern our actions: only *human* acts that emanate from the will suit us. But from the beginning of his *De actibus humanis*, Thomas encounters the problem of invincible ignorance and error, which can keep our acts from being human acts in the real sense (ST I-II, 6, 8). We call ontic evil any lack of a perfection at which we aim, any lack of fulfillment which frustrates our natural urges and makes us suffer. It is essentially the natural consequence of our limitation. Our limitation itself is not an evil—to be created to be limited—but, because we are thinking, willing, feeling and acting beings, we can be painfully hampered by the limits of our possibilities in a plurality of realities that are both aids and handicaps (ambiguity).

How does this situation concern our actions? By action, we do not mean here the inner act of the will, but the concrete act made up of the material and the formal element (means and end). We feel that we may take the position on this level that each concrete act implicates ontic evil because we are *temporal* and *spatial*, live together *with others* in the same *material world*, are involved and act in a *common sinful* situation.

Our Temporality

Our actions follow each other in the course of the different moments of time. It is true that we can do some things by force of habit while we deliberately keep ourselves busy with another thing. But from the moment our actions demand our full attention and endeavor, we can do them only successively, i.e., where ambiguity enters our freedom of choice (*liberum arbitrium*). Our ability to resolve which action we want to effect at a certain moment is an expression of our autonomy, of our self-determination. Henri Bergson very correctly stated that our freedom is "*la détermination du moi par le moi.*" In this sense the fact that we have the *ability* to decide and to determine what we do, is the positive aspect of our freedom. But there is also a negative side. When we choose a certain action, we must at the same time, at least for the time being, postpone all other possible acts. This is the meaning of Bergson's words: "*Tout choix est un sacrifice*"; or as the traditional terminology puts it, each *commissio* (act) includes an *omissio*. Usually this does not strike us as bad because we can postpone until another time what we cannot do now: all is not lost that is delayed. But the situation can be one which makes us painfully aware of our temporary limitation. The fact of an unavoidable *omissio* may even become a moral problem. The matter of the moral problems involved in the question of the *omissio* and the conflict of duties and values came up often in our textbooks.

However, the point of the question is not the conflict of the duties or the values—all duties and values by their own definition have some connection with the fulfillment of the human person and consequently, are not conflicting. The conflict is directly related to our temporality. A husband for example, can be very busy with his professional duties; he must also spend enough time in the company of his wife; as a father he must be interested in the education of his children; as a religious man he feels the need to spend time reading and meditating on religious topics; he has also to keep up his social life and he has a need of friendship, recreation, etc. All these realities are very valuable. But to do all this he needs time, more time than he has. He has the feeling he is lacking something when he becomes aware of his inability to realize all these different values as much as he pleases. So there is ontic evil. This ontic evil is *distinct* from moral evil—we speak here about limits and restrictions which force themselves upon man. But at the same time there is a *connection* between moral and ontic evil: it occurs every day that people who are busy in several ways experience the problem of the conflict of duty and of *omissio* to the degree of the sensitivity of their own conscience. This problem comes from the temporality of our existence and our activity.

Our Spatiality

By this way we mean that our *corporal being* and the reality of the *world* in which our activity is embedded are material and subject to physical laws that escape our freedom. Here, too, we are facing a fundamental ambiguity.

Our corporal being has a share in our subjectivity; it forms part of the subject we are. It enables us to communicate by way of social relations. It gives us the capacity for acting as a subject on the things of this world. But at the same time our body remains a part of the world, and because it is material, it is necessarily subject to the laws which govern matter. Our power to act on things is limited and graded by our corporeal capacities (which can always become more refined, stronger and wider with the help of technical aids). Our actions are unavoidably limited by the fact that we are subject to tiredness, need to sleep, sickness, physiological wear and tear etc. Our body is a means to action. But it is also a handicap which impedes our action. This hindrance may hurt us as an ontic evil.

But the ambiguity is not only present in our own corporal being; it becomes more intense when our activity deals with the *material* things of this world. These things are governed by laws which we have not created and which we cannot change by our free will. But the very fact that these things have their own nature and are governed by fixed laws makes them aids and means to our fulfillment. We can count on them: e.g., if by their own nature bricks did not retain their solidity, our free will could not use them as proper construction materials. Because we can count on things and because their laws are fixed, we can change with our work the world of nature into a cultural environment (objective culture) wherein we can live and continually improve the standards which correspond to the dignity of man's existence (subjective culture). This presupposes that we first become familiar with the things and their laws. Referring to Hegel, Marx wrote that necessity is only blind as long as it remains unknown. For instance, as long as man was ignorant of the laws of electricity, he could only fear it as the blind and destructive force of thunderstorms. Because scientific knowledge helped him formulate the necessary laws of electricity, man can use electricity as a source of light, power and heat. Generally speaking, we can say that the more we learn about the material reality, the better we can harness it as an aid to action.

But this knowledge remains limited. The material world, moreover, is pluriform and is subject to many and very diverse laws. We can make an efficient use of some of them as a means to certain ends of our existence because we have tapped their power in a scientific and technological way. But other forces and processes handicap our actions. To a certain extent things act with degrees of hindrance and usefulness for man and place him in a situation of ambiguity.

As temporality involves man in the problem of the *omissio* and the conflict of duties or values, so our spatiality involves him in the problem of acts with several effects. Scientific and technological progress have meant for man an enormous increase in the output of goods which has accompanied the rise of " Big Technology," yet we cannot manage this big-scale industry enough to prevent the pollution of the environment which threatens to engulf us. We have succeeded in organizing very high-scale traffic by air, land and sea which binds up the world in a web of communication routes at a rate of speed the world has never known, but the detrimental side-effects are the enormous number of traffic accidents and the psychological stress and strain caused by the noise level and the hectic pace of life.

We control our material reality only imperfectly and partially. Detrimental consequences flow from the use of things in the constant accompaniments of every day, e.g., a walk gives me rest and fresh air but it also wears out my shoes.

We do not usually pay attention to the ambiguity of our daily actions caused by our spatiality. But once ontic evil increases considerably, we start seeing very clearly that the problem of activities with many effects becomes a very important moral question. Who would still dare to deny that the problems of the pollution of the environment and the soaring statistics of traffic mishaps involve no need for moral thinking? It would be very hard to lose sight of the moral problems that crop up constantly in the field of medicine. They become more and more complicated since medicine introduces more and more *things of the material world* to work on the processes of our physical life, after having made them into products of science and technology; thus, the ambiguity of both our physical being and the material things manifests itself. The technological means (material things) used in the field of surgery serve the health and life of man, but a loss of integrity of the body may be the consequence of their incursion into the processes of life. More and more effective medicines are continuously available to man, but are there any medicines which are not detrimental at the same time?

Our Togetherness

Our human existence is also being *with, by, and for each other*; our life is togetherness. Ambiguity also runs through this dimension of man's life. Our being is open to the totality of the reality. Within this intentionality our openness to each other or our social being evidently plays an important role. Child psychology has sufficiently proven that only through the achievement of openness to others and integration into a human "togetherness" can the child become a human, responsible and self-asserting subject—only *with* and *by* those who are already human will man become human. Having become a responsible and self-asserting subject, man can by virtue of his essential openness unfold and achieve himself only by engaging himself in and for others in the forms of social relations which suit man. Our self-fulfillment can only be realized in our being *for* each other.

This sounds quite positive. Nevertheless, there is a fundamental ambiguity in our social life. Consider this example. Probably the most important aspect of the social dimension of life is that we must be able to share the cultural achievements, fruits of the collaboration. When we share the same *spiritual* values, we are not disturbing one another. On the contrary, an educated person does not become less educated when he transfers his knowledge to his students. When many share the same spiritual value, one's share is not made smaller by the sharing with others. What is said about the unifying power of spiritual values is so true. Think of the spiritual affinity and the ties of people who are interested in the same branch of science, share the same religious conviction, have a common love and appreciation of esthetic values. This too sounds very positive. But we find also a relationship to material things in social life. Social ties, too, grow out of a common sharing of interest in the material environment. If we did not have this sharing of interest, living-together would not become a working-together which produces these material goods. But, community life also means that all of us take something of the products of the corporate enterprise. Whatever is consumed or used by one member of the community is not available to another at the same time. In other words, although we profit from living for, by, and with others there remains a seamy side to the way society is related to the allocation of the resources made available to man. As to the need of regulating the use and the consumption of goods according to moral laws which guarantee the dignity of man, there is no doubt. The moral controls put on this aspect of social life will vary according to the nature of the use of these goods and of the goods themselves. For example, we use only a section of the highways for a certain time. Others use other sections before, after and near us. But when the traffic becomes very heavy because of the many dozens of vehicles which use the highway, a system of traffic laws becomes absolutely necessary. The controls will affect other fields still more. There are things which must always be available to our basic needs. They must be owned by us. Even Marx defended the right to own the useful goods and the consumer goods because it fits the dignity of man (personal property). Thus without social controls, man is constantly in the way of other men in a world where material goods must be shared. Without social controls, this state of confusion would make a decent social life impossible. Ethical controls must be imposed on individual freedom for the sake of the safety and the freedom of all who live in the human community.

Our Sinful Condition

The outstanding fact about these problems is that we cause ontic evil when we act immorally. And so we move to the question of the fundamental source of ontic evil—our sinful condition. There is no need to emphasize the obvious fact that a very great amount of ontic evil is caused or is tolerated by the immoral behavior of individuals or groups, e.g., the inhumanity of man to man, the evils of racial discrimination, the starvation of two-thirds of the population of the world, the destruction of life and property during wars, etc. All these forms of evil cannot be whitewashed by the claim that temporality, spatiality, the shortage of economical goods, etc., are sources of ontic evil. It is a sad fact that much ontic evil is the fruit of moral evil. If individuals and groups, in their mutual intercourse, always acted according to their inner inclinations (which Aristotle already said give moral goodness to the acting subject and his deeds), the level of ontic evil present in this world would drop considerably.[15]

IV. Distinction and Connection Between Ontic and Moral Evil

We have tried to show why ontic evil is *always* present in our concrete activity. If this approach is true, it cannot be concluded that it is inevitably morally evil to cause ontic evil or to allow it to remain in this world by our actions. If this were the case, there would not be any way to act morally. We must act. "Nous sommes embarqés," said Blondel. Our humanity is imperfect, it is a being-potentiality and at the same time it is a dynamic tendency pressing forward the fulfillment of this potentiality (to expound this we should make a study of our inclinations, but we take it for granted). As *open* reality we can realize our potentialities only as we realize our relationships with things, men, social groups to which we belong and God. The realization of all these relationships, within the measure of morality, of course, presupposes our effective engagement, our activity as an active intercourse with reality. To be man means to tend dynamically toward self-realization. Now self-realization can only be the fruit of our actions. We must act. Consequently, it cannot be said that all activity is essentially tied up with moral evil, although ontic evil is always present in the activity. Ontic evil and moral evil, hence, are not the same.

Yet, there is a connection between ontic evil and moral evil. As we have said, ontic evil is a lack of perfection which impedes the fulfillment of a human subject (this subject could be ourselves or other individuals or a group of individuals). In any case, it is harmful and damaging to human beings. And since morality is chiefly concerned with the human relationships and the well-being of human beings, it cannot remain unconcerned about the ontic evil which in all its forms handicaps and harms the development of individuals and communities. If we accept this view, we must ask ourselves: When and to what extent are we justified in causing or allowing ontic evil?

We have accentuated that, according to Thomas, a human act is morally good when the exterior act (material element, means) has a *debita proportio* within the measure of reason to the morally good end (formal element). It seems to us that a further examination of Thomas' understanding of this *debita proportio* will help us find the answer to that question.

The authors who try to answer the question in the light of the principles of the acts with more effects also appeal to the notion of *debita proportio*. One of the principles they start from is that the directly intended good effect must have a *debita proportio* to the indirectly willed bad effect: the value realized in the direct effect must at least counter-balance the bad, indirect effect. Mangan claims that this principle is a Thomistic one (Mangan 1949, 41-61). He refers to Thomas's article on self-defense: "*Illicitum est quod homo intendat occidere hominem ut seipsum defendat.*" Mangan asserts that *intendere* implies both end and means. Both of them are *directly* intended and so they must be morally good. Mangan is right when he maintains that according to Thomas *intendere* applies to the end and the means. But his affirmation will no longer serve when he juxtaposes end and means as though both of them were equally *direct* objects of the intention. According to Thomas, the end is intended *absolute secundum se*, and it is the reason and the cause of the willing of the means. In other words, the end is the formal element and the means or the external action is the material element. Well, as material element the means or the external action has to be a *materia bene disposita* or in due proportion to the end. Consequently, in Thomas' view due proportion is an *intrinsic* requisite in the one but composed action; it is a due proportion between means and end, between the material and the formal element of the action, while the principles of the acts with more effects require a due proportion between the direct and indirect effect.

According to another principle (the most important) of the moral evaluation of acts with several effects, the act must be good in itself or at least indifferent; in other words, the use of bad means to attain a good end is never permissible. This principle supposes that the external action (means) can be morally evaluated in itself without any consideration of the end or the effects. Our analysis of the structure and the morality of a human action has led us to our firm claims that this position is one of the currents of thought contested by Thomas. According to Thomas a moral evaluation is only possible about a concrete action, considered as a whole, composed of end and means. And two questions must be answered. First, is the end of the agent morally good? Second, is the external action a material element able to be actuated by the end as formal element or is it a *true* means? On account of its very definition, means involves being-related-to-the-end. Hence, it is not subject to a judgment that considers it as an absolutely unrelated thing. The judgment must judge the *debita proportio* of the means by virtue of which the totality of the act participates in the moral goodness of the end.

We should never overlook the *debita proportio* of the means to the end in a composite action. In order to explain it, we will examine successively different aspects (without distinguishing, it is not possible to describe), but even now we must say that it is necessary to grasp the interrelationship of all those aspects in order to define all the requirements of a *debita proportio*.

1) If ontic evil is *per se* intended, the end itself (object of the inner act of the will) is morally bad and, being the formal element (reason and cause of the exterior action), vitiates the entire action.

We have already stated that any dimension of ontic evil is a lack of perfection, a deficiency which frustrates our inclinations. We label it *evil* when it affects a human subject insofar as it appears to the consciousness as a lack and a want, and to the extent that it is detrimental and harmful to the development of individuals or communities. It follows from this definition that we should never *per se* will ontic evil. In the final instance, the entire set of moral laws and principles exists for the real well-being and the true development of man and society. Therefore, it is obvious that we would fall into immorality if we should strive for ontic evil itself and *for its own sake* because ontic evil necessarily impedes and precludes the development of man and society. In other words, ontic evil should never be the end of the inner act of the will if by end is meant that which definitively and in the full sense of the word puts an end to the activity of the subject (*finis* as *terminus*). In this sense, Thomas said that a private individual is never justified, not even in the case of self-defense, in willing the death of a human subject as an end, because this would make his act *per se* an act of murder (ST II-II, 64, 7 *in corp.* and ad 1). However, Thomas says, *under certain conditions* it can be right to intend an ontic evil as end of the inner act of the will, if that end is not willed as a final end, but only as *finis medius et proximus* to a higher end. Referring to this principle, Thomas teaches that the public authorities who are bound by their office to be responsible for the public good, have the right to *will* the death of a criminal as the immediate end (*finis medius*) if it is a necessary means to the higher good of the community (intendens *hominem occidere* . . . refert hoc *ad publicum bonum*) (ST II-II, 64, 7 *in corp*.). We can now establish the principle that we never have the right to will ontic evil *as the ultintate end of our intention*, because the formal element of our action, viz., the end, the object of the inner act of the will, would be morally evil, and the malice of the end determines and characterizes the grade of morality of the entire action.

Unless we remember this fundamental principle, it is not likely that we will understand Thomas's explanation of the sin of scandal. When someone sees that I am doing something which is sinful or which looks sinful to him (ST II-II, 43, 1 ad 1), my action "scandalizes" him (occasion of sin). What he sees me do can cause trouble for him; it can lead him into wanting to do the same thing. This set of circumstances is detrimental to him and is, therefore, an ontic evil. So my action causes ontic evil. But does that make it a special sin of scandal (*speciale peccatum scandali*)? According to Thomas, if we will only the sinful act we commit and if we do not intend to lead others into temptation (*non intendit alteri dare occasionem ruinae sed solum suae satisfacere voluntati*) we do not commit the sin of scandal. Because the ontic evil which has been effected has not been willed *per se* (as end). It stays outside the end of the inner act of the will (*praeter intentionem agentis*). But when we actually intend to lead others into sin (*intendit alium trahere ad peccatum*) we want the ontic evil for its own sake and so the end is immoral. Because the end is immoral (*ex intentione* specialis *finis*) we are guilty of the special sin of scandal (*finis enim dat speciem in moralibus*) (ST I-II, 43, 3 *in corp*.). Each sinful action can be the material element of a special sin of scandal, because its ontic evil is its potentiality of scandal. But the moral evil of the special sin of scandal only comes to the fore when the inner act of the will involves the intention to lead others to sin, because this end is the formal element which specifies the totality of the action (ST I-II, 43, 3 ad 1).

Leaving this example out of our study, we can formulate as a general principle that any action, insofar as it involves *ontic evil*, becomes the material element of an immoral act, if this is ontic evil is *per se* the end of the intention since this makes the end of the acting subject into an immoral end which, as a formal element, contaminates the totality of the action with its malice.

2) When the single and composite act is viewed from the point of view of reason (*secundum rationem*) it must be found without an intrinsic contradiction between *the means* (exterior act as material element) and the morally good *end* of the inner act of the will (formal element).

The first condition for a good act is the goodness of the end of the agent (*debitus finis secundum rationem*). However essential this condition may be, it is not yet sufficient. Thomas taught us that the moral end as formal element only deserves to be labeled as the reason and the cause of the exterior action if this action is a means which, in conformity with reason (*secundum rationem*) has a *debita proportio* to the end, which only in these conditions puts the stamp of its moral goodness on the totality of the act. I mean that no intrinsic contradiction between the means and the end may be found in the total act when the act is placed in the light of reason. Put into terms of the philosophy of values, this means that the means must be consistent with the value of the end. Or, according to a more abstract formulation, the principle which has been affirmed in the end must not be negated by the means.

By stealing something from my fellow man, I cause damage to him, and I do something he dislikes because it causes an ontic evil for him. If I take something away from him to keep it for myself and to enrich myself, my action is an act of immoral theft, because this act involves an intrinsic contradiction between the means and the end: my end is the affirmation of the right to ownership (for me), while the means I use is the negation of the same right to ownership (for the victim of the theft). Now suppose that I take something away from him because I need it to save myself from utter misery. This time there is no intrinsic contradiction. I only signify that the right to use has priority over the right to ownership. Viewed from the angle of morality, this act is not an act of theft. What ground underlies this different moral evaluation? Reason is fundamentally ordered to truth (*appetitus veri*). Given that I am sure that I have evidence of something or that it seems to me that I have it (because I can be mistaken in good faith), I cannot but register this evidence cognitively even when it concerns a truth which displeases me or which interferes with my own profit or pleasure. Reason is disinterested. Thomas calls it a *facultas liberalis*. It submits itself *necessarily* and gratuitously to the truth which it embraces as evidence or as something which has all the appearances of evidence. It affixes to the truth the strictest connotation of necessity, absoluteness and universality so that it rejects any suggestion of a negation of itself. When it is obvious to me that I, the subject of the whole action, use a means which is the negation of the value (or the principle) I am affirming in my idea of the end, I am forced to be aware of this contradiction. This contradiction is the source of my feelings of guilt: the awareness of the inner disunity of the subject which has turned its free will against its rational understanding when it aimed at an end it could not rationally sanction or when it used a means by which it negated the value it affirmed by the end. My self is a united self, a subject which is undivided, and I preserve this unity only when I apply my will to use the means and to realize the end to my reason. My reason is necessarily ordered to the truth. It is like a pivot on which everything hinges. My power to will is *free*. Hence, there is only one way to preserve myself as a united subject: I must order all the aspects of the act of my will to the disinterested understanding of my reason. That is the fundamental axiom of morality.

Knauer pointed out very well that the axiom of the *debita proportio* or of the unwarrantableness of the inner contradiction between means and end is the central norm of each human act;[16] and he applied that fundamental norm to a problem of conjugal morality (Knauer 1970, 60-74). According to *Gaudium et spes* the marriage act must be ordered to the conjugal love and to the human transmission of life, viz., to responsible parenthood. This must be the end of marital intercourse; each conjugal act must include a *debita proportio* to this end. Consequently, if the marriage partners engage in sexual intercourse during the fertile period and thereby most likely will conceive new life, the marital act may not be morally justifiable when they foresee that they will not have the means to provide the proper education for the child. The rhythm method, too, can be immoral if it is used to prevent the measure of responsible parenthood. But the use of contraceptives can be morally justified if these means do not obstruct the partners in the expression of conjugal love and if they keep birth control within the limits of responsible parenthood. Marital intercourse can be called neither moral nor immoral when it is the object of a judgment which considers it without due regard for its end. A moral evaluation is only possible if it is a study of the totality of the conjugal act, viz., when one considers whether or not the conjugal act (means) negates the requirements of love and responsible parenthood (end).

The question to which we refer here is known as the problem of the relation of the *debita proportio* and ontic evil. If the presence of ontic evil as such would always endanger the *debita proportio* of our action, it would be impossible to act morally, because it is impossible to prevent ontic evil. The danger lies in the fact that *moral* evil is mentioned too soon. This happens every time a moral judgment of an exterior act does not include a judgment of the end and of the agent. This is taking ontic evil for moral evil. For example, it is said that "to say something which is not true" is "to lie." and the generally accepted meaning of "to lie" suggests moral disapprobation. This judgment is not sufficiently discriminating to be true. It passes over the distinction between *falsiloquium* (ontic evil) and *mendacium*. Each *falsiloquium* is undoubtedly an ontic evil, and it clashes with the ideal of absolute truthfulness (an ideal which from a moral point of view is of the utmost importance as will be shown below). But is each *falsiloquium* (ontic evil) at the same time a *mendacium* (moral evil)? To answer this question, we must consider what reason tells us about the meaning of human speech.

We can deal with language as an objective reality, as a system of phonemes which has its own structure (structuralistic approach). But when a subject utters language, the utterance becomes a very human means of communication: one individual says something about something to *another person*. We are social beings and in our social behavior language plays a fundamental role. The question is then if each *falsiloquium* contradicts the objective meaning of our human relations.

No doubt we would use speech in the most commendable way if we always used it to utter only the truth. If we feel that a person does not care very much for the truth, we lose our faith in him. Faith in others is a necessary condition of good social relations. The rule about "never be untruthful" is valid in most cases: *valet ut in pluribus*. It suggests an ideal, and it certainly means that if it were always permissible to utter *falsiloquia* this would be the end of all faith in our fellow men which is a condition for truly human relations. Reason dictates that we use our speech to *reveal* truth, if truth is the means to the furtherance of truly human social relations and of the faith in others which leads to this kind of relation (end). But the same end will also often dictate that we *keep silent* about certain truths, e.g., the duty of keeping something a secret. If certain secrets, e.g., professional secrets, are not kept under certain circumstances (which are indicated by the standards of a truly human social life), faith in others which is so indispensable to truly social relations is also eliminated. To be silent is the best way to hide a secret. But it may happen that somebody wants us to reveal a secret and that silence may be interpreted as a revelation of the secret. When someone has no right to know our secret, we must defend our right of secrecy by the necessary means, even by a *falsiloquium* if it is the only means and although it includes an ontic evil. We could also speak about our relation to people who at least for the time being could not take a certain truth....

But it is sufficient to mention the example of secrecy to explain our intention. The ontic evil of a *falsiloquium* is not willed here *per se* as the ultimate end of our intention (we regret on the contrary that it is inevitable, because there are people who want to know something they have no right to know or who would not be able to take the truth should they know). Our end is morally good: we want to hide a truth insofar as this is necessary to make good human relations possible. We implicate ontic evil in our speech only insofar as we want to use an effective means. No contradiction exists between means and end. The meaning of the entire act is secrecy and consequently, we intend only to preserve the trustfulness of all who expect that their secrets be kept. This should not be called a lie, because every lie enters the ontic evil of a *falsiloquium* as an end or as a means to an immoral end, or its implication in an action causes this action to absolutely contradict a good end.[17]

It will be said that this opinion does not agree with the view of Thomas, although we take Thomas' idea of the structure and the morality of the activity as our starting point. This is an objection well taken.

But first of all, when Thomas begins his study of the lie, he grounds it immediately and explicitly on his view of the structure and morality of a human act:

3 ~ Ontic Evil and Moral Evil

A moral act is specified by two elements, viz., the object and the end, because the end is the object of the will which is the first principle (*primum movens*) of the moral act. But the faculty too which is put into motion by the will has *its own object*. This object is the immediate object of the voluntary act (*proximum objectum*, consequently ordered to the end as *objectum voluntatis*) and is related in the act of the will [in the singular!] to the end as a material element to a formal element (*se habet in actu voluntatis ad finem sicut matetiale ad formale*) (ST II-II, 110, 1).

How strikingly and succinctly Thomas sums up the fundamental givens of his *De actibus humanis* in very few sentences! These givens serve as basis of his definition of the lie. The material element of the lie is "to utter a falsehood" (*falsum enuntiatur*). This is not yet a lie. One can be mistaken in good faith. A mistake is not a lie: "*falsum materialiter sed non formaliter quia falsitas est praeter intentionem dicentis*" (ST II-II, 110, 1 ad 1). To be a lie, this material element must be embraced by the *formal* element, viz., the end of the inner act of the will, the *intention* to utter something that is not true (*intentio voluntatis inordinatae ... ut falsum enuntietur*) (ST II-II, 110, 1 *in corp.* and ad 1). Then and only then the act clashes formally and directly with the virtue of veracity: "*Sic ergo patet quod mendacium directe et formaliter opponitur virtuti veritatis.*" This contradiction appears from Thomas' definition of the *virtus veritatis* or veracity:

> *Potest dici veritas* qua aliquis verum dicit, *secundum quod per eam aliquis dicitur verax. Et talis veritas sive veracitas necesse est quod sit virtus quia* hoc ipsum quod est dicere verum *est bonus actus virtus autem est quae bonum facit habentem et opus bonum reddit* (ST II-II, 109, 1).

Thomas' argument is very logical. He argues that telling the truth—the obiect of the virtue of veracity—is a good act (*dicere verum est bonus actus*). Hence, when one has the *intention* (the object of the inner act of the will, end) of uttering a falsehood (*voluntas falsum enuntiandi*) (ST II-II, 1 10, 1 *in corp.*) he commits a sin against the virtue of veracity. Thomas calls this sin a lie.

However, Thomas adds restrictive clauses to his definitions. Talking about veracity, he admits that it is not good to utter any truth anytime: it is bad, he says, to talk without reason about one's own virtues, even if they are real (*etiam de vero*) or to talk about one's sins if nobody profits by this conversation (ST II-II, 109, 1 ad 2). Moreover, one of the reasons why Thomas advocates veracity is that "people must be sure that they can trust each other." Now it is obvious that trustworthiness can be preserved by keeping secrets or by revealing the truth (ST II-II, 109, 3 ad 1). Evidently Thomas encounters the same difficulties when he reflects about his definition of the lie. He understands very well that just keeping silence is not always a good means to hide a truth if the revelation of the truth has bad consequences or is immoral. We shall not speak about the ways Thomas, just like Augustine, juggles words to absolve certain biblical saints from mendacity (ST II-II, 110, 3 ad 3 and ad 4). It is not permissible to tell a lie in order to save somebody from a danger, but it is permissible to practice a bit of prudent dissimulation (*aliqua dissimulatione*) or to veil the truth with many figures of speech (ST II-II, 110, 3 ad 3 and 4). One gets the impression of veracity. Or let us consider the question of the secret of the confessional. Thomas says that the confessor even has the right to declare under oath that he does not know anything. Thomas claims this right for the confessor for the following reason: *qua* human being he does not know anything because he knows it only the way God knows it since he represents God. "*Et ideo absque laesione conscientiae potest jurare se nescire, quod scit tantum ut Deus*" (IV Sent., dist. 21, q. 3, art. 1 ad 3). It is a pity that Thomas does not speak anywhere about professional secrets. Would he perhaps have said that those who must keep professional secrets have the moral right to declare that they do not know anything because they *qua* private individuals, do not know anything and because they *qua* professionals, must defend the professional secret in the name of the rights of society?

Let us accentuate that these arguments of Thomas are brilliantly consistent with his views on the structure and the morality of the human act. But we dare think that he has not sufficiently analyzed the meaning of speech and consequently loses sight of the "speech behavior of man in society." In every form of speech something is said about something (*enuntiatio, locutio*) by somebody to somebody (*communicatio*). Thomas knows this. He writes that on Pentecost Day the Apostles received the grace of the Holy Spirit to pass it on to others. This is signified very well by the figure of the fiery tongues, he says, because the *tongue is instrumenal in the communication with others by way of speech (lingua per locutionem est communicativa ad alterum)* (ST III, 72, 2 ad 1). Now, in his definition of the lie, Thomas mentions only the *locutio*, the fact that something is said about something—so the material element of the lie is the utterance of a falsehood (*falsum enuntiare*) and the formal element is the *intention* to utter a falsehood (*voluntas falsum enuntiandi*). Evidently, Thomas is right when he says that a sin of lying is committed when the *end*, the object of the inner act of the will, is to speak a falsehood. To will *per se* an ontic evil as the end of the *intention* is sinful. But the question is whether the utterance of a falsehood—ontic evil—in a *voluntary* falsehood is always willed necessarily as end . If speech is viewed only as *enuntiatio*, the way Thomas views it in his definition of the lie, it must follow that "to say something about something" is the formal element of a human act. But this leads to a view which is at variance with reality. Is it not a fact that in many voluntary *falsiloquia* the end of the object is certainly not to say something which is false only because it is false (*intentio voluntatis inordinatae . . . ut falsum enuntietur*). In other words, in these cases there is a *voluntas falsum enuntiandi* but this *voluntas* cannot be identified as *intentio finis*, the way Thomas does. Thomas' distinction between a material and a formal element of the lie is excellent. The weakness of his view is in the fact that he applies this distinction to an incomplete analysis of human speech. In his definition of the lie he considers only the *enuntiatio* "to say something about something," and it slips his mind that he mentions elsewhere that speech is a social phenomenon—somebody talks to somebody about something (*lingua per locutionem est communicativa ad alterum*). This is the totality of the phenomenon in which we must look for the formal and the material element. Thomas applies this distinction only to a partial aspect of the phenomenon we call human speech. Therein seems to be his weakness.

Obviously, language is a social phenomenon—it reveals our social being, and it is at the same time a fundamental instrument of the realization of a truly human community. Think, for example, about the ways speech is indispensable to the common endeavors to realize a human culture and to give to all the opportunity to share in the cultural resources. This is actually the end we should aim towards as speaking subjects: the realization and the promotion of a truly human community life (social relations). It is evident that, in order to achieve this end, we need the *locutio* the utterance about something, as a means (material element) to turn this end into reality (*finis* as *terminus*). But what must we say? It is obvious that generally speaking our speech must truthfully *reveal* a reality. If it were not this, it could not be a *positive* contribution to truly human relationships, could it? But it will also happen that speech will *conceal* a truth, also for the good of social relations. This is its *negative* function, viz., to safeguard the conditions of a truly human community life against those who do not stay within the bounds of their rights (e.g., by attempting to know a secret they have no right to know) or in relationships with those who cannot yet take a truth. If keeping silent is not sufficient, a *falsiloquium* may be the only *effective* means to the end. The implication of an inevitable ontic evil in this act does not keep this act from having the sense of a rightful secrecy which benefits truly human relations.

We can establish as a principle that it is impossible to pronounce a moral judgment on an exterior action which contains ontic evil—e.g., to kill somebody, to utter a falsehood—if this action is viewed only as a factual and actual event (*secundum speciem naturae*) and without paying attention to the end of the inner act of the will. We can further establish that, in order to be able to make a moral evaluation, we must consider: 1) if the end of the agent, the object of the inner act of the will, is morally good; 2) if the exterior action has a *debita proportio* to this end or if, on the contrary, it contains the negation of the value or the principle which is affirmed in the end.

From all of this, it follows that it would not be morally justifiable to keep all forms of ontic evil out of our actions in such a way that we would make it impossible to realize morally good ends. This would be presumptuous; it would be a failure to see our human condition as it really is. It would be an illusion which paralyzes our moral life. Traffic accidents, for example, evidence a considerable amount of ontic evil—material damage, the mutilation of thousands of people, the death of many. This sad situation imposes very serious duties on public authorities—the construction of good highways, the enforcement of coercive measures against those who break traffic laws, adequate traffic laws, driver education, etc. But if the authorities should want to prevent this ontic evil, they would have to prohibit the use of the entire road system, and by doing this, they would paralyze economic and social life. The sad fact of traffic accidents also imposes serious moral obligations on those who use the road system—obedience of traffic laws, the practice of caution and courtesy. But if they too should be of the opinion that this ontic evil should be completely eradicated, they would have to give up all use of the road system, and in doing this, they would have to stop practicing essential rights and duties that are inherent in life. Another illustration. It is beautiful that people are giving all they have to the tasks of their chosen vocation or profession. But it happens often that very committed people are annoyed by the fact that they must set aside time to sleep, to rest, to relax, etc. But if they do not set aside time for leisure, they will become ill, weak, and too tense. In other words, they will lose their inner balance and their mental zest. And they will cause many other ontic evils which keep them in the long or the short run from accomplishing their work at all.

We can conclude that we must accept the inevitable fact that we will run into ontic evil when we act. We cannot do away with ontic evil without depriving our actions of their effectiveness and without sooner or later endangering the realization of our morally good ends. Within these restrictions, the implication of ontic evil in our actions does not mean that no attention should be given to the *debita proportio* of the means to the end.

3) We have the moral obligation to reduce as much as possible the ontic evil which comes about when we act.

This thesis is implied in the fact that ontic evil should never be the ultimate goal of our intention (point 1) and that we must preserve the proper proportion of the means to the end (point 2). We have already said that ontic evil always enters our consciousness as an impediment and a frustration of the ends of man and society. Since the very object of morality is to promote the truly human growth of the individual and the social communities, it is bad to will ontic evil which obstructs this growth. And this happens from the moment we bring about or tolerate more ontic evil than is necessary to make our actions into effective actions. If our actions contain more ontic evil than they must have to be the proper means, they are not ordered properly to the goals of man and society. Consequently, they are immoral.

At face value, this thesis sounds quite negative. But it has a very positive sense, and it is pregnant with stirring contents. Indeed, it throws light on the dynamic character and the need for the historical evolution of morality. The progress of science and technology makes it more and more possible to lower the level of the nocivity (ontic evil) of things and increasingly raises the level of their usefulness. To the extent that we have more cultural resources at our disposal, we can reduce more forms of ontic evil and actualize the positive chances for a truly human development of each individual and of humanity. If it is immoral to let ontic evil exist when it is possible to cause it to diminish, it is our pressing duty to actualize those possibilities for the well-being of each and every individual. That which can be used to further the development of individuals and society thereby becomes a moral dictate. Consequently, morality is dynamic. What Ricoeur calls "*le souhaitable humain*" becomes the object of a moral obligation from the moment it becomes possible to realize it.

At the moment it becomes economically possible to bring about a steady and very substantial output of products and a more equitable distribution of the consumer goods which would give to each and everyone the opportunity to live at a truly human level of prosperity, this possibility becomes a source of moral obligation; further, it is immoral to tolerate the ontic evil of hunger and misery. To the extent that medicine discovers increasing possibilities to prevent or to cure the ontic evil of sickness, it becomes a moral obligation to organize a system of social medicine which is motivated by "le souci de mettre à la portée de tous les ressources d'une médecine de qualité."[18] When it becomes possible in a country or all over the world to lessen the ontic evil of the lack of education, it becomes a moral obligation to provide the means of education to each and everyone....

We could say more about these topics, but these examples will suffice to explain that wherever ontic evil can be lessened it must be lessened. This obligation reveals the dynamic character of morality. There are two reasons for this obligation. The first one follows from the definition of morality: moral activity fundamentally concerns the truly human development of man and society and the struggle against ontic evil which impedes this development. The second reason follows from the meaning of our activity in the world: by our activity we must turn the world of nature into a world of culture. In other words, our activity is ordered to the realization of the objective culture for the promotion of the subjective culture of each and everyone. In this respect, ontic evil is anything which impedes the progress of objective culture and the increase of the share of each and everyone in the resources of objective culture. If we do not care to eliminate ontic evil to the best of our ability, we neglect our duty to ensure a truly human life in a truly human world for each and every human being.

4) In the actualization of a good end and the deliberation about the means to this end, the genuinely important question is what place this end has in the totality of human existence.

We have said that Thomas defines the ends of our actions as the proper object of the inner act of our will. Something becomes an end insofar as the subject aims at it. It should not amaze us, therefore, that Thomas carefully avoids the use of the expression *finis operis* in his *De actibus humanis*. To him, the exterior action is a means insofar as it is ordered by its object to the realization of the end of the subject. To act, consequently, means that a *subject* actualizes his intentions in and by an active contact with reality. If we begin this way from the acting and willing subject, it is possible to look at our actions as something more than a succession of isolated, diversified and scattered acts. As moral subject man can understand that he, as a dynamic being, must actuate, in a way which *in truth* fits his being-a-person, his spiritual consciousness and his openness to the totality of reality (things, fellow men, communities, God). Thus, his existence becomes a meaningful event, a history of acts that are unified and integrated into this event by his *ends*. Thomas has this destiny in mind when he places the subject at the center of the activity and when he concerns himself with the hierarchy and the reciprocal connection of the ends which the subject endeavors to realize in and by his acts. For this reason he starts his study of morality with a treatise on the total and ultimate end to which man must order all his acts. And for the same reason he examines—always in the light of this total end—how in daily life, on account of the hierarchy and interrelationship of ends (*finis proximus, medius, remotus*, etc.), human acts, in spite of their diversity and frequency, are not necessarily isolated and contradictory, but can and must be integrated into the meaningful totality of a human and decent life by way of their good ends.

This integration demands not only that the particular ends we aim at in our concrete acts be morally good, but also that we take their relativity into consideration. It demands that we aim at them in such a way that we do not lose sight of the place and the rank they have in the whole of a meaningful human existence. In other words, it demands that we do not lose sight of the intensity (the urgent character) and the hierarchy of values in our behavior. "Personal and social growth would be endangered if the true scale of values were lost."[19]

The full significance of this moral axiom can be best shown by a look at the problem which is nowadays called "world politics." We have already said that "*le soushaitable humain*" or the "desirable level of humanity" should be provided to each and every human being from the moment and to the extent that this becomes possible. *Populorum Progressio* gives us a clear perception of the stepping stones to the ideal (or utopia) which is called "increased level of humanity." They are:

> to move up from the level of misery to the level of the ownership of the basic necessities of life, to end the social wrongs, to raise the level of education, to engage in the pursuit of culture. They are also a growing appreciation of the dignity of the fellow man, an attitude of the spirit of poverty, the united efforts toward the common good, the will and the yearning to create peace. Even more significant is man's appreciation of the highest values and of God who is the source and the ultimate end of the highest aspirations of man. Of the highest significance are: faith, a gift of God to which man's good will responds and the unity in the love of Christ who calls all of us to be His children and to share in the life of the living God, the Father of mankind.[20]

Is this many-sided growth an object of real concern to us? For many years already the affluent countries have advocated economic expansion—a higher level of production of consumer goods which would lead to more job opportunities and to a higher consumption potential. But more and more this intent to expand the economy has become the butt of criticism. The question has been asked whether there is not a kind of idolatry of the improvement of economic conditions. It seems that many are only concerned with material wealth, riches, comfort, prestige and power based on the notion that what one *has* rather than what man *is* is the measure of his greatness. Is this not materialism? Is it not the tyranny of a one-dimensional life?

More and more, voices clamor for a mentality which is not shot through with a yearning which is slanted too much toward *prosperity*. They call for a quest for the true well-being of individuals and communities. Mansholt is advocating a thorough change and broadening of objectives. He is strongly in favor of a strong lowering of the *per capita* consumption of economic products, compensated by a considerable rise of interest for other objectives: social provisions, especially for forgotten groups; intellectual and educational provisions for the leisurely unfolding of reason or feeling, etc. (Mansholt 1972, 6-7). Theologians, too, react against the one track mentality of a theology of the activist type which regards man exclusively as a worker who changes the world and makes it fit to live in. Theology turns again its full attention to religious cult, prayer, meditation, contemplation, mysticism, suffering, joy, etc., which are realities that are on the outside of the useful and the profitable, but are of enormous significance in the practice of the faith.[21] At the same time the specialists of the problems of the development of the underdeveloped countries remind us of the old problems of asceticism and mortification of the natural inclinations, not only at the level of the individual life, but on the scale of the affluent countries which should lower the ceiling of consumption in order to have more goods available for projects that are directed to the "improvement of the human condition" in underdeveloped countries.[22]

The problems of the hierarchy of objectives and of the relationship of the objectives to the totality of a meaningful human existence, at the individual and social level, are becoming pressing problems at this time, when the dimension of the future moves more and more to the focal center of attention. The study of the future becomes a science (*futurology*). More and more means to plan the future are at our disposal, so that terms like prognosis, prospective, etc. come more frequently into use. All this has mainly to do with the future of man himself and of the entire range and scope of man's life in society. Undeniably, the sense in which we opt for our priorities and the exact nature of those priorities is of utmost importance. It has become a problem of *debita proportio* on a world-wide scale of the ends we set for ourselves and the means we are ready and willing to order toward these ends.

V. Conclusion

We have undertaken this study to explain the meaning and the significance of the *concrete material norms* of morality. This category of norms prohibits *ontic evil*. They show us that we should not kill, maim someone, utter falsehoods, harm others (e.g., by taking something which rightfully belongs to someone else, by failing to return something that has been entrusted to us: *deposita sunt reddenda* etc.), fail to act to eliminate ignorance, sickness, hunger, etc. They are reducible to: you shall *neither* bring about (cause by your *actions*) *nor* tolerate (allow to grow by your *omissions* by failing to act) ontic evil.

It clearly follows from the foregoing that the fundamental basis of these norms is an ideal. We must work toward a society wherein there is less and less need to kill, wherein all are so respectful of rights that there is no need for self-defense and the use of defensive violence, and wherein, at the level of international relations, conflicts can be prevented or, in any event, resolved without wars. In a truly human society there must be solicitude about moral education, so that everybody becomes able to cope with the truth he should hear and be discreet enough to keep from prying into the secrets of others, so that for the sake of the smooth course of truly human relations, ontic evil can be lessened more and more. Briefly, concrete material norms invite us to bring about the ideal relations which lessen more and more effectively all forms of ontic evil which by their definition hamper the development of human beings and communities.

I am of the opinion that it is quite necessary to accentuate these points, since, in this era, we are more and more equipped to "create" the future of man and of society by planning and prospecting. Nowadays the word "utopia" has a positive ring. These days very much is said and written about utopia. There is still a long way to go to a consensus of opinion about it. But in spite of the differences of opinion, it always appears from discussions that a positive and a negative meaning is assigned to the term utopia: the perfect and the absolute conditions of a dream which has not yet found its place in the present era and which is the wish and the hope of mankind to secure a place for a perfect world in the future. The utopian speculation is in the field of the polarity of the present and the future. It originates in a contrast conception: beyond the ills and the defects of the present times which disgust us, we see the opposite image of the truly human and attractive way of life which lies over the boundaries of the things which are now. This insight into a better world originates in the dynamic qualities of our human nature which is essentially tending toward the future. In other words, the utopian speculation is inherent in the history of man; what the past generations have already accomplished and have made into events of history does not satisfy us and cannot satisfy us because we are dynamic beings. This should not lead us into underestimating the positive results of the traditional and past endeavors, as often happens in the name of utopia when there is a criticism of the existing structures that goes too far afield.

The utopia is also an expression of the faith that history has a future; and it is an expression of the idea that we must feel responsible for the ideal of the betterment of the world when we act. The *concrete material norms* of morality hold the ideal of the utopia before us and continually suggest a future which is more suitable for man. These norms are a constant protest against the different forms of ontic evil, and as we have said already, they pronounce us guilty of immorality when we bring about or tolerate more ontic evil than is necessary to realize the moral objectives of our human existence. The negation of anything which hampers the development of man and society appears strongly from their negative terms: *no* killing, *no falsiloquium*, *no* tolerance of ontic evil, etc. Consequently they are the negation of the negation (= all forms and shapes of ontic evil). By way of this negative dialectic they point to the *formal norms* which turn attention to that which ought to be done positively, since they show which moral dispositions must inspire the agent and which moral ends the agent must realize by his contact with reality.

Insofar as they express *the ideal*, the concrete material norms concern the "desirable degree of humanity" (*le souhaitable humain*). Insofar as they are norms, they imply only the obligation to realize that which is possible for man. We have already demonstrated that it would not be right to try to do away with all the forms of ontic evil because it would become impossible to actuate moral objectives. We must make allowance for our human limitations. That is why Thomas already said that the concrete material norms (*precepta magis propria*) are not applicable in all cases: *valent ut in pluribus* (ST I-II, 94, 4). He illustrates this with an example that comes from Plato. Generally speaking it will be true that we must return something that has been entrusted to us if the owner claims it (*ut in pluribus verum est*): but when we know that he demands that we return a weapon because he plans to use it to commit murder, the restitution of the weapon would clash with the universal and constantly valid norm of morality; viz., that we must act reasonably (*apud omnes enim etiam hoc rectum est et verum, ut secundum rationem agatur*). Thomas even lists several exceptions to the rule "you shall not kill" which concerns the fundamental value of human life (licit self-defense, death penalty, deaths caused in a justified war). We could add some restrictions of our own to his. The concrete norms are *relative*: they only forbid that we cause or tolerate ontic evil which exceeds the boundaries of the measure of means to the actualization of good ends.

But we have shown that these boundaries are made smaller by cultural progress. More and more ways are at our disposal to lessen the ontic evil in this world and to keep us from bringing about or tolerating ontic evil. This fact casts light on the *historicity* of the concrete material norms. Historicity does not mean a negation of the past. On the contrary, long ago before our time, mankind had already made history and had discovered concrete material norms to preserve the riches of culture. The fundamental concrete norms which guard the essential values—life, human integrity, truthfulness in social relations—will always be valid. But historicity means also that we, dynamic beings with inexhaustible possibilities, never cease to plan and to construct new ways of truly human life. Consequently, in the measure that a possibility becomes an actuality of the desirable level of humanity, concepts of norms must be adjusted to the new state of affairs of humanity. We have already said that all forms of ontic evil hamper the development of men and society and that morality which is at the service of this development, consequently, demands that we should not bring about or tolerate ontic evil which can be kept out of this world. We also said that we should eliminate this ontic evil whenever possible. Morality tries to affirm this moral obligation and mission throughout history by new concrete material forms.

When Karl Marx wrote his *Communist Manifesto* in Brussels in the year 1848, children were put to work in Belgium at the average age of twelve. Only the children of rich families had the opportunity to study. At that time, too, the idea of giving all children a chance to procure a good education was an attractive idea; but it was also an "impossible dream" because the *primum vivere* was the most compelling urgency. Now, at least in the affluent countries, it is possible to postpone making a living until the eighteenth year. Consequently, it has become possible to give to each child a time of youthfulness, and at the same time it has become financially possible to expand the educational system and to differentiate it in such a way that the ontic evil of lack of education can be reduced and that each child has an opportunity to choose an education which suits his talents. This possibility becomes *ipso facto* a moral obligation; that is why morality establishes norms of the democratization of the system of education. We could mention other examples: it is more and more possible to prevent and to cure illnesses, to eliminate hunger and misery, etc. Morality establishes new norms for all those new situations, because it demands that ontic evil be eliminated whenever and wherever possible. This negation of the negation is the core of the utopian speculation and implies the exigencies of the human activity which in a dynamic morality is governed by norms which shine forth from an ideal.

NOTES

[1] A good analysis of the existence and the orientation of those two currents of thought can be found in F. J. Van den Berge, *De morele kwalifikatie van het menselijk handelen. Klassieke en scholastieke achtergronden van een modern probleem.* Doctoral thesis, Faculty of Theology. (Privately printed. Louvain, 1972).

[2] This has been demonstrated very well by W. van der Marck, *art. cit.* It seems to me that he does not sufficiently stress the significance Thomas attaches to the *voluntas* or *simplex actus voluntatis*, as order of the inner act of the will to the end by itself and for itself (*absolute et secundum se*) even outside the context of an action. To me, this element seems to be an essential one, because it accentuates even more that Thomas' starting point is the subject, the end of the inner act of the will, and because this point is of great importance in any study which concerns Thomas' doctrine on the virtues and the moral evaluation of an act.

[3] Thomas often compares the way the act is composed of a formal and a material element (end and means) with the way the agent himself is a composition of soul and body. This goes, of course, with his axiom: *agere sequitur esse*. This analogy has an important function in his description of the structure and the morality of human activity. For this reason we will look at it more closely.

Thomas disputes a *monistic* view of man. Man is not only material. He is more than matter; he is also spiritual. Consequently, there is a certain duality in his single being. Thomas puts this into a philosophical term. He says that the soul is *forma subsistens* (ST, I, 76, 1 ad 5). The analogical sense which is applicable to the human act is obvious: the proper object of the inner act of the will is the end which can be intended in itself and absolutely, even outside the context of an action. The end is the *forma* of the totality of the act in the way of a *forma subsistens* and therefore as the proper object of the will or the *simplex actus voluntatis*.

Although Thomas teaches that there is duality in the human being, he is strongly opposed to a dualistic view of man. Man is one single subject, one single beings a unified composite. In order to signify this unity of the unified composite Thomas says in philosophical terms that the soul *qua forma subsistens* is at the same time *forma substantialis* of the oneness of the human being: "The soul communicates its own *esse* in which it subsists to the corporal matter, so that both elements make up one single being in such a way that the *esse* of the unified composite is the *esse* of the soul. This is not the case for the *formae* which are not *subsistentes"* (*ibid*.: see also ST, I, 76, 5; art. 6 ad 3; art. 7 ad 3). On account of the communication of its own *esse* to a part of the material world the soul makes this material part into human corporality of a single human subject. In this way, the body remains a material part of the material world but it participates at the same time in the subjectivity and belongs to the single human subject. As the formal element, the soul gives to the compound whole the specification of humanity: the *forma* specifies a reality. Again the analogy of the human being and the human act is clear. Thomas repeats again and again that our actions are a unified composite: the formal element is the end of the inner act of the will (*actus interior voluntatis*). The material element is the exterior action (*actus exterior*). And as the soul is the *forma* of the human subject which specifies the human being, so the end is the formal and specifying element of the structure and the morality of the action; the end of the agent or of the inner act of the will makes the exterior action into a means (ST, I-II, l, introduction: *ex fine enim oportet accipere rationes eorum quae sunt ad finem*) and at the moral level it determines the *species moris* (the moral goodness or the malice) of the entire action (ST, II-II, 43, 3: *finis enim dat speciem in moralibus*).

[4] *Cf.* ST, I-II, 18, 5 *sed contra*; q. 19, 1 *sed contra*; q. 20, 3, second objection and ad 2; q. 21, 2 *sed contra*.

[5] Abaelardus already contributed this thought in *Dial. inter phil., iud., et Christ.*, (*PL*, t. 178, col. 1652B): "*Quaedam etenim bona aut mala* ex seipsis proprie *et* quasi substantialiter *dicuntur, utpote virtutes vel vitia; quaedam vero* per accidens *et* per aliud, *veluti operum nostrorum actiones, cum in se sunt indifferentes, ex intentione tamen ex qua procedunt, bonae dicuntur vel malae. Unde et saepe cum idem a diversis agitur vel ab eodem in diversis temporibus, pro diversitate tamen intentionum, idem opus bonum dicitur atque malum.*" Moral goodness is, in the strict sense of the word, a qualification of the virtues, the good dispositions which make the subject into a good subject and which are the sources of the orderly relation of the inner act of the will and the moral good which is the end that communicates its moral specification to the exterior action. Without any doubt Thomas thinks along these lines.

[6] ST, I-II, 43, 3. Cf. also ST, I, 48, 1 ad 2: "*Bonum et malum non sunt differentiae constitutivae nisi in moralibus, quae* recipiunt speciem ex fine, *qui est* obiectum voluntatis *a quo moralia dependent; et quia bonum habet rationem fnis, ideo bonum et malum sunt* differentiae specitiae *in moralibus.*"

[7] ST, I-II, 18, articles 2, 4, 5, 6 and 7; q. 19, 7 and 8; q. 20, 1, 2, and 3.

[8] Here Thomas uses the terminology of the line of thought he disputes: *id quod de se est bonum*. But his intention is obvious. Almsgiving is usually the *materia* which can be specifically made into a moral action by a good end of the subject (to help the needy). But no moral judgment can be made about the material event as such (*secundum speciem naturae*) and as an element which has been abstracted from the end which is the formal element. The example given here by Thomas shows that the material event "almsgiving" belongs to a bad action, if a bad end is the reason and the cause of the exterior act (*actus exterior*). According to Thomas' terminology in his commentary on Petrus Lombardus, the *finis operis* of almsgiving is the alleviation of misery. But "*finis operis semper reducitur in finem operantis.*" In other words, a goal, on account of its very definition, is the object of the inner act

3 - Ontic Evil and Moral Evil

of the will of the subject. Consequently, it relates to morality only if it is willed by the subject (*ab agente*) as the *ratio operis* (see note 13). The actions "*recipiunt speciem ex fine, qui est obiectum voluntatis a quo moralia dependent*" (see note 47). Almsgiving, consequently, is *per se* good on the condition that the subject makes it into the end of his inner act of the will. Only then can the *finis operis* be properly called "end" because *finis* is by definition *objectum voluntatis*. This is so in the case of the action Thomas describes here.

[9] ST, I-II, 1, 3; q. 4, 4; q. 17, 4; q. 18, 6 *in corp*. and ad 2; q. 19, 10; q. 20, 1 ad 3.

[10] *Finis* as *ratio*: ST, I-II, 8, 3; q. 9, 3; q. 12, 4; q. 13, 5; q. 19, 10. *Finis ut causa*: ST, I-II 19, 7 ad 1 and 2; q. 20, 1 ad 3.

[11] ST, I-II, 18, 7, *obiectio* and *in corp*. Cf. ST, I-II, 110, 3 ad 4: "*Non licet furari ad hoc quod homo eleemosynam faciat, nisi forte in casu necessitatis in quo omnia sunt communia.*"

[12] ST, I-II, 19, 3 ad 2; q. 20, 3 ad 2. Cfr. ST, I-II, 65, 1: "*Ad rectam electionem non solum sufficit* inclinatio in debitum finem *quod est* directe per habitum virtutis moralis, *sed etiam quod aliquis* recte eligat ea quae sunt ad finem *quod fit per prudentiam quae est consiliativa et indicativa et praeceptiva eorum quae sunt ad finem. Similiter etiam prudentia non potest haberi nisi habeantur virtutes morales, cum* prudentia *sit* recta ratio agibilium *quae sicut ex principiis procedit* ex finibus agibilium *ad quos aliquis recte se habet per* virtutes morales."

[13] ST II-II, 43, 3 ad 1: "*Omne peccatum potest* materialiter *se habere ad scandalum activum, sed* formaliter *rationem specialis peccati potest habere* ex intentione finis."

[14] ST II-II, 64, 7 *in corp.*, cf. ST, I-II, 1, 3 ad 3.

[15] We said that mental defects and spiritual deficiencies, such as ignorance and error, can be listed as ontic evil. We can leave them out of the study of the ontic evil of our *human* acts, since acts are not *human* when ignorance, error, mental disturbances, etc. are the *cause* of the behavior. Thomas would say that they keep an act from being *actus voluntarius*—an act which emanates from the will—and a human act. It is possible that certain defects—ignorance, error, etc.—are *voluntarii*, but this brings us back to the question of sin as a source of ontic evil. See ST, I-II, 6, 8; q. 19, 5 and 6.

[16] P. Knauer, "La détermination du bien et du mal moral par le principe du double effet," in *NRT* LXXXVII (1965) 356-376.

[17] Is this not always so in the case of a voluntary *falsiloquium*? It is true that each *falsiloquium* always runs counter to the faculty of cognition which by its own nature and consequently necessarily and directly is ordered to the truth. This is precisely the definition of ontic evil: each ontic evil runs counter to the aim of one of our *inclinations*. That is why we experience it as an imperfection. The problem of moral evil concerns *the activity*. The gratuitous cognitive act comes in here as a measure which examines: (1) whether the intended goal is really good, and (2) whether there is really no intrinsic contradiction between the means and the end.

[18] Letter from the Vatican to the chairman of the 38th "Semaine Sociale de France," in *Sante et Societe: Les découvertes biologiques et la médecine sociale au service de l'homme*, (Paris, 1951.)

[19] Paul VI, *Populorum Progressio*, March 26, 1967, n. 18.

[20] Ibid., n. 19.

[21] Cf. H. Schaeffer, "'Politieke theologie' in een tijd van 'religieuze renaissance'," in *Tijdschrift voor Theologie* XII (1972), 226242.

[22] J. Zinbergen, *Een leefbare aarde*. Amsterdam-Brussels, 1970.

Direct Killing/Indirect Killing
Bruno Schüller, S.J.

The treatment of the fifth commandment in any textbook of Catholic moral theology would show that the significance attached to the distinction between direct and indirect killing is very fundamental. Direct suicide, for example, would never be justified. Indirect suicide, however, could be morally justified in certain circumstances: for a proportionate good. Exactly the same would apply in the case of killing another man who is innocent. Only if it could be considered as indirect killing could it be allowed or even commanded for a proportionate good. If the killing were direct, it would have to be considered illicit in all circumstances.

One always hesitates a bit before casting doubt upon a distinction which has been accepted unanimously in a long tradition, and which is likewise so practically important. That is to say, there is hardly any reason for doubting that one could make a purely descriptive distinction between direct and indirect killing. But there is reason for doubting that traditional moral theology has been correct in attributing to this distinction the overwhelming significance that it has for establishing ethical norms. It is easy to recall that earlier moral theology distinguished just as sharply and carefully between direct and indirect sterilization. Someone who since then has judged for himself that the traditional moral assessment of methods of contraception could not be maintained no longer considers it necessary to fall back on the earlier distinction. He can, if he so desires, make the distinction, but he makes it purely descriptively. Since he now judges direct sterilization according to the same principle as the indirect method, allowing even direct sterilization for the sake of a proportionate good, he will understandably consider the distinction between the "direct" and the "indirect" to be morally irrelevant. This could come as a surprise, for all at once one can do without that tool which one previously considered indispensable. And from this surprise emerges the following question: How did it happen that in the traditional way of building norms so great a moral importance has been attached to this distinction?

Once one has reached this question, one becomes aware that moral theology has had to use this distinction between direct and indirect acts only in setting norms for a certain few types of acts. Among these are leading another into sin (*scandalum activium*) and cooperation in the moral failure of another (*cooperatio cum peccato alterius*), and also acts such as suicide, killing a man who is innocent, and contraceptive interventions.[1] The question raised before can then be expanded: What do the aforementioned actions have in common? Can a common means of establishing norms be discerned from these common traits? Does this means of establishing norms make it understandable on its own why moral theology has found it necessary to distinguish between direct and indirect acts in a morally meaningful way?

I. "Direct" and "Indirect" as Distinguishing Characteristics of Intrinsically Evil Activity

Traditional moral theology classifies all the acts mentioned above as intrinsically evil acts, as acts that are morally evil by their very nature. Clearly it does this for different reasons. It is fairly obvious why leading another into sin and cooperating in the sin of another should be considered evil by their very nature. Inasmuch as one leads another into sin or cooperates in his morally evil act, one affirms moral evil, one promotes another's doing it, or one performs it along with another. To affirm evil in this way and to bring it into existence can be nothing else but morally evil. This is immediately apparent. The intrinsic immorality results here simply from the morally evil quality of the intended result of the activity (sin).

Moral theology proceeds differently in establishing that suicide and the use of contraceptives are morally evil by their very nature. The respective consequences, namely the individual's death or the unfruitfulness of the marriage act, are not in themselves morally bad but are rather a non-moral evil. So far it is not readily apparent from the (intended) result of the acts why suicide and the use of contraceptives by their very nature should be considered morally evil. Actually, in these cases moral theology does not establish norms on the basis of the consequences of the acts, but from a special modality of the acts. Suicide is not allowed because it would occur without the required authorization (*ex defectu juris in agente*). The intrinsic immorality in contraceptive birth-control follows from the fact that these means would make the marriage act unfruitful in a way contrary to nature. The process for establishing each of these norms has been different. Keeping that in mind, it can be said that the normative sentence "no one may lead another into sin or participate in the sin of another" is to be considered as analytic, while the sentence "suicide and the use of contraceptives are always forbidden" is the expression of a synthetic judgment. Why is one required to distinguish between direct and indirect in the case of both the analytic prohibitions and the synthetic prohibition?

II. Direct and Indirect Leading Another to Sin

The sense of the normative sentence "one may not lead another into sin" is understood only if one knows exactly what is meant by the word "lead." Moral theology presents an exact account of the meaning of "leading another into sin." This account should not be simply repeated. Rather, we should make an attempt to reconstruct the problem and the considerations by which moral theology was eventually able to give the explanation of this concept as exactly as in fact it does. It is universally agreed that a man is responsible for all foreseen (negative) consequences of a free act. Working from this understanding of human responsibility, one could try to define "leading another into sin" as follows:

> To lead another into sin means to make a free decision from which one foresees that it will have as a consequence the sin of another man.

In light of such a definition, the prohibition would run as follows:

> You shall not make a decision from which you know that it will have as a consequence the moral transgression of another.

One can see at first glance that if measured by this norm many acts would have to be considered illicit which one would usually consider licit or even morally obligatory. For example, a civil legislator can foresee, on the basis of common experience, that every penal law will lead an indefinite number of people to use the knowledge they have obtained to blackmail people who have committed criminal acts which have not yet come to the knowledge of law enforcement agencies. Thus, according to the principle that one may not make a decision which he knows will result in morally objectionable acts of others, the legislator would not be allowed to pass any penal law. This is obviously absurd. On the other hand, one cannot exclude the negative consequences of an act from the responsibility of the one who performs the act. It would seem that one could not do anything if the negative consequence consisted in a sin, even if the sin is another's. Sin is an absolute non-value, another's sin no less than one's own. Therefore, it must be avoided unconditionally. It is unthinkable that one could justify condoning what is morally evil. But what does the phrase "to avoid sin unconditionally" mean? To wish unconditionally that sin not exist? But such a desire does seem to imply that one is resolved to avoid anything that could in any way help sin to come into existence. But then one would have returned to the prohibition that one knows is not acceptable: i.e., one may not make a free decision, from which one can foresee that it would result in the sin of another.

It is well known that for many years a solution to this dilemma has been sought in trying to distinguish in the free attitude of the moral agent toward moral evil a positive desire, intention, or working for the evil on one hand and an allowance, a toleration, an accepting something as a by-product on the other. The absolute non-value of sin demands only that one not positively desire or intend it in any circumstances or at any price; granting this, it is thoroughly consonant with the absolute non-value of sin that one permit it, if one has a proportionately grave reason.

This way of solving the dilemma remains a bit obscure in spite of its general trustworthiness. Be that as it may, one thing seems to stick fast: the distinction between an intending will and a merely permitting will becomes necessary when one is faced with the free attitude of the moral subject toward moral evil. The absolute non-value of sin—one might eventually conclude (without logical contradiction?)—would entail an absolute avoidance, which as absolute would be incompatible with any willing or intention of sin. But such avoidance of sin would lead to consequences which one could for good reasons consider to be absurd. And the Christian (the theist) has an absolutely cogent reason for so thinking. For such an avoidance of sin is incompatible with the will of the Creator to create a being that is moral and capable of sin. To avoid such a conclusion, one must introduce a tolerating or permitting will, of which we could say: Under certain conditions this attitude of permission is morally justifiable, allowed, or even commanded, even in the face of the absolute non-value of sin.[2]

It should be clear, then, that leading another into sin, as this is understood by moral theology, must be considered morally evil by its very nature. For it takes this term to mean an act which has the sin of another as its foreseen *and* intended consequence.[3] It calls an act so characterized a *direct* (formal) leading another into sin. If an act results in another's sin, but this is merely allowed, according to everything that has been said, this act can under certain conditions be allowed or can even be obligatory. It is called an *indirect* leading another into sin.

III. The Free Attitude Toward a Non-Moral Evil

From the preceding considerations it can be conjectured that a permissive will and an indirect act are required as ethically meaningful categories only for moral evil. As soon as one establishes the proper moral attitude toward non-moral evils such as error, pain, sickness and death, the decisive reason which led to the distinction between intended and allowed, direct and indirect, namely the absoluteness of the disvalue, disappears. If we judge that a disvalue ought to be avoided, removed, or prevented, it seems that a non-absolute, a relative disvalue is such that it is to be avoided only conditionally.

The condition under which a relative disvalue should be noted is this: if it does not concur competitively with another finite value but one that is to be preferred to it, or with an absolute value. An illness is to be avoided, but not at any price, e.g., not if it means that one would spend all his money for medicines and cures and would therefore reduce his family to most dire straits. One may not inflict pain on another, except in cases in which it is only through inflicting pain that one can gain a certain desired result, e.g., a therapeutic or even a pedagogical result.

In short, insofar as it is necessary for the realization of a preferable value, one is allowed to cause a relative disvalue and at times one causes it. But in such a case, isn't the causing like an indirect act, so that the disvalue that has been caused would be considered an indirect result, merely allowed and accepted as a side-effect of an act? Even if one wanted to accept that, he would still have to use such linguistic convolutions as would strike most men as downright unusual, if not nonsensical. One would have to say, for example, that a man who would give a spanking to his obstinate child with a purely pedagogical purpose would have not to desire and not to intend that the spanking also cause pain; he would accept this effect of the spanking only as a side-effect. One would be constrained to assert that the health police who force quarantine on someone who has caught typhus intend only to prevent an outbreak of typhus; the police merely allow or regretfully tolerate the isolation of the sick man which they forced on him. In ordinary speech, one would rather say in such cases that the causing of evil would serve a good end, would be a necessary means to this end. But one says of the use of a means that it proceeds from an intending will; that it is direct activity. So, too, the axiom: whoever desires an end desires also the means necessary to reach his end. It is not easy to see why one should abandon this way of speaking. On the contrary, this way of speaking expresses clearly the differing attitude one should have toward moral evil and non-moral evil. For the sake of a correspondingly important good, one may merely permit a moral evil or cause it indirectly. But he may intentionally desire and directly cause the non-moral evil.[4]

Apparently, this is also the interpretation of Catholic moral theology. It considers some acts which result in non-moral evil as morally allowable, without demanding as a condition that the effect or result not be intended. Some examples might help: one may expose the hidden faults of another, may even damage his reputation or honor, in order to ward off a proportionately grave harm from one's own person or from a third party (Mausback-Ermecke 1961, 582). One may break his word in violation of an oath if this is the only way one has of keeping a "proportionately grave" evil from his person (Schilling 1957, 70). Not to keep a promise is by any standards an evil for him to whom the promise was made. But "the duty of promised silence ceases if this is justified by the threat of greater personal harms ... if an innocent person would be condemned ... if the common good would be damaged" (Schilling 1957, 61). The breaking of a promised secret has the character of a non-moral evil for the one interested in having the secret kept. In none of the cases mentioned do moral theologians see themselves obliged to declare that the negative consequences of the acts may not be intended and that they are ethically acceptable only as permitted. One can consider this as a sort of confirmation for the acceptance of the idea that not a relative disvalue but only the absolute disvalue of sin forces the moral theologians to establish the category of "indirect act."

IV. Cooperation In the Moral Failure of Another

Exactly the same problems we encountered in the case of leading another into sin confront us when we consider the classic topic of cooperation in the moral failure of another. That direct (formal) cooperation cannot be allowed follows, as it were, from the definition of direct cooperation: it consists in one's approving the morally objectionable deed of another and thereby sharing in its performance. But what of the case where someone disapproves of the immoral act of another but nonetheless helps in its performance? One could say that the person concerned does not properly disapprove of the evil deed; otherwise he would resist cooperation in the deed at any price. How Catholic moral theology answers this is already well known: it is morally justifiable under certain conditions to accept the sin of another as a negative byproduct of an act.

It can be doubted that one has to fall back upon the category of the non-intended or indirect consequence of an act in order to justify material cooperation. Whether one lends material cooperation or refuses it has no effect on the sin of another but only on the evil consequences of this sin. A case may be useful to illustrate this. The cashier of a bank, threatened by a robber with a drawn pistol, is faced with these alternatives: either let himself be shot, or remove the stacks of bills from the safe and hand them over to the robber. Does his decision have any effect on the sin of the robber? Could he say to himself that a murder is a morally worse crime than a robbery, that therefore he must prevent the murder and allow the robbery, and therefore hand over the money? Actually in normal circumstances, he would have to hand over the money, not because in so doing he lessens the moral guilt of the robber, but because the loss of money which the bank suffers is a lesser non-moral evil than the loss of a human life. The measure of the moral guilt of the robber is determined by his determination to commit even murder if necessary. It is not possible for the decision of the cashier to lessen the degree of this moral guilt, but only the amount of non-moral evil which the robber is determined to commit. Therefore, the cashier in these circumstances may will the loss of the money for the bank for the sake of saving his own life. One need not view the harm to the bank as a negative result of the cashier's choice which he may accept only as a side-effect of his action. No, one may intend a relative disvalue as the consequence of his act, if only it occurs in the service of a proportionately important end.

But however one understands the negative consequences of material cooperation, whether as a moral or as a non-moral evil, it suffices as a response to the question raised at the beginning to establish that traditional moral theology saw itself obliged to fall back upon the category of the indirect effect of an act because it understood that the negative effect of such cooperation consists formally in the sin of another man. The first part of the question posed above has thus been basically resolved. The analytical prohibitions—one may not lead another into nor cooperate in the sin of another—have forced us to make the distinction between the direct and the indirect consequence of an act because the result of the prohibition seems to consist in the absolute disvalue of sin.

V. The Indirect Consequence of an Act in Cases Where Norms Are Established Deontologically

As was already established at the beginning, the intrinsic immorality of leading another into sin and of cooperating in the sin of another derives from the consequences intended in these acts. So far the method of establishing norms has been teleological. It is different in the case of suicide, of killing another person who is innocent, and of using methods of contraception. The consequence of these acts is a non-moral evil, a relative disvalue. Therefore, from the consequence of the act it cannot be immediately shown why these acts are intrinsically evil, why they must be forbidden in all circumstances. That is to say, Catholic moral theology does not use purely teleological means to establish norms for these acts in every case. It ascribes to these acts the further characteristics either of being an arrogation of a right (killing, suicide) or of being contrary to nature (contraception), characteristics which are not immediately derivable from the consequence of the act itself. One may long for his own death, if he does so for an unobjectionable motive. Likewise, one would be allowed to wish that the marriage act remain in fact unfruitful for a proportionate reason. But one may not promote either of these results by his own actions. Exactly this fact, that one may not intend as a result of his act what can be legitimately longed for and desired, makes it obvious that we are not establishing norms here teleologically. With C. D. Broad, we want to name this unique way of establishing norms "deontological."[5]

This leads to synthetic prohibitions such as: You may never kill yourself no matter what results this might have in an individual instance. Therefore, you may not do this even if you know that you could thereby save another man from certain death.

In the foregoing there was no question of proving whether this deontological method of establishing norms is conclusive. However, it is my opinion that it is not conclusive, as I have attempted to point out in earlier essays (Schuller 1970a, 1970b). The question here is merely this: Why does moral theology see itself obliged to distinguish in a morally relevant way between direct and indirect effects precisely where there is question of acts for which moral theology uses deontological norms?

To analyze this question, we will use the deontological prohibition against killing: You shall not kill either yourself or another innocent man. Once again, the practical importance of this norm depends on what should be understood by the word "kill" in this context. One can suggest that by "kill" is understood the knowing and willful causing of the death of oneself or of another. But this response merely transfers the problem to the word "cause." From a teleological standpoint, one would say that this word reaches just as far as a man's responsibility for his own life and for the life of others. One could give this definition: To cause the death of a man is to reach a free decision which one knows will result in his own death or in the death of another. Furthermore, for killing understood in this way, one could use norms that are mostly deontological on the grounds that man as a creature has no right to make such a decision. On first glance, this would seem plausible. Anyone who can decide whether a man lives or perishes seems in fact to be able to act as Lord of life and death. One would usually look upon this as appropriation of divine prerogatives. The prohibition of killing would then be worded as follows: You may never make a decision which you know will result in your own death or in the death of others. However, the consequences of such a prohibition of killing will appear to most as unacceptable and contradictory

To prove this it is sufficient to give a couple of typical examples of self-killing and of killing another. Some man, tired of his life, slits his wrists. Another man gives the last place in a lifeboat to someone else. A third man takes over the care of plague victims, realizing that he may soon infect himself and die of it. These cases all give examples of self-killing, according to the accepted definition of the word "kill" that is, a decision from which the subject knows that it will have as a consequence his own death. Another example? A doctor performs a craniotomy in order to save the life of a mother. Another doctor refrains from performing the craniotomy, knowing that his decision means the death of the mother. A third doctor performs a hysterectomy on a pregnant woman, which is warranted on medical grounds (carcinoma). In these three cases there would be an example of the killing of an innocent man according to the accepted definition of the word "kill." If one wanted to apply the principle here that no one may kill himself or another man who is innocent, then all the actions described in the examples would have to be judged as morally forbidden. But this appears to be thorough nonsense. Especially unacceptable is the notion that it makes no difference whether a doctor prescribe a craniotomy in order to save the life of a mother or refrains from the craniotomy knowing that it will result in the death of the mother, because in either case he makes himself guilty of the forbidden killing of a man.

How can one avoid these unacceptable or contradictory consequences and still retain deontological norms? In any case, we must define more precisely that killing which is generally considered to be unjust; we may not understand by this term every free decision which results in death. That can be done first of all by excluding the free decision for an omission with the foreseen result of death from illegal killing. In this way the classic distinction between killing and letting die took form. It is only killing that is considered to be generally unjustifiable, not letting die. Certainly a person must be morally responsible for the decision which he makes to let another die, but basically this decision admits a moral justification. If it takes place for a proportionate reason (*propter rationem proportionate gravem*), it is permissible or even obligatory. Hence we have the attitude, rather generally shared, that the doctor could not be obliged to prolong the life of an unhealthy sick person at any price and by all available means.

These discussions are familiar and seem to be self-evident. Precisely for this reason it is necessary to be aware of two things: (1) to do and to allow may have the same result: the death of a person; nonetheless—judged morally—they are very different. The ethical weight is shifted from either the free decision on one hand or from the value of a human life on the other to a middle position: to the different ways a man has to achieve definite results. There is something strange about this: that is, one would think that the only crucial matter is whether the life of a man is saved or lost. It makes no ethically relevant difference whether that happens through doing something or through "allowing" something to happen. (2) Since "allowing to die" is excluded from the category of unjustified killing, one creates the possibility of using teleological norms for it. Death, as a non-moral evil, is now seen in its relationship to another concurring evil. This is proved by the fact that if death is seen as the lesser evil, then it is morally permissible, if not obligatory, to omit everything which could delay or prevent death. It is important to establish this. The deontological prohibition of killing becomes more plausible precisely because "allowing to die" is removed from the prohibited category and is submitted to a teleological norm.

It could still be asked whether it is morally permissible to intend the death of a man as the consequence of a freely willed omission. The etymological affinity of the words "omit" and "permit" could lead to the assumption that a death which results from an omission is a morally responsible act only as a permitted death, as a not-intended death. But this assumption does not prove right. Only if the death of a man were an absolute evil in the sense of moral evil is it necessary to appeal to the notion of permission (*voluntarium indirectum*) to establish its moral licitness.

Catholic moral theology has excluded not only "permitting to die" from those killings controlled by deontological norms. Behind that, even among the acts which result in death, it has understood an exceptionally subtle distinction. It may happen that some act has an immediate second effect besides the death of a man, e.g. the healing of another man from a threatening disease. There is a question here of something like a double action, if we allow an act to be specified by its consequences: an act which has the character of a therapeutic operation and also the character of a killing. As a therapeutic operation, the norms for the act would be established teleologically in the view of moral theology, and in the majority of cases it would be morally permissible or even obligatory. As an act of killing, however, it must be considered morally evil, it seems, ex defectu juris in agente. Here a question occurs: May one resolve to perform such an act, which one could look upon as morally permissible and forbidden at the same time? Moral theology concludes that one may perform such an act, but under the condition that one intends only the therapeutic effect and merely permits the death. Thus such a killing—called "indirect"—would not fall under the prohibition that admits of no exception, but would be morally justifiable for a proportionate reason.

Again, it is apparent that it is the free attitude toward the moral evil that leads to the distinction between the direct and the indirect act. If moral theology were to consider the killing of an innocent person not as an act that is intrinsically evil, if it would see in this act the negation of a value which, though fundamental, is still a nonmoral evil and would attempt to establish norms from this starting point, then it would not have to carry through this distinction. We have a striking proof of this in the different ways and means that moral theologians use to explain killing in self-defense. They all consider such a killing to be morally justified. But—and this is noteworthy—some consider it morally justifiable because in their opinion such killing is *indirect*; others consider even a direct killing in the situation of self-defense to be allowed. How is this explained? By a different wording of the deontological prohibition of killing. Some propose the idea that the individual as a private person may not at any time kill anyone, not even an unjust aggressor.[6] Consequently, for them, killing in self-defense can be morally justified only if it can be understood as indirect killing. The others restrict the deontological prohibition to the killing of an innocent man,[7] but the unjust aggressor is *ex definitione not innocent*.[8] Thus killing him does not fall under the deontological prohibition. Hence there is no need to explain the killing of an unjust aggressor as an indirect killing.

Finally, the usual understanding of the teaching of the act with a double effect is a proof for the fact that it is the attitude toward moral evil that made the category of indirect effect necessary. In this teaching, the negative consequence of the act is seen either as a moral evil in itself, or at least as intended.[9] This can be seen most clearly from the ever present demand that both the good and the bad effects must proceed with equal immediacy from the act. If the good result proceeds from the bad, then the act would be forbidden, since a good end does not justify a bad means. Bad means can mean only a morally bad act. Since as often as a non-moral evil may be intended as the effect of an act, it is ethically irrelevant whether the good effect appears at the same time or only later, if only it is proportionate to the evil. For example, in the case of vaccination, the positive effect of immunization follows only from a negative act, an artificially induced infection. No moral theologian will object that vaccination must not be allowed because the good end does not justify the bad means. From this it can be established that one has to fall back on the category of indirect effect only where the effect of an act in itself (as with the sin of another) or at least the intending of the consequence of an act (death of an innocent) is to be considered as morally evil.

The distinction between direct and indirect relates to the prohibition of killing in a way similar to the distinction between acting and allowing. If indirect killing is exempted from the deontological prohibition, this prohibition's sphere of application is reduced a few degrees, and so it becomes more plausible. Indirect killing comes to be covered by teleological norms, that is to say, it is justified by a proportionate good. And so it is that a deontological establishment of norms becomes acceptable to the extent that it lets itself be restricted in favor of a teleological establishment of norms.

It should be mentioned only very briefly that moral theology judges contraceptive measures in exactly the same way. The marriage act can be unfruitful because one has decided for himself to omit something that would make it fruitful, e.g. a medical treatment. The moral norms in the case of this decision for an omission are established teleologically. The same is true of an act that is indirectly contraceptive. It is only for the direct use of contraceptive measures that norms are established deontologically, i.e., considered to be "contrary to nature." Presented schematically:

$$\text{Decision to} \begin{cases} \text{Omission} \longrightarrow \text{Teleological} \\ \text{Act} \begin{cases} \text{Indirectly} \longrightarrow \text{Teleological} \\ \text{Directly} \longrightarrow \text{Deontological} \end{cases} \end{cases}$$

4 ~ Direct Killing/Indirect Killing

One short glance at this outline is enough for one to recognize that if it be demonstrated that the deontological method of establishing norms for killing and for birth control cannot be maintained and should therefore be replaced with the teleological method of establishing norms, then it would be useless to continue to distinguish as before among omission, indirect act, and direct act. For whether it is a question of omission or action, in both cases the principles of teleological norms would have to be used. If one judges that contraception cannot be proscribed because of its supposed "contrary-to-natureness," one is abandoning for this instance deontological norms. This is the reason why one is able to get along very well without that tool which the teaching on the act with a double effect places in one's hand.

Even if one regards the deontological method of establishing norms for killing and birth control as erroneous, one cannot help but admire the ingenuity which led to the development of the teaching on the act with a double effect, an ingenuity surely in the service of an excellent purpose, as indeed any theologian must admit. The teaching on the act with a double effect restricts the scope of the deontological norm in favor of a teleological norm, as far as this is at all possible. But even this cannot prevent the deontological method of establishing norms from betraying its highly questionable character in certain situations. In their book *Respect for Persons*, R. S. Downie and Elizabeth Telfer call attention to this questionable character:

> If the deontologist is correct, it is theoretically possible that the performance of a duty could on a given occasion make the world a worse place than it would have been if the duty had not been performed. It might be argued that the very fact that a duty has been performed must mean that some good consequences will be brought about. But even if we grant that the mere fact of duty-performance is itself good, it still may be the case that the total state of the world after the duty-performance is worse than it would have been if the duty had not been performed. And if this is a consequence of the deontologist's interpretation of moral rules, his interpretation must be rejected as a bad case of rule-worship.[10]

A moral theologian could prove through actual examples the things that Downie and Telfer mention as theoretical possibilities. B. Häring takes the case of a doctor who had to operate on woman in the fourth month of pregnancy for an adnexal tumor (Haring 1967, 126). Because of complications, the doctor found himself faced finally with the following alternatives: either the removal of the uterus together with the fetus, or the removal of the fetus while saving the uterus. He decided in favor of the second alternative. In this case, the woman, who had not as yet had any children, was still able to conceive and give birth. Later the doctor, as he himself reports was told by a moral theologian that although the doctor had acted in good faith, objectively speaking, he had acted wrongly. He "would have been allowed to remove the bleeding uterus with the pregnancy, but not to interrupt the pregnancy and thereby save the uterus. The first would be an abortion for the sake of saving the mother, which is not allowed; but the other would be a permissible *prima intentio*, as in the case of cancer of a pregnant uterus. So the consideration that he would be saving the woman's fertility and thereby would possibly be saving the marriage in certain circumstances, would play no decisive role." Häring himself considers that the moral theologian in this case illustrates what Catholic casuistry ought not to be: "The application of principles of moral theology may not be confused with the manipulation of a slide rule. The act is much rather to be viewed in its entirety." With this comment Häring shows moral common sense, but he shows also that he has not grasped the problematic revealed by the report of the doctor—the problematic of deontological norms.

As far as a non-medical person can understand the operation performed by the doctor, this must actually be considered as a direct killing to save the life of the mother. He who is concerned, confused, or terrified by this cannot extricate himself from the affair by asserting that in this case the ethical principles which he himself espouses have to be used not as principles but merely as rules of thumb. There are only two possibilities left open to him: either to stand squarely by the consequences of his principles, or to become critical of them and to question whether there is not something wrong with them. In saying this, anyone who considers any direct killing of an innocent to be intrinsically evil says also that any such killing would have to be avoided in individual cases, no matter what the consequences. The permanent inability of a woman to bear children and the childlessness of a marriage are not the worst (non-moral) evils which can come from one's refusal on the grounds of his duty to directly kill another. To use deontological norms for killing *eo ipso* means that there can be situations in which adherence to one's duty results in a greater measure of non-moral evil than acting against one's duty.

One may not incorrectly overvalue this last assertion. It characterizes deontological norms but does not disprove them. A deontologist can answer pointedly that the moral value of acting according to one's duty should be valued unconditionally higher in every case than any non-moral evil which can result from acting according to one's duty. No theologian can contradict him in this, as long as he recognizes the unconditionality of moral value. One can refute deontological norms only if one can show that the reasons brought forward to validate them are not sound, for example, if one could establish that the so-called "opposition to nature" of using contraceptives cannot be ethically normative. Even the norm (grounded purely teleologically) "One may not lead another into sin" must obviously be considered with the condition "whatever the consequences may be." These consequences could be terrible for this norm also affirms that "one may not try to get another to act against his *erroneous* conscience." But this norm is analytically evident; its justification comes only from the meaning of the words used in it.

The conclusion of the preceding analyses can be summarized as follows:

1. If one establishes norms exclusively on teleological grounds, then the distinction between a direct and indirect act is ethically meaningful if, and only if, the consequence of the act is in itself morally evil. This holds true certainly in the case of leading another into sin.

2. If one establishes norms partly on teleological grounds, partly on deontological, one can still use the distinction in the case of acts for which norms are established deontologically. By so doing, one has the great advantage of being able to avoid many seemingly unsupportable consequences of this way of establishing norms.[11]

Notes

[1] O. Lottin, *Morale Fundamentale* (Tournai, 1954), 286ff names as the major cases of this: "scandale direct et scandale indirect, et cooperation au mal ... homicide direct et homicide indirect ... la luxure volontaire en soi et dans sa cause."

[2] Cf. J. de Vries, "Theodizee" in W. Brugger (ed.) *Philosophisches Worterbuch* (Freiburg 1967) 381: "God can 'not positively will' the morally evil. ... But it is indeed possible that God allows evil, i.e., does not prevent it, even though he foresees it and has the power to prevent it." J. B. Schuster, in W. Brugger, op cit. 49, "Why does holy God, who can never will, cause, or sanction evil, allow evil, or why does he not prevent the beings which he created from misusing their

freedom unto evil? This permission, which includes no positive sanctioning and responsibility for evil, is motivated by compensating values." The terminology used is not always the same. Cf. J. Hellin, *Theodicea* (Matriti 1957) 337: "Mala autem moralia Deus non vult per se nec per accidens; nam ob suam sanctitatem non vult peccata directe, nec vult ea indirecte (!) ut media ad fines bonos obtinendos." F. Diekamp, *Kath. Dogmatik* Bd. I (Munster 11 1949) 216: "Reason validates the notion that there is no good that outweighs the greatness of moral evil . . . Therefore God cannot will sin, he can merely allow it." Cf. also J. M. Dalmau, "De Deo Uno et Trino" in *Sacrae Theologiae Summa* Vol. II (Matriti 1955) 177.

[3] The question need not be explored here in what sense the moral of another can be called the result of my act. On this cf. A. Vermeersch, *Theologia Moralis* T. I (Romae 1947) 108.

[4] J. de Vries, op cit: "God can not only allow physical evil, but he positively causes it as a means to reach a higher goal." W. Brugger, *Theologia Naturalis* (Pullach 1959) 412, distinguishes as follows: to intend something as a goal (*in se et propter se*); to intend something as a means to a goal (*in se, non propter se*); to allow something, neither to intend it as a goal nor as a means, but also not to prevent it, although one be in a position to do so. He continues: an evil as such, whether a moral evil or a non-moral evil, one could never intend as a goal in itself, but only as a means or, not intending simply allow it. It would be morally justified to intend a nonmoral evil and to allow a moral evil, when this happens for the sake of a "*bonum praevalens*." In my opinion, one should also understand in this connection under the term "means" that non-moral evil that is necessarily entailed in an intended goal, even if it is only a side-effect of that goal. The decisive factor might be that the intended goal can be reached only if one pays a price for it. Whether the price must be paid before reaching the goal or after makes no morally significant difference.

[5] *Five Types of Ethical Theory* (London 1967) 206: "Deontological theories hold that there are ethical propositions of the form: 'Such and such a kind of action would always be right (or wrong) in such and such circumstances, no matter what its consequences might be.'"

[6] So, it seems, Thomas, ST II-II, 64, 7 c: "occidere hominem non licet, nisi publica auctoritate propter bonum commune . . . illicitum est quod homo intendat occidere hominem, ut seipsum defendat, nisi ei qui habet publicam auctoritatem." Very significantly, H. Merkelback, *Theologia Moralis*, Bd. 2 (Brugis 1962) 357: "Directa (occisio) non est iusta, nisi ex auctoritate publica, erga malefactores, et erga hostes nocentes in bello iusto, non autem erga innocentes, nec mere privatis (!); licita tamen esse potest occisio indirecta etiam mere privatis, iustae defensionis vel conservationis causa."

[7] So, among others, M. Zalba, *Theologia Moralis*, Bd. 2 (Matriti 1953) 275: "occisio vel mutilatio innocentis (!) directa est semper grave peccatum."

[8] The expression "not innocent" is in this context merely a synonym for "unjust" concerning which moral theology is known to be of the view that an attack justifies self-defense if it is unjust only objectively, though it may be subjectively innocent. This view is especially vulnerable and somewhat disquieting if one uses the following saying as an argument right need not soften upright. But that is not particularly germane here.

[9] A. Vermeersch, *Theologia Moralis*, Bd. 1 (Romae 1947) 105, clarifies the negative result of an act: "Effectus malus, i.e., talem hoc loco vocamus qui nec intendi nec

eligi honeste posset." According to this, one must accept that "*malus*" here means simply "morally evil." But the consequence of an act judged by deontological norms is not evil in itself, but only as the intended consequence of an act. From this it follows that not only evil such as death and sterility count as "effectus mali:' but even the *pollutio* which should hardly be qualified as evil. It counts as "*effectus malus*" because it is contrary to nature and therefore it is morally evil to intend it as a consequence of one's actions.

[10] R. S. Downie and Elizabeth Telfer, *Respect for Persons* (London 1970) 34; see also G. E. Moore, *Ethics* (London 1912, Oxford Paperback 2 1966) 93.

[11] On the same, cf. B. Schüller, "Zur Rede von der radikalen sittlichen Forderung ' in *ThPh* 46 (1971): 321-341, esp. 327ff. As to the moral relevance of the distinction between killing and letting die, cf. my essay "Various Types of Grounding for Ethical Norms" in *Readings in Moral Theology No. 1: Moral Norms and Catholic Tradition*, ed. Charles E. Curran and Richard A. McCormick, S.J. (New York: Paulist Press, 1979) 184-198.

Ambiguity in Moral Choice
Richard A. McCormick, S.J.

The distinction between what is directly voluntary and indirectly voluntary has been a staple of Catholic moral thought for centuries.[1] It has been used to face many practical conflict-situations where an evil can be avoided or a more or less necessary good achieved only when another evil is reluctantly caused. In such situations the evil caused as one goes about doing good has been viewed as justified or tolerable under a fourfold condition. (1) The action is good or indifferent in itself; it is not morally evil. (2) The intention of the agent is upright, that is, the evil effect is sincerely not intended. (3) The evil effect must be equally immediate causally with the good effect, for otherwise it would be a means to the good effect and would be intended. (4) There must be a proportionately grave reason for allowing the evil to occur. If these conditions are fulfilled, the resultant evil is referred to as an "unintended by-product" of the action, only indirectly voluntary and justified by the presence of a proportionately grave reason.[2]

The practical importance of this distinction can be gathered from the areas where it has been applied in decision making: killing (self-defense, warfare, abortion, euthanasia, suicide), risk to life (dangerous missions, rescue operations, experimentation), sterilization, contraception, cooperation in another's evil action, scandal. Its appeal is attested to by the long line of prominent theologians who have used it in facing problems of the first magnitude such as the conduct of war. The most articulate contemporary exponent of the just-war theory (Paul Ramsey) appeals to it frequently in his writings, as did John C. Ford, S.J. in his excellent work on obliteration bombing.[3] Many other theologians fall back on the distinction, sometimes unwittingly, sometimes when it suits a rather obvious purpose. So settled, indeed, had the usage become in theological circles that the direct/indirect distinction has achieved a decisive prominence in some of the most influential and authoritative documents of the Church's magisterium.

For instance, in discussing the problem of abortion, Pius XI asked: "What could ever be a sufficient reason for excusing in any way the direct murder of the innocent (*directam innocentis necem*)?"[4] Pius XII repeatedly condemned the "deliberate and *direct* disposing of an innocent human life"[5] and insisted that "neither the life of the mother nor that of the child can be subjected to an act of *direct* suppression."[6] Similarly Pius XII employed the distinction in dealing with sterilizing drugs. He noted that:

> if the wife takes this medication not with a view to preventing conception, but solely on the advice of a physician, as a necessary remedy by reason of a malady of the uterus or of the organism, she is causing an indirect sterilization, which remains permissible according to the general principle concerning actions having a double effect. But one causes a direct sterilization, and therefore an illicit one, whenever one stops ovulation in order to preserve the uterus and the organism from the consequences of a pregnancy which they are not able to stand.[7]

Where the conduct of war is concerned, recent documents of the magisterium have insisted on what theologians refer to as noncombatant immunity or the principle of discrimination. Thus Pius XII, after stating that an aggrieved nation may licitly turn to warfare as a last defensive resort, immediately rejected a use of nuclear weapons which "entirely escapes from the control of man" and represents "the pure and simple annihilation of all human life within the radius of action."[8] The Second Vatican Council condemned as a crime against God and humankind "any act of war aimed indiscriminately at the destruction of entire cities. . . ."(Abbott 1966, 294). The principle of discrimination proposed in such statements has commonly been explained and applied through the distinction direct/indirect (Ramsey 1961, 34-59).[9]

In 1968 Pope Paul VI made explicit use of the distinction between direct and indirect in *Humanae Vitae*. He stated:

> We must once again declare that the *direct* interruption of the generative process already begun, and above all, *directly* willed and procured abortion, even if for therapeutic reasons, are to be absolutely excluded as licit means of regulating birth.

He immediately added:

> Equally to be excluded, as the teaching authority of the Church has frequently declared, is *direct* sterilization, whether perpetual or temporary, whether of the man or of the woman.[10]

More recently the "Ethical and Religious Directives for Catholic Hospitals," approved overwhelmingly by the American bishops in November 1971, refers repeatedly to the distinction between direct/indirect. Directive 10 reads: "The directly intended termination of any patient's life, even at his own request, is always morally wrong." Similarly, prohibited abortion is described as "the *directly* intended termination of pregnancy before viability." Furthermore, the revised Directives define what direct must be taken to mean: "Every procedure whose sole immediate effect is the termination of pregnancy before viability is an abortion."[11]

It is safe to say, therefore, that the rule of double effect has had an honored and very important place in the formulation of Catholic moral theology and teaching. However, in the past four or five years, there have been rumblings of dissatisfaction, uncertainty, disagreement—or all three.[12] These sentiments have surfaced in several studies which reapproach the distinction between direct and indirect, to test its traditional understanding, to challenge its decisiveness, or even to deny its moral relevance. Clearly we have here an issue of the greatest theoretical and practical importance, one that deserves most careful reflection. The purpose of this essay is to review critically several recent studies on direct/indirect voluntariety and to offer some personal reflections in an attempt to identify the present state of the moral question.

It should be said at the outset that these reflections should be regarded as no more than gropings and explorations undertaken with the confidence that others more competent will carry them further and bring greater clarity to the question. A distinction with a history as imposing and long-lived as that between the direct and indirect voluntary should not be abandoned unless its inadequacy is rather clearly and systematically established. I say this because in these our times there are far too many ready and eager to turn a theological question into a new discovery, and to promulgate this *urbi et orbi* in

5 - Ambiguity in Moral Choice

terms which the professional theologian can only regret, and most often disown completely.

The recent discussion was, I believe, largely put in motion by the writings of Peter Knauer, S.J.[13] Knauer, it will be recalled, began with the insistence that moral evil consists in the permission or causing of a physical evil without commensurate reason. In explaining this, Knauer relied heavily on St. Thomas's analysis of self-defense. The defense of one's life against an assailant is not exactly an effect, but rather an aspect of the act. Therefore, the *finis operis* or meaning of an action is not derived simply from its external effect but is really that aspect of the act which is willed. For example, almsgiving is not simply a physical act; it gets its sense and becomes a moral act through the intention of the donor.

Knauer argues that it is with this in mind that we must understand the terms direct and indirect. In the past, we have tied these terms too closely to physical causality (Curran 1970, 237ff). Actually, "the permission or causing of a physical evil is *direct* or *indirect* as there is or is not present a commensurate reason," for when such a reason is present, it

> occupies the same area as what is directly willed and alone determines the entire moral content of the act. If the reason of an action is commensurate, it alone determines the *finis operis*, so that the act is morally good (Knauer see above 34).

What, then, is a commensurate reason? This is crucial to Knauer's presentation. It is not just any reason, meaningful or important as it may be. Rather a reason is commensurate if the value realizable here and now by measures involving physical evil in a premoral sense is not in the long run undermined and contradicted by these measures but supported and maximized. Thus, "a refusal to bear children is only commensurately grounded if it is ultimately in the interests of the otherwise possible child" (Knauer 1970, 73). Or again,

> to prove that a particular act is contraceptive in the moral sense it must be shown that the act in the last analysis does not serve the end of preservation and deepening of marital love, but in the long run subverts it (Knauer see above 55).

To the objection that this amounts to proposing that a good end justifies an evil means, Knauer would reply that a means can be judged to be evil only if it is caused without commensurate reason. One cannot, in other words, isolate certain physical evils and say of them that they are, in all circumstances, moral evils. The distinction between physical and moral evil is not, of course, new. For instance, in discussing the principle that a good end does not justify an evil means, the late and renowned Gerald Kelly, S.J., wrote:

> This principle, so simple in itself, can be very complicated in its explanation. It does not mean that no evil may be done in order to obtain good. It refers primarily to *moral* evil; and in this respect it is absolute, because *moral* evil may never be done to obtain any kind of good.
>
> The principle is not absolute as regards *physical* evil, because there are some physical evils that we have a right to cause in order to obtain a good effect. An example of this latter that is very common in medicine is mutilation. Mutilation is certainly a physical evil; yet as we shall see, there are some circumstances in which man has a right to mutilate himself or to authorize such mutilation (Kelly 1958, 4).

This explanation of Kelly is absolutely correct. What is not clear is what is to count (and why) for *moral* evil. Kelly clearly regarded contraceptive interventions and directly sterilizing interventions, for example, as falling in this category. Knauer has questioned—and I believe rightly—just that type of conclusion and insisted that what is morally evil can only be determined after we have examined the reason for the procedure. What is to be said of Knauer's understanding of direct and indirect intent? My earlier reaction was critical. Since that time, however, I have come to accept the substance of Knauer's presentation, though not without serious qualifications about his use of the terms *direct* and *indirect* as will become clear in the course of this study.

Germain Grisez says of Knauer that he "is carrying through a revolution in principle while pretending only a clarification of traditional ideas" (Grisez 1970a, 331). As Grisez sees it, Knauer's basic failing is that he overlooks a very important mode of obligation. He

5 - Ambiguity in Moral Choice

ignores the obligation that we not turn directly against the good. This omission opens the way for his redefinition of "directly intended" in a way that bears no relation to any previous use of the expression. To support his position, Knauer also finds it necessary to claim that moral intent is completely distinct from psychological intent (Grisez 1970a, 331).

I shall discuss later the notion of "turning directly against the good" as proposed by Grisez. However, his criticism of Knauer's neglect of psychological intent is, I believe, justified. The notions of direct and indirect intention have become so utterly identified with the existence of a commensurate reason in Knauer's thought that direct and indirect really do not function. This is not to deny the decisive nature of commensurate reason or to challenge the substance of Knauer's approach. It is only to note that Knauer seems to give no meaning to psychological intent. One can only wonder why Knauer retained the terminology at all. Secondly, Knauer does not satisfactorily indicate the limitations of intention in determining the meaning of concrete human actions and therefore he is unable to deal convincingly with cases like that of Mrs. Bergmeier who committed adultery to free herself from prison and rejoin her family.[14]

The next theologian to turn a critical eye to the direct/indirect distinction was William Van der Marck (Van der Marck 1968). His critique is intelligible only within the larger framework of his thought. Van der Marck's treatment is anchored in the notion of intersubjectivity. He notes:

> The fact that human action is intersubjective means that it necessarily has consequences favorable or detrimental to the mutual relationship of the persons concerned. To state this more directly, intersubjectivity is a form of either communication or the disruption of communication; it is a form of either community or the destruction of community. When we now speak of act and consequences, of act and effect, of means and end, we are, in the first place, not speaking of something that happens *now* and has results, consequences, or effects, or that achieve an end *later*; rather, we are speaking of a particular corporeal action that, precisely as a human act, has immediate implications with respect to the relationship between subjects (Van der Marck 1968, 61).

Now the essential meaning of *good* and *evil* is simply a qualification of the implications, effects, consequences. In other words, it is only a qualification of the human content of the act. Good and evil, he insists, refer to the success or failure of intersubjectivity,

> and for this reason there cannot be any question of good and evil unless there is first a question of intersubjectivity; furthermore, we may speak of good and evil only to the extent that we speak of intersubjectivity.

Van der Marck feels that the disease of traditional moral theology is that it began to maneuver among categories of good and evil before it touched intersubjectivity. Thus traditional theology would characterize something as a means and a bad one prior to consideration of intersubjectivity. For example, it would say that to have children is good, but artificial insemination is a bad means to it.

Van der Marck does not deny the usefulness of the categories object-circumstances, means-end. But he argues that the

> reality itself, however, is much more important than categories and the tools they provide, and when we do gain insight into the reality itself, these categories and other ways of approach will themselves become more intelligible (Van der Marck 1968, 54).

Thus Van der Marck sets out to criticize the categories in light of the reality.

What is the reality of a human being? A human being is both corporeal and intersubjective. "Corporality qualifies man under all aspects in which he coincides with and forms part of the nonhuman world." Intersubjectivity, on the other hand, points him out in his human uniqueness. Now if this is true of a human being, it is true of his action also. Therefore, the most fundamental thing to be said about human action is the distinction between corporeity and intersubjectivity. Human action is a reality which is wholly corporeal, yet we see its uniqueness only when we view it as intersubjective.

A few examples offered by Van der Marck will throw light on his analysis. The physical, bodily reality of killing can be as an intersubjective reality, murder, waging war, administering the death penalty,

5 - Ambiguity in Moral Choice

self-defense, suppressing an insurrection and so on. Taking something from another can be intersubjectively stealing, borrowing, satisfying dire need, repossessing one's property. Removing a nonviable fetus from the womb can be intersubjectively abortion (murder), removal of the effects of rape, saving the life of the mother and so on. Van der Marck feels that too often the reality of action is identified with one single form of intersubjectivity to the total exclusion of others. Why? Because the qualification good and bad is derived from the corporeal act as such, the physical act, in spite of the explicitly made distinction between *esse physicum* and *esse morale*. The criticism he levels against traditional manuals of moral theology is this:

> That the same material, bodily act may possibly have a *different* intersubjective significance is something that, in principle, lies outside its field of vision (Van der Marck 1968, 56).[15]

Van der Marck then applies the corporeity-intersubjectivity distinction to the means-end and act-intention categories. Thus, means is related to end in the same way as corporeity is related to intersubjectivity. That is, just as intersubjectivity is the ultimate determinant of *human* action, so the end is the ultimate determinant of *human* action.

> For example, termination of pregnancy could be called "means," and intersubjectivity would be indicated by "end," whether it be murder, removal of the effects of rape, or saving the life of the mother.

Similarly with act (object) and intention.

> Act refers to the whole action as a physiological reality, while intention refers to the same action, but precisely as human and intersubjective.

In summary, intersubjectivity demands special consideration before we can speak about good and evil, for "what is material in human action is able to be intersubjective in the most diverse and varied of ways" (Van der Marck 1968, 59).

Against this background, Van der Marck approaches the principle of double effect. The double effect principle is very helpful, according to Van der Marck, in overcoming the tendency to ascribe a meaning to an action independent of intersubjectivity. For the double effect principle, in distinguishing between action and effects, thereby distinguishes between corporeity and intersubjectivity. However, the problem with the principle according to Van der Marck, is that

> a twofold intersubjectivity is ascribed to the act (two effects) and then one aspect is immediately canceled out ("indirectly willed" for "sufficient reason") (Van der Marck 1968, 58).

According to him, both effects or aspects constitute the intersubjectivity of the act, its human meaning. They are there and are determinative of the meaning (and morality) of the act whether I will them or not. To hold that one is only indirectly willed (unintended) he sees as "canceling it out."[16] And he seems to find that objectionable. What Van der Marck approves in the double effect idea is not, then, its validity as an adequate account of the human meaning (and morality) of our actions, but rather the fact that it moves a step away from assigning meaning independently of intersubjectivity. For effects are the intersubjective aspects of acts and to take them seriously is to take intersubjectivity seriously.

Ultimately, then, Van der Marck would abandon the distinction between direct and indirect. It is not an adequate tool to get at the meaning of our actions, and for two reasons, if I understand him correctly. First, it "cancels out" as indirect one aspect of intersubjectivity—the evil effect. Secondly, the morality of our actions requires a larger setting than that present in the assessment of immediate effects—that of community-building or destruction of community. Every action, as an intersubjective reality, is either a form of community or destruction of it. That *determines* its objective moral quality.

> To call something *good* or *evil* is therefore, in the first instance, a highly pragmatic statement that can be made only after the event, after one has been able to establish the "results" actually produced by the action (Van der Marck 1968, 61).

5 - Ambiguity in Moral Choice

Van der Marck's argument is basically this: we must first describe our conduct and its meaning in categories which respect our social nature before speaking of this conduct as good or evil. The conduct so described is then judged to be good or evil depending on whether it is community-building or not. This judgment is not adequately elaborated out of the categories of direct and indirect intent. His analysis, while a helpful corrective at key points, reveals, I believe, the symptoms and problems of a reaction. I see three serious problems in his approach.

The first difficulty raised by Van der Marck's analysis is the problem of the application of the categories corporeity-intersubjectivity to the categories of means-end and act-intention, and the implications of this application. As for the application itself, the author says means and end are formally, not materially distinct. They are related to each other just as corporeity and intersubjectivity. Therefore, it is the end which contributes human meaning to action. This is true, it seems, with regard to those effects which are rather the immediate implications of one's activity than genuine, later-on effects. Van der Marck is aware of this distinction. For in writing of means-end, act-effect, he says:

> When we now speak of act and consequences, of act and effect, of means and end, we are, in the first place, not speaking of something that happens *now* and has results, consequences; rather, we are speaking of a particular corporeal action that, precisely as a human act, has immediate implications with respect to the relationship between "subjects."[17]

Therefore he does distinguish "later-on effects" from "immediate implications." It is these latter which are only formally distinct from the action and which give human significance to my action.

But how does one make this distinction in practice? Perhaps saving the life of the mother is not a later-on effect, but an *immediate implication* of the action giving it its basic human description and meaning. But Van der Marck has given us no satisfactory criterion for distinguishing the two. Grisez, as I shall indicate later, uses the criterion of indivisibility. But as I understand him, Van der Marck gives none. In other words, perhaps a case can be made for saying that terminating pregnancy to save the mother is actually not a use of a means to achieve an end, a means-to-end act. Rather the saving of the mother is an immediate implication of the act, its intersubjectivity. Van der Marck should have attempted to show why in this instance we are not dealing with a true means at all, but with the immediate intersubjective implications of an act which define its basic human meaning. If one fails to do this, then eventually any intended effect can be grouped under title of end and be said to specify the act in its human meaning. In summary, there is a cutoff point between the physiological description of the action and the consequentialist (or intentional) description. It is this cutoff point that is not clear in Van der Marck. And it is this cutoff point, I think, that is precisely the practical problem.

Secondly, there is the matter of canceling out the evil effect. *Canceling out* is terribly loose theological language and it is not clear what Van der Marck intends by it. But it seems to convey the idea of not counting, ignoring. I do not believe that the evidence justifies the statement that the rule of double effect was denying that one aspect (the evil) of the action had intersubjective significance. To say that it was canceled out by indirectness implies this. The rule was rather insisting on just the contrary, and for this reason demanding a truly proportionate reason. If the evil effect had been canceled out by use of the double effect, no proportionate reason would have been demanded. One can argue that Van der Marck's fear of a merely physiological analysis of the meaning of an act has brought him to a contrary extreme—where physiological realities are totally dominated by intent, and therefore, where he is the one who cancels out the evil. For instance, to redescribe emptying the womb of a nonviable fetus as "destroying or removing the effects of rape" could be a rather hasty way of depersonalizing the fetus. The intention is, indeed, removing the effects of rape. But the most immediate, obvious, irrevocable implication of this removing is the destruction of nascent life. The language of intention dare not disguise this fact and suffocate the full implications of our conduct. To be consistent intersubjectivity must include all the subjects, and the fetus cannot be that easily verbalized out of significance. We may characterize the action as "removing the effects of rape," but the question remains: is this morally appropriate when these effects are a person, or nascent human life?

The third problem is the criterion of community-building. There is, of course, a sense in which one cannot quibble with such a criterion. That is, if an action is, in its *full* intersubjective reality, eventually destructive of community, then clearly it is immoral and any criterion which approves it is inadequate. But at this point one asks: has experience and reflection given us no practical presumptive judgments about what is community-building? I think it has. Van der Marck suggests the contrary when he says that good and evil are pragmatic statements "that can be made only after the event." Clearly we have more to learn, but by that same token we have learned something already. We know, for instance, that killing of others is, except in the most extreme and tragic circumstances, destructive of the *humanum* in every way, and is therefore destructive of community. And there are other things that we know before the event. Otherwise experience and reflection generate nothing by way of valid (I do not say exceptionless) generalization. In summary, if in the past we have identified good and evil too narrowly with the physical structure of the action, Van der Marck has backed off so far from this shortcoming that intention seems to swallow up the physical reality of the action. A balance is missing.

Another interesting discussion of the principle of double effect is that of Cornelius J. Van der Poel, C.S.Sp (Van der Poel 1968, 186-210). His thought-structure is very close to that of Van der Marck. Van der Poel believes that the standard interpretation of the double effect has two weaknesses. First, it fragments the human action. For instance, in the tragic case where termination of pregnancy is the only way to save the mother's life, traditional casuistry has spoken of the "direct killing" of the child in order to save the mother. Van der Poel rejects this as the proper reading of what is going on. He notes:

> The termination of the pregnancy is seen as a negative value, the saving of the mother as positive. One effect viewed as a completely independent human act in itself seems to be weighed against the other effect, also viewed as a completely independent human act in itself.... Thus we get the impression that the unity of the human act of saving the mother (which includes the most regrettable but inseparably connected element of the death of the child) is divided into two independent realities (Van der Poel 1968, 193).

Obviously, the thought of Van der Marck hovers over this rendering.

Secondly, the traditional understanding overemphasizes the importance of the *physical* effect in judging the *moral* value of the human action. Thus, in determining what is directly intended, moralists narrowed their focus too much to the physical structure of the act. If the *finis operis* of the act was killing, then that action was direct killing. The weakness of this approach is manifested, Van der Poel believes, in the moral discussion of organ transplants. Transplantation of organs demands the direct physical excising of an organ from the donor. However, this physical structure of the action must be put into its total context.

> The physical exertion of the organ is a part of the total human action of transplantation. The example shows that the physical structure of the act is merely a premoral consideration, and not itself determinant of morality (Van der Poel 1968, 194, and Fuchs see below 60-99).

Thus physical occurrences which represent intermediate stages of a human action get *moral* determination from the totality of the human action. What gives this totality or unity? "The total intention or reason of the action." It is precisely this intention or purpose which unites the intermediate stages and makes the action human. For example, "the intermediate action of surgical intervention... is in totality directed toward the saving of the mother's life."[18]

At this stage of his analysis Van der Poel makes two important points. First, not any material effect can be used to obtain a good result. There must be a proportionate reason which makes the occurrence of physical evil acceptable within the whole act. Thus of an abortion to avoid shame or inconvenience, Van der Poel says that these purposes enter "into the act of terminating the pregnancy" and are the goals that "determine the human meaning of it." But they are (I presume he would say, though he nowhere says it) disproportionate, not sufficient to render the evil caused acceptable.

Secondly, the intermediate stages within a total action are certainly voluntary, but they are "willed only in relation to the purpose." The agent wills and wants "the means of the intermediate stages only insofar as the final goal *is contained in these means*." Van der Poel gives the example of a person who loves nature and beauty and wants to view the countryside from the highest mountain peak in the area. The climb is long, fatiguing, and perhaps dangerous. But the inseparable fatigue and danger do not constitute a separate object of the will. "There is only one object, the vision, which communicates its

5 - Ambiguity in Moral Choice

meaning to all the intermediate stages of the one *human* act." If we consider the fatiguing and dangerous climb as an independent entity, we rob it of its specific *human* determination and ascribe a human value to an abstract physical entity.

This same analysis should be applied, he argues, to those actions which have a double effect. Thus,

> the amputation of a leg may be an absolute requirement for the life and health of a person. In such a case the act of the will directs itself not to two different actions of amputation and cure, but the one act of curing including the amputation unavoidably and defines the *human* meaning of the amputation itself.[19]

In all such instances, we should not speak of an effect which is in *itself evil* but which can be permitted for that ascribes a human meaning to the material effect independent of the total human action. Thus, once we concentrate our attention on the total human action and the proportion between the evil caused (means) and the purpose (end) within this single action, we need not speak of direct and indirect willing. Rather the evil is voluntary *in se sed non propter se*.

Van der Poel, therefore, rejects the classical methodology that would face conflict situations by appeal to the notions of direct and indirect. But the question remains: how do we know whether the end or good of the action is proportionate to the evil caused within it? Here Van der Poel states that the "ultimate moral criterion is the community-building or destroying aspect of the action." Thus

> the means for a particular action may never be so grave that the total result of the whole action would be damaging for the community (Van der Poel 1968, 209).

Van der Poel's analysis raises several problems. For instance, when are occurrences (of evil) to be viewed as only intermediate stages of a single action? May every premoral evil that occurs in any way in conjunction with my activity be reduced to an "intermediate stage"? For example, is the killing of innocent children to get at the enemy's morale simply an "intermediate stage" of the action describable as *national self-defense*? What is the criterion here? Somewhat similarly, because if seems legitimate to intend some premoral evils *in se sed non propter se*, does it follow that all evils which occur in conjunction with one's activity can be said to be intended *in se sed non propter se*? For instance, does one intend and choose the death of the fetus in a cancerous uterus situation in the same way one intends and chooses the fatigue and danger involved in a mountain climb? This can be doubted, as I will attempt to show later. How one intends premoral evil would seem to depend on how that evil relates to the action—whether as effect, aspect, or integral and inseparable means.

It is, however, the matter of proportionate reason to which I wish to attend here. Van der Poel seems quite ambiguous on what this term should mean. When he says that not any good will justify any evil, he seems to suggest that proportionate reason is found in a balancing of the identifiable values immediately at stake. For instance, one may not abort a pregnancy simply to avoid shame. Yet at another point, he backs off from such a calculus and insists that

> there needs to be a proportionate reason which makes the occurrence of the physical evil acceptable *in view of the total human existence*.

Or again:

> This total human action should be projected against the background of the whole of human existence in this world, to see whether it is contributing to it or destructive in its results.

The evil in the action "may never be so grave that the total result of the whole action would be damaging for the community" (Van der Poel 1968, 198). Briefly, the proportionate reason is determined by whether the action is community-building or not.

Van der Poel is, I believe, both right and wrong. First the good news. Obviously—as was pointed out above where Van der Marck is concerned—if an action is reasonably foreseen or eventually known to be ultimately community-damaging, it is, regardless of its immediate meaning and rewards, immoral. The criterion is clearly correct in this rearview-mirror sense. But now for the bad news. To propose as the only criterion of the morality of an act a measure so utterly ultimate is to suggest (at least) that more proximate criteria are useless or invalid. That is, in my judgment, to bypass a good deal of

5 – Ambiguity in Moral Choice

accumulated experience and wisdom. Furthermore, pastorally it is a general invitation to creeping exceptionism and to all kinds of self-serving and utilitarian decisions under the guise of community-building.

The problem, then, is not the validity of the ultimate criterion of community-building. It is rather the existence of more proximate norms. For instance, Van der Poel says:

> When the life of the mother is certainly threatened by the fetus, the moralist (following the community-building criterion) can conclude to the taking of the life of the fetus in these circumstances (Van der Poel 1968, 207).

Just how *that* criterion leads to *this* conclusion remains almost totally mysterious. This is not to deny the conclusion, not at all. It is only to say that unless one specifies a bit what counts for community-building and how we know this, then that criterion can be squeezed to yield almost any conclusion—for instance, the immorality of all abortions, or the morality of abortion on demand.

A criterion is like a weapon. If not carefully and precisely constructed, it can impale its user. This has happened, I believe, to Van der Poel. Speaking of self-defense, he says:

> We do not weigh the independent value of the human life of the unlawful attacker against the independent value of the life of the person who legitimately defends himself against the attack. We place the total action in the social setting of human existence and we call the whole action morally good provided that this was the only way to defend himself (Van der Poel 1968, 210).

Here Van der Poel is left dangling helplessly on his own *petitio principii*. For the precise point of his own criterion is not whether "this was the only way to defend himself," but whether self-defense in such desperate circumstances is community-building or not. I believe self-defense is a legitimate Christian response. And I know of no studies that tell us that this response is more community-building than its opposite. Once again, I believe that behind this difficulty in Van der Poel is an overreaction. His legitimate dissatisfaction with a narrow physicalism has led him to presume too readily that once he has shown that an action ought to be viewed and described as mother saving, self-defense, or transplantation, it is community-building. It may be, but that is precisely the issue.

Against Van der Poel, I think we must also and first wrestle realistically with proportion in much narrower terms. That is, if the more immediate good achieved by the total act itself is not at least proportionate to the evils within it or accompanying it, then we must conclude that the action will be *de facto* community-damaging. This type of calculus could turn out to be shortsighted and wrong. But it should not be overlooked. For instance, if the purpose of a truly dangerous mountain climb is simply a view of natural beauty, one might easily conclude (in lack of other criteria) that such a climb represents an unjustified risk and is immoral. If, however, the same climb and same danger is undertaken to rescue another, a different assessment of proportion would be in place. Van der Poel himself suggests, perhaps unwittingly, that we need not always go foraging in the community-building forest but that the morality of an action which causes premoral evil can be found in a less sweeping and more modest criterion. In dealing with abortion of a pregnancy to avoid shame or burden or an unwanted child—an abortion I presume he considers immoral—he says:

> The ultimate goal (in this case avoidance of shame or burden) enters into the act of terminating the pregnancy. It is this goal, therefore, that determines the human meaning of it (Van der Poel 1968, 201).

Granted, the intention does shade the meaning. But the question remains: is an action with this meaning morally acceptable? If he considers the act immoral (as he seems to), it can only be because there is no proportion between "avoiding shame or burden" and destroying fetal life. The perception of this disproportion is not secured by reference to community-building or destroying. Indeed, it seems clear that anyone who does such disproportionate things does *thereby* something that is likely to be community-destroying.

Philippa Foot approaches the double effect from a different perspective.[20] After admitting the legitimacy of the distinction between "direct intention" and "oblique (or indirect) intention," she claims that the distinction plays only a very subsidiary role in determining what is right in difficult situations. Much more important is the distinction between avoiding injury and bringing aid, a negative duty and a positive duty. The former weighs on us more strictly than the latter.

Foot uses several examples to illustrate her thesis. First there is the case of a runaway tram which the driver can steer only on either of two tracks. Five men are working on one track, only one on the other. Anyone working on either track is bound to be killed if the tram comes through. The second example is that of a group of rioters demanding that a culprit be found for a certain crime and threatening to kill five hostages if he is not. The real culprit being unknown, the judge sees himself as able to prevent the death of five by framing one innocent person and having him executed. Foot says that we would unhesitatingly steer the tram down the track where it killed but one rather than five. But we would balk at framing one innocent man to save five. "Why can we not argue from the case of the steering driver to that of the judge?"

To that question Foot admits that the double effect provides an answer. The death of the innocent man framed by the judge would have to be intended. Whereas if he refrained, the deaths of the hostages would be unintended by him. But she believes that such situations should be solved in another way: by distinguishing positive and negative duties. In both cases we have a conflict of duties, but the steering driver faces a conflict of *negative* duties. His duty is to avoid injuring five men and his duty is also to avoid injuring one. "It seems clear he should do the least injury he can." The judge, however, is weighing the duty of not inflicting injury (negative) against the duty of bringing aid (positive). If our only choice is between conflicting negative duties or conflicting positive duties, we reasonably opt for the least harm or most good. But when the conflict is between negative (inflicting injury) and positive (bringing aid) we do not inflict injury to bring aid.

This is a thoughtful and intriguing study. I would agree with Foot that the double effect probably plays a lesser role in at least some conflict decisions than we have thought. Furthermore, her distinction between positive and negative duties is certainly valid and meaningful, although it is not new. It has been known for centuries. But tidy as it is, it still leaves unanswered questions. First of all, in applying the distinction to the case of abortion to save the mother (where nothing can be done to save mother and child, but where the mother can be saved), Foot states that "it is reasonable that the action that will save someone should be done." I would agree, but it is not clear how the distinction between bringing aid and avoiding injury functions here. Presumably Foot would say that abortion in this instance is "bringing aid." However, it is precisely the contention of traditional moralists that taking the child in this instance is "causing injury," even though the child is to perish. Foot nowhere shows why the operation should not be called "causing injury." Similarly, it is difficult to see how Foot would argue the moral legitimacy of self-defense and warfare if her overarching categories are "bringing aid" and "avoiding injury."

Secondly, and more importantly, Foot states that her

> conclusion is that the distinction between direct and oblique intention plays only a quite subsidiary role in determining what we say in these cases, while the distinction between avoiding injury and bringing aid is very important indeed.

What is this "subsidiary role"? This is not clear. Indeed, it would seem that it is ultimately no role at all. For at one point she states: "If you are permitted to bring about the death of the child, what does it matter how it is done?" If Foot had clarified the moral role of intention in human conflict situations, perhaps she would have clarified *why* and therefore *where* it is or is not permissible to inflict injury to bring aid. Not having done so, she retreats to the statement that "to refrain from inflicting injury ourselves is a stricter duty than to prevent other people from inflicting injury." Is it? That is precisely the point.

One of the most ranging and profound recent discussions of the double effect is that of Germain Grisez (Grisez 1970a, 307-46). Grisez's analysis is developed with relentless consistency and subtlety. His treatment of the distinction between direct and indirect intention interlocks logically with his overall moral theory. This moral theory is developed somewhat as follows. The basic human goods (life, knowledge pursued for its own sake, interior integrity, justice, friendship, and so on) present themselves as goods-to-be-realized. They appeal to us for their realization. Thus these goods are the nonhypothetical principles of practical reason. "As expressions of what is-to-be, the practical principles present basic human needs as funda-

5 – Ambiguity in Moral Choice

mental goods, as ideals" (Grisez 1970a, 314). But the appeal of these goods is not the direct determinant of moral obligation. They clarify the possiblities of choice but do not determine why some choices are morally good and others evil.

What determines this? The attitude with which we choose. What, then, is a right attitude? A realistic one.

> To choose a particular good with an appreciation of its genuine but limited possibility and its objectively human character is to choose it with an attitude of realism (Grisez 1970a, 315).

The right attitude does not seek to belittle the good that is not chosen, but only seeks to realize what is chosen. This open, realistic attitude shapes itself into specific moral obligations. For instance, we must take all the goods into account in our deliberations; we must avoid ways of acting which inhibit the realization of any one of the goods to the extent possible; we must contribute our effort to their realization in others. A final and most important mode of obligation is this: we must never act "in a way destructive of a realization of any of the basic goods." For to act *directly* against a good is to subordinate it to whatever leads to that choice. And one may not morally do that, because the basic goods are equally basic.

But clearly not every inhibition of a good that occurs as a result of my action is directly destructive of this good. Some inhibitions are unsought and unavoidable side effects of an effort to pursue another value. Thus one *directly* goes against a basic good when its inhibition is directly intended.

When is the destruction of a basic good directly intended? Here Grisez modifies the textbook understanding of the double effect. He believes that the modern formulation is too restrictive. It insists too much on the behavioral aspect, the physical causality, in determining the meaning of the act. In the textbook tradition, if evil is the sole immediate effect of the physical act, then it is directly produced and hence directly intended. For example, one may not "shell out" an ectopic fetus that represents a mortal threat to the mother, though one may excise a pathological tube which contains a fetus. Similarly one may not abort the fetus to save the mother.

Grisez rejects this understanding. Rather he insists that

from the point of view of human moral activity, the initiation of the indivisible process through one's own causality renders all that is involved in that process equally immediate. . . . For on the hypothesis that no other human act intervenes or could intervene, the moral agent who posits a natural cause *simultaneously* (morally speaking) posits its foreseen effects (Grisez 1970a, 333).

For instance, the saving of the mother is an aspect of the abortifacient act equally immediate, morally speaking, to the death of the child. Thus he writes:

The justification is simply that the very same act, indivisible as to its behavioral process, has both the good effect of protecting human life and the bad effect of destroying it . . . the entire process is indivisible by human choice and hence all aspects of it are equally present to the agent at the moment he makes his choice (Grisez 1970a, 340).

Central in Grisez's analysis is the indivisibility of the action or behavioral process. It is this indivisibility which allows one to conclude to the equal immediacy of the good and bad effects—and therefore to direct intent of the good and indirect intent of evil. If, however, the process is divisible and the good effect occurs as a result of a subsequent act, we are dealing with means to end, or with effects not equally immediate. Thus one may not commit adultery to save one's children from a prison camp "because the saving effect would not be present in the adulterous act, but in subsequent human act—that of the person who releases them." Similarly, organ transplants that will involve deprivation of life or health to the donor are immoral because the two aspects (excision, implant) are factually separable.

Grisez applies this analysis to many instances involving killing. He contends that it is *never* permissible *directly* to take human life. For him, capital punishment cannot be justified. The argument from deterrence, even if factually defensible, is "ethically invalid, because the good is achieved in other human acts, not in the execution itself." Similarly, Grisez argues that killing in warfare is indirect (and must be to remain morally tolerable) much as it is in self-defense.

Thus far Grisez. His ranging analysis of the direct/indirect distinction is by far the most subtle, consistent, and plausible defense of that distinction that I have seen in recent literature. What is to be said of it? First of all, Grisez's notion of an indivisible process seems certainly correct. If the evil effect or aspect occurs within an indivisible process, then "the moral agent who posits a natural cause *simultaneously* (morally speaking) posits its foreseen effects." In other words, the evil effect is not a means, morally speaking, to the good effect. Hence, it is not, or need not be, the object of an intending will. So far so good. What is not clear is why one must be said to turn against a basic good when the evil occurs as a means, and is the object of an intending will. This is the very problem posed by Schüller, as we shall see. The problem I am raising centers around the notion of proportionate reason. A closer examination of proportionate reason might have forced Grisez to admit that it need not be ultimately decisive whether the will is intending or permitting, but whether the reason in either case is proportionate. Grisez's reluctance to examine proportionate reason more thoroughly allows him to concentrate his full attention on the posture of the will with reference to the evil in a narrow sense and to frame the problem of unavoidable evil in these terms. If he had discussed what constitutes a proportionate reason more adequately, perhaps we would see a different understanding of what it means to go directly against a basic good.

Behind Grisez's failure to examine more thoroughly the notion of proportionate reason is his deep repugnance to anything resembling a utilitarian calculus. In discussing the four conditions for use of the double effect, Grisez says of the last (proportionately grave reason):

> The last condition can easily become a field for a covert, although limited, utilitarianism. However, that is not necessary. Though human good is not calculable and though diverse modes of human good are incommensurable, the basic human goods do require protection when possible. Human life may not be destroyed frivolously or gratuitously . . . where safer methods of achieving desirable objectives are readily available (Grisez 1970a, 329).

After this brief statement, Grisez fairly runs from the notion of proportion and returns to it only to indicate here and there what reasons are not proportionate. However, the heart of the matter has been passed over a bit too quickly here. If one insists—as we should—that there must be a proportionate reason, we ask: what is a proportionate reason for taking another human life? Or in Grisez's terms above: what does *when possible* mean concretely in the phrase "the basic human goods do require protection when possible"? When is destruction of human life not "frivolous or gratuitous" and why? We know that lesser goods such as convenience, avoidance of shame, and health are not to be preferred to life. But what goods are to be preferred, or at least are of equal status? Grisez does not clarify this because on his own terms he cannot. The basic goods are simply incommensurable, and to start weighing and balancing them is to succumb to utilitarianism.

Perhaps. But I agree with Stanley Hauerwas that ultimately Grisez cannot "avoid the kind of consequentialist reasoning that our human sensibilities seem to demand in such (conflict) cases."[21] For if a good, like life, is simply incommensurable with other goods, what do we mean by a proportionate reason where death is, in Grisez's terms, indirect? Proportionate to what? If some goods are to be preferred to life itself, then we have compared life with these goods. And if this is proper, then life can be weighed against other values too, even very basic values. Granted, there are real dangers and genuine difficulties in a merely utilitarian calculus. But I believe that some such calculus can be avoided only at the cost of artificiality and contrivance. Our problem is rather to do all we can to guarantee that our calculus will be truly adequate and fully Christian.

Let me put the matter very concretely. In cases (admittedly rare) where abortion is necessary to save the mother's life, Grisez writes:

> The justification is simply that the very same act, indivisible as to its behavioral process, has both the good effect of protecting human life and the bad effect of destroying it . . . the entire process is indivisible by human choice and hence all aspects of it are equally present to the agent at the moment he makes his choice (Grisez 1970a, 340).

This is not, in my judgment, the *justification* at all. It is only one way of explaining how the evil that I do is not direct, according to one understanding of what that term means. In other words, this is the justification only on the assumption that an intending will necessarily involves one in turning against a basic good, that is, if directly intended killing is evil *in se*. What is the true justification for allowing abortion here? It cannot be that one may prefer the life of the mother to that of the fetus. For that preference is simply not clear. Furthermore, such a preference gets one into the functional and utilitarian valuations of life that Grisez so rightly abhors. What is the justification—or proportionate reason? Is it not that we are faced here with two alternatives (either abort, or do not abort)? Both alternatives are destructive, but one is more destructive than the other. We could allow both mother and child (who will perish under any circumstances) to die; or we could at least salvage one life. Is it not because, *all things considered,* abortion is the lesser evil in this tragic instance? Is it not precisely for this reason, then, that abortion in this instance is proportionate? Is it not for this reason that we may say that the action is truly lifesaving? And is it not for this reason that abortion in these circumstances does not involve one in turning against a basic good?

The matter can be urged in another way. Suppose we are faced with a situation (suggested by Philippa Foot) with the following alternatives: an operation which saves the mother but kills the child, versus one that kills the mother but saves the child. In either choice Grisez's use of double effect would seem to apply. That is, there is a single indivisible process one of whose aspects is good, one evil. And the act is lifesaving. But unless one uses functional criteria (the "greater value" in some sense of the mother's or child's life), is there a proportionate reason for choosing mother over child, or child over mother? If Grisez would say that in this instance we may save the mother, I ask: why? Why *prefer* the mother to the child when I have a choice? On the other hand, if Grisez says that I may do neither since to do either would involve one in a preference of one life over another, then it seems that what has functioned as proportionate reason in instances where he allows abortion to save the mother is this: it is better to save one life than to lose two. Or more generally, a proportionate reason exists because that choice represents the lesser evil.

Frankly, I do not know what Grisez would say to an either/or case of this kind. But I suspect he would hesitate long and hard. But he would not and does not hesitate in the simple instance where abortion (of a fetus who will perish under any circumstances) is necessary to save the mother's life. Does this not indicate that in this latter instance the crucial and decisive consideration is that it is better on all counts in such circumstances to save one life where my only alternative is to lose two? Does it not indicate that the procedure is legitimate precisely for this reason? And does it not then follow that "acting directly against a basic good" need not be interpreted within the deontological understanding of direct and indirect that Grisez provides?

Ultimately, then, Grisez has provided only an ingenious criterion to loosen the notion of direct killing to accommodate the instances where common sense seems to allow it. This is a further relaxation of a deontological norm. But it still presupposes that direct killing is evil *in se* and necessarily involves a morally reprehensible attitude. As I shall indicate later, it can be argued that our moral posture must be measured by a broader intentionality that relates it to a plurality of values. In brief, it is the presence or absence of a proportionate reason which determines whether my action—be it direct or indirect psychologically or causally—involves me in turning against a basic good in a way which is morally reprehensible.[22] Or as Hauerwas puts it:

> Grisez does not seem to provide the necessary theoretical account of why so many of our moral arguments take the form of choices between "lesser evils" (Hauerwas 1971, 413).

The most precise and searching challenge to the distinction between direct and indirect voluntariety is that of Bruno Schüller.[23] Schüller notes four areas where the distinction has been used by traditional theology: scandal, cooperation, killing, and contraception. But according to Schüller it was used for different reasons where scandal and cooperation are involved. These reasons must be isolated.

The sin of another, Schüller notes, is a moral evil and as such is an absolute disvalue. It would seem to follow that an action (scandal) which has such a disvalue as a foreseen effect must be absolutely avoided. But this would lead to impossible consequences. No lawmaker, for example, could attach a punishment to a violation of law because he would know in advance that this would be the occasion of sinful bribery for a certain undetermined number of people. More fundamentally, it is hard to reconcile an absolute duty to avoid foreseen evil with the will of the creator who created a being capable of sin. The way out has always been sought in distinguishing will, intention, and purpose from permission and toleration—or direct from indirect. The absolute disvalue of sin demands only that one not will and intend it under any circumstances. However, for a proportionate reason it may be permitted.

5 - Ambiguity in Moral Choice

The reason the distinction is necessary is that we are dealing here with moral evil. The absoluteness of the disvalue forces some such distinction. However, when we are dealing with nonmoral evils (error, pain, sickness, death), the reason for the distinction between directness and indirectness disappears precisely because these disvalues, fundamental as they are, are *relative* disvalues. These we must, of course, also avoid—but conditionally. The condition under which we must avoid a relative disvalue is that it does not concur with a greater relative disvalue or an absolute one. For example, sickness must be avoided but not at any price, not, for example, at the price of plunging one's family into destitution. Schüller argues that when we justifiably cause a relative disvalue in our conduct, we should not call it *indirect*. Thus when health officers quarantine one with typhoid fever, should we say that they intend only the prevention of its spread and "merely permit" the isolation of the sick individual? Hardly. The isolation is a necessary means to an end. And where means are concerned we speak of an intending will, a direct choice.

We should not abandon this usage. Indeed it brings out the difference between the attitude to moral evil and that to nonmoral evil. For a proportionate reason we may *permit* a moral evil, but we may directly will and directly cause a nonmoral evil if there is a proportionate reason for doing so.

This has been a tenet of Catholic moral theology for centuries. For instance, one may reveal the hidden defects of another and thereby hurt his reputation "to ward off a relatively important harm from oneself or the neighbor." Similarly with a promise. But this breaking of a promise is experienced by the one to whom the promise was made as an evil. In such cases we do not demand that the negative effect be unintended.

Schüller next turns to killing and contraception. Why did traditional theology feel it necessary to use "direct" and "indirect" when dealing with these subjects? It was because it viewed them as evil *in se*. This can be sustained, however, only if the death of a person is an absolute evil in the sense of a moral evil. Once it is granted that the killing of an innocent person is the destruction of a fundamental but nonmoral value, there is no need for the distinction direct/indirect. Rather the assessment is made teleologically, that is, from presence or absence of proportionate reason.

Schüller concludes, therefore, that death and contraception must be judged according to teleological, not deontological norms (these latter being norms independent of proportionate reason). He further concludes that since this is so, it is superfluous to distinguish between indirect and direct action. All of them must be judged according to proportionate reason.

My first reaction to Schüller's analysis was that it is absolutely correct (McCormick 1972, 71). After further reflection, I think that there is still some unfinished business in it. Here I should like to raise a question which is not clearly resolved in his study.

Schüller concludes that the distinction between direct and indirect is necessary and functional only where the *sin* of another (scandal) is concerned. In other instances the distinction is merely descriptive. This suggests the following problem. If one says there is a crucial difference between an intending and a permitting will where *moral* evil is concerned—as one must—then that must mean that the will relates differently to what it intends and what it permits. Otherwise the distinction is meaningless and arbitrary. But if the will relates differently to what it intends and merely permits in this one instance, then it must do so wherever that distinction is legitimately made. That is, there is a different relation to the will when it intends and merely permits even where *nonmoral* evil is concerned. The only question then is the following: is this different relationship of moral significance where *nonmoral* evil is concerned? As I read him, Schüller says it is not, because in all instances the action (whether one intends or merely permits the nonmoral evil) is to be judged teleologically (that is, by proportionate reason). However, it can be doubted that, because both indirect and direct causing of nonmoral evil are to be judged teleologically, the same teleological judgment applies to both.

Here something more must be said. Because direct (descriptively) killing must also be judged teleologically, it does not seem to follow that the same proportionate reason which would justify what is indirect (descriptively) would always justify what is direct. In other words, there may be a proportionate reason for doing something in one way which is not proportionate to doing it another way.

Let us take the death of noncombatants in warfare as an example. Traditional theology has concluded that it can be permissible (proportionate) at times to attack the enemy's war machine even though some noncombatants (innocents) will be tragically and regretfully killed in the process. The difficulty of applying this distinction in practice (that is, determining the noncombatants) does not affect its theoretical legitimacy. It has also concluded that it is not morally permissible to make these noncombatants the target of one's attack, to kill them as a means to bringing the enemy to his knees and weakening his will to fight. This latter conclusion is, I believe, a teleological judgment (one based on proportionate reason defined by foreseeable or suspected consequences in the broadest sense), not a deontological one. Equivalently it means that direct attacks on noncombatant civilians in wartime, however effective and important they may seem, will in the long run release more violence and be more destructive to human life than the lives we might save by directly attacking noncombatants. But this teleological assessment is concretely different from the teleological assessment made where the deaths are incidental. The difference is not in the number of deaths here and now. They could be numerically the same—for instance, one hundred civilians killed incidentally, one hundred directly killed. The deaths are equally regrettable and tragic simply as deaths and *in this sense* how they occur does not affect their status as nonmoral evils. But how they occur has a good deal to say about the present meaning of the action, the effect on the agent and others, and hence about the protection and security of life in the long run. These considerations are certainly a part of one's teleological calculus. There are those who argue that it makes little difference to a person whether he is killed by a direct or indirect action, hence that a "love ethic" abandons this distinction. I would urge, contrarily, that it is precisely a "love ethic" which demands the distinction; for a love ethic is concerned not simply with this or that effect, but also with the *overall* implications and repercussions of human conduct. And these implications and repercussions are affected very much at times by whether a certain evil is visited by an intending or merely permitting will.

In summary, Schüller's effort has been to show that the norms governing killing and contraception must be built and interpreted teleologically, not deontologically. In this I believe he is correct. But his study leaves the impression that therefore the distinction between direct and indirect is totally superfluous in these areas, and others too. I am not persuaded of this. The nonmoral evil is, to be sure, quantitatively the same whether it is chosen or merely permitted. But the act is not necessarily thereby the same. The relation of the evil to the will, how it happens, not only can tell us what kind of act we are performing, but can have enormously different immediate and long-term implications, and therefore generate a quite different calculus of proportion. I am suggesting, therefore, that the terms direct/indirect are not superfluous, or at least not at all times, but only that a different teleological calculus may apply in each instance.

This problem can be restated in terms of Schüller's analysis of cooperation in another's evildoing. Schüller argues that the distinction between direct and indirect is not necessary here. For whether one performs or refuses the cooperation has no influence on the *moral* violation of the other, but only on the effects of this moral violation. Schüller takes the example of a bank cashier during a robbery. The cashier may and should hand over the money not because this leaves the robber less morally guilty, but because the loss of money is a lesser nonmoral evil than loss of life. The moral guilt of the robber is in his determination to kill during the robbery if necessary. The cashier, Schüller notes, cannot lessen this. But he can lessen the nonmoral disvalues that the robber is prepared to commit. In this instance the cashier can *intend* to cause the harm to the bank to save his own life. There is, says Schüller, no need to appeal to indirectness here. The problem is analyzed teleologically.

I agree with this analysis, but I believe that something more must be said. Schüller says the cashier should hand over the money because the loss of money is a lesser nonmoral evil than loss of life. That is certainly true. But must we not add also that preserving one's life in this way will not in the long run threaten more lives and undermine the very value I am protecting in this instance?

Let us return to the case of the rioting mob and the judge. In Schüller's analysis we would have to say that the *moral* guilt of the mob is already there in its determination to kill five men unjustly if the judge does not frame one innocent man and execute him. Therefore this moral evil cannot be lessened. But the judge can lessen the nonmoral disvalues the mob is prepared to commit by executing one innocent man. Certainly the death of one innocent man is a lesser evil than the death of five innocent men. Schüller (if his analysis stops where it does) would be forced to conclude that the judge should execute the one innocent man. Yet I think we are appalled at this conclusion. Is it not precisely because we sense that taking the life of this innocent man in these circumstances would represent a capitulation to and encouragement of a type of injustice which in the long run would render many more lives vulnerable? Yet our judgment would be different if the death of the one innocent man were incidental. In summary, proportion must be measured also in terms of long-term effects. And in terms of such effects, whether one directly intends (or not) certain nonmoral evils what one now does may make quite a difference.

In other words, the teleological character of all our norms does not eliminate the relevance of the distinction between direct/indirect where nonmoral values and disvalues are involved. Rather precisely because these norms are teleological is the direct/indirect distinction relevant. For the relation of the evil-as-it-happens to the will may say a great deal about the meaning of my action, its repercussions and implications, and therefore what will happen to the good in question over the long haul. If one asks why, I believe the answer is to be found in the fact that an intending will represents a closer relation of the agent to the disvalue and therefore indicates a greater willingness that the disvalue occur.

These are some of the recent attempts to deal with conflict situations in a sinful and imperfect world. All of these studies make valid and necessary points and I have found all of them illuminating. If a single thread or theme is common to all of them, it is, as Charles Curran has repeatedly pointed out, dissatisfaction with the narrowly behavioral or physical understanding of human activity that underlies the standard interpretation of direct and indirect. I agree with this dissatisfaction. On the other hand, in making their points they all seem in one way or another incomplete, and even misleading when dealing with the distinction between direct and indirect intention.

For instance Knauer rightly rejects the use of *moral* evil to describe actions independently of the reasons for which they are done, hence independently of their context and intention. However, in interpreting the direct/indirect distinction in an exclusively moral way (that is, with no relation to psychological intentionality), he underestimates the real differences in the meaning of our conduct that could be generated by psychological intentionality. Grisez provides a satisfying account of the origin of moral obligation with his analysis of basic human goods. But his interpretation of what it means "to turn directly against these goods" seems too contrived and incapable of accounting for the complexity of reality, especially of the conflict situations we have been considering. This is traceable to his reluctance to examine more realistically the notion of proportionate reason, a reluctance rooted in his nervous fear of any utilitarian calculus.

Van der Marck and Van der Poel rightly insist that the meaning of our actions must take account of intersubjectivity (Van der Marck) and intentionality (Van der Poel). However, both authors seem too readily to accept the idea that once an action is described in terms of its dominant intentionality (for example, "removing the effects of rape") it has been justified, or that the only calculus which is of any help in weighing the moral quality of the decision is community-building or destroying.

Schüller is certainly correct in his insistence on the difference between moral and nonmoral evil and therefore on the profound difference between actions occasioning the sin of another and actions visiting nonmoral disvalues on the neighbor. Similarly, I believe he is correct in insisting that the meaning of moral norms concerning nonmoral evils must be interpreted within the confines of a teleological calculus (as long as a greater evil would not result). However, his preoccupation with this point leads him to suggest that direct and indirect intention are altogether morally irrelevant where nonmoral evil is associated with our activity. This fails to take seriously enough the real contribution of intentionality to the significance of human actions. In doing so it could leave him somewhat vulnerable to the weaknesses of a merely numerical calculus of proportionality.

In conclusion I should like to attempt a synthesis that takes advantage of the above positions but seems identifiable with no one of them. Such a critical synthesis will remain incomplete, and even vulnerable, I am sure. Not only does the problem we are dealing with involve one's whole moral theory (an area where there is considerably less clarity and certainty than is desirable), but it also brings this theory to bear on practical day-to-day problems. One is asked to be both theoretically consistent and practically sensitive to the complexity and intransigence of reality—in other words, to plug all the loopholes in a prudent and persuasive way. This is particularly difficult in times where theologians have different views on how the loopholes ought to be plugged, if they should be plugged at all! The following reflections must, therefore, remain a thought-experiment and will represent above all a useful invitation to other theologians to correct

5 - Ambiguity in Moral Choice

the shortcomings, inconsistencies, and even errors they may contain. My own very tentative conclusions would be summarized in the following statements:

1. There is a difference between an intending and permitting will, and therefore in the human action involving the one or the other.

2. In a conflict situation, the relation of the evil to the value sought is partially determinative of the posture of the will (whether intending or permitting).

3. The basic structure, however, in conflict situations is avoidable/unavoidable evil, the principle of the lesser evil.

4. Both the intending and the permitting will (where evil is involved) are to be judged teleologically (that is, by presence or absence of proportionate reason).

5. Proportionate reason means three things: (a) a value at stake at least equal to that sacrificed; (b) no other way of salvaging it here and now; (c) its protection here and now will not undermine it in the long run.

6. The notion of proportionate reason is analogous.

An explanation of each of these will provide the context for my own modified understanding of the moral relevance of the direct/indirect distinction.

1. *There is a difference between an intending and permitting will.* If the distinction between an intending and permitting will is utterly essential and profoundly meaningful where the moral evil (sin) of another is concerned, as Schüller rightly maintains, that can mean but one thing: there is a real difference between an intending and permitting will. Otherwise we are dealing with mere words, as was pointed out above. Now if there is a real difference between an intending and permitting will, then this difference must show where nonmoral evil is concerned. That in turn means that the human action involving an intending will (of evil) is or at least can be a different human action from that involving a permitting will. To say anything else is to say that intentionality does not affect the meaning of human activity, a tenet that becomes inconsistent if one reverses it where sin is concerned. This difference between an intending and permitting will generates two important conclusions, one negative, one positive. First of all, it is not simply and exclusively the existence or nonexistence of an evil effect that determines the meaning of the

action that occasioned it. *How* this evil relates to the human will is also relevant. A love ethic is, indeed, concerned with effects; but it must also be concerned with how they occur. Why? Because secondly, actions which are different because of differing intentionality have a different immediate meaning and may lead to different social and long-term effects.

To admit that there is a difference between an intending and permitting will within an action is not to deny that the overall significance of the action is affected by intention of the end, a point clearly made by Van der Marck and Van der Poel. Nor is it to deny a certain unity of the action rooted in this intentionality. It is simply to say that within such ultimate purposefulness the will can assume at least two different postures vis-à-vis the evil that is associated with one's choice. That this difference can be morally significant is suggested by the instance of the intention or permission of the *sin* of another. How should this difference be explained? The matter remains somewhat mysterious, as Schüller notes. But we can say this much at least: the intending will (hence the person) is more closely associated with the existence of evil than the merely permitting will. Furthermore I believe we must say that an intending will is more willing that the evil be than is a permitting will. That this can have morally significant repercussions I shall attempt to indicate later.

2. *In a conflict situation, the relation of the evil caused to the value sought is partially determinative of the posture of the will (whether intending or permitting).*[24] It seems that nonmoral evil can be immediately associated with human activity in at least two distinguishable ways: as an aspect of the act with no causal relation to the good effect and as a means with a necessary causal relationship to the good envisaged. That which stands in a relationship of means to end is necessarily the object of an intending will, even if not *propter se*. That which is merely effect or aspect need not be. When is the evil in a causal relationship to the good, a means to it, and therefore necessarily the object of an intending will? I would be willing to accept Grisez's criterion: if the evil occurs within an indivisible process, then in the moral sense it is equally immediate with the good effect, and hence not a means. If, however, the process is divisible so that the good effect occurs as the result of a subsequent act, we are clearly dealing with a means, and an intending will. There are difficulties in this criterion because it moves a step away from our psychological experi-

ence of permission. Concretely, it is much clearer that we are dealing with a means when there is divisibility than it is that we are not when the process is indivisible. For some evils that are part of an indivisible process do seem to be means. Be that as it may, Grisez's criterion can be accepted provisionally.

An example will bring out the difference between the intending and permitting will. If a woman has cancer of the ovaries, a bilateral oophorectomy is performed. The result: sterility. If a family has seven children, the wife is weak, the husband is out of a job, the woman may have a tubal ligation on the occasion of the last delivery. The result: sterility. The immediate effect (nonmoral evil) is the same in both cases—sterility. Obviously these actions are different human actions in terms of their overall intentionality—the good sought. One is a lifesaving intervention, the other a family-saving or family-stabilizing act, so to speak. But even within this larger difference, the bearing of the will toward the sterility is, I believe, distinguishable in the two instances. For the moment no moral relevance will be assigned to this difference. But it seems that there is a difference and the difference originates in the relation of the nonmoral evil to the good sought. In the one instance, the nonmoral evil is chosen as a means; in the other it is not. Van der Marck and Van der Poel have been reluctant to admit the category of means in this regard. But one need not unduly fragment the wholeness or unity of the overall action to allow the validity of this distinction within it.

Because the forms of associated evil are distinguishable within our actions, the psychological experience of "intention" is somewhat different in each case. General reluctance that the evil must be brought about (whether "intended" or "permitted") is presumably common to both instances. Still when the evil is an effect or aspect with no necessary causal relationship to the good being pursued, one does indeed have a different psychological awareness of the evil involved than one does when there is a necessary causal relationship between the evil and good achieved. I have suggested that this psychological difference is traceable to the fact that an intending will is more closely associated with the evil, more willing that the evil exist. The crucial question is whether (and why) this single form of psychological awareness—that associated with evil as aspect—is normative for a proper human intentionality. The traditional answer has been yes, at least in the instances involving human life and our sexual faculties. That is, the evil involved must be unintended *in that one psychological sense.* I believe that there are good reasons to doubt this conclusion and to assert that the meaning of human intentionality toward nonmoral evil is to be determined by reference to a larger canvas.

3. *The basic analytic structure in conflict situations is the lesser evil, or morally avoidable/unavoidable evil.* The rule of double effect is a vehicle for dealing with conflict situations. When we see the situations it was trying to meet, we can discern its essential elements. It was facing conflict situations where only two courses are available: to act or not to act, to speak or remain silent, to resist or not to resist. The concomitant of either course of action was harm of some sort. Now in situations of this kind, the rule of Christian reason, if we are governed by the *ordo bonorum*, is to choose the lesser evil. This general statement is, it would seem, beyond debate; for the only alternative is that in conflict situations we should choose the greater evil, which is patently absurd. This means that all concrete rules and distinctions are subsidiary to this and hence valid to the extent that they actually convey to us what is factually the lesser evil. This is true of the distinction between direct and indirect voluntariety. It is a vehicle, not a principle—and a vehicle as useful as its accuracy in mediating and concretizing the more general principle. Now, if in a conflict situation one does what is, in balanced Christian judgment (and in this sense "objectively"), the lesser evil, one's intentionality must be said to be integral. It is in this larger sense that I would attempt to read Thomas's statement that moral acts "*recipiunt speciem secundum id quod intenditur*" (ST II-II, 64, 7). Thus the basic category for conflict situations is the lesser evil, or avoidable/unavoidable evil, or proportionate reason.

Because the evil caused was so often genuinely incidental and associated with a permitting will (psychologically), the distinction between direct and indirect came to be identified with proper intentionality. That is, from being a subordinate vehicle in service of the determination of the lesser evil, it became a principle of this determination. Awareness of its broad rootage gave way to a concentration on the actions, their causality and the psychological posture of the will in explaining the idea of twofold effect. Actually, where nonmoral evil is concerned, direct voluntariety says but one thing: the evil has a causal relation to the good and is willed as a means. This becomes morally decisive only when the posture of the will affects

5 ~ Ambiguity in Moral Choice

the determination of what is, all things considered, the lesser or greater evil.

I am arguing, therefore, that the essential ingredients that led to the formulation of the rule of double effect are two: (1) the legitimacy, desirability, or above all necessity of a certain good (self-defense, saving the mother, resisting national aggression, rescuing another, and so on); (2) the inseparability of this good from harm or evil in the circumstances. But evil-as-effect (or aspect) of the action is only one form of this inseparability of evil from a desirable good. Another form is evil-as-means.

Concretely, it can be argued that where a higher good is at stake and the only *means* to protect it is to choose to do a nonmoral evil, then the will remains properly disposed to the values constitutive of human good (Griesez's basic goods, Schüller's *ordo bonorum*). That person's attitude or intentionality is good because he is making the best of a destructive and tragic situation. This is to say that the intentionality is good even when the person, reluctantly and regretfully to be sure, intends the nonmoral evil if a truly proportionate reason for such a choice is present.

To face conflict situations exclusively in terms of a psychological understanding of the terms *direct* and *indirect* could be to give a narrow and restrictive reading to the overall intent of St. Thomas. Be that as it may, we know that later theologians moved away from this analysis of self-defense and stated that some conflict situations could legitimately involve one in intending (reluctantly) nonmoral evil as a means. For instance, M. Zalba, S.J., in his treatment of capital punishment, defends the *direct* killing of criminals by appeal to the common good: "Without it (capital punishment) the public common good cannot survive, if one considers the malice and daring of criminals...." (Zalba 1957, 272). The factual validity of this argument can be denied; but what is important here is the theoretical structure of the argument. Zalba, with many other theologians, is arguing that there are greater goods than an individual human life and when they are threatened, and there is no other way to circumvent this threat, then it is reasonable to choose to do the evil to achieve the good, or avoid the evil.

Similarly Zalba (with many others) holds that in situations of self-defense against unjust aggression, one may legitimately intend the wounding or death of the assailant as "a legitimate and upright means instituted by God for the prosecution of one's right...." (Zalba 1957, 278). The appeal to the double effect, he says, appears "*obscurior*" precisely because "the preservation of one's own life is achieved *through* the wounding of another life rather than as a concomitant of this wounding." Once again, the structure of the argument is similar: one may intend nonmoral evil as a means if it is the only way of protecting a good judged to be at least proportionate.

There are other instances where we see a similar teleological model operative. One may legitimately intend the deception of another through falsehood to preserve a professional secret. To say that the deception is indirect and unintended (psychologically) as Zalba does, is unnecessary—and, in his case, inconsistent if he argues as he does where self-defense and capital punishment are concerned. Why did he not argue that deliberate, intended deception of another is a legitimate means to a proportionately grave good otherwise unobtainable? In the recent past theologians argued (correctly in my view) that women could directly sterilize themselves against the very real possibility of pregnancy by rape.[25] Once again, what is this but an avowal that I may reasonably choose to do nonmoral evil (as a means) if it is justified by a truly proportionate reason?

These reflections suggest that the moral integrity of one's intentionality cannot be restrictively defined in terms of the psychological indirectness associated with evil-as-an-effect (or aspect) of an indivisible process even where the basic goods are concerned. Psychologically unintended evil effects are but an example of legitimate intentionality. But if the unintended effect is but one example of integral intentionality, and if intended means can be another, then it seems clear that integral intentionality traces not to psychological indirectness as such when evil occurs, but exclusively to the proportionate reason for acting. If there is a truly proportionate reason for acting, the agent remains properly open and disposed toward the *ordo bonorum* whether the evil occurs as an indivisible effect or as a means within the action. However, since evil-as-means and evil-as-effect are different realties, they may demand different proportionate reasons. What is sufficient for *allowing* an evil may not in all cases be sufficient for *choosing* it as a means.

4. *Both the intending and permitting will are to be judged teleologically (that is, by presence or absence of proportionate reason)*. Even though there is a real difference between an intending and permitting will,

and hence a real difference between actions involving the one or other, the moral relevance of this distinction must be approached delicately. In the past it was too readily concluded that if an evil occurred in conjunction with an intending will it was thereby immoral. This was especially true where the values of life and sexuality were concerned. The present reaction against this is a statement to the effect that it is simply the existence of the evil, nor its relation to the intending or permitting will, which has moral significance. Both positions are, I believe, one sided, and, if urged, extreme. The mediating position suggested here is that there is a difference between an intending and permitting will where concomitant premoral evil is concerned, but that both must be judged teleologically.

Concretely, the supposition behind the assertion that certain evils are morally tolerable only if they are indirect with regard to human intentionality is either one of the following two: there are no higher values; or if there are, they are never in conflict with lesser values. For if there are higher values and if they will be lost or threatened unless one sacrifices the lesser values, and if this choice will not subvert the relevant values in the long run, then what is wrong with choosing, reluctantly to be sure, to do the nonmoral evil that the greater good may be achieved? Is there a reasonable, defensible alternative to this? If there is, I do not see it. This leads to the conclusion that in those instances where nonmoral evil has been viewed as justified because it is indirect, the psychological indirectness was not radically decisive at all. What was and is decisive is the proportionate reason for acting. Similarly, in those instances that have been traditionally viewed as immoral because the intentionality was direct, the psychological directness itself is not decisive. The immorality must be argued from lack of proportionate reason. An example of each instance will clarify the point of the argument.

In discussing indirect sterilization, Edwin Healy, S.J. presents the following case:

> The patient has had many vaginal deliveries and as a result lacerations, infections, and erosions have occurred in the *cervix uteri*. Moreover, there has been subinvolution of the uterus and the organ itself has become heavy, boggy, enlarged and weakened, and is now causing the patient great physical debility, pain and distress. May the physician excise the uterus for the present relief of the patient? (Healy 1956, 179).

The operation will, of course, result in sterilization—an evil effect, a disvalue when viewed abstractly. Healy approves the operation as a justified indirect sterilization, for "the condition described above would be sufficiently grave to justify this operation if less radical treatment would not prove effective." Is this not simply at root a calculus which asserts that the pain, debility, and distress caused by the uterus are greater disvalues than the loss of fertility entailed in its removal, and that sacrificing fertility in this instance will not subvert its value in the long run? Indirect here means one thing: the sterility is not chosen as a means. The term should not imply that one may never choose infertility as a means.

The principle of discrimination in the conduct of war (noncombatant immunity) may serve as the second instance. This principle has traditionally been presented as a moral absolute, and the direct killing of innocent persons viewed as intrinsically evil, evil *in se*. That is, such killing is morally evil regardless of the circumstances and independently of the consequences. Here I should like to suggest that it is precisely because of foreseen consequences that such a principle is a practical absolute. In this perspective its meaning would be: even though certain short-term advantages might be gained by taking innocent life in warfare, ultimately and in the long run, the harm would far outweigh the good. Taking innocent human life as a means, for example, to demoralizing the enemy, totalizes warfare. The action is radically different in human terms from the incidental death of innocents as one attempts to repel the enemy's war machine, even though the evil effects are numerically the same. It is radically different because of the intentionality involved, and to deny this is to deny to intentionality any realistic place in determining the meaning of human choice. Taking innocent human life as a means removes restraints and unleashes destructive powers which both now and in the long run will brutalize sensitivities and take many more lives than we would now save by such action. We cannot prove this type of assertion with a syllogistic click, but it is a good human bet given our knowledge of ourselves and our history—at least good enough to generate a practically exceptionless imperative, the type of moral rule Donald Evans refers to as "virtually exceptionless" (Evans 1971, 184-214).

What is responsible for this difference? This is the crucial question, of course, and one that cannot be answered (or at least has not been) with full satisfaction. Above it was suggested that the intending will

5 ~ Ambiguity in Moral Choice

(hence the person) is more closely associated with the evil than is a permitting will. This bespeaks (in some admittedly obscure way) a greater willingness that it occur. Now such a willingness is morally acceptable only to the extent that such an intention represents a choice of what is the lesser evil.

This analysis is not without its weaknesses. Suppose, for instance, two situations where one and the same good could be realized. In the first situation it can be realized only by intending the evil; in the second it can be realized by permitting the evil. If someone is ready to bring the good into existence only by permitting the evil, it has been suggested that he is less willing that the evil exist. Yet it must be said that he is also less willing that the good exist. Furthermore, the person who is prepared to realize the good even by intending the evil is more willing that the evil exist, but only because he is more willing that the good exist. Ultimately, therefore, to say that the intending will is more closely associated with evil than a merely permitting will is somewhat circular and considerably less than satisfying.

Joseph L. Allen views the principle of noncombatant immunity from direct attack as one generated teleologically, by a consideration of consequences. Of this principle he states:

> Such limits represent the fact that in the overwhelming number of cases, the strategist will be far more destructive by transgressing the rule than by following it (Allen 1963, 167-78).

Therefore the rule of noncombatant immunity is a virtually exceptionless moral principle not independently of a calculation of consequences, but precisely because of an adequate calculation. Thus Allen writes:

> Calculation over whether to obliterate a city is too narrow if it asks only whether this action would "shorten the war" or assist in the attaining of military objectives. The strategist must also consider several other possible effects of the proposed action, if he is actually concerned for the total result: the destruction of people who have little direct relation to the war effort; the destruction of the social fabric of the city and its surrounding area; the invitation the raid gives, both to the opponent and to one's own side, to conduct more and more attacks of this sort, perhaps out of revenge and often out of all proportion to some "better peace"; and the increased callous-

ness to creaturely beings that tends to accompany such acts.... The effect of an act on the whole range of creaturely beings must be considered, not merely its effect on a narrowly conceived military goal (Allen 1963, 171-2).

What Allen is saying is that killing innocent people *as a means* in warfare is wrong because there is no proportionate reason for doing this, if our calculation of proportionality is adequate. This leads him to conclude that the end does not justify the means, but that the ends do. That is, before an adequate moral assessment of an act can be made, its effect on all the ends or values must be weighed. In the case of indiscriminate warfare, our experience and reflection tell us that all the ends or values will not be best served by such actions. Or, as Charles Curran puts it, "all of the moral values must be considered and a final decision made after all the moral values have been compared" (Curran 1970, 239). It is this weighing of all the moral values that has made of noncombatant immunity a virtually exceptionless moral rule. Proportionality is always the criterion where our actions cause damage. Our major problem is to make sure that we do not conceive it narrowly. The strength of our moral norms touching concrete conduct is an elaboration of what we judge, within our culture, with our history and experience, to be proportionate or disproportionate.

If there are norms that are teleologically established and yet are "virtually exceptionless"—as I believe there are—the remaining theological task is to clarify those metaethical assertions in view of which these norms are held as exceptionless. Above I referred to the fact that "we sense that taking the life of this innocent man in these circumstances would . . . in the long run render many more lives vulnerable." Of the direct destruction of noncombatants in warfare, I have said that it would "in the long run . . . take many more lives than we would now save by such action." These are nondemonstrable calculations, prudential judgments based on both the certainties of history and the uncertainties of the future. Our sense of what we ought to do and ought not to do is informed by our past experience and a certain agnosticism with regard to our future behavior and its long-term effects. This leads to the suggestion—and it is only that—that where we view norms as "virtually exceptionless," we do so or ought to do so because of the prudential validity of what we refer to technically as *lex lata in praesumptione periculi communis* (a law established on the presumption of common and universal danger).

The notion of a presumption of universal danger is one most frequently associated with positive law. Its sense is that even if the action in question does not threaten the individual personally, there remains the further presumption that to allow individuals to make that decision for themselves will pose a threat for the common good. For instance, in time of drought, all outside fires are sometimes forbidden. This prohibition of outside fires is founded on the presumption that the threat to the common welfare cannot be sufficiently averted if private citizens are allowed to decide for themselves what precautions are adequate.

It seems to me that the exceptionless character of the norm prohibiting direct killing of noncombatants in warfare might be argued in a way analogous to this. The risk in alternative policies is simply too great. There are enormous goods at stake, and both our past experience of human failure, inconstancy, and frailty, and our uncertainty with regard to long-term effects lead us to believe that we ought to hold some norms as virtually exceptionless, that this is the conclusion of prudence in the face of dangers too momentous to make risk tolerable.

5. *Proportionate reason means three things*: (a) a value at least equal to that sacrificed is at stake; (b) there is no less harmful way of protecting the value here and now; (c) the manner of its protection here and now will not undermine it in the long run. If one examines carefully all instances where the occurrence of evil is judged acceptable in human action, a single decisive element is at the heart of the analysis: proportionate reason as here described. Under scrutiny this term must include the three elements mentioned. This understanding of proportionality is very close to that of Knauer. However, he maintains that when the reason is proportionate in the sense stated, the evil caused or permitted is indirect. I would prefer to say that the evil is direct or indirect depending on the basic posture of the will, but that it is justified in either case if a genuinely proportionate reason (in the sense stated) is present. The position suggested here is an attempt to incorporate into our moral reasoning all aspects of proportionality, immediate and long term, in contrast to a position that would appeal exclusively to the criterion of community-building, or

rely too narrowly on psychological directness and indirectness as decisive without further ado.

The foregoing could be put negatively. An action is disproportionate in any of the following instances: if a lesser value is preferred to a more important one; if evil is unnecessarily caused in the protection of a greater good; if, in the circumstances, the manner of protecting the good will undermine it in the long run.

It is with reference to this third aspect of proportionality that the difference between an intending and permitting will (direct and indirect) reveals its potential moral relevance. Thus where nonmoral evil is involved, even if the good at stake is quantitatively proportionate to or greater than the loss, protecting it *in this way* could in the long run undermine this good. The principle of noncombatant immunity would seem to be an example of this.

The judgment of proportionality in conflict situations is not only a very decisive judgment; it is also a most difficult one. To see whether an action involving evil is proportionate in the circumstances, we must judge whether this choice is the best possible service of all the values in the tragic and difficult conflict. What is the best possible promotion of all the values in the circumstances will depend on how one defines *in the circumstances*. A truly adequate account of the circumstances will read them to mean not just how much *quantitative* good can be salvaged from an individual conflict of values, but it will also weigh the social implications and reverberating after effects insofar as they can be foreseen. It will put the choice to the test of generalizability ("What if all persons in similar circumstances were to act in this way?"). It will consider the cultural climate, especially in terms of the biases and reactions it is likely to favor in a one-sided way. It will draw whatever wisdom it can from past experience and reflection, particularly as embodied in the rules peoples of the past have found a useful guide in difficult times. It will seek the guidance of others whose maturity, experience, reflection, and distance from the situation offer a counterbalance to the self-interested tendencies we all experience. It will allow the full force of one's own religious faith and its intentionalities to interpret the meaning and enlighten the options of the situation. This is what an adequate and responsible account of the circumstances must mean. So informed, an individual is doing the best he can and all that can be expected of him. But to say these things is to say that an individual will depend on communal discernment much more than our contemporary individualistic attitudes suggest.

6. *The notion of proportionate reason is analogous.* The comments made above should not lead us to believe that the concept of proportionate reason is reducible to a simple utilitarian calculus. Far from it. The notion is much more difficult than traditional casuistry would lead us to believe and, I believe, somewhat more fruitful and Christian than deontologists would allow us to imagine. Perhaps the problem can be introduced by a concrete instance. Moral theologians have judged as heroic charity the choice of a soldier to throw himself, at the cost of his own life, on a live explosive to save the life of a fellow soldier or soldiers. This means that they have asserted that, in technical terms, there is a proportionate reason for doing this. On the other hand, they have also asserted that an individual is not obliged to do this. In other words, there is a proportionate reason also for not making such a choice.

Somewhat similarly, if one has a proportionate reason for throwing himself on an explosive to save the life of his friend, then he also has a proportionate reason for allowing an assailant to kill him in preference to defending himself. Indeed, an unjust assailant is in a legitimate sense, precisely in his injustice, one's neighbor in greatest need. What then does proportionate reason mean if it can yield either conclusion?

The criterion of proportionality is that *ordo bonorum* viewed in Christian perspective, for it is the *ordon bonorum* which is determinative of the good one should attempt to do and the criterion of the objectively loving character of one's activity. In the light of this *ordo bonorum* there are three distinct possible and general senses of "proportionate reason."

First, there is the situation where the only alternative to causing or permitting evil is greater evil. This is the instance where both mother and fetus will certainly die without an abortion but where at least the mother can be saved with an abortion. It is also the case of the drowning swimmer where the hopeful rescuer cannot be of help because he cannot swim. The mother cannot save the child; under no condition can she do him any good. Similarly the bystander cannot save the drowning man. He can do him no good. It would be immoral to try. One who cannot save another but still tries is no longer governed by the *ordo bonorum*. For love (as involving, besides *benevolentia*, also *beneficentia*) is always controlled by the possible. There is no genuine *beneficentia* if no good can accrue to the individual through my sacrifice. An act of love (as *beneficentia*) is not measured by the mere desire or intention (*benevolentia*). Therefore, in instances like this, abortion and not attempting to save the drowning swimmer are proportionately grounded decisions precisely because the harm cannot be avoided, whereas harm to the mother and prospective rescuer can and should be avoided. Into this first category of proportionality would fall also the standard case where falsehood is uttered as the necessary means to protect a patient's confidence and reputation.

Secondly, proportionate reason in a different sense is realized in situations where the alternatives are not so obvious. This is the instance where I lay down my life for another (or others). In this instance a good equal to what I sacrifice accrues to another and is the only way of securing that good for him. This is proportionate not because his life is preferable to mine—they are equally valuable as basic human goods—but because in case of conflict, it is a human and Christian good to seek to secure this good for my neighbor even at the cost of my life. Indeed, other things being equal, such self-sacrifice is the ultimate act of human love. It is an assertion-in-action that "greater love than this no man has than that he lay down his life for his friends." To deny that such sacrifice could be proportionately grounded would be to deny that self-giving love after the model of Christ is a human good and represents the direction in which we should all be growing.

By saying that self-sacrifice to save the neighbor can truly be proportionate, traditional theology has implied that the goods being weighed, the alternatives, are not simply physical human life, my life versus that of another. Rather it has implied: (a) a world in which conflict occurs; (b) a world in which we are not mature in charity; (c) that the most maturing choices in such a world of conflict and sin are, other things being equal, those which prefer the good of others to self after the example of Christ. Preference of another to self is only thinkable as a good in a world both *objectively* and *subjectively* infected by sin and weakness: objectively in terms of conflict situations where death and deprivation are tragic possibilities that cannot be prevented except by corresponding or greater loss; subjectively in terms of the fact that being immature in grace and love, we tend to view such situations in terms of our own personal good exclusively and primarily—whereas our growth and perfection as human beings are defined in terms of our being, like the triune God himself, *ad alterum*, a being for others.

Thirdly, some actions or omissions were said to be proportionately grounded because the preference of a good for or in another at the cost of that good in or for myself should not, in view of human weakness and immaturity, be demanded. To say anything else would be to impose perfect love on imperfect creatures under pain of separation from divine friendship. This would be disproportionate because it would crush human beings and turn them from God. We know that the manuals of moral theology were often designed with confessional practice in mind. This means that casuistry was often concerned with what is sinful to do or omit rather than whether it was Christianly good to aspire to a particular value. Is it not to be expected that this perspective would also appear at the level of "proportionate reason"? Understandably, therefore, scholastic tradition has always maintained the axiom: "*Caritas non obligat cum gravi incommodo.*" In other words, there is a proportionate reason for not aiding my neighbor in his distress or need. This axiom must be carefully understood if this third sense of proportionate reason is not to compromise genuine Christianity.

Could we approach it as follows? It is important, first of all, to admit that the allegation that Christ knew nothing of "excusing causes," "extraordinary measures," "excessive inconvenience," and so on, where fraternal love was involved, is assuredly correct. However, Christ was proclaiming an ideal after which we should strive and which we will realize perfectly only after this life and the purgations preparatory to eternal life. "Love one another as I have loved you" is a magnificent ideal. Our growth and maturity depend on our continued pursuit of it. But nobody has ever achieved it. This disparity between ideal and achievement suggests an explanation of the maxim under discussion which will show that it is not incompatible with, but even demanded by, the gospel message. That is, it suggests the imperfection of our charity in this life. What I have in mind is something like this. To propose a deep knowledge of physical science as desirable, as an ideal, is one thing. To demand of a ten-year-old that he master the subtleties of atomic physics under pain of deprivation of further instruction probably means that I will put an end to the individual's whole educational process. To propose bodily health as an ideal is proper and necessary. To demand that a tubercular patient recover his health all at once under pain of relapse into serious illness means that he is condemned to ill health. Similarly, to propose the Savior's love as an ideal is helpful and necessary. But to demand of human charity the perfection of virtue exemplified and preached by Jesus under pain of deprivation of charity itself (mortal sin) would be to condemn human beings to life in mortal sin. This can hardly be thought to be the message of One who knew human beings so thoroughly that He came to redeem them. Hence, when one asserts limits to charity, he is not emasculating the gospel message; he is rather asserting it, but insisting that it was proclaimed to imperfect beings who must grow to its fullness. One dare not forget this. For if charity can be minimalized out of existence, it can also be maximalized out of existence. When proclamation and immediate demand are confused, the proclamation can easily be lost in the impossibility of the demand.

The adage we are dealing with, therefore, simply recognizes human limits and the consequent imperfection of our charity. It is saying that we do not lose divine life for failing to have and express its fullness now. The ideal remains. It is there—to be sought, pursued, struggled after. But it is precisely because its achievement demands constant pursuit that it would be inconsistent with the charity of the gospel message to assert that its demands exceed the limitations of the human pursuer. This is the third sense of proportionate reason.

This study would very tentatively conclude, therefore, that the traditional distinction between direct and indirect is neither as exclusively decisive as we previously thought, nor as widely dispensable as some recent studies suggest. As descriptive of the posture of the will toward a particular evil (whether intending or permitting), it only aids us in understanding what we are doing. Whether the action so described represents integral intentionality more generally and overall depends on whether it is, or is not, *all things considered*, the lesser evil in the circumstances. This is an assessment that cannot be collapsed into a mere determination of direct and indirect voluntariety. Hence the traditional distinction, while morally relevant, cannot be the basis for deontologically exceptionless norms—which is not to say that there are no virtually exceptionless norms, quite the contrary in my judgment.

This conclusion no doubt will appear rationally somewhat untidy. But it is, I believe, a reflection of the gap that exists between our moral sensitivities and judgments, and our ability to systematize them rationally. Moral awareness and judgments are fuller and deeper than rational arguments and rational categories. They are the result of evidence in the broadest sense—which includes a good deal more than mere rational analysis. While moral judgments must continually be submitted to rational scrutiny in an effort to correct and nuance them, in the last analysis, rooting as they do in the intransigence and complexity of reality, they remain deeper and more obscure than the systems and arguments we devise to make them explicit.[26]

NOTES

[1] See Joseph T. Mangan, S.J., "An Historical Analysis of the Principle of Double Effect," *Theological Studies* 10 (1949): 40-61; J. Ghoos, "L'Acte à double effet: Étude de Théologie Positive," *Ephemerides Theologicae Lovanienses* 27 (1951): 30-52.

[2] See G. Kelly, S.J., *Medico-Moral Problems* (St. Louis: Catholic Hospital Association, 1958), 13ff.; G. Grisez, *Abortion: The Myths, the Realities, and the Arguments* (Washington: Corpus Books, 1970), 329.

[3] Paul Ramsey, *The Just War* (New York: Charles Scribner's Sons, 1968); Paul Ramsey, *War and the Christian Conscience* (Durham: Duke University Press, 1961); John C. Ford, S.J., "The Morality of Obliteration Bombing," *Theological Studies* 5 (1944): 261-309.

[4] *Acta Apostolicae Sedis* (AAS) 22 (1930): 563.

[5] *AAS*, 43 (1951): 838-39.

[6] Ibid., p. 857.

[7] *AAS*, 50 (1958): 735-36.

[8] *AAS*, 46 (1954): 589.

[9] See Ramsey, *War and the Christian Conscience*, pp. 34-59.

[10] See Peter Harris, et al., *On Human Life* (London: Billing & Sons, 1968), p. 129. This book gives both the Latin text and an English translation.

[11] *Ethical and Religious Directives for Catholic Health Facilities* (Washington: United States Catholic Conference, 1971), p. 4.

[12] Earlier the distinction had been challenged by authors such as Joseph Fletcher, *Morals and Medicine* (Boston: Beacon Press, 1954); Glanville Williams, *The Security of Life and the Criminal Law* (New York: Alfred A. Knopf, 1951).

[13] P. Knauer, S.J., "The Hermeneutic Function of the Principle of Double Effect," see below, 25-59. This is a revised version of his earlier article in *Nouvelle revue théologique*, "La détermination du bien et du mal moral par le principe du double effet," 87 (1965): 356-76.

[14] See ibid., and Noonan's footnote question to Knauer in "The Hermeneutic Function of the Principle of the Double Effect."

[15] The sweeping character of Van der Marck's statement must be denied. Otherwise traditional theology would have proscribed all taking of another's property, all falsehood, all killing, etc. Obviously it did not.

[16] This is a point of view expressed recently by Nicholas Crotty, C.P., in "Conscience and Conflict," *Theological Studies* 32 (1971): 208-32. See also my critique in "Notes on Moral Theology," *Theological Studies* 33 (1972): 68-119.

[17] Ibid.

[18] Where Van der Poel, says "totality," Van der Marck speaks of "immediate implications" and Grisez of "indivisible aspects."

[19] Van der Poel, "Principle of Double Effect," p. 201. See Fuchs, "Absoluteness of Moral Terms."

[20] Philippa Foot, "The Problem of Abortion and the Doctrine of Double Effect," in *Moral Problems*, ed. James Rachels (New York: Harper and Row, 1971), pp. 29-41. The essay appeared originally in *Oxford Review* 5 (1967): 5-15.

[21] Stanley Hauerwas, "Abortion and Normative Ethics," *Cross Currents* (Fall 1971), 399-414. This is a very thoughtful critique of the work of Daniel Callahan and G. Grisez on abortion.

[22] This does not imply that direct and indirect are indistinguishable realities and morally irrelevant. It merely means, as I shall argue later, that both forms of intention are subject to a theological judgment.

[23] Bruno Schüller, S.J., "Direkte Tötung," *Theologie und Philosophie* 47 (1972): 341-57.

[24] I say "partially" because even a disvalue which has no necessary causal relation to the good can be, perversely indeed, desired.

[25] See Ambrogio Valsecchi, *Controversy* (Washington: Corpus Books, 1968), 26-36. Valsecchi presents a thorough bibliography in this test case and digests the relevant articles fairly.

[26] This monograph was composed at and supported by the Kennedy Center for Bioethics, Georgetown University, Washington, D.C.

Morality by Calculation of Values
Paul M. Quay, S.J.

Many widely known moralists of recent times have been seeking to eliminate "absolutely binding" moral norms. They deny, that is, that any norm known antecedently to the ultimate assessment of the agent's existential situation and of what appears to him his full set of alternative lines of action can specify either the moral goodness or moral badness of the line of action actually chosen. In other words, they assert that no antecedently binding moral norms can be universally applicable; none are unconditional and independent of the situation and the subjective dispositions of the agent.

Presumably because this tendency first gained notoriety through the "situation ethics" of Sartrian existentialism and certain forms of Protestant sentimentalism, attacks upon it have focused largely upon its demand for a moral judgment based on the entirety of a concrete situation including all subjective elements. But in fact the flaws lie elsewhere. For St. Thomas and, I think, the whole Catholic tradition have maintained that every component of reality concretely contained in or related to a given moral choice and its alternatives needs in principle to be considered in one fashion or another in the formation of the moral judgment.

The question then is this: are there any concrete (not purely formal, not tautological) prohibitions and/or precepts of Christian morality which bind a duly informed conscience antecedently and universally? Of the many arguments for the negative, only one is considered here that based on the philosophy of values as more or less recently elevated into a theology of values. Whatever may be said from a purely speculative point of view as to the possibility or usefulness of such a theological approach, this article will center exclusively on the principle use to which a number of current moralists are putting it,[1] i.e. to "relativize" so-called "absolute prohibitions" against defrauding laborers, adultery, abortion, and the like.[2]

I. A Theology of Values

The main elements in their argument from values can be summarized as follows:

1) Every element of the concrete moral situation facing a particular human agent (most particularly, possible courses of action, both in themselves as modes of activity and in their previsioned consequences, what he sees of circumstances and relationships, his interior dispositions and purposes, his ends and goals, his moral and religious convictions, the social, political, and cultural contexts operative) is (or has) a value, positive if helpful to man, negative (and then often called "disvalue" or "physical evil") if hurtful or injurious. Most elements will contain more than one value and often may have aspects of both value and disvalue.

Moral norms embody and protect the particular values which a society has learned to esteem and has made its own through past observation of their helpfulness; thus these norms protect and foster the society itself. They enter into the moral evaluation precisely as value-affirmations deeply rooted in historical experience.

While not absolute or determinative, they represent values which experience has shown to be so great within this cultural context that it is highly unlikely (in that same context) that any congeries of oppositely directed values which might arise because of circumstances, intentions, and the rest will ever countervail their worth. Nonetheless, on principle, the possibility of such countervailing value must always be left open until the concrete moral situation has been evaluated.

2) The over-all value, then, of each alternative course of action is grasped through a moral calculus in which the human agent, after assessing the values of each of the elements belonging to that alternative, sums these values and, in a moral judgment, perceives and asserts the aggregate worth of each course of action physically open at the moment. That is judged to be bad which has a negative total value; and that to be good which has a positive total value.

All the values thus far discussed are considered to lie at the premoral level, i.e., to be physical goods or evils for man, society, family, etc. They are values which, even when summed by the moral judgment, are as yet antecedent to moral good or moral evil, which enters only with the engagement of one's liberty in an act of free choice.

Positive total value intended

3) Having judged as best one can the total value of each alternative, one is then obliged to intend and choose that particular action which has the greatest total value or, at least, some action whose net value is positive. The intention is to be directed to the positive total value, considered as a whole, which is attainable through the particular action. To intend a negative total value is always morally wrong.

Because of the mixed nature of most situations, the intention will usually bear on a line of action that contains a certain number of disvalues as well as of positive values. In such a case, if indeed the aggregate value of the whole is positive, still, for the action to be morally good, the intention must bear on the totality only, without intending directly, or as such, any negative elements. Thus, such heavily negative premoral elements as killing the innocent, sex with another's husband or wife, and the like, form part of a morally good action whenever, rare as the case may be in practice, they are incorporated into and coalesce in a single act of choosing a net positive value.

One may rightly will an abortion, for example, but only when the death of the child is seen as but one of many premoral elements whose values when summed result in an overriding positive value for the action as a whole. Since all the values present, positive and negative alike, are premoral values, there is no question of first making an evil moral choice, directly intending to kill the infant and then using that evil choice or its results as means to one's good end. There is only one human action, one which has—in this presumably rare situation—a net positive premoral value; hence, the action is good. There is no morally bad action anywhere in the process which one might order to some good end.

4) It is then pointed out that no human or created value can be absolute; none is such as to weigh infinitely in the balance regardless of what is placed in the other pan. This follows not merely from reason but also from the fact that no human value has ever been recognized as absolute by the Scriptures or by the Church. God alone is absolute. Nothing and no one else can have absolute weight. Hence, no one may ever choose anyone or anything in direct preference to God. Since most moral choices, however, are not between God and a creature but between one line of creaturely conduct and another, one

must say that, apart from direct blasphemy, no value-judgment can be antecedently determined by appeal to some absolute value supposedly present.

5) Often an ultimate relativization is obtained by restricting the values to be considered to intra-worldly ones, those which bind individuals or societies to their world-of-experience. It is then argued that Christianity does not appreciably change even the weights to be ascribed to the various values entering into the moral assessment. Apart from the moral "forms" of faith, hope, and charity, revelation has directed its concrete imperatives only to the culturally conditioned and highly mutable value-systems of its day, instructing us that, as Christians of that day were to avoid the things then quasi-universally regarded as immoral, so the Christians of our day are to adapt their conduct to the moral judgments of their cultural milieu.

In Section II we shall indicate some of the key elements in any moral situation or in the alternative responses open to free choice which cannot be reduced to any complex of values whatever: physical good, physical (or ontic) evil, qualitative differences between values, relations of cause and effect, persons, and personal relations. Then, in Section III, we shall consider some of the unfortunate consequences of confounding such irreducible elements with values.

II. Elements Not Reducible to Values

Now, is it possible to reduce to values all the elements needed for the making of a moral judgment, as these positions assume, and thus reduce the moral judgment itself simply to evaluation? Alternatively, is a correct moral judgment possible if and only if it is based on consideration of all the premoral *values* concretely present, and only these?

Some aspect of value can doubtless be distilled from most elements in the moral situation. But the full reality of that situation and, consequently, its significance for moral choice cannot be adequately described by any listing of its values. This is obvious *a priori*: for, unlike the good, value is not transcendental; hence, it is not convertible with being; hence, there are aspects or modes of being which must perforce escape any discussion in terms of values. But the matter is too important to leave at this level of generality.

Value vs. good

1) How, in detail, does a value differ from a good? Obvious as the answer may be, we must discuss it, since perhaps the commonest error is to think that a physical or indeed any premoral good can be treated simply as a positive value.

Now, the good is whatever is (i.e., any being or mode of being whatever) considered under those aspects in which it is all that it ought to be, i.e., perfect and, therefore, evoking in any intellectual being who knows it in its existential totality a willed response of love, complacency, or desire.

A value, on the other hand, is that which can be, is, or ought to be prized, esteemed, or thought to have worth by some human agent (whether an individual, a group, or a collectivity such as state, society, or culture); more abstractly, a value is that formal aspect of a being which is the ground of its being thus prized. Thus, value theologians call human life a value in the former sense and, in the latter sense, speak of the capacity for loving, interpersonal relationships as the value of human life. A value, then, may rightly be subjected or, at least, can be subjected to a weighing of its worth by men. In the sense of that which ought to be prized, a value is something of intrinsic worth to man, which of its nature is related to human advantage or the furtherance of human ends. For example, an activity which leads to or constitutes a given mode of self-realization is such a value.

A value, then, is not simply convertible with what is good for man but with that which is good for him in terms of his needs, desires, or purposes. To be free is a metaphysical good for man, whether he knows or admits the fact or not; food is good for him physically, again independently of his awareness of the fact; but values require his consciousness, his own perception, estimation, and choice of what he will consider good for man. It is, I believe, the recognized need for just such personal assimilation of the morally good that has been chiefly responsible for the current exaggeration of the role of values in moral choice.

Thus, a value is not merely valuable *to* some prospective agent but is of value to him *for* some purpose or goal. A value stands in relation, therefore, not only to man in his physical and metaphysical constitution, like the good, and to his conscious and subconscious views of reality, but to his already accepted goals. The more a being contributes to a desired goal, the greater value it has. But the goal itself must already be given. *Qua* goal, it is good, but not of value; obviously, though, most goals receive a value when considered in relation to yet further and more nearly ultimate ends.

Worth for exchange

If a value differs from a good by its web of qualifying relations, it is also these relations which define the value concretely, which give an object its value. Hence, anything else so related is equally valuable— *value implies the possibility of exchange*. So long as one object has as great effectiveness for the attainment of given ends as some other, it is of equal value with it or with anything else which is no more, no less effective in the same respect. Thus the commercial origins of the word in English are still evident; and "value" never wholly sheds its denotation of a worth-for-exchange. Thus the valuable as such is the interchangeable, not in the sense of identity and, so, of anonymity, as of one penny for another, but in the sense in which a nickel has the same value as five pennies, i.e., in all that matters for the given context, there exists complete interchangeability or convertibility.

Further, it is a common experience to find good and value in conflict. Who has not had to part with things because they are of no value to him whatever and yet which he recognizes as truly good, e.g., a fine old mansion, now far too expensive to maintain? Conversely, who has not felt disgust or sadness on seeing some trifling good become the center of men's attention and interest, taking on enormous value, or even some evil thing becoming a major value?

The good can be of value under many different aspects; but since it grounds and, in some sense, contains not only all these values but an infinity of other, merely possible ones, the good cannot be reduced to any finite set of values. More simply, the good, since it is not defined by any relationship to human advantage, cannot be adequately replaced by any set of elements, such as values, which are in this way relative. On the other hand, values can be exhaustively described in terms of complex goods and so be reduced to them, hence, the traditional concern of moral theology with the good, physical as well as moral, rather than with value.

Disvalue vs. evil

2) If, then, positive value and good are not equivalent, we may expect to find that negative values (disvalues) are not the same as premoral (ontic) evils. Thus, it might be for me a negative value in the defense of a client in court that I cannot simultaneously attend a performance of an opera that I should very much like to hear. But that is not an evil, not even a physical one. It may be retorted that "negative value" is the wrong way to put the matter; rather, defense of my client at this time is merely of slightly less, aggregate, positive value than were it compatible with my also hearing the opera. Yet the very notion of aggregation and balance of values renders this an evasion. That which, when added to anything, makes this latter less than it would otherwise be is just what is meant by a negative quantity.

Nor can one avoid the point by arguing that I might in time do both. Perhaps but the quintessential drama of all moral existence is precisely that of those great choices (and their lesser analogs) where the taking of any option destroys in choosing the very possibility of all others, e.g., marriage now to this woman.

How premoral evil differs

A physical (or premoral) evil is quite different. It represents not merely a contingent aspect of a good as a result of which its advantage to me is or seems diminished, i.e., a negative value, but contains a true privation of a good called for. The good that naturally belongs to or is intrinsically part of some being is, in fact, destroyed or prevented. Operas are no essential part of pleading a case or of human life; I am deprived of nothing, therefore, in the example above, no matter how great the negative value. Removing, on the other hand, a human fetus, "animated" or not, from the nourishing shelter of its mother's womb is to deprive it of its natural conditions for and possibility of life and growth—a negative value indeed, but worse than that, a grave evil. The difference between physical evil and disvalue can be made still more evident by obvious modifications of the arguments given above concerning good and value.

3) A third element also recalcitrant to value reductionism is that of qualitative difference. To attempt to judge an action solely by the aggregate of value it contains leads logically to seeing the determination of moral good as a merely quantitative process—a "moral calcu-

lus" as these moralists say—a quasi-algebraic addition of plusses and minuses. For things cannot be added save insofar as they are of one kind. Two apples and three oranges can be added only if one ignores their diversity and regards them as "pieces of fruit." Hence, the addition of values must lead ultimately to the discarding of all elements of uniqueness and nonconvertibility even among diverse kinds of values.

Thus reduction to values is a reduction to the quantitative but without the carefully wrought methods of quantifying the qualitative which have been the hallmark of science. It is less a calculus than a mercantilism of values, an exchange and weighing for trade. Everything can in principle be evaluated and scaled in accord with utility, worth, and price; as values are balanced, exchanged, and traded off for one another, the moral judgment becomes a commerce and merchandizing in human conduct and Christian behavior.

It is the mercantilist spirit applied once again to human behavior, defending its present relativism with essentially the same arguments as those with which it once defended trading glass beads and brass buttons for the wealth of furs in the Pacific Northwest: Indians valued the beads more than the furs; the white man, the reverse; each got the things he valued. So what is this talk of injustice?

Intention and relations

4) Though the matter is not entirely clear, apparently a majority of value-moralists, rightly, do not regard the moral intention as one among the premoral values entering into the determination of the moral judgment. Yet often they seem overly insistent that all intentions concretely present at the time of a choice be considered in order adequately to grasp the human meaning of the act (opposed usually to grasping merely "its physical nature"). Such language is at least open to misunderstanding in its context. This position is called "new" or "newly recovered." Yet, who of moral theologians of past or present has held that the intention of the agent is less important concretely than the physical structure of his action? Who has regarded an unintended killing, say, as murder? In any event, it will be helpful to make the point entirely clear, since the untangling of some serious confusions will depend upon it.

The intention is the intellectually grasped end or *finis* to which an action, if chosen, will be directed (or, about as commonly, the intellectual act which grasps this end). It serves primarily to map out and delimit the precise elements which will constitute the moral activity I choose. I can choose freely and so am responsible solely for that which I in some way intend (both positively and negatively—that is, I am responsible for intending A; I am responsible as well for not intending B along with A).

So, then, the intention is not one factor among others in the concrete situation or concrete alternative actions but is that by means of which I delimit and bind together all the elements needed to form the pattern of possible action which constitutes such an alternative. It determines net values (and all else) from the outside, not as an element or component of the alternative but as that which defines the alternative to have such and such components.

The crucial tie-in between intention and value-morality lies in the fact that the reduction of all internal aspects of the moral judgment to values or relations among values renders impossible or irrelevant consideration of other intrinsic connections between the different elements, connections which, however, have an essential role in the specification of one's intention.

In particular, the relation of cause to effect cannot be expressed solely in terms of values, though it is essential for the moral judgment. The values, individual and aggregate, of someone's dying and my escaping with my life would seem to be the same, all else being equal, whether there is a causal link between them or not. But the moral importance of his death's being the cause of my survival is not negligible. As we shall see in Sect. III, a radically false view of moral intention is generated by ignoring causal relations.

Persons neglected

5) Finally, let us look at what are for the Christian the most basic and important elements omitted in the attempt to carry all by the way of values: human persons and their relations, especially with God. Now, the value-moralists do often assert that the human person is the most basic or fundamental of values. Yet, while it is evident that a person may well be designated a "fundamental good," these moralists never tell us by what right he may be regarded as a "fundamental value."

That he is not an "instrumental value" is also clear—but why "value" at all?

At the level of fact, it need not be true. Many a person—tragedy though it is—has lived for months or years without being a concrete value for anyone; he is unknown or despised by all. Yet this person need not be less good because he is valued less by anyone or by all others, save God.

At the level of possibility, can a person as such be evaluated? There is already a theoretical problem in evaluating a person merely as an athlete or as a scientist, still more as a lawyer or a mother. For a person's "performance" as any of these never depends merely upon his observable abilities and skills but also upon his basic character, virtues, and personal relationships. These latter suffuse all he does in a manner which does not permit sharp separation of his worth as "man," as "physician," as "otolaryngologist." Yet here one only has to answer such questions as: how well does he do this work or relate to particular people in certain specified manners? But how judge his value as person? Indeed, it is not easy even to say what we might mean by "the value of a person." His value to whom? For what ends?

It would seem precisely this attempt to assay our fellows as persons which the Gospel excludes when it forbids us to "judge" them, i.e. to make a judgment about their goodness in God's eyes, on the basis of their conformity with our values, even when these seem to be based on revelation. No one can be weighed or evaluated as a person, nor can the attempt legitimately be made to do so, by anyone but God himself.

The person is unique

Even were it possible truly to evaluate a person as such and licit to do so, would seeing him as of value to man, as one who ought to be esteemed, be a morally sound way to see him?

First of all, equivalence for exchange and convertibility are simply incompatible with a Christian understanding of the person. For the person, in what makes him truly such is unique and irreplaceable and unexchangeable. He is literally invaluable; for whatever is the only one of its kind cannot be evaluated from that aspect in which it is unique. Quantitative measure, even of the fairly indefinite sort involved in premoral values, requires at least two of a kind, one of which can be used to furnish a measure for the other. Hence, no person can be adequately regarded for any human simply as a value, as "for others."[3] Indeed, the central problem of a Christian morality is just the opposite: namely, how is it possible to have objectives and universal norms for beings who are precisely non-universal and unique? Since Christ died for each man, not just for a global "all," a satisfactory response can be given; but it cannot lie in direction of denying the uniqueness and the irreplaceability of the person, as value-moralists seem to allow.

Yet do we not sense that a truly good person is of great value to society? We see him as a good example, know him to be reliable in danger or difficulty. He is of service to all, for all good ends. Yet he is not a means to anyone's ends. One cannot use him in order to have good example, though each can profit by the example he offers. His "value" is gratuitous; there is no predetermined way in which he will be of value to anyone or to society. And he is unique; even his work in this world is not replaceable by others'. Is it not clear, then, that the greater the good, the greater the variety and magnitude of the values it can ground and sustain—but that it is the good at which we are looking, and that our proper response to it is not evaluation or esteem but love? And is not the evil that afflicts family life so widely today just this, that parents *value* their children and that husbands *value* their wives, with reasonable accuracy, indeed, and "love" them accordingly?

Valuing and esteeming are, at best, ancillary virtues in the moral life of the Christian, where charity has primacy. It is the unique quality of charity to love a person—because God loves him and in Christ—who is not (yet? ever?) worthy of love at his deepest level. It is the love with which God loved us when we were still in our sins and worthy only of damnation, valuable only as a vine-branch for burning. Charity is a love which seeks indeed to give value and worth (in relation to God, however, and not in relation to man directly) to a person who lacks all worth, or to increase it beyond its present measure where it already exists; further, charity seeks to help him become good, to call forth from chaos, as God did at the first Creation, the unique goodness of this person whom we must love before he has in himself any ground for our love.

Induced desirability

6) We may note here in passing a further difficulty which this example of charity raises for a value-theology: not only is it true that all morally relevant elements of a situation cannot be expressed as values in a self-consistent manner, but a highly pertinent class of values is not to be found at all in the antecedent situation and possible courses of action, so that it is impossible to make the moral judgment on the basis of all the values which are chosen in the free act.

This is the phenomenon of "induced" desirability, whereby my free choice itself becomes the source of at least part of the value of the object chosen—the simplest case being found in the choice of one among several identical chocolates, stamps, or the like (Buridan's ass died for failing to realize this). But in fact, this investing of something with value by the very act of liberty which chooses it enters into all free choice. It is this which explains some of the destructive power of sin to blind the sinner, in the act itself, to his own sinfulness, preventing repentance through disguising the need for it: for the mind seeks justification for the sinful action by objectifying this increment of value as if there were true grounds for it in the antecedent reality. In a good action, the person tries rather to bring into being (or at least into consciousness) the element of goodness which could ground such an increment of value within the real situations where this value was not grounded (or perceived). And, as mentioned, this sort of induction of value reaches its transcendent and higher-than-human perfection in charity.

In brief, then, neither the persons involved in the moral situation nor their relationship with one another nor, least of all, those relations to the Persons of the Trinity which are charity, hope, and faith, can be dealt with adequately in a moral framework concerned primarily with human values.

III. New Problems Arise

Though any moral system must devote an appreciable place to problems concerned with values, there arise novel and serious problems wherever the assignment of values to the elements of the action-in-context is made to carry the entire burden of the moral judgment.

Whose values count?

1) Assuming, then, for the sake of discussion, that a morally good action is one which is of net positive value to man as man, we must still ask: how can the values belonging to the elements of this concrete action be *uniquely* prescribed?

For, any element of premoral good may have, and properly so, very different values for every different person—even for the same person at different times. For example, the good that my continuation in life represents at a given time could be more or less objectively discovered by each person who wished to do so, regardless of his own situation, so long as the same definition of good was used. The same is not true of value. My life may be much more valuable to one person than to another, though both understand "value" identically; it may be a disvalue to yet others.[4] Are their moral obligations not to shoot me down equally diverse?

Whose values then are to count? Since we are speaking of the moral quality of some individual's free choice, presumably these values must be those of this moral agent, though evidently they will be so shaped as to include some sort of reference to those of other people. But do his actual values count? Or the values he ought to have?

If the former, we should have to approve Hitler as morally good since he clearly chose fairly effective means for developing the "pure Aryan" stock which he valued; and in general he seemed to act consistently with his value-system. That this value-system itself was monstrous and that he was acting immorally when acting in accord with it can be shown only if one admits that his value system was, ultimately at least, a matter of free choice. And since no values can be assigned at all till some value-system has already been chosen, one cannot determine the moral quality of any choice of a fundamental value-system by summing the values which would be realized through the choice of this system rather than of some other. Further, if it is the agent's actual values which determine the morality of his action, by what right may the state pass laws to force him to act otherwise? Law becomes nothing more than a device for behavioral conditioning, and fundamentally unjust.

If, on the other hand, we insist that a man act in accord with values he does not hold but ought to hold, at least in these circumstances, this sounds suspiciously like an antecedent moral norm of universal applicability. Whence else comes the "ought"? It clearly is meant to represent a moral obligation, binding in conscience. Nor is it a grudge against Hitler personally, for no one at all can rightly hold such values. If someone knowingly refuses the values he should have, we consider him to be acting immorally. But on the basis of what values would he make the moral judgment that he ought to reject the fundamental values he holds and embrace others which he sees only as disvalues at present?

Other people's values

Further, does the reference one person's values *should* show towards those of others relate to others' actual values or to the ones they ought to have? Or to both? Again, if something is of great value to the agent but a disvalue for the great majority of people, how should the agent take these values of others into account?

Suppose I am a sodden and single derelict, but innocent of misdeed against others. Have I the right to defend myself against an attacker who is a pillar of society, one who is, apart at least from his hostility to me and the dispositions from which it springs, of great value to millions of people? It has been urged by value-moralists that killing in self-defense is still permitted because, in the long run, such killing best protects the value it seems to harm: human life for as many as possible. But whose value is this? Not mine; I may defend my life against the two other survivors of a nuclear holocaust. Not, clearly, my attacker's. Then society's?

But how can other persons, even a whole society, demand, in any way obliging on my conscience, that I shift my value-system to conform to theirs, unless there is within my value system (therefore, in principle, universally) one value greater than all other possible values together, namely, to follow the basic values of the society in question—something for which there seems little enough evidence. Why should I feel obligated to conform, especially if in my actual value-system the key values of society count for little—as true of St. Paul vis-à-vis both his native Judaism and the Graeco-Roman world as, in a less worthy manner, of some individualistic struggler for wealth and power?

The one against the many

Moreover, the quantitative summing of values has this inconvenience, that whoever is acting for the state, that is, in the name of or for the benefit of the people as a whole, has automatically a factor of millions with which to multiply one or other relatively minor value. If the value of my life, drunken bum that I am, is to be laid in a scale against the far smaller values of, say, good business and avoiding offense to the sensibilities of many millions of citizens, then, innocent though I be of crime, how could the value of my life ever prevail? The objection that to give such power to the state in one case would, by implication, give it such power in all others and that this would be a negative value large enough to block an assault on me, presumes a state acting irresponsibly. But suppose a responsible statesman who would, every time, assiduously weigh the appropriate values in accord with suitably accurate laws before snuffing out some fellow citizen, so that indeed the values of all others were truly served. How could he be faulted?

An obvious response would be to deny that the values of different agents are additive, to insist rather that every agent must make the common good of all a major value of his own. "Must . . . ?" Do his antecedent values necessarily and in all cases determine this to be the choice of greatest net value for him? Is this knowable antecedently to any knowledge of his case? In any event, is it not cheating a little to invoke the common *good* here rather than some common value—else, why should good not replace value everywhere? The problem recurs: how *ought* I to take into account the values of others if the grounding of all my moral activity lies not in the good but in my values?

One final and more fundamental difficulty may be noted in this context. If other people's good, as well as their values, are to have weight in the formulation of my moral judgment only insofar as they can be transformed into values of my own, then I would seem to be inescapably locked into a wholly self-centered moral attitude. For again, unlike the good, even if it is only good-for-me, a value-for-me has no necessary implication of value for anyone else. Nothing, then, would be admitted into my moral judgment except in terms of my own advantage and perspectives—an approach to morality incompatible not only with the God centered orientation of Christianity but even with a psychologically sound attitude towards reality.

Ignoring causal relations

2) As mentioned in Sect. II.4, the tendency to see all in terms of value leads to nearly complete neglect of the implications for morality of the metaphysical structures of causation, most particularly, that of efficient cause and effect. It is in connection with the intention of the agent that this neglect becomes crucial.

In the real order, an intention cannot, save by ignorance or mistake, bear on only one or other link in a single causal chain. If I know that this (valuable) effect comes about only through the placing of this (premorally evil) cause, then it is simply hypocrisy to pretend that I can will *only* the net value, the cause somehow vanishing in the addition. Rather, the exact opposite obtains. My moral intention bears upon and makes me responsible for *all* the individual elements that are, to my knowledge, interrelated by causal necessity. Whoever wills the effect wills the cause, or else his willing the effect sinks to the level of velleity. After all weighing of values, for example, suppose that I decide that the greatest net value is obtainable by a line of action taking me on a pleasure-cruise by means of money obtained by the mercy-killing of my slowly dying and cancerous father. All the "willing" in the world of this net value is of relatively little moral consequence unless I decide finally to kill him. And if I so decide, the basic moral quality of the act is fixed, whatever modifications are introduced by other elements.

On the other hand, what is not connected causally with the desired end need not enter my choice, though its value be the same as if it were so connected. Recall the permission classically accorded me to run down a child playing in the middle of a narrow road between cliff and chasm as I flee from those intent on killing me. The running down is physically necessary (so the case assumes) if I am not to lose my own life; but it is not the cause of my staying alive and I, therefore am able and, indeed obligated, while confronting the whole reality of what will keep me alive, to avoid intending that child's death. If (as in the old Saturday-afternoon "serials" at the movies) it happens that there is a hidden escape-mechanism available for the youngster at the last moment, I am delighted, once I learn of it, and nothing has happened to prevent my escape.

But change the case a bit. Let the road be wide enough at this point for me to get by without either hitting the child or slowing down; let me recognize him as my pursuer's only son, innocent entirely of his father's misdeeds; and let me know for certain that running him down would cause my enemy to call off his pursuit, indeed, that at this juncture there is no other means to escape death. In no way could I be justified in killing this boy. His death would now be the means of my escape and there is no way I could intend the global "escape-from-my-enemy-by-killing-his-son" without bearing the full guilt of intending to kill an innocent man.

It is this clear regard for reality in all its relationships that lies at the heart of the principle of double effect—rejected by a majority of value-theologians or restated in terms of that same dreamy unreality, the undiscriminating global intention. This principle does not merely state, as some seem to think, that if there exist two effects, one good, one bad, of a single action, I can will the good and permit the bad. Rather, I may will or choose only the good and must, by my willing, reject the bad, even if I see no way of avoiding it concretely (and, of course, have sufficient reason for acting anyway). The question is not whether I cause the bad effect or not (I do, by supposition) but whether the bad effect is causally related to the good intended.

The Global Intention

Consider the matter from a slightly different point of view. It is always the agent's option to intend as large or small a domain of choice as he wishes, provided that, in drawing his boundaries, he always respects the real relationships, especially those of causality, linking what he is doing with all else; for freedom involves among its functions the specification, in and by the free act itself, of this domain. But if, as the value-moralists would have it, the intention need not attend to causal linkages, provided only that the net value of whatever domain is chosen is concretely positive, then we may well inquire into the criteria for drawing the boundaries of one's intention. Might I pull the trigger on a loaded gun which happened to be pointing at someone's head, intending only the exercise of my trigger-finger and practice in the steadying of my hand? If one looks only this far, till the bullet is in the air and no further, then is not the value-summation positive and the act good? The case is not absurd. One may severely restrict one's intention, coming to intense, often deadly concentration on the very present act, assiduously not looking so far as its first consequences lest the horror there surmised freeze the heart and weaken the determination, as Althaea did when she burned the log on which her son's life depended—and how many murderers since! Only knowledge of cause and effect justifies us in calling such ostensible limitation of intention insincere and morally ineffective.

Or, what of those Marxist enthusiasts who do not hesitate to loose destruction for millions in the hope of a better humanity in the future, rising rejuvenated from the ashes of its former self? "We must break eggs if we wish an omelet." So long as the intention need bear only on the total value of all that it embraces, without being constrained by the relational configuration of reality, then whenever a given span of intention is insufficient to provide a positive counterbalance to one's presently envisaged premorally evil act, one can shorten or extend the intention, shrink the range of elements included or broaden it even to all things known and foreseeable.

Intrinsic Consequences

It is strange, with their strong emphasis on the moral significance of foreseen extrinsic consequences of an action, that these moralists do not grasp more clearly the still greater importance of intrinsic consequences—those which, by the nature of the action, are produced, for good or ill, in the one acting, independently of whether he knows of them or not (premoral good or evil), though having a far stronger impact and making a far deeper modification of his being when lifted to the moral level. Thus as I have shown elsewhere (Quay 1961), an act of sexual perversion, even if we suppose it to be carried out in good conscience, still damages the properly human personality of the agent, conforming it to the falsity such an act symbolizes. Now, if one knows the evil of such an act, there is still no way his intention can truthfully separate the act from its inner and immediate effects—if he intends the act, he intends these. To call these negative values and to perform the action for some extrinsic good is simply to do evil that good may come.

A Shabby Empiricism?

3) If the metaphysical grounding of the value-theologies is this weak, one may expect their epistemology to be little better. Indeed, the

same false notion of intention will be operative here also to prevent them from extricating themselves from situations to which they are not necessarily bound by other demands of consistency.

Central to their argumentation is the assertion that no single element can antecedently determine the moral quality of a proposed course of action independently of all other factors; for if the element has a non-infinite value, then sets of circumstances must be conceivable with aggregate value sufficient to outweigh it. It is conceded, indeed, that this would not have to be the case were we able to know every possible set of circumstances, consequences, and the rest; but this is patently impossible in principle, still more so in practice.

Now, such a position seems no different from the crudest sort of empiricism, according to which we can know only what has been directly given us in our experience. Even in the physical sciences, till recently so dominated by both British empiricisms and Continental positivisms as to seem their source, it has always been admitted that proper deductions can be made, *via* abstract thought and logic, to conclusions of strict impossibility. Given some set of empirically valid principles, e.g., Newton's laws or the principles of quantum mechanics, one can immediately deduce all sorts of "absolute" statements (i.e., which do not depend on further circumstances at all) about objects of specified properties. No circumstances could combine to make certain prescribed behaviors possible for these objects.

True enough, some sort of "back ground knowledge," "theoretical framework," or "contextual presupposition" is always necessary for such deduction. But it was just the empiricists' difficulties-in-principle with this background for deduction that have contributed in large measure to the recent total collapse of positivist philosophies of science.[5] It would be a shabby empiricism that could not sustain deductions of this sort in moral questions as well. And, of course, once made and checked and tested for validity, such deductive conclusions can be taught to others as sure guides, enabling the concrete morality to be determined as soon as this or that feature is discerned, regardless of the range of other elements and values involved.

Vitiating defects

Yet one might expect even an empiricist ethics to advert to the asymmetry between the good, with its requirement of integrity, and the evil, which can result from a multiplicity of possible defects, even if not every defect is such as to convert the good to evil. Even values, especially intrinsic ones, can reflect such asymmetry with regard to disvalues. Almost daily we experience how single defects can reduce dramatically or even destroy both great goods and great values. Some defects may only render an object less good and less valuable, but others spoil it altogether, making it to be of no value or positively to be rejected or even bad. Nor is this a matter of the size of the defect to the eye of the non-expert, but only of the real effectiveness in damaging the object in question. A nut only an imperceptible fraction of a millimeter too large is useless for its bolt. An icepick can make as deadly a hole in someone as a meat-cleaver; an invisible crystal of botulinus toxin is deadlier than either.

So then, in morality one element of evil, not necessarily obvious or easily discernible, can vitiate a whole act. If I cannot choose to do something without willing directly, even if implicitly, what is evil, then the concrete act is evil. If, further, the evil is an intrinsic consequence of the action, then the action is intrinsically evil. It must surely be obvious that a bad intention can by itself vitiate any action, even what would otherwise be the holiest, e.g., saying Mass, with the intention of profanation. It is possible, likewise, to think up circumstances or extrinsic consequences that would render any normally good act evil. Why, then, cannot the act itself be intrinsically vicious, as, e.g., sexually perverse acts, or conditionally vicious, e.g., if the person I am about to kill has not forfeited his right to life? Recognition of intrinsic evil in actions in no way restricts one to discussing only the "objective act" or confines morality to an essentialist level. To say that would be merely a dodge to avoid seeing or admitting that if the act is bad, then no extrinsic consequences, circumstances, or intentions can remedy the situation any more than any amount of good in the act itself can remedy a malicious intention or vitiating consequences or circumstances.

If all this is unclear to the theologians in question, the root reason seems to be, again, their insistence on regarding all in terms of *additive* positive and negative values, so that the components melt together as indistinguishably as abstract numbers do. Just as no mathematician can tell whether a net sum of + 10 was reached from summing +6 and +4 or from -100,000 and the product +10,001 times +10, so for the value moralist. Having abstracted from physical evil merely the one aspect of negative value and having similarly denatured the good, he is left with abstractions which are, indeed, wholly symmetric with one another but therefore, utterly inadequate to deal with the moral drama of human good and evil.

Why positive values?

4) A further element missing from the value-approach is some indication of why it is morally necessary for man to choose a net positive value or to avoid direct choice of a negative one. Whence comes the moral link? What is there in what is for me the *most valuable* (in any of its senses) which forces me to consider its choice to be *morally good*? The omission is the more serious in that most of the moralists in question argue that no created value can be absolute; that consequently, no concrete moral norm can bind without exception (cf. Sect. I.4). Problems of internal consistency arise at once.

Is not the requirement that one choose directly only positive values itself a moral norm? A norm, moreover, according to these theologians, antecedent to every concrete choice and universally applicable? It will be objected that this norm is not concrete. True, perhaps, in an "ordinary language" sense. But it is certainly not a merely formal or tautological norm,[6] the only alternative to "concrete norms" which these moralists offer. For "most valuable" and "morally good" are not even roughly equivalent in their vocabulary—it is the *pre*moral good and evil which they claim to be the elements of the final, summed, and still premoral value.

Further, and even more strikingly, this norm is considered absolute in the sense of admitting no exceptions, whatever the circumstances or extrinsic consequences. A free and direct choice of a net, premoral, negative value (which is not absolute in any sense) is said to be always morally evil; and, so far as I can tell, even according to these moralists, I am never free to do a morally evil thing for the sake of any consequent and separately conceived good or value. Thus moral evil is absolutely forbidden; and my free assent has somehow mysteriously removed the relativity of the negative value.

On the other hand, the argument drawn from the non-absoluteness of created values seems to leave out of account the fact that God is personal and has a mind and will. Not merely is God the Absolute; his will is absolute also, though he need not will absolutely all that he wills. Hence, any truly moral act involves, at least implicitly, a judgment that something is good or bad or, in a value-context, positively or negatively valuable, and that God forbids or permits or desires or commands it accordingly.

But God does not forbid whatever it is that might be meant by the term "absolute evil" nor protect a putative "absolute value." But he forbids absolutely that we choose evil, albeit relative; he may command absolutely that we do some relatively minor good. And any refusal to act in accord with his will thus signified, even though we seek only created and limited values, is a rejection of the Absolute. Some at least of the value-moralists are in explicit agreement with this position. For them, the question is rather how to discover what *is* God's will in matters of moral values.

Values under judgment

While it seems clear enough that God wills things that are for our good and forbids things that would harm us, what he wills as to our human values is not so clear. Our human values are rarely in full consonance with what he desires our values to be; hence the need of continuous conversion of mind and heart, of continually submitting to his judgment. And, as the value-moralists rarely fail to remark, our human values are always highly relative to our particular cultural context and are highly mutable. Obviously then, these men are right in thinking that no assessment of values alone is sufficient unconditionally to determine moral good or evil. But that shows only the inadequacy of their value-approach.

The Christian moral theologian has as a major charge, perhaps his chief one, to assess all human values in the light of the Gospel, to judge them by his own norms of faith (with all it gives us of concrete moral norms), hope, and charity, accepting what is compatible with these, rejecting the rest. To subject the moral conduct of the Christian as prescribed in the New Testament (with all that this implicitly takes over from the Old) to a weighing against human values would be to undo the Gospel.

Only intra-worldly values?

5) The restriction to intra-worldly values would seem to nullify the morality built thereon. It is possible, indeed, to draw out of our ex-

perience and from Christian teaching that law of nature which shows what is good or bad for man in virtue of his nature and to know that this is not overturned by grace though the latter's demands may be more exigent. Yet it is not possible—as the very argument about the cultural, social, and individual relativity of values presumes—to do a "natural-law analysis" of values, which, at least so far as our weak human knowledge goes, are always contingently modifiable and inextricably linked with our entire, sinful history.

Thus, one cannot deal usefully with such an abstraction as "intraworldly values" (taking it to mean true values but belonging to the order of nature alone) nor licitly take the concrete and actual "intraworldly values" of our morally purblind society as normative for men as such. Nor, since actual human values are largely suffused by sin and the refusal of grace, is it possible to consider them as values formed by faith, hope, and charity in interaction with the "purely human" or the "concretely human."

The scriptural argument will not concern us here, since it needs special treatment. But the questions the value-theologians must answer in that regard are now clear: where in Scripture do they find support for the value-imperative at the base of their whole system? How can they show that the concrete moral norms of the New Testament are intended not to identify what is morally good or bad for the children of God but only to reinforce particular and contingent values or value-systems? Since, however, the rest of the framework of value-morality seems untenable, it is not clear that Scripture scholars need undertake the task.

Notes

[1] The moralists whose writings are directly of interest here are: Josef Fuchs, Richard McCormick, Giles Milhaven, John Dedek, Charles Curran, and Bruno Schüller.

[2] Something should be said about the purpose and method of this paper. Its purpose is to disengage one single thread which runs through the writings of many, not always concurring, moral theologians, to show its influence upon the moral theories into which it has been woven and to indicate the errors to which such theories are exposed if wholly self-consistent. I am primarily concerned, therefore, with certain generic modes of argumentation and only secondarily with details, though to the best of my ability I seek to preserve the integrity of the arguments given by these authors. My effort is to highlight a flaw which, to different degrees and in different manners, is found in the works of each of these men, some of whom perhaps attribute to it no other importance than that of a shift of language. I seek here to show that, whatever their intentions, the shift is

important, inept, and often deleterious. This is, then, a summary paper, a digest of many articles, on the one side and an outline of generic response on the other. Direct refutation of an individual's arguments would clearly call for a different method; my concern here is rather to give warning with regard to a global tendency.

[3] Sensitivity to this uniqueness of the person has always been the distinguishing characteristic of the professions, which are concerned with services to persons in the invaluable, inestimable aspects of their existence. And to the extent that money or personal advantage becomes a goal of the professional man, to that extent he begins to treat his clients as interchangeable sources of income or prestige and to that extent he falls away from his profession.

[4] I am speaking here solely of "objective values." Thus, anyone who objectively considers me and my life-situation adequately would see that my life has a greater value for my parents than for some total stranger. A "subjective value," on the other hand, is imposed or ascertained only by the valuing subject. I am not concerned with subjective values save where explicitly indicated.

[5] For a detailed analysis of the structure of empirical thought, cf. my "Estimative Functions of Physical Theory," *Stud. Hist. Phil. Sci.* 6 (1975): 125-157. Much of what is developed there finds easy application to questions of the epistemological structure of morality.

[6] "Good is to be done; evil, to be shunned" is commonly supposed to be tautologous or true by definition.

Against Consequentialism
Germain Grisez

I

In this article, I attack a general theory of moral—and jurisprudential—judgment which I refer to as "consequentialism." In this section, I clarify what consequentialism is, suggest why it is plausible, and outline the remainder of the article. Although I do not articulate and defend an alternative to consequentialism in the present article, a schematic review of alternative theories of moral judgment will help to clarify what consequentialism is.

Some accounts of moral judgment—that is, of what most people call "moral judgment"—are noncognitivist. Such theories claim that linguistic expressions which usually are thought to articulate moral judgments never actually do express judgments or statements or anything cognitional at all. Instead, such expressions are said by noncognitivists to do important tasks such as expressing feelings, attitudes, wishes, commitments, or something else; inciting feelings, actions, expectations, or something else; or some combination of these and other properly noncognitional tasks.

Consequentialism differs from all such theories, for it is cognitivist. A consequentialist maintains that linguistic expressions which are thought to express moral judgments at least sometimes do articulate moral cognitions. Like other cognitivists, consequentialists maintain that acts of a cognitional type bearing upon moral questions can be correct or mistaken—for example, that judgments about what is morally right and wrong can be true or false.

Some cognitivist accounts of moral judgment claim that all the principles of moral knowledge are perceptions of particular and concrete moral realities. On such accounts, primary moral cognition is nondiscursive and nonrational. One may be said to "intuit" moral quality, perhaps by using a "moral sense." Theories of conscience according to which one's conscience receives guidance in each unique case from some transcendent source and theories which treat conscience as a kind of immanent and infallible oracle belong in this category.

Consequentialism differs from all such theories for it proposes a method of moral reasoning. The consequentialist holds that there are some general principles of morality from which moral judgments about particular cases can be drawn. Like others who consider moral reflection to be a rational process, consequentialists hold that there can be sound and unsound arguments for moral judgments.

Some accounts of moral judgment both hold that there are general or universal moral principles which are not derived from moral perception and hold that these principles of morality—which shape morality from within—are irreducible to any principles which are supramoral. For such accounts, moral rightness and duty do not depend upon anything transcendent to the moral domain itself, and moral uprightness is an end in itself. Kant's formalistic theory of moral law is the clearest example of such a theory. Some versions of stoicism and some natural law theories also belong here, as do those divine-command theories which ground the force of divine commands in divine holiness—which is thought of as a constitutive principle of morality—rather than in mere divine power.

Consequentialism differs from all such theories, for it proposes a method of deriving moral judgments from goods which ultimately are not entirely of the moral order. The consequentialist holds that moral uprightness should serve other personal and interpersonal human goods, and that moral rectitude and the doing of one's duty can be understood as a function of the fulfillment or flourishing or well-being or happiness of human individuals and communities. Like others who hold that there is a transmoral source of morality, consequentialists hold that there can be a sound or unsound method for seeking the grounds of moral judgments in the human goods which are regarded as the basic, transmoral principles of morality.

Any theory which maintains that moral judgments can be reduced to transmoral goods involves a distinction between basic human goods, which are ends immanent (at least by participation) in persons and communities, and other goods which are means that can exist apart from persons. No one attempts to ground morality in merely instrumental goods such as wealth. Certain consequentialists, such as Bentham, have maintained that pleasure is the sole basic human good, and they have tried to make morality depend upon this one principle. But consequentialism is not defined by so narrow a view of what the basic human good is. Consequentialists and others who think that morality depends upon human goods which are not exclusively moral can agree that such goods include knowledge of truth, esthetic experience, excellence in skilled performance, good fellowship, and perhaps many other goods which persons can seek without ulterior purpose and enjoy for their own sake.

But not all who think moral judgments can be reduced to principles of human good which are not exclusively moral accept the same theory. Nonconsequentialists can locate the distinction between moral right and wrong in the manner in which a person freely disposes himself or herself towards the basic human goods. On such a view, one can dispose oneself in an attitude of realistic and open responsiveness towards all the basic human goods, or one can arbitrarily limit one's appreciation and respect for them.[1] In either case, one establishes a personal hierarchy of commitments to goods, and this hierarchy shapes an individual's life-plan or self-constitution.[2] But an attitude of openness puts one's own projects and satisfactions in the service of wider human possibilities and a more perfect life in community, while exclusive and arbitrary self-limitation reduces others to the status of instruments of self-fulfillment. Thus nonconsequentialist theories of moral judgment which reduce it to transmoral principles of personal good can use as a methodological key the diverse modes in which persons orient themselves towards these goods.

Consequentialism differs from all such theories, for it proposes efficiency in promoting measurable good results—and/or in preventing measurable bad results—as the methodological key by which what is qualified in moral terms is related to the transmoral goods of persons. In a consequentialist theory, "the good is defined independently from the right, and then the right is defined as that which maximizes the good" (Rawls 1971, 24). Although technically too restrictive—as we shall see—to embrace all consequentialism, the preceding statement does suggest consequentialism's central idea—conduciveness to measurable results as a criterion of morality.

Consequentialism does not demand a sharp distinction between acts (or whatever else is taken to be the primary subject of moral evaluation) and consequences. Consequentialists, for example, can define right and wrong in terms of the good and the harm one will cause both *in* acting and *through* one's acts. Thus consequences immediately present in one's behavior can be considered along with those expected to follow from it, even remotely.

A typical, simple consequentialist theory of moral judgment can be stated as follows: "Moral judgment is a comparative evaluation of alternative courses of action. Each alternative is appraised—if a sound method of moral judgment is used—in terms of the results it can be expected to bring about. One tries to predict with reasonable probability the measurable good and bad results, where 'good' and 'bad' are defined by the causing or protecting, the destroying or preventing of greater or lesser instances of basic human goods. The right act is the one which is expected to yield the greater good—that is, the greatest net good or, in case there is no desirable prospect, the least net evil."

Not all consequentialists specify their position so simply and clearly. For example, some suggest that good consequences are not relevant to morality; they maintain that the right act is one which minimizes evil. Others hold that one can make a consequentialist judgment upon a possible course of action considered in isolation from any alternative; any act may be judged right if it does more good than harm. The arguments I propose against consequentialism are not affected by these variations. Hence, in what follows I use "greater good" and similar expressions to refer to any outcome of the comparative weighing of goods and/or evils which any consequentialist considers appropriate to ground moral judgment. Thus "greater good" is to be taken to include in its meaning "lesser evil," "proportionate reason," and like expressions as they are sometimes used by consequentialists.

Some philosophers and theologians adopt consequentialism not as a complete theory of all moral judgments but only as an element of a theory of all or of some moral judgments. For example, a few philosophers hold that there is an independent standard of justice and that one may never do what is unjust, but that when justice is not at stake, consequentialist judgment ought to be followed. A widely adopted variant is that one may do injustice only if one can thereby bring about *much* more good than would eventuate if one satisfied the strict demands of justice. Many theologians maintain that in general one ought to abide by the moral wisdom which has been articulated in the religious community and passed down to the present by tradition, but that in difficult cases of various sorts, a morally responsible person will decide that it is permissible and even obliga-

7 - Against Consequentialism

tory to act in ways which were traditionally considered intrinsically and gravely immoral. Many philosophers and theologians who hold some form of intuitionism with respect to personal morality accept consequentialism as the appropriate method for making judgments in the field of jurisprudence and social policy in general.

Mixed theories of these and other kinds gain theoretical plausibility by their concessions to common moral opinion. But in gaining plausibility, they lose theoretical simplicity and perhaps even consistency. The arguments I propose against consequentialism do not tell against mixed theories to the extent that they are nonconsequentialist. But if consequentialism must be rejected as inherently incoherent— as I am going to argue—then so must every mixed theory precisely to the extent that it gives consequentialism an irreducible and indispensable role. Nevertheless, in what follows I make no claim to refute theoretical elements of mixed theories which are contingently, rather than logically, related to consequentialism.

Some consequentialists introduce a factor which mediates between the results which are expected and the acts whose morality is to be determined. For example, acts might be evaluated by rules, and rules by the expected consequences of adopting and generally following them. It has often been argued that many forms of indirect consequentialism do not differ very much in practice from direct consequentialism, and that forms of indirect consequentialism which really do differ from direct consequentialism lack plausibility.[3] I agree with this view.

But there is a different point I wish to make here. All forms of indirect consequentialism can be regarded as mixed theories which assert consequentialism with respect to certain special classes of acts. For example, the act of adopting or accepting a rule is itself a particular act, which a rule consequentialist must judge in the same direct way in which an act consequentialist urges that all acts ought to be judged. Hence in what follows I deal with direct consequentialism, for I think that arguments which are effective against it are equally effective against every form of indirect consequentialism precisely at the point at which such theories consider it appropriate to employ a consequentialist methodology.

Why is consequentialism plausible? I think the primary reason why consequentialism is plausible is that it seems self-evident. A typical consequentialist attack on a rival theory is: "Do you mean to say that doing what is right might leave the world worse than doing what is wrong?" In this vein, Richard A. McCormick, S.J., says that in conflict situations

> ... the rule of Christian reason, if we are governed by the *ordo bonorum,* is to choose the lesser evil. This general statement is, it would seem, beyond debate; for the only alternative is that in conflict situations we should choose the greater evil, which is patently absurd. [4]

A second reason why consequentialism is plausible is that there seems to be no good alternative to it. Many current ethics textbooks first classify theories on principles which clarify the characteristics which define consequentialism, then criticize its alternatives, and finally conclude that it is the last resort for reason in morals. Some people deny that there is an objective criterion of morality. But subjectivism appeals to few moral theorists, and relativism blocks one from criticizing one's own society. A direct appeal to intuition to justify moral norms seems arrogant, for intuitions conflict, and an intuitionist is forced to call those who disagree with him "morally blind." Any ethics of objective moral norms which are not based on human well-being seems inhuman. Thus, traditional theism seems to many today to offer a set of taboos, some of them irrational. Kantian ethics is dismissed as too formalistic and also as too idealistic for flesh-and-blood individuals. Thus, consequentialism gains plausibility from the weakness of familiar alternatives to it.

A third reason why consequentialism is plausible is that we do settle some practical questions by measuring, counting, and weighing. "Deliberation" etymologically means *weighing*. Justice is represented as a blindfolded woman holding a scale. Even those who reject consequentialism admit that the greater good of society outweighs private interests, that a proportionate reason can justify doing an act with bad side effects, and so on. Moreover, when public officials must decide whether to proceed with a given project, they count the expected costs and benefits, and weigh them against each other.

A fourth reason why consequentialism is plausible is that its most common forms appeal to the impartiality and unselfishness of good persons. Classical utilitarians popularized consequentialism as the ethics of "the greatest happiness of the greatest number." Some Christian consequentialists say one should do "what Christian love requires." Thus, one who opposes consequentialism seems to disregard the happiness of others and to substitute legalism for charity.

These factors which render consequentialism plausible will be treated more fully below. But the following can be said at once.

First, the seemingly obvious statement that it is right to bring about the greater good or the lesser evil assumes what is not obvious, namely, that goodness is measurable and that diverse forms of it are commensurable. If there are nonmeasurable goods, toward which human acts should be oriented, then acting only in view of measurable goods will mean ignoring goods which cannot be measured but should not be ignored. If the consequences of one act include several goods and evils, how can one tell which good is greater, which evil is lesser?

Second, not all theories of the moral criterion are reviewed in the dialectic from which consequentialism emerges as the last resort. Many scholars think that Aristotle's ethics defies the usual classification. So does my own. I define moral right and wrong in terms of human goods, but not in terms of the *amount* of good one expects to bring about.

Third, I shall show in section four that the measuring, counting, and weighing usual in practical reasoning do not imply consequentialism. Sometimes the judgment one reaches depends upon presupposed moral norms. The scales of justice weigh facts, not goods. Sometimes the judgment one reaches concerns nonmoral value and does not presuppose moral norms. A cost-effectiveness study clarifies the advantages and disadvantages of possible projects. But such a judgment concerns the efficiency of techniques, not the morality of acts.

Fourth, there is no necessary relation between consequentialism and unselfishness. An egoist can be a consequentialist; most consequentialists argue independently that one should not be an egoist. A theologian who appeals to Christian love in support of consequentialism usually also admits that Christian love requires that one do what is morally right. Thus, if one assumes that the requirements of Christian love are defined by consequentialism, one begs the question in its favor.

Utilitarian impartiality also appears less attractive if one considers the imaginary counterexamples philosophers propose against utilitarianism. These are usually drawn from the fields of justice and personal integrity. Would it be right to secure the greatest happiness for the greatest number by isolating one innocent person in a perpetual life of horrible torture? Would it be right to save a dozen suspects from a lynch mob by offering one other—not more probably guilty than the dozen—as a victim to the mob's wrath? As John Rawls points out, utilitarianism does not take seriously enough the distinction between persons; it merges the benefits and harms to everyone into a totality:

> Thus there is no reason in principle why the greater gains of some should not compensate for the lesser losses of others, or more importantly, why the violation of the liberty of a few might not be made right by the greater good shared by many (Rawls 1971, 26).

Consequentialism implies that there are no intrinsically evil acts. This view can seem attractive if one considers kinds of acts one holds to be morally acceptable. Most college students today easily accept consequentialism in the field of sexual ethics. But consider: Would it ever be right for a professor to assign grades in a course, not according to the work the students have done, but rather according to the extent to which they agree with him? Confronted with this question, students usually begin to see that acts of some kinds are always wrong.

Many critiques of consequentialism—or of various specific forms of it—hardly go beyond proposing counter examples. Such arguments cannot be decisive. A consequentialist balances his own moral intuition against his willingness to defy common moral opinion. If the intuition is strong, the received norm is declared to be an irrational taboo. If common moral opinion is too powerful to defy, the proposed counter example is declared to lack an adequate consequentialist justification.

My thesis is that consequentialism is rationally unacceptable because the phrase "greater good" as it is used in any consequentialist theory necessarily lacks reference. I do not reject consequentialism merely because I think it dangerous; I reject it because I think it dangerous *nonsense*—nonsense in the sense that inasmuch as expressions essential to the articulation of consequentialism necessarily lack reference, the theory is meaningless.

To speak of the "greater good" as consequentialists do is to imply that goods are measurable and commensurable. But goods cannot be measured unless there is an available standard applicable to them as goods. They cannot be commensurable unless all of them are called "good" in one and the same sense, and one and the same measure can be applied to all of them. I deny that "good" said of the alternatives to be judged morally can have a single sense and in this sense signify anything which can be measured by a common standard.

In section two, I review the difficulties with respect to the measurement of goods which consequentialists themselves have recognized and failed to overcome. In section three, I argue that these difficulties are inevitable, not contingent, because a consequentialist account of moral judgment is incompatible with essential features of the morally significant choices which moral judgment (on any theory) is intended to direct. In section four, I analyze several legitimate uses, often mistakenly confused with consequentialist uses, of expressions such as "greater good." In section five I expose the character of consequentialism, not as an ethical theory, but as a practical method of thinking about right and wrong.

II

In an extensive survey of work in utilitarianism from 1961-1971, Dan W. Brock points out that utilitarianism requires that utility be calculable. After suggesting that there are obvious difficulties in making such measurements, Brock adds:

> More important and perplexing, however, is how the necessary calculations can, even in principle, be made and whether the logical foundations necessary to the intelligibility of these calculations exist.
>
> Moral philosophers have paid surprisingly little attention to these two problems. Most discussions of utilitarianism in recent books and journals simply assume that it is possible to determine in any situation what is required by utility-maximization, and then go on to consider whether this always coincides with what is required by morality (Brock 1973, 245).

Brock's remarks might be discounted as the view of an unsympathetic student of utilitarianism. But this would be a mistake.

J. J. C. Smart, a leading proponent of unrestricted, direct utilitarianism, admitted in an article published in 1967 that because of obstacles to calculation

> . . . the utilitarian is reduced to an intuitive weighing of various consequences with their probabilities. It is impossible to justify such intuitions rationally, and we have here a serious weakness in utilitarianism (Smart 1967, 210).

Similarly, A. J. Ayer, who defends a form of consequentialism with respect to the formation of social policies, criticizes Bentham's attempt to apply consequentialism to the moral judgment of individuals. Ayer concludes:

> In virtue of what standard of measurement can I set about adding the satisfaction of one person to that of another and subtracting the resultant quantity from the dissatisfaction of someone else? Clearly there is no such standard, and Bentham's process of "sober calculation" turns out to be a myth (Ayer 1959, 268).

It also is worth noticing that Bentham himself recognized difficulties in an area related to that considered by Ayer, for in an unpublished note Bentham wrote that the

> . . . addibility of the happiness of different subjects, however when considered rigorously it may appear fictitious, is a postulation without the allowance of which all political reasonings are at a stand: nor is it more fictitious than that of the equality of chances to reality on which the whole branch of the Mathematics which is called the doctrine of chance is established. [5]

In other words, Bentham regards the postulation of commensurability as one *necessary* for practical purposes. He justifies the interpersonal comparisons challenged by the objection he is considering by saying that when there is no reason to consider incommensurable goods more or less than one another, it is quite rational to consider them equal. Bentham's position is unassailable, provided that "equal" can be used meaningfully in this context. This I deny.

If "greater good" is to be meaningful in the formulation of a criterion of morality, three conditions must be fulfilled: 1) "good" must have a single meaning; 2) what is good in this unique sense must be measurable; and 3) the result of measurement must settle moral issues either directly or indirectly.

Clearly, the necessary meaning of "good" cannot be specified in moral terms. What Rawls says of utilitarianism is true of all consequentialism: Its point is to define "good" independently of "right" and to define "right" in terms of "good." And, in general, consequentialists see this requirement and try to meet it (Frankena 1963, 63-77). If consequentialists said that ethical considerations determine what a good consequence is, they would either be going in a circle or setting off on an infinite regress.

If the single meaning of "good" which consequentialism needs cannot be specified by moral principles, how can it be specified?

If human persons have a single, well-defined goal or function, set for them by nature or by God, then "good" has the necessary, univocal meaning. Acts are right or wrong insofar as they do or do not bring one to this goal or fulfill this function.

On one interpretation, Aristotle's ethics are of this sort. But Aristotle's ethics, understood thus, have been challenged. Most modern philosophers deny that humankind has a definite goal or function. In this dispute, the moderns seem to be in the right. If persons are ends in themselves, they cannot be ordered to a good as any part to a whole or any means to an end. Aristotle either subordinates the lives of the many to the actualization of a few, or he admits the intrinsic value of lives other than the contemplative. If the latter, "good" lacks the univocal meaning consequentialism needs.[6]

Many Christians have thought of personal salvation as a single, well-defined goal.

Consequentialist thinking based on this conception of the good led to the abuses for which modern humanists condemn Christianity: excessive otherworldliness, religious fanaticism, inhuman asceticism, and so on. Of course, these abuses are not entailed by the view that personal salvation is a single, well-defined goal. But this view does entail that the goodness of a Christian's acts is specified by their efficiency as means of getting to heaven. Those who accept this moral theory face a dilemma. If they consider human acts in and of themselves to be effective means of salvation, they are pelagians. If they consider human acts to be effective means of salvation by divine fiat, they are voluntarists. The latter position implies that this life is inherently meaningless, but is meaningful as a time of temptation. This concept respects divine power, but ignores divine wisdom.[7]

Anyone who holds that all human persons have a single goal which defines "good" univocally also confronts facts one cannot easily explain. People who seem equally able, intelligent, and healthy have different goals in life. If one says that all humans have the same goal, one will find almost everyone else disagreeing as soon as the goal is specified. Even those Christians, who in theory take an otherworldly and voluntaristic position, in practice treat an incommensurable variety of goods as determinative of the moral goodness of human acts, for they admit the legitimacy of a variety of Christian life styles and they try to show the immorality of various kinds of acts, not only by their incongruity with holiness and grace, but also by their incompatibility with goods immanent in human persons—goods such as life, truth, justice, love, and peace.

Shortly after World War II, a British economist, Lionel Robbins, reflected upon the simplifications introduced into the making of socioeconomic policy during wartime. A single objective counts; all else is instrumental. If there is no victory, there is no future. All decisions are technical. Unity of purpose "gives a certain unity to the framework of planning which at least makes possible some sort of direct decision which is not wholly arbitrary." [8]

Robbins is correct about the wartime psychology of Britain and the United States. The unconditional surrender of the enemy became a fixation with the leaders and people of both nations. This fixation partly explains the adoption of ethically questionable tactics, such as obliteration bombing. It also helps to explain why Soviet leaders, who took a longer view, were more prudent than Anglo-American leaders in gaining post-war advantages before the war ended.

Most philosophical consequentialists have been liberals. Instead of saying that all humans have the same goal, they have tried to define "good" univocally, to leave room for differing concrete goals, but to make them commensurable with one another. Many utilitarians, following Bentham, define "good" in terms of happiness. Others define "good" in terms of the maximum satisfaction of desires, less the minimum of unavoidable frustration. Since different people have different enjoyments and desires, either approach allows for differing goals. To ensure commensurability, those who take either approach must deny that any sort of pleasure or desire differs from any other sort in a way which would make their inherent *goodness* differ. Desire theorists, for example, often say that all human desires have the same initial claim to satisfaction.

If happiness is used to define "good" univocally, "happiness" itself must be used univocally. If it is, the theory becomes implausible.[9] For example, if happiness is taken to be a certain quality of consciousness, how can one explain certain people's dedication to causes which are irreducible to states of consciousness? For them, happiness is participation in something bigger than themselves.

A consequentialist can use "happiness" in a very wide sense to allow for the diverse life styles people regard as intrinsically good. But if this maneuver makes it plausible to say that everyone desires happiness, "happiness" ceases to be univocal and thus becomes useless for the consequentialist. People not only get happiness by different means, but "happiness" as an end is different things to different people.

Attempts to define "good" univocally in terms of satisfaction of desire also fail.

Do all human desires really have the same initial claim to satisfaction? Some people desire sadistic pleasure. Many people desire death for criminals. Pornography sells better than the best literature; more people desire the former than the latter. Some people desire feminine deodorant spray. It sells. Most people have what some economists call "artificial desires." Keynes, for instance, distinguishes the needs people have of themselves from the needs they have insofar as they wish to get ahead of others. Galbraith talks of wants created by production and advertising. He points out that the desire for increased expenditure may be stronger than any need which can be satisfied by it.[10] Are all these desires to be counted uncritically in calculating moral right and wrong?

A desire theorist can answer that desires must be criticized. If someone desires what is logically impossible, his desire should be ignored. If someone has a desire which would go away if her false belief about matters of fact were corrected, the error ought to be corrected. But these criteria do not dispose of all the examples mentioned in the previous paragraph. The desires of sadists, of proponents of capital punishment, of dirty old men, and of status seekers are not for anything logically impossible. Nor is it always the case that such desires arise from errors about matters of fact.

The desire theorist must find additional principles of criticism. Since moral criteria cannot be invoked without circularity or infinite regress, the desire theorist might seek a scientific criterion from psychology. Clearly, the desires of the insane do not have the same initial claim to satisfaction as do the desires of the mentally healthy. Sadists, proponents of capital punishment, dirty old men, and status seekers need not be insane, but perhaps they are not mentally healthy. Therefore, let mental healthfulness of desires be the criterion.

But there are just as many schools of psychology as there are philosophical and religious conceptions of the good life. Psychologists are not proceeding as scientists when they go beyond the consensus about insanity to give a full account of "mental health." Opinions about the good life do not become science simply because they happen to be the opinions of Freud, Jung, Adler, Allers, Horney, Maslow, Allport, Erikson, Fromm, Menninger, or some other person of scientific competence. If the opinions of such persons about the good life were science, they would offer a common, detailed account of "mental health." They do not.

Attempts to define "good" either in terms of happiness or desire also must fit in pain and frustration. If the disvalues are the same in kind as the values, merely negative in degree, the value and its opposite can be measured on a single scale as one measures heat and cold with the same thermometer. But this assumption has been questioned.[11] It is not at all obvious that a disvalue is simply a low level of a value, as cold is lack of heat. Disvalues such as pain and frustration are not mere privations; they have a positive character of their own. Thus, "good" is not univocal if it is defined either in terms of happiness and avoidance of pain, or in terms of satisfaction and frustration of desire. The calculation of the "greater good" is blocked by the incommensurability of the opposites in either pair.

Another difficulty with these theories of value is that enjoyments and desires differ in kind, not only in degree. As I said above, "happiness" means different things to different people. One can compare the enjoyment of drinking a Coke with that of eating a candy bar or the desire for the one with that for the other.[12] But how many appetizing meals in a French restaurant give enjoyment comparable to that of a happy marriage? How many satisfactions of desires for particular objectives are comparable to the satisfaction of one's desire to be a good father, an excellent philosopher, or a faithful follower of Jesus?

Jeremy Bentham, who took calculation seriously, dealt with the problem of commensurability in a characteristically straightforward way:

> Money is the instrument for measuring the quantity of pain or pleasure. Those who are not satisfied with the accuracy of this instrument must find out some other that shall be more accurate, or bid adieu to Politics and Morals.
>
> Let no man therefore be either surprised or scandalized if he find me in the course of this work valuing everything in money. Tis in this way only we can get aliquot parts to measure by. If we must not say of a pain or a pleasure that it is worth so much money, it is in vain, in point of quantity, to say anything at all about it, there is neither proportion nor disproportion between Punishments and Crimes. [13]

Since one must calculate, one can. So "good" is reduced to pleasure and avoidance of pain, and these are reduced to money. Bentham's leap-of-faith is breathtaking.[14] He is no cynic saying that every person has his or her price. He is a moralist saying that the best things in life simply cost more than a Coke or a candy bar.

The definition of "good" in terms of enjoyment faces another objection. Enjoyment is a conscious experience which normally arises but is distinct from some activity which extends beyond consciousness. Let us imagine a device which could record total experiences as they were being lived and then play them back in the brains of other persons. One might enjoy receiving such a recorded experience—for example, of one's favorite athlete winning one's favorite game. But would one wish to spend the rest of one's life receiving such recorded experiences, however enjoyable they might be? This thought-experiment isolates enjoyment as a conscious experience from the whole of real life which one enjoys. If one agrees that one would not wish to spend the rest of one's life receiving recorded enjoyable experiences, one can still value enjoyment, but only insofar as it is part of a real life in which goods transcending consciousness also are participated (Grisez and Shaw 1974, 25-27; Nozick 1974, 42-45).

Those who define "good" in terms of desire can point out that the preceding argument does not touch them. "Satisfaction" is said of whole persons interacting with their total environment. Moreover, while "desire" often is used in a wider sense than "enjoyment," it also is used in a more precise sense than "happiness."

But even if desire theorists can solve other difficulties, they still must admit incommensurable kinds of desires if they are to avoid something like Bentham's postulate that the best things in life merely cost more. If desire theorists admit incommensurable kinds of desires, then in the present matter I have no quarrel with them. The goods remain incommensurable, and consequentialist calculation is blocked.

Why do so many intelligent and serious people think that all forms of desire are commensurable? I think the reason is that it seems obvious that each individual has a rational system of preferences.[15] "Isn't it evident," a desire theorist might argue, "that any sane person faced with a choice can say which alternative he or she prefers? If so, one always knows what one *wants more*. Thus individuals, at least, somehow manage to make all their desires commensurate."

One of the conditions necessary for a rational system of preferences is that if one prefers *A* to *B* and *B* to *C*, then one must prefer *A* to *C*. But the dispositions underlying choice making need not be rational in this sense.[16] One can prefer a Plymouth to a Chevrolet and a Chevrolet to a Ford, yet also prefer a Ford to a Plymouth. For when one chooses an automobile, one is interested in several factors—for example, price, available options, and expected quality of service. Comparing the three makes of cars in respect to these three factors, one might arrive at a preference-ranking as follows:

Rank	Price	Options	Service
1.	Chevrolet	Plymouth	Ford
2.	Ford	Chevrolet	Plymouth
3.	Plymouth	Ford	Chevrolet

The Plymouth outranks the Chevrolet in two respects (options and service), and the Chevrolet similarly outranks the Ford in two respects (price and options). These rankings seem to imply that the Plymouth will be preferred to the Chevrolet and *a fortiori* the Plymouth to the Ford. But the Ford also outranks the Plymouth in two respects (service and price), and these rankings seem to demand a preference of the Ford to the Plymouth. In such cases, the dispositions underlying choice making are not rationally ordered. One's initial wishes must be harmonized by a choice of the aspects one will accept as determinative. For example, if one sets price aside, the Plymouth wins.

Why does one set price aside? Perhaps one has sufficient reason for doing so. But an analysis of the dispositions underlying this choice will uncover previous choices and eventually reach an individual's commitments to the goods he or she regards as intrinsically worthwhile. For a given individual, these commitments do have a definite order. For example, the religious person puts religion first, the liberal humanist puts freedom first, the Marxist puts justice first, the existentialist puts authenticity first, many people put peace of mind first. But no matter how one constitutes one's personal hierarchy of goods, one's basic commitments are not to particular goals which can be pursued by suitable means in an efficient way. Rather, one is interested in working towards particular goals because of one's basic commitments.

At the level of basic commitments, the economic model is useless. Here one comes to the goods which shape different styles of life. Many people are not dedicated to anything, but all who live their own lives must have a sense of identity, an idea of what their life is about. If a word like "commitment" connotes too formal and reflective an act for the way most people set the direction of their lives, one can say more modestly that all who live their own lives must think in terms of some concerns to which they are most deeply *attached*. These are goods in which one wishes to participate for themselves, not for anything ulterior. For these goods, one would give anything, yet money cannot buy them. This is as true of goods such as being contented, being somebody, and being liked—by which many people one would hardly call "committed" shape their lives—as it is of goods such as being a Christian, being a liberal, being a reformer, and being authentic by which some people quite consciously constitute their own identities.

The point of the preceding explanation can be made specific by considering the limits of cost-benefit analysis. The economic advantages and disadvantages of a proposed public project can be quantified. But people also want freedom of speech and of religion, equal protection of the laws, privacy, and other goods which block certain choices, yet which cannot be costed out. Cost-benefit analysis can tell one the most effective way of attaining certain objectives, assuming one accepts the objectives and has no concerns about the means and the side effects of the means required to attain them. But such analysis cannot tell one whether the objectives one seeks are objectives one ought to seek, or whether nonquantifiable factors should be ignored.[17]

If a consequentialist admits that justice and theoretical truth, or any other two goods, are fundamental and incommensurable, then the consequentialist also admits that "greatest net good" is meaningless whenever one must choose between promoting and protecting or impeding and damaging these two goods in some participations. For if these goods really are incommensurable, one might as well try to sum up the quantity of the size of this page, the quantity of the number nineteen, and the quantity of the mass of the moon as to try to calculate with such incommensurable goods.

Different kinds of quantity do have something in common with each other. About all of them, one can ask: "How much?" Each can be measured using a measure homogeneous with itself. But different kinds of quantity are *objectively* incommensurable. One can relate them to one another only by *adopting* a system of weights and measures. Similarly, diverse modes of basic human goodness do have something in common with each other. About all of them, one can ask: "Is this something I would give anything for?" Participations of each good can be measured by an instance one accepts as a standard. But the many basic human goods are objectively incommensurable. One must *adopt* a personal hierarchy of values in order to relate them to each other.

Of course, goods which are not basic but derivative can be commensurable. Means or useful goods are measured by ends or intrinsic goods, because the former are subordinate to the latter. However if one is dealing with basic goods, which are intrinsic to the full being of human persons, one cannot make them commensurable by relating them to something more basic.

Someone might object that theologians must admit the possibility of measuring, counting, and weighing all created goods, for God has "disposed all things by measure and number and weight" (Wis. 11:20).

Plato pointed out that the gods quarrel over issues of right and wrong, because such issues cannot be settled by measuring, counting and weighing. If such issues could be settled by calculation, the gods would hardly quarrel over them.[18] But Plato's gods, like humans, lack insight into the Good Itself.

According to traditional Jewish and Christian faith, God orders everything by reference to the only absolute: His own goodness. Yet even God's perfect knowledge of the goodness of various creatures does not eliminate their incommensurability with each other, for the created participations of divine goodness mirror in their very irreducible diversity the richness of perfection which is united only in the Creator.

Thus, God, who knows His own goodness in itself, cannot help loving Himself with an infinite love. However, God creates freely, because creatures are unnecessary for His perfection, and He freely chooses the world He is creating, for no created world could be perfectly good in every respect.

Similarly—according to a plausible Christian theology—a human person who saw God face to face could not help loving Him above all things. But in this life, human persons constitute themselves freely because none of the goods by which they can integrate and direct their lives exhausts the totality of goodness to which a human person is open. If any particular good did exhaust a person's capacity for good, such a person would not be open to sharing in divine life. Our hearts would have been made for a finite good and they would rest in that good for which they had been made.

III

The arguments in the preceding section showed that attempts by consequentialists to give "good" a univocal meaning have not succeeded. But those arguments were based upon assumptions—though ones I think a consequentialist would accept—which could be false. Moreover, an optimistic consequentialist always can hope that despite past failures someone eventually will show how the theory can be made to work. The argument I am about to state is based not on assumptions, but on facts and analysis. If this argument is sound, any reasonable person can learn from it that consequentialists never will be able to make their theory work. No one will show how to do the calculations consequentialism requires, because such calculations are impossible. "Greater good," as the consequentialist needs to use it, inevitably lacks reference, and so consequentialism is meaningless.

As I explained in section one, consequentialism is a method for reducing moral judgments about possible options to transmoral basic human goods. If "good" were defined in moral terms, then "One ought to take that option which promises the greater good" would be trivially true, but this truism does not express the consequentialist theory. I also explained in section one that although one must distinguish consequentialist theories which bear directly on the whole range of morally significant acts from indirect consequentialist theories, even the latter bear upon a certain range of acts—for example, the acts by which rules are adopted, or institutions established, or certain traits of character cultivated. Consequentialists, like other moral theorists, sometimes recognize that there are derivative cases of moral judgment bearing upon the moral results of moral acts and upon the past moral acts of oneself or of others. But the primary case of moral judgment, according to any consequentialist, is a practical directive to adopt one proposed course of action (which may itself be the acceptance of a rule, and so forth) rather than some alternative to it.

According to this view, a moral judgment as to what one ought to do can make an immediate practical difference only when one is considering what one could do. In other words, moral judgments can shape one's action only when one is deliberating. I begin my critique of consequentialism from this point by clarifying, with a brief summary of the phenomena of deliberation, what is involved in that mental process.

Deliberation begins only if one experiences a conflict of desires or interests. One becomes aware of incompatible possibilities, such as sitting still or leaving the room, beginning to read a different book, or visiting a nearby spa. Something in oneself draws one to each of the alternatives. The conflict makes one stop and think—something one does not do if there is no problem. Each alternative is somehow attractive, but none promises complete satisfaction. One checks to see if one has some previously established principle which clearly dictates which alternative is to be carried out. If one has such a principle, there is no need to make a choice. But when one is aware of no such established principle which seems unquestionable, then one feels that a choice will have to be made. One feels one's spontaneous behavior blocked; one finds oneself in a practical impasse. Deliberation is the thinking which begins at this point. It is a quest for a way out.

One deliberates, considering various proposals, and examines the advantages and disadvantages which probably will follow from the adoption of each. While one deliberates, one regards the alternative proposals as genuine possibilities. One expresses this possibility, perhaps, by saying to oneself: "I could adopt this alternative, and then again I could adopt that one." This "could" expresses more than mere logical possibility or causal contingency; it expresses a *practical* possibility. One is projecting a use of one's capacity to act in a context in which one thinks its use requires only one's choice to use it.

Thus, persons in deliberating are aware of alternative courses of action and are confident that they can and must settle among these alternatives. One perhaps says to oneself: "The choice is mine and I must make it."

If some possibility did not seem attractive in any respect at all, then that possibility would be of merely theoretical interest. Only what is somehow attractive can become the subject of a practical proposal which must be chosen or rejected. The proposal which is adopted at the end of deliberation is chosen precisely because of the good or apparent good which kept it in the running to the end. Hence, when one has made a choice, one always can give a reason for this choice by citing the good for the sake of which one adopted this alternative.

Now, the consequentialist holds that the goods involved in each alternative are commensurable—that is, that they can be weighed or measured by a common standard. The proof that consequentialists are committed to commensurability is that they talk in terms of the "greater good," which would be meaningless if the goods were not commensurable.

The consequentialist also holds that one ought to adopt the proposal which promises the greater good. Clearly this "ought" is vacuous if one cannot adopt some alternative proposal. My criticism of consequentialism is that it is inconsistent to hold both that the goods involved in various alternatives are commensurable and that a person can deliberately adopt an alternative which promises a lesser good than the alternative which ought to have been adopted.

Let us suppose that a person makes a consequentialist moral judgment and acts upon it. By hypothesis, such a person *does* adopt the proposal which promises the greater good, but *could* instead have adopted a different proposal promising measurably less good. The question is: How could anyone knowingly choose the lesser good?

Whether or not one is a consequentialist, a choice by a person of an alternative apparently thought to promise measurably less good would be puzzling indeed. One might suppose that the wrong choice is made by mistake. But this supposition provides no escape for consequentialists, for they hold that the morality of one's act is determined by the facts as one sees them; moral evil is not merely an honest error in computation. One also might suppose that the wrong choice is made by virtue of the influence of unconscious factors upon choice. However, this hypothesis also provides no escape for consequentialists, for they propose their theory as a method of adjudication between values and disvalues which they claim can be intelligently measured and compared in the process of deliberation.

Therefore, the consequentialist must hold that one *could* purposely adopt a proposal which promises measurably less good than an alternative proposal which one *should* adopt. Nevertheless, as the data of deliberation already described establish, there never is any reason for choosing the alternative which one does choose except the good it promises. It follows that if one alternative promises a measurably greater good than another, one who is deliberating has all the reason for choosing the alternative which promises the measurably greater good which he or she has for choosing the other, and has the further reason for choosing the former provided by the greater good it promises.

Thus, given the commensurability required by the consequentialist's theory of judgment, no one can do what one ought not, since no one can deliberately prefer the lesser good. The reason for choosing the greater good—assuming the goods are commensurable—is not merely a good reason, it is a sufficient reason.

In other words, given the commensurability required by the consequentialist's theory, no one *can* deliberately adopt any proposal other than that which the consequentialist says one *should* adopt—the proposal, namely, which promises the greater good. But this means that no one can do moral evil. Yet consequentialism is advanced as an account of moral judgment. A theory of moral judgment must leave open the *possibility* that someone deliberately makes a morally wrong choice.

An analogy will help to make clear the force of this argument. If one were literally interested in nothing whatsoever except acquiring money, whenever one considered possible courses of action, one would look for only a single thing: how much money one might acquire if one chose each course. When one saw that a certain possibility was not the best bet, one could not choose it. Likewise, since one who chooses can be interested in various possibilities only insofar as they promise good, whenever one deliberates, one considers what good one can hope for by choosing each possibility. If one could see that a certain possibility promised measurably less good, one could not choose it.

Someone might object that the foregoing argument presupposes that choices are free, and that this supposition is question-begging against consequentialists, who can reject free choice and defend some form of determinism or compatibilism.

Before answering this objection I offer an historical observation. As a matter of historical fact, many consequentialists have rejected the libertarian conception of choice. Bentham, Mill, and Sidgwick are examples, and others come easily to mind. Many such consequentialists base their determinism upon a psychological theory of motivation according to which one must choose that to which one has the stronger motive. This theory has the same assumption as consequentialism: that prospective goods are commensurable. The same symbol has played a principal role in the history of both psychological determinism and consequentialism—the symbol of the balance scale.

Now to the objection. I do think that people can make free choices.[19] However, the argument I offer here against consequentialism does not rest upon this controversial position. All I need for the present argument are the *phenomena* of deliberation and choice. Someone like Mill who is both a psychological determinist and a consequentialist holds both that one necessarily chooses what appears to be the greater good and that one ought so to choose. The two positions are incompatible. Undoubtedly there are consequentialists who do not accept psychological determinism. But I think that if goods really were commensurable as consequentialism requires, then just to that extent psychological determinism would be true.

As we know by experience, we do make choices. How can we make them? I submit that we can make them because "greater good" has no definite meaning *antecedent to* the choice which ends the deliberation. Prior to choice, the goods which are promised by different proposals are diverse and incommensurable. For this precise reason, one's always unquestionable antecedent principle, "The more good the better," is inapplicable. Thus one can and must choose. At this point, the consequentialist's advice to adopt the proposal which promises the "greater good" is meaningless; those who are deliberating know that they do not know in what the "greater good" will lie.

Someone might object that it must be possible to know what is better and yet to choose what is worse, for such perverse choice is at the heart of immorality on any account of it, nonconsequentialist as well as consequentialist. I grant that one can know what is morally better and yet choose what is morally worse, and I find no difficulty in accounting for this fact. What is bad from a moral point of view can be good from another perspective—for example, that of self-fulfillment. Provided that morality and self-fulfillment are incommensurable forms of good, my problem is solved. But consequentialists cannot solve their problem in this way, since for them choice bears upon premoral goods which are commensurable with each other, the preponderance of which *defines* what is morally good.

Again, someone might object that one can know what will produce the greater good for everyone concerned, but choose a lesser good which happens to be a greater good for oneself. My answer to this objection grants for the sake of argument two assumptions without which the objection does not make sense: first, that egoism is a matter of choice, not merely a personality disorder generated by heredity and environment; and second, that the choice to be or not to be an egoist is a morally significant one of a sort that a consequentialist theory tries to regulate, rather than an option at the frontier of morality by which one constitutes oneself amoral or accepts one's role as an actor in the moral institution. On these assumptions, if one chooses to be an egoist, one must have a reason for this choice. For example, one expects more enjoyment for oneself. If the greater good is good in precisely the same sense as one's own good is good, but also is regarded as measurably greater, then one has no reason for not opting for the greater good. This is the case, for example, when enlightened egoists see that they can have everything they can get for themselves in certain situations by either of two courses of action, but also benefit others by one of them. Not being malicious, enlightened egoists choose to benefit others as well as themselves. But if the supposedly greater good does not promise an egoist every benefit for himself or herself which an alternative promises, then the egoist can choose the so-called lesser good, because, at least for the egoist, one's own good and the good of others are not commensurable.

Even gross egoists have reasons which seem to themselves good enough for their egoistic choices. "I'm going to get what I want, and to hell with the rest of them," one might say to oneself. This reason would not seem to others a good reason, for gross egoists introduce into their notion of "good" an egocentric reference. This reference is not universalizable andshareable with others by means of rational discourse. But an egoist need not be stupid or crazy. One can even offer a plausible reason for one's general egoistic policy: "I'm looking out for number one, because you can bet your life nobody else is going to." Thus, egoists are both rational, in the sense that they act not without reason, and unreasonable, in the sense that they have no reason they can expect others to accept by way of justification for their egoistic choices.

Someone might further object that even apart from choices involving moral good and evil, one can know of a greater good and a lesser good, yet deliberately choose the lesser. For example, a boy might have learned in health class that an egg nog has more nutrients in it than a Coke, and he might also understand that the food with more nutrients is better for him. Yet he can choose the Coke. But this choice is possible only because the good of nutrition is competing with another good. The boy wants the Coke and will feel better just now if he gets it. The sense of "feeling better" is an aspect of harmony within the self, which is a basic human good incommensurable with health.

Whenever one chooses, one determines whether one will be the sort of person for whom this or that potentially greater good shall be *the* greater good. The consequentialist assumes that the decision about the controlling value is a judgment of what *is* greater, not a choice of what *shall* be greater. But the ability to make a choice precisely is the prerogative to adopt the goodness of one alternative rather than the goodness of another as the principle by which one determines oneself and shapes the action which expresses oneself.

Once one has chosen, the alternatives which have not been chosen often seem to pale in significance. The viewpoint of the alternative which has been chosen tends in retrospect to alter the attractiveness of the others. Not long after having made a difficult choice, one often wonders what could possibly have appealed in alternatives which were not chosen.

Looking back upon a choice, it is easy to suppose that one chose the alternative which seemed to offer the greater good. This retrospective distortion provides a key argument for psychological determinism. If this good seemed greater, how could one not have chosen it? What must be kept in mind is that during deliberation just prior to choice, each alternative seemed better in its own way, but none seemed better in every way. Otherwise, one would not have been perplexed; one would not have felt that one had to make a choice. Only rational indeterminacy *between alternatives* calls for a choice between them.

Someone might object that not all morally significant action follows upon deliberation and conscious choice. For example, a morally good woman is inclined to help others; she sees someone in need of her help; she thinks of nothing but their need and what she can do to satisfy it; she acts spontaneously—without thinking, without consciously choosing. Surely, such an act is good; a sign of its goodness is that the woman might be praised for it, even more highly praised than less good persons who carefully considered their own interests before deliberately choosing to render assistance.

I admit that such spontaneous acts can be morally good. They do not follow upon deliberation and conscious choice. But my thesis is not that all morally good acts are deliberately chosen. Rather, it is that the acts which consequentialists seek to regulate by their purported criterion are thus chosen. Clearly, the consequentialist is not talking about spontaneous acts such as the one described, for in these spontaneous acts only one course of action is considered and it is done without choice. Commensuration cannot begin unless there is some deliberation.

Someone also might object that there are situations in which the "right" choice is defined by completely determinate goals, so that "greater good" does have a definite meaning. If one accepts the goals and nothing interferes, then one does what is wrong only by mistake. For example, "good" might be defined nonmorally in descriptive terms: "good" is that which is accepted as good in one's society, and the "greater good" is that for which one will be most highly praised. The right act then becomes the one which an intelligent person with a normal desire for approval sees to be necessary.

I admit that there are systems such as that described by this objection, and that the language of morals often is used both within such systems and in talking about them. Children old enough to talk but too young to think of themselves as responsible agents in some sense make choices, but such choices do not have the same moral significance as do the choices of adults. A sign of this is that we do not hold such children criminally liable for their conduct which violates criminal laws. Children can nevertheless understand that it is better to please the adults on whom they depend than to displease them. The right act is the obedient act. A naughty child is one who rebels.

However, what is at stake in a case such as this is not morality in the full sense; it is conventional standards of behavior. What is right by conventional standards of behavior need not be morally right at all. My thesis is not that "right" in a nonmoral sense cannot be defined in terms of commensurable, nonmoral values, but that "right" *in the moral sense* cannot be so defined. Consequentialists cannot disagree, for they offer their theory not as a descriptive hypothesis about conventional morality but as a normative theory of objective morality by which conventional morality can be criticized. Both consequentialists and I are at odds with subjectivists and relativists who confuse morality in the full sense—which is reflective and critical—with conventional morality, which is a datum taken as final only by the uncritical, such as children and those adults who do not develop beyond a childish way of thinking about their own lives and the real world in which their lives must be lived.

If the foregoing criticism of consequentialism is correct, then consequentialism is not merely a theory with difficulties (a fact admitted by even the most earnest proponents of the theory), nor is it merely a theory which is false (the possibility generally envisaged by those who reject consequentialism), but it is one of those philosophical theories which is literally meaningless. The meaninglessness of consequentialism follows from the conclusion that the goods are not commensurable in the way the consequentialist requires, for this lack of commensurability eliminates all possibility of reference for the expression "greater good" as the consequentialist uses this expression.

If consequentialism is meaningless, it also follows that any ethical theory which admits it is defective to that extent. An ethical theory might be sound in other respects, but if it allows any role for consequentialism—for example, in the resolution of conflict cases—it is incoherent in this respect. Some moralists reject consequentialism and adopt a moral criterion based on personal relationship and covenant, yet maintain that in a world broken by sin, situations occur in which moral ideals must be compromised. In these cases, a lesser evil may be done to avoid a greater one. Such theories admit consequentialism without realizing it, and to this extent become incoherent.

As I mentioned in section one, philosophers often argue against consequentialism by citing plausible counterexamples. Since consequentialism is meaningless, it becomes clear why the dialectic of intuitions and counterexamples cannot be decisive. One who proposes a counterexample argues that in some case an act which brings about a greater good is wrong. This assumes two things: (1) that right and wrong can be determined by nonconsequentialist criteria, and (2) that it is meaningful to say in this context that one alternative brings about a greater good than another. Since consequentialism is meaningless, (1) is true but (2) is false. Thus the opponent of consequentialism who depends upon counterexamples accepts an impossible burden of proof.

Consequentialists easily defend themselves. They either admit that the act proposed as a counterexample brings about the greatest net good and deny that it is wrong, or they admit that it is wrong but deny that it can ever bring about the greatest good on the whole and in the long run, or they assert that the example in question is a very difficult one. The consequentialist taking the last alternative might claim that different calculations can be expected to yield different results in close cases, since measurement is not yet precise.[20] One cannot argue with this, since measurement is impossible.

IV

As I said in section one, one reason consequentialism is plausible is that measuring, counting, and weighing do have a place in practical reasoning. We do use such operations to decide what to do. "Greater good," "proportionate reason," and like expressions can be used meaningfully. But if they are, the context is one of two types. In one, a practical but nonmoral judgment is made. One calculates, not to determine what is right, but to decide what is better in some nonmoral sense. In the other type of context, one does reflect to determine which alternative is morally right, but one does not measure, count, and weigh the amount of premoral good promised by each alternative. Rather, one reflects within a framework of moral assumptions, which determine the measure of each of the relevant goods.

My purpose in this section is limited. I do not try to prove consequentialism meaningless by showing that no possible use of such expressions as "greater good" will serve its purpose. I assume that the argument in the preceding section has settled the question of the meaningfulness of consequentialism.

However, a refuted position can still keep some plausibility. My purpose here is to disperse such residual plausibility. Otherwise, a reader attached to consequentialism is likely to think that there *must* be some way around the argument against it. Therefore, I take up legitimate uses of expressions such as "greater good" and "proportionate reason" only to clarify the muddle between the consequentialist's attempted use of such expressions and their legitimate uses in other contexts.

I first consider uses of "greater good" and similar expressions in contexts in which calculation leads to a practical, nonmoral judgment.

Sometimes one can compare the extent to which one or more basic goods would be participated in particular instances, and see that the participation of the good by one alternative includes all that the other includes and more. (For simplicity I omit cases with more than two possibilities.) In such cases, a practical judgment in favor of the more extensive participation is made, provided that no other factor enters consideration. But this practical judgment is not a moral judgment. One has no choice.

For example, if one is aware of two possible courses of action between which one sees no difference except that the one protects and promotes a basic human good in a single instance while the other does this and also promotes or protects the same or another good in another instance, one necessarily prefers the second course of action to the first. One might say that one "chooses" the second course of action, but such choices are not proper to human persons. A computer can make them.

In cases of this sort, one is "killing two birds with one stone." One can choose not to kill two birds with one stone, but only if some other factor comes into play. A hunter might wish to practice conservation. If one is a malicious egoist, one can choose an act which benefits only oneself rather than an act which similarly benefits oneself and also benefits others, but only because one's malice leads one to see denying a good to others as an additional good for oneself.

Again, life is a greater good than health, since life includes health, and health is a greater good than merely avoiding the pain which is caused by a disease. Thus, if no other factor comes into play, one necessarily prefers a remedy which cures a disease and removes pain to a remedy which only removes pain, and one prefers life as a cripple to death. One who chooses death in preference to life as an invalid is considering some other factor— for example, that death will end sadness. In this case, the good of avoiding the disvalue is not part of life and health. Thus there are incommensurable goods, and one can choose.

The famous case of the careening trolley car provides another example. One is steering a trolley down a steep hill, notices that the brakes have failed, knows there is a switch at the bottom of the hill which will allow one to steer onto either of two tracks, and observes a few people on one track and a large crowd of people on the other. If no other factor comes into play, the larger group includes all the instances of good—several human lives—included in the smaller and more. One has no choice but to steer away from the larger group. But if one sees only strangers in the larger group and members of one's own family in the smaller, then friendship also is involved. The goods are incommensurable. If one has time to deliberate, one can choose.

What about cases in which one might be tempted to kill one person to save two or more? Sometimes, what is involved is indirect killing, as in the example of the trolley car, in which steering *away from* the larger group is causally but not morally equivalent to steering *toward* the smaller. I find it hard to think of any clear example in which the killing of one or of a few *certainly* will save the lives of two or of many where the killing and the saving occur in distinct actions related to each other as means to end. Usually, the choice of certain death renders the life-saving only *probable*. If there are cases in which one has the choice of killing one person or some persons for the ulterior purpose of saving two or more, the life or lives one might choose to sacrifice are *not* counted among those to be saved, even if one notes no objective difference except in number between the two groups. For to choose to use some for the benefit of others reduces those who are used to the status of mere means. One has a choice precisely because one can regard those who would be sacrificed as sharing in a priceless dignity which one should not subordinate to any purpose extrinsic to themselves.

In politics, there is another use of "greatest good" which is meaningful but useless to the consequentialist. One can say that a public official is pursuing the greatest happiness of the people if he tries to find out what they want and to give it to them.

However, "the greatest happiness of the most people" as defined by a census of their desires does not settle what is morally right. I criticized the desire theory of value in section two. The majority often is unhappy with decisions upholding minority rights; demagogic politicians often sacrifice minority rights to majority prejudices. But the social covenant expressed in the society's constitution can demand that the happiness of the majority yield to justice for the minority.

Bentham's reflections on morality began from his attempt to rationalize law. He imported a meaning into "the greatest happiness" formula quite different from that later imported into it by social Darwinism. Twentieth-century socioeconomic liberalism is Bentham's heritage, while individualistic conservatism owes much to social Darwinism. Neither policy has shown itself unequivocally better than the other; each uses standards by which it excels to compare itself with the other. Thus, political debate between socioeconomic liberals and conservatives is endless, yet questions about human goods remain unresolved. The moral questions cannot even be stated in the consequentialist language in which political debate usually goes on.[21]

"Proportionate reason" can refer to an acceptable level of probability that a certain means will secure a desired end. The proportion is of means to end; the suitability of the means is measured by the end. If one is folding parachutes, one has reason to be fussy to an extent that would be disproportionate if one were folding linens. Premoral goods are not weighed against one another here. If the judgment has some moral force, that is only because moral evaluations of risking life and risking unsightly wrinkles in one's linens are presupposed.

Again, one weighs evidence to arrive at a judgment. One proportions one's confidence in the judgment to the weight of the evidence. But even if the conclusion concerns a moral issue, the proportionate reason for accepting it with a certain degree of confidence need have nothing to do with morality. One has weighed evidence, not goods. Perhaps the values are considered afterwards, the facts are measured.

"Greater good" has a legitimate place in technical judgments. If one has a well-defined objective and knows the cost of various ways of achieving it, one can rate a certain means best. "Best" here means most efficient. Cost-benefit analysis yields judgments of this sort. There is nothing wrong with efficiency; it is wrong to be wasteful. But whether it is right to do what is efficient depends upon the moral acceptability both of one's end and of the means one uses.[22]

For example, if one's well-defined objective is the elimination of Jews, one can proceed efficiently. Waste of scarce resources would be wrong. There is a best way of achieving one's objective. But "best" here refers to technical value, not to moral value.

One's goal can be acceptable and one's means efficient, yet the means morally questionable. The goal of freeing one's people from a colonial exploiter can be morally right and the use of terrorism can be efficient. Yet Gandhi regarded guerilla warfare as immoral; he stressed nonviolence precisely because "impure means" would contaminate the justice for which he was striving.

In his discussion of the morality of killing in self-defense, Thomas Aquinas uses "proportionate" in another sense. He holds that one may repel an unprovoked attack with proportionate force.[23] One might say there is a "proportionate reason" for using such force.

But "proportionate reason" in this context does not imply commensuration of goods leading to moral judgment. The proportion is between the force used and the purpose of self-defense, which Thomas considers justifiable on other grounds. One need measure only degrees of damage to the attacker. Killing is more damaging than wounding, wounding than stunning, and so forth. As I explained early in this section, one can make such judgments without trying to measure the incommensurable. Thus one can see which force is proportionate by seeing which of those likely to be effective also is likely to be least damaging. A man unjustly defending himself against a provoked attack also can choose proportionate or disproportionate means.

This is a good place to begin considering uses of expressions such as "proportionate reason" in reasoning which does lead to moral judgment. Although these uses point to a moral justification of one alternative, they must not be confused with consequentialism, for in each case moral presuppositions contribute meaning to the expressions which imply comparison of goods. Consequentialism requires that premoral goods be commensurated.

It is reasonable enough to suppose that one does a morally evil act if one chooses as a means an act which impedes or damages one or more basic human goods and which of itself does not promote or protect any such good. But what about an act which in itself has a good and a bad aspect, an act which does not impede or damage a good for the sake of an *ulterior* good? In this case, the performance of the act itself—considered as a unit indivisible by the agent—impedes or damages some participation of a basic human good. But the very same act promotes or protects a good. Can it be morally right to choose such an act?

Such a choice is not excluded by the general principle that evil may not be done that good might follow therefrom, since in this case the good does not *follow from* the evil. Both are indivisibly joined in one act. A person intent upon the act's good aspect can choose it, not choosing the bad aspect as a means, but only accepting it as an unavoidable side effect. One steers the trolley *away from* the big crowd; it is incidental to one's intent that one steers *toward* the small group of people. In this case the so-called "principle of double effect" applies.

I have written elsewhere about double effect. In received formulations, it includes a requirement that there be a proportionately grave reason for doing an act which has a side effect which it would be wrong to seek as an end or choose as a means. I accept this requirement, and this leads Richard McCormick to say:

> But I agree with Stanley Hauerwas that ultimately Grisez cannot "avoid the kind of consequentialist reasoning that our human sensibilities seem to demand in such (conflict) cases" [note omitted]. For if a good like life is simply incommensurable with other goods, what do we mean by a proportionate reason where death is, in Grisez's terms, indirect? Proportionate to what? If some goods are to be preferred to life itself, then we have compared life with these goods. And if this is proper, then life can be weighed up against other values too, even very basic values.[24]

I admit that if an act has two aspects, one needs a proportionate reason for choosing it. I deny that "proportionate reason" can be specified by measuring life against other nonmoral values, or the goodness of some instances of life against the goodness of other instances of it. How, then, do I answer the question: "Proportionate to what?"

My own view—which I have not stated clearly enough in previous works—would be better expressed by saying one needs a "morally acceptable reason" more than a "proportionate reason." My answer to McCormick is that one must have a morally acceptable reason for doing the good one is doing, considering the evil one is accepting as an unavoidable side effect. But is this not to admit that one measures the good against the evil? Yes and no. One can compare these if one has a moral standard. One cannot measure these against each other and reach any moral judgment if one considers them only as premoral values and disvalues.[25]

In my view, a person considering an act having a twofold aspect and noting that the act is not excluded by the principle that the end does not justify the means, still might think about other moral grounds on which the act under consideration might be forbidden. I distinguish eight modes of responsibility, only the last of which dictates that one does not turn directly against a good. The first seven articulate other necessary conditions for moral judgment (Grisez 1970b, 317-319; Grisez 1974, 107-137).

For example, my second mode of responsibility is a version of the universalizability criterion. A man who is considering putting poison around his garden to control the rabbits which are eating his lettuce ought to ask himself how he would react if he were in his neighbors' shoes. Perhaps the gardener has no children, there are no fences, and children sometimes wander nonmaliciously into the gardener's yard. If he were in his neighbors' place, would he not be concerned enough about the safety of the children to exclude as too dangerous the use of poison to control the rabbits? If an honest answer to this question is that if it were his children and their lettuce, he would not be willing for the sake of rabbit control to endanger the children, then the reason is not morally acceptable—in traditional language, proportionately grave—when it is his lettuce and their children.

It would take too much space to go through all the modes of responsibility, illustrating how each of them can contribute meaning to "morally acceptable reason" or "proportionate reason" (if the latter, misleading expression is to be retained). However, the basic idea of my view of this condition of double effect should be clear from this one example. The good one is doing must be such as to justify the evil one is accepting as a side effect, not in the sense that premoral goods must be commensurable, which is meaningless but in the sense that one's doing and one's accepting must be permissible according to every relevant moral criterion.[26]

Sometimes one is required not to permit a certain evil, though one does not directly do it.

Someone might object that a morally good person sometimes refrains from doing an act with two aspects, not citing any other mode of responsibility, but rather saying something like: "I won't do it. It would result in this good, but considering the harmful side effects, it is just not worth it."

Upright people do talk like this and it sounds consequentialist. But I do not think they mean they have reached a moral conclusion by measuring premoral goods. Rather, they use consequentialist language to express a *moral intuition*. Morally good persons will not do what they feel it would be wrong to do. They might say that they will not act because their conscience "tells" them not to. If one feels it would be wrong to do something and refrains for this reason, one *thereupon* judges that the good one would be doing would not justify the evil one would have to accept. One establishes a proportion between premoral good and evil by one's moral judgment; one's moral judgment is not reached by measuring, counting, and weighing premoral goods.

But if upright persons are expressing a moral intuition, not the conclusion of a calculation, why do they use consequentialist language? There are at least three reasons.

First, the ordinary morally upright person does not carefully segregate—as do moral theorists—the premoral and the moral uses and connotations of evaluative language. One may not even be aware of the distinction which a consequentialist interpretation of one's remarks leads into them.

Second, everyone tends to use language as it is used. As I have explained, calculative language is appropriate in the evaluation of techniques. It also is widely used by consequentialists. Thus even the upright person naturally tends to talk like a consequentialist.

Third, children obviously learn the language of technical activity at an earlier age than they learn the language of morals. Moreover, their initial conception of morals is not of morality in the full sense but of conventional standards of behavior, which I discussed near the end of section three. Knowing how to be a "good child" is itself a technique to be mastered, before moral reflection begins. Thus, technical language sets a pattern for ethical language. This also is true of moral theory. Aristotle, for example, often uses the language of *techné* when discussing *phrónesis*, although he clearly distinguishes them.

Upright persons use their intuition as a negative criterion in cases such as that of the lettuce gardener. Having found no articulate moral objection to what one is considering doing, the upright person can still be warned by conscience not to proceed.[27] This situation is altogether other from one in which a person thinks with some reason that a course of action is immoral, yet appeals to "conscience" to justify it. Thus, "proportionate reason," as it is used in the principle of double effect, ought not to open the way to consequentialist arguments against hitherto accepted moral norms.

Goods intrinsic to human persons and communities can be compared with those which are not. Goods intrinsic to persons take priority. If an animal is sick and its disease is a threat to humans, the animal should be destroyed. This is not to say that creatures other than humans have no intrinsic worth. Rights to property insofar as it is a good extrinsic to persons must yield to rights to a good such as life which is intrinsic to persons. Institutions which are merely instrumental to human goods and practices which are only particular ways of serving human goods should not be vested with the inviolable dignity which belongs to persons.

Consequentialists have been keenly and rightly aware of this point. Their emphasis on it lends credibility to their theory. The Sabbath is made for humankind, not humankind for the Sabbath. My right of ownership to my excess wealth is outweighed by the right of the poor to survive; if their lives are at stake, they need not wait while I prudently plan my philanthropies, although this is my right. But judgments like these cannot be extended to justify the destruction of goods intrinsic to persons, without reducing these goods to the status of mere possessions, and thus implicitly denying the dignity of persons as ends in themselves.

"Greater good" also can be used meaningfully in the context of legal processes. Judgments reached through legal processes should be morally just, and legal processes obviously involve measuring, counting, and weighing. Justice is symbolized by a blindfolded woman with a scale.

However, a legal judgment has moral force only insofar as the legal system has a moral foundation and uses morally justifiable procedures. Conflicting claims and relevant facts, not competing goods, are weighed in the scales of justice. The scales of justice is the whole set of norms and the entire procedure for applying them to the facts and the claims. One must make prelegal judgments as to what norms are just, what procedures fair. These norms and procedures reflect a society's basic commitments; they are only as sound as these commitments are right.

The United States Constitution, for example, expresses a society's basic commitments. The self-constitution of the political community by reference to basic human goods is explicitly stated in the Preamble. In many respects the Constitution is a morally admirable document. But in its initial form it included the choice to compromise the dignity of some human persons—Negro slaves and native Americans—for the good end of obtaining consensus sufficient to launch the new nation.

Obviously, in cases in which legal norms and procedures are adopted for the sake of justice—as they sometimes are—one must have a prelegal way of telling what is just. Whatever can be determined using the scales of justice, these scales are of no use at this stage, for the prelegal problem is how to construct the scales. Once it is constructed, moral norms are built into it. One cannot get any commensuration of goods out of the law which is not built into it by the society's commitments to basic human goods.

Natural law theory is concerned with the prelegal principles which should guide the construction of the scales of justice. The legal positivist, noting that there is no commensurability of goods before the scales of justice are constructed, but defining justice in terms of commensurability, says that there is no justice prior to positive law. The natural law theorist can admit the incommensurability of the goods which ought to be protected by the law, but hold that there are moral norms which should guide the *choices* which must be made in constructing the legal system. Once the system is constructed, it can make goods morally commensurate by applying morally defensible legal norms and procedures to the facts and conflicting claims.

In the light of the foregoing distinction, consequentialism is revealed to be a legalism. The consequentialist takes the way in which legal judgments are made by reference to prelegal, morally specified factors as a model for a method of making moral judgments by reference to premoral goods. I showed in section three why the analogy is unsound.

With its constitutional and other law constructed, decisions by a society on issues of public policy and on particular cases often are expressed in language which sounds consequentialist.

For example, the policy of common law with respect to negligence in some respects sounds consequentialist, but reference to the "reasonable man" clearly is an appeal to moral intuition. My earlier example of the gardener using poison to prevent rabbits from destroying his lettuce while incidentally endangering his neighbors' children reveals the moral considerations which underlie the law of negligence.

An example involving a particular, public act is the following. A legal process is carried out taking a piece of private property for public use. The decision states—in seemingly consequentialist language—that "the public interest outweighs the private interest of the individual concerned." Farmer Jones must give up his land so that an adjacent highway can be straightened, eliminating a dangerous curve. Upon reading the decision, Farmer Jones might well balk. Interviewed while sitting at his lane gate with a shotgun at hand, Farmer Jones might explain: "I have lived on this land all my life. My father homesteaded it. My wife is buried on it. It would tear my heart out to leave it. Don't tell me that some other good—the safety of the drunken drivers who have accidents on that curve—outweighs what you want to do to me."

Farmer Jones is right. The goods are incommensurable. The justification of the public act is not expressed by the language of the decision. The real justification of the public act is that the process by which Farmer Jones is required to give up his land is part of a fair system of living together, a system of mutual commitments to one another and to certain basic human goods. Farmer Jones usually has been satisfied with this system. He cannot reject as unjust a judgment against himself when he has accepted as just similar judgments against his fellow citizens. Farmer Jones might well appreciate the force of this argument. If the judge had been careful to avoid consequentialist language, the sheriff might have been spared having to disarm the old man and carry him bodily off his property.

Like a society, individuals have normative systems *which depend upon* their basic commitments. Having made these commitments, each person has his or her own hierarchy of goods. One's values flow from one's self-constitution.

In previous works I have urged that play and esthetic sensibility are basic human goods along with such other goods as theoretical truth and life itself. Many people disagree. The two former goods seem to them much less important. I think this reaction reflects most people's commitments, not any objective hierarchy of goods. A scholar is likely to think that theoretical truth is more important than play. But a fine musician can well believe that his or her art—which is a form of play—and esthetic sensibility to it are more important than theoretical truth. This reversal of the scholar's priorities is not immoral. If one respects all the goods, one is morally free to commit oneself in a special way to some of them. In fact, one is morally obligated to do so.

Life itself can seem both more important and less noble than the other basic human goods. This view is not unreasonable, but it does not reflect objective commensuration. It reflects, on the one hand, the interest we mortal animals have in our own survival and, on the other, the rather low place human life as such has in most people's commitments. However, if one has devoted many years to promoting and protecting human life as such—for example, by writing and lecturing against abortion, capital punishment, and nuclear warfare—then one acquires a sense of the nobility of "mere" human life.

A Jew or Christian might object that between some basic human goods there is *an objective* hierarchy. Is not the good of religion, which is a harmonious relationship with God, infinitely more important than other basic human goods?

Some Christians have held that the ethical sphere as a whole must give way to the religious. I think this position arises from a confusion between the created, immanent human good of religion—which is neither more nor less absolute than other basic human goods—and the goodness of God Himself. The good of religion is a finite participation in divine goodness, but so are other basic human goods, and the latter are neither reducible to nor commensurable with the good of religion.

However, though there is no objective hierarchy which places religion above other basic human goods, it is reasonable to make one's religious commitment overarch one's whole existence. A commitment to the right sort of religion is an excellent principle by which to integrate one's identity. It gives ground to the highest hopes, yet at the same time allows wide scope to promote and protect other basic human goods.[28]

Christians believe that all other basic human goods take on a new meaning from the existential integration of other goods with the basic Christian commitment. This commitment is to share in the redemptive work of Christ; the pursuit of other basic goods becomes an effort to build up the Body of Christ. Of course, non-christians do not see things in this light, nor should they.

Moreover, Christians should not confuse the importance religion has for them—because of their God-given, but freely accepted, faith and hope—with the importance which religion has as one basic human good among others. If these are confused, one is on a short road to religious fanaticism.

Aristotle's ethics involves a confusion between the status of theoretical truth as one fundamental human good among others and the status of this good as the chief purpose of the philosophic life. His confusion is facilitated by the ambiguity of "reason," which both points to a basic human good and to a species-specific nonmoral human function without the exercise of which human behavior lacks moral significance. But, in addition to the difficulties I mentioned in section two, Aristotle slighted play and esthetic experience, which are also specific to human persons. Human bodily life itself and human bodily processes are not generically animal. Antecedent to any judgment or choice of ours, they are human, personal, one's own. Those who deny this fall into dualism.[29]

Aristotle himself is not a consequentialist, at least not a consistent one. He holds that the judgment of the person of practical wisdom (*phrónesis*) is the standard for concrete moral judgments. Such a person is uniquely fitted to tell what is more and less important. But one does not do it by measuring, counting, and weighing premoral goods. One does it by insight. The ability of the good person to make accurate moral appraisals *depends upon* the fact that he or she has a virtuous character. Technical insight (*techné*), by contrast, is separable from good character, and hence can be used wrongfully.

Aristotle's persons of practical wisdom have right desire. Their hearts are fixed upon every human's true end. Their entire character and personality is integrated with this sound orientation. Their judgment as to what ought to be done is an expression of the good with which they have fully identified themselves. This judgment *cannot* be mistaken. Thomas Aquinas developed Aristotle's teaching on practical wisdom and the manner in which a good person judges by it.[30]

Aristotle thought that the good person can settle concrete moral issues by the insight of practical wisdom. Frequently in recent years, common moral opinion has been used to justify the revision of hitherto accepted moral norms. Some moral theologians appeal from traditional Christian moral beliefs to the *sensus fidelium*. This appeal has the defects of any form of intuitionism used as a principle in moral theory. Intuitions differ and the intuitionist is reduced to calling those who disagree "morally blind." Similarly, the *sensus fidelium*—as distinct from the *sensus fidei*—is divided. Using widespread opinion as a criterion implies that those who disagree with the revisionist's proposals are to be reckoned among the *infideles*.

I have argued in this section that expressions such as "greater good" and "proportionate reason" have a number of legitimate uses but that none of these uses implies the possibility of commensurating goods as consequentialism requires. It has not been my purpose in this section to show consequentialism meaningless, but only to disperse any residual plausibility it might have retained after the argument of section three.

V

Consequentialism in moral theory must be distinguished from consequentialism in deliberation leading to moral choice. I have considered the former. Now I turn to the latter. In doing so, I assume that consequentialism as a theory is meaningless and that its plausibility has been dispersed. Therefore, the objections a theorist who accepts consequentialism would make against what I am about to say will be ignored. In ignoring them, I beg no question. The moves a theorist makes in defending a position are pointless when there is no position to defend.

Since consequentialist theory is meaningless, what can consequentialist moral reasoning possibly be?

As I explained in the preceding section, it is not the calculation one does in technical reasoning. Nor is it the weighing and balancing good persons do intuitively as they judge by their personal hierarchy of values. Nor is it the social analogue of such personal intuition: the weighing of facts and claims by a just legal process.

Consequentialist moral reasoning occurs in situations such as the following. A possible course of action seems attractive; one is inclined to choose it. But a norm which one has hitherto accepted forbids the choice. One feels existential stress. One would not feel such stress if the course of action to which one is attracted did not at least seem likely to lead to some partial aspect of some basic human good. At the same time, one would not be inclined to act contrary to a norm if one had wholly identified oneself with the good which—if the norm is a sound one—the forbidden choice will somehow violate. In this situation, one's reasoning can take either of two directions. One can say to oneself: "This attractive course of action would not be forbidden were it not against a good of which I am losing sight." One can try to see what this good might be. One can try to dwell upon it *as a good* to offset the temptation to violate it.

But one can also say to oneself: "Perhaps my inclination is sound, but the moral requirement which forbids me to satisfy it is not. Let me see which is right." So far, so good. Hitherto accepted moral norms can be false. But one can proceed either impartially or with bias.

To proceed impartially, one must ask oneself the questions another person, as clever as oneself would ask, if he or she did not wish one to choose the course of action to which one is inclined. In this way, one attends to the goods involved and the relevant modes of responsibility. One who is impartial often seeks moral advice from others who are chosen not for their sympathy with one's inclinations but for their insight into and commitment to a worldview which one believes to be true.

But if one proceeds with bias, one does not search out the goods and modes of responsibility. Instead, one considers the act to which one is inclined and its significant alternatives from a single point of view. "Significant alternatives" often reduces to a single live option: not doing as one wishes. The single point of view is that of the good which makes attractive the course of action to which one is tempted. This good defines the situation and sets a standard by which other goods involved in it are measured.

Proceeding with bias, one does not ask the questions which would be raised by someone who disapproved of the course of action to which one is tempted. If moral advice is sought, the advisor is chosen for the support one needs to follow one's inclination. Such advisors are not spokespersons for a worldview one believes to be true; they are spokespersons for one's wishes. On this basis, many people today look for a permissive, reassuring confessor or psychological counselor. Such a counselor helps one to deal with guilt feelings.

Just as consequentialist theory is meaningless, consequentialist moral reasoning is incoherent. Considering a course of action to which one is tempted, one seeks to justify *freely choosing* this course of action by adopting a viewpoint from which one will seem to have *no choice* but to take this course of action. One makes definitive the good on which one has set one's heart. But one avoids, if possible, awareness of one's bias. One wishes to feel compelled by objective demands *of the situation*, not to feel oneself arbitrarily pricing goods to fit one's inclination. Careful reflection can deliver the required result by a seemingly objective calculation. The more rational the process appears at the moment it produces the right answer, the better it is.

Consequentialist moral reasoning is a method of rationalization. Still, the conclusions reached by such rationalization can be true. An illicit rational process sometimes accidentally produces true conclusions. It can happen that the norm set aside by one who proceeds with bias does not express a true requirement of human goodness; the action chosen happens to be the very one a good person with clear moral insight would have chosen. The truth of such a conclusion seems to vindicate the consequentialist procedure.

Consequentialist moral reasoning gains additional plausibility from the use of consequentialist language to express personal or public judgments reached by legitimate moral intuition or sound legal procedures. In section four I gave examples of this use of consequentialist language and reasons why this unsuitable language is used to express sound moral judgments.

If consequentialist moral reasoning is either mere rationalization or an inept way of articulating sound moral judgments, still consequentialist theory need not be mere reflective justification of rationalization and of bad rhetoric. Of course, it is possible that proponents of consequentialist theory can be rationalizing. We moralists are not immune from self-deception. At least I see no reason why philosophers and theologians as a group should be expected to be any more or less upright than doctors, lawyers, merchants, or chiefs of state. And, naturally, if one whose profession is the unfolding of moral theory happens to be immoral, one is likely to construct extraordinarily sophisticated rationalizations which will embrace all of one's practical and theoretical reflection in a single outlook.

Still, honest moral theorists adopt consequentialism for the reasons which render it plausible—several of which have been summarized in previous sections.

Since consequentialist moral reasoning is a method of rationalization, certain problems with consequentialist theory become clearer.[31]

First, how can the *good* signified by "greatest net good" (and similar expressions) be defined? (I considered this problem in section two.)

Second, how does one decide which alternatives must be examined in a consequentialist survey of possibilities? At any given moment, one not only can do or not do a particular act, one also can do that act in many ways, and one can do anything else within one's power.

Third, where can one draw the line in the investigation of consequences? The consequences of any act go on forever. Predictable consequences are limited, but extend very far. How can so extensive a set of consequences be taken into account, especially when the probability of each consequence can seldom be expressed numerically?

Fourth, how can one decide whose welfare is to be considered? Egoism is seldom defended, but the question, "Why should I be moral?" which is taken to mean, "Why shouldn't I be an egoist?" continues to plague consequentialists. Nor is egoism the only alternative to universalism, as most consequentialists assume. One can propose that one's country or one's family should come first. If a utilitarian says that one should consider every person impartially, the question remains: Who is included in "every person?"

These four problem areas have been used against consequentialism by its opponents. Those who have seriously tried to explicate and defend consequentialism have been troubled by them. One who uses consequentialist moral reasoning as a method of rationalization will not be troubled by these problems. I do not say "need not be troubled," but "will not be troubled." Why not?

Because, in the first place, the *good* is specified in each situation by the good of the alternative to which one is inclined. Accepting one good as the standard by which all else in a situation will be measured is the first step in rationalizing.

Moreover, in the second place, the good to which one is inclined defines a very small set of possibilities as live options. If one is tempted to do away with one's senile grandfather to put the old man out of his misery, one does not consider most of the alternative actions one might do—for example, to take him for a walk, to share a bottle of wine with him, and so on. One considers killing and not killing the old man, and perhaps considers a few alternatives such as putting him in a public institution or abandoning him at an airport.

Then too, in the third place, the consequences to be considered are limited by the good one has chosen as a standard. Consequences favorable to one's purpose are considered; some unfavorable ones which cannot be ignored also will be noticed. If one's first view does not make one feel that one has no choice but to do as one wishes, then one can look for further consequences of the right sort until one reaches a satisfactory view of the situation.

For example, if one wishes to justify the use of terrorism in a guerilla war, one notes the deterrent effect of terrorism on the enemy. One does not think of the effects upon oneself and one's own society of adopting terrorism as a policy.

Finally, in the fourth place, one would not be inclined to do the act to which one is tempted if it did not seem likely to benefit some definite persons. Thus the magic circle is drawn. It need not be drawn about oneself alone; even immoral persons need not be gross egoists. Anyone with whom one identifies can be included in one's magic circle. So it can include one's pets, members of any group important to one's identity, persons for whom one feels sympathy, even a non-living feature of the natural world with which one enjoys communing. Those in the helping professions such as physicians and clergymen, are tempted to draw a circle to include the clients who present themselves for help and to exclude other parties who are absent and unable to stir one's sympathy. The magic circle can include humanity—humankind as a whole—safely distant if not abstractly universal. At the same time, living human individuals whom one is willing to damage or destroy can be excluded from one's magic circle. They can be said delicately to have no significant potential for personal existence or less delicately to be mere gooks or mere animals or mere vegetables or mere blobs of protoplasm or mere pieces of fetal matter.

The preceding explanation of how consequentialist moral reasoning works, although consequentialist theory is meaningless, also clarifies the use of "situation" by some moralists. Actually, situations are not predefined. Situations relevant to moral choice are not like clearly distinguished scenes in a play; they are rather like scenes in a continuous landscape from which one composes a photograph. But the situation ethicist talks as if situations were predefined and as if such situations could specify the morally right action.

Consequentialist rationalization does define situations. Consequentialist moral reasoning avoids the difficulties of determining goods, alternatives, consequences, and beneficiaries precisely by taking what one wishes to do as a defining principle for the situation. Once all relevant factors are specified, there is a situation, and it makes sense to say: "Do what love demands *in this situation*."

Of course, it is wise not to define "love." To define anything is to limit one's future freedom to do as one pleases. One can counterfeit moral idealism by demanding that love be selfless. Since no intelligent, sane person is a gross egoist, one can always act out of unselfish love while immorally fulfilling oneself in the goods one brings about in those with whom one is identified. "I did it for my country." "I did it for humanitarian reasons." "I did it to preserve the balance of nature." "I did it for the child's own good. No unwanted child should ever be born." In view of considerations such as these, I do run from consequentialist calculus, as Richard McCormick says I do (McCormick see above 188). I am indeed reluctant to admit proportionate reason in McCormick's primary sense into the justification of moral judgments. But I think my attitude is not one of nervous fear, as he suggests. Rather, it is an attitude of reasonable terror. For, as I see it, consequentialism is not merely a meaningless theory, it also is a pernicious method of rationalization. No matter how personally upright proponents of theoretical consequentialism happen to be, the theory encourages the practice.

If immorality were a mere breaking of a taboo, there would be little reason for concern about the immorality to which consequentialism lends aid and comfort. But authentic morality—which is less a theory than a style exhibited in moral heroes such as Socrates, Jesus, Thomas More, and Joan of Arc—is not mere conformity to a set of rules. Moral goodness is necessary for the full being of human persons as individuals and in communities.

Consequentialism regards the moral agent as a producer of goods. Moral action and moral rules are means to ends. Authentic morality manifests the moral agent and the moral community as a self-creating process. Moral action by individuals and groups is participation in goods which fulfill constantly unfolding human possibilities. Thus moral actions and moral norms are constitutive of persons and communities. Moral norms are the plan of the good life and are to be built into it.[32]

Since consequentialism regards moral action as production, it must deal with the problem of allocation. Goods produced must be distributed to those who will possess them. Thus consequentialism fosters the attitude of *having*. Authentic morality manifests goods in which moral agents participate as constitutive principles of what humans are and what they can be. Individuals and communities can be committed to goods which are greater than each individual, greater than the whole group. The proper attitude is one of *being*, not one of *having* (Marcel 1965, 154-174). Consequentialism begins with the question, "What do I want?" or "What do we want?" Authentic morality begins with the question, "What shall I be?" and "What shall we be?"

Consequentialism is compatible with the view that nature has no meaning or value prior to human interests and desires. Yet consequentialism demands that human needs, wants, whims, and wishes determine what is meaningful and valuable prior to personal reflection and choice. Reason is a slave of the passions. Human moral agency is an inefficient way of doing for humans what instinct does for other animals: shape behavior toward the satisfaction of all one's specific desires to the extent that heredity and environment permit such satisfaction (Kant 1959, 12).

For authentic morality, basic human goods not only perfect a person but are entrusted to each person. Humans by nature are inclined to these goods, but human persons must unfold them creatively. What truth, friendship, play, or religion is to be depends in part upon human creativity. Commitment to basic human goods initiates a process by which something of the boundless plenitude reflected by these outlines of human possibility is introduced by human creative effort into the day-to-day lives of human persons, as individuals and in communities.

The radical existentialism of Nietzsche and others can be seen as a reaction—excessive but intelligible—against the narrowness of consequentialism, which is found in many forms of pagan philosophy, Christian apologetics, and modern social and political ideology. Nietzsche is right in thinking that persons who are not participating in their own creation are less godlike than human persons ought to be. Radical existentialism is right in holding that there should be a dialectic of human existence. It is wrong in rejecting the indispensable presuppositions of such a dialectic: the basic human goods and the modes of responsibility which arise from the truth of our being as creatures, as persons and social beings, and as bodily entities.

Consequentialism promotes enthusiasm for plans and projects, but it stifles profound dynamism. Consequentialist rationalizations begin only after the goods which are assumed to be ends are posited and conceded. Thinking about what should be accepted as an end is divorced from inquiry into the means. If the goals are settled, one can plan efficiently. If something gets in the way of carrying out the program, it is merely an obstacle to success. Technical thought systematically excludes reexamination of ends.

The Japanese wish to surrender *conditionally*. That will never do; drop the bombs. How can you do such a horrible thing? It will save lives, not only of American boys, but also of Japanese boys, who will die if the invasion has to be carried out. *But why should the invasion be carried out?* The Japanese must be forced to surrender unconditionally. Why not blockade the Japanese home islands? The war might drag on for years. So what? They will never surrender unconditionally.

Technical reflection invents more and more horrible ways of dealing with interfering factors. If one cannot collectivize the Ukraine without killing several million kulaks, the kulaks are liquidated. If one cannot keep South Vietnam out of communist hands without carrying on an immoral war, one continues the war.[33] If one cannot maintain a strategic balance of terror without being willing to kill millions of people, one commits oneself to the horror of nuclear extermination. One hopes that the mass murder to which one is committed never will be necessary, but this velleity and the consequentialist calculus which accompanies it does not alter the fact: America as a nation and the Soviet Union as a nation, most of their leaders, and many of their people *already have committed* nuclear extermination in their hearts, even if the buttons never are pressed.[34]

Sound moral reflection involves a constant dialectic between one's fundamental commitments to basic human goods and possible ways of participating in them. The consideration of possibilities in the light of the transcendence of the goods to any particular participation of them moderates enthusiasm and blocks fanaticism. Meditation on the goods which are the content of one's commitments leads to deeper commitment and arouses the creativity necessary to find new ways to protect and promote these goods. Love finds a way, and the way love finds respects all the basic human goods and opens upon as yet unimaginable unfoldings of them.

Consequentialism, as a method by which anything can be rationalized, is laxist. But in theory it is rigorist. According to the most plausible forms of consequentialism, there is only one right act in any situation: the act which is likely to yield the greatest net good. There is no room for a hero, for everyone either does what is best or does what is wrong. A theory as rigorist as this promotes the rationalization that being upright must be distinguished from being morally perfect; one is upright if one is only as immoral as most people (Williams and Smart 1973, 48, 128).

According to consequentialism, all of one's obligations are *defined* by premoral goods and objective states of affairs. One cannot freely assume a moral obligation.[35] In lives of authentic morality, few definite moral obligations fall upon persons willy nilly. The most important of these are negative: not to turn directly against basic human goods. Most affirmative moral obligations arise from one's own commitments. By these commitments, one constitutes oneself and enters into covenants with others. Since one makes promises, one must keep them. Since one is a philosopher, one must think a problem through when one is challenged to do so. Since one is engaging in sexual intercourse, one must want the child one might conceive. Such are the responsibilities of freedom.[36] In many cases, several alternatives are morally acceptable, some morally better than others. One can choose what is best when an alternative also would be blameless.

An ethics whose basic norms are negative might seem too minimalistic and legalistic. But this objection ignores the beauty of a sound ethics. "Never turn directly against basic human goods" says what "Respect the dignity of every person" says and more. A sound ethics demands the indispensable foundation for a creative moral life. The good which can be is more important than the evil which should be avoided; there was no evil in the nothingness out of which the world was made. To want an ethics composed entirely of affirmative norms is either to want to be told precisely what to do, or it is to want to be free to create oneself from nothing in a vacuum and with the stipulation that "create oneself" shall remain undefined until the process is completed.

If any person or community could possibly live according to consequentialism, such a person or community would have no stable identity. If there were a fixed human nature, a stable identity could arise from that, just as the "personality" of one's dog arises naturally. But human nature is not fixed in that way. It is not amorphous as subjectivists, relativists, and historicists suppose, but it is stable only to the extent it must be to allow men and women to participate in their own creation.

Thus, consequentialism means that what one must be willing to do and to be, to produce today's greatest net good, can require one to be and to do something totally different tomorrow. No commitment can be permanent, no covenant indissoluble. A person or community which accepts consequentialism ought in all consistency to avoid any firm self-definition. The consequentialist ideal is that the person be a utensil, an all-purpose tool, available to be to do whatever is necessary to bring about the "greater good." One is at the mercy of evil men, for one must always be ready to do what is necessary to bring about the least evil in situations they create.[37] Consequentialists will be what their enemies make them be: obstructers of justice, droppers of napalm, targeters of hydrogen bombs.

A sound ethics should help one to establish one's self-identity. It should encourage one to make commitments and to form indissoluble covenants. In this way it should provide the foundation for faithfulness and open up a possibility of magnificent creativity. A sound ethics leaves room for persons and communities to unfold themselves with continuity, to act with authenticity, to defend their own integrity.

Humans seem to sense that all the goods they can realize in particular instances can never satisfy the yearning of their hearts. Consequentialism, if it were meaningful and consistent, would rule out a religious faith which promises that this yearning can be fulfilled by the more than human love of God and for God, poured forth in human hearts by the Holy Spirit. A sound ethics at least will hold open the possibility that if human persons are called to share as adopted members of God's family in His very life, they shall be free to answer the call, no matter what the consequences.[38]

Notes

[1] I have attempted to articulate an ethical theory along these lines in several previous works: "The First Principle of Practical Reason: A Commentary on the *Summa Theologiae*, Question 94, Article 2," *Natural Law Forum*, 10 (1965): 168-201; *Contraception and the Natural Law* (Milwaukee: Bruce Publishing Co., 1964), 46-75; *Abortion: The Myths, the Realities, and the Arguments* (New York and Cleveland: Corpus Books, 1970), 267-346; "Toward a Consistent Natural-Law Ethics of Killing," *American Journal of Jurisprudence and Legal Philosophy*, 15 (1970): 64-96; with Russell Shaw, *Beyond the New Morality: The Responsibilities of Freedom* (Notre Dame and London: University of Notre Dame Press, 1974); "Suicide and Euthanasia," in Dennis J. Horan and David Mall, eds., *Death, Dying, and Euthanasia* (Washington, D.C.: University Publications of America, 1977), 742-789.

[2] Cf. John Rawls, *A Theory of Justice* (Cambridge, Mass.: Belknap Press of Harvard University Press, 1971), pp. 407-446, and the works Rawls cites on life plans, for ideas close to my notion of self-constitution. My view is nearest to those of Josiah Royce and Charles Fried. See the latter's *Anatomy of Values* (Cambridge, Mass.: Harvard University Press, 1970), pp. 7-101.

[3] See David Lyons, *Forms and Limits of Utilitarianism* (Oxford: Clarendon Press, 1965), for arguments showing that many seemingly restricted consequentialist theories are reducible to direct— "act"—consequentialism. J.J.C. Smart and Bernard Williams, a leading proponent and a leading opponent of consequentialism, argue that direct consequentialism is the only plausible form of it: *Utilitarianism: for and against* (Cambridge: Cambridge University Press, 1973), 9-12, 81, and 118-135.

[4] Richard A. McCormick, S.J., *Ambiguity in Moral Choice: The 1973 Pere Marquette Theology Lecture* (Milwaukee: Marquette University Press, 1974) see above 200. Readers will note that in a few places in the present article I single out McCormick's views for criticism. The reason is not that I have any special quarrel with McCormick, but that this article was written as a contribution to a volume edited by Paul Ramsey and Richard McCormick, taking the cited lecture of the latter as its point of departure. When the edited volume was not published as hoped, I revised my contribution for publication here, but have not eliminated all vestiges of the context for which it was originally designed.

[5] Bentham papers, University College, London, box 14, folder 1, no date, sheet 3, section 3. I am indebted to John M. Finnis, University College, Oxford, for transcribing material from this folder.

[6] A useful introduction to the ambiguities of Aristotle's view is W. F. R. Hardie, *Aristotle's Ethical Theory* (Oxford: Clarendon Press, 1968), 317-357; see also Whitney J. Oates, *Aristotle and the Problem of Value* (Princeton, N.J.: Princeton University Press, 1963).

[7] See my "Man, the Natural End of," *The New Catholic Encyclopedia*, vol. 9, pp. 132-138; *Beyond the New Morality*, pp. 27-30. Vatican Council II considerably moderated otherworldliness in its *Pastoral Constitution on the Church in the Modern World*, part 1, ch. 3.

[8] Lionel Robbins, *The Economic Problem in Peace and War: Some Reflections on Objectives and Mechanisms* (London: Macmillan & Co., 1957), 49-50. Cf. Henry Fairlie, *The Kennedy Promise: The Politics of Expectations* (New York: Dell

Publishing Co., 1974), 93-94, where Robbin's point is applied to the politics of the Kennedy administration. Fairlie's book makes clear what consequentialism in politics means.

[9] An implausibility of Bentham's theory dealt with by Mill in a way which makes the utilitarian criterion incoherent; see Anthony Quinton, *Utilitarian Ethics* (London: Macmillian, 1973), 39-47.

[10] See a number of works on this point, John Maynard Keynes, *Essays in Persuasion* (New York: Harcourt, Brace and Co., 1932), 365-373; John Kenneth Galbraith, *The Affluent Society* (Boston: Houghton, Mifflin Co., 1958), 152-162; James S. Dusenberry, *Income, Savings, and the Theory of Consumer Behavior* (Cambridge, Mass.: Harvard University Press, 1949), 28; see also David Braybrooke, "Scepticism of Wants and Certain Subversive Effects of Corporations on American Values," in Sidney Hook, ed. *Human Needs and Economic Policy: A Symposium* (New York: New York University Press, 1967), 224-239.

[11] A recent treatment is Robinson A. Grover, "The Ranking Assumption," *Theory and Decision*, 4 (1974): 277-299.

[12] Richard B. Brandt *begins* from such examples in his "Interpersonal Comparison of Utility," a paper presented at the meeting of the American Philosophical Association, Western Division, Spring, 1971. (Professor Brandt kindly supplied a copy of this paper and a section from a draft of a forth-coming book in which he develops an enjoyment approach.) Brandt states that he would want to define "utility" or "welfare" only in terms of criticized desires; in materials I have seen, however, he does not show how to criticize desires while avoiding moral assumptions in a way which would yield a plausible theory. It is important to note that Brandt wishes to include only desires for intrinsic goods which one could enjoy for their own sake; see his "Personal Values and the Justification of Institutions." in Hook. ed., *op. cit.*, pp. 22-40.

[13] Bentham papers, University College, London, transcribed in Élie Halévy, *La Formation du Radicalisme Philosophique*, vol. 1, *La Jeunnesse de Bentham* (Paris: Felix Alcan, 1901), 412-414.

[14] This leap of faith is still made. See Garrett Hardin, "The Tragedy of the Commons," *Science*, 162, (1968): 1244: "Comparing one good with another is, we usually say, impossible because goods are incommensurable. Incommensurables cannot be compared. Theoretically this may be true; but in real life incommensurables *are* commensurable."

[15] Brock, *op. cit.*, 245, says it is "relatively noncontroversial that it is possible to determine" the order of preference of a single person; he proceeds immediately to the attempts which have been made to combine different persons' orders of preference. If the preferences in question were actual choices, Brock might be right, but the desire-theorist is not concerned with choices, but with desires, which are *dispositions* for choices. The ambiguity of "preference" conceals the fact that desires have nothing like the determinacy which is assumed by consequentialists who have wrestled with this problem, and whose writings Brock reviews (245-249).

[16] It is well known that majority voting can lead to intransitive group preferences—see S. K. Nath, *A Reappraisal of Welfare Economics* (London: Routledge & Kegan Paul, 1969), 135; Herman Kahn, *On Thermonuclear War*, 2nd ed. (Princeton, N.J.: Princeton University Press, 1961), 119-123. What is ignored is that although the analogy is not sound in other respects, in respect to the present difficulty, an individual's underlying desires are to his or her choices as the votes

of members of a society are to the common decision. For ethics, choices cannot be accepted as brute facts; they are justified by reasons which refer to the goods which would satisfy one's desires. In any choice situation, the desires are many and to some extent conflicting; the perplexity which requires choice arises precisely because the goods which arouse these desires are not already integrated into a single, harmonious set.

[17] E. J. Mishan, *Cost-Benefit Analysis: An Introduction* (New York and Washington: Praeger Publishers, 1971), makes clear both the legitimacy and the limitations of this technique. He points out that ethics must come into play to determine which external effects are to be considered (108), that the inevitable death of a particular person or persons normally cannot be finitely priced (161), and that welfare economics as a whole and cost-benefit analysis in particular has a social basis which presupposes ethical premises (307-321). Mishan also points out that while "there is always a strong temptation for the economist, as for other specialists, to come up with firm quantitative results. . .the economist should resist this temptation" (175). Of economic activities there are spillovers which elude the calculus: "After measuring all that can be measured with honesty, he can provide a physical description of the spillovers and some idea of their significance" (*ibid.*). Paul L. Joskow, "Approving Nuclear Power Plants Scientific Decision Making or Administrative Charade?" *Bell Journal of Economics and Management Science*, 5 (1974):320-332 points to an abuse of the technique to provide pseudo objectivity for decisions as to whether the calculable advantages of nuclear power plants justify the incalculable risks of disaster associated with them. These difficulties arise within the economic sphere itself; if one considers goods such as personal integrity and faithfulness, one finds problems which elude even Mishan's good advice.

[18] Plato, *Euthyphro*, 7 c-d; cf. Philo, *De Somniis* ii, 29, 193, who quotes with approval an earlier Jewish writer saying that "the plant of folly is in Sodom, for Sodom means blinding or making barren, since folly is blind and unproductive of excellence, and through its persuasions some have thought good to measure and weigh and count everything by the standard of themselves, for Gomorrah by interpretation is 'measure.' But Moses held that God, and not the human mind, is the measure and weighing scale and numbering of all things." The last sentence contains an obvious allusion to the famous dictum of the early consequentialist, Protagoras: "Man is the measure of all things."

[19] For an attempt to establish this position, see Joseph M. Boyle, Jr., Germain Grisez, and Olaf Tollefsen, *Free Choice: A Self-Referential Argument* (Notre Dame and London: University of Notre Dame Press, 1976). If human persons can make free choices, and if consequentialism is incompatible with the *phenomena* of choice—as I am arguing here—then consequentialism is *a fortiori* excluded by any position which affirms the reality of free choice. Among the positions affirming the *reality* of free choices are most forms of Jewish and Christian theology, for the mainstream of Jewish and Christian faith regards the human ability to respond freely to the divine offer of the Covenant or the Gospel as an essential principle of religion.

[20] A typical example of such consequentialist dialectics is Kai Nielsen, *Ethics without God* (London: Pemberton Publishing Co., 1973), 65-103. Like many consequentialists in the empiricist tradition, Nielsen seems to think he has demonstrated consequentialism if he has shown it not to be meaningless. The

argument I offer here is intended to satisfy the requirements set by such consequentialism for an acceptable refutation of their position.

[21] Sidney S. Alexander, "Human Values and Economists' Values," in Hook, ed., *op. cit.*, pp. 101-116; Nath, *op. cit.*, pp. 138-152; show that all applied economics such as that which figures in political debate presupposes ethical value judgments. Nath argues that these should be made explicit and suggests that questions about whether a wage or an international economic arrangement is just ought not to be regarded as too value laden for disciplined treatment while other issues are erroneously assumed to be value free.

[22] Nath, *op. cit.*, 152-158; Mishan, *op cit.*, 175-178. The contributions of several of the philosophers to the volume edited by Hook make the same point; see the essays of Ernest Nagel, Kurt Baier, Paul Kurtz, and John Ladd.

[23] Thomas Aquinas, *Summa Theologiae*, II-II, q. 64, a. 7, c.; see my "Toward a Consistent Natural-Law Ethics Or Killing," pp. 73-79.

[24] McCormick, *op. cit.*, p. 48; he is commenting on the version of my view of double effect in my *Abortion*, pp. 321-334. The version cited in note 4, above, is somewhat clearer, but still in my present view inadequate.

[25] Bruno Schüller, S.J. "Zur Problematik allgemein verbindlicher ethischer Grundsätze," *Theologie und Philosophie* 45 (1970): 3, claims that all moral norms save those concerned with God and those which are trivially true were grounded by traditional moral theology by a principle of preference for the greater good and the lesser evil. He offers no proof for this universal statement, and I regard it as false. As I shall explain shortly, upright persons often do express sound moral judgments in consequentialist language, and one can find plenty of examples of language which sounds consequentialist in classical moral theology. Also, there is surely some consequentialism in the arguments of these authors. But one must bear in mind that they did not have the benefit of the light which has been thrown on this matter by the elaboration of consequentialism by modern secular humanists, and they did not see consequentialism used in jurisprudence and politics as it has been used in our day. Catholic moralists writing since 1965 and embracing consequentialism do not have the excuse their predecessors had. Moreover, the classical moralists were not specialists in ethical theory and it is odd that anyone should rely on their authority in questions of theory while disregarding it in substantive matters to which they gave almost all of their attention.

[26] Paul Ramsey, "Abortion: A Review Article," *Thomist*, 37 (1973): 174-226 at 226, in a generally perceptive article, seems to have misunderstood my conception of modes of obligation (responsibility) and reduced all but the eighth to duties of charity. In my view, immoral acts which violate other modes of obligation often are rationalized because they happen not to violate the eighth mode: I by no means regard the first seven modes as less binding, although several of them are less specific about what they bind one to. A traditional moralist might object to my explanation of the requirement of proportionate reason by saying I am reducing the fourth requirement of the principle of double effect to the first— that an act not be evil in itself. But I am not, for the first requirement pertains to the object of the act, while I am reducing proportionate reason to what the traditional moralist would have treated under the morality of circumstances.

[27] Socrates' reference to his *daimon* (Plato, *Apology*, 31 c-d) is an example. Why is the *daimon* always only negative? Because the context of articulate moral norms is taken for granted. If upright persons feel they ought to do something when no other moral norm but their feeling of duty is relevant, they simply do it, because

good people have no inclination to omit doing what seems morally right to do. No moral choice is made at this point. In general, very good and very bad people do not struggle with temptation as most of us do.

[28] For a brief sketch of Christian morality integrating commitment to the religious good with other basic human goods, see Ronald Lawler, O.F.M. Cap., Donald W. Wuerl, and Thomas Comerford Lawler, eds., *The Teaching of Christ: A Catholic Catechism for Adults* (Huntington, Ind.: Our Sunday visitor, 1976), 275-354.

[29] Examples of blatant dualism are found in Joseph Fletcher, *Morals and Medicine* (Boston: Beacon Press, 1954), 211 (the passage quoted from Buber should be read in its context); and in documents of the majority of the Commission of Pope Paul VI on Population, Family, and Birthrate. In a working paper, the latter state that human biological fecundity *must be assumed into the human sphere and regulated in it* (see Robert C. Hoyt, ed., *The Birth Control Debate* [Kansas City, Mo.: National Catholic Reporter, 1968], 71), which obviously implies that the sexuality of men and women is not in and of itself human. See my "Dualism and the New Morality," in *Atti del Congresso Internazionale Tommaso d'Aquino nel suo Settimo Centenario*, vol. 5, *L'Agire Morale* (Napoli: *Edizioni Domenicane Italiane*, 1977): 323-330.

[30] What is operative here is something more than what is usually called conscience. See my "Logic of Moral Judgment," *Proceedings of the American Catholic Philosophical Association*, 36 (1962): 67-76, where I treat this matter in Aquinas and cite recent relevant works.

[31] Brock *op. cit.*, reports much recent work in which these problems have been explored.

[32] An excellent article which helps to clarify this point is B. J. Diggs, "Rules and Utilitarianism," in Michael D. Bayles, ed., *Contemporary Utilitarianism* (Garden City, N.Y.: Doubleday & Co., 1968): 203-238. In many works, Lon L. Fuller has articulated a similar point with respect to law; a typical and good example is *The Morality of Law* rev. ed. (New Haven and London: Yale University Press, 1969).

[33] Arthur M. Schlesinger, Jr., *A Thousand Days: John F. Kennedy in the White House* (Boston and Cambridge: Houghton, Mifflin Co. and The Riverside Press, 1965), describes (312-319) from a sympathetic viewpoint the application by Robert S. McNamara of management techniques for making decisions. He also cites (549) the famous remark McNamara made when he first went to Vietnam in 1962: "Every quantitative measurement we have shows we're winning this war." Since Schlesinger's book appeared, it became clear that McNamara's cost accounting overlooked a few factors. The decision to stay in the war was made repeatedly on a consequentialist calculation, as is pointed out by Leslie H. Gelb, "Vietnam: the System Worked," *Foreign Policy*, 3 (1971): 145: "The importance of the objective was evaluated in terms of cost, and the perceived costs of disengagement outweighed the cost of further engagement.... The question of whether our leaders would have started down the road if they knew this would mean over half a million men in Vietnam, over 40,000 U.S. deaths, and the expenditure of well over $100 billion is historically irrelevant. Only Presidents Kennedy and Johnson had to confront the possibility of these large costs. The point is that each administration was prepared to pay the costs it could foresee for itself. No one seemed to have a better solution. Each could at least pass the baton on to the next." Gelb was Chairman of the Vietnam Task Force in the Department of Defense which prepared the Pentagon history of the war in Vietnam.

[34] William V. O'Brien, *Nuclear War, Deterrence and Morality* (Westminster, Md.: Newman Press, 1967), pp. 8-16 and 84-86, shows that it is only willingness to do the last act which makes the threat effective. He bases his analysis in part upon testimony by Defense Secretary Robert S. McNamara before a Congressional committee; such testimony, published in the documents of Congress each year, is the means by which the threat is officially communicated. One of the many merits of Herman Kahn, *op. cit.*, is that he is forthright in stating the unthinkable and making clear exactly what the consequentialist logic of deterrence means; see, for example, his famous chapter (40-95), "Will the Survivors Envy the Dead?" Kahn's conclusion is that they need not, if one is really prepared to fight and survive a nuclear war.

[35] This line of argument is developed by W. D. Ross, *The Right and the Good* (Oxford: Clarendon Press, 1930), 22.

[36] See my *Beyond the New Morality*, the central theme of which is that we have responsibilities only insofar as we are free, and most of our responsibilities arise from our own acts.

[37] Bernard Williams, in Smart and Williams, *op. cit.*, 108-118, and in his own work, *Morality: An Introduction to Ethics* (New York: Harper and Row, 1972), 96-107, makes this point.

[38] Research on this paper was supported by grants from the Medora A. Feehan Charitable and Educational Trust and from Campion College, University of Regina. Baruch Brody and Paul Ramsey allowed me to see drafts of papers they were preparing. Richard McSorley, S.J., provided some research help. Kenneth Goodpastor and Ralph McInerny offered suggestions before the first draft. So did Joseph M. Boyle, Jr., Philip E. Devine, and John Ziegler, who also made comments on at least parts of the first draft as did the following: Francis Canavan, S.J., John M. Finnis, John C. Ford, S.J., James Gallagher, James Kevin McDonnell, K. L. McGovern, William E. May, Rabbi David Novak, Richard L. Purtill, and Olaf Tollefsen. With the usual disclaimer of any responsibility on their part for the defects which remain in this study, I thank all of them most heartily for their generous assistance.

Catholic Ethics: Has the Norm for Rule-Making Changed?
John R. Connery, S.J.

The above question is an inquiry into the norm underlying the traditional rules of Catholic ethics. Often referred to as "secondary rules," the latter are generally identified with the so-called Ten Commandments of the Old Testament (Exod 20:1-17), e.g., "Thou shalt not steal," "Thou shalt not commit adultery," etc. These rules have been interpreted and developed over the centuries through the combined efforts of the Fathers, theologians, and the official Church on the local and universal level. The rules of sexual morality, for instance, have been developed in reference to what Roman Catholics call the Sixth and Ninth Commandments, although numerous other passages from Scripture have played an important role in this development. Although these sources are accepted as "revelation," there is no doubt that the rules derived from them coincide with human experience and that reflection on this experience was an essential element in formulating them. In this respect, the experience not only of the Jews and Christians but also of neighboring cultures was influential.

When the question is raised about the norm for making rules, the concern seems to be about a "primary" rule or norm underlying all of these "secondary" rules, which will explain them. More concretely, the question would be: What makes an act morally good or morally bad? Or: Why are stealing, adultery, murder, etc. morally bad? One must be careful, however, when discussing this question not to assume that there was a chronological development of secondary rules from some basic primary rule or norm on which they depended. There is good evidence to show that the kind of inquiry we are speaking of was of much later vintage. In the Old Testament one finds little philosophizing about rules. To the Jews the rules were part of God's covenant with Israel; they were His law. No further explanation was needed. The early Christians inherited much of this attitude toward the rules. We even find among them a certain suspicion of philosophy and philosophizing. A coherent, rational explanation of the basis of Christian rules began to develop only at the end of the first millennium.

This study will attempt initially to explain a new norm for making rules, commonly known as proportionalism, which some theologians are advocating today, and show how it differs from the traditional norm. Since some of the advocates of the new norm claim that it has its roots in St. Thomas, the study will examine this claim to see whether it can be verified. It will continue with an examination of the impact a change in the basic rule or norm of morality would have on secondary rules and on Church teaching regarding such rules. It will conclude with a critique of proportionalism.

Norms of Morality

Over the course of history many theories about primary rules, or what is often called the norm of morality, have been proposed and defended. The fundamental question comes to this: What makes an act morally good or bad? It is not possible or pertinent in this brief presentation to enumerate even in summary form all the responses that have been made to this question. Peter Knauer, S.J., who was the first in recent times to suggest a new approach to rule-making, reduces all these opinions to three categories (Knauer see above 25-30). They classify as morally good (1) that which leads man to his last end, (2) that which corresponds with human nature, and (3) that which is "simply good." This may be an oversimplification, but with a little explanation it will suffice for our purposes.

Those who identified moral good with that which leads man to his last end were never able to attract many followers, because it always seemed that a judgment that an act would lead man to his last end would depend on whether the act was already morally good. This presumes the existence of a prior norm of morality. The second opinion, which identified the morally good with that which corresponded with human nature, has been, and still is, more generally accepted. This norm has been proposed in different ways by different proponents, but all agree in making man's rational nature the basis of morality. Thomas Aquinas spoke of *recta ratio* as the norm, but this was also anchored in man's rational nature. Knauer objects that this norm does not distinguish adequately between physical and moral evil; in fact, it will really identify only physical or premoral evil.

Proportionalism

The third norm of which Knauer speaks is the norm under discussion in this article. The statement that it is "the simply good" is somewhat cryptic as it stands; its meaning is a little more nuanced. There is no doubt that if one could perform an act that was "simply good" in all its aspects, it would be a morally good act; it is presumed, of course, that it would be a human act, arising from deliberate consent. Unfortunately, it may be practically impossible to place an act which is simply good, at least if one has to consider all the effects of one's act. As human beings, it is our unfortunate lot that our acts are generally mixtures of good and evil, and since this is the case, they will not be simply good. To Knauer it is sufficient for a morally good act that only the good be intended and that any evil connected with the act be beyond the intention of the agent. He maintains that the evil in an act will be beyond the intention of the agent if there is a proportion between the evil and the good to be achieved (Knauer see above 30). Thus, even if the evil is a means to a good end, it will not be intended if it is proportionate to this good. Others do not give the same importance to intention. While they rule out intending an evil end, they see no moral significance in intending an evil means. Schüller, for instance, argues that there is no moral difference between permitting evil and intending evil as a means (Schuller 1978, 165-92). As long as there is a proportionate good to be achieved, whether it is achieved through an evil means or with concomitant evil effects is of no moral significance. What is of moral significance is that the good be proportionate, since that is what makes the difference between a morally good and morally bad act.

Because of the emphasis put on proportion, this norm is often referred to as proportionalism.[1] Frequently it has been put in terms of a proportionate reason (good) justifying the use of some evil means. This is probably because it is in this area that the chief problem lies; it is here that it comes into conflict with the tradition. But if it is to be a general norm, it must cover other possible combinations of good and evil, e.g., where the evil is an effect rather than a means.[2] Briefly, it would have to assess all the evil in an act, including the effects, and the proportionate reason would refer to all the good expected from a particular act. The moral judgment would depend on the balance. Prior to this balancing, the evil in the act would be premoral or ontic, as it is sometimes called. Similarly, the good in the act would be premoral or ontic. The act would be morally good if the ontic good outweighed the ontic evil, morally evil if the ontic evil outbalanced the ontic good.

When the question is asked about changing the norm for rule-making, the meaning in the present context seems to be whether we are moving from a norm which related the moral goodness of an act to its conformity with man's rational nature to one which relates it to a proportionate reason, or a balance of good over evil. A clearer picture of the meaning of this change can perhaps be obtained from a consideration of the elements of the human act. Traditionally, these elements have been classified as the object, end, and circumstances of the act. If one followed the traditional norm, one would conclude that if all these elements were in accord with the demands of right reason, or man's rational nature, the act was morally good. If any of these elements was contrary to right reason, the act was morally bad. This was all epitomized in the axiom *bonum ex integra causa, malum ex quolibet defectu* (ST I-II, 18, 4, ad 3). Thus a bad end or intention could vitiate an act that might be good *ex objecto*. Similarly, an act could be morally bad *ex objecto* in spite of a good end or intention. The latter was frequently expressed in another axiom: the end does not justify the means (Rom 3:8). Ordinarily the comparison was made with secondary rules rather than with the basic norm of morality. Thus, if what you were doing was stealing (object), it would be wrong in spite of a good intention. It should also be mentioned that if the circumstance in question was an unintended effect, while it might vitiate the morality of the whole act if it were bad, it would not necessarily do so. More about this later.

If the basic rule were changed, the morality of an act would not be determined by comparing its various elements with the demands of man's rational nature. At most, this would tell you whether there was some premoral or ontic evil in any of the elements of the act. To make a moral judgment of the act, one would have to weigh all the good in the act against all the evil to see where the balance lay. Such weighing would include unintended good and evil effects, at least if they were foreseen. Ultimately, an act would be judged morally bad only if the bad outweighed the good. One could not say, according to this approach, that an act would be bad *ex quolibet defectu*; it would be morally bad only if the evil it contained outweighed the good it was expected to accomplish.

What this is saying is that a moral assessment cannot be made of any isolated aspect of the human act. It can be made only of the whole act on the basis of the balance of good and evil in its combined elements. There is indeed an underlying assumption that evil may never be intended as the end of the act; the intention must be directed at a good end. Granted that the intention is directed ultimately at the good in the act, the latter will be morally evil only if the good intended is not sufficient to offset the evil.

It should be obvious that the key to this kind of moral assessment is the proportionate reason; the good to be achieved must be proportionate to the evil involved. Knauer admits that it is impossible to do this kind of quantitative weighing when one is dealing with qualitatively different values (Knauer 1979, 11-12). It is like comparing apples and oranges. His position is that the reason for an act will not be proportionate if there is a contradiction between the act and the reason, or if in the last analysis what one does to achieve one's goal is self-defeating. He gives the example of traffic limitations. Generally, speed regulations should be such as to facilitate traffic and prevent loss of life. But how does one weigh the value of life against the value of faster traffic? He seems to argue that you can make an evaluation only if you can reduce the issue to one factor, the loss of life. Slower traffic might reduce the loss of life from traffic accidents but might increase the loss of life from other causes, e.g., people would not be able to get to an emergency room on time. The best limit would be that which resulted in the lowest overall loss of life. Traffic regulations that are too severe in limiting traffic would actually be self-defeating.

He also gives the example of the student who wants to learn the greatest possible amount in the shortest time. The more time he spends at study, the more he learns. But if he goes beyond a certain limit, he will undermine his health and have to give up study altogether. What he actually does by his actions is defeat his whole purpose. So Knauer argues that one's acts will not be proportionate if ultimately they are self-defeating or contradictory to his goal.

Proportionalism in St. Thomas

Some of the proponents of proportionalism maintain that this is basically a Thomistic approach. If this is true, adopting it will not involve changing the traditional approach but recovering it. The most serious study on this point was made by Louis Janssens (see above 100-147). He develops his argument from Thomas' concept of the rational will as the basis of human acts. The will aims at good, which it pursues as an end. But not every good the will aims at will be a moral good. To be a moral good, it must correspond to reason. If it does not, it may still be a good in reference to some lesser appetite, but it will be morally vitiated because it is contrary to man's rational nature.

Janssens admits that according to Thomas there is an exterior aspect to the moral act as well as the will aspect, but he argues that in Thomas they are one act, and a moral judgment of the exterior act cannot be made apart from the interior act, and hence from the will of the agent. He gives the example of killing. If one viewed just the exterior act, one could not make a judgment on the morality of the act. The same exterior act, killing, may be moral or immoral according to the intention of the agent. If it is an expression of a will for justice, it is a good act. If it is an expression of anger, it is a bad act. Janssens then takes up a difficulty, which seems to be a contradiction in Thomas. In one place he says that the goodness or badness of an act is determined by the end, the object of the inner act of the will. In another he asserts that the morality of the external act depends on whether or not it is in keeping with reason. Is he not saying that the morality of the exterior act can be evaluated by itself and apart from the end of the inner act of the will? Janssens feels that this problem is solved by the distinction Thomas makes between the formal and material element in the moral act. The inner act of the will is the formal element in determining morality, since it is through the will that the exterior act becomes moral. So the moral species of the act depends formally on the end (of the inner act of the will) and only materially on the object of the exterior act. Janssens feels that this substantiates his understanding of Thomas, i.e., that it is the willing of the end that is decisive in determining morality.

Janssens finds confirmation of this interpretation in several passages of the *Summa Theologiae*, but his chief support comes from

Thomas' article on self-defense. In that article Thomas says clearly that moral acts acquire their species from what is intended. His argument then is that since the intention in using violence against an unjust aggressor is self-defense, it is permissible even though injury or even the death of the aggressor might result. These would be *praeter intentionem*. According to Janssens, this treatment of self-defense shows that in Thomas it is the intention that determines the morality of the act. In support of this position he keeps quoting St. Thomas' statement: "*finis dat speciem in moralibus.*"

In the article Thomas sets down another requirement for the liceity of self-defense which seems to support the proportionalist position. It is the requirement that the means (the violence) be proportioned to the *finis* of the act. If the violence used goes beyond the needs of self-defense, the act is wrong. St. Thomas does not say so explicitly, but the reason for this requirement seems to be related to the intention. The use of more violence than necessary would imply an intention beyond that of self-defense, e.g., vengeance or anger. The injury or killing would hardly remain *praeter intentionem* under these circumstances. To the proportionalist the requirement of a proportion between the means and the end seems to put Thomas in their camp.

According to Janssens, then, in St. Thomas it is the end that is the key to the morality of the human act. All that is required of the means is that it be proportioned to the end. If this is the correct interpretation, it seems to follow that Thomas was a proportionalist. Is this an accurate interpretation of Thomas' analysis of the moral act? I think there is serious reason to question it. There is no doubt that Thomas says an act can be human or moral only in so far as it proceeds from man's rational will (ST I-II, 1, 1). It seems quite clear that a human act by definition must be the product of the will. Nor can one doubt that the end of the act (the object of the will) will give it a "moral species" (ST I-II, 1, 3). But if one studies the treatise on the goodness and badness of human acts in Thomas, one will find that ordinarily there is more to the human act than just the act of the will; there is the exterior aspect of the act. Although this is all one act, if one is going to analyze its morality, one must consider the whole act, that is the object and circumstances as well as the end. And Thomas says explicitly that an act receives its moral species from the object and circumstances as well as the end (ST I-II, 1, 3). Therefore, when he says that the human act receives its moral species from its end, this is not to be understood in an exclusive sense. He is not denying that it can acquire its moral species from other sources.[3]

Actually, Thomas tells us that a moral act can have two moral species: one from the object, one from the end. He gives the well-known example of the man who steals to get money to commit adultery. His act includes two moral species, stealing and adultery, one from the object, the other from the end. It is true that Thomas considers him more an adulterer than a thief; in Thomas' language, he is formally an adulterer, materially a thief (ST I-II, 18, 6). But this does not mean that he is not really a thief or that his only sin is adultery. His act contains a double malice, although the more basic problem is the sexual failure.

A proportionalist might argue that the above does not prove that Thomas was not a proportionalist. All it shows is that adultery is not a proportionate reason for stealing—which a proportionalist would admit. A proportionalist would have no problem with the immorality of the adultery, since it involved the intention of an evil end. So the proportionalist could admit a double malice in an act, one of which might be *ex objecto* in a sense, without abandoning his position.

But there is a difference between Thomas' analysis and that of a proportionalist. While both admit a double malice in an act, the proportionalist relates it all to the end of the act; the stealing is wrong because of the absence of a proportionate reason. Thomas would not agree. He asks specifically whether the goodness or badness of the exterior act depends on the goodness of the will (ST I-II, 20, 2). In his response he presents with approval the Augustinian thesis that there are some things which cannot be justified by any good end or good will. He goes on to explain that moral evil in the external act can come from two sources: from the matter of the act (object and circumstances) or from the end. That which comes from the ordering of an act to the end depends on the will, but that which comes from the matter or circumstances comes from reason, and on this the goodness of the will depends. He then goes on to say that the badness of an act can come from any one defect, but that its goodness depends on the goodness of all its elements. So, for the goodness of the external act, a will which is good only by reason of the intention of the end is not sufficient. The external act can be bad either by reason of the intention or by reason of what is willed. According to

Thomas, therefore, an act can be bad apart from a good intention, i.e., a proportionate reason. The stealing in the above example, then, is wrong apart from the intention.

In the preceding article Thomas touches on the same issue (ST I-II, 20, 1). He asks whether the goodness or badness of an act is found primarily in the will. His answer is that moral good and evil are found primarily in the will. He then explains that goodness or badness can be found in the exterior act in two ways: by reason of the matter or circumstances, e.g., almsgiving, or by reason of the intention (end), e.g., almsgiving out of vainglory. The goodness or badness which the exterior act has by reason of its end is in the will first and redounds to the exterior act. That which it has by reason of the matter or circumstances does not come from the will but from its conformity with reason.

All of the above seems to make it clear that in Thomas there is moral goodness and badness in actions apart from the will or intention of the end. It is a simplification, then, to say that according to Thomas it is only the end that specifies the moral act. This is only part of the story. The moral act can be specified by its object and circumstances as well, and these specifications are independent of the intention of the end. He does not deny, of course, that some acts may be morally bad by reason of the intended end. But in his general analysis of the morality of human acts, he asserts clearly that some acts have an objective morality that is independent of the end of the act.

We have already pointed out that Janssens finds confirmation of his interpretation of Thomas in the latter's article on self-defense (ST I-II 64, 7). The same is true of Knauer. There seems to be no question that Thomas' basic justification of killing in self-defense comes from the intention. It is definite also that he calls for a proportion between the violence used and the needs of self-defense. So one must ask: Does this make his explanation of the morality of self-defense proportionalistic? In saying that it is the intention that determines the moral species of the act of self-defense, Thomas seems to be arguing along proportionalistic lines. It is less clear, though, that the other side of this statement, that what is *praeter intentionem* does not affect the morality of the act, reflects proportionalism. This should become more apparent as the discussion goes on.

Furthermore, there is some difference between the Thomistic requirement of proportion in self-defense and that of the proportionalist. Thomas calls for proportionate means; the proportionalist speaks more of a proportionate reason (end). Knauer makes the claim that these requirements mean the same thing. Whatever one may think of this claim, Thomas' interest in proportion is related to the means, and his concern is that excessive violence would be aimed at the death of the assailant rather than self-defense. This would invalidate his original justification, since the killing would no longer be *praeter intentionem*. The proportionalist is more concerned with the original justification of self-defense. Is it a proportionate reason for killing? Thomas is satisfied with the simple explanation that it is natural for a person to defend himself.[4] The proportionalist would look for some kind of proportion between the good and evil in the act of self-defense—between what is saved or defended and the damage done. For Thomas, such a comparison is unnecessary. The damage done is acceptable to him not because it is a lesser evil or because there is a proportionate reason for it. It is acceptable because it is *praeter intentionem*; it has no moral bearing on the act.[5]

Even if one could give a proportionalist interpretation to Thomas' treatment of self-defense, in view of his general analysis of the moral act, there is no basis for universalizing this explanation. This is clear even in his treatment of other kinds of killing. It is clear, for instance, that he considers taking the life of an innocent person wrong *ex objecto* (ST II-II, 64, 6). "Nullo modo" is his response to the question regarding its permissibility. There is no implication at all that it would be permissible for a proportionate reason. Explicit confirmation of this may be found in his treatise on baptism (ST III, 68, 11, ad 3). He is dealing with the question of doing a caesarean section on a dying mother to baptize the fetus. It was argued that this should be permissible even though it meant the death of the mother because the eternal life of the fetus was more important than the temporal life of the mother. This seems a clear case where a proportionalist would admit a proportionate reason for causing the death of the mother, even if it had to be considered a means to an end. But Thomas refuses to allow it. Quoting St. Paul (Rom 3:8) that one may not do evil that good may result, he says simply that one may not kill the mother to baptize the child. He does not deny that the eternal welfare of the child is more important than the physical welfare of the mother, but simply does not consider it a decisive factor. The decisive factor is that taking innocent human life is wrong apart from whatever reason one might have for doing it.

Proportionate reason does not even seem to play a part in St. Thomas' treatment of killing which is *praeter intentionem* (accidental killing) (ST II-II, 64, 8). In other words, he does not make any demand that it be balanced by a proportionate good. In q. 64, a. 8, he takes the position that one will not be responsible for such killing if what he is doing is licit and there is no neglect, that is, if the killing is not the result of neglect. Initially, the principle he was using called for some kind of necessity, but before the time of Thomas it was softened to a requirement of liceity.[6] As long as the act was licit, one would not be responsible for any death resulting from it, presuming, of course, that it was *praeter intentionem*. It would be clearly wrong to intend such a death.

This is not the place to develop it, but I think a strong case can be made to show that the principle of double effect as formulated in the nineteenth century was more dependent on this article in St. Thomas than on the article on self-defense. What is missing in the article is any mention of proportionate reason. Thomas makes no demand for a proportionate reason to justify accidental killing. All that is required, apart from the demand that the killing be *praeter intentionem*, is that the act from which the killing results be licit and that there be no neglect. The liceity of the act from which the evil effect results is, of course, an important condition of the principle of double effect. The proportionate reason requirement was added by J. P. Gury, S.J., when he formulated the principle in the nineteenth century.[7] There is good reason to believe, however, that this requirement was added not to balance the evil effect but rather to guarantee that it would remain *praeter intentionem*. As already seen, this condition was a requirement in Thomas and was basic to his justification of accidental killing. The requirement of proportionate reason, then, did not call for a careful comparison of values. All that was required, as Knauer rightly says, was that the proportionate reason be serious. This was enough to make sure that the intention would be directed at it rather than at the evil effect. The concern in accidental killing, therefore, is not primarily a balance of good over evil; it is rather the intention of the agent.

Putting everything together, it is hard to detect any convincing evidence of proportionalism in Thomas. It can hardly be argued, therefore, that those who are proposing this norm today are really recovering a Thomistic methodology. In stating that Thomas was not a proportionalist, however, I am not implying that he held that all moral evil is in the object, or that an act cannot receive its moral species from the end. What is meant is that he held that acts can receive their moral species from their objects and that therefore some acts can be morally bad *ex objecto* (since they can become morally bad *ex quolibet defectu*). This means that they are morally bad apart from the reason behind them. Not all objective evil, then, is ontic or premoral. While every act must come from the will, it can be morally wrong by reason of its object and apart from an ultimate good intention.

In answer, therefore, to the question whether the norm for rule-making has changed, we would have to say that a number of present-day theologians have adopted a new rule, proportionalism. This rule is often stated as follows: an act will be morally bad (1) if it has an evil end or (2) if it causes evil without a proportionate reason (or if it causes more evil than good, or if it causes more evil than it should). Apart from these two instances, any evil in an act will be only ontic or premoral; it will not be moral evil. As is clear, this approach differs from the traditional approach according to which an act can be morally evil *ex objecto*, that is, apart from the reason behind it.

The proportionalist also rejects the distinction between "direct" and "indirect" that has been traditional in Catholic ethics. The distinction is between intending some moral evil as a means or an end and permitting it. To the proportionalists this distinction has no moral significance unless one is thinking of intending evil as an end. As long as one has a proportionate reason, it is just as permissible to intend evil as a means as it is to permit it. In the tradition it was just as wrong to intend evil as a means as it was to intend it as an end. I will have more to say about this later.

Impact on Secondary Rules and Church Teaching

More important perhaps than the original question about a change in the basic norm of morality is the question regarding the impact such a change would have on secondary rules. How would it affect such rules as: "Thou shalt not steal," "Thou shalt not commit adultery," etc.? Perhaps the key change would be in the concept of the rules themselves. Traditionally, the understanding has been that these rules, as they are interpreted, deal with moral evil. A change in the basic norm would change this understanding. The rules would no longer deal with moral evil as such but only with ontic or premoral evil. Such things as adultery, stealing, killing an innocent person are in themselves only ontic evil, so a rule prohibiting them can only be dealing with ontic evil. One violating these rules, then, would be causing only ontic evil. He would be guilty of moral evil only if he violated them without a proportionate reason. Every rule, therefore, would have to carry an implicit rider "unless there is a proportionate reason," and this rider would add the moral dimension to the rule.

For the proportionalist, then, secondary norms as they stand do not deal with moral evil. To give them moral force, one would have to rule out all possible proportionate reasons, and to do this, one would have to be able to foresee all possible combinations of object, circumstances, and effects both intended and unintended (Fuchs see below 80-95). Since this is an impossibility, a secondary norm proscribing such acts as adultery, stealing, etc. as immoral is also an impossibility. Proportionalists hold that this is true even of Church moral teaching, especially since it is generally not infallible. Even the special guidance of the Holy Spirit will not give the Church the omniscient perspective necessary to set up unconditioned norms.

In fairness to the proportionalists, however, it must be admitted that they are speaking here on the level of theory. They are willing to admit that in practice norms do deal with moral evil. The fact that the human mind cannot foresee all possible combinations of object, end, etc. in which a norm might apply does not mean that it cannot foresee any such combinations. The human mind is not without all foresight. And where Church teaching is concerned, the guidance of the Holy Spirit may well give it more than ordinary foresight. Therefore, when the Church teaches that something is morally wrong, even a proportionalist would have to admit that it would apply to foreseeable circumstances. Actually, in the past, when controversy has arisen over the application of a particular norm, the Church has not hesitated to teach that the norm would apply in particular circumstances, e.g., abortion to save the life of the mother.

Consequently, a change in the norm of morality to proportionalism would demand that a conditional clause be an implicit part of every secondary rule dealing with evil.[8] A proportionate reason would allow one to violate the rule. Or perhaps it is preferable to say that a proportionate reason would exempt an act from the rule or law. All this sounds much more liberal than current thinking (according to the present norm) seems to allow; current thinking does not admit exceptions in certain rules. Whether it will really be more permissive will depend on what one considers a proportionate reason. One could be a proportionalist, for instance, and still deny that a proportionate reason existed, e.g., for adultery, taking innocent human life, etc. In that case, although the rule in theory would still yield to a proportionate reason, in practice it would stand as it is and a violation would constitute moral evil, since there is no proportionate reason. So a change in the norm for rule-making would not necessarily bring about a practical change in the rules themselves. At most, such a change would provide a theoretical allowance for exceptions. One might be able to fantasize or conjure up cases where a proportionate reason might exist, but the rules would still bind in the ordinary case, and this could include cases where observance would cause considerable hardship. The practical problem with proportionalism is that some might want to make every difficult case an exception. But this would hardly be condoned by conscientious followers of proportionalism. I do not think they would subscribe to the principle that a rule obliges only when it is easy to observe it. On the other hand, the greater the difficulty, the more the pressure to find in the difficulty itself a proportionate reason.

Even if the Church were to adopt proportionalism as its basic norm, it would not necessarily change the secondary rules it teaches and has taught in the past. It might continue to condemn without exception adultery, abortion, etc. What would change is that instead of claiming that these acts are morally wrong in themselves, it would simply say that they are morally wrong because there is no proportionate reason to justify them. It could do this even though it held the theoretical position that a proportionate reason would justify them. It would be a mistake, therefore, to presume that a change in ecclesiastical metaethics would lead to a change in Church rules.

It might be well to make the point here that the question of changing the norm for rule-making is not the same as allowing for exceptions to rules. There is a history of exception-making in the Church that goes back to Aquinas. One did not have to wait for proportionalism to provide for exceptions. Thomas himself advised that the more remote a rule might be from first principles, the greater the likelihood of exceptions (ST I-II, 94, 4). He gives the familiar example of the duty to return a deposit. Ordinarily this is what one must do. There may be circumstances, however, in which this would not be a duty, and might even be morally wrong, e.g., to return a sword to someone who had suicidal or homicidal intentions. And the more detailed the rule, the greater the likelihood of exceptions, e.g., if the rule prescribed not only the return of the deposit but also a detailed procedure for doing so.

Thomas does not say that all rules will allow for exceptions. We have already seen how absolute was his condemnation of the killing of an innocent person. It may be enlightening to see how he deals with a possible exception to the precept against fornication (ST I-II, 154, 2). The exception has to do with a man who will guarantee the education of the child that might result from his nonobservance of the law. Thomas' response is that rules are formulated on the basis of what ordinarily happens, not on the basis of a rare possibility. Presumably, then, it would oblige even in this case. But even if one wanted to maintain that Thomas would allow fornication where such a guarantee existed, it would not be on the basis of a proportionate reason. It would have to be because such an act would not be evil, since it would not be *contra bonum prolis*. It would not be a violation of the rule, and hence would not need a proportionate reason. Today, of course, one wonders how the good of the child could be provided for adequately outside of a marriage commitment. One also wonders whether it is only the good of the offspring that is at stake in fornication.

Critique of Proportionalism

To recapitulate in terms of means and end, it must be said that to the proportionalist a means has no independent morality of its own; its morality comes from its relation to the end of the act. Traditionally, an ethics of means has been strongly asserted. Traditionalists would certainly agree that there are means which receive their morality from the end of the act, e.g., violence, mutilations, etc. But this is not true of all means. Some means have a morality of their own and a good end will not justify them. All this has been summarized in the axiom "The end does not justify the means." Proportionalists will deny that their method is a violation of this axiom. They argue that the axiom has always applied to an immoral means and that they still hold it true in this sense (Fuchs see above 80-95). I do not think this defense can be questioned, at least theoretically. In practice, however, the proportionalist deprives the axiom of real meaning. If there is no independent morality of means, that is, if the morality of the means always depends on the end, the axiom loses any meaning or force it might have had. The proportionalist has to admit that the end really justifies the means. If one were to give the axiom a proportionalist meaning, it would have to be expanded to read: the end does not justify a means which is immoral by reason of the end. In this sense it becomes a circular statement. A proportionalist may certainly continue to use such an axiom, but it serves no useful purpose. Many proportionalists today seem willing simply to say that it is permissible to do evil to achieve a good purpose.

Intending Evil

Although proportionalists allow one to intend evil as a means, they do not allow one to intend it as an end. One wonders whether this is a consistent position. Presumably, the reason one is allowed to intend evil as a means is that the evil is only ontic and a proportionate good may be achieved. But if this is true, one wonders why it would not be allowed to intend evil as an end as long as it was related to some proportionate good end (also intended). If the proportion between good and evil is the essential criterion of moral good and evil, why is it wrong to intend evil as an end in a situation in which it is balanced by a proportionate good? In itself, the evil end constitutes no more than ontic or premoral evil, just as the means. Or if it is wrong to intend evil in such a situation, why is it permissible to intend it as a means as long as it is balanced by some good end? In other words, if it is the proportion that is the primary criterion, why will it not justify the intention of evil as an end as well as the intention of evil as a means?

It seems, then, that in proportionalism the traditional distinction between intending and permitting loses any significance it might have had. As long as the evil in an act is balanced by the good, it does not matter whether it is permitted or intended, whether it is intended as a means or an end. So the proportionalist does not have to have special concern for evil which is intended. But freedom from the distinction between permitting and intending may not be an unmixed blessing. While the proportionalist may be less bound by intended evil, he will be more bound by permitted evil. Any evil in the act will have to be weighed. Permitted evil will weigh into his moral judgment just as much as intended evil, and the fact that it is not intended will not be pertinent. He must face the problem, then, of assessing all the evil connected with a particular act, as well as all the good. We will pursue this difficulty later.

Ontic Evil

A more basic objection to proportionalism aims at the "demoralization" of all the good and evil that is found in human acts. In proportionalism such good and evil in themselves can only be ontic or premoral. A judgment of moral good or moral evil can be arrived at only by balancing this ontic good and evil. So it is not enough to judge that what one does goes against right reason to conclude that it is immoral. Before a moral judgment can be made, one must go a step further and compare it with the good to be sought as well as other goods and evils connected with it. The tradition has been that such things as adultery, killing an innocent person, stealing, etc. could be judged morally evil in themselves. They were contrary to right reason and could be judged morally wrong apart from a consideration of the reason behind them and/or the other goods or evils connected with them in a particular act. One could generally presume that such acts would produce more evil than good, but the moral judgment did not depend on this factor and one did not have to wait for an assessment of all the good and evil connected with the act to make it. On the same basis a rule could be formulated prohibiting such acts, and the understanding was that this rule dealt with moral evil. Proportionalism denies a moral dimension to such judgments and the rules derived from them and for a moral judgment requires a comparative assessment of all the good and evil in a particular act. This calls for such a radical revision of one's whole moral outlook that one is forced to question the validity of the system which demands it.

Weighing Good and Evil

The relativization of morality involved in proportionalism also imposes on the moral agent the extremely elusive task of weighing good and evil. Knauer, as pointed out earlier, calls attention to this problem and concedes the impossibility of weighing qualitatively different values. He suggests the possibility of reducing them to one factor and gives the example of traffic regulations. The criterion would be the number of deaths connected with a specific regulation. Certainly, there is a point where slower traffic would be self-defeating in this respect. Fewer deaths might occur from automobile accidents, but the number might be less than the number of deaths caused by the delays the regulations caused. Admittedly, the latter number would be very difficult to calculate. But even if it were calculable, one wonders whether all the evil effects resulting from slower traffic could be reduced to this one category. What about the loss of revenue resulting from slower traffic? What about the loss of jobs? Some of these losses might be put in terms of resulting deaths, but surely not all of them. Realistically, one can seriously question whether the kind of reduction Knauer speaks of is a possibility.

Knauer also suggests the possibility of using long-term effectiveness as a criterion of proportionate reason. We have already cited the example of the student who studies day and night to learn as much as possible in the shortest time. Knauer argues rightly that this would be self-defeating since eventually it would not achieve the desired good. He is speaking, of course, in terms of proportionate means rather than proportionate reason or end. One can agree with him that if an evil means is not productive of good, it is not permissible to continue to use it. But can one argue that because it may be self-defeating over the long haul, it is not permissible to use it here and now when it is still effective? For instance, is it wrong for a student to study all night for an examination because if he did this every night he would undermine his health and not be able to study at all? Studying all night seems to be self-defeating only where the individual intends to make a practice of it. So one must at least make a distinction between a proportionate reason for a single act and one for a practice.

But even if a means were effective, and would continue to be effective in producing some good on a long-term basis, is this an adequate criterion of its morality, even from a proportionalist viewpoint? If one is a proportionalist, it seems that some comparison between the good and evil involved is still called for. Even if an evil means would effectively produce some good and continue to do so, it is possible that the good produced would not outweigh the evil. So one wonders whether Knauer's criterion really provides an escape from a comparison of values. As pointed out above, St. Thomas avoids this problem in his article on self-defense by focusing on the intention of the agent rather than a comparison of values. As long as the evil in the act is *praeter intentionem*, it does not affect the morality of the case. One does not have to weigh it against the good to be achieved to make a moral judgment about the legitimacy of self-defense.

The problem of weighing to which Knauer calls attention is accentuated when one considers the possibility of weighing a whole set of good and evil effects. What weight, for instance, does one give to evil effects that may be seen only as a remote possibility? What weight does one give to effects that may be a result of a concurrence of causes? Are all similar effects given the same weight whether they are certain or only a remote possibility, whether they are traceable to a particular act or the result of a concurrence of causes? If not, how does one estimate the different weights of such evil (and good) effects? On the surface, it seems to be a herculean task.

A proportionalist might argue that he is no worse off in this respect than a traditionalist applying the principle of double effect. The latter also has to consider proportionate reasons and must therefore weigh values. This may seem true, at least if one follows recent formulations of the principle. They call for a proportion between the good and bad effects of an act as a condition for its licit application. As already shown, however, the approach of the traditionalist to the proportionate reason differs from that of the proportionalist. The main concern of the traditionalist is that the evil in the act be *praeter intentionem*. The requirement that the good effect be *proportionate* to the evil effect is meant to guarantee the proper direction of the intention; it must be of some importance to provide this guarantee. But it is on the intention rather than the weighing of good and evil that the morality of the act depends. The weighing of values is of only secondary importance. In proportionalism, however, where the morality of the act depends basically on the proportion and therefore on the weighing, the weighing is of primary significance. So the seeming similarity between proportionalism and the traditional approach to double effect is somewhat deceptive.

Certainly, even a proportionalist will not be responsible for unforeseen effects if they are not overlooked through neglect. His judgment of the morality of a particular act may not represent objective reality in this case, but he will not be responsible for what through no fault of his own he failed to see. But he must take account of all foreseen effects in making his calculus. He cannot fall back on the distinction between permitting and intending, since he cannot make a moral judgment unless he weighs all the effects. The traditionalist must also consider unintended effects, but he is freed from the kind of analysis the proportionalist must make, since the more basic question is not whether the evil effects outweigh the good effects but whether they are intended. One who follows the traditional approach does not have to do the kind of impossible weighing proportionalism seems to demand.

To conclude briefly, I believe that the proportionalist, by shifting the basis for moral judgment to a comparative standard, makes moral decision making more difficult than is healthy for moral life. While it may seem to simplify the moral enterprise by eliminating the distinction between permitting and intending evil, it imposes on the moral person a kind of calculus that will make moral assessment largely inaccessible, if not impossible. For reasons such as these, I do not believe that a shift to proportionalism is in the best interests of a healthy moral life.

Notes

[1] In a previous article I identified proportionalism with consequentialism (see *Theological Studies* 34 (1973): 396-414). Richard A. McCormick, S.J., criticized this identification in his "Notes on Moral Theology" *Theological Studies* 36 (1975): 93-99. Although from the standpoint of traditional morality, proportionalism and consequentialism present the same problem, denying the possibility of an independent morality deriving from the object of the act, it may be more accurate to say that proportionalism involves an assessment of all the good and evil in an act rather than just the consequences. Even when proportionalists speak of an act getting its morality from the *finis* or end (the

intended consequence), they still call for a proportion between the means and end, and, presumably, other unintended consequences. Bruno Schüller has written a more extended critique of the above article in "Neuere Beiträge zum Thema 'Begründung sittlicher Normen,'" in *Theologische Berichte* 4 (1974): 164-80.

[2] One gets the impression that those who follow proportionalism often short-cut the process of making a moral judgment of an act. They apply the proportionate-reason criterion only to the intended effect, the end of the act. If the intended good outweighs the evil means, they judge the act morally good. Little or no attention is given to other effects of the act. It is difficult to see how a system that makes the moral judgment depend on a balance of the good and evil in an act can overlook any good or evil that might in any way be connected with it. Such failure runs the risk of making a false moral judgment. In a system, however, in which the moral judgment is closely bound to the intention, unintended effects play a less important role.

[3] Thomas' special concern about the moral influence of the end of the act comes from the fact that it seems to be extrinsic to the act. One might want to argue that anything extrinsic to the act should not influence its morality. Thomas simply insists that the end is not totally outside the act. Far from excluding other aspects of the act as sources of morality, he is merely arguing that the end must also be included (ST I-II, 1, 3, ad 1).

[4] That Thomas does not regard it merely as a matter of proportion seems to follow also from the way he responds to an objection about fornication or adultery. The objection is that if killing is allowed in self-defense, these acts should also be allowed, since they are less evil than killing. Thomas responds that even so they are not permitted because they are not defensive acts. Actually, they are closer to surrender than self-defense. As such, they would encourage aggression rather than discourage it. It is true, of course, that the victim may save her life, but one might have to conclude that to Thomas it is not the saving of life as such that justifies what is done, but the prevention of aggression.

[5] Thomas says nothing about any requirements of proportion between what is defended and the damage done. Later authors will discuss this issue. But there is no requirement that there be a life-for-life proportion. In other words, there is no requirement that the life of the person attacked be at stake to justify taking the life of the aggressor. All that is required is that it be some important value, even though less than life itself. These authors argue that if self-defense is permissible only when one's life is at stake, one is at a serious disadvantage when other goods are attacked. The subsequent loss of life to the aggressor results primarily from his own actions. If he wants to save his life, he can always stop the aggression. It is not quite accurate to say that he loses his right to life in these circumstances. He never had a right to life that would give him a right to attack others or protect him in such an attack. His right to life gives him a right to pursue his life by just means and protect himself against unjust attack. It is not a right to attack others unjustly. The obligation to respect his life is his own, not that of his victim. Similarly, the failure to respect life, his own as well as that of his victim, is his own.

[6] The principle was stated in the Council of Worms (868) c. 29 (*Mansi*, 15, 874).

[7] *Compendium Theologiae Moralis* 1, 9th ed. (Paris: 1857), n. 9. Gury is not the first to mention proportionate reason, but he is the first to formulate the principle of double effect.

[8] Proportionalists maintain that present norms are the product of a proportionalist refinement (see McCormick, "Notes on Moral Theology," *Theological Studies* 36 (1975): 98). They give the example of killing. Self-defense was considered a proportionate reason for killing, and so the latter was justified. Similarly, killing combatants in a just war and capital punishment were considered morally good because of a proportionate reason. Direct killing of an innocent person was considered morally bad because there was no proportionate reason to justify it. They argue that if we wish to be consistent, we must admit that a proportionate reason would at least theoretically justify such killing. In other words, if the norm is a proportionate reason, every secondary norm must yield to it. It is quite true that in Thomas the moral judgment regarding killing depended on the intention of the agent, but as shown there is no clear evidence that any weighing of good and evil was basic to the judgment. And such acts as adultery, stealing, etc. were judged morally wrong apart from the intention of the agent. So there was no room for any kind of comparative assessment. To postulate some prior comparative assessment on which the moral judgment of adultery etc. depended is to assume what must be proved. Such a comparison is not necessary to show that something is contrary to *recta ratio*. And once the moral judgment is made, there is no place for such an assessment. A comparative assessment is possible only if one is dealing with ontic or premoral evil.

Moral Absolutes: A Critique of the View of Josef Fuchs, S.J.
Germain Grisez

I. Introduction

Until recent years, all Catholic theologians held that there are moral absolutes, in the sense that there are true universal moral norms, such as "Contraception is always morally wrong" and "Adultery is always morally wrong." Such moral absolutes are included in received Catholic teaching and have been reaffirmed by the magisterium in documents such as *Humanae Vitae*, *Persona Humana*, and *Familiaris Consortio*. Yet some Catholic theologians now reject these and other moral absolutes. The purpose of this paper is to defend such moral absolutes by criticizing an important example of the dissenting view.

That view usually includes a number of related theological opinions. 1) There are no specifically Christian moral norms, added to the norms of common human morality, among which one might find moral absolutes. Of course, everyone is absolutely bound to make a right fundamental option toward God, but this option is not a particular moral act, for it is not made by any particular free choice. 2) Received moral teaching of absolute norms includes historically and culturally conditioned elements. Thus, it is not necessarily valid in the changed conditions of today. 3) When one must choose and any available option will involve bringing about some harm, the right choice is of that action which promises to realize a favorable proportion of good to bad. 4) Thus, no norm which morally characterizes a definite kind of action (such as contraception or adultery) is always and everywhere true, and so no such norm can be infallibly proposed as part of Catholic teaching.

Josef Fuchs, S.J., has rejected moral absolutes and defended the preceding theological opinions, especially in one important article, "The Absoluteness of Behavioral Moral Norms." This article, first published as "The Absoluteness of Moral Terms" in 1971, has been republished in a 1983 collection of some of Fuchs' recent works:

Personal Responsibility and Christian Morality. (Unless otherwise noted, all page references to Fuchs within this article correspond to Fuchs' article in *Proportionalism For and Against.*)

The article is unique in its brief articulation of all the elements of the view Fuchs espoused when he published it. It also is unusually important because of its influence since its first publication and because of Fuchs' professional stature — well deserved by his many previous, valuable publications and years of service at the Pontifical Gregorian University. Hence, I have chosen this article as a focus for criticism, although I also refer occasionally to other items in the recently published collection.

In part II, I will expound Fuchs' view concerning moral absolutes, including what he thinks about the four interrelated theological opinions. In subsequent parts I will criticize Fuchs' view with respect to the relationship of morality to salvation (III), historical and cultural relativity (IV), proportionalism in moral judgement (V), and the use of theological sources (VI).

Many who have continued to defend and to try to live by received Catholic moral teaching are tempted to dismiss contrary theological opinion as mere rationalization of surrender to contemporary, post-Christian culture. To give in to that temptation in criticizing Fuchs' view would be unjust. Fuchs was struggling with real theological problems that were not faced adequately by Catholic moral theologians before Vatican II. Fuchs' work has helped me in my own effort to face these problems, although I have come to conclusions very different from the dissenting positions of which Fuchs' view is a typical instance. In the present paper, I suggest my own view incidentally; it is developed at length in a recently published book.[1]

II. Fuchs' View On Moral Absolutes

Recent Catholic moral theology has reacted against a legalistic conception of morality, which thought of natural moral law as a set of precepts to be recognized and applied by each individual's conscience. The proper response was obedience to the law thus grasped by conscience. The immediate end of obedience, on this view, was moral uprightness itself or, negatively, avoidance of mortal sin. The ultimate end of obedience to moral law was that by it one would gain the reward of heaven, while those who died in grave sin would suffer everlasting punishment in hell.

9 – Moral Absolutes: A Critique of the View of Josef Fuchs

Fuchs considers unsatisfactory "the conception of natural moral law as an all-embracing set of invariable norms." (Fuchs see above 61-62). He firmly rejects as "a 'preceptive' understanding of the moral law" and the notion that the function of conscience is simply "the application of the moral law, or its norms, to the concrete cases. Rather, Fuchs holds: "The function of conscience is to help man, as agent, make his action authentic (i.e., self-realizing). Hence conscience ought to assist action toward objectivity, toward truth, in conformity with the concrete human reality. It is necessary above all that action be conformable to the evaluating judgment (of conscience) with respect to the given concrete moment and its options" (Fuchs see above 74). Morality is not an end in itself: "The moral task proper to man is not to fulfill norms so that in the final analysis life's reality would serve merely as material, so to speak, for actualizing moral values —that is, obeying norms. Inversely, the concrete reality of life itself—that is, its actualization—is the real task" (Fuchs see above 94). Moral norms are not imposed by God on human persons but emerge as insights into the intrinsic conditions which must be met for human self-realization and self-development (Fuchs see above 78; Fuchs 1983, 59, 97, 178).

Fuchs firmly rejects the inversion of the priority of grace to morality: "Christ's mission was not to establish a new moral order, new moral laws. Nor was it his primary intent to teach a moral doctrine corresponding to creation. The significance of his coming was rather to redeem sinful mankind, to transform man interiorly by grace, to make him one who believes and loves." Loving faith must bear fruit and be manifested in right conduct. But "faith, love, and salvation do not depend upon the rectitude of the norms of living that are basic to one's life practice." (see above 60).

It follows, Fuchs thinks, that one must take *cum grano salis* the usual explanation of the Church's teaching in the moral field: that she "has to teach the way to salvation and true morality is the way to salvation." (Fuchs see above 67). For, Fuchs holds, the concrete content of moral life "is not directly concerned with salvation, or union with God; only faith and love, together with the effort to incarnate this materiality in the 'true' way in the reality of life are thus concerned." From this, Fuchs tries to draw a further conclusion: "That the material mode of this incarnation can represent only a *secundarium,* already makes it reasonable that within certain limits moral pluralism might well be possible" (Fuchs see above 67).

Fuchs distinguishes among various sorts of moral norms. Some—such as the requirement to obey God and follow Christ—are central to the Bible, for they directly concern conversion and salvation. These are absolute. "But *these* moral-religious imperatives are transcendental—that is, they refer to the personal human being as a whole and not to specific moral conduct" (Fuchs see above 63). Other absolute norms—for example, to be meek and compassionate —commend certain attitudes and values, but do not specify which actions embody these attitudes and values. Finally, there are "operative norms of conduct" which morally characterize kinds of action precisely described in a way that does not presuppose the moral evaluation to be given. Fuchs holds that while such norms can be absolute in the sense of being objectively true and binding in a given instance, they cannot be absolute in the sense of holding universally (Fuchs see above 64; Fuchs 1983, 141, 143). Examples of "operative norms of conduct," as Fuchs uses the expression would include the received norms concerning contraception and adultery, assuming that "contraception" and "adultery" refer not only to *wrongful* birth prevention and *wrongful* extramarital intercourse, but to forms of conduct which can be described in morally neutral ways and then characterized as always morally wrong.

Fuchs denies that there are specifically Christian operative norms of conduct, added to the norms of common human morality, among which one might find moral absolutes: "Christian behavioral norms, in their material content, are not distinctively Christian norms that would hold only for Christians, but "human" norms, i.e., corresponding to the (authentic) humanness of man, which we have traditionally called norms of the natural moral law, or moral law of nature" (Fuchs see above 76). In support of this position, Fuchs cites the teaching of St. Thomas Aquinas, who holds that in virtuous works Christians are guided by natural reason, the common standard of morality (Fuchs 1983, 73-74, 95; ST I, 108, 2).

One might suppose that Fuchs' denial that there are specifically Christian operative norms of conduct entails an absolute separation of grace from human nature and its fulfillment through moral action. But that is not Fuchs' view. Rather, he relates the two domains

9 - Moral Absolutes: A Critique of the View of Josef Fuchs

by his theory of fundamental option. According to Fuchs, the fundamental option has two aspects.

On the one hand it is an act, inaccessible to conscious reflection, by which the person as such realizes himself or herself before the Absolute (Fuchs 1983, 56). It is acceptance or rejection of an original intimate revelation, involving "either a fully accepted self-surrender to or a self-despairing rejection of the personal God" (Fuchs 1983, 94). This option thus corresponds to the absolute transcendental norms of Christian life and is irreducible to the particular choices and actions which are governed by operative norms of conduct.

Yet, on the other hand, while grace does not specify operative norms of conduct within moral life, the right fundamental option does transform the whole of moral life, for the fundamental option is made *through* the many acts of free choice, which must be integrated with it to bring it to maturity (Fuchs 1970, 96). Hence, while Christian morality has no new moral precepts, it is "the content of the new man who does not remain in the life of the sinner (*sarkikos*) but rather is converted to the grace of being redeemed—in faith, in love, in the following of Christ—and who expresses his being redeemed by living true human morality and Christian religious life as a new man in Christian manner" (Fuchs 1983, 76).

Insofar as Christian morality is nothing but true human morality, Fuchs holds that the operative norms of conduct in Christian life are necessarily conditioned by human historicity. For instance, Fuchs thinks that given the experience necessary to understand sexual behavior, it is immediately evident "that sexuality has to be viewed in relation to a particular culture" (Fuchs see above 76). Fuchs favors the view that ""absoluteness", understood as "immutability" and "universal validity" yields to the principle of change and historical conditioning" (Fuchs see above 61). Against the position that there are "numerous precepts of natural law, which, because rooted in an unchangeable nature, are unvarying and universal" (Fuchs see above 72), Fuchs insists that "the human state may differ in different epochs and cultures" (Fuchs see above 72).

While affirming the historicity of morality, Fuchs firmly rejects individualistic subjectivism: "There is a human orientation to moral questions only in terms of a group, a community, a society, conceived as a whole" (Fuchs see below 93). He also rejects radical cultural relativism by positing a constant, transcultural standard. Because human self-realization is a historical process, the constant criterion of morality is "a steadily advancing 'humanization'" (Fuchs see above 76). For each person: "Self-realization entails that he himself must discover the available possibilities for his action and development, and determine on the basis of his present understanding of himself which of these possibilities are right, reasonable, human (in the full and positive sense of these words), and so contributive to human progress" (Fuchs see above 73). In short: "Whatever leads to our unfolding, in the fullest and best sense of the word, is good" (Fuchs see above 73).

Hence, in Fuchs' view, moral norms which try to be universally valid by that very fact fail to reach the human reality they were meant to direct. The historically conditioned character of operative norms of conduct must be admitted precisely for the sake of their truth: "The critical question, then, is not one of relativism but of objectivity, or the 'truth' of the action which must be in conformity with the whole concrete reality of man (of society)"(Fuchs see above 80).

It follows that when a behavioral norm is being formulated, all the human values and disvalues must be considered in the total human situation. On Fuchs' view, these values and disvalues do not of themselves belong to the moral sphere; rather, they become morally significant only insofar as reason, taking them into account, reaches a judgement as to what way of acting *under the actual conditions* is likely to contribute to human progress:

> To arrive at a behavioral norm regarding premarital intercourse or birth control, for example, a whole complex of factors obviously has to be considered. (It should not be necessary to add that this takes place in an explicit manner only in scientific reflection). What must be determined is the significance of the action as value or nonvalue for the individual, for interpersonal relations and for human society, in connection, of course, with the total reality of man and his society in view of his whole culture. Furthermore, the priority and urgency of the different values implied must be weighed. By this procedure, man as assessor (the evaluating human society) arrives at a judgment, tentatively or with some measure of certitude, as to which mode of behavior might further man's self-realization and self-development (Fuchs see above 77).

Fuchs believes that only a norm arrived at in this way is likely to fit concrete reality and so have the relevant absoluteness of objectivity

9 - Moral Absolutes: A Critique of the View of Josef Fuchs

and moral truth. There are constant human values (such as life and truth) and disvalues (such as death and error), but these values and disvalues do not immediately entail moral norms. Rather, the premoral human values and disvalues must be considered in the concrete situation relative to the overall human good of "self-realization and self-developments."

But even norms formulated in this way, Fuchs believes, are nonabsolute. Societies are not homogeneous but include diversity; cultures themselves gradually change (Fuchs see above 66). Any norm formulated before the choice to be made has a certain generality. Confronted with the actual situation, unexpected factors may be found which require an exception or restriction to a previously assumed norm (Fuchs see above 68-69). Thus, although in principle there are no exceptions to an adequately refined moral norm, Fuchs thinks that no norm can be assumed to be adequate until one has considered the values and disvalues in the situation one actually confronts.

For this reason, Fuchs does not define the moral goodness of the particular action by its conformity to a true moral principle. He formulates and answers the central question:

> Here we take up the question: when is human action, or when is man in his action (morally) good? Must not the answer be: when he intends and effects a human good (value), in the premoral sense—for example, life, health, joy, culture, etc. (for only this is *recta ratio*); but not when he has in view and effects a human nongood an evil (nonvalue) in the premoral sense—for example, death, wounding, wrong, etc. What if he intends and effects good, but this necessarily involves effecting evil also? We answer: if the realization of the evil through the intended realization of good is justified as a proportionally related cause, then in this case only good was intended (Fuchs see above 84).

Thus, Fuchs introduces the notion of "proportionally related cause." He spells it out further as a requirement for rightness of action: "The evil (in a premoral sense) effected by a human agent must not be intended as such, and must be justified in terms of the totality of the action by appropriate reasons" (Fuchs see above 84).

Fuchs grants that the end does not justify the means if the means in question is already admitted to be morally evil. But he holds that the intention and realization of a good can possibly justify the doing of any premoral evil (Fuchs see above 86). In such cases, Fuchs insists, the bringing about of the evil cannot be morally evaluated by itself: "An action cannot be judged morally in its materiality (killing, wounding, going to the moon), without reference to the intention of the agent; without this, we are not dealing with a human action, and only of a human action may one say in a we sense whether it is morally good or bad" (Fuchs see above 84).

In Fuchs' view, it follows that there can be no absolute behavioral moral norms and so, theoretically, no intrinsically evil acts. "The reason is that an action cannot be judged morally at all, considered purely in itself, but only together with all the circumstances and the intention. Consequently, a behavioral norm, universally valid in the full sense, would presuppose that those who arrive at it could know or foresee adequately all the possible combinations of the action concerned with circumstances and intentions, with (premoral) values and nonvalues (*bona* and *mala 'physica'*)" (Fuchs see above 88). Such knowledge, Fuchs observes ironically, is not easy to come by.

Of course, Fuchs affirms that there are universal ethical statements—for example, that one ought to be just, chaste, merciful, and so on—but these are merely formal, since they stop short of specifying the actions which would fulfill them (Fuchs see above 91). Thus, Fuchs counts life as a human good and recognizes the moral norm which protects it: "But 'Thou shalt not kill' is obviously too broadly stated, it would be better to say, 'Thou shalt not commit murder'— that is, 'Thou shalt not kill unjustly'" (Fuchs see below 88). The latter, truly universal formula, however, leaves open the question what killing counts as murder. Fuchs thinks that the method of formulating norms and making judgments he accepts might today lead to drawing the lines between lawful and unlawful killings differently than in the past—for example, with respect to capital punishment and some instances of suicide (Fuchs see above 89).

Fuchs also holds that universal norms can be useful in practice. Formal norms call attention to values. Behavioral norms developed in view of the actual conditions can suffice for ordinary cases, but remain open to refinement when necessary. Also, Fuchs admits: "There can be norms stated as universals, with precise delineations of action to which we cannot conceive of any kind of exception—e.g., cruel treatment of a child which is of no benefit to the child. Despite misgivings on the level of theory, we get along very well with norms of this kind" (Fuchs see above 89).

In the light of the proceeding, it is not surprising that in Fuchs' view no true moral absolutes, in the sense of universal behavioral norms, are

9 ~ Moral Absolutes: A Critique of the View of Josef Fuchs

to be found in Scripture or the Church's teaching. But it is worth noticing how Fuchs handles these theological sources when they seem to falsify his theory.

Fuchs says that Christianity has tended to take moral norms in Scripture as absolutes (universal, ever valid and unchangeable), inasmuch as Scripture is God's word. But since this word is spoken in a human mode, "the moral imperatives appearing in Holy Scripture should not be interpreted as direct divine 'dictates.'" Thus, there remains the problem of interpretation, and so "moral theology will have to go to school to contemporary exegesis, to avoid lapsing into unauthorized good-will reading" (Fuchs see 63).

Fuchs illustrates this view with a few examples from the New Testament. He thinks that the demands of the Sermon on the Mount probably should be interpreted as having absolute validity as models of behavior, but not as universal behavioral norms (Fuchs see below 64). He says recent discussion of the Lord's word on the indissolubility of marriage opens up questions as to whether what is involved is an imperative or something more, and if an imperative whether an operative norm or an ideal (Fuchs see above 64).

Fuchs suggests that St. Paul presupposes and "accepts the moral wisdom of the 'good' men of his time, both Jew and Gentile, one thinks, among other things, of the tables of domestic rules and the catalogue of vices." Thus, "Paul does not present himself as a teacher of moral living, still less as a teacher of specifically Christian norms of conduct." Paul represents a Stoic, Judaic, and Diaspora-Judaic ethos which can hardly be supposed timeless (Fuchs see above 64). St. Paul's moral "directives concerning woman's position in marriage, society and the Church... are to be regarded as conditioned by his time" (Fuchs see above 64). Since these directives given by Paul are considered dated, all the rest—including "the affirmation that certain explicitly mentioned modes of conduct ban one from the kingdom of God"—may be true only in the sense that "these modes of conduct are to be judged negatively, in accordance with the moral evaluation proper to that age and accepted by Paul. Paul therefore did not teach such evaluation as thesis, but admitted it as hypothesis in his doctrinal statement on the Christian mystery of salvation" (Fuchs see above 66).

Fuchs admits that these considerations do not mean that norms of behavior found in the New Testament are no longer valid. But he thinks that the criterion of their possible universality cannot be found in Scripture itself, and concludes: "The moral behavioral norms in Scripture are directed to actual persons of a definite era and culture. Hence their character of absoluteness would not signify primarily universality, but objectivity; and the latter can denote either the objectively right evaluation in a particular culturally conditioned human situation or necessary conformity to the moral views of the morally elite in a given society" (Fuchs see above 66).

In dealing with the moral teaching of the Church and with natural law, Fuchs deploys his theories, already summarized, about the relationship of moral life to salvation and about human historicity. With an evident allusion to polygamy, he argues that whether marriage is to be understood and lived in a Congolese or a Western European style is an important question, "but not in itself determinative of salvation" (Fuchs see above 66; Fuchs 1983, 132). True, amidst pluralism, there must be unconditionality in stating precepts. "However, it could follow from what has been said that this quality of absoluteness does not represent primarily the universality of a norm, but an antithesis to arbitrary judgment; or, positively stated, orientation toward concrete human (total) reality, and, in this sense objectivity, truth" (Fuchs see above 67-68).

With respect to the assistance of the Holy Spirit promised to the Church, Fuchs denies that "the Holy Spirit slowly began to impart via the Church what he had not conveyed through Scripture—a vast collection of moral behavioral norms proclaimed for the whole world and for all times (Fuchs see above 69). The "Spirit is merely 'incarnated' in the Church" which remains very human despite his assistance (Fuchs see above 69). The Spirit only "guarantees that error, which in human comprehension-discovery-evaluation-listening-deciding can never be absolutely excluded, will not become in the end an essential component of the Church." From the preceding statement, Fuchs proceeds at once to draw the conclusion that there is room for dissent from behavioral norms received in the Church: "It stands to reason, then, that the same ecclesial community or a particular cultural group within it—pluralistic, therefore—will at times begin to experience and evaluate in a new and different way, regarding specific points. In this connection it is noteworthy that in the Church's two thousand years, seemingly no definitive doctrinal decision on moral questions has been made, at least insofar as these would be related to natural law, without being at the same time revealed" (Fuchs see above 70).

Fuchs affirms that nondefinitive moral guidelines of the Church come under the assistance of the Spirit and should enjoy a presumption of truth (Fuchs see above 70). But for him that only means that received behavioral norms are nonarbitrary guidelines, which remain open to review by conscience confronted with a concrete situation including elements not envisaged by the general norm (Fuchs see above 75). Even if moral norms were proposed infallibly, Fuchs thinks, "it can be imagined and probably demonstrated, if need be, that a strict behavioral norm, stated as a universal, contains unexpressed conditions and qualifications which as such limit its universality" (Fuchs see above 75).

III. Critique With Respect to the Relationship of Morality to Salvation

Without using the expression "fundamental option," Vatican II clearly teaches that the act of faith is the fundamental option of Christian life: "'The obedience of faith' (*Rm* 16, 26; cf. 1, 5; 2 *Cor* 10, 5-6) must be given to God who reveals, an obedience by which man entrusts his whole self freely to God, offering 'the full submission of intellect and will to God who reveals,' and freely assenting to the truth revealed by him" (DV 5). While saving faith depends upon the mysterious working of grace, the teaching of Trent, Vatican I, and Vatican II clearly implies that the submission of faith is made by a free choice, a moral act of assent, in conformity with conscience.[2]

Fuchs says that faith (*fides qua*) is the fundamental option. However, he thinks this act is not a free choice, but pertains to basic freedom and is inaccessible to conscious reflection (Fuchs 1983, 92-94). This view depends upon an arguable theological theory of grace (Fuchs 1983, 94; Fuchs 1970, 109). Whatever one thinks of that theory, in reality faith as a particular moral act of assent by free choice can be located by conscious reflection. Not only do many converted as adults remember the precise moment when they made that choice, but many baptized as infants can recall a moment at which they freely committed themselves to their faith in rejecting a temptation to abandon it or freely recommitted themselves after having sinned directly against it.

Moreover, Fuchs elsewhere treated fundamental option as if it were charity rather than faith (Fuchs 1970, 109). Whether faith or charity is considered the fundamental option is important. A Christian can be in mortal sin and have true faith at the same time, since not every mortally sinful choice involves changing one's specific choice to believe (DS 1336-1339/804). Charity, however, should inform the whole of Christian life and is incompatible with mortal sin.

As soon as one admits that the fundamental option of Christian life is faith and that one takes this option by a particular free choice, one begins to see difficulties in Fuchs' view of the relationship of the content of morality (conscious choices) to salvation (the transcendental). By Christian faith one enters the communion of the new covenant and so accepts the personal and communal responsibilities of friendship with God in Jesus' Church. A covenant has definite stipulations and life in any human community has many operative implications. Thus, faith requires one to keep the commandments (DS 1336-1339/804).

Faith also leads to specifically Christian operative norms. In denying that there are such norms, Fuchs uses the authority of St. Thomas, but does so selectively. For Thomas holds that there are specific responsibilities, such as love of enemies, which flow from the properly Christian virtue of charity.[3]

Thomas also holds that Christian life requires specifically Christian moral virtues which differ in kind from the virtues which can be acquired through human acts formed by natural reason alone. According to Thomas, natural virtues equip one only for life in civic community in this world. Specifically Christian virtues are needed precisely because by faith human persons become fellow citizens of the saints and members of God's household. Natural virtues will end with this life, but specifically Christian virtues will continue to shape appropriate actions in the heavenly fellowship (ST I-II, 63, 3-4).

Christian virtues bear on the same matters as the civic virtues they correspond to, but, according to Thomas, sometimes make specific demands different from those of human reason. For instance, the rule set by reason for eating is that one's diet be healthful and not block the use of reason. But the rule of divine law is that one chastise one's body and make it docile by abstinence from food, drink, and other satisfactions. Thomas expressly argues that something excessive according to the rational norm of civic virtue can be appropriate according to the norm of specifically Christian virtue—for example, to willingly lay down one's life in defense of the faith.[4]

Is Thomas' teaching on infused virtues inconsistent with his position, cited by Fuchs, that in virtuous works Christians are guided by natural reason, the common standard of morality? Hardly. For if one does not consign faith to the transcendental domain, as Fuchs does, it can generate Christian operative norms by specifying the content of a life conducted according to the principles and processes of natural reason. One can see how this specification works by considering an example: love of enemies.

Jesus says: "Love your enemies, do good to those who hate you, bless those who curse you, pray for those who treat you badly" (*Lk* 6, 27-

28). In explaining the reason for this norm, Jesus appeals to a generally accepted moral principle: "Treat others as you would like them to treat you" (*Lk* 6, 31). Everyone takes care of friends and deals fairly with others when that is advantageous. But Christians should do more. As God's children, they are called to act as he does: "Be compassionate as your Father is compassionate. Do not judge, and you will not be judged yourselves; do not condemn, and you will not be condemned yourselves; grant pardon, and you will be pardoned" (*Lk* 6, 36-37).[5]

The parable of the merciless official in Matthew's Gospel makes the same point. A king forgives a high official a huge debt, but the official refuses the same mercy to a subordinate who owes a small amount. The king thereupon insists on full payment, and Jesus draws the moral: "That is how my heavenly Father will deal with you unless you each forgive your brother from your heart" (Mt 18, 35).

The moral principle underlying these arguments is the Golden Rule, which is available to everyone. Christian faith makes a claim about the human situation: that although sinful men and women are God's enemies, they are offered fellowship with him by his mercy. One who believes this claim and accepts the offered fellowship therefore has specific moral responsibilities toward others, including enemies: to treat them with similar mercy.

Is this moral norm accessible to any upright nonbeliever who proceeds reasonably? Fuchs thinks so, but his argument assumes that loving enemies is the only alternative to hating them (Fuchs 1983, 61). Of course, nonbelievers can know that revenge is immoral, that kindness to enemies is godlike, and even that such beneficence can at times be morally required.[6] But in many cases nonbelievers will faultlessly follow the policy of keeping their distance from enemies in order to avoid both suffering and doing evil. Only faith in the divine initiative of reconciliation provides a reason for loving enemies—for example, by making repeated, risky, and often seemingly fruitless approaches to them.

In consigning the specifically Christian to the transcendental, Fuchs tends to reduce salvation to union with God (Fuchs see above 67-68). Much old-fashioned spirituality favored that reduction, despite the New Testament's teaching that redemption includes all human goods and the cosmos itself (Rm 8, 21; 1 Cor 3, 22-23; Eph 1, 10). The teaching of Vatican II firmly excludes such reductionist spirituality.

The work of redemption, according to Vatican II, is not limited to saving souls. The mission of the Church extends to the temporal order. The spiritual and temporal orders "although distinct, are so connected in the plan of God that he himself intends in Christ to appropriate the whole universe into a new creation, initially here on earth, fully on the last day" (AA 5). Christians will find perfected in heaven the very good fruits of human nature and work which they nurture here on earth (GS 39).

Thus, when Fuchs says that Christ's mission was neither to establish a new moral order nor primarily to teach a moral doctrine corresponding to creation, we can agree with him. Faith and love do not depend on the rectitude of norms of living. But the material mode in which Christians "incarnate" faith and love is not so much a "*secundarium*" as Fuchs suggests. Morally good actions not only manifest faith and love but prepare the material of the heavenly kingdom (GS 38). Thus, Christian moral teaching concerns not merely extrinsic effects and signs of saving grace but intrinsic and partially constitutive means to the integral fulfillment for which Christians hope.

Fuchs is right in rejecting legalism and what he calls a "preceptive" understanding of natural law. The genuine good of humankind is the ultimate principle of morality. But that good will never be fully realized within history and this world, for while our work prepares the material of the heavenly kingdom, earthly progress is not identical with the growth of the kingdom (GS 38-39). As Vatican II teaches, the selves and relationships built up by our actions are more important than the technical results we achieve: "A man is more precious for what he is than for what he has" (GS 35). Persons and their relationship, souls in loving communion, already mysteriously share in the kingdom which will last. "Hence, the norm of human activity is this: that in accord with the divine plan and will, it should harmonize with the good of the human race, and allow men as individuals and as members of society to pursue their total vocation and fulfill it" (GS 35).

In short, Christians are called to do what Jesus did and add to it, to bear real and abundant fruit, not by themselves but in him. Without Jesus we can do nothing; in him we can and ought to do great things. Thus, Christian ethics should guide us in communal cooperation with Jesus. The work of Jesus bears upon human salvation, begun in this world but completed only in heavenly fulfillment. Hence, Christian ethics primarily should be an other-worldly humanism. It should direct Christian life here and now as a real sharing in the kingdom (which is not of this world) and preparation for everlasting life (still to come).

Furthermore, while a life according to Christian faith must conform to the moral truth the non-believer can know, for each believer faith excludes many options which would be available to an upright nonbeliever. For, according to faith, diverse personal talents and opportunities are so many different gifts which Christians must put to work in the cooperative effort of building up the Church or preparing the material of Jesus' expected kingdom (AA 3).[7] Jesus' followers are to make their different personal contributions to the work he began. Hence, there is a specifically Christian norm which binds every Christian and no nonbeliever: One should discern one's personal vocation, accept it, and faithfully fulfill it.

This norm emerges very clearly from St. Paul's teaching concerning the Church, considered as one body of Christ, having many members with diverse and complementary functions (*1 Cor* 12, 12-26). In his encyclical, *Redemptor hominis*, John Paul II refers to the teaching of St. Paul in emphasizing the principle of personal vocation:

> For the whole of the community of the People of God and for each member of it what is in question is not just a specific "social membership;" rather, for each and every one what is essential is a particular "vocation." Indeed, the Church as the People of God is also—according to the teaching of St. Paul mentioned above, of which Pius XII reminded us in wonderful terms— "Christ's Mystical Body." Membership in that body has for its source a particular call united with the saving action of grace. Therefore, if we wish to keep in mind this community of the People of God, which is so vast and so extremely differentiated, we must see first and foremost Christ saying in a way to each member of the community: "Follow Me."[8]

Thus, each Christian, following Christ according to his or her personal vocation, has specific responsibilities with respect to a small part of the whole work of redemption.

The fulfillment of one's vocation by no means guarantees success in realizing the human goods one attempts to serve. Indeed, in the fallen world, one can expect only limited results. The perfection of the redemptive work will come about by God's act of recreation, which accepts and answers the sacrifice of faithful obedience, according to the model and in continuity with the death and resurrection of Jesus.

Hence, for each Christian, a morally good action is one marked by faithfulness, whether or not it actually effects innerworldly good. Jesus did not say: If anyone wants to be a follower of mine, let him intend and bring about more premoral human good than bad. Rather, he said: "If anyone wants to be a follower of mine, let him renounce himself and take up his cross every day and follow me." (*Lk* 9, 23).[9]

Fidelity to personal vocation is specified by true moral norms. Since the human fulfillment to which they direct is the heavenly kingdom planned by God and expected through his re-creative act, these true norms cannot be reduced to the principle of the human self-realization and self-development possible within this world. Hence, Fuchs is mistaken in thinking that the right option is the one which contributes to human innerworldly progress or makes for steadily advancing humanization in the course of history.

The Christian needs something more modest in order to be able to choose responsibly in view of his or her unique but very small role in the divine plan of salvation. For example, the morally decisive question about extramarital sexual intercourse is not whether it contributes to self-development and steadily advancing humanization, but whether it can faithfully fulfill anyone' s personal vocation by bringing souls into that loving communion which is the kingdom – a loving communion not only of human but of divine persons.

In sum, Fuchs is right in rejecting legalism and seeking the basis of morality in integral human fulfillment. However, he overlooks the place this fulfillment has in the work of redemption, which will be completed only by God's re-creative act. Hence, Fuchs accepts as part of an oversimplified criterion of morality how well acts effect goods in this world and history. He thus neglects the importance of faithful service to the goods pertaining to each Christian's personal vocation, a service which remains significant even when failure seems to render faithfulness pointless. At the same time, Fuchs too rigidly divides the "transcendental" from the "operative" dimension of Christian life. Thus he makes the relationship between Christian moral life and salvation too loose.

Whether Fuchs' view of that relationship does full justice to Catholic doctrine concerning the merit of good works is a question which need not be considered here. However, it is worth noting that Fuchs' conception of the relationship between moral life and salvation is not the only alternative to the legalistic view of it. One also can understand merit in relationship to God's faithfulness to his covenantal promises – as the appropriateness of God's ultimate work or re-creation and glorification in response to the obedience of men and women united in Christ, fulfilling their personal vocations within Jesus' redemptive mission. On this view, faithful service to human goods in this life merits what it cannot effect – their integral realization in the kingdom, where "we will find them again, but freed of stain, burnished and transfigured" (GS 39).

IV. CRITIQUE WITH RESPECT TO
HISTORICAL AND CULTURAL RELATIVITY

A radical historical or cultural relativism treats as ultimate the set of norms commonly accepted as morally obligatory at a given time and place. This reduction of morality to social convention leaves no room for moral criticism which transcends culture sand epochs. Radical relativism also presupposes a unity and harmony in culture one does not find in any actual society or epoch. Thus, radical relativism is not so prevalent among professional anthropologists as it once was. David Bidney aptly summarizes the antirelativist view: "In the last analysis, *culture is not* the measure of things, *but nature is*, and there are more things in nature than are ever grasped through our human cultural symbols. Culture is but our best human means of adjusting to nature and utilizing its powers in the service of mankind. This postulate of a *metacultural reality* renders scientific progress possible and saves us from the *culturcentric predicament* of historical idealism, historical materialism, and evolutionary positivism" (Bidney 1968, col. 544).

In general, Fuchs' view does not involve a radical historical or cultural relativism. For instance, when he dismisses as culturally conditioned "the Pauline directives concerning women's position in marriage, society and the Church," one might think he is committed to radical relativism, especially when he proposes as a conclusion: "Such directives cannot be normative for a period in which the social position of women is essentially different." But Fuchs' basic nonrelativism appears when he adds that a judgment is possible "at least in principle—as to which suits the nature of women in society better, and hence is the moral ideal, the social position of women in Paul's cultural milieu or that of women in our cultural milieu—along with corresponding moral demands" (Fuchs see above 64-65).

Nevertheless, there are passages in which Fuchs' suggests that there might be a profound relativity of morality to social reality. For instance, he refers to polygamy in an African tribe, and sketches two ways of viewing it. One is that the social reality is defective, which raises an issue at the pastoral level but not one concerning moral truth. The other raises a more basic question: "But might it not be assumed also that on the basis of dissimilar experiences, a heterogeneous self-concept and varying options and evaluations on the part of man (humanity) projecting himself into the future in human fashion—*secundam rectam rationem*—are entirely possible, and that these options and evaluations within the chosen system postulate varied forms of behavior?" (Fuchs see above 79).

Without admitting radical relativism, there are several ways in which one can make room for historicity and for the relativity of morality to contingent social reality.

First, factual judgments often lead to an altogether fresh insight into moral responsibilities. That is how the Christian faith's teaching concerning the fallen and redeemed human condition generates specifically Christian norms, such as the requirement treated above of mercy toward enemies. At a much lower but still significant level, modern knowledge of communicable diseases leads to morally binding norms of hygiene inaccessible to less well informed societies

Second, social and cultural entities are not discovered by us in the natural world. Rather, they are constituted by human practical reflection. Thus, relationships of tenants to landlords and charging interest on loans had different moral significances in the Middle Ages than they do today, because the socioeconomic system was so different that outwardly similar actions actually involved very different relationships between the wills of those doing them and the relevant human goods.

Third, societies like individuals have options which both generate and limit moral responsibilities. There is no relativism in the fact that a husband and wife should express their affection for each other in ways which would be inappropriate for a couple who are not married. Different moral responsibilities follow from different morally acceptable antecedent options. Similarly societies can have options—for example, whether to press harder for the development of useful techniques or to live a simpler style of life. Options such as this one can make a profound difference in certain moral responsibilities such as those bearing upon communal property.

Fourth, conceptual clarification can transform the options with which one is faced by distinguishing what had appeared a single choice into two or more. Fuchs points out an example: "The Church's opposition in the past to religious freedom is understandable if religious freedom and indifferentism are equated conceptually" (Fuchs see above 71). One might be tempted to say in such cases that an error in moral judgment is detected and corrected. But it would be more accurate to say that a correct judgment on one inadequately understood alternative has been replaced by two correct judgments on more adequately understood alternatives.

Fifth, moral insight often is blocked by bias and released by changed social conditions. Thus, when all the members of a society with the leisure to engage in critical reflection benefit from an institution such as slavery, it is difficult for anyone seriously to entertain the moral truth. However, when slavery is no longer so expedient, the truth about its unfairness easily appears. In this way, changing social reality alters available knowledge of moral truth and thus changes people's subjective moral responsibility, although the moral truth remains what it was. Slavery has not become wrong in the past century or two, but its wrongness has become known.

Contingent social reality makes a difference to the morality of behavior in these five ways and perhaps in other ways as well. Clearly, growing knowledge of moral truth (the fifth way) is compatible with there being moral absolutes. That leaves the first four ways. But all of these also are compatible with moral absolutes—that is, with certain universal norms, such as those concerning adultery and contraception, being true. For such moral absolutes refer not merely to patterns of behavior but to human acts specified by definite intentions: Contraception is a choice to do something to prevent conception, and adultery is a choice to engage in extramarital intercourse involving a married person.[10] These specifications will not be changed by further factual information, differing interpretations of similar outward behavior, changing options with respect to social priorities, or conceptual clarification. Acts specified by intentions remain the same despite such variable factors, because their basic interpretation is identical with their constitution as human acts, and so they are not open, as behavior is, to reinterpretation.

Thus, if one wishes to hold that contraception and adultery are not necessarily wrong for Christians today but were necessarily wrong for Christians in earlier times, one must hold either that only our *knowledge* of the moral truth rather than the truth itself has changed or that contingent social reality makes a difference to what is morally right and wrong in some more radical way. When Fuchs emphasizes historical and cultural relativity, he obviously wants to say something other than that Christian morality always has been erroneously strict. Thus, he is supposing some way more radical than any of those listed above in which the concrete historical and cultural situation determines moral truth.

When Fuchs suggests as criteria of morality standards such as "steadily advancing 'humanization'" (Fuchs see above 76) and "man's self-realization and self-developments" (Fuchs see above 131), he evidently wants them to be more than formal and empty concepts.

When he insists upon the social ("the evaluating human society") to exclude individual arbitrariness, he points to the de facto "total reality of man and his society" as the principle which provides determinate content (Fuchs see above 78). Clearly, he wishes to avoid relativism: "The critical question, then, is not one of relativism but of objectivity, or the 'truth' of the action which must be in conformity with the whole concrete reality of man (of society)" (Fuchs see above 80). But how can Fuchs avoid relativism if he accepts as determinative of the formal concept of human self-realization the *whole* concrete reality of society, with its actual historical and cultural conditions?

One could say that the whole concrete reality of persons and their societies must be taken into account in developing moral norms, but that not everything should be accepted uncritically as determinative of what is morally right and wrong. That position is available to anyone who holds that critical reflection can invoke operative norms with transhistorical and transcultural validity. But Fuchs, to avoid moral absolutes, proposes a concept of *recta ratio* which empties it of such content:

> We shall continue to employ the traditional term *recta ratio*. The human is in it, that which is humanly right. Whatever is not *recta ratio* is necessarily nonhuman not worthy of man, antithetic to a steadily advancing "humanization." *Recta ratio* does not mean innate discernment or moral truth, "inscribed" somehow, somewhere. Hence it does not denote a norm of conduct "inscribed in our nature" at least not in the sense that one could read off a moral regulation from a natural reality. The "nature" upon which the moral law is inscribed is preeminently and formally nature as *ratio*, but only, of course, as *recta ratio*. From this viewpoint, the preferred expression would probably be that of Paul in Romans: the moral law is "engraved on the heart" (*Rm* 2,15). Apart from this, realities of the natural order, *ratio* excepted, can neither provide a basis for, nor affirm, any moral laws. Considered positively, then, the task of *homo-ratio* in discovering or projecting behavioral norms consists in understanding man himself, his own total reality, together with his world, in order to assess the significance of the alternatives for action available to him and so arrive at a moral affirmation (Fuchs see above 76-77).

While this account of *recta ratio* is not without its ambiguities, it clearly excludes the sort of content which would be needed to determine what should and what should not count as morally determinative when one fills the formal concept of human self-realization with the *whole* concrete reality of persons in society and their world.

Thus, in rejecting moral absolutes Fuchs is driven to do two things: to appeal to the whole historical-cultural reality to find content for the formal notion of human self-realization, and to exclude from natural law anything beyond the formal requirements of reason which might serve as a principle of criticism. He probably did not intend indiscriminately to accept as morally determinative actual, socially functioning views of human self-realization. He certainly did not consider the implications of doing so. But only the relativity of morality to actual, socially functioning views of human self-realization seems to involve sufficiently radical relativity to exclude moral absolutes. Therefore it is worth considering in the concrete what such relativity amounts to, even though Fuchs surely would wish to introduce limiting principles.

One actual, socially functioning view of human self-realization is the Marxism which is accepted by the leadership of the Soviet Union. Those who espouse this ideology are not constrained by the ethical absolutes of other eras and cultures, such as the Stoic, Judaic, and Diaspora-Judaic ethos which Fuchs thinks St. Paul assumed as hypothesis from his cultural milieu. Nor does any Marxist wonder about what is required for steadily advancing humanization. For a convinced Marxist, human self-realization and self-development are no mere empty concepts. What contributes to the revolution and emergence of the new society is good; what resists the course of historical inevitability is bad. Thus, while Marxists deny moral absolutes which would bind always and everywhere, regardless of the concrete historical and cultural conditions, they insist on moral absolutes of the sort Fuchs accepts—norms which guide behavior in the actual situation to true self-realization and self-fulfillment.

Fuchs might reply that although Marxism is the established worldview in the Soviet Union, it can be criticized on factual and logical grounds, and thus does not represent the whole concrete reality of anyone's historical-cultural situation. Whether such a critique could be carried through without assuming some moral standards will not seem so clear if one considers the ideological differences between the findings of social scientists in the Soviet Union and the West. Moreover, will the situation be improved if one sets aside Marxism as one's example of a socially functioning view of human self-realization and takes instead the liberal worldview common to the democratic nations of the West?

Here social norms also are predicated on a definite view of steadily advancing "humanization." Human self-realization ideally means material wellbeing for all and maximum liberty for each. Among the normative implications of this conception are approval of contraception, abortion, and easy divorce and remarriage. By limiting population growth and the cost of social welfare programs, contraception and abortion contribute to the attainment of a high and rising standard of living. By freeing individuals from burdensome family responsibilities, these practices together with easy divorce contribute greatly to individual liberty.

Theologians of the West who appealed to public opinion polls (the "*sensus fidelium*") and the academic climate of opinion ("*consensus theologorum*") against recent reaffirmations by the magisterium of received Catholic moral teaching are hardly in a position to disown the specification "self-realization" receives from the actual social reality of the contemporary West. Indeed, Fuchs seems to appeal to this reality.

Undoubtedly it is full of inconsistencies, and so can be criticized on logical grounds. But logical criticism can only show that *some* position is false; it is impotent to determine which, if any, of an inconsistent set of positions is true. Moreover, because of the libertarianism and pluralism characteristic of the West, frequently anyone who sought moral specification from social reality would be sent back to individualistic subjectivism: On that question, what is right for you depends upon what you want out of life. But Fuchs appealed to society precisely to avoid that sort of arbitrariness and relativism.

Of course, when the very survival of a society is at stake, those who admit no moral absolutes do tend toward unanimity in their judgments concerning what ought to be done. Shortly after World War II, a British economist, Lionel Robbins, reflected upon the simplifications introduced into the making of socioeconomic policy during wartime. A single objective counts; all else is instrumental. If there is no victory, there is no future. All decisions are technical. Unity of purpose "gives a certain unity to the framework of planning which at least makes possible some sort of direct decision which is not wholly arbitrary" (Robbins 1957, 49-50).

Robbins surely is right about the wartime psychology of the leaders and people of Britain and the United States. Absolute victory, the unconditional surrender of the Axis nations, became an obsession. That it precisely why virtually everyone accepted the strategy of obliteration bombing as harmonious with the whole concrete historical-cultural reality of those societies. Against that strategy, two decades later Vatican II articulated a moral absolute of the sort Fuchs considers theoretically impossible: "Any act of war aimed indiscriminately at the destruction of entire cities or of extensive areas along with their populations is a crime against God and man himself. It merits unequivocal and unhesitating condemnation" (GS 80).

During World War II Germans also had a clear sense of the requirements of concrete social reality. Although subsequently hardly anyone could be found who had supported Nazi ideology, at one time some Germans were certain that racial purification required that all Jews be eliminated. Of course, Nazi ideology can be criticized. The most obvious criticism is that it is *always* wrong to try to kill all the Jews in the world. No doubt Fuchs would agree with that moral absolute. But for him absoluteness is not universality. It is "the objectively right evaluation in a particular culturally conditioned human situation or necessary conformity to the moral views of the morally elite in a given society" (Fuchs see above 66). In other words, the relevant absolute is merely what we must think about Nazi genocide. Or, at best, it is one of those "norms stated as universals, with precise delineations of action to which we cannot conceive of any kind of exception" (Fuchs see above 89).

Martyrs in general, not only Christian ones, often lay down their lives for what they think are moral absolutes at odds with social demands which themselves claim absoluteness in Fuchs' sense. The fictional Antigone and Plato's Socrates appealed to moral absolutes. John the Baptist lived too soon to know how to provide "internal forum solutions" for difficult marriage cases. Thomas More, thinking it always wrong to swear falsely, died "the King's good servant, but God's first."

Had Jesus, in discerning his own responsibilities, used the criterion of the whole concrete historical-cultural situation of his society, he might have sided with the leaders, like Caiphas, who judged that "it is better for one man to die for the people, than for the whole nation to be destroyed" (Jn 11, 50). Of course, Caiphas was assuming that the end justifies the means. But unless one supposes that killing the innocent is *always* wrong, how can one disagree with Caiphas' evaluation of the premoral goods of one innocent life and the whole nation's survival? Indeed, what happened a few decades later might be taken to verify the realism of Caiphas' policy of collaboration with the Roman authorities.

For the Christian there is a way of escaping from the limitations of the concrete totality of particular historical-cultural situations. The ultimate horizon of good action need not be settled by what contributes to human progress in one's actual, earthly society. For while natural virtues promote the good life of earthly society, Christian virtues equip one for life in the kingdom. The kingdom is no mere abstraction but a reality which relativizes the particularities of historical epochs and cultures.

That is why Vatican II, having stressed the tremendous changes which mark the modern world, affirms: "The Church also maintains that beneath all changes there are many realities which do not change and which have their ultimate foundation in Christ, who is the same yesterday and today, yes and forever. Hence in the light of Christ, the image of the unseen God, the firstborn of every creature, the Council wishes to speak to all men in order to illuminate the mystery of man and to cooperate in finding the solution to the outstanding problems of our time" (GS 10).

When it approaches urgent questions about war, the Council specifies this teaching to affirm moral absolutes: "Contemplating this melancholy state of humanity, the Council wishes to recall first of all the permanent binding force of universal natural law and its all-embracing principles" (GS 79). These principles are not merely transcendental norms; rather, they are operative norms drawn from the gospel's vision of human self-realization and progress. Hence, "The good news of Christ constantly renews the life and culture of fallen man. It combats and removes the errors and evils resulting from sinful allurements which are a perpetual threat. It never ceases to purify and elevate the morality of peoples. By riches coming from above, it makes fruitful, as it were from within, the spiritual qualities and gifts of every people and of every age. It strengthens, perfects, and restores them in Christ" (GS 58).

Obviously, the content the gospel provides for the notion of human self-realization does not give Christians a goal which would enable them to calculate what sorts of actions are likely to effect the most good or contribute most to human progress. Moreover, as explained above, success in effecting goals, even those involving the most genuine goods of persons, is far less important than faithful obedience in serving goods, whose realization ultimately depends upon God's re-creative act. How, then, can the gospel's vision of integral human fulfillment generate any operative moral norms?

According to the Preface of the Feast of Christ the King, which Vatican II quotes, the goods of the kingdom are truth and life, holiness and grace, justice, love, and peace (GS 39). Each of these is an irreducible aspect of human fulfillment. Each contributes to the image of God whose fullness will be found only in the whole Christ.

9 ~ Moral Absolutes: A Critique of the View of Josef Fuchs

Yet each of these goods can be served by our work in this world. Such service gives content to love of neighbor, and loving service to one's neighbor is service to Jesus. In carrying on such service, partiality is excluded, except that partiality to others characteristic of the mercy of Jesus, who came not to be served but to serve.

However, not all Christians have the same gifts and opportunities for service. Hence, apart from their common religious duties, the affirmative operative norms of Christian life flow from finding one's personal vocation, committing oneself to it, and faithfully fulfilling it. In doing so, one promotes the good fruits of human nature and effort. The neighbors one serves will attain truth only imperfectly, will die, will fall short of perfect holiness, will suffer from injustice and share in it. Still, the redemptive work of Jesus will continue in the world and the coming of the kingdom will continue to be merited.

In cases in which it would seem to a nonbeliever necessary to destroy, damage, or impede some instance of one of the human goods, the Christian will remember that these are irreducible aspects of persons made in God's image. Love of neighbor excludes any choice to harm; that is why it fulfills the commandments (*Rm* 13, 8-10). Reverence for the person rules out, always and everywhere, a whole series of abuses. For example, one may never choose abortion, willful self-destruction, slavery, or prostitution (GS 27). Within the limited perspective of human knowledge, no one can ever know that choosing to destroy, damage, or impede a human good truly would contribute to human self-realization. The Christian has the certitude of hope that God will crown faithfulness with the perfection of all the human goods in the heavenly kingdom. Hence, it never is necessary to make the best of a broken world by sacrificing some persons (or aspects of persons) to other persons (or aspects of persons). The preceding explanation of the place of absolutes in Christian morality may be clarified by considering the example of marital love.

Marital love is a good intrinsic to the persons of husband and wife in their communion. This good is not merely a means to some further end. Unlike an automobile or a dose of medicine, marital love is an ultimate principle— though not the only one—which specifies the acts of married life. Beyond marital love lies only the ultimate and full human good — the heavenly communion, of which Christian marriage itself is the sacrament, in which Jesus is united with his Church.

The meaning of the good of marital love is not exhausted by anyone's present understanding of it. All couples who truly love grow constantly in their understanding of their love. As they do so, they look back with the realization of how little they understood at earlier stages (Some of this growth in understanding certainly can be articulated and handed on from age to age. It would be a mistake to think that husbands and wives today have no more responsibility to and for one another than did married people in Old Testament times).

Precisely for the sake of marital love's growth, we must not attempt to define it in positive terms. To say, once for all, what marital love is and must be, would be to mummify it. Yet if married people have no way of identifying authentic love, they cannot pursue and foster it. Thus, marital love is "defined" negatively, in terms of exclusive and permanent rights, mutually given and received, to marital acts. Thus, negative moral norms which absolutely exclude divorce (with remarriage) and adultery hold open the way for the constant growth and creative newness of marital love.

Remove the moral absolutes which make marital love possible without delimiting its possibility, and marital love then will be redefined positively, in terms of certain skillful performances (such as simultaneous orgasms), psychological satisfactions (such as secure affection), or social advantages (such as economically beneficial family ties). Even if people succeed in the pursuit of such goods, they will only complete projects, not receive a continuous and inexhaustible gift.

Maintain these absolutes and others like them. Human self-realization and progress have content which can generate operative norms. These do not ideologically define a this-worldly social goal, historically and culturally conditioned and constantly changing. But they do direct one to the service of the various goods of the person, to reverence for persons, and to preparing the material of the kingdom. Conforming to moral absolutes, one sometimes will pay the price of not effecting certain good results or of suffering certain evils. But one may confidently hope that God's re-creative act will respond to one's faithfulness.

V. Critique with Respect to Proportionalism in Moral Judgment

Of course, Fuchs has reserved a way out of the inadequacy of socially articulated moral norms with their dependence on the actual historical-cultural situation to provide content for the otherwise merely formal concept of human self-realization or steadily advancing "humanization." That way out is through conscience. For, according to Fuchs, behavioral norms formulated in advance, which are necessarily abstract and somewhat generalized, never can be wholly adequate to the concrete human reality to which authentic, self-realizing action should conform. Hence: "As only the *ratio* (*recta ratio*) of conscience judges the reality ultimately and comprehensively in terms of the concrete element in it that is to be actualized, the *ratio* (*recta ratio*) of behavioral norms exercises merely an auxiliary function" (Fuchs see above 76).

Still, it was important to see the inadequacy of Fuchs' view of the historical and cultural relativity of behavioral norms. Otherwise, when the unworkability of moral judgment as he understands it becomes clear, one might have supposed that the individual conscience could look to society for support. However, what has been shown above with respect to historical-cultural relativity makes it clear that society is in no better position to support conscience than a bankrupt nation is to support its impoverished citizens. Fuchs' view of the relationship between conscience and norms means that the individual must in principle be able to review the work of the evaluating society in formulating general norms.

Thus, in theory, at least, concrete moral judgment, if it is to arrive at moral truth, somehow must be able to reconsider everything involved in societal evaluation: "the significance of the action as value or nonvalue for the individual, for interpersonal relations and for human society, in connection, of course, with the total reality of man and his society and in view of the whole culture. Furthermore, the priority and urgency of the different values implied must be weighed" (Fuchs see above 78). Beyond this, conscience must consider what human good and nongood—in the premoral sense—will be effected by each action possible in the actual situation. Whenever the action will effect both good and bad, conscience must determine whether "the realization of the evil through the intended realization of good is justified as a proportionally related cause" (Fuchs see above 84).

It is important to notice that the case in which an action intends and effects a good but also effects an evil is by no means an exception. Whenever anyone undertakes to bring about a certain good something is lost; at least, valuable resources such as time and energy are used and they will never be recovered. Moreover, no one sets out to effect evil (in the premoral sense) precisely as such. Even malicious people seeking revenge intend some premoral good—for example, what seems to them just satisfaction for the wrong another has done. If we think of a possible action and notice nothing bad about it, no choice is necessary; we proceed spontaneously. And if a possible action is suggested to us and we see nothing good about it, we do not entertain it as a real option.

Therefore, when Fuchs introduces the notion of "proportionally related cause," he embraces a general theory of moral judgment: proportionalism. According to this theory, the moral judgment of conscience can and should be reached by making a comparative evaluation of benefits and harms promised by available possibilities. The right choice is the one which offers the best proportion of premoral good to nongood.

Since Fuchs is not alone in holding proportionalism, I shall first offer a general—and, I believe, decisive—criticism of the theory, and then deal with some of the peculiar features of Fuchs' presentation of it.

The first point to notice is that we can and often do make practical judgments in the way proportionalism suggests. In cases where one has a definite, firmly accepted goal in view, deliberation seeks to determine the easiest or least costly route to this objective. After considering the possibilities, one often finds only one remaining and proceeds to take it. Here "more good" and "less bad" have definite meanings, for one is not thinking morally but technically: Only instrumental good is at stake. The morality of what one is doing and of the various ways of doing it is either taken for granted or ignored for the time being. One reaches a conclusion about the best course from a comparative evaluation of premoral goods, but the conclusion is not a moral judgment. For example, if someone is only concerned to reach a destination as quickly as possible, "I ought to take the night plane to Rome" is not a judgment about moral rightness but about efficiency.

If individuals could simply accept their moral framework from society, their judgments of conscience could be limited to technical questions, and they could proceed as proportionalism suggests. However, since no merely earthly society is in a position to give moral support to its members' consciences, proportionalism requires conscience to evaluate the promise of different options not in view of particular goals but in view of human fulfillment as a whole.

In many cases, one makes a moral judgment, eliminating possibilities by using previously recognized moral norms. For instance, a mother who believes she ought to divide her estate evenly among several children may consider and reject several possible ways, until she finally finds the way which seems least inequitable. She then makes the division in this way, saying it is less bad than the alternatives—that is, less uneven than the discarded possibilities. Here the moral good of fairness is at stake, and reflection concludes in a moral judgment. But the judgment is different from those proposed by proportionalists. The proportion here is determined by a moral principle (fairness). By contrast, the proportionalist thinks moral judgments are reached by a comparative evaluation of human goods, without assuming a moral principle to settle the proportions.

When they break promises and do other things which they consider justifiable exceptions to accepted norms, people often explain themselves in a way which sounds like proportionalism: "I broke my promise to my friend and wouldn't let him have his gun because, regardless of any harm to our friendship, it would have been much worse to let him go out and kill somebody." However, the nonabsoluteness (open to exceptions) characteristic of most moral norms can be explained without adopting proportionalism, by pointing out the absolute norms in which others are grounded.

For instance, the Golden Rule—treat others as you would have them treat you—both grounds the norms that one should keep promises and justifies exceptions. An upright person who breaks a promise when the Golden Rule requires this judges that fairness is a greater good than dependability. This judgment is by no means proportionalist; it does not involves the proportionalist's weighting and balancing of goods and bads prior to a moral norms in order to justify a judgment that some goods can be attacked for the sake of promoting others or preventing "greater evils." Fairness is a greater good than the dependability of keeping promises because the latter has moral value from the former: One ought (usually) to be dependable because it is (usually) unfair not to be. The Golden Rule itself does not admit of exceptions. What could justify one who treated others in a way he or she would not want to be treated in a similar situation?

Many proportionalists accept some absolute moral limits, such as the Golden Rule, on the use of proportionalism. They do this precisely to prevent their theories from justifying judgments like that of Caiphas. Fuchs does not explicitly make any reservations of this sort. But even if he admitted some absolute moral limits, he would have to face the issue of the workability of proportionalism within those limits.

That issue is: How can one commensurate the premoral benefits and harms promised by available possibilities to determine which of them offers the best proportion of good to nongood? In trying to explain how the goods and bads can be weighed against one another, proportionalists who are clearheaded have tried to find some way consistent with their theory to commensurate premoral benefits and harms. But they have never succeeded in doing so.[11]

Analysis of moral action shows that proportionalism is in principle unworkable because the problem of commensuration is logically insoluble. This is so because proportionalism requires that two conditions be met, and the two conditions are incompatible. The two conditions are: 1) that a moral judgment is to be made, which means both that a choice must be made and a morally wrong option could be chosen; 2) that the option which promises the definitely superior proportion of good to bad be knowable. The following consideration makes it clear that these two conditions cannot be met at the same time.

If the first condition is met and the morally wrong option could be chosen, then its morally acceptable alternative must be known. Otherwise, one could not choose wrongly, for one chooses wrongly only when one knows which option one ought to choose and chooses a different option.

But when the first condition is met, the second cannot be. The option which promises the definitely superior proportion of good to bad cannot be known by a person who chooses an alternative which promises less. If the superior option were known as superior, its inferior alternative simply could not be chosen. Any reason for choosing it would be a better reason for choosing the superior option. Whenever one really knows that one possibility is definitely superior in terms of the proportion of good to bad it promises, any alternative simply falls away, and there is no choice to make.

Thus, although proportionalism is proposed for cases in which one must choose between morally significant alternatives, all that proportionalists really say is that it would be wrong to choose precisely that which practical judgment (as they understand it) would exclude as a possibility for free choice, namely, an alternative measurably inferior in terms of the relevant good and bad. The truth of the matter is that when such an alternative is recognized in deliberation no choice about it is possible; it drops out of consideration. Hence, whenever proportionalist judgments are possible, they exclude choices contrary to them by preventing them, not by forbidding them. But a judgment which prevents one from choosing otherwise is not a moral judgment. Therefore, proportionalism is inherently unable to serve as a method of moral judgment.

If the preceding analysis is correct, why has it seemed to Fuchs and other intelligent and reflective people that it is possible to carry out the commensuration of goods and bads proportionalism requires? There are several causes of this mistake.

Proportionalists who are not clearheaded often try to use scales which their theory makes unavailable to them. One such scale is a definite objective, which reduces the moral question to one of technical calculation. This mistake is involved in the common practice of leaving to experts the evaluation of means to an end, once the end has been accepted as morally valid. For instance, given that a war is just, there is a tendency to approve whatever means military leaders consider most effective. Even those who are amoral often learn that this is disastrous, because no expert takes account of all the interests involved. Military leaders, for instance, often forget that politics will go on by other means after a war is over. Morally sensitive people take for granted that the morality of means cannot be settled merely by considering their technical effectiveness. That is precisely why Fuchs holds that the "truth" of an action "must be in conformity with the whole concrete reality of man (of society)" (Fuchs see above 80).

Another scale often assumed by proportionalists is a moral principle. For instance, when Fuchs tries to offer an example of a behavioral norm involving action so precisely delineated that we cannot conceive any kind of exception, he suggests "cruel treatment of a child which is of no benefit to the child" (Fuchs see above 89). Here the word "cruel" has an unmistakable moral connotation. Undoubtedly, Fuchs had a certain pattern of behavior in mind, but his good moral sense overwhelmed his bad ethical theory when he tried to describe what he had in mind.

Another possible cause of the mistaken belief in the workability of proportionalism is suggested by a significant clause Fuchs adds at the end of one of his formulations of the theory: "Causing an 'evil for man' is not morally wrong in every case. All that seems necessary is that it be justified by a comparative evaluation of all the elements of the total actual situation, without such evaluation having necessarily to take place on the plane of conscious reflections (Fuchs 1983, 164-165). Here the appeal is to intuition.

No doubt, everyone has intuitions about what is appropriate to do. The moral intuitions of a truly upright and well-integrated person— the person who has the virtue of "prudence" as St. Thomas understands it—will be sound, for they will embody the moral principles by which such a person was formed. The equally compelling intuitions of someone who is not vicious but simply morally immature will reflect the immediate resonance of human values and disvalues in a more or less healthy sentient nature. That will be so because the character of the morally immature person is not yet determined through intelligence and free choice to life in accord with reality as a whole. Thus, the value response of the immature person results from what is determined by nature. The proportionalist who appeals to the intuition of the prudent begs the moral question; the one who appeals to the intuition of the immature abandons it.

Decent people sometimes have intuitions at odds with moral principles to which they are committed. For example, a compassionate priest who believes in the indissolubility of marriage can feel that it would be best in a particular case if a divorced and "remarried" couple continued to live in their adulterous relationship. The question is whether that intuition reflects some sort of subconscious "comparative evaluation of all the elements of the total actual situation," as Fuchs might think, or whether it reflects decent feeling about some of the elements of the situation but fails to reflect the whole truth of human fulfillment, which goes not only beyond sentiment but even beyond intelligent wishes unintegrated by faith. The priest's intuition is not self-validating; it requires criticism. And so the critical question which is the task of ethical theory cannot be settled by appealing to such intuition.

Another possible cause of the mistaken belief in the workability of proportionalism is confusion between moral judgment and free choice. Unlikely as it might seem that Fuchs would confuse the two, there is some evidence of this confusion in his favorable reference to what Karl Rahner, S.J., wrote about "a moral faith-instinct" (Fuchs see above 93). Rahner advanced this notion in an article concerned with genetic manipulation (Rahner 1972, 243). He asserted that there are aspects of the essential morality of human acts which are nonconceptual, but belong to experienced reality and to practice which is in a "darkness" beyond theory. He also pointed out that people (including moral theologians) have a hard time articulating good arguments for their moral convictions. On this basis Rahner posited his "moral faith-instinct."

What Rahner had in mind is somewhat unclear; perhaps he only intended an appeal to intuition similar to that already criticized. But it seems he meant to propose a version of individual voluntarism, for in the summary of the article he wrote that "this 'instinct' justifiably has the courage to say *Stat pro ratione voluntas* because such a confession need not necessarily be overcautious about making a decision" and that the whole theoretical argument is based on "we do not *want* to manipulate" (Rahner 1972, 251).

9 ~ Moral Absolutes: A Critique of the View of Josef Fuchs

No doubt, choice does commensurate objectively noncommensurable values and disvalues. However, to make choice the principle of moral determination is to surrender to subjectivism. The point of ethical reflection is to determine what is right and wrong before one chooses, so that one's choice will be right. Subjectivism reverses the roles of judgment and choice: First one chooses and then one finds a reason for one's choice. That process overcomes the unworkability of proportionalism, but, unfortunately, it does so by replacing conscience with rationalization.

Having criticized proportionalism as such, I now turn to some peculiar features of Fuchs' presentation of the theory. Examination of these features will confirm the preceding criticism by further pointing up the incoherence of Fuchs' view. Fuchs uses the word "intention" in two senses without distinguishing them, and thus rests part of his argument on equivocation. He uses "intention" in one sense to refer to that willing without which there is no human act at all (Fuchs see above 83-84). He uses "intention" in another sense to refer to the willing of the precise good for the sake of which one acts (Fuchs see above 83-86). These two are not logically identical and often are distinct in fact. For example, a couple who deliberately and freely contracept can have only one "intention" in the first sense, namely, to impede the coming to be of a possible new person. (That contraception is a definite human act is clear, since a wide range of somewhat different performances can count as the same human act). But the human act of contraception can be carried out with many different "intentions," in the second sense. For instance, some couples contracept for the sake of freedom from parental responsibilities while others do so because they fear having another child would make it difficult for them to fulfill their parental responsibilities.

Proportionalists do not wish to admit that intention in the first sense can be morally determinative by itself—that is, apart from intention in the second sense, and perhaps other factors as well. They are entitled to try to defend that view. But they ought to be clear that they are approving choices to destroy, damage, or impede (premoral) goods, and that any such choice is an intention in the first sense.

Fuchs does not wish to admit that his view approves intending (premoral) evil. For this reason, he suggests that the moral justification of an action can affect what one intends (Fuchs see above 83-85). By using "intention" in this odd way, Fuchs makes his view appear much closer than it actually is to received Catholic teaching's concern about the morality of the means one uses to gain one's ends. However, he pays a price to gain this advantage: He loses the subject matter of ethical reflection. For, if there is no act without intention and no intention without moral characterization, there is no act without moral characterization, and hence there is nothing whose moral character can be in question.

The preceding confusion affects Fuchs' remarks about the morality of killing. He asserts that a morally significant action "can be performed only with the intention of the agent. One may not say, therefore, that killing as a realization of a human evil may be morally good or morally bad; for killing as such, since it implies nothing about the purpose of the action, cannot, purely as such, constitute a human act. On the other hand, 'killing because of avarice' and 'killing in self-defense' do imply something regarding the purpose of the action, the former cannot be morally good, the latter may be" (Fuchs see above 83-84).

Here Fuchs oversimplifies the complexity of the situation. There are cases in which one brings about death without choosing to kill and there are cases in which one chooses to kill. The former class includes those killings which received Catholic teaching called "indirect" (Killing in self-defense, had to be indirect to be justified, according to some, though not all, Catholic moralists). Direct killing—that is, killing which carries out a choice to destroy a life—can be done with many different intentions: out of avarice, for revenge, to end a burdensome life, and so forth. By rendering it impossible even to consider direct killing prior to its moral characterization as an important kind of moral action, this oversimplification lends plausibility to Fuchs' claim that the commandment forbidding killing must be understood as forbidding unjust killing (Fuchs see above 88-90).

I think that as a matter of historical fact, Christian tradition did treat direct killing as an important kind of moral action.[12] True, it did not characterize all such killing as morally evil. However, the factor believed to make killing immoral was not the injustice involved in most killing—suicide violates the commandment but need not be unjust—although the injustice of killing usually aggravates its malice. Rather, direct killing was considered immoral in the absence of divine authorization, both because unauthorized killing violates God's lordship over life and because it violates the reverence due to the person made in God's image. As St. Thomas says: "Considering man according to himself, it is not licit to kill anyone, since we ought to love in everyone, even the wrongdoer, the nature which God made and which is destroyed by killing" (ST II-II, 64, 6).

One can challenge the traditional view of killing on various philosophical and theological grounds. But whatever its strengths and weaknesses, its approval of some choices to kill provides no precedent for Fuchs' interpretation of the commandment, which amounts to saying: Thou shalt not kill unless the choice to do so seems "justified by a comparative evaluation of all the elements of the total actual situation, without such evaluation having necessarily to take place on the plane of conscious reflections" (Fuchs 1983, 164-165).

Fuchs' oversimplified analysis of the moral act, which follows from his equivocation on "intention," also facilitates his exploitation of cases which moral theology formerly dealt with as instances of indirect killing, indirect mutilation, and so forth (Fuchs see above 83-86). These were cases in which the destruction, damaging, or impeding of a good (life, bodily integrity, and so forth) is not chosen but is freely accepted as a side effect incidental to carrying out a choice to bring about a good. Fuchs points out, I believe correctly that there were certain confusions in the traditional statement of the principal of an act with a double effect (Fuchs see above 86). While no extended treatment of that principle is required to complete the present critique, a few clarifications are in order.

Proponents of the principle of double effect presupposed moral absolutes. There would have been no point in their trying to distinguish cases in which a side effect may be accepted had they not been convinced that some kinds of acts are always wrong and that such a kind is specified by a choice to bring a certain premoral evil. The articulation of the principle was an effort to discriminate instances in which it is permissible to bring about what it would always be wrong to choose.

Fuchs does his best to submerge choosing in the overall movement of the will toward good. One might ask: Why was choosing formerly thought to be so important? The answer, briefly stated, is that in the Christian tradition, morality is in the heart. God cannot choose evil but he can and does permit certain evils. Similarly, the human will sometimes can permit what it could never choose without losing its goodness. One determines oneself in respect to what one chooses in a way one does not with respect to what one freely accepts. Unless one changes one's mind—in case of a sin repents—one's choices, being self-determining, endure to constitute one's lasting self.

Hence, an upright person such as Jesus might freely accept death incidental to the carrying out of a choice to do something good without that acceptance qualifying a constant love of the good of human life. But no one can choose to kill without qualifying that love. Traditional justifications of killing qualified it by subordinating it to reverence towards God. Proportionalist justifications of killing qualify it by subordinating it to considerations of quantity of lives (Hiroshima), or quality of life (Baby Doe), or to various other finite goods.

Besides requiring that one not choose evil, the principle of double effect in its usual formulations set other requirements for the uprightness of an act having a bad side effect. One of these was that there be due proportion between the good sought and the evil accepted. Proportionalists frequently argue that this requirement is evidence both that traditional moralists were at least half-hearted proportionalists and that they assumed the commensurability of goods which proportionalism requires.

The answer to this challenge is that when traditional moralists talked about "proportionality" they referred to *moral* criteria, over and above the moral absolutes which forbid certain direct acts, which govern the acceptance of side effects. For example, a pediatric physician prepared to accept the harsh side effects of some form of therapy for her patients when she would not approve the same sort of treatment for her own children shows immoral partiality. In such a case, although other conditions of a standard understanding of double effect would be fulfilled, there would be lack of proportionate reason for accepting the harmful side effects, and so the choice of that type of therapy would be immoral. Of course, since what is in question here is a genuine moral judgment according to a rational principle, prudent persons often know intuitively when the requirement of proportionality is met and when it is not.

Fuchs accepts the dictum that the end does not justify the means, but only with the qualification that the excluded means is the morally bad one (Fuchs see above 86). The qualification would seem to render the dictum nugatory: A good purpose does not morally justify what cannot be morally justified. However, Fuchs' view does not leave room for even this vacuous interpretation of the dictum. For, as explained above, Fuchs thinks that there is no act at all until the purpose for acting is specified. If so, what he calls a "morally bad means" would not be a complete human act so long as there were a further possibility of its serving as a means to some ulterior good end. Hence, on Fuchs view, the dictum loses all sense.

St. Paul articulated this dictum when he confronted precisely the question whether what would otherwise be evil—a lie or refusal of truth—might not be justified if it promotes God's glory (*Rm* 3, 7-8). I neither wish nor need to use Paul as a proof text against proportionalism. Fuchs probably would argue that Paul's rejection of violating truth to promote God's glory was simply another instance of his acceptance as hypothesis of a moral evaluation proper to his time.

However, the following *reductio ad absurdum* makes it clear why Paul took the position he did. If he holds 1) that one may do evil that good might come of it together with 2) Paul's doctrine of divine providence (God permits what is bad only to draw good from it), then one also must accept as a moral principle: If in doubt about what is right, try anything. For if one accomplishes what one attempts, one can be certain that one the whole and in the long run it was for the best, since it must fit into the plan of providence. And if one does not accomplish what one attempts, one learns that would have been wrong, but no harm is done.

This suggests proportionalism's central theological inadequacy: It confuses human responsibility with God's responsibility. We however are not responsible for the overall greater good or lesser evil, for only God knows what they are. Our responsibility requires not success in effecting goods and preventing evils but faithful fulfillment of our personal vocation, according to which we serve human persons as we can, refraining from choices to violate them, and hope for God's re-creative act to complete the work of redemption.

VI. Critique with Respect to the Use of Theological Sources

Like parts of a house of cards, the opinions which make up Fuchs' view lean upon one another for support. Hence if even one part of the preceding criticism has succeeded, Fuchs' effort to exclude moral absolutes from Scripture and the Church's faith loses virtually all of its initial credibility. Still given the dependence of theological dissent on a method of using theological sources exemplified in Fuchs' recent work, a direct consideration of this matter is necessary to round out this critique.

With respect to interpreting Scripture, Fuchs tells us "to go to school to contemporary exegesis, to avoid lapsing into unauthorized good-will reading" (Fuchs see above 63). That is good advice, but Fuchs' advice is better than his example.

Noting the difficulty of understanding the Sermon on the Mount, Fuchs expresses the opinion that the absolute validity of its demands probably is not as universal norms but as "models for the behavior of the believing and loving citizens of God's kingdom who will be ready for such modes of conduct, perhaps, under certain conditions not individually specified by the Lord" (p 118). Fuchs offers no exegetical evidence for this opinion. No doubt he could find it. However, there is equally good exegetical support for the view he wishes to exclude and for a number of others, because there are at least a dozen different and respectable ways of reading the Sermon on the Mount (McArthur 1960, 106-27).

In his book, *The Moral Teaching of the New Testament*, Rudolf Schnackenburg rejected the opinion Fuchs considers probable (Schnackenburg 1965, 82-89). Other competent exegetes argue cogently that the moral teaching in Matthew's Gospel is not merely incidental—a "*secundarium*," to use Fuchs' expression.[13] Moreover, through the monumental work of Jacques Dupont on the Beatitudes, one verse of the Sermon on the Mount recurs like a refrain: "It is not those who say to me, 'Lord Lord,' who will enter the kingdom of heaven, but the person who does the will of my Father in heaven" (Mt 7, 21). Nor does Dupont understand this verse in a way compatible with the interpretation Fuchs favors.

About Jesus' teaching on the indissolubility of marriage, Fuchs asks: "Is the moral imperative to be understood as a norm to be followed as universal practice or as an ideal?" (Fuchs see above 63-64). Schnackenburg discusses this question and does not even consider the opinion that Jesus' prohibition of divorce is only an ideal; he concludes that it is a universal norm.[14] E. Schillebeeckx, in his work on marriage published in 1963, considered the relevant passages of Scripture and drew the same conclusion (Schillebeeckx 1963, 141-155). Moreover, against the opinion that the prohibition of divorce is only an ideal stands the weight of the whole Christian tradition including the tradition of those who admitted an exception in the case of adultery, for that claimed exception would have been pointless had Jesus merely announced an ideal.

In dealing with St. Paul, Fuchs focuses on "the Pauline directives concerning woman's position in marriage, society and the Church" and takes it as self-evident today that these "are to be regarded as conditioned by his times" (Fuchs see above 64). No doubt, distinctions must be made among Paul's "directives," for some are rules of Church order while others are teachings, and canon law must not be confused with moral truth. But given these distinctions, substantial recent work calls into question what Fuchs considers self-evident (Clark 1980, 209-220).

Fuchs uses the example of Paul's teaching on man and woman to support a more general thesis: "It could hardly be supposed that the Stoic, Judaic, and Diaspora-Judaic ethos which Paul represents was in all respects a timeless ethos" (Fuchs see below 64). If that reference is to anything having more than intentional unity, it hardly could be timeless, for cultural houses so thoroughly divided are as fragile as houses of cards. More important, if Paul "represented" either Judaism or Stoicism, more typical participants in either tradition might have wished for better representation.

Of course, Paul did draw on Judaism; he did not believe that divine revelation began with himself. But like Jesus himself, Paul was careful to discriminate what Christians had to accept from the earlier tradition of Israel. The diligence he shows in liberating his converts from unnecessary requirements of the law argues strongly that any demands Paul assumes from the Judaic tradition are believed by him to be essential for the salvation of Christians. Paul believes that the greatest possible transformation of human nature has occurred in Jesus; anything which survives this transformation can hardly be in his eyes a mere expression of the Jewish ethos.

The thesis that Paul borrowed heavily from Stoic and other popular morality of the time needs to be proved, and Fuchs offers no proof for it. Against it stand very substantial exegetical studies, which minimize the borrowings of the authors of the New Testament Epistles, including Paul, from Greek sources, and find in the Epistles a pattern of moral teaching which suggests that underlying them is a primitive Christian catechism, probably developed for the instruction of the catechumens and the recently baptized.[15] Forcefully opposing pagan corruption and carefully prescinding from elements of the Judaic law not essential to Christian life, the apostolic Church appropriated the revelation in Jesus of what persons should be; the result was moral formation in the way of Christ which is valid always.

In handling the question of moral norms in Scripture, Fuchs proceeds as if his audience consisted of persons who had been brought up as fundamentalists and who have no living community of faith to rely upon when they encounter difficulties in interpreting Scripture. He admits that the behavioral norms of the New Testament might remain valid today, but adds: "Only, we must reflect whether the criterion of their possible absolute (i.e., universal) validity is Holy Scripture itself, whether it can be and was intended to be" (Fuchs see above 66). Similarly, in dealing with the Church's moral teaching, Fuchs proceeds as if the Church were a merely human community which had no access to God's word when it encounters difficult moral questions: "Is the claim of absoluteness for the norms transmitted by the Church a claim of universal norms? Does the Church give us thereby a system of universal morally valid norms which God has not given us in Holy Scripture?" (Fuchs see above 67).

That way of dividing theological sources does not comport well with Catholic teaching and practice. Vatican II, in its magnificent Constitution on Divine Revelation, makes it clear both that Scripture must be read within the Church under the guidance of the magisterium and that the Church entirely depends upon divine revelation whose handing on the magisterium serves. As if directly rejecting the view implicit in Fuchs' methodology, the Council concludes. "It is clear, therefore, that sacred tradition, sacred Scripture, and the teaching authority of the Church, in accord with God's most wise design, are so linked and joined together that one cannot stand without the others, and that all together and each in its own way under the action of the one Holy Spirit contribute effectively to the salvation of souls" (DV 10). If one adopts a methodology more in harmony than Fuchs' with this Catholic principle, one will have no trouble discovering some moral absolutes in Scripture and the Church's teaching.

The Ten Commandments have a unique place within the Mosaic law; they are represented as being the very words of the covenant, dictated by God (see *Ex* 34, 27-28) (Hamel 1969, 18-20). Their religious and liturgical significance makes them no less functional as a moral foundation for legal enactments (Hillers 1969, 88-89). Within the New Testament, Christian morality is presented as the perfection and superabundant fulfillment of the Decalogue.[16] In the Sermon on the Mount, Jesus broadens and deepens several of the commandments and demands their interiorization (see Mr 5, 21-37). All the synoptics, moreover, present Jesus as affirming the commandments as a necessary condition for entering eternal life (see Mt 19,16-20; *Mk* 10, 17-19; *Lk* 18, 18-21). St. Paul, in asserting that Christian love fulfills the law, assumes the truth of the Decalogue and its permanent ethical relevance, extols the superiority of love, and rejects any suggestion which would empty love of its operative normative implications (see *Rm* 13, 8-10).

The prohibitions of the commandments were no doubt understood more narrowly in their original context than in their unfolding in later Jewish and Christian tradition. Still, no reasonable reading of the Decalogue can deny it the status of fundamental revealed moral truth—a status always recognized by common Christian practice in moral instruction.[17] To say that the Decalogue has the status of fundamental, revealed moral truth is not to deny that it needs interpretation and development. This process begins in the Old Testament itself and, as indicated, is continued in the New. The same process is carried on today by the living magisterium, whose competence extends as far as revelation's protection and exposition requires

9 – Moral Absolutes: A Critique of the View of Josef Fuchs

(LG 25). However, the continuous process of interpretation and development does not justify the claim that Decalogue is mere moral exhortation to follow an existing code, which always must be read with proportionalist riders—for example, Thou shalt not commit adultery, unless it seems to be the greater good.

In considering the moral teaching contained in Scripture one must bear in mind that most moral norms are nonabsolute. Moreover, as already explained in respect to the commandment prohibiting killing, some important norms taught in Scripture are limited in ways taken to be divinely revealed. For these reasons, instances in the Bible of norms which admit of exceptions do not argue against the truth of absolute norms which are proposed there as absolute and certainly true. (Moreover, nonabsolute norms proposed in Scripture as certainly true are not falsified by their exceptions).

Moral absolutes are found in divine revelation. It is fitting that they are for, as was shown in part III, moral absolutes guide human acts and protect the intrinsic goods of human persons, and these acts and goods are constitutive elements of the kingdom, in which alone integral human fulfillment will be found. Moreover, as was shown in part V, proportionalism is unworkable in principle as a method of guiding human actions to integral human fulfillment because human providence is inherently limited. And, as was shown in part IV, by faith the Christian is in principle both liberated from the moral bondage of the historical-cultural relativity of this world's ideologies of human self-realization, and enabled to live with Jesus in a communion which remains the same always and everywhere. Living in that communion, one benefits from both the definiteness and the openness of having one's faithful obedience defined by negative norms. Thus, the word of God includes moral absolutes to provide the guidance we need to play our own small but irreplaceable role in the drama of salvation and to play it with originality and creativity.

Moral absolutes also contribute to the economy of revelation itself. This can be seen by considering adultery.

Fuchs and others who reject moral absolutes seldom take adultery as an example. The commandment against it has not been proposed with divinely authorized limits, as has the commandment against killing. Also, it seems ridiculous to claim that the true meaning of the commandment has always been: Thou shalt not engage in *wrongful* extramarital sexual intercourse involving a married person. The commandment absolutely forbidding adultery, moreover, is proposed consistently throughout Scripture and tradition, and surely still reaffirmed by a morally unanimous magisterium. Transparently, the commandment was not conditioned upon the ethos of New Testament times. Both St. Paul and Trent include adultery among the immoralities—a list obviously based on the Decalogue—which will exclude unrepentant Christians, even if they die in faith, from the kingdom (DS 1544/808; 1 Cor 6, 9-10).

To understand the importance of adultery to revelation and the life of faith, one must notice that the revelation we have actually received would have been impossible had God not created sex: "God created man in the image of himself, in the image of God he created him, male and female he created them" (Gn 1, 27). For if we had no experience of familial relationships based on sexual generation, we could not understand the meaning of "Father" and "Son" and without these concepts we could not begin to understand what we believe about the Trinity, the Incarnation, and our adoption as children of God.

Marriage is the created reality before all others by which God reveals to us the communion of divine and human persons for which he has created us and to which he calls us in Christ. Marriage is a union of utmost intimacy (the two become one flesh) which yet preserves the individual identities and different roles of those who share in it. As husband and wife, so divine and created persons are united in communion while retaining their personal dignity, because the covenant relationship is formed by mutual, free commitments. One can see how unique the Christian vision of divine-human communion is if one compares it with other religions which either exclude such intimacy or submerge the individual personalities of creatures.

God's faithfulness to the covenant relationship is one of the most central revealed truths, for this truth is the ground of our trust in God's mercy and our hope of glory. Take away our assurance that God is faithful and the gospel ceases to be good news. Faithfulness in marriage is the created reality before all others by which God reveals his faithfulness to us. The moral absolute forbidding adultery makes marital faithfulness possible. Therefore, this moral absolute belongs to the economy of revelation itself. The revelation we have actually received is necessarily linked with marital faithfulness.

Someone will object that even if there were no moral absolute forbidding adultery, some husbands and wives might still be absolutely faithful to one another, and so there would still be available the experience required for the revelation of God's faithfulness. But the objection fails, for two reasons.

First, faithfulness is not a contingent fact: that this man and woman happen to have intercourse only with one another. The faithfulness is in making and keeping a commitment to a self-giving which is both mutual and exclusive. From one point of view, that commitment is a free choice. But from another point of view, it has in it a necessity which excludes contingency. This necessity is the only sort of necessity compatible with free choice: moral necessity. This moral necessity is the bindingness of the commitment, the obligation one accepts in making it. Just as an ordinary promise is more than a prediction because it is a moral undertaking, so covenantal promises are more than both predictions and ordinary promises because of their more profound moral undertaking. That undertaking is a pledging of oneself, its violation is moral self-destruction. Here is moral necessity.

In fact, of course, we can be unfaithful; we can destroy ourselves morally. But we know what that means only by recognizing the moral absolute which forbids it. Knowing our faithfulness and unfaithfulness, and believing that God cannot destroy himself morally, we begin to conceive what God's faithfulness is. Thus, the moral absolute forbidding adultery, not merely some examples of exclusive sexual communion, is necessarily linked with the revelation of God's own faithfulness.

Second, created realities by which God reveals pertain to the image of God in creation. The means God uses are not mere means, they always have their own intrinsic value. That is so because whatever goods God makes belong within his plan; they are part of the fullness he intends to complete in Christ. Therefore, marital fidelity contributes to the building up of the reality it signifies—the faithful communion of husbands and wives is within the faithful communion of divine and created persons. After they serve the Lord here on earth, faithful spouses will find the good of their fidelity again in the kingdom, freed of stain, burnished and transfigured. In sum, marital fidelity is no mere conventional sign of the fidelity of Christ and the Church, but a true sacrament. For this reason too, the moral absolute excluding adultery, not merely contingent examples of exclusive sexual communion, is necessary.

The final topic for criticism is Fuchs' opinion about the moral teaching of the Church. To criticize it, one must first consider a certain assumption about infallibility. The assumption, widely shared in recent years, is that what is not solemnly defined is not infallibly taught.

If this assumption were correct, infallibility would attach quite contingently to some propositions pertaining to faith, namely, to those which for one reason or another happen to be solemnly defined. But this is a mistaken conception of the relationship between infallibility and the revealed truth which faith accepts.

To see why, one must consider what infallibility adds to the absolute truth of God's revealed word and the absolute certitude of the divinely given faith by which Christ's faithful accept, hold, and hand on God's word. Although God can neither deceive nor be deceived, individual believers, even those whose faith is true and generous, can err in matters of faith. For example, St. Thomas Aquinas mistakenly thought that Mary was conceived in original sin—an opinion we now know to be an error contrary to the truth of faith. How is such error possible?

The answer is that such error is possible because the individual believer can confuse what is not revealed with what is, can mistake either a nonrevealed and possibly false opinion for a revealed truth, or a revealed truth for a nonrevealed and possibly false opinion. This confusion and mistaking is what infallibility—the certain gift of truth—excludes. The Catholic Church as such has this gift, although no individual Christian as such, not even the pope as an individual Christian, has it.

To see why the Church as such has the certain gift of discerning revealed truth, it helps to begin with the apostles. The Church is founded on them, because they were the authorized recipients of God's revelation in Jesus, who is the reality and truth by whom the Church lives.

Revelation is communication, and there is no communication without a recipient. An attempt at communication which goes unreceived is just that— a failed attempt, not a communication. But God, revealing in Jesus, communicates perfectly and in no way fails. Therefore, God's revelation in Jesus was perfectly received by the apostles. Perfect reception of a communication excludes confusing anything which belongs to the communication with anything extraneous to it. Therefore, the apostles could not make such mistakes. However, of themselves they were fallible men. Therefore, they needed and received a certain gift of discerning God's revelation in Jesus: infallibility.

Revelation in Jesus, however, was not for the apostles alone, but for all humankind, including us men and women. Even to us, God continues to communicate. His revelation in Jesus—infallibly received, witnessed, and handed on by the apostles—continues to reach people as the apostolic communion continues to spread to all nations and eras. Thus, men and women today share in revelation by living within the apostolic communion, the Church.

The Church, however, would not hand on revelation to us if she were not infallible. Rather, at best, she would hand on fragments of a mutilated revelation mixed with much merely human and possibly

9 - Moral Absolutes: A Critique of the View of Josef Fuchs

erroneous extraneous matter. Since revelation cannot be verified or falsified by any outside standard, such as experienced facts, the residue of God's authentic communication could never be reclaimed and purified. If that were the situation, God's undertaking to reveal to us would be a botched attempt.

But God cannot fail in his undertakings. Therefore, the Church as such—the apostolic communion still continuing in the world and in history—continues to share in the apostolic gift of sure discernment. She infallibly accepts, holds, and hands on as revealed all and only what truly is revealed thus, as Vatican II teaches:

> The body of the faithful as a whole, anointed as they are by the Holy One (cf. Jn 2, 20.27), cannot err in matters of belief. Thanks to a supernatural sense of the faith which characterizes the people as a whole, it manifests this unerring quality when "from the bishops down to the last member of the laity" (note to St. Augustine omitted), it shows universal agreement in matters of faith and morals.
>
> For, by this sense of faith which is aroused and sustained by the Spirit of truth God's people accepts not the word of men but the very word of God (cf. I *Ths* 213) It clings without fail to the faith once delivered to the saints (cf. *Jn* 3), penetrates it more deeply by accurate insights, and applies it more thoroughly to life. All this it does under the lead of a sacred teaching authority to which it faithfully defers (*LG* 12).

Thus, whatever the Church as such received, holds, and hands on infallibly believed and taught.

But the Church hands on more than solemnly defined doctrines. As Vatican II teaches:

> Therefore the apostles, handing on what they themselves had received, warn the faithful to hold fast to the traditions which they have learned either by word of mouth or by letter (cf. 2 Ths 2,15), and to fight in defense of the faith handed on once and for all (cf. Jn 3). Now what was handed on by the apostles includes everything which contributes to the holiness of life, and the increase in faith of the People of God, and so the Church, in her teaching, life, and worship, perpetuates and hands on to all generations all that she herself is, all that she believes (DV 8).

Therefore, infallibility does not attach in a merely contingent way to certain truths of faith.

The conclusion which was to be proved follows: The widely shared assumption that what is not defined is not infallibly taught is false. The truth rather, is that whatever the Church as such believes and hands on as part of revelation is infallibly taught.

Of course, many will deny this. But the ultimate cost of denying it will be to deny that God still does reveal to us in Jesus, for if the Church is not infallible, nothing in the world to which we have access will be able to bring God's communication to us intact.

But if infallibility characterizes all that the Church as such believes and teaches, what distinguishes the infallible Church from her fallible members? When does the Church as such act, in distinction for the particular acts of believing and teaching which belong to her members?

The Church is a human community. Like any human community, she has a leadership. A human community acts as such when its leaders act in certain official ways. These ways of acting which constitute the acts of a community as such are called "authoritative." Therefore, the Church as such acts when her leaders act according to their proper authority. Specifically, the Church as such teaches when her leaders teach according to their proper authority.

The revelation which is handed on is the whole reality of the Church—all that she herself is, all that she believes. This whole reality is the communion of divine and human persons in mind, in will, and in performance. Therefore, the Church's belief and teaching, her sacramental communion with God in Jesus, and her revelatory living out of the gospel before the world are not three separate sets of acts, but only one integrated set of acts.

Jesus founded the Church upon the apostles; they were her initial leaders. They led her in respect to the one set of acts which constitute her life by preaching the gospel, presiding over the eucharistic assembly, and building up and guiding the Christian community in its responsibility of bringing the light of Christ to the world.

In every aspect of the life of the Church, all of her members were called to participate according to their gifts. Thus, the apostles were not the only teachers, priests, or apostolic workers. But since the single life of a community requires unified leadership, the apostolic office included leadership in the Church in teaching, worship, and government. Thus, when the apostles taught according to their proper authority as leaders of the Church, they taught infallibly.

With respect to their role of leadership, the apostles had successors: those still recognized as leaders of the Church, namely, the bishops. There are many bishops, and they can act individually and inconsis-

9 ~ Moral Absolutes: A Critique of the View of Josef Fuchs

tently, even when they are trying to fulfill their official duties as leaders of the Church. When that happens, one cannot say that their official acts constitute acts of the universal (Catholic) Church as such.

However, when the bishops act officially, together, and in harmony, the Church as such acts. When the Church as such teaches, she teaches infallibly. Therefore, when the bishops teach officially, together, and in harmony, they teach infallibly. Therefore, as Vatican II teaches:

> Although the bishops individually do not enjoy the prerogative of infallibility, they nevertheless proclaim the teaching of Christ infallibly, even when they are dispersed throughout the world, provided that they remain in communion with each other and with the successor of Peter and that in authoritatively teaching on a matter of faith and morals they agree in one judgment as that to be held definitively (LG 25).

Study of the development of this conciliar text clarifies it.[18] The first condition—that the bishops be in communion with one another and with the pope—does not mean that they must act as a single body, in a strictly collegial manner. It is necessary and sufficient that they remain bishops within the Catholic Church. The voice of the Church is identified, and distinguished from various voices within the Church, partly by the sacramental ordination and bond of communion which unite the bishops who share in uttering the Church's teaching.

The second condition—authoritative episcopal teaching *on a matter of faith and morals*—requires that the bishops be acting in their official capacity as teachers, not merely expressing their opinions as individuals or as theologians. As for the subject matter of their teaching—"faith or morals"—the formula has a long history.[19] It is sufficient here to say that nothing in the pertinent documents limits "morals," in the sense intended by Vatican II, in such a way as to exclude moral absolutes, such as that forbidding adultery.

The third condition—that the bishops agree in one judgment—identifies universality as a requirement for an infallible exercise of the ordinary magisterium. What is necessary, however, is the moral unity of the body of bishops in union with the pope, not an absolute mathematical unanimity such as would be destroyed by even one dissenting voice.[20]

Furthermore, if this condition has been met in the past, it would not be nullified by a future lack of consensus among the bishops. The consensus of future bishops is not necessary for the ordinary magisterium to have taught something infallibly or to do so now. Otherwise, one would be in the absurd position of saying that it is impossible for there to be an infallible exercise of the magisterium until literally the end of time; since at any given moment one cannot tell what some bishops in the future might say.

The fourth condition—that the bishops propose a judgment to be held definitively—obviously does not refer to the formulation and promulgation of a solemn definition, since what is in question is the bishops' day-to-day teaching. The condition does mean at least this: that the teaching is not proposed as something optional, for either the bishops or the faithful, but as something which the bishops have an obligation to hand on and which Catholics have an obligation to accept. In the case of moral teaching, however, it is unlikely that those proposing the teaching will explicitly present it as something to be intellectually accepted as true; it is more likely that they will leave this demand implicit and will propose it as a norm which followers of Jesus must try to observe in their lives.

The Church as such also teaches when a truth of faith is solemnly defined, either by a general council or by a pope teaching *ex cathedra*. Solemn definitions presuppose, pick out, and officially formulate particular propositions from the infallibly received and handed on reality of the Church. Thus, an act of solemn definition does not add infallibility to a truth previously taught noninfallibly, but adds only the canonical expression of the truth — the "irreformable definition" (DS 3074/1839). Moreover, such definitions are "irreformable" only in this: The language used in the sense in which it is used in that act of defining accurately expresses an infallibly believed element of the content of faith.

In one passage, there is a suggestion that Fuchs shares the erroneous assumption that what is not solemnly defined is not infallibly taught. Fuchs says:

> It is noteworthy that in the Church's two thousand years, seemingly no definitive doctrinal decision on moral questions has been made, at least insofar as these would be related to natural law, without being at the same time revealed. On the other hand, this is not to say that the nondefinitive authoritative guidelines of the Church are meaningless, as if one might ignore them, oblivious to the fact that they also come under the assistance of the Spirit of Christ abiding with the Church. Hence a certain presumption of truth must be granted them. Yet one may not see in such instances any conclusive legislation or doctrinal definition of an ethical norm

whose validity would be guaranteed by the Holy Spirit (Fuchs see above 70).

This argument seems to overlook the category of nondefined but infallibly taught moral truths. In doing so, it reduces the status of common, constant, and very firm moral teachings to that of noninfallible judgments on moral questions offered by leaders of the Church acting without the consensus of the body of bishops in communion with one another and the pope.

Fuchs qualifies his denial that there have been solemn definitions of moral truths probably to leave room for Trent's definitions of polygamy and divorce (DS 1802/972, 1805/975, and 1807/977). But his denial raises the question of the significance of the fact that there is not a body of solemnly defined moral norms comparable to the body of solemnly defined dogmatic truths.

I think this fact can be explained easily in a way compatible with confidence in the infallibly taught common, constant, and very firm moral teaching of the Church. As has been explained, solemn definition does not add infallibility to what was noninfallible, but only adds a canonical expression of the truth. Why is such canonical expression important? Because the Church has the task of handing on revelation, a process which involves both words and deeds—the words which proclaim the gospel and the deeds which carry it out. Sometimes doctrinal confusion makes a canonical expression of a dogma necessary so that Christians will all speak in the same way, and thus be able to convey the same gospel message. But canonical expression of moral norms generally will be of little help in cultivating the communal, living witness to Christ which will convey God's love and make the truth of the gospel credible.

Therefore, to counter moral disarray among Christians, the Church has not resorted to solemn definitions of moral norms but has taken other, more relevant measures: declaring certain very grave sins to be canonical crimes, exhorting the faithful to do penance for certain sins, approving certain rules of life for the more devout living of the gospel, providing catechisms which help the faithful learn how to live the Christian life, canonizing saints who exemplify certain virtues, requiring that confessors be trained in moral theology according to the content of approved textbooks, using certain passages of Scripture in the liturgy, and so on.

If one approaches the Church's teaching without an a priori conviction that no moral absolutes could possibly be found there, one will not have any difficulty in finding such norms. Many of them, like the norm forbidding adultery, have been universally, constantly, and very firmly handed on in moral teaching proposed as revealed in the Decalogue, its deepening, and development. Such norms clearly are infallibly taught, for the Church as such has accepted, held, and handed them on through the centuries. The conditions articulated by Vatican II to identify infallible teaching by the bishops were met as they exercised their moral leadership. Hence, although such norms were never solemnly defined, their status is unmistakable from the many other relevant acts, analogous in morals to definition in dogma, proposing these norms as absolutely essential conditions for Christian living.

If one sets aside the peculiar developments of the twentieth century and considers the entire previous Jewish and Christian tradition, its massiveness and unity in witness to the moral teaching centering on the Decalogue are overwhelmingly impressive. For example, not only no Catholic but no other Christian and no Jew ever would have dared to say of adultery and killing the innocent anything but: These are wicked things, and they who do them can have no part in God's kingdom. Thus the whole People of God stands against contemporary theological speculation to the contrary. That speculation has accepted the burden of showing that even until yesterday the whole People of God profoundly and thoroughly misunderstood how to do his will. Can such a claim find any possible ground in faith? Is it not, rather, patently a claim whose whole plausibility derives from contemporary cultural factors wholly alien to Jewish and Christian faith?

But Fuchs contrasts what pertains to natural law morality with what pertains to revelation. Some norms commonly, constantly, and very firmly taught by the Church—for example, that concerning contraception—do not so obviously pertain to divine revelation as does the norm, say, concerning adultery. Might such norms be taught by the Church without being infallibly taught?

The answer, clearly, would be yes, if the norm in question is not taught by the Church as such. For example, various bishops and groups of bishops have expressed different opinions concerning the morality of a nuclear deterrent which involves the threat to kill noncombatants. Some of these differing judgments, even if they were proposed to be held definitively, might be in error.

But norms such as that concerning contraception pose a different problem. That norm surely has been held and handed on by the Church as such (Grisez and Ford 1978, 277-282). That is precisely the point made by the popes who have said that the norm has been "handed down uninterruptedly from the very beginning" (Pius XI), "is as valid today as it was yesterday; and it will be the same tomorrow and always" (Pius XII), "has been proposed with constant firmness by the magisterium" (Paul VI), and is reaffirmed "in continuity with the living tradition of the ecclesial community throughout history" (John Paul II).

Very often those who proposed the Catholic teaching concerning contraception appealed to Scripture. Sometimes, the norm concerning contraception was reduced to the commandment concerning homicide or to that concerning adultery. In other cases, appeal was made to another text, such as that concerning Onan. Whatever more recent exegesis makes of such uses of Scripture, those who taught in this way made it clear by doing so that they were convinced that the teaching belongs to revelation and must be accepted by Christians with faith.

Those who invoked or alluded to particular texts in Scripture did not interpret them in isolation from the whole body of Christian moral convictions. These latter in turn were grounded more in the meditation of Christians upon the whole of divine revelation, contained both in Scripture and in the concrete experience of Christian life, than in an exact reading of isolated texts. Holding a body of moral convictions, which they were confident expressed God's wisdom and will for their lives, Christians invoked particular Scripture texts as witnesses to the truth and obligatory character of the moral norms they believed to belong to the law of God.

If one looks at matters in this way, it is easy to believe that the principles explicitly contained in revelation implicitly include whatever Christians need to shape their lives in Christ. Still, some theologians have thought that while the Church must be able to teach definitively on the whole natural law, not all of it can be found in revelation. In an early draft of Vatican II's text on the infallible teaching of bishops, there was an important limiting clause: "in handing on the revealed faith." This clause was deleted to accommodate the view that infallibility is not thus limited, and instead the qualification was made that the truth must be proposed as one to be held definitively—that is, as certain or absolutely binding (Grisez and Ford 1978, 267).

At the same time, both Vatican I and Vatican II make it clear that in defining doctrine, there is no question of adding to divine revelation (LG 25; DS 3070/1836). The infallibility of the Church, Vatican II teaches, extends just as far as divine revelation extends—that is, it extends to all those things and only those things "which either directly belong to the revealed deposit itself, or are required to guard as inviolable and expound with fidelity this same deposit" (LG 25). The clarification in the phrase, "or which are required to guard as inviolable and expound with fidelity this same deposit," was provided by the commission responsible for Vatican II's text; it excludes a restrictive theory of the object of infallibility, which would limit it to truths explicitly contained in already articulated revelation, and so prevent the Church from developing its doctrine and rejecting new errors incompatible with revealed truth (Ford and Grisez 1978, 264-269).

I think this clarification solves the problem of how moral truths, such as that concerning contraception, taught by the Church as such do belong to divine revelation. They need not be expressed or even implied in Scripture. For revelation includes more than is in Scripture and more than truths. It includes the whole reality of the new covenant communion. This communion is what the Church herself is, what she hands on. Sometimes it is necessary to articulate a moral norm in order to guard as inviolable and expound with fidelity that aspect of covenant communion which is following Christ and bearing witness to him by doing the truth. So if the Church as such teaches some moral norms, they pertain at least in this way to divine revelation.

Those Jews and Christians who first began to set aside the tradition on contraception had no intention of setting aside the entire received morality concerning sex and innocent life. The majority of Paul VI's Commission on Population, Family, and Birthrate, and other Catholics who denied the moral absolute concerning contraception before *Humanae Vitae* almost unanimously insisted that the approval of contraception would have no effect upon received teaching concerning fornication, adultery, homosexual relations, abortion, or the indissolubility of marriage. But today there are few indeed who approve contraception on any sort of theoretical ground who have not also rejected at least some of the moral absolutes more obviously included in revelation. Hence the moral absolute concerning contraception pertains to the deposit of revelation at least in this sense: The body of received teaching concerning sex and innocent life is so tightly integrated that all of it must be firmly held to guard as inviolable and expound with fidelity those parts of it which are most clearly revealed. Hence, the norm concerning contraception could be solemnly defined as pertaining to divine revelation.

So much, then, for Fuchs' view of moral absolutes and for the opinion that Catholics may dissent from the Church's common, constant, and very firm moral teaching.

In 1965 I argued that one cannot approve contraception without more generally abandoning traditional teaching on moral absolutes. After *Humanae Vitae* I argued that a Catholic cannot accept the legitimacy of dissent from such teaching without more generally abandoning the Catholic conception of the Church, so freshly articulated by Vatican II. Now I am arguing that no believer can accept dissenting theology' s conception of Jewish and Christian life without altogether abandoning faith in divine revelation. More quickly than I ever expected, events have shown that the logic of the first two arguments was sound.

Notes

[1] Germain Grisez, *The Way of the Lord Jesus* vol. 1, *Christian Moral Principles*, (Chicago: Franciscan Herald Press, 1983).

[2] DS 1554/814, 1559/819, 3010/1791; DH 2-3; Cf. *ST* I-II , 113, 3.

[3] See *ST*, II-II, 25, 8; 83, 8; *De perfectione vitae spiritualis*, c.14. Cf. S. Pinackaers, "La morale de saint Thomas: est-elle chrétienne?" Nova et Vetera 51 (1976): 93-107.

[4] See *Sent.* IV, d. 33, q. 1, a. 2, qu.la 4, ad 2; *De virtutibus cardinalibus*, a. 4

[5] For an exegesis of *Lk* 6,27-38 supportive of my reading: Joseph A. Fitzmyer, S.J., "The Gospel According to Luke (I-IX)" *Anchor Bible* 28 (Doubleday, Garden City, N.Y 1981), 630, 637-641.

[6] See Pheme Perkins, *Love Commands in the New Testament*, (New York: Paulist Press, 1982), 27-40 and 89-95, for further background and exegesis of New Testament texts, which make it clear that the Christian norms regarding love of enemies are tightly based on faith.

[7] Cf. Paul VI, *Populorum progressio*, 59 (AAS [1967] 263-265).

[8] John Paul II, *Redemptor hominis*, 71 (AAS [1979] 517).

[9] Cf. Fitzmyer, 241-43 and 783-90.

[10] See Grisez, *op.cit.*, ch. 9, for an analysis of human acts which makes this point clear. Fuchs takes a contrary view, of course; his view on this point will be criticized toward the end of part V.

[11] See Grisez, "Against Consequentialism" in this volume; Alan Donagan, *The Theory of Morality* (Chicago: University of Chicago Press, 1977), 149-209; John Finnis, *Fundamentals of Ethics* (Georgetown University Press, Washington, D.C. 1983), 80-120; John R. Connery, S.J., "Morality of Consequences A Critical Appraisal," *Theological Studies* 34 (1973): 396-414; "Catholic Ethics: Has the Norm for Rule-Making Changed?"originally in *Theological Studies*, 42 in this volume; Ferdinando Citterio, "La revisione critica dei tradizionali principi morali alla luce della teoria del 'compromesso etico'" *Scuola cattolica* 110 (1982): 29-64; Dario Composta, "Il consequenzialismo: Una nuova corrente della 'Nuova Morale'" *Divinitas* 25 (1981): 127-56; Marcelino Zalba, S.J., "Principa ethica in crisim vocata intra (propter?) crisim morum," *Periodica de Re Morali, Canonica, Liturgica*, 71 (1982): 25-63 and 319-57.

[12] See St. Augustine, *City of God* I, 20-21; XIX, 7.

[13] See John Meier, *The Vision of Matthew: Christ, Church, and Morality in the First Gospel*, (New York: Paulist Press, 1979), 42-51; W. D. Davies, *The Setting of the Sermon on the Mount*, (Cambridge: Cambridge University Press, 1964), 94-108.

[14] E Schillebeeckx, *op. cit.* 132-43.

[15] Philip Carrington, *The Primitive Christian Catechism: A Study in the Epistles*. (Cambridge: Cambridge University Press, 1940), 88-89 (summary); Edward Gordon Selwyn, *The First Epistle of Peter: The Greek Text, with Introduction, Notes, and Essays*. (London: Macmillan, 1958), 437-439 (summary); David Daube, *The New Testament and Rabbinic Judaism*. (London: Athlone Press, 1956), 90-105, 102-103: "Everything points to the existence of early Christian codes of duties in Hebrew, from which the principles of correct practice crept into the Greek of the epistles. Freedom in the spirit did not relieve the Church of the necessity of insisting on a definite moral order."

[16] See Matthew Vellanickal, "Norm of Morality according to the Scripture," *Bible Bhashyam: An Indian Biblical Quarterly* 7 (1981): 121-146, for a remarkably clear and balanced synthetic statement of the biblical teaching of moral truth, centrally in Christ, but also including specific and unchanging norms.

[17] See ST I-II, 100, 1,8; 107, 2, ad 1. For a very detailed study of this point in the Fathers of the Church, see Guy Bourgeault, S.J., *Décalogue et Morale Chrétienne: Enquête patristique sur l'utilisation et l'interprétation chrétiennes du décalogue de c. 60 à c. 220*, (Paris: Desclée, 1971), 405-418 (summary conclusions). An important textual study: Patrick Lee, "Permanence of the Ten Commandments: St. Thomas and his Modern Interpreters" *Theological Studies* 42 (1981): 422-43.

[18] The present interpretation of the conciliar text is based on the study of it presented by John C. Ford, S.J., and Germain Grisez, "Contraception and the Infallibility of the Ordinary Magisterium," *Theological Studies* 39 (1978): 263-77.

[19] See M. Bévenot, "Faith and Morals in Vatican I and the Council of Trent" *Heythrop Journal*, 3 (1962) 15-30; Piet Fransen, S.J., "A Short History of the Meaning, of the Formula 'Fides et Mores' ," *Louvain Studies* 7 (1979) 270-301. The formula in Vatican I and II certainly includes reference to specific moral norms under "mores," and in Trent and before, we "fides" was understood more existentially and less rationalistically, under "fides." See Teodoro López Rodriguez, "'Fides et mores' en Trento," *Scripta Theologica* 5 (1973) 175-221; Marcelino Zalba, S.J., "'Omnis et salutaris veritas et morum disciplina' Sentido de la expresión 'mores' en el Concilio de Trento," *Gregorianum* 54 (1973) 679-715.

[20] At Vatican I, Bishop Martin of Paderborn, speaking for the Deputation of Faith, explained the unanimity required for the infallibility of the ordinary magisterium (which Vatican I teaches: 3011/1792) by using the following example: All Catholic bishops believed in the divinity of Christ before the Council of Nicea, but this doctrine was not defined until then, therefore up to that time it was taught by the ordinary magisterium: J.D. Mansi et al., ed., *Sacrorum conciliorum nova et amplissima collectio* 51: 224-25. As everyone knows, there hardly was anything like unanimity about this doctrine either before or even after Nicaea, except to the extent that those who denied it may have ceased to be Catholic bishops, having lost communion by their heresy.

Christian Witness
John Finnis

I. Free Choice: A Morally Decisive Reality

Everyone has the experience of choosing, and of constraints—physical and psychological, logical, cultural and social—which block choosing what one wants or doing what one chose. But outside the cultures formed by the Old and New Testaments, few have acknowledged with clarity or firmness the reality of *free choice*.

There is free choice where one really does have *motives* for choosing and doing each of two or more incompatible options, but these motives are not determinative, and neither they nor any other factor whatever, save the choosing itself, *settles* which alternative is chosen.

Because nothing—not even the motives which are necessary though not sufficient conditions for making the choice—settles the free choice, save one's own very act of making it, that act is truly creative. It is creative of personal character, and thus of a most significant aspect of the reality of each person who is capable of meaningful relations with other persons, human and divine, because capable of establishing some meaningful relationship between his or her feelings, understanding, judgments, and actions.

The transcendence of God to the created universe, the utter originality of the act of divine creation, and the independence of that act from every kind of necessitating condition are impossible for us to conceive save on the analogy of the human free choice. Conversely, only those cultures which proclaim divine creation and meditate on its significance display a firm grasp of the reality of human free choice. And, apart from that reality, interpersonal relationships such as those in the heavenly communion looked for by Christian faith are equally inconceivable. For the reflexive goods of friendship, inner tranquillity, authenticity, and love of God, are all constituted by free choices or the dispositions which such choices establish. It is no coincidence that the Enlightenment, which denied divine transcendence and causality and the hope of heaven, denied also the reality of free choice (Finnis 1991b, 20-24).

And they also denied specific moral absolutes. The profound inner connection between free choice and the tradition's specific moral absolutes is this article's theme. I shall not here defend the reality of free choice. But it is worth remarking that the incoherence in proportionalism was first clearly identified, by Boyle and Grisez, in the course of elaborating their potent argument that the rational denial of free choice is self-refuting.[1]

II. Evil: Not to be Chosen That Good May Come

Some of Christian tradition's most decisive witnesses to the truth of moral absolutes have been mentioned (Finnis 1991b, 6-12), particularly the Decalogue in its reaffirmation and paradigmatic interpretation by Jesus, so manifest in the Synoptic Gospels.[2]

John's Gospel, in which no word is at random, places before us not once but twice, the rhetorical question of Caiaphas: "Is it not better that one innocent person be put to death than that the whole people perish?" (John 11:50; 18:14) The question is general. But since one particular person's fate hangs on the answer, the evangelist's careful articulation of the question, in that particular context, clarifies and powerfully reinforces the faithful reader's acknowledgment of the norm (and the underlying principle) embodied in faith's inevitable answer, No!

But John presents us also with another image: the man who not only, like Peter, offers to lay down his life for his friend (John 13:37), and not only describes laying down one's life for one's friends as the greatest of human acts of love (15:13) but actually himself, knowing all that was to befall him (18:4), and in fidelity to the mission for which he came into the world (18:37), accepts the great wrong (19:11) of crucifixion. The particular relevance of this image, this careful representation of the reality of a particular human choice and act, consists in the distinction which it implicitly presupposes: between Jesus' choice (freely to accept death[3] without in any way joining his will with his accusers' sinful will) and any choice that could rightly be described as suicidal, as choosing, intending one's own death.[4]

Some people, in the first ferment of belief in humankind's definitive redemption through Christ by grace, opined that wrongdoing is tolerable or even desirable because it affords occasion for God to accomplish his redemptive work: compare Romans 6:1 and verse 15.

And as Romans 3:8 makes clear, some people actually claimed that St. Paul's own preaching of redemption carried that implication. The line of thought is developed quite clearly from verses 5 to 8:

> (5) If our wickedness serves to show the justice of God, shall we say that God is unjust to inflict wrath upon us? . . . (7) if through my falsehood God's truthfulness abounds to his glory, why am I still being condemned as a sinner? (8) And why not do evil that good may come?—as some slanderously charge us with saying.

Human faithlessness (v. 3), unrighteousness, denials of the truth have a good side effect: they give God glory by affording the opportunity of demonstrating his fidelity, holiness and truthfulness. That good effect is surely greater than the evil in the actions! How then (v. 7) can God, in his final judgment on those actions, regard them as evil? Indeed, why should not those who notice this connection between their actions and God's glory pursue that greater good directly, by choosing to do what would otherwise be sin as a *means* of bringing about that greatest good?

Such is the general line of thought which Paul is concerned to display and reject. On this, there is impressive agreement by modern translators and exegetes. True, almost all modern exegetes leave the thought "Evil may be done for the sake of good" no further elaborated than: "antinomianism,"[5] "libertinism,"[6] *pecca fortiter* (Robinson 1979, 34). But their own agreement on the sequence of thought allows us to be more precise. This is antinomianism with a difference; it is a rejection of moral norms on the precise ground that to depart from them will yield, not merely what I happen to want here and now, but precisely an *intelligible* good which is *greater* than any bad moral or nonmoral involved in my action. The intelligible good in question in Romans 3:8 is God's glory. But Paul's brusque and total rejection of this line of thought entails certain conclusions.

The first conclusion is that rightly drawn by Augustine and by Grosseteste, Albert, Thomas (Finnis 1991b, 20-24, 55-57)—and then by the entire Catholic moral preaching and theological tradition down to Pius XI in *Casti Connubii* (1930)[7] and Paul VI in *Humanae Vitae* (1968).[8] Since St. Paul does not dispute that sin brings about the incomparably great good of God's glory, his teaching entails that the question whether an act is wrongful is *not to be settled* by trying to show that in a given case it would bring about consequences greater in goodness, or lesser in evil, than the goods attained or evils avoided by alternative acts. *Nor* is it settled by showing that the act in question can be regarded as a part of some totality than which no greater created good can be conceived.

A second conclusion is this: One of the reasons why the first conclusion is justified is that the opposed, proportionalist view involves the intolerable paradox (Finnis 1991b, 12-16). Combined with Christian faith in providence, proportionalist moral method yields, willy-nilly, the all-purpose practical norm, Try anything. Divine providence involves the permission of evil (of any and every kind) only so that out of it God may draw a somehow greater good (Aquinas, *In Sent.* II, d.29, q.1, a.3, ad 4). So, if the supreme or decisive moral responsibility is to pursue a state of affairs embodying greater good, the moral norm for every problem-situation would be, quite simply, Try anything. For if you accomplish what you attempt, you can be certain that what you chose tended toward overall long-run net good (since God's providence permitted it), whereas if you fail to accomplish what you attempt, you can be certain that your failure tended toward overall long-run net good since God's providence excluded the success of your effort. It seems to me that, in Romans 3:5-8, Paul was virtually articulating that implication and identifying it as what it is: a *reductio ad absurdum* of attempts to understand morality in terms of *effectiveness* (intended or actual) for good.[9]

We may conclude, third, that Grisez summed up the position accurately enough when he wrote, concerning Romans 3:8:

> Proportionalists deny the relevance of this verse of St. Paul as a proof text against their position. They claim that Paul only excludes the choice of a moral evil, not of a premoral evil proportionalism seeks to justify. However, the preceding verse is raising precisely the question whether what otherwise would be evil—a lie or refusal of truth—might not be justified if it promotes God's glory. Still, *I do not use Rom 3.8 as a proof text against proportionalism,* for without an *independent and conclusive critique* of proportionalism, its proponents could plausibly argue that Paul's rejection of violating truth to promote God's glory is a specific norm whose extrapolation into a general principle is question begging.[10]

But, as we have seen, independent and conclusive critiques of proportionalism are indeed available. One of those is the theological critique, identifying the incoherence of proportionalist moral method with belief in providence (Finnis 1991b, 12-16). What is striking is how far that critique is anticipated by Paul's rapid critique of (what the exegetes now, too vaguely, call) "antinomianism."

St. Augustine knew as well as any modern exegete that Paul's primary concern in Romans 3:8 is not with any specific moral norm but with a precise though far-reaching argument for a wide-ranging "antinomianism."[11] But Augustine also saw that the logic of Paul's position tells against other arguments seeking to justify choices against a human good. The human good in issue in Augustine's treatises on lying is, of course, the good of truth—participation in truth through knowledge and communication of it.

Augustine's first treatise on lying, *De mendacio* (written about 395 A.D., before he became a bishop) is an extraordinarily energetic, and not wholly conclusive, philosophical and theological exploration of the most powerful arguments and examples which can be mustered to defend the rightness of "necessary lies." In it he confronts the opinion of "those who say that no deed is so evil that one ought not to do it to avoid a greater evil, and that what one does," that is, what one is responsible for, "includes not only what one actually performs but also what one willingly suffers," in the extended sense of "willingly" in which the martyr suffers death willingly rather than do wrong.[12] Augustine, in other words, knew the characteristic consequentialist (now we might say "utilitarian" or, similarly, "proportionalist") thesis that no act can be judged wrong unless one has weighed up the totality of its foreseeable consequences against the totality of foreseeable consequences of alternative available options—and that one's responsibility for the *side effects* of fidelity to a moral absolute often makes that fidelity paradoxical or morally foolish. We see again what we began to see in Paul: that the theological tradition's adherence to moral absolutes was made with an awareness of the alternatives.

Augustine's later work on lying, *Contra mendacium*, was written in 420 A.D., against the activities of Catholics who infiltrated heretical circles to discover and later denounce covert heretics. On the opening page, he formulates the core of his response: the zeal to eliminate heresy is admirable, but unearthing heretics by lying, amounts to saying "Let us do evil that good may come," something "which you see how the Apostle Paul detested."[13] In developing his response, Augustine portrays with great frankness all the inner feelings and popular suasions which move him, like anyone else, to want to lie. In the storm of objections and temptations which he puts to himself, his life raft, the consideration he judges will hold firm for all his Christian readers, is the moral absolutes against denial of faith and adultery.[14] If the arguments defending lying, as the lesser evil were valid and true, the same would have to be said of adultery.[15]

Thus something going far beyond the theological opinions of Augustine himself becomes clear. In the Christian community of his day, although there was confusion about lying, there was practical unanimity on two points, One may never do wrong in order to prevent a greater wrong.[16] And the norm excluding adultery (any choice of extramarital sexual intercourse involving one or more married person) is one of a number of exceptionless moral norms, identifying in nonevaluative terms a type of act which will always be wrong even when done to prevent great wrongs.

In the middle of Augustine's tract is the page of general moral theory (7, 18) which became foundational for Catholic moral theology from the thirteenth to the twentieth century. For when Peter Abelard, in the second quarter of the twelfth century, argued (ambiguously) that behavior is morally indifferent and the morality of acts depends entirely on intention and was understood or, perhaps, misunderstood as contending that there are no specific moral absolutes, the decisive reply was given, within a decade or two, by Peter Lombard (2 *Libri quatuor sententiarum* d.40). And the reply consists of a quotation of this passage from the *Contra mendacium*, together with the injunction to take it very seriously, and some sentences of paraphrase.

Intention and purpose, Augustine is here saying, are of great importance in judging acts good or bad. But there are some things, he immediately adds, which are clearly wrong and may not be done, not for any plea of good cause, for any seeming good end, for any supposedly good intention. These are per se wrongful. Examples are thefts, fornication, blasphemies, lies in the witness box, forgeries of wills so as to divert money to the poor or ransom captives or build churches, playing gigolo to rich women so as to give one's gains to the needy. In relation to something wrongful (*malum*) per se, Lombard infers and says, we should deny that its wrongfulness comes from purpose or will (*ex fine et voluntate*, or *secundum intentionem et causam*).

With Lombard's last-mentioned view Aquinas disagrees, magisterially, in his first work touching morals. His disagreement is not with the judgment that there are acts which, as he states, are wrong in themselves and cannot in any way be rightly done (*de se malus, qui nullo modo bene fieri potest*). It is with Lombard's denial that such acts are wrong by reason of will, intention, purpose (*finis*). Such acts, says Aquinas, are wrongful by reason of the acting person's will. There need be nothing wrong with his *intentio* or *voluntas intendens*, his ultimate motivating purpose (*finis ultimus*), for example, to give money to the poor. What is wrongful is, rather, his choice, his *electio* or *voluntas eligens*, his immediate purpose (*objectus proximus* or *finis proximus*), for instance, to forge this testament (Aquinas, *In sent.* 2.d.40 a.2). The goodness or badness of what Aquinas calls the "exterior act" (which signifies everything one does to carry out one's choice, even what lies entirely within one's own mind, as in sins of thought) depends entirely on the goodness and badness of one's will, choice, immediate purpose, that is, on what one chooses and tries to do, including what one chooses and attempts as a means to one's ultimate purpose (Aquinas, *In sent.* 2 d.40 a.2c). From all this, though his later analyses are more complex, Aquinas will never deviate. The rightness or wrongness of behavior is totally dependent on the rightness or wrongness of the deliberating and choosing which makes that behavior voluntary and thus morally significant action of some specific sort (Finnis 1991b, 1-27).

From Peter Lombard down to the Second Vatican Council, the position so forcefully expressed by Augustine and so clearly explained by the young Aquinas was peacefully accepted in Catholic theology.[17] I need not repeat the council's solemn articulation of the specific moral absolute against every act of "indiscriminate" bombing of cities, that is, bombing not intended exclusively to affect combatants and their operations. Here I shall simply recall the council's reflective restatement of the Socratic "Better to suffer than to do wrong." In *Gaudium et Spes* 27, having condemned various acts which "are opposed to life itself, such as homicide of every kind, genocide, abortion, euthanasia, and willful (*voluntarium*) suicide," together with other acts which violate the integrity of the person or human dignity, the council observes that such acts "do more harm [or: are more degrading, *inquinant*] to those who carry them out than to those who suffer the wrong."

III. ACTIONS: MORALLY SPECIFIED BY THEIR OBJECTS (INTENTIONS)

Underlying these strategic Christian testimonies to the truth of moral absolutes are beliefs and dispositions which I have already emphasized-above all, trust in divine providence, and the distinction between the loving service of human good and the effecting of good states of affairs (Finnis 1991b, 12-16). I want now to reflect on something partly implicit, partly explicit, in these testimonies: the rejection of certain types of *choice* or *intention*.

The tradition teaches, as these witnesses show, that certain types of choice and intention are incompatible with love of God and with seeking the Kingdom, because incompatible with love of human good. Whatever may be said about persons who do such acts believing them to be justified, or without the clear understanding that sufficient reflection would induce, such choices and intentions must simply be excluded from one's own deliberation and choice. Accepting death as a foreseen and humanly certain result of one's choice to remain faithful to one's mission to save others can be spoken of as laying down one's life for one's friends, but it is not an act of suicide, of intending to kill myself (or of intending that others kill me) as a means to an end (Finnis 1991b, 59-67). Killing noncombatants as a side effect, which one clearly foresees and thus accepts, of one's properly motivated military operations can be acceptable; but killing noncombatants, by the very same devices, as a means of demoralizing enemy combatants or of impeding them with crowds of terrified refugees is never to be intended, chosen, done.

This sort of distinction matters because free choice matters. Let me indicate, first, how it is entailed by the reality of free choice and, second, why free choice has the moral significance it does.

Choice is between intelligibly appealing options. But an option is not yet the state of affairs one hopes to bring about by action. Rather, an option is a *proposal* for action, and choice is precisely the adoption of that proposal rather than alternatives. Being intelligibly appealing, the proposal includes all, and only, that which makes it seem worthwhile to attempt whatever one will attempt in trying to carry out the proposal. Thus the proposal includes both one's "ultimate" purpose (say, restoring one's health, giving expression to one's friendship, restoring peace with justice) and all the means one judges appropriate to effecting that purpose (taking bitter medicine, acquiring thus-and-thus a gift to give one's friend, undertaking military operations thus-and-thus). The means are included in the proposal, not under some description which makes them seem compatible with some legal or moral rule but under that description which makes them intelligibly attractive *as means*—that is, the description under which they enter into one's deliberation toward choice (not one's rationalizing of attempts to square that choice with one's conscience or with the law). Thus, if one decides that such-and-such a military operation is needed in order to block the enemy's tank columns with crowds of refugees, and that the way to make noncombatants become refugees is to destroy or injure some of them in their homes, then killing or injuring noncombatants in their homes is intelligibly attractive and is the relevant true description of what one chooses and does. That description does not alter just because one tells oneself and others that what one is doing is "bombing military targets" in the sense of targets whose destruction will have an effect on military operations.

Choice, then, is of proposals, and the proposals one shapes in one's deliberations include one's ends and one's means. Deliberation is for the sake of action, and in one's acting every means one has adopted in one's proposal has the character of an end, something one must set out to achieve. So, everything included within one's proposal has the character of *end*, of purpose, of objective. The distinction between ends and means is only relative: all one's means are intermediate ends, subordinate objectives on the way to one's further end or ends, to the ultimate point, simple or multiple, of the choice and action.[18] To use the classical terminology of Thomas, used again in *Reconciliatio et paenitentia*, one's proposal, end and means (remote objective(s) and proximate objectives), is the *object* of one's choice and act.[19] If one is asked, or asks oneself, *what* one is choosing and doing, one answers accurately by describing the proposal one is adopting and carrying out. Acts, in their human reality as creations and expressions of one's reality as a person, are identified by or *specified by their objects*.[20]

That famous phrase is used by Aquinas interchangeably with another, equivalent phrase: *acts are specified by their intention(s)*.[21] For, although Aquinas often distinguished between "intention" in the sense of one's ultimate or remote objective and "choice" in the sense of one's proximate objective, that is, one's chosen means (as in his commentary on Peter Lombard: III.2), he also often abandoned that distinction as irrelevant when he was considering the precise boundaries between right and wrong. For, to repeat: the object, the proposal adopted by choice, includes the end and the means alike; "intending" an end and willing the means are, he says, a single act of will, and moral reflection and analysis considers that whole act of will (ST I-II, 12, 4; 19, 2 ad 1).

In this perspective, *merely* behavioral differences fall away as morally irrelevant to identifying the type of wrong involved. For example: the behavioral difference between so-called actions (or positive actions) and omissions is morally irrelevant where each is chosen as a means. If we decide to kill our child or our aged aunt to collect on the insurance or the will, we may then settle on doing it with a pillow or a needle, or on achieving the same end simply by omitting to supply food. Either way, we have chosen an act of murder; bringing about death-was built into the proposal, as the means we adopted in adopting that proposal by choice.

Conversely, states of affairs which are connected, perhaps even very closely and directly, with the carrying out and the outcome of one's action, but which are neither needed nor wanted as part of one's way of bringing about what one proposes to do and bring about, are unintended effects, side effects. Though they are caused by one's choice and action, they are not chosen, that is, are not intended, even if they are foreseen (even foreseen as certain). Rather, they are permitted, that is, (as I shall say), *accepted*. Certainly one has moral responsibility for what one thus knowingly and "deliberately" causes or brings about. But that responsibility is not the same as one's responsibility for what one chooses (intends) as part (whether as end or means) of one's proposal. Why is it not the same?

Every choice and action has some more or less immediate or remote negative impact-in some way tends to destroy, damage, or impede-some instantiation(s) of basic human goods. One can always refrain from the *choice to harm* an instance of a good. But one can never avoid *harming* some instances of human goods. Since it is inevitable that there will be some such harm, it cannot be excluded by reason's norms of action. For moral norms exclude irrationality, over which we have some control; they do not exclude accepting the inevitable limits we face as rational agents.

Thus, though one is responsible for the side effects of one's action, there can be no rational norm of the form, Do not cause harm, even as a side effect. But there is always a reason not to *intend* to harm human beings in any basic aspect of their good, and since that reason cannot be outweighed by a weightier reason established prior to moral judgment and choice (Finnis 1991b, 54-57), there is no reason to override that first reason, which, therefore, is simply reason. In short, there is a principle of the form, Do not intend harm to a human being, either as an end or as a means. More precisely (and more precisely than Romans 3:8, though not outside its range): Do not do evil-destroy, damage, or impede a basic human good-that good may come.

Thus the morally significant distinction between intention and acceptance of side effects is clear even when common speech obscures it. A woman who chooses to have her womb removed out of hatred of human procreation or as a means (perhaps reluctantly adopted) to enjoying sex without fear of pregnancy which would prevent the acquisition of a holiday house makes a different choice, performs a different act, from the woman who chooses to have it removed to avert the spread of a cancer. The acts are different, even though the behavior is identical; even though in common speech she could be said in each case to "be being sterilized," or even to be "getting herself sterilized," only the first two choices were choices *of sterilization*. Common speech, which is not systematically oriented toward precise moral understanding and is impressed by behavioral and consequential similarities and by legal categories, is not a safe guide. It uses all the action-related terms, including even *act* and *intention*, with an ambiguity which can be overcome only by careful attention to the importance of the end and means united in a proposal shaped by intelligent deliberation (however rapid) and adopted by choice.

The significance of the distinction between choosing (intending) ends or means and accepting side effects can be further clarified by considering directly the significance of choice. The form of "voluntariness" involved in knowingly causing side effects may well be culpable. But it cannot have the same self constituting effect as the form of voluntariness we call intending (choosing). For choosing is adopting a proposal, and what one thus adopts is, so to speak, synthesized with one's will, that is, with oneself as an acting subject. One *becomes* what, seeing reason to, one chose: what one intended.

Forming an intention, in choosing freely, is not a matter of having an internal feeling or impression. Nor is it a matter of following a desire, in the sense of a feeling; even if quite reluctant, it will be self-constitutive, since intelligence and will are more constitutive of personal life than are feelings or emotions. Forming an intention is a matter of setting oneself to do something. Thus, for example, if one fails to do what one set oneself to do, *one has failed*. But if the foreseen side effects fail to materialize, one has in no way failed, indeed, if one adopted means with an eye to minimizing bad side effects, the nonoccurrence of those side effects enhances the worth and success of one's attempt.

And every choice, once made, lasts in one's character. As behavior, performance, or cause, one's choice and action may be frustrated and utterly fail. But unless and until one repents of it—that is, reverses it by some contrary, incompatible choice—one retains the character which one specified and created for oneself by intelligently shaping and freely adopting the object of that choice, the proposal one synthesized with one's will by choice. The lastingness, the persistence, of choice is something which the tradition of philosophical and theological reflection did not make sufficiently explicit until recently.[22] It is very important for an understanding of the relation between this worldly actions and the completed Kingdom in heaven, and of the sacramental continuation of Christ's salvific acts, and, as I am now indicating, of every morally significant choice's self constitutive significance. Thus it is important to understanding the significance of moral norms, particularly specific moral absolutes, which specify acts by their shaping intention rather than by reference to their side effects (even in the case of those norms, particularly concerning sex, where built-in side effects are intrinsically related to the wrongness of a type of act).

To summarize: The *intention* of an act has the significance it has in the identification and evaluation of the act, precisely because *choice* has the creative self-constitutive importance it has. That importance is so great that Aquinas placed the whole of his mature work on ethics under this prologue: "Since man is said to be made in the image of God because 'image' here refers to intelligent and free choice..., let us consider man, that image, precisely insofar as he is himself the origin of his own deeds, through having free choice and power over those deeds" (ST I-II, prol and 1, 1, c).

IV. INTENDING HUMAN HARM: NEVER ACCEPTABLE FOR GOD OR MAN

But perhaps our human status as images of God tells against my argument? For if human persons are in the image of God, and if God can intend evils for the sake of the good of the universe, why should not we, too, intend evils as means to greater good? Perhaps Romans 3:5-8 has a message other than we discerned; perhaps it means that God can do whatever redounds to his greater glory, even if Paul and the rest of us are subject to some scarcely intelligible law against emulating our creator?

As Paul would say: By no means! Christian thought has insisted that God does not intend evils, not even as means, and that he only permits them, as a side effect of what he does intend for the sake of the good of the whole universe (the expression of his own goodness, his glory).

The distinction between intention (including of means) and permission (that is, accepting the foreseen side effects of one's own choices) is employed definitively by the Council of Trent, in one of its canons on justification, in the course of defending the reality of free choice: "If anyone says that it is not in man's power to make his ways evil, but that God performs the evil works just as he performs the good, not only permissively but also properly and *per se. . . .: anathema sit*."[23] What does *per se* mean here? There can be no doubt about its meaning in the terminology stabilized for the scholastic theological tradition by Aquinas, on the basis of Aristotle's *Physics* 8,4. Aquinas explains it thus: In relation to purposeful actions [*propter finem*], "something is spoken of as *per se* when it is intended [*intentum*], and is said to be *per accidens* when it is outside the intention [*praeter intentionem*]."[24] Or again: "In moral matters.... what is intended is *per se*, whereas what follows *praeter intentionem* may be regarded as *per accidens*" (ST II-II, 39, 1, c). There are many passages in which Aquinas draws this same distinction between the *per se* and the *per accidens*, and in which the linking idea is the distinction between what is intended and what, for one reason or another, lies outside the agent's intention.[25] And of these numerous passages, many make it clear that, in these contexts, "intention" extends not only to ultimate ends but also to proximate means.[26]

Trent's similar use of per se manifestly means the same thing. Neither as end nor as means does God in any way intend human evil (the canon gives an instance: Judas' treachery); God merely permits it.

The defined dogma of faith pertains to God's permission of human sin; a foreseen and permitted side effect of his creation of human free choice. And some proportionalists, following Schüller, wish to draw a sharp distinction: God's holiness (they oddly call it his "moral will" as distinct from his "creative will") is incompatible with his in any way intending human sin; but God, and therefore also human persons, can rightly intend premoral evils.[27] We need not recall here the unanswered difficulty which Schüller and others face in explaining why, on proportionalist principles, one may not rightly intend the sin of another as a means to reducing the overall number or gravity of sins (Finnis 1991b, 47-51). More significant here is a related question. Why should the difference between intending and permitting be relevant, as Schüller admits, in relation to one's involvement in the wrongdoing of other people, but irrelevant, as he insists, in relation to one's involvement in any and every other kind of evil? But what is most significant here is this: The proportionalist willingness to intend premoral human evil (the destruction or damaging or impeding of human persons in basic aspects of their reality and fulfillment)[28] jars against the massive tradition of theological reflection on the divine will and providence, expounded by Aquinas and before him by St. John Damascene, the last of the Fathers (c. 745 A.D.). For that tradition insists, vigorously, that for God to will per se (that is, intend) anything which intelligence would call an evil is inconsistent with his holiness.[29]

Christian reflection on God and his holy will, and Christian reflection on the morality of human choosing and doing, thus develop together in mutual support. Together they mark a large advance in differentiated understanding over pre-Christian philosophy and philosophical theology. Philo Judaeus, Christ's contemporary, will insist (like Plato) that God is not the cause of evils and is not responsible for them; but Philo's explanations derail into a strange theory of agency in which the principal is not answerable for the acts of his agents; corruption and destruction are brought about not by God but "by certain others as ministers [of the sovereign King]."[30] Christian reflection advances decisively beyond the undifferentiated concept of "cause," replacing it with the act-analytical distinctions between choosing or intending and permitting or accepting. As one reads through the writings of sophisticated proportionalist moralists of the late twentieth century, one sees with amazement that they everywhere lose their grip on the distinction. They have fallen back into the undifferentiated problematic of "causing" evils (including, of course, the Enlightenment extension of "cause" to include whatever one could have prevented but did not, a concept incompatible with Christian understanding of divine holiness).[31]

V. Counterexamples

Still, can it really be true that one may never rightly intend human harm even as a means to human good? Garth Hallett, S.J., intends a decisive one-sentence argument against the whole traditional distinction between intention and side effect when he insists: "Love not only permits but repeatedly requires nonmorally evil means: disagreeable medicine, distressing criticism, painful punishment, fatiguing labor, and so forth" (Hallett 1983, 112). The criticism simply overlooks the distinction it claims to criticize. The fatigue induced by labor, the bitterness of medicine, the distress occasioned by honest criticism-all are side effects, not means.

Richard McCormick, S.J., makes a more careful attempt to show that the tradition was inconsistent with any principle of the form, Do not intentionally harm human good. Do not do evil for the sake of good. His list of intended harms allowed in the tradition encompasses (i) intended deception of another when necessary for the protection of, for example, the confessional secret; (ii) intended amputation of a leg to prevent spread of cancer; (iii) intended death of the criminal in capital punishment; (iv) intended death of assailant in cases of self-defense; (v) intended pain of the child whom we spank pedagogically.[32]

Item (iv) should be removed immediately. As McCormick half concedes, Aquinas denies that one who is defending himself may rightly intend the death of his assailant, even as a means of self defense, though one may, if necessary, adopt means of self defense which one knows will cause death as an unintended side effect (ST II-II, 64, 7).

Quite a few in the tradition have disagreed, but many have agreed, as I do. Item (i) should equally be removed; the tradition does not judge that one may rightly lie to protect a confessional secret, nor that one may intend more than that inquirers with no right to the truth should remain in their ignorance. Then item (ii) should go; therapeutic amputation is not doing harm but preventing the further harm that a limb already doomed would do to the health or life of the person. Moreover, the basic goods to be respected in every choice are aspects of the fulfillment not of this or that organ but of the whole human individual; that individual's bodily health is integral, not merely instrumental, to that fulfillment, but it is measured as the good of an organic whole. So the transplantation of a duplicated organ such as the kidney, leaving the whole substantially unimpaired, need not be regarded as doing harm for the sake of good.

Then item (v) should fall away, too. Pain is not itself an intelligible evil; indeed, it is itself an intelligible good, as one can understand by considering the difficult, usually short lives of those born with no sense of pain. Pain is experienced as a sensory evil; the horror it arouses in us is essential to its intelligible function. But it is an intelligible human evil only insofar as it causes disturbance to the inner harmony of one's feelings with each other and with reason, and to all the other harmonies dependent on inner harmony. Spanking a child (and Hallett's "painful punishment"), when rightly done, is done precisely to restore that harmony and the interpersonal harmonies dependent on it. It need involve no harm to health or life, no intelligible evil at all, and therefore no intention to do harm for the sake of good.

There remains, then, item (iii): capital punishment. It will be helpful first to reflect on the concept of punishment. Insofar as it is intended only to be preventive or reformative, punishment can be chosen without including in its precise object any negative impact whatsoever on any good; the negative impact on various goods valued by offenders can be accepted as a side effect of benefits sought for them and for society. Insofar as it is chosen precisely for the sake of deterring others, the justifiability of punishment is, to say the least, entirely questionable. But there need be nothing wrong in welcoming the deterrent side effects of punishment otherwise justified. The justification of punishment, as a practice distinguishable from preventative or reformative control of the insane or infectious, must always be retributive. Punishment is not revenge. It is the restoration of a balance of fairness which the offender's crime, being essentially a willful choice to prefer his own freedom of action to the rights of others, has necessarily disturbed. Restoring that balance requires that offenders undergo something contrary to their will, just as they voluntarily imposed on others what was contrary to *their* will (Finnis 1980, 262-64).

However, punishment does not require more than that offenders be deprived of something they value or desire, such as instrumental goods like property or liberty, or sensory satisfactions which are not inseparably connected to basic human goods. The principle which excludes choosing to destroy, damage, or impede basic goods does not forbid a retributive penalty focused on instrumental and sensory goods as a means to blocking not the realization of any basic human good, but only some of the desires and some aspects of the willing of the one punished.

But does not the infliction of capital punishment entail a choice to destroy a basic human good, human bodily life itself? Here there is room, it seems to me, for debate and further reflection, such as that on which the church itself, I think, is engaged. It seems possible to hold that, just insofar as the action chosen immediately and of itself instantiates the good of retributive justice, the death of the one punished is not being chosen either as an end in itself or as a means to an ulterior end. Others disagree. All, however, should agree that the truth of the great principle that evil may not be done for the sake of good cannot be made to turn on its conformity to some prior judgment (such as the church has never definitively made) that capital punishment is a justifiable exercise of the right and responsibility of rulers to punish, a right which the church certainly has proposed as a truth to be held definitively.

VI. Responsibility for Side Effects:
Other Principles and Norms

How, then, should one regard the consequences which one foresees one will or may well bring about, and which one in that sense "chooses to cause" though does not intend, that is, does *not* choose (whether as end or as means)? What is one's moral responsibility for these?

Often great. But it is not measured by the principle that evil may not be chosen, whether for the sake of injury (revenge) or of good.

Therefore, one's responsibility for consequences is not measured by the specific absolute moral norms which express that principle's implications in relation to particular basic human goods. Instead it is measured by the principle of fairness (the Golden Rule), and by all the other basic moral principles. (These further principles, which I have not here explored, call for creativity and fidelity in making and carrying out commitments, a certain detachment from particular goals, and all the other virtues needed to bring feelings and actions into harmony with reason's grasp of the basic human goods) (Finnis 1980, ch. 5; Grisez 1983, ch. 8).

Fairness is an objective measure, requiring rational impartiality as between persons. It imposes reason's sway over all the feelings which deflect one toward a partiality not rooted in the intelligible requirements, in this finite world, of the basic human goods themselves. But though it is a rational and objective standard of judgment, fairness's implications, and the standard's applications, depend on feelings which others may not share and commitments which others may not have made.

Indeed, to apply the Golden Rule, to make sense of "as you would have others do to you," one must be able to commensurate burdens and benefits as they affect oneself, in order to know what one considers *too great an evil to accept*. One carries out this commensuration by reference to factors more or less peculiar to oneself, particularly one's prior commitments and one's intuitive awareness ("discernment") of one's own differentiated feelings toward various goods and bads as concretely remembered, experienced, or imagined. (This is not, of course, the sort of commensuration proportionalists need, for their claim is to employ a rational and objective premoral commensuration, and one which could override [other] moral principles and norms.) The feelings of good persons are, for the most part, integrated with their prior commitments, their sense of vocation. That one adopt some such vocational commitments is certainly a requirement of reason, but reason rarely if ever directs the choice of vocation toward a single, rationally determined option.

Analogously, in the life of a community, the preliminary commensuration of rationally incommensurable factors is accomplished not by rationally determined judgments but by *decisions*.

Thus all the institutions and practices shaped and regulated by the principle of fairness are more or less relative to times and places-unlike the moral absolutes (including, of course, the *principle* of fairness itself). Is it fair to drive at a speed which can kill? In our society it is. For by the fair procedures of custom and legislation, we have chosen to accept for ourselves these risks, imposing like risks on others, as a side effect of goods we esteem. But if a society chose by fair procedures to restrict vehicles to walking pace, we could scarcely criticize the fairness of the decision, just as members of that society could not criticize the fairness of ours. The good and bad consequences of such decisions, and of such ways of life, are truly not commensurable by reason. Here, as in countless lesser decisions, only the feelings of the prudent provide the measure.

But the "prudent," whose feelings are the right measure, are not the worldly wise, or the cautious and risk averse, but the *phronimoi* or *spoudaioi*, the *prudentes*, mature people of practical wisdom. Part of their prudence, their justice, their love of neighbor as themselves, their seeking the Kingdom first, is precisely their firm integration of character around *all* the moral absolutes, their unwillingness even to deliberate about departing from one or other of them.

Notes

[1] Joseph Boyle, Germain Grisez and Olaf Tollefsen, *Free Choice: A Self-Referential Argument* (Notre Dame Ind.: Notre Dame University Press 1976) for a brief sketch of the main argument see John Finnis, *Fundamentals of Ethics* (Washington, D.C.: Georgetown University Press, 1983), 137 and *Moral Absolutes* II.5.

[2] Especially Mark 10, Matt. 19, Luke 16 and 18.

[3] "a death he freely accepted": *Roman Missal*, ICEL translation 1973, Second Eucharistic Prayer (translating *voluntarie*).

[4] The comprehensive Christian rejection of suicide is well elaborated by Augustine, *De civitate Dei* 1, 17-27; exploiting for his own purposes the Roman love of role-models (*exempla*: see c.22, 2), Augustine's first move (in c.17) is to point to the suicide of Judas Iscariot.

[5] E.g., Matthew Black, Romans, *New Century Bible Commentaries* (London: Marshall, Morgan & Scott, 1973) 62; W. S. Campbell, "Romans iii as a Key to the Structure and Thought of the Letter," *Novum Testamentum* 23 (1981): 22 at 35-36 Isaac J. Canales, "Paul's Accusers in Romans 3:8 and 6:1," *The Evangelical Quarterly* 57 (1985): 237 at 244; Raymond F. Collins, *Christian Morality: Biblical Foundations* (Notre Dame, Ind.: Notre Dame University Press, 1986) 246, 248; C. E. B. Cranfield, *A Critical and Exegetical Commentary on the Epistle to the Romans* (Edinburgh: T. & T. Clark, 1975), 186 n. 4; David R. Hall "Romans 3.1-8 Reconsidered," *New Testament Studies* 29 (1983): 183 at 194; William Sanday and Arthur C. Headlam, *A Critical and Exegetical Commentary on the Epistle to the Romans* 4th ed. (Edinburgh, T. & T. Clark, 1900), 74; E. P. Sanders, *Paul, the Law and the Jewish People* (Philadelphia: Fortress Press, 1983), 31; Frank

Stagg, "The Plight of Jew and Gentile in Sin: Romans 1:18-3:20," *Review and Expositor* 73 (1976): 401 at 411-12.

[6] E.g., Ernst Kaesemann, *Commentary on Romans* (Grand Rapids, Mich.: Eerdmans, 1978), 85; Collins, *Christian Morality*, 246, 248.

[7] The encyclical states that to justify a direct abortion by its consequences would violate "the divine precept promulgated in the words of the Apostle: *Evil is not to be done that good may come of it.*" *Acta Apostolicae Sedis* 22 (1930): 541 at 546; Denz.-Schoen. 3721.

[8] See, para. 14; *Acta Apostolicae Sedis* 60 (1968): 481 at 491.

[9] Robinson, *Wrestling with Romans* 34, observes that the same thought may well be discernible in Wisdom 15:1-2: "But thou, our God, art kind and true, patient, and ruling all things in mercy. For even if we sin we are thine....; but we will not sin, because we know that we are accounted thine." Robinson notes that the error in question is of confusing the moral relationship (or love of God and responsibility before him) with "the standpoint of the spectator." Cf. *Moral Absolutes* II.4.

[10] *Christian Moral Principles* 168 n. 32 (emphases added). Giving a fine example of proportionalist manipulation, Raymond F. Collins, *Christian Morality: Biblical Foundations* 238 quotes the first three sentences but omits the fourth and immediately states, "In the exposition of his own position, Grisez unabashedly cites Rom 3:8 as a proof text or Scriptural warrant for the moral adage that the end does not justify the means"! The passages from *Christian Moral Principles* which Collins then cites each in tact take Rom. 3:8 to be supporting "the moral adage" (actually, that "we may not do evil that good may come of it": 155) by advancing quite specific lines of thought derived from the context of Rom. 3:8 (a context which, Collins insinuates, Grisez overlooked), viz. (i) that we do not have the same responsibility God has for the good he wills (155), and (ii) that Paul excludes rationalizations which would seek to justify evil doing for the sake of religion (220). Grisez's treatment of the passage is everywhere consistent with the exegetical learning assembled by Collins.

[11] See, e.g., Augustine, *De fide et operibus* (circa 413) xiv, 21.

[12] *De mendacio* ix, 12. This tract also contains his own formulation of the Socratic saying (see *Moral Absolutes* II.4): Although murder is worse than theft (by, for example, forging a will), committing theft is worse than being murdered (ix, 14). *Contra mendacium* ix, 22, contains the dictum itself: It is better to suffer wrong than to do it.

[13] *Contra mendacium* i, I; see also the echoes throughout 18 and very plainly in the penultimate sentence of xv, 32.

[14] See, for instance, xix-xxi, 40-41.

[15] As Augustine notes in vii, 17.

[16] See especially ix, 20-21.

[17] So Richard McCormick was really rejecting a central strand in the whole tradition in remarking that, when St. Thomas appeals to the axiom that good ends do not justify evil means, he "had to be referring to morally evil acts, as his use of the term 'lie' would suggest; or else Thomas needs correction": *Notes on Moral Theology 1965 through 1980*, 763. Aquinas's definition of lie (*mendacium*) is free of evaluative terms, i.e., does not presuppose that lying is morally evil; his statement that evil means are not justified by good ends is therefore not the empled "morally wrong acts cannot be justified," and therefore "needs correction" if it is to be brought into line with McCormick's proportionalism (which must treat Rom. 3:8 as empty, erroneous, or grossly misinterpreted by the tradition).

[18] As Aquinas says in *De veritate* q.5 a.4 ad II [10] (in some editions, see the corpus of the article itself): "in the set of means to an end, all [means] intermediate [between the agent and the end] are ends as well as means [*in ordine eorum quae sunt ad finem omnia intermedia sunt fines et ad finem, ut dicitur in 11 Physica* (II, 5: 194b5) *et Metaphysica* V (V, 2: 1013a35)]." His commentaries on the *Physics* 2 lect. 5 (no. 181: "each intermediary between the prime mover and the last end is, in a way, an end [*omnia quae sunt intermedia inter primum movens et ultimum finem, omnia sunt quodammodo fines*] . . .") and the *Metaphysics* V (no. 771: "*non solum ultimum, propter quod efficiens operatur, dicitur finis respectu praecedentium; sed etiam omnia intermedia quae sunt inter primum agens et ultimum finem, dicuntur finis respectu praecedentium* . . .") give a vivid and careful illustration of this from medical practice.

[19] "Considered as a certain state of affairs [*res*], the end is an object of the will different from the means, but considered as the reason for [and meaningful content of one's] willing [*ratio volendi*], the end and the means are one and the same object": ST 1-2. q.12. a.4 and 2.

[20] ST 1-2. q.18 aa.2c, 4c, 5c, 6c, 7c, 10c; *De malo* q.2 ads ad 9 ("*finis proximus actus idem est quod objectum et ab hoc recipit [actus] speciem*").

[21] ST 2-2 q.64 a.7c; equally, in effect, q.43 a.3c, 1-2 q.72 a.1c.

[22] See now Germain Grisez, *The Way of the Lord Jesus* vol. I *Christian Moral Principles* (Chicago: Franciscan Herald Press, 1983) 52, 70; Karol Wojtyla, *The Acting Person* (Dordrecht, Boston, London: Reidel, 1979) 13, 19,1495z, 160, on the "persistent" "intransitive" effects of chosen action; Finnis *Fundamentals of Ethics* 139-44, 153. The idea is certainly present in the tradition, in the idea that sinners need a new heart, in the theological ideas of mortal sin and the stain of sin, and in notions about virtues and vices. What these elements in the tradition fail to articulate is the constitutive and dynamic aspect of the lastingness of choice. Grisez analogizes this to intellectual knowledge, which lasts by constituting a dynamic framework, making one capable of and disposed to further knowledge.

[23] See, Sess. 6 (1547 A.D.), can. 6; Denz.-Schoen. 1556.

[24] ST 2-2 q.59 a.2c. "[something is done] *per accidens* insofar as it happens *praeter intentionem operantis*.... For we are said to do *per se* and not *per accidens* those things which we intend to do. Nothing is specified in terms of what is *per accidens*; things are specified only by what is *per se* . . .": *In eth.* 5 lect. 13, nn. 1035-36; see similarly 7 lect. 9 n. 1438.

[25] And Aquinas sometimes links *directe et per se*, as opposed to *indirecte vel per accidens*, the distinction being precisely that in the former case what is willed *directe* et *per se* is willed as a means. Cf. ST 1-2 q.76 a.4.

[26] E.g. ST 1-2 q.76 a.4c; 2-2 q.37 a.lc; q.39 a.lc; q.43 a.3c; q.64 a.7c. See likewise Cajetan on the last-cited text.

[27] Thus James J. Walter, "Response to John Finnis: A Theological Critique," in Thomas G. Fuechtmann, ea., *Consistent Ethic of Life* (Kansas City: Sheed & Ward, 1988) 186-87, thinks that Aquinas in ST 1-2 q.19 a.9 accepts that God wills the evil of natural defects for the sake of the preservation of the natural order; Walter then exclaims that neither he himself "nor any other proportionalist can see here how God's moral will is only disposed indirectly or permissively vis-a-vis non-moral evil (natural defect)." Walter misreads a.9 by ignoring the ad 3m, which establishes that God does not will evils to be, and that the only sense in which he wills even natural defects is that he wills to permit them. Walter also thinks, mistakenly, that *per se* means, in effect, *propter se* (as an end in itself), and

is thus contrasted with *propter aliud* (i.e., with "as a means"); in fact, however, the everywhere more usual and here certainly the relevant contrast is with *per accidens*, and that contrast is precisely between the intended and the "outside intention."

[28] Some proportionalists, notably Josef Fuchs, are unwilling to admit that they countenance intending such harm and speak instead of causing, occasioning, provoking, allowing, "indirectly intending," and so on. But analysis of the acts which they countenance but the tradition excluded as *intrinsece mala* shows that, even for these authors (as for other, less squeamish proportionalists), the difference between intending a result and causing a result plays no real part in reaching their judgment on the morality of acts.

[29] See John of Damascus, *De fide orthodoxa* 2, 29; Aquinas, ST I q.19 a.9; Patrick Lee, "Permanence of the Ten Commandments: St. Thomas and His Modern Commentators," *Theolological Studies* 42 (1981): 422 at 435-36. The thought is compactly expressed, without the differentiation, in Hippolytus around 225 A.D. in his *Philosophumena*, book 10,33; the differentiation between results of which God as creator is "altogether the cause" and results of which, though foreseeing them, he is "not altogether the cause," is made in the same decade in Origen's *Commentary on Genesis* book 3,6; the distinction of permissive from intending will emerges in Augustine and is clearly stated by Fulgentius around 520 in his *Ad monimum* 1,13. Especially illuminating is Aquinas *De veritate* q.5 a.4, obj.10 and ad 10, arguing that doing evil/causing harm (*facere malum*) is wholly foreign to good persons, whether human or divine, but that "ordering" evil/harm, by permitting it on account of some good that can thereby ensue, is consistent with divine goodness. In a.4c he stresses that natural defects (e.g., congenital deformities) are "means" only in the sense that God turns them to good effect; they are not "means" in the sense that every intended means is (viz. not only a means but also an [intermediate] end).

[30] Philo, *Questions and Answers on Genesis* I, q.23; see also qq. 68, 78, 89 loo; 2, q.13; *De confusione linguarum*, c.36, pare. 180.

[31] See, e.g., Bruno Schüller, S.J., "La moralite des moyens," *Recherches de Science Religieuse* 68 (1980) 205 at 211 (*causing* moral evil is never justified, *causing* nonmoral evils is justified in pursuit of nonmoral good of corresponding importance), 221-22 ("*pour tous les biens dont la possession contribue au bien-être de l'homme . . . [q]uoi que l'on choisisse . . . Les conséquences négatives qui resultent du choix vent un pur moyen en vue des conséquences positives qui en résultant*"); Peschke, "Tragfähigkeit und Grenzen des Prinzips der Doppelwirkung," *Studia Moralia* 26 (1988) 101 at 110-12, where Peschke states the "principle of double effect" (which he ascribes to Catholic theology and attacks) in terms not of what is directly or indirectly willed or intended or chosen or done but in terms of what is directly/indirectly "caused"; Josef Fuchs, *Christian Ethics in a Secular Arena* (Washington, D.C.: Georgetown University Press; Dublin: Gill & Macmillan, 1984) 85 ("prohibitive moral norms ... forbid an act because it causes a pre-moral wrong...").

[32] McCormick, *Notes . . . 1965 through 1980*, 647. Franz Scholz treats as decisive the pain a mother causes her child when she puts disinfectant on his wound: see ibid., 808.

Proportionate Reason and Its Three Levels of Inquiry: Structuring the Ongoing Debate

James J. Walter

Anyone familiar with the recent developments in contemporary Catholic moral theology is aware of the continuing debate over proportionate reason. Over the past decade and a half the proponents of the theory have established the basic foundations for such an approach to moral reasoning.[1] Although I consider myself to be a proponent of the theory, my intent in this essay is not to offer justifying reasons for its legitimacy in solving conflict situations. Rather, my primary aim is to call for further conceptual clarity in the discussion. More specifically, the clarity which I will be seeking concerns the necessary distinctions among the following levels of inquiry: (1) the *definition* of proportionate reason, (2) the *criteria* that guide and establish the assessment of proportionate reason, and (3) the *modes* by which we know that the criteria have been fulfilled and thus that a proportionate reason has been obtained. My argument will be that these three levels of inquiry are related but conceptually distinguishable from one another.

When compared with other debates of such magnitude within the discipline, this one is relatively short-lived. One only has to recall the lengthy debate over probabilism in the 17th and 18th centuries to gain some perspective. The proponents of proportionate reason have groped to articulate the essential characteristics of the theory and how they relate to the traditional position on double effect. They have been aided in their search for clarity, no doubt, by the persistent objections of the opponents of the theory. However, one perceives in the literature a certain breakdown or impasse, which I see partially as a lack of structure within which to carry on further debate. Some of the misunderstandings and even misrepresentations of the theory can be traced back to misunderstandings and confusions among the three levels of inquiry which I have enumerated above. The structure which I offer for the continuing debate is addressed not only to the proponents of the theory but also to the opponents. The questions which I raise lack settled answers in my own mind, but I raise them in order to indicate further concerns that need to be attended to in the debate.

I. The Definition of Proportionate Reason

The first level of inquiry concerns the proper definition of proportionate reason. It might be more profitable if I were to proceed by analyzing in turn the notions "reason," "proportionate," and then the general notion of "proportionate reason."

Negatively, one should not mean by "reason" some serious reason which one might offer in order to justify the premoral evil in the act. Such a position "would indeed be the most evil form of ethical relativism" (Knauer see above 49). Although the Catholic manualists of the twentieth-century were not ethical relativists, some of them at least were quite prone to interpreting the notion "reason" in the fourth condition of double effect in ways that are consonant with the offering of "serious or excusing reasons."[2] Positively, most proponents of the contemporary theory mean by "reason" a concrete value which is at stake in the act of an agent. Take the familiar example of the surgical removal of a limb. The value which is at stake is the overall health of the patient or even his/her life. Although it is important that the surgeon morally intend the value at stake in the act, this fact is only a necessary but not sufficient condition for the moral determination of the act. A proper moral determination of any act can only be made once another factor is investigated, namely, whether or not the value at stake is proportionate to other elements in the act. Thus, we must turn to an understanding of the meaning of "proportionate" as it is used by contemporary Catholic ethicists.

Many Catholic ethicists today argue that every human act involves some premoral evil, whether this evil be in the means or in the consequences of the act.[3] If this is the case, there is the necessity to assess the relationship between the concrete value at stake in the act and the foreseen premoral evils. In its broadest sense, "proportionate" means a formal structural relation between the premoral value(s) and disvalue(s) in the act. More specifically, the term signifies a proper structural relation (*debita proportio*) of the means to the end or of the end to further ends. Although we must wait until the next section to discuss the precise criteria that establish proportionality, it is important to state at this time that the determination of a proper relation (*debita proportio*) between the premoral value(s) and disvalue(s) in the act is the second and final condition for the determination of morality. Indeed, it is precisely the determination of a proper relation which makes the premoral disvalues stand beyond the intention of the agent in a moral sense.

Proportionate reason, then, is both a concrete value (reason or *ratio*) in the act and its proper structural relation (*debita proportio*) to all of the other elements (premoral disvalues) in the act. The definition of this term illuminates a number of claims made by the proponents of the theory. First, there is the claim that proportionate reason cannot be identified with the intention (end) of the agent as this was understood in the Catholic manualist tradition (McCormick 1982, 83-4). In the manualist tradition the intention of the agent was something distinct from the object of the act. In a recent article John Connery, S.J. has misconstrued what the proponents of this theory have been saying by identifying the intention (end) of the agent with proportionate reason. Connery wants to show that there is a basic difference between Thomas' analysis and that of the "proportionalist." He argues that the "proportionalist" holds that stealing is not wrong in itself but becomes such on the basis of a lack of proportion of the end of the agent. He fundamentally disagrees with this sort of reasoning and finds it at variance with Thomas' own view of the matter. Then Connery concludes: "According to Thomas, therefore, an act can be bad apart from a good intention, i.e., a proportionate reason. The stealing in the above example, then, is wrong apart from the intention" (Connery see above 303). Here Connery's critique of the theory of proportionate reason is skewed by his misunderstanding of the very definition of proportionate reason.

A second but related claim made by the proponents of the theory that proportionate reason constitutes the very definition of what an agent is doing in an act (McCormick 1982, 84). In other words, proportionate reason is not something which is added to the description of an act already defined. Thus, one does not define the act of the surgeon as amputation or mutilation of the body *and* then add the description of "saving the life of the patient." If the surgeon morally intends the value of life (reason or *ratio*) *and* there is structurally a proper relation (*debita proportio*) between this value and the premoral disvalue of loss of limb, then the proportionate reason itself becomes constitutive of the very description of the *moral* act. Here again, a correct understanding of the proper definition of proportionate reason is important. For if proportionate reason is misunderstood as something added over and above an act already defined, e.g., either as "intention" in the classical manualist tradition or as some "serious reason," then one will continue to misrepresent the theory of proportionate reason at a very fundamental level, i.e., at the level of definition.

II. Criteria That Guide and Establish Proportionate Reason

We now turn our attention to a criterion or set of criteria that guide and establish the assessment that a proper relation between the value (*ratio*) in the act and all of the premoral disvalues does indeed obtain. The criteria should not be confused with the object which they are attempting to establish, i.e., a proper relation, nor should both of these be conceptually confused with the modes by which we know that the criteria have been fulfilled.

Proponents of the theory of proportionate reason have not always been clear in distinguishing the definition of proportionate reason and the criteria that guide and establish the assessment of a proper relation (*debita proportio*). No doubt one of the reasons why this is so is because they have felt that the relation of premoral value(s) to premoral disvalue(s) can occur in a vast number of differently structured situations. As true as this may be, there are two reasons why clarity is necessary. First, it is imperative to make the distinction between definition and criteria in order that those who oppose the theory of proportionate reason can as honestly as possible articulate which criteria they reject without rejecting the basic theory of proportionate reason itself. Second, this distinction would be helpful because it might provide the possibility for authors (pro and con) to discuss whether some form of hierarchy ought to exist among the criteria or whether some form of lexical or serial order ought to be established among them.

When one turns to a review of the literature, one finds that the authors offer a variety of definitions or criteria dealing with proportionate reason. Thus, one finds the following candidates: (1) a non-contradiction between the means and the end or between the end and further ends,[4] (2) the means do not undermine the end,[5] (3) the means do not cause more harm than is necessary,[6] (4) in the action as a whole the good outweighs the evil,[7] (5) the means are in a necessary causal relation to the ends,[8] and (6) the means possess the inherent ability to effect the end.[9] Now, it is possible that many of the proponents of the theory do not make a sharp distinction between the definition of proportionate reason and its criteria because they view the above six categories as specifying explanations of proportionate reason. A good example of this view would be Richard McCormick. In one place he states:

> Proportionate reason means three things: a) a value at stake at least equal to that sacrificed; b) no other way of salvaging it here and now; c) its protection here and now will not undermine it in the long run (McCormick see above 198).

If one were to interpret McCormick's use of the word "means" in the above quotation to signify a specifying explanation of proportionate reason, then one could align his "three things" with the categories which I have enumerated above in the following way: (a) is the same as or some form of (3); (b) is the same as or some form of (5); and (c) is the same as or some form of (2). I believe that McCormick is offering specifying explanations of proportionate reason here, and this can be borne out by reference to another place in his writings. He says:

> To see whether an action involving evil is proportionate in the circumstances, we must judge whether this choice is the best possible service of all the values in the tragic and difficult conflict (McCormick see above 209).

By his use of the word "judge" he seems to mean that we must judge by means of criteria; in this case, by the criterion of "the best possible service of all the values" (see § 4 above).

Notwithstanding McCormick's attempt to offer specifying explanations of proportionate reason, I would proffer that the six categories listed above should be looked upon as criteria that guide and establish the assessment that a proper relation (*debita proportio*) does indeed obtain. Once this conceptual distinction is made, two further questions no doubt arise. First, whereas it is possible to argue that all the criteria are teleological in nature, i.e., they all relate to the value sought in the act, it might be questioned whether all the criteria are indeed valid as they stand, or at least equally valid. Thus, it might be questioned whether criterion § 4 (in the action as a whole the good outweighs the evil) is some form of utilitarian teleology and therefore should be rejected. This criterion need not necessarily be construed in terms of a utilitarian teleology, especially when the criterion is placed within the contact of an *ordo bonorum* which transcends the purely subjective calculation of the agent.[10]

Second, a further question arises concerning the necessity of arranging the criteria within some kind of hierarchy or lexical order. Thus, one might want to say that the criterion of noncontradiction (§ 1) and the one closely related to it, viz., § 2 (the means do not undermine the end), must be looked to first and, if possible, employed before proceeding to some of the others. Even if McCormick and others want to continue to view these six categories as specifying explanations of proportionate reason, it still remains possible that some of these categories might represent more closely the nature of the theory and thus take some precedence over the others. It should be clear, however, that to argue for some type of hierarchy, lexical order or precedence does not necessarily entail the view that any of these six categories can be logically reduced into another. So, for example, to argue the proper relation between the value(s) (*ratio*) and premoral disvalue(s) in an act on the grounds of non-contradiction is not to argue the point on the basis that in the action as a whole the good outweighs the evil; to argue the proper relation on the basis that the means do not undermine the end through the association of goods is not to argue the point on the basis that the means are in a necessary causal relation to the ends, etc. Thus, my point here is not that one ought necessarily to eliminate any of the six categories of criteria or to reduce some of them into others; rather, it is to make the point that a preference might be given to some of these criteria over others.

III. Modes By Which We Know

The third related but distinguishable level of inquiry in the discussion of proportionate reason is concerned with the modes by which we know that the criteria have been fulfilled and thus that a proportionate reason has been obtained. I will begin with some general remarks about knowing and then proceed to a discussion of the various modes that come to bear on the theory of proportionate reason.

All of the modes of knowing enumerated below have some reference to the general Catholic position on *recta ratio*. However, to say that we come to know that the criteria of proportionate reason have been fulfilled *secundum rectam rationem* is not to suggest that this implies some abstract ahistorical vantage point. There is no such point from which we humans can judge. Reason, even in the sense of *recta ratio*, is always historical reason which seeks truth within an historico-cultural situation.[11] The desire for absolute certitude on moral matters will be unreasonable and utopian on this side of the eschaton. Therefore, when one claims that a proportionate reason has been established, what one is claiming is that a proper relation between a concrete value in an act and the concomitant premoral disvalues has been obtained in the light of historical reason. To make such claims about the nature of reason cannot imply that the nature of ethics must be relativistic in either a personal or cultural sense. The Catholic tradition has been long-standing in its attempt to show that *recta ratio* is capable of arriving at moral truth, albeit today we understand maybe more clearly that this truth is always open to further elaboration and clarification in the light of historical and cultural circumstances of the knower.

Several proponents of the theory of proportionate reason have made serious attempts to locate and describe in some depth the ways by which we might know that a proportionate reason obtains. A significant fact to note is that the opponents of proportionate reason have been less critical of the theory at this level of inquiry than at the other two levels.[12]

In his "Notes on Moral Theology: 1980," *Theological Studies* 42, Richard McCormick attended to the epistemological level of the theory. At the end of his discussion on the interchange between Germain Grisez and Peter Knauer over the issue of human experimentation, he noted that the basic question between these two scholars seemed to be epistemological in nature, i.e., how does one know that a proportionate reason obtains. If McCormick is correct here, and I think that he is, then one must not only attend to the definition of proportionate reason and the criteria that guide and establish it, but one must also attend to the epistemological level of this theory.

McCormick himself offers three categories or modes of knowing at the end of this section of the "Notes." He prefaces these categories with the statement that the judgment of counterproductivity (lack of proportion) is probably made in different ways depending on the issues at stake. First, he suggests that human experience is a way or mode of knowing. He offers a number of examples as a way to illustrate his point. "For instance we know that private property is essential to the overall well-being of persons, hence that robbery is counterproductive. We know that those who live by the sword die by the sword, hence that violence is most often counterproductive" (89). His conclusion is that experience itself can provide a sound basis for making such judgments. Second, he maintains that we can know prediscursively through a sense of profanation, outrage or intuition that some actions are disproportionate. Third, he believes that we can come to know some actions to be disproportionate only gradually by the method of trial and error, e.g., whether or not DNA recombinant research should be allowed. The reason why we must proceed by this method in such areas is because no real experiential history is available to instruct us at the present time (89-90). I think that McCormick is correct on all three counts, but I would offer further modes by which we can come to know that the criteria have been met.

In addition to the three offered by McCormick, I would suggest that we can know through: (1) discursive reasoning, i.e., analysis and argument, (2) long-term consequences and, (3) our experience of harmony or of guilt over our actions. I will only say a few things about each one of these modes of knowing and then proceed to show briefly that there is still a need for conceptual clarity at this level of inquiry.

First, there is our ability to reason discursively about whether or not a proportionate reason can be or has been attained. The function of reason in its discursive mode is to analyze as best it can what we prediscursively apprehend. Thus, we marshal the evidence and in the light of logic we attempt to formulate arguments and concrete material reasons to support and substantiate what we have only prediscursively apprehended. Now, the arguments and concrete reasons which we offer should be confused neither with the intentions of our acts nor with the criteria which guide and establish the assessment of proportionate reason. Take again the case of the amputation of a cancerous limb to save the life of a patient. It seems wrong prediscursively to allow the patient to die from such a condition when a surgical procedure can be done to save the life. The surgical operation involves premoral evil for the patient because the operation entails the amputation of a limb. One must now search for a structure of moral reasoning in order to justify the premoral evil in the act. Once again, the fact that the surgeon morally intends the value of life (*ratio*) in the act is only a necessary but not sufficient condition for the determination of morality. One must also determine whether there is a proper relation (*debita proportio*) between the value of life and the premoral disvalue of amputation in the light of historical reason. The surgeon might employ the criterion that the means stand in a necessary causal relation to the end as a way to guide and establish the assessment of proportionate reason. Now, one must marshal the evidence and offer concrete reasons as arguments devised by discursive reason in order to support and substantiate the fact that the criterion can be employed and fulfilled. Once again, these concrete reasons can be neither simply elided descriptively into the intention of the act nor into the criteria which guide the assessment of proportionate reason. Thus, one might offer evidence and reasons why there is no other way available to contemporary medicine to achieve the saving of the patient's life than by amputation. The reasons offered in this case are nonmoral in nature, and their thrust is to show the medical counterindication of any other procedure. It seems to me "medical counterindication" supports and substantiates the fact that the criterion that there is a necessary causal relation between the means and the end can be employed and fulfilled, i.e., a true and proper relation exists between the value and disvalue of the act. This being the case, the only proper moral description of the act is the saving of life: indeed, the determination of a proportionate reason constitutes the very moral object of the act. Now, one might argue that this criterion itself is not valid as a guide for the assessment of proportionate reason, but that is to argue a point at the second level of inquiry, viz., at the level of criteria.

There are other ways in which discursive reason can serve as a mode of knowing for determining that a proportionate reason can be or has been obtained. In some circumstances one might reason that a *debita proportio* is obtained or lacking on the basis of an analysis of associated goods which are called into the picture when it is determined that the means do not stand in a necessary causal relation to the end. Because all of the basic human goods which define our flourishing are equally underived, they are quite naturally associated with one another in both our moral characters and acts. Due to this close association of basic human goods, McCormick has convincingly claimed that an indirect contradiction can occur in our acts, when we undermine associated goods (McCormick 1978, 251-254). Thus, it would be the role of discursive reason to discover disproportions in situations wherein fundamentally related goods might be undermined.

In addition, by the use of discursive reason, one might weigh instrumental values against basic values. This weighing quite clearly recognizes an *ordo bonorum* and thus is not subject to the somewhat common brand of utilitarianism.[13] Now, whereas one may prediscursively apprehend the basic values, it is the role of reason in its discursive mode to weigh these values against instrumental ones. Therefore, if it can be argued that, other things being equal, an agent has chosen an instrumental value over a basic one, then one can know that more harm than is necessary will result and thus that a disproportion has occurred. Once again, to question the validity of the criterion (more harm than is necessary) is not a proper question to raise at this level of inquiry. Rather, what is at stake here is whether one can offer valid reasons to support and substantiate the fact that the criterion can be employed and fulfilled.

Besides the use of discursive reason other modes of knowing can be listed. McCormick himself has stated that whereas long-term consequences do not constitute the disproportion itself they can illuminate that such a disproportion has probably occurred.[14] Furthermore, Janssens has correctly suggested that we can discover a disproportion through our feelings of guilt, i.e., "the awareness of the inner disunity of the subject which has turned its free will against its rational understanding when it aimed at an end it could not rationally sanction or when it used a means by which it negated the value it affirmed by the end" (Janssens see above 130). Thus, the experience of the disunity of the self can become a source of knowing disproportion, and the experience of unity can be a source for knowledge of proportionality. Caution must be taken here so that a careful distinction is made between an authentic and inauthentic sense of guilt. With this caveat in mind it seems that the experience of guilt can itself be an illuminator of disproportion.

Whereas I believe that the proponents of proportionate reason have made some substantial headways in the area of how we can know that a *debita proportio* has been obtained, further clarity is called for. I turn briefly to McCormick's writings for an example. He states, "Thus, I see 'association of basic values,' 'proportionate reason,' and 'adoption of a hierarchy of values' as attempting to say the same thing, or at least very closely related" (McCormick 1978, 253). It could be argued, as I have above, that the "association of basic values" and the "adoption of a hierarchy of values" more properly relate to the discussion of the general level of how we know that a proportionate reason can be obtained and more particularly to the mode of discursive reasoning.

Conclusion

The aim of this study has been to call for greater clarity in the discussion of proportionate reason. This can be achieved most appropriately by properly distinguishing three levels of inquiry viz., the definition of proportionate reason, the criteria that guide and establish proportionate reason, and the modes by which we know that a proportionate reason has been obtained in the light of historical reason. The ensuing debate among proponents of the theory and between the proponents and the opponents could more profitably take place if the agreements and disagreements alike could be organized according to these three levels of investigation. Although clarity will not resolve any of the differences among contemporary authors, it is at least a further step in structuring the ongoing and fruitful discussion.

Notes

[1] Three volumes continue to be the best resources for investigating original publications on proportionate reason. Charles E. Curran and Richard A.

McCormick, S.J., eds. *Readings in Moral Theology No. 1: Moral Norms and Catholic Tradition* (New York: Paulist Press, 1979); Richard A. McCormick and Paul Ramsey, eds. *Doing Evil To Achieve Good : Moral Choice in Conflict Situations* (Chicago: Loyola University Press, 1978); and Richard A. McCormick, S.J. *Notes on Moral Theology: 1965 Through 1980* (Washington, D.C.: University Press of America, 1981). A good summary of the theory can be found in Richard M. Gula,, S.S. *What Are They Saying About Moral Norms?* (New York: Paulist Press, 1982).

[2] For example, H. Noldin, S.J., stated, "Ad obtinendum igitur bonum effectum quandoque licitum est permittere malum, *si adsit ratio excusans proportionate gravis*." *Summa Theologiae Moralis, Vol. I* (Rome, 1914), 101, emphasis Noldin's.

[3] Louis Janssens has forcefully made this point in his article "Ontic Evil and Moral Evil." See below 100-48.

[4] Knauer and Janssens have adopted this candidate. See their articles in this volume. By the word "contradiction" both authors seem to mean a straight-forward contradiction, i.e., the means *directly* contradict the end.

[5] McCormick has persuasively adopted this candidate in *Doing Evil*, especially pp. 193-265. Because McCormick argues his point not on the basis of a straight-forward contradiction (candidate § 1 above) but rather on the basis of the associated goods which are called into question when there is not a necessary causal relation between the means and end, one could argue that this candidate is not the same as § 1, albeit closely related.

[6] Janssens and McCormick have adopted this candidate. It seems that what both of these authors mean by "causing more evil than is necessary" is that an agent would choose a lesser value over a higher one, other things being equal. Although Albert DiIanni does not adopt this candidate for his discussion of direct and indirect effects, he nonetheless does make a distinction between what he calls "dignity-values" and "welfare-values." "Dignity-values" for DiIanni are of a higher order because they relate to such values as self-respect, autonomy, fidelity, justice, etc. On the other hand, "welfare-values" refer to the fulfillment of potentials for action and enjoyment, e.g., life, health, pleasure, power, etc. One might assume that for DiIanni, other things being equal, to prefer a "welfare-value" over a "dignity-value" would cause more harm than is necessary at least partially because such a preference involves the choosing of a lower value over a higher one. See his "The Direct/Indirect Distinction in Morals," in *Readings in Moral Theology No. 1*, pp. 215-43, especially pp. 229-33.

[7] McCormick adopted this view in his *How Brave A New World?: Dilemmas in Bioethics* (Garden City: Doubleday & Co., 1981), 428. It is also possible that Philip Keane has adopted this view in his *Sexual Morality: A Catholic Perspective* (New York: Paulist Press, 1977), 217, n. 95.

[8] McCormick offered this as a candidate in *Doing Evil*, especially pp. 237-40. It seems that what McCormick means by this view is that there is no other way to salvage the value lost here and now.

[9] I offer this as a candidate for consideration. It seems that in order for some action to become a true means to an end it must possess the inherent capability to achieve the end. If the action does not possess this quality, then one can assume that the agent is either only wishing (*velle*) and not willing (*voluntare*) the end or simply mistaken about the efficacy of the action. Whereas some immoral means can effect the end in a physical sense, they are not able to achieve their end in a moral sense because they are disproportionate by definition. Thus, an action cannot be

a *true* means to an end if (1) it is not capable of realizing the end in a physical sense and (2) it is not proportionate to the end in a moral sense.

[10] Janssens and McCormick have argued the place of an *ordo bonorum* in the theory of proportionate reason. See Louis Janssens, "Norms and Priorities in a Love Ethics," *Louvain Studies*, 6 (1977 -1978): 207-38; and McCormick in *Doing Evil*, especially p. 251-54. In addition to Janssens' and McCormick's attempts to show that the theory of proportionate reason is not utilitarian in nature, studies by Charles E. Curran and Lisa Sowle Cahill seek to prove this same point. Charles Curran, "Utilitarianism and Contemporary Moral Theology: Situating the Debates," in *Readings in Moral Theology No. 1*, 341-62; and Lisa S. Cahill, "Teleology, Utilitarianism, and Christian Ethics," *Theological Studies* 42 (1981): 601-29.

[11] Josef Fuchs, S.J. has also made this point in two of his recent essays. See his "The Absoluteness of Moral Terms" in this volume pp.60-99 and "The Sin of the World and Normative Morality," *Gregorianum* 61 (1981): 51-76.

[12] Although this fact can be substantiated from the literature produced by the opponents of proportionate reason, it still remains a question of how much a role these opponents want to give to the hierarchical magisterium of the Roman Catholic Church in discerning moral truth in concrete situations. Several essays in a book edited by William E. May attempt to deal with this issue. See William E. May. ed. *Principles of Catholic Moral Life* (Chicago: Franciscan Herald Press, 1981). Philip Keane, who is a proponent of the theory, also has called for more clarity at this level. See his "The Objective Moral Order: Reflections on Recent Research," *Theological Studies* 43 (1982): 260-78.

[13] See, for example, Frederick Carney's claims in his "On McCormick and Teleological Morality," *The Journal of Religious Ethics* 6 (1978): 81-107.

[14] McCormick originally claimed in his *Ambiguity in Moral Choice* (Milwaukee: Marquette University, 1973) that it was the long-term consequences which constituted the disproportion. He has subsequently changed his mind on this matter in *Doing Evil*, p. 250.

Proportionalism: One View of the Debate

Edward V. Vacek, S.J.

I approach the debate over the adequacy of proportionalism with great hope and little hope: great hope because this discussion of the theoretical foundation of the moral life promises profound insight into the human condition; little hope because over the past ten years I have watched how time and time again intelligent persons read the views of the other side, report them rather accurately, then shake their heads at how someone so smart could be so benighted.

I. Some Definitions

I will try to present what is called the proportionalist (*P*) view; but, as will be obvious, what follows is my own position. There is no theologian so pre-eminent in the *P* school that others understand themselves by reference to his or her position.[1] We have no Kants or Mills, no one like Aquinas or Plato. Throughout this paper the contrasting school will be called deontology (*D*). I will be talking more *about P* than developing it systematically. My desire is to summarize issues, clarify misunderstandings, show convergences, and push the debate forward. For convenience, I lump together respected thinkers like Grisez, May, Connery, Quay, and Ramsey as active advocates of *D*, and McCormick, Fuchs, Keane, O'Connell, and Hallett as proponents of *P*. I take only scant consolation in the fact that far better minds than mine have run aground in these waters. I fear contributing to the truth of Alasdair MacIntyre's perception that Roman Catholic theologians seem only "mildly interested in God or the world; what they are passionately interested in are other Roman Catholic theologians" (McCormick 1983, 92). (MacIntyre seems to miss the ecclesial nature of moral theology. Theologians argue not only about the nature of reality but also, though derivatively, about the identity of their community—hence about the views of their colleagues.)

Perhaps it is best to begin with two clarifications. First, *P* is not some new, upstart ethical theory trying to overthrow "traditional" ethics (Janssens see below). An appeal to tradition, it has been noted, is often no more than an appeal to "what I was taught...." Thus the principle of double effect is considered traditional, even though it achieved prominence only in the 19th century (Cahill 1981, 608). Hallett may or may not have been successful in trying to show that P is the one theory most used by Christians throughout their history, but at least he shows that it has been one of their traditional approaches (Hallett 1983, 205). Secondly, the advocates of *P* not only do not think it is opposed to a natural-law theory, but usually count it as one of the leading forms of natural law. The problem is that "natural law" has many meanings. If it means an objective ethic, or an experience-based ethic, or an ethic that pays special attention to the structures of human existence (O'Connell 1978b, 165-73), *P* certainly strives to be just that.

I presume that most readers are aware of one or more expositions of *P* and *D*. However, for purposes of a common starting point, let me quote Frankena's classic description of these two theories (*P* is one form of Frankena's teleology [*T*]):

> A teleological theory says that the basic or ultimate criterion or standard of what is morally right, wrong, obligatory, etc., is the nonmoral value that is brought into being.... Thus, an act is *right* if and only if it or the rule under which it falls produces, will probably produce, or is intended to produce *at least as great a balance of good over evil* as any available alternative; an act is wrong if and only if it does not do so....
>
> Deontological theories deny what teleological theories affirm.... They assert that there are other considerations . . . certain features of the act itself other than the value it brings into existence, for example, the fact that it keeps a promise, is just, or is commanded by God or by the state.... Deontologists either deny that this characteristic [comparative value] is right-making at all or they insist that there are other basic or ultimate right-making characteristics as well (Frankena 1963, 14-16).

Four comments on these descriptions are in order. First, they are drawn in opposition to one another: *D* denies what *T* affirms. In practice, however, both theories typically do not break into "only consequences" or "only right-making characteristics of acts." Rather, a "broad deontologist" might say that duty also requires attention to benefits, while a "broad teleologist" might say that it is part of the good that it must be distributed fairly (Cahill 1981, 604; Sen 1983, 30-32). The "broad *T*" I am defending is one in which the values of *persons* and their *acts* and *relations* are included among the values to be "weighed."

Secondly, *D* and *T* have come to mean many things (Schuller 1978, 167). In its contemporary version, *D* frequently means that there are certain "right-making or wrong-making characteristics" of acts which are decisive *regardless of circumstances or consequences* (e.g., the inviolability of "basic goods"). When there is a clash between two or more right/wrong-making characteristics, some forms of *D* will permit a person to compromise, but there can be no compromise between these characteristics and circumstances or consequences. Present-day Roman Catholic teaching, with its concern over "intrinsic evil," is a most stringent form of *D*, since it adds that one can never deliberately do an act with a wrong-making characteristic. It allows one to prescind from achieving certain intrinsic goods as long as one never acts against them. Perennial problems such as whether it can ever be moral to be dishonest (deliberately tell an untruth) divide these ethical systems. The debate is twofold. Are there some goods/evils that are morally decisive independently of all consequences? And are there intrinsic goods/evils that cannot be weighed even against other intrinsic goods/evils?

Thirdly, according to Frankena, *T* is said to concern itself only with nonmoral goods, and he takes this to mean that "moral" attributes of an act such as "being honest" or "being just" therefore do not count for *T*. Admittedly, in some non-Christian versions of *T*, there is a demand to maximize either material goods or subjective pleasures such that a sacrificial love or a costly honesty might be excluded. *P* is not this kind of *T*. Unlike utilitarianism, as we shall see, *P* insists on the virtues of honesty, justice, etc. These virtues, I will argue, can be understood as values of personhood.

Fourthly, the modern form of *T* described by Frankena seems distant from a classical natural-law *T* which looked to the fulfillment of basic human tendencies. In fact, Frankena's *D* and *T* are both "act-centered" to such a degree that they omit what is the mainstay of traditional Christian ethics: a theory of the person. A vision of the person must ground the meaning of "right" or "moral." Most contemporary versions of *P* and *D* side with classical *T* in giving pride of place to the person and the virtues.

As a broad theory, *P* tries to incorporate the insights of Frankena's *T* and *D*. *P* asserts that the free realization of "at least as great a balance of good over evil as any available alternative" is the moral criterion. Where it disagrees with or at least modifies Frankena's portrayal of *T* is in the range of values it envisions. Thus, it agrees with *D* that features of acts such as honesty or loyalty have moral significance. The term "value" applies not just to results. It also pertains to the agent, to expressive and evolving natural tendencies, to intentions, acts, and manners of acting, to the circumstances as well as social situations (e.g., fair arrangements) and to the religious context (e.g., command of God). It departs from *D* when it does not allow certain right/wrong-making characteristics to be either necessary or sufficient for determining morality. *P* is a middle position (McCormick 1981b, 314) between an ethic concerned only with external consequences and an ethic which determines the right in total independence of consequences. *P* asks not less than Frankena's *T* or *D* but more.

II. Moral Experience

Rowntree has, I think, accurately noted that both sides of the debate try to be faithful to moral experience (Rowntree 1982, 450). The problem is that moral experience is very complex. Our moral experience includes times when we know we work to improve the world, times when we are aghast at some misdeed, times when we act in fidelity to and fulfillment of our own nature, times when we worry about consistency in our decisions, times when we submit in obedience to God or others, times when we stand resolutely on principle, times when we compromise, etc.—and all of these are part of moral experience. The ethician's task is to integrate all these moments in one system. There are at least four levels to our moral experience.

Concrete Level

On the immediate level, we have at least some strong judgments that certain acts or ways of being are usually wrong. We hold these views because of some experience or reflection of our own (McCormick

1979b, 163) or, more usually, through the mediation of social/ecclesial conventions. Whatever their origin, a theory is generally expected to justify, not destroy, our confidence in these judgments. If a moral theory blessed slavery or rape, that fact would be a strong argument against the theory (Connery 1979, 257).

Much of the debate between *P* and *D* consists in "hard cases," e.g., the standard "Southern sheriff case" or the "Bergmeier case," in which our spontaneous judgment seems to refute one or other theory. The hard cases are important for validating a theory, because on the easy cases most theories agree and thus seem valid (Sen 1982, 15). At the present stage of the debate, each theory has stock examples which, it thinks, undermine the other theories. In response, each theory has developed some explanation of those hard cases. Such explanations show either that our moral intuitions can be justified within the favored theory—even if sometimes rather tortuously—or that the spontaneous judgment is itself wrong. In the "Southern sheriff" case, some proportionalists have noted that the whole criminal justice system is at stake, while others have remarked that, if the "unjust" penalty was something like a slap on the wrist, surely we should choose the unjust penalty in order to save hundreds of human lives.

Moral Decision-Making

In addition to immediate judgments about particular acts, we also have the experience of *making* moral judgments. We make such judgments all the time, and through a reflexive sort of awareness we are able to grasp how in fact we do go about making such judgments. Often our judgments are "instantaneous" (Gleick 1983, 23-4), but occasionally we may go through a somewhat orderly process of deciding.

Hallett rightly insists upon a crucial distinction (Hallet 1983, 171-98). On the one hand, there is criterion for right and wrong; on the other, there are various methods an individual uses to discover what to do. One person might guess the answer to a mathematical calculation, another might consult an expert, a third might use a computer; still, the criterion for rightness is independent of the path traveled to discover that answer. In moral matters a Hegelian citizen may discover what to do simply by following the laws and customs of the state, just as a Christian might consult norms in Scripture, tradition, or Church teaching. How a person comes to a judgment of right and wrong is different from a criterion that would justify whether a deed is right or wrong.

Is there a method or style of thinking that characterizes *P* and another that characterizes *D*? An ethical theory will in part be judged inadequate to the extent that it seems to employ a distorted style of thinking about practical matters. When parodied, what to *P* looks like its own open mindedness looks to *D* like a crass mindset that "knows the price of everything and the value of nothing." When parodied, what to *D* looks like its own principledness looks to *P* as a fearful closed-mindedness that cannot deal with the complexity of reality.

Image of Human Existence in Creation

In his recent book, Ogletree insists that a perfectionist theory must be added to *D* and *T* (Ogletree 1983, 28-34). By perfectionism he means a theory that attends to virtue and to the person in addition to acts. We must ask what it means to be a decent or moral human being. We are aware that not only do we choose to do this or that particular act, but also that in so doing we are actualizing our humanity either authentically or inauthentically (Fuchs 1983, 56).

Different views of our temporal being-in-the-world often underlie *T* and *D*. In its consequentialist form, only the future exists for *T*. Acts are judged according to the increase of good they bring about in the physical, personal, and social worlds. By contrast, *D* theories typically concentrate on present and past realities. The structures or basic tendencies of human existence are already present and not to be violated; past social relations are already formed and not to be severed. According to Ramsey, the future can be left to God.

A moral theory will be embraced to the extent that it well articulates a vision of being human in this world. *P*, as I hope to show, tries to account for all three phases of this temporal structure of human and creaturely existence (Ogletree 1983, 34-41).

Ultimate Ground

On a fourth level, moral experience includes some sense of a moral order or universe whose horizon is God. We enter into a relation with this moral order, whether co-operating with it or resisting it.

This moral order acts as an absolute horizon for our decisions, and like all horizons it is not able to be definitely grasped. Nonetheless, differences in horizons can make for differences in concrete decisions.[2] And what God enables and requires is the religio-ethical task (Gustafson 1981, 235-50).

At this fourth level an individual or group recognizes its basic or fundamental relation to God. One may experience God as a lawgiver, a ground for a stable world, a source of creativity, a direction in the future, a person to obey or co-operate with, and so forth. A moral theory must not contradict this experience of God's self-communication (Fuchs 1983, 94).

Theoretical Adequacy

For a moral theory to be embraced, it has to ring true to all these levels of experience. If a moral theory shows that there is a need for God, as Kant's tries to do, then that counts *prima facie* in favor of such a theory. If Grisez's claim that consequentialism logically excludes religious existence is true, then all of us who are theists have a good reason to reject consequentialism (Cahill 1981, 629). If Skinner's behaviorism shows that to understand the determinism of actions is to forgive all, then most of us would say that such a theory is inadequate because it does not fit our experience of freedom and guilt.

On the other hand, we also recognize a dialectical movement in our reflection. Sometimes one level of our experience becomes more refined and points to a needed purification or reformation of the other levels of our experience. In the West our acceptance of slavery was challenged by the Enlightenment's view of what it means to be human. More recently, in medicine, ethical sensitivities which used to favor paternalism now favor patient autonomy; and this remarkable change has come about through a theoretical critique, a critique that initially seemed to fit neither the doctor's nor the patient's customary experience. It also happens that changes in our experience of concrete issues lead to alterations on other levels. An argument could be made that *Humanae Vitae* has fueled the development of P in Catholic thought, and that the birth control debate has been so drawn-out and intense precisely because it is really a debate over a style of moral reasoning and a vision of what it means to be human, not to mention over what God is doing in the world—therefore over much larger matters than the use of a pill.

In sum, as we discuss these issues, all of us appeal to experience. We should be careful to note which level of experience we are concerned with. Some, for instance, support *P* because it accounts for how they actually make or justify moral decisions. Others reject it because they think it leads to false practical judgments or to a false view of humanity or away from a religious ground. Christians who embrace either *P* or *D* or any other theory need to show its adequacy to all four levels. Let us now look at the contemporary debate in the light of these four levels.

III. Comparisons

Contrary to what its critics say, *P* is not opposed to the use of the terms "intrinsic evil," "duty," or "absolute," but it uses these terms only for concrete acts. One ought not— "absolutely" ought not—do an act that is wrong. Such an act is "intrinsically evil."[3] In the sphere of concrete moral decisions, *P* often is experientially indistinguishable from classical act-deontology (Frankena 1963, 16). What *P* refuses to do is use these terms for norms or for classes of acts viewed independently of the agent or the circumstances. "Absolutes" commonly refer to a class of acts that are always prescribed or proscribed, i.e., in all circumstances, at all times, in all places, and for all persons without exception. For *P*, the word "absolute" is reserved for a particular contingent deed that is objectively required (Fuchs 1983, 113-52). Since no behavioral norm can foresee or include all the possible combinations of values involved in a concrete deed, absolute behavioral norms unjustifiably exclude consideration of features of an act that may be relevant.

The epistemological issue here is certitude about an intricately interrelated and evolving world. One can, and indeed must, strive for moral certainty. But theoretically one can never be sure that one has properly seen all the values resident in act. Hence one can never be theoretically certain that a given act is always wrong. Further, an "absolute" would have to be formulated in such a way as to ensure in advance that the uniqueness and development of individuals, the variations of cultures, the changes of history, and the involvement of God in the world will never introduce any significant differences.

This seems impossible if one takes historicity seriously. New situations, conceivably, may appear which will introduce new values that would tip the balance or recharacterize, i.e., give a new *ratio* to, an action. With this in mind, Fuchs gives a modern interpretation to a Thomistic observation: "because it is necessary that human behavior vary with different personal and temporal conditions and with other circumstances, therefore conclusions drawn beforehand from the first precepts of natural law are not always valid, but only for the most part (*ut in pluribus*)" (Fuchs 1983, 193).

To say that absolute behavioral norms arbitrarily cut short an examination of all that is involved in a concrete choice is not to deny that there are universally relevant values. A theory of objective value should assert that at least values such as those of life, love, and beauty are always and everywhere valuable. It may be that an individual, e.g., a terminally ill patient, need not actively strive to realize some of these. But they remain objectively valuable *in se* and can be acknowledged as such even by those who do not have an obligation to realize them on this or that occasion. Conversely, disvalues remain disvalues even when they are tolerated. Grisez and Boyle get at this notion: "the basic requirement of morality is that one choose and act for some human goods, while at the same time maintaining one's appreciation, openness and respect for the goods one is not now acting for" (Grisez and Boyle 1979, 364). Celibates should do this toward marriage, and those who practice birth control should do it for fertility and children.

One of the areas where there should be far less misunderstanding between *P* and *D* is the status of the good that is omitted or even harmed in pursuing a greater good. Grisez argues that a moral choice must "not attempt to transform and belittle the goodness of what is not chosen, but only to realize what is chosen" (Grisez 1970b, 315). *P* readily agrees. Grisez adds: an immoral choice "presumes to negate what it does not embrace in order to exalt what it chooses.... Principles ... are brushed aside as if they wholly lack validity."[4] The latter claim in no way reflects what *P* proposes. The metaphors of "balance" or "sum" imply that the loss of a good is recognized as a disvalue. The loss of a good decreases the "total amount" of good, and thus such a loss should never be chosen for itself. As McCormick notes, "To say that something is a disvalue or non-moral evil is to imply thereby the need to be moving constantly and steadily to the point where causing of such disvalues is no longer required. To forget that something is a non-moral evil is to settle for it, to embrace it into one's world" (McCormick cited in Gula 1978, 106). To be sure, persons can grow comfortable in permitting evil. Such a process is a forgetfulness of one's starting point. This forgetfulness might be reason for insuring that exceptions do not become the rule; it might be reason for strong social policy, based upon the "moral decline" version of the wedge argument (Beauchamps and Childress 1979, 112-113); It is not, however, a theoretical basis for a universal proscription of all exceptions.

P is often charged with relativism. The charge is ambiguous. If it means that *P* is arbitrary, "merely subjective," or groundless, the charge is false. *P* is, however, relativist if that term is taken to mean that the subject and its intentions plus the circumstances and all other objectively given facts are interrelated with one another and relevant to the morality of a decision (Sen 1982, 19-32). Objectivity or fidelity to reality requires as much. The relational character of reality is not synonymous with relativism.

P affirms that the circumstances must count in moral evaluations. Such a position seems hardly novel. That the situation makes a difference does not mean that it makes all the difference. There never has been an act without circumstances. The act of "taking money" begs for a specification of its conditions before one can make a moral evaluation. So, too, does getting married, speaking the truth, and so forth. A type of act may be describable apart from any context, but one needs to know the context of a concrete deed before one can evaluate the deed performed. We shall return to this issue of wholistic assessment.

Again, *P* is not subjectivistic (Grisez and Boyle 1979, 340-45), if that term means arbitrary. The popular "situation ethics" was really an ethics of "good intentions"; and frequently the intentions were only loosely related to the deeds that flowed from them. Maiming a disobedient child out of love for that child is an inconsistent act. There is a misfit between the intention and the deed which flows from it. Only a material act which is congruent with the intention adequately expresses the intention. Having said this, however, we can still assert that the intentions of the subject are part of the objective act. The difference between "killing out of self-defense" and "killing out of jealousy" is an objective difference. A "merely subjective" act is an act wherein the intentions of the subject do not correspond with the other objective determinants/values of that act (Keane 1982, 275-77). In the eyes of *P*, traditional ethics too often spoke of (material) actions apart from intentions as if intentions were a distinct and perhaps only mitigating factor. But depositing money with a charity is not a human act until it is further and intrinsically specified as done out of vanity or out of generosity. Different intentions constitute different human acts.

Making Moral Decisions

MacDonald has noted that the category of "appropriateness" or *convenientia* is more characteristic of *P*-thinking than a strictly deductive approach (MacDonald 1983, 541). The latter approach, he claims, characterizes that form of *D* which dominated Catholic thought. This same observation has also been made by Gustafson in his analysis of the Roman Catholic position on abortion (Gustafson 1970, 102-6). For *P*, ethical reasoning is not like speculative reasoning (Fuchs 1983, 93). It demands that practical conversion called wisdom—an evaluative sensitivity to relative importances, their interrelation, their densities, their urgencies, and an assessment of their probable consequences. Ethical demonstrations often proceed by appeal to example, and they depend greatly on the richness or poverty of character of the discussants. Stories, images, and traditions inform our decisions by their power to reveal, constellate, and prioritize values and disvalues (McCormick 1981b, 310; Spohn 1983, 52). Above all, as a prerequisite for doing ethics, love is required. If love can be described an as emotional, participative union with the dynamisms of beings and Being moving in the direction of their value-enhancement (Vacek 1982, 177), then love is necessary not only for living ethically—as almost all religious persons agree—but also for doing ethics. Much of the aura of "cold calculation" that surrounds *P* could be dispelled if this idea of love as the pioneer into the value realm (plus the idea of reason as *ratio*-grasping) received greater emphasis in *P*.

Not Consequentialist Reasoning

Contrary to the views of its critics, *P* should not be identified with the sort of reasoning that goes on in consequentialism. Six differences can be noted.

First, *P* has to reject Ramsey's dichotomy between acting for value and acting for persons (Ramsey 1978, 238-39). *P* is concerned, above all, for the supreme value of persons (Scheler 1973, xxiv). Again, *P* rejects the Grisez-Boyle contention that *P* is closed to the richness and growth of persons (Grisez and Boyle 1979, 369). *P* agrees that the usual value-theory of utilitarianism is reductionistic. There is more to being human than "maximizing pleasure," "preference-satisfaction," or "happiness for the greatest number."[5] These common utilitarian criteria acknowledge only certain subjective values and are incomplete with respect to the full range of values. *P* aims at the enhancement of all values. In the best of all possible worlds, that aim would lead to human happiness; but even in such a world happiness would be the result, not the criterion, of moral living. The enhancement of value, including human value, is the criterion of the morally good.

Secondly, consequentialism sometimes, e.g., in the hands of Joseph Fletcher, takes the short view, considering only immediate results. *P* insists that we must exercise "commensurate reason." Reason is not commensurate if in the long run the values chosen (or other equal or more basic values) are undermined by the choice. To choose in this way indicates that we are not really interested in those values. A judicial murder ruins respect for life or for law, and therefore it cannot be commensurately chosen. In the long run, sex-just-for-pleasure, in the absence of higher reasons, loses its appeal, and ever greater means have to be taken just to keep the original amount of pleasure. It becomes self-defeating.

Thirdly, a mindset bent on "getting results" overlooks the intrinsic (yet nonabsolute) value of many human activities. We sit faithfully by the side of a comatose spouse. We forgo advancement in order to spend (even "waste") more time with friends. We choose to do hands-on work with the poor rather than do political work to modify social structures, even if the latter might be more effective. *P* shares with consequentialism its concern for the future. After all, we are future-oriented beings; what we do alters the future, and thus is our responsibility; besides, we or other human beings will have to live in that future. But *P* also is concerned with values that lie in our past, e.g., divorce tends to devalue years of life shared in love; and with the present values of who we are and what we are doing, e.g., becoming a killer in order to get vital organs to save five sick persons. Present covenantal relations of marriage, friendship, society, or nation are worth our time and energy, love and devotion, regardless of any further good that comes of them. The very exercise of our faculties, as Aristotle noted, is an act of intrinsic worth, quite apart from any results. Such exercise constitutes "the point" of a liberal education. As Scheler has noted, Christianity became overly consequentialist when it made children the primary meaning of sexual intercourse, thereby failing to see the worth of the expressive and unitive aspects of that act.

Fourthly, in contrast to consequentialism, *P* can recognize that the manner in which consequences are achieved can greatly affect the moral meaning of an act. The concerned social worker may get no more food stamps for a client than the indifferent bureaucrat, but the former performs in a more valuable manner and therefore, other things being equal, more ethically.

Fifthly, the focus on "consequences" implies a narrow, even technological understanding of reason. Indeed, the term "proportionalism" should be read as a theory of "proportionate reason." Consequentialism neglects reason's power to grasp or form natures and unities of acts. The determination of the nature of a particular act can be the crucial task. Is one a prostitute or a "working girl," performing an abortion rather than removing diseased fallopian tubes, stealing an apple or liberating it? Prior to any summation or comparison of values, reason and emotive consciousness must grasp the nature of the act.

Lastly, *P* need not follow those forms of consequentialism which claim that we must maximize goods or minimize evils (O'Connell 1978b, 152-54). There is a range of morally good alternatives which may be different in value without one being obligatory and all others being wrong. Thus, McCormick indicates that one may throw oneself on a grenade to save others and one also may run.[6] Both are positive acts, one heroic but not obligatory, the other ordinary but also not obligatory. *P* is not committed to a mindset which knows only a simple criterion of maximalization of value.

Uses of Rules

Practical reasoning frequently makes use of rules. Rules thematize a recurrent pattern of value or disvalue and thus function as summaries of *P*-thinking.[7] Some rules have the appearance of being always valid. From a *P* perspective, all behavioral rules contain the implied qualifiers "under normal circumstances," "unless there is a sufficient reason," or "all other things being equal." W. D. Ross's prima-facie duties are exceptionless qua *prima facie*. They have the same status as universally valid values in *P*. By designating certain rules as *prima facie*, Ross can say that it is always the case that they are relevant, even when some other rule overrides them.

Rules may also be so formulated as to apply in certain specific conditions (e.g., tell the truth to "persons owed the truth") or to the exclusion of certain other conditions (e.g., do not "directly" kill "the innocent"). For a theory in which morality is coextensive with rules, it is necessary to infinitely multiply rules to cover every condition or exception. Thus the efforts of Catholic casuistry. Thus, too, Ramsey argued that whenever a legitimate exception to a rule occurs, we need to reformulate the rule so as to include the "exception" as part of the rule, with the result that the exceptional case is no longer an exception (Ramsey 1968, 67-135). For *P*, this move is unnecessary since moral reasoning can never be purely deductive. Insofar as concrete actions are never exactly the same, some (potentially relevant) aspect of reality will always be omitted by pure universals. The proper role of conscience is not merely to "apply" moral rules to decisions; it also judges whether and to what extent a rule is relevant (Fuchs 1983, 128-29). Having said this, however, *P* quickly adds that some evils are so monstrous that countervailing exceptions can hardly be envisioned. Rules prohibiting these evils are described as "practical absolutes" or "virtually exceptionless."[8]

Like its half sister utilitarianism, *P* can even affirm the *necessity* of some rules. Rules create social practices or institutions, and they establish patterns of social expectation. Social ethics develops an analysis of the *values* of these patterns, structures, roles, laws, etc. Rules are also *useful*. Armed with rules, we do not need on each occasion to consider all possible values and disvalues. They have a pedagogical function as guides enabling us to see more clearly what needs to be done. For example, otherwise "good people" today copy software because no commonly accepted rule including these acts under stealing has been established. Rules offer a great service to decision-making by pointing out patterns of disvalues/values which must be considered if we are to act responsibly.

In sum, rules are themselves valuable for human beings, and so their value counts in a system that tries to weigh values. What *P* tries to do is to give a theoretical grounding to these rules, laws, commandments, and so forth. It tries to answer two questions: Why this rule rather than another? What should we do when the rules clash?

Enhance Value-Realm

P often spends much of its time defending itself against its attackers. Because it has at bottom a simple criterion, its own set of questions to opposing theories seems rather rhetorical: Are you opposed to enhancing the good and eliminating the evil? Are you opposed to a wholistic view of agency? Are you opposed to taking into account all of reality? As Maguire once remarked, such questions have the ring of "I'm for truth. What are you for?" Nonetheless, the questions may help clarify the discussion. We begin with the notion of value.

Premoral and moral values. Values may be experienced as ideal or already realized; as inviting or obligating; and as concretely impossible, realizable, or realizable-by-me. Behind the notion of premoral values lies a metaphysical view: every object, act, person, relation, institution, and so forth is valuable or disvaluable in a great variety of ways. Beings are good in themselves; usually they are also good for others; and they may also be means to still other goods. Beings may be good/bad for the senses, the body, the psyche, the mind, or the religious soul. When values and disvalues are considered in relation to freedom, they are called "premoral values." "Premoral" in this phrase means "relevant to moral goodness or badness, but not *in se* constitutive of that goodness or badness." The term "premoral" is employed to indicate that a value has yet to be realized, but is contemplated as an aspect of a free act.

The term "moral value" commonly has at least two meanings. Theorists of *P* speak of moral value (human fulfillment) being created when premoral value is realized, but they also speak of moral values apart from such actions.[9] Among these latter moral values, they include such characteristics of the person and his/her acts as being just, chaste, honest, faithful, etc. Reflection, I think, shows that this second sense of moral value may not be essentially different from the first. Just arrangements and honest communication are not moral values when found in dogs or birds, even though among animals these "habits" are good. When consented to or freely developed by a person, these habits or virtues form our character and are called moral values. That is, they are moral values because they are *realized* virtues of the person. Moral values are premoral values of the *person* which have come to be in freely realizing other premoral values. As Aristotle observed, "The virtue of man [and woman] will be the state of character which makes a man [or woman] good and makes him [or her] do his [or her] work well."[10]

Though Frankena (Frankena 1963, 14-16) acknowledges that utilitarianism is not wed to any particular theory of values, he and others (Ramsey 1978, 239) claim that justice cannot be a premoral value, cannot be a good to be included among the values to be enhanced. The crucial question of our debate reappears: Why, for example, do we act justly? Because the world is "better off" when just, or because even if the world is worse off, it is right to be just? (Brandt 1983, 43; Sen 1983, 30-32). Rawls's difference principle argues that it is moral that some people be better off if that improves the lot of the least well off. Why is it that Rawls's intuition fits many of us? Is it possible that some would prefer equal poverty to a system that allowed inequalities where the lot of all was improved? To be sure, some characteristics are more central to humanity and therefore of high and usually overriding value, without reducing other values to the morally irrelevant. Thus, a world in which no one was honest but in which everyone had a high material standard of living would not be a "better off" world. Still, a social system that was so rigidly structured that no one was tempted to be dishonest, but also no one desired to improve his/her material well-being would not be a "better" world. One cannot lexically take care of moral values and only then attend to welfare values.

A secondary reason behind the use of the term "premoral" is to avoid a linguistic or logical difficulty, found more often in Protestant authors but also occasionally in Catholic authors.[11] These authors sometimes say that an act is sinful or intrinsically evil, but that morally we must do it. *Pecca fortiter*. Similarly, other theorists solve the problem of conflicts by a weighing of rightness and wrongness rather than goods and evils (Frankena 1978, 154). And W. D. Ross's device of *prima-facie* duties explains occasions where our (final) duty is not to do our (*prima-facie*) duty. In all of these theories there seems to be confusion of meanings. An obligation to sin is a contradiction; a wrong act cannot be made right; a duty either is or is not a duty. By using "premoral disvalue" instead of "intrinsic evil," "sinful," "wrongness," or "duty" for aspects of a deed, *P* is able to say that at times we may, when necessary, deliberately will a disvalue because it is only premorally disvaluable. By telling a lie to a murderer, we are less than perfectly honest, but on the whole we have enacted a positive relation to the realm of value.

Weighing Values. It is no secret that the most underdeveloped aspect of *P* is its value theory. Here the critics of *P* are quite correct. Parallel to an analogy of being, there should be an analogy of value. Accompanying the near obsession of epistemologists with analyzing conceptual judgment, there should be an in-depth analysis of value assessment. Values are not added like dollars and cents. Loyalties and vocations configure the concrete values that one individual but not another perceives and must realize or avoid. Some goods, such as food, are valuable relative to our changing hungers. Other goods, such as a relation to God, are universal demands of our existence, though even here there are variations in types. Biological, psychological, mental, and religious development modifies the range and depths of the values one can perceive and should respond to (Keane 1982, 274).

Various schemas, such as the elaborate one of Brandt (Brandt 1979, 46-69) or the simpler one of Hallett (Hallett 1983, 165-69), aid in understanding how we might go about a rational assessment of value priorities. Since at least many of the acts we perform contain a mixture of value and disvalue, *P*-reasoning needs to establish what will represent an increase of the good and a decrease of the bad. Needless to say, such assessments are not easy, at least if we try to make them in a theoretical way. Obviously, we muddle through: people do not need to study epistemology before they learn about their world; so, too, people adequately evaluate the risks of crossing the street without first formulating a theory of value and value assessment. Nonetheless, for philosophical and theological adequacy, such a theory is greatly needed. Wisdom, not more sophisticated computers, is necessary for making these judgments. Compassion and depth of feeling are more important than calculation. *P*—to its detriment—continues to use metaphors that imply a quantitative enterprise, but at bottom it demands a qualitative sensitivity to the depth and breadth of value.[12] As Scheler insisted, it is the well-ordered heart that is both the origin and result of ethical decisions.

Grisez and Boyle, among others, oppose *P* not because (or not only because) it yields wrong answers but because it is "altogether unworkable" (Grisez and Boyle 1979, 349-51). It is, they charge, a "calculative method," and this "calculation simply cannot be done unless the values of various outcomes" can be measured against one another; but such outcomes are "simply incommensurable." Five things might be said in response.

First, Grisez and Boyle seem to presuppose that either the human mind would have to be a computer which processes data by reducing the data to multiples of some common denominator, or else it cannot make comparisons (Grisez and Boyle 1979, 350-57). They argue that by definition the "better" alternative must include "all" that lesser alternatives possess plus an extra. For commensurability to work, they say, one might compare "prayer" and "prayer with a meal," but there is no "good plus more good" in "prayer" as compared to a "meal." Grisez and Boyle (1979, 354-55) argue that we cannot properly choose between goods, e.g., between a Julia Child meal and a van Gogh painting; we can only pick either a nourishment or an aesthetic standard, and then one or the other good accordingly becomes superior (Grisez and Shaw 1974, 113). Since there is no common denominator, the calculator will not work. To this argument one might reply that human beings function more complexly than a computer. Even other animals do.

Secondly, we all do make such value assessments. *Ab esse ad posse*. The human mind, like the human body, is fortunately able to choose between "apples and oranges" (McCormick 1979a, 32). We are sure that loving a friend is in itself more valuable than tasting peaches, even if the former is fraught with pain and the latter consistently gives pleasure. Anyone who could not make such a comparison of these "incomparables" would have to be value-blind, bereft of value judgment. It is up to the epistemologists to explain how we do so, not to declare that such judgments are impossible.

Thirdly, and more to the point, there is a common standard which we call "value" and which, like the analogy of being or intelligibility, is not strictly a quantifiable standard but does nonetheless yield comparisons. If beings or actions are in fact incommensurable, then one cannot say that God or human beings are more valuable than stones.

Aquinas' Fourth Way for proving the existence of God presupposes the possibility of comparisons. The fourth condition of the principle of double effect also demands comparisons. Like being, value, though it is indefinable, is the analogously "common" facet. Grisez and Boyle acknowledge that people speak comparatively in ethical matters (Grisez and Boyle 1979, 357-58, 372). They reply, however, that people do not understand what they are saying when they make such judgments. *P* thinks that people know what they are talking about. We just may be smarter than some theories say we can be.

Fourthly, Grisez and Boyle assert that where people do compare goods, such evaluation is a function of practical judgment concerning "some nonmoral sense of 'better'" (Grisez and Boyle 1979, 356). Practical judgment, they say, decidedly is not moral judgment. Since the comparison of nonmoral goods is what *P* proposes as the criterion of morality, *P* has to ask why such a sharp distinction is drawn. Grisez and Shaw continue: "where there is no other moral issue," one can and indeed must be a utilitarian (Grisez and Shaw 1974, 113). *P* rejects the necessity for this two-step process: first moral issues, then nonmoral issues. To be sure, in practice we often do check our proposed act against various standard rules, then in default of prohibitions at this stage go further to see if there are additional considerations. But for *P*, in theory we must weight even the values/disvalues thematized in these initial *ut in pluribus* prohibitions and we must ask whether the peculiarities of the situation (the so-called nonmoral factors) warrant overriding even these prohibitions. The whole must be considered from the outset in order to be objective.

Fifthly, Grisez and Boyle say that when *P* examines alternatives, it must do so in the light of prior commitments and therefore it is subjectivist (Grisez and Boyle 1979, 352-55, 365). They fail to make clear why a person's commitments must be subjectivist. Any human choice of standards must, analytically, be subjective, without for that fact necessarily being subjectivistic. The criterion for selecting between the meal and the painting is their respective power to promote human flourishing, but the aptness at a particular time of one over the other is objectively true. More importantly, "my commitments" to a friend rather than to peaches, or to peace and justice rather than profit and comfort, are, I hope, objective-value revealing commitments.

Conflicts. P can also take the offensive in this debate. Some questions it continuously asks of D, without receiving a satisfactory answer, are: How do you know that such and such an act is always wrong? How do you justify your norms? With what justification can you say that the presence of one factor obviates the need to look at other factors? If there is such a property of acts that *in se* marks them as always right or always wrong, what, so to speak, does that property look like? Concerning any behavioral norm, P asks a series of why-questions in the hope that D will finally admit that we must not do this or that, e.g., not kill innocent people, because there is a great premoral disvalue in doing so and because no proportionate value is achieved by so doing. P may point out to D that all or almost all of the traditional "intrinsic evils" have over time been modified. At one time, lying, birth control, taking of money as interest, active disobedience, and divorce with remarriage were absolutely forbidden. Now under special conditions all are tolerated. For example, St. Paul considered a peace-filled faith life to be a higher value than the sheer permanence of the marriage, and so he legitimated divorce and remarriage. If, in answer to the why-question, D gives reasons in the sense of some good enhanced or protected or of some evil eliminated, avoided, or diminished, then it embraces P-reasoning.

Proportionalists typically continue the offensive by asking what one is to do in the case of conflicting "duties." If I "must" return the borrowed knife and I "must" protect my family, what should I do? What should I do when I am forced to choose between loyalty to a friend and being honest about revealing some fault of that friend? Grisez and Shaw are consistent when they argue that in the face of conflicting duties there are "no general principles by which one can say that the weight of moral responsibility lies in the direction of one duty or the other" (Grisez and Shaw 1974, 124-126).[13] In fact, following their formal criterion of morality, "consistent inclusiveness," they suggest that if one consistently favors one duty over another, one acts unreasonably (Grisez and Shaw 1974, 91). It would appear that a flip of a coin should be a moral device for solving conflicts of duty.

The tack of saying that duties are *prima-facie* duties follows a pattern similar to the weighing of premoral values. These are "duties" because *normally* the acts they describe contain a preponderance of value or, more usually, disvalue. They are *prima-facie* because the values enshrined in these duties may be overridden or outweighed by the values enshrined in other duties. Duties are not ultimate, theoretically speaking; rather, values are the solid foundation of the moral life (Scheler 1973, 163-237).

Idea of Person in Creation
Wholistic Assessment

The richness of human value and the complexities of individual and social histories demand a more sophisticated analysis than that ordinarily provided by utilitarianism. Ashley and O'Rourke stress the dangers of utilitarianism:

> To many it seems based on a very superficial, overly economic view of the needs of human persons and human communities. It makes its calculations of cost and benefit consequences by treating human values as quantitatively comparable items, without taking adequate account of the unified, hierarchical, interdependent structure of the human person or the person's relation to a community sharing higher values (Ashley and O'Rouke 1997, 159).

P should agree. Classical teleology, at its best, makes wholistic assessments. (Again, the epistemology of the whole-part relations needs to be developed.) Moral theorizing must begin with persons/agents and not merely with acts. In the words of Grisez and Boyle, "the goodness of the person . . . lies in realizing, not all potentialities for action, but rather in realizing those which are conducive to fuller and fullest self-realization" (Grisez and Boyle 1979, 363; Grisez and Shaw 1974, 85-87). Here we have a self-fulfillment ethics which makes the realization of the self—or, better, a community of selves—the goal of our actions.

Therefore, to make wholistic judgments, ethics must insist that every act be understood and morally evaluated within the whole dynamism of that person (Gustafson 1970, 109). *Agere sequitur esse*, or ought to. But this *esse* is that of personal being which transfuses all particular tendencies and facets of a person. Acts receive their significance (*ratio*) in part from the agent who performs them. To take a common example, sexual activity does not have a morality all to itself. Human sexual activity is human, and therefore it must be assessed in part by how it contributes to human individuals and communities. One does not simply establish the biological nature of the sexual organs and then set down rules for their use. Any theory that considers only one aspect of human nature does not take seriously the "being" of human persons. At least when it comes to human beings, one must avoid a crude pin-cushion substance theory which envisions human beings as unchanging substances in no way modified by their accidents. To be sure, each of the various dynamisms of a human person has its own semi-autonomy which an objective ethic must respect. At the same time, each dynamism must be integrated within the developmental dynamism of the whole person (Ruf and Cooper 1982, 142-59) and, once again, within social and religious relations (Rigali 1983, 252-57). *Agere informat esse.*

Where *P* disagrees with *D* is that it thinks *D* absolutizes human tendencies as separate items; *D* offers an inadequate account of the unity of the person, a unity which is a structure of hierarchically ordered and interdependent dynamisms; and *D* gives insufficient attention to a person's relation to community. Put sharply, for *D* any serious disvalue must lead to an overall weakening, if not destruction, of the "unified, interdependent structure" of human existence. For *P*, however, a loss in one "item" of human experience might be the condition for a gain in the whole of the human-growth process or in communal relations. *D* says certain acts are wrong "regardless" of any fulfillment of other basic goods (Grisez and Boyle 1979, 336). For *P*, the fulfillment of other basic goods may mean the fulfillment of the whole person, and thus the dynamism of the whole may compensate for a loss in the dynamism of a "part."

Basic Goods

Mention has just been made of "basic goods." McCormick (1981b, 305) gives the following partial list of basic tendencies: preserve life, mate and raise children, explore and question, friendship, use intelligence in guiding action, be religious, develop and exercise skills in play and the arts.[14] The classical natural-law tradition spoke of basic human tendencies and noted that the fulfillment of these tendencies is our moral obligation (McCormick 1989b, 164). Still, some questions can be asked. First, how is this criterion of "basic" established? Surely some aspects of human life are more basic than others. However, whether there is some clear line dividing eight or ten basic tendencies from all others seems uncertain. For *D*, of course, it seems essential to establish such a line. On one side of the line are those tendencies that can never be violated, while on the other more latitude, if not also moral indifference, is appropriate. In my view, the issue is more susceptible to the image of a continuum, with some tendencies very basic, others less so, and still others of small import.[15]

Normally these basic tendencies or goods override other values both because these tendencies are so valuable in themselves and because they are the conditions for the realization of other values. That is, there are various essential and contingent interrelations between these grounding tendencies and the values that would not be without them (Hallett 1983, 155-58; Sen 1982, 15-18). Thus, prayer and life are both intrinsically valuable and the conditions for other goods.

P does not, as we have seen, subscribe to the optimistic thesis that these basic goods can never conflict with one another or with the thesis that these basic values have a lexical priority over all other values.[16] Life is sadly full of tragic choices.

The present debate centers on the fact that *D* asserts at this juncture that any act inconsistent with a basic human good is by that fact immoral (Grisez and Boyle 1979, 360-68). If *D* says that this sort of act is immoral because it thwarts human flourishing, *P*'s question is, does it necessarily and always do so? If it does, then *P* would normally[17] agree that such an act is immoral, and on *P* grounds. That which on the whole leads to lesser value than its alternative is wrong. If it always does so, it is always wrong.

Still, there is a question lurking. How can one make the is/ought leap from a "basic human good" to "always" or "necessarily" wrong to violate? *D*'s reply might be either empirical ("that's the way it works out") or conceptual (either a tautology, e.g., "unnecessarily self-limiting" (Grisez and Boyle 1979, 363), or a demonstration that any inconsistency with a basic good must lead to human diminishment). We have just seen that if the former is true, then such an act is wrong on *P*-grounds. Considering the finite and often tragic nature of life, I fail to understand why the latter (unless tautological) must be true (McCormick 1978, 228-30, 253). (McCormick's "association of basic goods" seems to me to be open to the same question.) It seems quite possible to choose in an instance to diminish a basic good (health in organ donation, e.g., or a particular friendship) in order to affirm some greater good (e.g., loyalty to one's child, family, nation, or God).

Aquinas was willing to subordinate each of the basic human tendencies to some higher good, whether of the individual or of the common good (McCormick 1978, 317).

Directly against

Grisez describes the basic goods as "equally ultimate" (Grisez 1970b, 315). For him, the word "equal" presumably is not meant as a term of comparison, but rather is meant negatively, i.e., incommensurable. He further claims that we can never act directly against a (basic) good (Grisez and Boyle 1979, 386). Respect for a basic good means in practice refusing to violate any fundamental good in order to achieve another. According to Grisez, one can omit a good if "that omission is essential to realize another good," or one need not act to preserve one of the equal goods since another equal good may be "very pressing." We might ask: On what rational basis might one choose to realize one incommensurable good, omit another, and not preserve still another, if in fact they are incommensurable?

Much seems to rest on the qualification "direct." If by "direct" one means "deliberately" or with "full knowledge," then we often act "directly" against various goods for the sake of other goods. For example, Ignatius of Loyola had to suppress his urge to pray so that he could devote himself to study. We, on the other hand, may forbid playing during class. According to McCormick, "the mistake of the tradition was to believe that intending as a means necessarily involves approval" (McCormick 1978, 264).

If, however, by "direct" one means either that the disvalue is desired for itself or is at least a welcome concomitant to another desired goal, then all agree that one should never act directly for such a goal. The moral act is informed by intention; it receives part of its *ratio* from what the agent thinks he/she is doing. If I make a major medical discovery solely in order to embarrass a colleague, the moral act performed is that of doing a harm to my neighbor. Thus the language of directness seems to imply the following test: If I could achieve an enhancement of value without going against a value, would I do so? If the negative effect is also desired, then I am acting directly for it, whether or not it precedes, accompanies, or follows other effects.[18]

For *P*, to choose against any good or for any evil is *ipso facto* a premoral disvalue; the terminology of direct or indirect is not morally apposite (McCormick 1978, 241). If there is a good to be realized, the evil permitted (or good lost) can be morally willed only as "part of the whole story." (And even if part of the whole story, the act is still not morally justifiable until a determination of proportionality and "commensurateness" has been made and, importantly, other alternatives have been considered.) One who has a legitimate reason for an abortion—say, to save a life—cannot choose an abortion if some alternative course would save a life without the abortion. McCormick summarizes:

> Further reflection by practical reason tells us what it means to remain open and to pursue these basic human values. First we must take them into account in our conduct. Simple disregard of one or other shows we have set our mind against this good. Second, when we can do so as easily as not, we should avoid acting in ways that inhibit these values, and prefer ways that realize them. Third, we must make an effort on their behalf when their realization in another is in extreme peril. If we fail to do so, we show that the value in question is not the object of our efficacious love and concern. Finally, we must never choose against a basic good in the sense of spurning it. What is to count as "turning against a basic good" is, of course, the crucial moral question. Certainly it does not mean that there are never situations of conflicted values where it is necessary to cause harm as we go about doing good (McCormick 1979b, 102).

Intention

A similar analysis can be made through a consideration of intentions and intentionality. Some theorists divide foreseen consequences into intended and merely accepted consequences (Grisez and Boyle 1979, 381-92). One is morally responsible for the former, but not necessarily for the latter since "it is no part of that to which they commit themselves" (Grisez and Boyle 1978, 385). The notion of "intention" used here seems to be that of volition in the sense of desired. What is permitted is also willed, but not desired in itself and therefore not "intended." It seems to me that some phenomenological refinement is called for.

When we perform an act that has consequences which we otherwise do not want, we identify ourselves with those consequences differently than when we desire those consequences. We do not align our heart in favor of their negative value. We are, nonetheless, aware that we are responsible for their coming to be, for without our action they would not be. We cannot be indifferent to evil of any stripe, but particularly not for evil that we cause, however unwillingly.

While we welcome the connection between ourselves and positive values, we distance ourselves from disvalues. When we are foreseeably the cause of any disvalue, we are in the tension of both involving ourselves with what we are causing and yet distancing ourselves from that evil. This experience, I believe, is the phenomenological basis of Grisez and Boyle's observation that any action against a basic good tends to "disrupt our inner harmony" (1979, 44). An analogous disharmony, I would contend, is present even in merely accepted evil (unless we have hardened ourselves to the evil which we accept, e.g., killing animals for our food). This disharmony is, however, experienced differently than the evil chosen for itself. We are able to consent to this tension if we judge that on the whole we are moving toward the good in general and that the accepted evil is necessary to sustain that movement which at bottom is love. The tension is not overcome, but is experienced as a regrettable necessity entered upon only because it is the necessary cost for sustaining our union with the good to be achieved. If we could be united with the same good without the tension, i.e., without being simultaneously involved with and repelled by evil, then there is an obligation to do so if only because inner division is itself a disvalue.

For the disordered heart, however, as Augustine's famous meditation on stolen fruit reveals, participating in evil is the union we seek, and the good is repulsive. St. Ignatius' discernment of spirits reflects the same insight. For a disordered heart, good may be accepted so that greater evil might result. For the ordered heart, a disvalue or the absence of value is experienced as something to be overcome where possible. In the case of evil accepted with good, such possibility conflicts with the greater good to be achieved. Once the decision in favor of the greater good has been made, there is no moral regret for having realized (premoral) disvalue, since one has acted on the whole (morally, therefore) in favor of the good. Still, as the above long quotation from McCormick indicates, there is regret that the good without qualification could not be realized, and even the good realized wears tattered clothes (McCormick 1978, 43; Grisez and Boyle 1979, 373).

The attempt to consider basic tendencies or goods separately as each decisive leads to a selectivity or narrowness of intentionality in considering the whole moral situation. Ramsey has criticized Grisez (1979, 406) for allowing that most abortions are not "killing in the strict sense" because most people who kill the fetus may in fact intend only to be free of the pregnancy and its subsequent responsibilities. In assessing the issue of research on infants, Ramsey has himself been criticized for saying that we cannot be concerned with future benefits to the human race but must look only at the act itself. Critics of such positions point out that in each case intentionality is too restricted. Intention in their sense of "desired in a morally upright way" has led to a partial blindness. Full intentionality requires a consciousness of the whole reality present to us.

Although there are gradations of personal identification between intended and merely accepted consequences, still we experience both as part of the whole act. Because, for Grisez and Boyle (1979, 365-66) basic goods are incommensurable, the omission of one is said to be "merely irrelevant" to the choice of another. The traditional view that in removing part of the fallopian tube in an ectopic pregnancy, one only does legitimate surgery on a threatening organ and that therefore one need not think of oneself as performing an abortion, seems to be mind-befuddling mental gymnastics (McCormick 1978, 207-8). The same could be said for claims that by putting a bullet through the head of an attacker we are merely defending ourselves with an "incapacitating mortal wound" (Grisez and Boyle 1979, 368-394).

P tries to take into account all foreseen consequences (McCormick 1978, 36-38, 149-52). It strives to be objective, faithful to whatever might make a relevant difference. Phrases such as "regardless of" or "merely irrelevant" are red flags to *P*. They indicate that some part of our experience is being sacrificed to our moral theory. Thus to *P*, a theory of *D* appears capricious, arbitrary, and nonobjective. Some part of reality is banned from consideration.

Ultimate Grounding

The fourth experiential level—divine grounding of morality—has, I fear, received insufficient attention by both *P* and *D* (Vacek 1984, 370-36). O'Connell, for example, uses the doctrines of the Incarnation and redemption to declare that we need pay no further attention to specifically theological warrants in establishing our ethics, but rather need only devote our attention to universally grasped human nature (O'Connell 1979b, 39).

Nonetheless, both *P* and *D* in various ways affirm that we can participate in the eternal law. Our ethics can be experientially as well as metaphysically theocentric. Ethics need not be anthropocentric ethics—though the classical teleology of natural law makes this mistake somewhat likely.[19] Both *D* and *P* are prone to the error of considering human value as the only value worthy of fulfillment. Ramsey rightly puts forward the old Calvinist corrective to anthropocentric ethics: "Are you willing to be damned for the Glory of God?" (Ramsey 1978, 151). It seems unlikely that a natural-law theorist would ever raise such a question. However, one can, as in Gustafson's recent emphasis on theocentrism, go to the other extreme (Gustafson 1983, 88-98).

For *P*, the life of a snail darter in a Tennessee stream and *a fortiori* the holiness of God are relevant to moral living. Stated religiously, God is concerned for more than human flourishing and therefore so should we be (Vandervelde 1983, 257-71). Theodicies which try to explain human suffering and loss often take a *P* form, justifying evil by the greater good God intends to achieve. The material world about us and, even more, the uncharted universe have a value beyond what they contribute to human beings. Humans can make sacrifices for the environment, and not simply because it will make their lives better. Humans most especially can and do make sacrifices for their God, and again not simply *because* it will make them better. A value ethic affirms rose buds wherever they may be found.

The usual anthropology behind a *P* view is that of a religious, developmental-relational model of human existence. To conclude this essay, we can sketch something of that model. Human nature is not an isolated or once-for-all-time nature. In phenomenological terms, our knowing, loving, and willing is able to be ever freshly directed to an evolving world within an ultimate horizon. Our existence is human and religious coexistence. At our depths we are related to God and to what God is doing in the world. Hence the primary ethical task is fidelity not to rules or norms but to changing worldly realities and Ultimate Reality. As Fuchs has pointed out, it is a mistake to think that that which is in the "eternal law" of God is itself eternal

(Fuchs 1983, 209). In God's eternal law the present is present as changing. Understood religiously, then, personal growth is, under God, human responsibility. But world history, again under God, is also our responsibility. Teilhard de Chardin, with his usual broad strokes, excoriated ethics that try to keep human beings faithful to a static nature. Where there is no progress, there is immorality. Because of God's love, God is bringing about change. Resisting change is resisting God. Teilhard had no patience with views that hold we are not responsible for making a better world. Rather, he insisted, we are responsible under and with God for evolution itself. We are responsible for the enhancement of value and the elimination of disvalue, wherever humanly possible. We are responsible because that is what the Alpha and Omega is doing.

Notes

[1] Richard McCormick, S.J, is perhaps the one who has spent most time in the trenches; accordingly, he has been most often shot at. In "Bioethics and Method," *Theology Digest* 29/4 (winter 1981): 313-14, he names 23 internationally known authors and adds that there is "a whole host of others."

[2] McCormick, "Bioethics and Method" 308-10; James Gustafson, *The Contribution of Theology to Medical Ethics* (Milwaukee: Marquette Univ., 1975); Hallett, *Christian Moral Reasoning*, 199-223.

[3] Philip Keane, S.S., "The Objective Moral Order" *TS* 43 (1982): 269-70. The word "intrinsic" seems both here and in recent Catholic thought to be a synonym for "moral." For an older and different Roman Catholic meaning cf. McCormick, "Notes 1982" 86.

[4] Similarly, May writes that one must never, in an objective ethic, "Say of these goods here and now that they are non-goods, no longer worthy of my love and respect" ("Ethics and Human Identity," *Horizons* 3 (1976): 36-37; also (Germain Grisez and Russell Shaw, *Beyond the New Morality* (Notre Dame Univ of Notre Dame, 1974), 88-90. No *P* need so deny reality.

[5] Many authors suggest this, among them: Richard B. Brandt, "The Real and Alleged Problems of Utilitarianism," *Hastings Center Report* 13/2 (April 1983): 39-40; Dan Brock, "Can Pleasure Be Bad for You?" ibid. 13/4 (August 1983): 30-34; Benedict Ashley, O.P. and Kevin O'Rourke, O.P., *Health Care Ethics* (St. Louis: Catholic Health Association, 1978): 174: Grisez and Boyle, *Life and Death* 347.

[6] Richard McCormick, S.J., and Paul Ramsey, ed., *Doing Evil to Achieve Good* (Chicago: Loyola Univ., 1978), 46; William Frankena, "McCormick and the Traditional Distinction," ibid. 159.

[7] Edward Vacek, S.J., "Values and Norms," *Annalecta Husserliana* (Boston: Reidel, forthcoming).

[8] Hallett, *Christian Moral Reasoning* 110. W. E. May (quoted in Gula, *Moral Norms* 96-97) gives the following examples of absolutes: coition with a brute animal, or using public monies to pay one's mistress. It does not take much imagination to think of possible, though unreal, exceptions. Suppose that AIDS could only be

12 ~ Proportionalism: One View of the Debate

cured through bestiality (of course, a typical next move by May might be to rename the act a form of therapy; but would not this sort of move erode the force of the word "absolute"?). Or suppose that part of the publicly approved compensation for public office was a mistress (the act of having a mistress might still be wrong, but not using public monies for this purpose.) *P* may use its imagination too freely, but *D* could use a bit more imagination.

[9] Franz Bockle, *Fundamental Moral Theology* (New York: Pueblo, 1980), 239-40, uses the word "good" for what we call premoral value, and "value" only for moral values.

[10] For more, see John Langan, S.J., "Values, Rules and Decisions" in Haughey, *Personal Values* 56.

[11] Cf. Fuchs, *Personal Responsibility* 135; McCormick, *Doing Evil* 222; McCormick, "Notes 1982" 86.

[12] One of the most challenging criticisms of *P* comes from an Episcopalian student of mine. She notes that *P* is filled with what I might call "sober Greek moderation." It is all prudence with little emphasis on the joy and enthusiasm of being in love with God—or anyone else, for that matter. It resolves tensions of competing loyalties rather than exulting in such tensions. It downplays symbolism, art, wonder, music, and poetry. Cf. Hallett, *Christian Moral Reasoning* 116-17; Scheler, Formalism in Ethics xxiii.

[13] Cf. McCormick, *Doing Evil* 224-25.

[14] Cf. Grisez and Boyle, *Life and Death* 359-61, for a slightly different list (also Finnis, in Cahill, "Teleology" 621 22). They, however, explicitly exclude pleasure from the basic goods. After Freud, that hardly seems wise, though doing so enables Grisez and Boyle to accept the obvious necessity of going against pleasure in some in-quinces. In a *P* system, the vast array of pleasures is an array of goods.

[15] McCormick, *Doing Evil* 201, 261, seems to take a narrower view. He says that the word "proportion" refers to a basic good, and he explains that the term "proportionate reason" means that "the value being sought will not be undermined by the contemplated action."

[16] Fuchs, *Personal Responsibility* 151. Grisez and Boyle, *Life and Death* 371, establish something of a lexical priority when they add three secondary principles to their deontological principles. These three, in my words, are benevolence, impartiality, and accepted role-duties.

[17] I say "normally" because it is not clear how acts such as martyrdom or self-sacrifice count in a system that emphasizes human flourishing; cf. 115 below.

[18] Thus the third condition for the principle of double effect collapses into the second (intentionality). The first condition (an act good or indifferent in itself) must be understood as a premoral judgment. Frankena rightly notes that if "one gives up exceptionless principles, there is not much reason, if any, for retaining the principle of double effect" (*Ethics* 155).

[19] Rowntree, "Ethical Issues" 453; Ashley and O'Rourke, *Health Care Ethics* 173-74 McCormick, "Bioethics and Method" 307; and Fuchs, *Personal Responsibility* 127—all come close to such an ethic. Grisez and Boyle at times slide toward this mistake acting for transcendent principles is accepted only if it records with self-fulfilment, and other persons seem a secondary consideration (*Life and Death* 362-68).

The Impracticality of Proportionalism
Bartholomew M. Kiely, S.J.

1. Introduction

The term "proportionalism" as used in the title refers to an approach that, in various forms, has become important in Catholic moral theology since the latter half of the nineteen-sixties.[1] "Proportionalism" seems to be the name most commonly used; "consequentialism" is a designation that seems to be falling from favor; sometimes a longer description like "the teleology of proportionate reason" is assigned.[2]

The present article is concerned with the feasibility or practicality of the step at which an assessment of proportionate reasons enters the process of deciding what should be done in a particular situation of moral choice and decision. It is first necessary to outline the meaning of this step as here understood; and (to avoid misunderstandings) it should be explained at once that the focus is narrow and is only concerned with the practical step of assessing proportionate reasons, "disembedding" an analysis of this step from the various contexts which different authors may provide. It is on this level that the attempt is made to generalize about a "proportionalist approach," in the hope of achieving some limited degree of clarification.

In the proportionalist approach,[3] then, the act-as-means no longer has an independent moral quality of its own (which could in principle preclude the use of certain means as intrinsically evil and at the same time be the basis of certain absolute negative moral norms).[4] Goods or evils accomplished as means are considered as "premoral," "nonmoral," "ontic," or "physical." "Ontic goods are, for example, health, life, property, knowledge of the truth; and ontic evil consists in the privation of such goods. Ontic goods may be goods of any kind that contribute to the fullness of human living; as such they do not yet possess a moral quality" (Pinckaers 1982, 193). Ontic goods or evils realized as means cannot be given a moral evaluation by themselves, even if accomplished directly, knowingly, and willingly. An act cannot (in the proportionalist approach) be judged on the basis of its own independent moral intelligibility and prior to a consideration of its consequences; it can only be judged as part of the larger process to which it contributes, and the larger process will of course include the consequences of the initial act. The object of moral judgment becomes the totality of the process under consideration. If this totality can be judged as positive, in terms of a prevalence of ontic goods over ontic evils, then any action bringing about such a positive totality will be justified. Rather than saying that the end can justify the means, it seems more accurate to say that the whole can justify any of its parts, if in the final outcome there is the desired prevalence of ontic goods over ontic evils. Any action whatsoever might in principle be justified if a proportionate reason for its performance can be found within the larger process which the action in question initiates. Moral evil will enter if ontic evil is accomplished in the absence of such a proportionate reason.

Since the act-as-means is not allowed an independent moral quality of its own, but can only be judged as part of the larger process involved, the traditional distinction between the direct and indirect causation of evil ceases to be relevant. If things turn out as desired in the long run, the order (chronological or causal) in which the various ontic goods or ontic evils enter the process is not of decisive importance.

The shift to the totality of the larger process as the proper object of moral judgment, and the assessment of proportions within this totality, seems to be the step which, on the practical level, characterizes proportionalism as such. The shift in question is part of quite a large number of contemporary theories. It occurs in various contexts; it is advocated with greater or lesser degrees of caution or limitation. The reflections which follow largely prescind from the context in which the assessment of proportionate reasons is proposed; they also rescind from the degree of caution accompanying the proposal; rather they focus on the practical possibility, in principle and in general, of assessing proportionate reasons at all.

The point to be discussed is part of a change of far-reaching significance. In the words of Pinckaers, rendered here in English,

> ... a profound change has been introduced, a change of axis: a shift from a morality centered on the relation of the act to its object, this

relationship giving to the act a moral quality that is intrinsic and independent of the intention of the agent, to a morality centered on the intention of the agent, an intention which constructs the object itself by means of the proportionate reason. The theory of the cause with a double effect, which in traditional casuistry had only a limited application in the solution of certain difficult cases, becomes a universal moral category; its interpretation no longer begins with its first condition, the principle that one may not do what is evil in itself to attain some good, but begins instead with its last condition, the proportionate reason, which subsequently determines what is good and what is evil. We are therefore witnessing a kind of revolution within post-tridentine Catholic moral theology.

The consequences for the problem of intrinsically evil acts are immediate: there are no acts that are intrinsically evil prior to judging if there is a reason proportionate to the end involved, as has been explained; and prior to this judgment, there exist only ontological goods and evils (Pinckaers 1982, 188).[5]

In other words, the application of any moral norm to a concrete situation is contingent upon a judgment regarding the presence or absence of a proportionate reason which could justify an exception to the general norm.

The enormous variety of concrete situations means that such a judgment cannot be general and a-priori. A norm may be "virtually exceptionless" insofar as a proportionate reason justifying its suspension is unlikely to be found; but "virtually exceptionless" in this sense is not the same as "absolute" in the traditional sense in which it was simply impossible that there be any proportionate reason to justify certain acts, such as adultery, which could be qualified as morally evil prior to a consideration of their circumstances or consequences.[6]

It can be seen even from this rapid outline that proportionalism offers the principal components of a moral system. It provides for the evaluation of concrete courses of action in the manner indicated. It offers a way of evaluating the intention of the agent: a positive balance of ontic goods over ontic evils in the intended process justifies the claim to a good intention. Further, the proportionalist approach seems to have the merit of being highly practical. It would replace a-priori judgments of moral good and evil with more concrete considerations of a totality of facts that includes the consequences of proposed acts. It would also seem to offer a way of solving difficult human situations calling for moral compromise.

Indeed, experience shows that it can be quite acceptable to evaluate an act simply as part of a process with heavy or exclusive emphasis on the consequences, as in the following cases:

i) if only a single value is involved, one chooses a course of action designed to maximize that single value;

ii) in situations of forced choice between courses of action, each of which involves some evil, and when even with the best of efforts one can find no further possibility, one chooses the course of action involving the lesser evil. Thus, if an airplane must crash in either a densely populated or a thinly populated area, with no chance of crashing in an unpopulated area, then one should choose to crash in the thinly populated area.

iii) when choosing among good courses of action, one seeks the greater good. Such a choice may be based solely on the foreseen consequences: as when a hospital or school is founded in a city rather than a deserted region.

iv) indifferent acts in general may be evaluated on the basis of foreseen consequences; strenuous exercise may be a good choice for one man, and a highly imprudent choice for another.

So there are cases in which an evaluation based largely or exclusively on foreseen consequences is clearly admissible.

Therefore the proportionalist approach has a definite appeal, and perhaps most of all in its claim to practicality.

However, the reflections of the present author have led him to the conclusion that, the more closely one examines the matter, the more that the proportionalist approach turns out to be impractical, and this to a degree which (to the best of my knowledge) has not been pointed out before, especially where the nature of statistical knowledge and its basis in non-systematic processes are concerned, besides the introduction of various considerations from contemporary psychology. Not all of these points are original; nevertheless it has seemed useful to assemble them and present them for the consideration of the reader. These reflections will be presented as directly as possible; this will have the advantage, apart from brevity, of enabling the reader to identify more easily the points with which he disagrees and the reasons for this disagreement.

A series of difficulties will thus be considered, which stand in the way of applying proportionalist assessment. These difficulties are largely variations on a single theme and so they will make more sense if considered together, rather than separately or in isolation.

2. Difficulties in Invoking Consequences in the Evaluation of an Act

If some ontic evil is to be directly accomplished for the sake of a proportionate reason, where can this proportionate reason be found? Clearly in this case the good must come about indirectly and therefore it must necessarily lie among the consequences of the ontic evil with which the process has begun: in some further good to be attained, or some further evil to be avoided. [7] (The paradigmatic situation with which this article is concerned is that of an individual, contemplating some concrete act, looking into the future, and attempting to foresee the outcomes.) The question of foreseeing outcomes leads to a first series of difficulties in the application of the proportionalist approach.

2.1 Foreseeing Consequences

If the evaluation of an act is to include future consequences, then those consequences must be foreseeable. But, in general, many of the consequences of human acts cannot be predicted, and the difficulty in prediction becomes all the greater as the consequences become more remote from the initial act.

Any event that occurs may involve two kinds of processes, the systematic or the non-systematic.

Systematic process repeats itself with perfect regularity: the movements of the stars and planets, for example, or the movement of a perfect clock. Such total regularity is accompanied by complete predictability of the future; it depends on a relatively simple system of causes and effects, isolated from outside interference.

Non-systematic process is quite different. Any event in such process results from the intersection of different lines of causality. The single event depends on a number of series of antecedent happenings; the different series are ordinarily divergent, as one traces them backwards; they interact in complex, fluctuating, non-coordinated, and therefore unforeseeable combinations.

Astronomers can foretell with precision the times of future eclipses, because these are part of systematic processes; weather-forecasting is much less precise, especially at long range, because the lines of causality involved can fluctuate independently and interact in so many ways. Roughly speaking, any future event about which one could place a bet (even having all the information that is in principle available in advance) belongs to a non-systematic process; events not suitable for gambling, such as the time of tomorrow's sunrise, belong to a systematic process.[8]

The great majority of historical events, including the consequences of human acts, have prevalently the characteristics of nonsystematic process.[9] The causality exercised by the human agent will immediately begin to intersect with other lines of causality, which are not under the agent's control. So consequences cannot be clearly foreseen; and the more remote the future, the greater the uncertainty of prediction.

Since any consequence of a human act is, in the proportionalist approach, *per se* only an ontic good or ontic evil, it must *in its turn* be judged in connection with further consequences which it causes or occasions or prevents. So an infinite regression is logically involved in the evaluation; and for that one should know all the consequences of the act. A short-range limit can be set only in an arbitrary (and so unjustified) way. But the totality of the consequences of any act simply defy prediction. It is not a matter of a great deal of reflection or prudence being required; the task is intrinsically impossible. Therefore the information on which a complete proportionalist assessment should be based cannot be attained.

2.2 Proper and Improper Consequences

The complexity of non-systematic process gives rise to the unpredictability of the future; and it also results in our needing to be able to distinguish between the proper and improper consequences of an act.[10]

A good act can have some negative consequences. Abel's sacrifice was pleasing to God; Cain grew angry and slew Abel. So Abel's sacrifice became an occasion of homicide. It can also happen that an evil act can have good consequences: Joseph was sold into Egypt by his brothers, and so was able to come to their rescue in time of famine.

Both examples illustrate the idea of improper consequences. Evil can result from good and good from evil because of the complexity of non-systematic processes. After the initial act has been performed, extraneous factors can enter in, like the character of Cain, or the ability of Joseph and the wealth of Egypt.

It is clear that such improper consequences have nothing to do with the moral quality of the initial act. Abel was not guilty as he would have been had he attacked Cain and provoked him to self-defense. Joseph's brothers did not deserve any credit for the good that Joseph did after reaching a position of power in Egypt.

A distinction between proper and improper consequences is thus necessary. One can make such a distinction only if one can first evaluate an act on the basis of its own moral intelligibility, and then proceed to classify the good consequences of a good act as proper, the evil consequences of a good act as improper, etc. Unless the act-as-means is allowed an independent moral quality of its own, the terms "proper" and "improper" can have no useful meaning; and such seems to be the case with proportionalism.

A distinction between proper and improper consequences will also enable one to see the difference between two ways of invoking consequences in the course of a moral argument: first, a genuinely consequentialist approach in which consequences are seen as conferring upon an act its moral quality; secondly, a form of argument in which consequences are used merely to *illustrate* the moral quality which an act is considered as already having, these consequences having been classified (at least implicitly) as consequences proper to the act itself.

2.3 The Logical Order in Our Customary Prediction of Outcomes

Conceding that responsible action involves taking account of such consequences as are probable, yet we do not ordinarily decide by first knowing the range of future consequences as facts and then, in a mainly empirical or inductive way, evaluating the proposed act. Ordinarily we go in the opposite direction and proceed by deduction.

It is true that, in special cases, one begins by simply measuring consequences in an empirical way, as when a new medicine is being tested for its effects and side-effects. But this is a highly specialized and time-consuming process, and further it is made necessary by ignorance of the basic processes involved; the more the relevant biochemistry is already known and understood, the less that purely empirical research remains to be done.

Our usual way of linking an act with its consequences seems remarkably like the approach used in traditional moral theology being deductive rather than empirical. We assume that acts that are intelligibly good will have good consequences, and acts that are intelligibly bad will have bad consequences; in other words, we attempt to see what the proper consequences of an act will be. One assumes that a favor will be welcome and that a slap in the face will be unwelcome; and one makes the assumption prior to taking action. That is to say, we begin usually by considering the intrinsic intelligibility of the act and then predict the consequences, deductively; we do not begin by considering the consequences as foreknown facts from which an inductive evaluation can be made. (Here it is not a question of moral intelligibility alone, but of intelligibility in general.) One anticipates that an armed policemen will resist an attempt to remove his pistol by force, because there is an intelligible relationship between such an assault and the policeman's concern for his own duty and his own safety. It is not necessary to make one hundred such assaults and then (if the experimenter is still alive) perform a test of statistical significance.

As McCormick notes, the experience of consequences over the centuries has surely played a role in the formulation of traditional norms, such as that prohibiting extramarital sexual intercourse (McCormick 1981, 363-365). But great stress must be laid on the difference between two ways in which a conclusion can emerge from experience. One way would be as the result of an empirical and *a posteriori* approach. The other way would be fundamentally different and indeed opposite; the understanding that, given the intelligible nature of an act such as adultery, it must have negative consequences. The opposition again is that between a deductive and an inductive-statistical approach. Deduction implies an insight into the nature of the act involved. A crucial difference is that the deductive approach can permit the formulation of absolute negative norms. An empirical approach applied to complex problems can at most lead to a statistical type of generalization, and accordingly must allow for many exceptions. (A very passive person, for example, might not object to unfaithfulness on the part of his or her spouse, especially if such behavior was frequent in the given culture.) But since the traditional norm prohibiting adultery (like various other negative norms) was seen as absolute, it cannot have been derived from an essentially statistical approach.

The immediate point here is that ordinarily we follow the deductive line, as when one assumes that a broken promise will cause resentment, the breakdown of trust, and so on. A man might go through his whole life believing this without ever putting it to the test by actually breaking a promise, and the more clearly he was convinced of this, the less likely he would be ever to break a promise. The empirical or statistical approach is too uncertain, given the unpredictability of consequences, as argued above; it is imprecise as to the outcome to be expected in the single case; and far too cumbersome for routine use. But proportionalism has an empirical component insofar as the proportionate reason is linked to the consequences of an act. This is a further reason for saying that proportionalism is impractical.[11]

2.4 Reflexive or Immanent Consequences

Among the consequences of any act are the consequences in the agent. In killing, Cain became a killer. In kissing the leper, St. Francis came to a new freedom (Jorgensen 1955, 37-40). Such a consequence in the agent is the first consequence of any act, and in a sense the only guaranteed consequence: it will result even if the attempt in question is a failure, as long as a genuine effort has been made.

Regarding the general sense of the principle in question, many authors might be invoked; Lonergan is chosen for the sake of his brevity:

> By his own acts the human subject makes himself what he is to be, and he does so freely and responsibly; indeed, he does so precisely because his acts are the free and responsible expression of himself.[12]

Whatever a person does, then, affects the person himself. In this sense one may speak of the reflexive or immanent consequences of acts. Especially, a person will tend to become habituated to repeated actions of a given kind, so that such actions become a kind of second nature to him. History shows that people have been able to become accustomed to the strangest kinds of behavior.

Is it a good or a bad thing to be the-person-who-has-done-X? The question requires an answer and a method that can provide the answer. It all depends on how one evaluates X, whatever X may be. If one can evaluate X on the basis of its own intrinsic moral intelligibility (that is, in the traditional way), then the answer is straightforward: it is bad to be such a person if X is bad, good if X is good, and indifferent if X is indifferent.

On the other hand, if one prescinds from the intrinsic moral intelligibility of X, it will be very difficult or impossible to evaluate reflexive consequences in terms of some measurement of the consequences themselves. Psychological realities are notoriously difficult to measure, even using the most specialized methods; and reports offered by the subject involved are of very limited value.[13] People can become accustomed to virtually anything; slavery was long accepted as a normal part of life, even by Aristotle. The desire to think well of oneself is a powerful motive to think well also of all one's actions.[14] It is possible that the agent himself will find even destructive behavior to be "normal" (Bursten 1972, 318-321). At the same time, the agent can be subject to unreasonable scruples.[15] Since both kinds of error are frequent, and quite familiar to the practicing psychologist, an evaluation based on the agent's own self-perception is not reliable. Here there is an analogy with the distinction made earlier between the proper and improper consequences of an act; there can also be proper or improper reactions to what has been done, that is to say, appropriate or inappropriate reactions. To be able to make this distinction, the act must be evaluated prior to examining the agent's reactions. But if the act-as-means is not allowed an independent moral quality of its own, as in the proportionalist approach, there is no adequate basis for a distinction between appropriate and inappropriate reactions to the instrumental action. As to the immediate consequences there is the same difficulty, and so on regarding more remote consequences; one has entered the infinite regression pointed out in section 2.1 above.

A reply to this point, deriving from the general logic of the proportionalist approach as outlined in the first section of this paper, might run more or less as follows: the agent's intention regards not only the instrumental act with which he initiates some process, but the larger process with its balance of ontic goods and evils. Accordingly, reflexive or immanent consequences must be conceived in terms of this larger process and not in terms of any of its parts taken alone.[16]

But, if the analysis of non-systematic process given above is admitted, it follows that the agent must accept a special responsibility for the act by which he initiates some process. It is only the beginning that he fully controls, so it is at this point that he is most fully identified with what he does or causes. Further outcomes depend on the fulfillment of further conditions which are less under the agent's own control, so subsequent results are more and more the objects of the agent's *hope* rather than of his intention or causation. So, in thinking of reflexive or immanent consequences, one may not circumvent the agent's identification with the act-as-means in favor of the evaluation of a larger process with its balance of ontic goods and evils, without running into the various difficulties with which this article is concerned.

Further, at least in the opinion of this author, it is remarkably difficult to identify an intention as evil without working backwards from the quality of the concrete expression to which the intention leads. The principle, "by their fruits you shall know them" (Matthew 7:16) applies also to one's own intentions; especially the first-fruits. Otherwise the powerful human urge to defend one's self-esteem will encounter little opposition.

2.5 In Summary

The traditional approach of Catholic moralists according to which an act could be judged directly on the basis of its own moral object or moral intelligibility can easily meet all four of the difficulties just presented. Such an evaluation did not depend on an impossible knowledge of future facts extending indefinitely forwards.[17] It corresponded to common-sense in that good consequences were expected from good acts and evil consequences from evil acts. It allowed for a distinction between the proper and improper consequences of acts, for the case in which a good act has some evil consequences or an evil act some good consequences. It also provided for a distinction between appropriate and inappropriate reactions to what has been done and so for an evaluation of the reflexive or immanent consequences of acts. But the proportionalist approach does not provide an adequate solution to any of the four difficulties; hence its impracticality. (It should be noted that, in the four kinds of cases outlined in the first section of this article, in which evaluation of acts by their consequences is accepted, the properly moral question has been settled first in each case, the acts being classified in advance as inevitable, good, or indifferent.)

3. The Human Good as an Organic Unity

Before taking up the question of the commensurability of different ontic goods or evils, involved in the assessment of proportionate reasons, it will be useful to provide some background and context.

The human good has qualitatively different parts, whose interrelationship is one of organic unity, not merely of addition. An organic unity is something that is intelligible rather than measurable; it is formal and not merely quantitative. These statements must now be given some justification.

The human good has qualitatively different parts. De Finance, in his *Éthique Générale* (section 23) has classified human values as follows: first, there are infra-human values including pleasure and health; secondly, there are human values that are infra-moral, including economic prosperity and success in general, also including spiritual values such as knowledge of truth, artistic beauty, social cohesion, and qualities of talent, temperament, and character; thirdly, there is moral value; fourthly and finally, there is religious value.

Without regarding this as the only possible classification, it is clear that any such analysis of values must recognize qualitative differences. Robust health will not by itself make a man erudite, erudition by itself will not make a person morally or religiously good, and so on. One way of emphasizing the existence of qualitative differences is to point out that often one kind of good will not take the place of another. Sometimes substitution is possible; one might eat spaghetti instead of potatoes, bread, or bananas as a source of carbohydrates; in that case no important difference is involved. But in general one kind of good will not take the place of another. Food and sleep, in their contribution to health, remain qualitatively distinct. You cannot take a second supper at midnight and so dispense with the need for sleep; nor will extra sleep make eating superfluous.

For the sake of further illustration, consider the goods that conscientious parents will provide for a child. One sees immediately that several different kinds of good are involved: food and drink, a place to sleep, emotional security, education of various kinds, opportunities for play, and so on; there is no one-and-only thing that parents must provide, as it were in the maximum quantity.

These two examples will also serve to illustrate the idea of organic unity. The value of health involves an organic unity of components such as food and sleep and exercise, which are qualitatively different. The same holds for the various goods provided for a child; they too have an organic unity, since their common effect is in the child, and the child itself is a unity.

An organic unity is a formal unity, not a merely quantitative summation. Qualitatively different goods must play qualitatively different roles of a complementary kind; together they constitute an intelligible or formal unity, which as such must be understood rather than measured. Such understanding may be highly complex;[18] it is not to the present purpose to go into further details; the main point is that an organic unity cannot be reduced to an algebraic sum of parts.

The coexistence of qualitatively different parts of the human good, in some organic unity, has various implications:

i) Qualitatively different goods are not subject to any common measure. You cannot ask, "how many suppers are equivalent to a night's sleep?"; such a question has no meaning. This points up another aspect of the impracticality of proportionalism, since a common measure is required if all the positive and negative results of an act are to be part of a single objective assessment. Otherwise one has to proceed without an explicit method of assessment (Grisez 1983, 158-9), or proceed on the basis of a consensus, or else attempt to consider outcomes related only to a single good, all of which lead to further difficulties to be considered below. The impossibility of a common measure has often been argued[19] and it has been recognized by Knauer since the beginning of the controversy (Knauer 1979, 11). Here it need only be added that hierarchy or ranking of values as first, second, third, etc., in order of importance (a ranking essentially of the kind used in non-parametric statistics) is not an adequate solution either. It still leaves one without an answer to the question, "in relation to what vision of the integral human good is importance being assigned?" (see points ii and v of this section; also sections 4 and 5 farther on in the article.)

ii) If the concrete good for a particular person consists in a synthesis of qualitatively different parts, it follows that the basic moral norm must take account of this synthetic or formal unity. Fagothey (Fagothey 1981, 125-130) provides a useful formulation: the norm of right reason must look to the whole, to human nature taken adequately or completely, with all its parts and with all its relations (with God, with other human persons, with the infra-human goods of the world, and—one may add—with oneself) being taken simultaneously into account. This principle is applied both to the person who is agent and the person who is the "object" of action.

Fagothey's formulation is not a tautology, as it would certainly be if any good were a good for the person-as-a-whole. On the contrary, temptation typically takes the form of some partial good that is desired at the expense of the integral good of the person. Any possible course of action will have something positive about it, since, metaphysically speaking, pure negation cannot exist. There is some good in adultery: pleasure and a transitory intimacy. Even suicide, as a desire "to cease upon the midnight with no pain"[20] can appeal as a partial good. With a little imagination, one can see some advantage in any conceivable course of action. But do such advantages constitute potentially proportionate reasons or are they merely temptations? The proportionalist approach, for reasons that have in part been already outlined, while further reasons follow, does not seem to provide a sufficiently clear basis for distinguishing between temptations arising from the appeal of a partial good and, on the other hand, proportionate (justifying) reasons, as a qualitative and not merely quantitative distinction.

iii) Without the recognition of qualitative differences between components of the human good, moral freedom would not be possible, as Grisez has pointed out (Grisez 1978, 41-9). If the criterion of choice is to be some essentially quantitative maximum, only one course of action can recommend itself, unless by coincidence of quantities. As a minimal condition for the possibility of properly moral deliberation, one would have to distinguish between satisfactions and values as objects of choice, to allow for the possibility of choosing values over satisfactions when conflict arises.[21]

iv) It is now possible to comment on the attempt to apply proportionalist assessment to some single value considered by itself. This is the approach taken by Knauer in a more recent article (Knauer 1980). Knauer again recognizes that qualitatively different goods are incommensurable (Knauer 1980, 328). Accordingly, he would begin with the consideration of some single value, thus avoiding the difficulty of comparing different values. If the proposed course of action will turn out to be prevalently counter-productive or self-defeating, in the long run and all things considered (*auf die Dauer und im Ganzen*) (Knauer 1980, 328-337) with respect to the single value in question, then the action is wrong. The course of action would be right if the consequences, for the single value in question and in the long run, were to be prevalently positive.[22] To this approach two objections may be made. First, the future is not foreseeable to the extent required for such calculation to be made in advance, even with respect to a single value, as argued in section 2.1 above. Secondly, different values do not run along parallel lines in such a way as not to affect each other. As parts of an organic unity they interact constantly, and so it is not realistic to claim that a single value can be considered in isolation.[23]

v) Even if proportions between different goods could be calculated in some clear, satisfactory, and complete way, a further problem would remain. The assessment of proportions would still have to consider the question, "what *is* the good life?"; that is to say, in terms of what vision of the integral human good are proportions being assessed? Either one would need to presuppose some generally-accepted vision of the integral good of the person, or else go further and claim that proportionalism could, of itself, generate a vision of the integral good worthy of general acceptance.

But history shows that there has been much disagreement concerning the human good. Philosophers have advanced many ethical theories, each with some master-idea as the core of a synthesis; psychologists also have, in a shorter time, produced a variety of theories.[24] Differences are most easily recognized by considering the "ideal person" expressing a theory. The Homeric hero is not the same as the Aristotelian sage, and both are different from the Christian saint.[25] In the area of psychology, the Rogerian emphasis on self-fulfillment is different from the Freudian emphasis on the discovery and mastery (or endurance) of conflict.[26] There have been many different anthropological theories grounding different visions of the integral good of the human person, as a synthesis or composition of different partial goods.

Lonergan, in his analysis of differences of horizon (complementary, genetic, and dialectical), and of the difference made by the presence or absence of intellectual, moral, or religious conversion, has provided a framework for the analysis of such differences between anthropological visions (Lonergan 1973, ch. 10). Conversion is needed—if a moment of rhetoric may be pardoned—to arrive at the point of departure, intellectual, moral, or religious, if such a point of departure is lacking. Proof appeals to an abstraction named right reason. Conversion transforms the concrete individual to make him "capable of grasping not merely conclusions but principles as well" (Lonergan 1973, 338).

A point of particular importance in any such anthropological vision is the question of being able to cope with the loss or renunciation that may accompany any decision (Demmer 1974, 72-80 and 215-227). Ernest Becker has argued with force that the origin of human evil lies in the inability to accept loss. People cling to the objects of their desire as "symbols of immortality" which they need in order to see themselves as guarantors of their own present and future well-being, which they have great difficulty in renouncing, as loss brings them face-to-face with the horror of their own mortality.[27] Only a religious solution seems adequate to free people from this fear of death that constrains them.

A religious view of life affects a moral theory in at least two ways. First, it provides a context in which the integral good of the person can be understood.[28] Secondly, it provides a meaning and a hope that help the believer to cope with present privations. The major religions have all addressed these problems:

> ... there is at least one scholar on whom one may call for an explicit statement on the areas common to such world religions as Christianity, Judaism, Islam, Zoroastrian Mazdaism, Hinduism, Buddhism, Taoism. For Friedrich Heiler has described at some length seven such common areas: ... that there is a transcendent reality; that he is immanent in human hearts; that he is supreme beauty, truth, righteousness, goodness; that he is love, mercy, compassion; that the way to him is repentance, self-denial, prayer; that the way is love of one's neighbor, even of one's enemies; that the way is love

of God, so that bliss is conceived as knowledge of God, union with him, or dissolution into him (Lonergan 1973, 109).

Ernest Becker, although not himself a believer in any religion (Becker 1975, 15), recognized in the Christian vision a particularly apt solution to the problem of human finitude and mortality (Becker 1973, 204).

These excessively brief reflections on the anthropological basis of any moral theory lead to this point: the evaluation of some course of action has first of all to regard the intelligible or formal relationship of the action to the relevant vision of the integral human good.[29] Such a vision has never been the object of universal agreement as something self-evident, and the underlying disagreements come to the surface in various ways.[30] It is hardly possible to prescind from such basic differences and engage in comparison of goods, directly and on their own merits, as if a basic context for such comparison could be presupposed as clear and accepted; nor is it clear that such a method of comparison can ever generate by itself an adequate anthropological basis. The insufficiency of the proportionalist approach is seen again.

4. SUBJECTIVISM AND THE ASSESSMENT OF OUTCOMES

If ontic evil might be realized directly for a proportionate reason, there is (as already argued) a necessary link between the proportionate reason and the consequences. But consequences as experienced are necessarily relative to the individual. As the proverb has it, one man's peach is another man's poison. The variability of consequences-as-experienced is recognized in the application of proportionalism to sexual morality made by Kosnik (Kosnik 1977, ch. 3 and 4); following the approach of these authors, one might reasonably experiment with various kinds of sexual behavior to find out the effects upon oneself of those kinds of behavior.

The same holds for other areas of life: one person may be greatly attracted by wealth, while another prefers idleness at the price of poverty; one person may be greatly drawn to power, while another prefers a quiet life without the responsibility going with authority. In general, the way given consequences are experienced will vary with the individual; as St Thomas put it, following Aristotle, *qualis est unusquisque, talis et finis videtur ei* (ST I, 83, 1, ad 5; I-II 10, 3, ad 2). If given consequences were experienced in exactly the same way by everyone, there would result at least a great simplification of the discussion; but such is not the case.

Here one is faced with two possibilities. Either one allows consequences as subjectively experienced to constitute potentially proportionate reasons, or else (as the only alternative) one calls for an objectification of the consequences and says that given consequences should be experienced in a certain way, beginning with the instrumental act itself and its reflexive effects, as the only "consequences" that are immediately within the agent's control and hence responsibility. This latter possibility would reintroduce the distinction made earlier (section 2.4) between appropriate and inappropriate reactions, and there it was argued that such a distinction is not possible unless the act-as-means is allowed an independent moral quality of its own. The same difficulty would accompany the attempt to base the evaluation of proportionate reasons upon some consensus. Either the consensus is claiming an objectivity that can over-rule individual and subjective preferences, or it is not. If it is not, why should the individual subordinate his own perception of outcomes to the consensual view? And if the claim is to be made, the consensus encounters basically the same difficulties as the individual would.

The point has considerable importance. Any person tends to remain in a particular way of living because it suits him and he tends to find the corresponding pattern of consequences convenient.

> [H]abits are inertial. The whole tendency of present perceptions, of present affectivity and aggressivity, of present ways of understanding and judging, of deliberation and choosing, speaking and doing, is for them to remain as they are.[31]

This applies to sinners as well as to saints: *qualis est unusquisque, talis et finis videtur ei*. And we regularly assume constancy of character, when a man is elected Superior General of a religious order, or sentenced to a long term of imprisonment as a criminal, as also in less extreme cases.

The problem of subjectivism in the evaluation of outcomes becomes especially acute when some moral crisis arises. There can be considerable subjective pressure in favor of abortion when an unmarried girl gets pregnant; such pressures being usually of a social rather than a medical nature (Freidman et al. 1974, 1332-1337). The temptation to dishonesty can be strong when one's own reputation is at stake. The urge to justify oneself can be powerful when a person has weak impulse-control and still desires to save his self-esteem. "Reasons of state" or "political necessity" have been urged as justifications for appalling violations of human rights.[32] When a person is under the pressure of a moral crisis, to encourage him to constitute his own moral object in terms of proportionate reasons[33] would be to allow him little chance of retaining a sense of direction. Consequences are relative to the individual or group, and one's own advantages will be more evident than more distant considerations, since there is always an effect of perspective by which one's own interests tend to take on an exaggerated importance. As Chesterton put it, "a permanent possibility of selfishness arises from the mere fact of having a self, and not from any accidents of education or ill-treatment."[34]

A further aspect of this point will be explored in the next section.

5. Stimulus to conversion?

It follows from the preceding section that there also exists a problem concerning the existence of a stimulus or challenge to on-going conversion.

If a person evaluates a course of action from his own present viewpoint, and in the absence of some objective challenge going beyond this horizon, then he is at the mercy of all the present limitations of his outlook; limitations that may be cognitive or affective, conscious or subconscious,[35] whether these be part of normal (but as yet incomplete) development, or whether they be pathological. It seems all too likely that such limitations will enter into claims to have found proportionate reasons exempting one from moral norms that clash with his present way of living. (Here it is assumed, as in the preceding section, that he evaluates outcomes from his own viewpoint, and does not recognize another criterion as objective, binding, and transcending his own present outlook.)

The issues here are complex, and may be reduced to three principal points.

i) Psychological limitations exist in many or all persons, and have been abundantly documented. A variety of population studies,[36] including one made on Catholic priests (Kennedy and Heckler 1972), indicate that, in round numbers, about 20% of any large group show difficulties in living that are usually classified as psychiatric symptoms; 60% show some degree of (non-pathological) immaturity or incomplete development affecting the range of their freedom; and only about 20% may be considered relatively free of psychological limitations of the kind in question.

Kohlberg and his colleagues have done much research on moral development and found that the moral reasoning of most adults does not rise beyond a conventional level,[37] which leaves individuals rather at the mercy of the outlook of the group to which they belong.[38] (Kohlberg himself is quite brusque on the question of consequentialism.)[39] The fact that Kohlberg's test measures only reasoning about problems of justice does not weaken the force of his finding about the prevalence of conventional moral reasoning, since the problems posed in his test have a relatively simple structure (Colby et al. 1983, 7 n.3 and 9-13); limits on reasoning-capacity should be more evident in more complex situations (Levine 1976, 41-46).

Rulla has shown the existence of a dimension of subconscious inconsistencies between needs and values, found in all subjects studied, which is not to be considered pathological in the psychiatric sense, but still limits to a lesser or greater degree the freedom of persons to realize the values they have adopted. [40]

ii) Such psychological limitations in general increase the normal inertia of habits of feeling, thinking, and doing. "Repetitive patterns and leitmotifs" emerge in each person's life:

> The basic themes are more readily detected in emotionally disturbed persons because they are more set, more clearly repetitive, and perhaps more familiar to the practiced ear that has heard similar themes so often before. Still, repetitive ways of reacting and relating occur in all lives. The meaning of an episode in a life can often be grasped properly only through understanding how it furthers, impedes, or disrupts essential themes (Lidz 1968, 509-510).

Fixity or resistance to change does not apply only to psychopathology; the dimension of subconscious inconsistencies between a person's needs and his values, affecting his freedom to live out adopted values, is also persistent.[41] And Kohlberg and his colleagues have shown that the level of moral reasoning in a given person changes slowly (Colby et al. 1983, n.59).

iii) One way of outlining briefly the complexity of human motivation is to recall the definition of attitude (important in social psychology) and also a distinction of four functions that attitudes serve.

An attitude is a mental and neural state of readiness to respond, organized through experience, exerting a directive and/or dynamic influence on behavior.[42]

Attitudes, thus defined, are clearly important in the directing of action, including moral action. Four functions of attitudes may be distinguished in terms of the motivation involved: the utilitarian function, the ego-defensive function, the value-expressive function, and the knowledge-function.[43] This fourfold distinction condenses a good deal of psychology in a conveniently brief way.

An attitude serving the utilitarian function regards its objects in the light of satisfactions or frustrations associated with those objects.

An attitude serving the ego-defensive function is held by the individual to protect himself from threatening aspects of himself or of the environment. Such an attitude is rooted in the conflicts or insecurities of the person and expresses the workings of mechanisms of defense.

An analysis of the value-expressive function of attitudes is provided by Rokeach (Rokeach 1968, n.70). A person has relatively few values of a terminal or instrumental kind, and further such values are rather abstract. Attitudes are much more numerous and are related to concrete objects and situations. Attitudes thus play an indispensable role in mediating between abstract values and concrete situations.

Finally, attitudes may serve a function of knowledge, in providing the individual with a more or less organized, and usually simplified, view of his world. There is a correspondence here with Lonergan's idea of "commonsense judgments" (Lonergan 1958, 289-293).

A single attitude may serve different functions at the same time. A prejudice against some group may be held as true (so serving the knowledge-function), and at the same time be ego-defensive (one has a group upon which to project blame); utilitarian (if there are advantages in opposing that group), and even apparently value-expressive (it is right and good to oppose this group!).

13 – Impracticality of Proportionalism

Proportionate reasons, justifying exemptions from moral norms, might be urged by an individual in relation to any of these four functions of his attitudes. All can involve advantages or disadvantages for him. This holds even for the ego-defensive function, because defenses *do* defend and protect a person from distress. It is possible for one form of pathology in a person's life to stabilize his personality and limit the expression of other symptoms (Socarides 1978, 441-26); and this can apply even if the behavior involved is manipulative and destructive.

To return to the main theme, can advantages related to the utilitarian and ego-defensive functions of attitudes constitute proportionate reasons over-ruling in certain cases the value expressive function? It seems that they can, *unless* a qualitative difference between the functions of attitudes is recognized that would give value-expression an intrinsic priority. But the proportionalist approach, for reasons given above, does not seem to be able to ground such a distinction. Even ego-defensive advantages are classifiable as ontic goods; a person may find consolation and peace of mind in the conviction of being Napoleon,[44] and consolation and peace of mind are surely classifiable as goods of some kind.

This brings us to the question of a stimulus to on-going conversion. Conversion in general implies a change in the criterion of evaluation (Lonergan 1973, 237-8), and as regards moral conversion in particular, giving priority to values over satisfactions (Lonergan 1973, 240). If someone recognizes that something that he is doing is simply wrong, then he can be challenged to change his way of living, a change that may be far-reaching. A way of life can be called into question by a single fact whose meaning is seen as contradicting the significance desired, much as a scientific theory can also be upset by a single finding. Such a change in one's way of living means rising above the probably painful consequences of changing, especially in the short run, in favor of some criterion not conditioned by experience of difficulty. To be able to do this, the person would have to recognize a moral order that is objective and not subordinate to feared consequences; some challenge in which the individual encounters a criterion other than, and independent of, the inertial habits of his own feeling, thinking, willing, and doing. Without such a challenge, how can he begin to emerge from the vicious circle defined by the inertia of his habits, an inertia increased by whatever psychological limitations he is subject to, and in which he may feel comfortable (*qualis est unusquisque, talis et finis videtur ei*)? Of course, the individual is in general not responsible for his own psychological limitations, nor for their effects insofar as these escape his present control (Kiely 1980, 243-247). But without an independent criterion to assess his actions, he will find it hard even to discover that such limitations exist, and in such discovery lies the first step towards greater freedom.

In other words, proportionalism would have a greater claim to practicality if we were able to see the future extensively and in detail; if our spontaneous evaluation of reflexive and other consequences were always appropriate; if our attitudes had no utilitarian and ego-defensive functions threatening the value-expressive function; if (in Lonergan's terms) we were fully converted, free from bias, and quite authentic; and if we were never inhibited by the fear of loss attendant upon doing our duty. These conditions are not fulfilled in reality. Even if they were fulfilled, the first step in the proportionalist approach, the moral neutralization of the act-as-means, would still be a problem (making it also difficult to define many of the terms in the conditions just listed); but a problem that, at least, would be less likely to cause practical confusion in the ideally-endowed beings which we, unfortunately, are not.

6. Different Approaches to Moral Compromise

It can and often does happen that a person suffers from the inability to fulfill some norm, a difficulty that may derive from limitations upon his effective freedom,[45] or from difficult circumstances, or from an interaction of both. In such cases the question of moral compromise arises.

Two basic approaches to compromise in such cases may be distinguished, following *Familiaris Consortio*, no. 34.

One approach corresponds to the idea of a "gradualness of the law," "as if there were different degrees or forms of precept in God's law for different individuals and situations." I take the idea of "gradualness of the law" as corresponding to the proportionalist approach, since the effect of a proportionate reason is to modify the application of the norm as long as the proportionate reason exists. Even if it were not the focus of this section of *Familiaris Consortio*, the case of artificial contraception would come to mind.

If an obligation is recognized to attempt to overcome whatever obstacles exist, then one is dealing with a different approach (in terms of *obstacles* and not *proportionate reasons*); "the law of gradualness, or step-by-step advance." This approach, in context, leads to the conclusion that "it is part of the Church's pedagogy that husbands and wives should first of all recognize clearly the teaching of *Humanae Vitae* as indicating the norm for the exercise of their sexuality, and that they should endeavor to establish the conditions for observing that norm."

I take it that the distinction between a "gradualness of the law" and the "law of gradualness, or step-by-step advance" may be generalized and applied to any moral norm. The essential difference between the two approaches (while both recognize the existence of possible difficulties) is that in the former approach, the law itself is modified, while in the latter approach the law remains valid in itself, even though effective freedom may at present be too limited to allow its observance; while the law as remaining valid stands also as a permanent call to the overcoming of existing limits upon effective freedom.[46]

The concept of the "law of gradualness" provides a framework for a theory of moral compromise; when a genuine inability to observe the norm exists, the person is obliged to "endeavor to place the conditions for its observance." A person is always free to make an attempt, even when he is not sufficiently free to succeed.[47] If "gradualness of the law" is accepted, then the person seems to be exempted even from the attempt to overcome existing obstacles; for if that were not the case, the two approaches would no longer be distinguishable.

Taking it then that "gradualness of the law" corresponds to the proportionalist approach, it is vulnerable to all the objections made against proportionalism in general. But the concept of the "law of gradualness" can meet all the objections raised in the course of this article, especially in sections 4 and 5. It does not allow the norm itself to be conditioned by the individual's present viewpoint, nor by consequences feared from within the limitations of that viewpoint. The norm remains as a challenge that stands outside any vicious circle defined by the inertia of personal habits; there remains a tension between the ideal and the real that offers a stimulus to continuing conversion. But if a norm can be modified or suspended for some alleged proportionate reason, that tension is weakened, and perhaps it collapses totally.

It seems fair to say that contemporary depth-psychology, in the sense of psychology recognizing the existence of subconscious motivation, with all that this implies in terms of human fallibility, (Kiely 1980, n.77) adds much emphasis to the importance of the difference between "gradualness of the law" and "the law of gradualness." Recognition of the importance of subconscious motivation ought logically to lead towards one of two extremes: either a renewed recognition of the importance of an objective moral order to protect people from the unrestricted influence of the subconscious (accompanied, of course, by a clear awareness of human frailty), or else an extreme relativism, where the right thing to do is simply whatever provides the most economic solution to one's conflicts. [48]

7. In conclusion

Various arguments have been advanced against the practicality of proportionalism. They are all, in the last analysis, aspects of a single difficulty.

Proportionalism, as compared to the traditional approach, introduces a change both in the object and in the criterion of moral evaluation. Rather than allowing an independent moral quality to the act-as-means by which the agent intervenes in the course of events, it makes the totality of a larger process into the only adequate object of moral evaluation. The criterion of evaluation, prescinding from the moral quality of the act-as-means, becomes a balance between ontic goods and ontic evils in the totality of the larger process. The proportionalist aim is that of reconstituting a viable morality after this shift has been made. Reconstitution would require that the new object and the new criterion be capable of providing adequately clear evaluations. If the arguments here presented are valid, such clear evaluations are not possible; instead, the change in object and criterion leads into such a maze of difficulties that one no longer sees how evaluations can be made. The clarity needed to make moral living possible does not seem to be provided. It may be that sufficiently large residues of tradition still remain in our "cognitive unconscious" to have kept this limitation of proportionalism from becoming, as yet, fully clear; proportionalists perhaps allow to traditional norms a general force that their own approach, strictly speaking, is not in a position to justify.

Notes

[1] This approach has become so widespread that R. M. Gula, *What Are They Saying About Moral Norms?* (New York-Ramsey: Paulist Press, 1982), 101-104, can suggest its acceptance on grounds of probabilism. D. J. Keefe, "Ecclesiological Implications of Consequentialist Theory," *Fellowship of Catholic Scholars Newsleller*, 6 (March 1983), 10-13, suggests that followers of this approach now include "perhaps a majority of Catholic moralists."

[2] This is the title of an article by J. R. Connery, *Theological Studies* 44 (1983): 489-496.

[3] In lieu of Kiely's third footnote, see the bibliography of this volume-ed.

[4] I follow Connery, "Catholic Ethics: Has the Norm for Rule-Making Changed?," *Theological Studies* 42 reprinted in this volume in identifying this as the point where proportionalist theories begin to diverge from the traditional Catholic approach. Knauer "Fundamentalethik: teleogische als deontolgische Normbegründung," *Theologie und Philosophie* 55 (1980): 348, has expressed this very point: "Wenn dagegen das Mittel zur Erreichung eines Zwecks zwar in der Verursachung oder Zulassung eines Schadens besteht, aber keine eigene Handlung mit gesondertem 'finis opens' darstellt, sondern nur den Talvollzug einer umfassenderen Handlung, dann kann das Mittel nur in dem Fall ethisch schlecht sein, daß die 'ratio boni' der Gesamthandlung kein 'entsprechender Grund' ist und somit der 'finis opens' der Gesamthandlung ethisch schlecht ist". A. Di Ianni, "The Direct/Indirect Distinction in Morals," *Readings in Moral Theology, No. 1, Moral Norms and Catholic Traditions*, ed. C.E. Curran and R.A. McCormick, (New York-Ramsey-Toronto: Paulist Press, 1979), 216, summarizes: "These authors [a group including Knauer] prefer to treat the posited act or means as a constitutive part or stage of a larger whole, which whole is the primary object of one's intentions, and thus is the only true unit of moral significance."

[5] McCormick, with reference to the article of Knauer, *op.cit.*, now recognizes that there *is* a revolution involved, the only remaining question being "Is it justified?" ("Notes," *Theological Studies* 42 (1981): 88-89)

[6] Connery, "The Basis for Certain Key Exceptionless Moral Norms in Contemporary Catholic Thought," *Moral Theology Today: Certitudes and Doubts* (report of a workshop of Bishops of North and Central America and the Caribbean, Dallas, Texas, 6-10 February. 1984), the Pope John Center, St. Louis, 1984, 121-135.

[7] There is nothing to prevent a proportionalist from considering traditional norms as usually valid; but when such a norm is suspended for some proportionate reason, then two criteria stand in opposition: the general norm, and some proportionate reason related to the consequences of the intended act. There is thus in proportionalism a component of pure consequentialism which may (when a reason is considered proportionate) prevail over the general norm.

[8] B. J. F. Lonergan, *Insight: a Study of Human Understanding*, revised students' edition, (London: Longmans Green, 1958), chapters 2, 3, and 4; especially 48-53 and 93-97. See also Macintyre A., *After Virtue* (Indiana: University of Notre Dame Press, 1981), 89-96.

[9] Lonergan *ibid.*, p. 107, points out that statistical methods serve to distinguish between the systematic and non-systematic components of complex processes.

But statistical methods commonly require very specialized experimental designs (such as large samples matched as far as possible on all variables other than the variable being examined); further, statistical methods may reveal surprisingly little about the outcome to be expected in the single case.

[10] Cf. C. S. Lewis, *The Weight of Glory and Other Addresses*, revised edition, ed. W. Hooper, (New York: Macmillan, 1980), 3-19. In these pages, Lewis makes a distinction between proper and improper rewards of good action, which suggested the analogous distinction made here.

[11] The points developed in the last three sections have been expressed with admirable brevity by Clive James, writing as a television-critic: "Television is simultaneously blamed, often by the same people, for worsening the world and for being powerless to change it. That the world is what it is has never been easy for sensitive souls to accept, and gets harder as faith ebbs. This is not to say, however that television, or anything else, is without effect. It is just that the effect is never easy to isolate from the cataract of events. People in television must live to the same rule as people who write articles and books. You can't change things as you would like, but nothing you do will be quite without result: that the consequences of your actions are strictly incalculable should make you more responsible, not less. That is what it means to act from principle." C. James, *Glued to the Box: Television Criticism from "The Observer" 1979-82* (London: Pan Books, 1983), 21.

[12] B. J. F. Lonergan, "The Subject", *A Second Collection: Papers by Bernard J. F. Lonergan S.J.*, ed. W. Ryan & B. Tyrell, (London: Darton, Longman & Todd, 1974), 79. Essentially the same point is made by P. Quay, "Morality by Calculation of Values," *Readings in Moral Theology, No. 1*, ed. C.E. Curran & R.A. McCormick, (New York-Ramsey-Toronto: Paulist Press, 1979); he speaks of "intrinsic values" (286). See also Quay, "The Unity and Structure of the Human Act," *Listening* 18 (1983): 245-259.

[13] See, for instance, I. L. Janis & L. Mann, *Decision Making. a Psychological Analysis of Conflict, Choice, and Commitment*, (New York: The Free Press; London: Collier Macmillan, 1977), 10-11.

[14] M. B. Smith, "The Self and Cognitive Consistency," in R. P. Ahelson et al. (ed.), *Theories of Cognitive Consistency: a Sourcebook* (Chicago: Rand McNally, 1968), chapter 27, see also M. J. Rosenberg, "Depth, Centrality and Tolerance in Cognitive Consistency", *ibid*, chapter 68.

[15] For example, see A. Plé, *Chastity and the Affective Life*, trans. M. C. Thompson, (New York: Herder & Herder, 1966), 164-167.

[16] Cf. the critique, along lines effectively similar to these, made by McCormick of the article of Pinckaers cited above; "Notes," *Theological Studies* 44 (1983): 76-80.

[17] Since we have limited knowledge and control of the future, it follows that our attempts to cooperate with the Providence of God are made within these same limits. The point has been re-stated by Grisez, *The Way of the Lord Jesus*, Vol. I, pp. 151 and 155. The same point is made by G. K. Chesterton his *Ballad of the White Horse*, book 1. In this connection it is worth recalling how such a careful and capable planner as Ignatius of Loyola could be so habitually, one might say stubbornly, about the future. Polanco, in his letter on the death of Ignatius, says that Ignatius' assertion that he would soon die was only the second time he had heard Ignatius with certainty about the future (*Monumenta Ignatiana, Fontes Narrativi*. I, 767). What was apparently the other instance is reported by Ribadaneira (*ibid.*, II, 342). And in both cases, Ignatius' words contain qualifying

clauses. At the other extreme, claims to far-reaching knowledge and control of the future may be considered as expressions of a Gnostic mentality (see E. Voegelin, *The New Science of Politics: an Introduction* (Chicago: University of Chicago Press, 1952), 107-161, especially 120.)

[18] For example, Lonergan has provided a very useful, although not exhaustive analysis of the interrelations of the different goods of marriage in terms of three different kinds of finality, horizontal, vertical, and absolute; see the article "Finality, Love and Marriage" in *Collection.- Papers by Bernard Lonergan S.J.*, ed. F. E. Crowe, (New York: Herder, 1967), 16-53.

[19] E.g., G. Grisez, "Against Consequentialism," *American Journal of Jurisprudence* 23 (1978): 29-41. Also, A. MacIntyre has pointed out that "different pleasures and different happinesses are to a large degree incommensurable; there are no scales of quality or quantity on which to weigh them." (*After Virtue*, as in note 9 above, p. 62.)

[20] Keats, "To a Nightingale." See also H. S. Olin, "Dying without Death: Third Wish in Suicide," *American Journal of Psychotherapy* 32 (1978): 270-275.

[21] "Moral conversion changes the criterion of one's decisions and choices from satisfactions to values" and "consists in opting for the truly good, even for value against satisfaction, when value and satisfaction conflict" (B. Lonergan, *Method in Theology*, 240).

[22] McCormick reports this article of Knauer with approval (*Notes, Theological Studies* 42 (1981): 85-89), and indeed this approach is like one made earlier by McCormick himself; see "A Commentary on the Commentaries" in *Doing Evil to Achieve Good: Moral Choice in Conflict Situations* (Chicago: Loyola University Press, 1978), 265, 201, 261, and 233-234; cf. Grisez, *The Way of the Lord Jesus*, Vol. 1, 162.

[23] Janis & Mann, in their extensive study of the psychology of decision-making, cited in note 16 above, set aside the case of the decision involving only a single objective as being marginal and providing no useful model for the analysis of decisions in general (p. 10 and *passim*.)

[24] For a survey of philosophical approaches, see De Finance, *Éthique Générale*, chapter 2; for a review of psychological theories, see S. R. Maddi, *Personality Theories: a Comparative Analysis*, fourth edition (Homewood, Illinois, Irwin-Dorsey, Georgetown, Ontario: The Dorsey Press, 1980.)

[25] For a development of this point and further examples, see A. MacIntyre, *A Short History of Ethics* (New York: Macmillan, 1966.)

[26] See Maddi, *op. cit.*, pp. 89-104 on the Rogerian approach; also S. Freud, *New Introductory Lectures on Psychoanalysis*, trans. J Strachey, (New York: W. W. Norton, 1965), lecture 35.

[27] E. Becker, *Escape from Evil* (New York: The Free Press; London: Collier Macmillan, 1975); also *The Denial of Death*, same publishers, 1973.

[28] What is important is "an integral vision of man and his vocation, not only his natural and earthly, but also his supernatural and eternal vocation"; Paul VI, *Humanae Vitae*, 7; see also John Paul II, *Familiaris Consortio*, 32. Non-Catholic works laying a similar stress on the importance of an integral vision of the human good are, for example, C. Dykstra, *Vision and Character* (New York: Paulist Press, 1981), and C.S. Lewis, *The Abolition of Man* (Glasgow: Collins, 1978). Such a vision of the integral human good seems necessary as a "heuristic structure" in relation to which reflections deriving from scripture, tradition, contemporary moral thinking, and the human and natural sciences can meet each other; as well

as being a product of such interaction. Concerning "heuristic structures," see Lonergan *Insight*, 33-69, 217-244, 390-396, 451 487, 530-594, and *Method in Theology*, 287.

[29] Rather than locating the controversy about proportionalism in a difference between teleology and deontology (taking "deontology'" with its Kantian connotations), I would prefer to follow Pinckaers and see the more important difference as that between a teleology that is technical or utilitarian and a teleology that is properly moral (Pinckaers, *op. cit.*, pp. 197-202).

[30] Even limited matters of technique can have deep and hidden roots; see R. L. Woolfolk & F. C. Richardson, "Behavior Therapy and the Ideology of Modernity," *American Psychologist* 39 (1984): 777-786. Further, even like-sounding terms and principles can carry opposite meanings and lead to opposed conclusions; see C. Bresciani, *Personalismo e Morale Sessuale, aspetti teologici e psicologici* (Rome: Edizioni Piemme, 1983).

[31] Lonergan, *Insight*, 477. See also I. B. Weiner, *Principles of Psychotherapy* (New York: Wiley, 1975), especially 119-120 and 155-159.

[32] See G. Orwell, "Politics and the English Language," in *Inside the Whale and Other Essays* (Penguin Books, 1957), 143-158, also Orwell,"Notes on Nationalism", in *The Decline of the English Murder and Other Essays* (Penguin Books, 1965), 155-179.

[33] Pinckaers, *op. cit.*, p. 188, as quoted above (see note 6).

[34] G. K. Chesterton, *Heretics* (London: The Bodley Head, 1960), 73. See also Lonergan, *Insight*, 191-232, for an account of venous kinds of bias; and (once again) E. Becker, *Escape from Evil*, on the significance of "symbols of immorality."

[35] See, for example, J. Piaget, "The Affective Unconscious and the Cognitive Unconscious," *Journal of the American Psychoanalytic Association* 21 (1973): 249-261.

[36] A useful survey is provided by D.C. Leighton & A.H. Leighton, "Mental Health and Social Factors," in *Comprehensive Textbook of Psychiatry*, ed. A. M. Freedman & H. I. Kaplan, (Baltimore: Williams & Wilkins, 1967), 1520-1533.

[37] A. Colby, L. Kohlberg, J. Gibbs, M. Lieberman, *A Longitudinal Study of Moral Development*, Monographs of the Society for Research in Child Development 48:1-2, (1983): especially 46-56.

[38] "... the conventional level has a vast amount of 'stretch' to absorb arbitrary but socially authoritative content," L. Kohlberg, *Essays in Moral Development Vol. 1* (San Francisco: Harper & Row, 1981), 127. (This poses a difficulty for any reliance on consensus or on tradition for an assessment of proportions between goods, or for a definition of the good in general, unless one recognizes some privileged authority and tradition among the competing traditions and authorities one encounters.)

[39] "Textbook psychology preaches the cliche that moral decisions are the product of the algebraic resolution of conflicting quantitative affective forces" (*ibid.*, p. 187.) The remark must be taken in the context of the whole chapter.

[40] L.M. Rulla, "Discernment of Spirits and Christian Anthropology," *Gregorianum* 59 (1978): 537-569; experimental backing is given in Rulla et al., *Entering and Leaving Vocation: Intrapsychic Dynamics* (Rome: Gregorian University Press; Chicago: Loyola University Press, 1976).

[41] Rulla *et al.*, *Entering and Leaving Vocation*, as in note 64; especially chapter 7, 8, and 9.

[42] The definition comes from G. Allport; it is cited by W.J. McGuire, "The Nature of Attitudes and Attitude Change", in *The Handbook of Social Psychology*, ed. G. Lindzey & E. Aronson, second edition, (Reading, Massachusetts: Addison-Wesley, 1969), chapter 21, 142.

[43] McGuire, *ibid.*; D. Katz, "The Functional Approach to the Study of Attitudes," in *Readings in Attitude Theory and Measurement*, ed. M. Fishbein, (Wiley, New York: 1967), chapter 49; M. Rokeach, *Beliefs, Attitudes, and Values: a Theory of Organization and Change*, (San Francisco: Jossey-Bass, 1968), 129-132, 156-178.

[44] Not that someone holding himself to be Napoleon is to be blamed for that; but it would be better if his peace of mind had some more genuine basis.

[45] On the distinction between essential and effective freedom, see Lonergan, *Insight*, 619-627.

[46] Such as, perhaps, the difficulties in communication between husband and wife that can cause difficulties with periodic abstinence: "The natural methods [of regulating births] can develop communication. Conversely, those who have already developed communication skills find it much easier to work with the methods." (M. A. Shivanandan, *Natural Sex* [New York: Berkley Books, 1981], 94.)

[47] It is in his antecedent willingness that a person is most free; cf. Lonergan, *Insight*, 622 ff. See also Paul VI, "Address to the Pilgrims of the Équipes Notre-Dame," *AAS* 62 (1971): 428-437; especially nos. 15-16 of this address.

[48] Cf. Kohlberg, *Essays in Moral Development, Vol. 1,* as in note 38 above, 105-114, for an analysis of this and other forms of ethical relativism.

Proportionalism & the Pill: How Consistant Application of Theory Leads to Contradiction to Practice

Christopher Kaczor

One may be tempted to think that after some 30 years of debate over proportionalism and *Humanae Vitae* scholars have heard almost every argument for and against proportionalism and almost every argument for and against contraception. Authors on both sides of both matters have pointed out the connections between the theory of proportionalism and the practice of contraception. All proponents of proportionalism argue that this theory justifies the use of contraception in at least some circumstances, and most but not all critics of proportionalism hold that contraception is an intrinsically evil act that cannot be justified. As Edward Vacek notes:

> An argument could be made that *Humanae Vitae* has fueled the development of P[roportionalism] in Catholic thought, and that the birth control debate has been so drawn-out and intense precisely because it is really a debate over a style of moral reasoning and a vision of what it means to be human, not to mention over what God is doing in the world—therefore over much larger matters than the use of a pill (Vacek see above 412-13).

Vacek notes that *Humanae Vitae* led to a greater and greater questioning of traditional formulations about many matters (Hoose 1987, 37). If one surveys the literature that began what is now called 'proportionalism,' one will find a recurring pattern; first basic principles are laid down and defended, and then, invariably it is shown that these principles justify the use of contraception.[1] John Finnis puts the point as follows:

> The formal attack on the moral absolutes emerges, among Catholics, in response to the problem of contraception. Not in response

to the desire to maintain a counterpopulation deterrent strategy of annihilating retaliation, or to tell lies in military, police, or political operations, or to carry out therapeutic abortions; or to arrange homosexual unions; or to relieve inner tensions and disequalibria by masturbation; or to keep slaves; or to produce babies by impersonal artifice. Those desires were and are all urgent enough, but none of them precipitated the formal rejection of moral absolutes. The desire to practice and approve of contraception did (Finnis 1991, 85).

For dissenting revisionist theologians, that traditional moral principles characteristically justify a prohibition of contraception is reason to adopt proportionalism as an alternative. For those who accept the Church's teaching in *Humanae Vitae*, the belief that proportionalism justifies contraception is reason for rejecting proportionalism. Contraception and proportionalism seem to be comfortable bedfellows.

What has been overlooked, however, is how the development of proportionalism itself and a consistent application of its principles leads to the conclusion that the use of contraception is, for the most part if not entirely, illicit. In other words, proportionalism itself given a developed understanding of proportionate reason and the goodness/rightness distinction leads one to a rejection of the use of contraception.

Unlike consequentialism or act-utilitarianism, proportionalism is not mere maximization of premoral goods or minimization of premoral evils. Though maximization of premoral goods and minimization of premoral evils *primarily* define proportionate reason, there are other *secondary* conditions that establish it as well.[2] These conditions were worked out through the responses to critics who suggested that proportionalism justifies any sort of behavior whatever, even for example allowing a sheriff to frame and execute an innocent person to prevent a riot. Proportionalists responded by clarifying that proportionalism does not advocate the maximization of non-moral goods irrespective of all other considerations. Certain secondary conditions must also be met for the reason to be considered truly proportionate. What are these secondary conditions of proportionate reason?

First, proportionate reason includes a *condition of necessity of cause* (McCormick 1981a, 718-719, McCormick 1978, 238). The premorally evil means used by the agent must stand in a necessary causal relationship to the premoral good sought. Hence, in the often cited case of abortion to save the life of the mother, one may legitimately effect the death of the child in order to save the life of the mother because the killing and the saving stand in a necessary relationship to one another. On the other hand, a sheriff may not frame an innocent person for a murder he did not commit even in order to prevent a riot that will kill many others. There is no necessary connection between framing an innocent person and preventing a riot; hence the act contemplated by the sheriff lacks a proportionate reason. Secondly, proportionate reason has a condition of *chronological simultaneity*. Proportionate reason is present only in the preservation of a good here and now, not some future good. One cannot have an abortion because one wants to avoid paying the unborn child's tuition; one cannot sleep with the prison guard to be reunited with one's family. On the other hand, one can kill in self-defense, since the killing preserves the good of life here and now. Finally, proportionate reason excludes causing *more evil than necessary*. If one can defend oneself by injuring rather than killing, then one should only injure. If one can defend oneself without even injuring, then one is obliged to take this course of action. This final secondary condition excludes the causing of *superfluous evil*. According to revisionists, these three secondary conditions of proportionate reason (namely, the causal necessity of the evil to achieve the good, chronological simultaneity, and the curtailing of superfluous evil) sharply delineate proportionalism from straight-forward consequentialism, especially if each is construed as a necessary rather than as a sufficient condition.[3] Finally, of course, proportionalism demands that one must choose the lesser of two evils and in this it does not differ from consequentialism.

How do these conditions relate to the use of contraception? That there must be a causal necessity between the evil used and the good achieved excludes, for example, the possibility of terror bombing, bombing innocent civilians to terrorize the enemy into submission. There is no necessary connection between these deaths and the capitulation of military leaders.

> [E]xtortion by definition accepts the necessity of doing nonmoral evil to get others to cease their wrongdoing. The acceptance of such a necessity is an implied denial of human freedom. But since human freedom is a basic value associated with other basic values (in this case, life) undermining it *also thereby undermines life* (McCormick 1978, 260).

In this context, "necessity" means that there is no other way imaginable to prevent greater loss of life, save the taking of life. If there is another way available, for example, the cessation of wrongdoing by others or heroic efforts on one's own part, then there is no necessary connection.

However, this causal necessity excludes many common grounds for the use of contraception, including financial well-being, a stable family life, and the desire to pursue a fulfilling career. There is no necessary connection between these goods and the use of contraception. Some who use contraception never achieve the goods of stable family life, financial well-being, and career fulfillment. Some who do not use contraception do achieve these goods. Certainly securing these goods can be thwarted or promoted by many persons involved in the situation—family members, spouses, and communal support to cite a few examples. The only case in which there is the requisite necessary connection between contraception and some good would be use of contraception in cases in which a pregnancy would endanger a woman's life or health. Here, it is the *pregnancy itself* that is the problem and not negative effects accidentally related to pregnancy. Hence, either proportionalism is inconsistent by invoking the necessity condition as an *ad hoc* measure in some cases (terror bombing) but not in other cases (contraception) or, if the necessity condition is consistently applied, the proportionalism leads one to reject many common justifications for the use of contraception, leaving only contraception to preserve the life or health of the mother.

Another secondary condition of proportionate reason is chronological simultaneity of the good and evil effects. Richard McCormick puts the point in the following way:

> Here [in the work of a critic of proportionalism] we have evil *now*—good *to come*. Thus it is sometimes said that adultery now justifies a future good. This misrepresents what Fuchs-Schüller-Böckle-Janssens-Scholz-Weber-Curran and many others are saying. What they are saying is that the good achieved *here and now* (though it may perjure into the future) is sometimes inseparable from premoral evil. Thus, an act of self-defense achieves *here and now* the good of preservation of life. A falsehood achieves *here and now* the protection of a professional secret. Taking property (food) of another saves the life of the taker *here and now* (McCormick 1984, 3).

When the condition of chronological simultaneity of good and evil effects is applied to the case of contraception, the result is that most uses of contraception become unjustified. For example, contraception used to avoid the costs that will be incurred at the birth and upbringing of a child is a case doing evil here and now for the good of preventing an evil feared in the future. Contraception for the sake of family stability or career advancement likewise is doing evil now so that one may have some good in the future. Once again the only cases of contraception which would be justified would be cases in which the health of the woman would be threatened.

Thirdly, proportionate reason demands that one cause as little premoral evil as possible to secure the end in question. One should use falsehood in self-defense rather than injuring another if both means will secure safety. One should not kill in self-defense if merely injuring the adversary will achieve the same goal.

Since one may not bring about superfluous evil in achieving the end, certain methods of contraception would be excluded on this basis. For instance, the pill, Norplant, and IUD can act as abortifacients. Women using these forms of contraception also report numerous side-effects including higher risks of blood clotting, strokes, and heart attacks. Other forms of contraception such as a diaphragm and the condom do not have these disadvantages. They are neither abortifacients, nor do they risk women's health. If one is obliged to avoid causing superfluous evils, then one is obliged not to use many of the most common forms of contraception, the univalent pill, the IUD, and Norplant.

Thus far, if consistently applied, no case of contraception would be licit on grounds given by proportionalists save for contraception used in cases in which a woman's life or health is endangered by pregnancy and the only form of contraception that would be licit in these cases would be condoms or diaphragms.

However, one must not forget the primary condition of proportionate reason demands the maximization of premoral goods and minimization of premoral evils. The requirement is sometimes formulated as follows: given the choice between two evils, one must choose the lesser of two evils. The only alternative would seem to be that in such conflict situations, one chooses the greater of two evils which is clearly absurd.

A fortiori given the choice between an evil and something good or indifferent, one must choose the indifferent or good over something that is evil, even if only premoral evil. Condoms and diaphragms are not entirely free from premoral evil. In the words of Richard McCormick:

> Contraception represents a type of intrusion, a nuisance, an interference. That is clear from the description of the "perfect contraceptive": it must be inexpensive, effective, without side-effects, aesthetically acceptable, and easy to use. Lack of these qualities would spell evils of some kind (McCormick 1987, 98-9).

Unlike condoms and diaphragms, Natural Family Planning (NFP) would seem to fulfill all the criteria laid down by McCormick for the "perfect contraceptive." Its only necessary expense is perhaps the time taken out from work or play to learn the method. Echoing the finds of numerous scientific studies, McCormick notes: "Natural family planning is a highly effective method." When used properly, NFP's failure rates are roughly the same as the pill used properly. Method related pregnancies reported in various studies range from 0% to 2.8%.[4] NFP has no side-effects on male or female health. It is aesthetically acceptable insofar as it does not disturb the natural structure of the sexual act. Finally, NFP is easy to use, requiring no specialized technique or knowledge. James P. Hanigan acknowledges additional advantages of NFP over contraception:

> Ironically, if one considers the virtues and relational dynamics needed to practice NFP effectively, one discovers many of the values and virtues advocated for marital relationships, by revisionist and feminist theologians who emphasize 'quality of relationship' norms to evaluate the morality of sexual behaviors. NFP, more than any other means of birth control, calls for honest communication, for mutual equality, for shared responsibility and joint decision-making between the sexual partners. The burden of responsible parenthood through the techniques of NFP, while still heavier on the woman than on the man, is not placed exclusively on the woman (Hanigan 1995, 212).

Given the advantages of NFP over all forms of contraception, considered purely within the framework of premoral goods and evils, the greater good is not difficult to discern. If one is required to choose the greater good or the lesser evil in avoiding pregnancy, NFP is obligatory and contraception impermissible.

Usually, revisionists acknowledge that NFP is an obligatory ideal, but this ideal, like many other ideals, must be tempered by realistic considerations. These considerations are of two kinds. First, NFP requires knowledge of the female reproductive system as well technical devices that may be too expensive or unavailable to some, such as thermometers for measuring body temperature to check for ovulation or calendars to record signs of fertility (Hanigan 1995, 212-213). Secondly, and much more importantly, NFP "requires a high degree of motivation and mutuality on the part of the couple which cannot be readily presumed, training in the practice of the method and a good deal of self-knowledge and self-discipline on the part of the couple" (Hanigan 1995, 212). Not all couples can meet these demands, hence given the practical alternatives, contraception may be justified.

The first objection offered by Hanigan has the theoretical drawback that it applies much better to other forms of contraception than it does to NFP. Like NFP, the proper use of contraceptives requires knowledge, at least minimal, of the reproductive system. One must also learn how to properly use condoms or diaphragms. Presumably, a doctor before prescribing the pill or Norplant teaches the patient something about the drug so as to allow the patient an opportunity to knowingly consent. And again, in terms of technical devices, the requirements of NFP are much more modest than other forms of contraception. If buying a thermometer or a chart for NFP taxes the family budget, certainly a visit to the doctor, pill prescriptions, condoms or diaphragms would be too expensive. This first argument against NFP has an even greater application against contraception.

Hanigan's second argument is more substantive. NFP is simply too demanding for couples. Not all couples have the heroic virtues necessary to abstain from intercourse the requisitely typical 9-12 days per month. Morality does not demand the impossible. I *ought* to do such-and-such implies I *can* do such-and-such. Some people, good people, just cannot bring themselves to such a long period of abstention. Not everyone is called to heroism, and a lack of moral perfection should not be considered evil doing in a moral sense.

To understand why this argument too fails on proportionalist grounds, one has to invoke a further distinction common to their writings, the distinction between goodness and rightness. Although in the early seventies, proportionalists spoke of good and bad actions, through the intervention of William Frankena and more importantly Bruno Schüller, proportionalists came to insist on distinguishing moral goodness and badness from rightness and wrongness. What is this distinction precisely?

Unfortunately, there is no precise definition upon which all authors agree. In *Goodness and Rightness in Thomas Aquinas's Summa Theologiae*, James Keenan explains the distinction as follows, "Goodness means that out of love we strive to live and act rightly. Rightness means that our ways of living and acting actually conform to rational expectations set by the ethical community."[5] Others describe goodness as a disposition or striving to do and know what is right and rightness as action in accordance with nature or reason. "Acting from love (*agape*) is morally good," writes Bruno Schüller, "Doing what on the whole is impartially beneficial to all persons concerned is morally right. Therefore, an action may be morally bad because performed from pure selfishness, but nonetheless be morally right on account of its beneficial consequences" (Schuller 1978, 165-92 and 183). Josef Fuchs offers this example of how to parse the distinction between goodness and rightness in a practical case:

> Perhaps someone makes a great contribution to the well-being of humankind but is only motivated in his activity by egotism—for instance, in order to be honored. He has done the morally *right* thing, for he has created premoral human goods or values; but he is not morally *good* (Fuchs 1984, 81).

What is common to all the ways in which the distinction is made is this: Goodness and badness refer to persons in their motivations and in their striving or failing to strive to do what is right; rightness and wrongness refer to acts. According to this view, one cannot resolve any question of the rightness or wrongness of an act by reference to virtues, that is, the interior dispositions of a person. The virtues are habits of seeking and desiring to do what is right; they cannot determine what is right.

How is the goodness/rightness distinction (GRD) justified? Many arguments are given in its favor, but one is that the GRD accords with our common sense intuition that good people seeking to do the right thing can nevertheless do the wrong act. In a gruesome example, Todd Salzman notes that an act can be objectively wrong while the agent is nevertheless good. He writes:

> UNICEF estimates that up to a million infants perished annually from dehydration and malnutrition due to improper bottle feeding. Clearly this was an instance where the mothers who purchased and used infant formula instead of breast milk had the health and

well-being of their children in mind. Their intention to provide the best possible care for their children was a good intention. Objectively, however, the act of bottle feeding with infant formula was wrong because it led to the death of countless numbers of infants. Could we say that these women's actions were right considering the devastating consequences? This would be ludicrous and against all moral sensitivities (Salzman 1995, 208).

The women's acts were wrong, since they brought about so many bad consequences, but the women were nevertheless good people because they acted out of a desire to protect and nurture their children. Despite these desires, one cannot deny that objectively wrong actions were done in light of the results. Rightness is determined on the basis of the premoral goods and evils involved, but goodness is determined by the agents seeking to do what is right.

How does the goodness/rightness distinction relate to contraception? People lacking the requisite virtue of temperance and self-denial will find it difficult if not practically impossible to abstain during times when they judge abstinence is called for. However, given the goodness/rightness distinction, one could readily admit this is the case, and it would not alter the character of contraception as right or wrong in the least. Right or wrong, according to those who hold the GRD, is a matter of the objective premoral goods and evils brought about by a given act. Virtue, seeking what is right, pertains to goodness not rightness. Hence, that someone has not or cannot seek what is right is irrelevant to determining whether or not the act is in fact right or wrong. That many, most, or all people fail to achieve what is right does not alter the character of the right. However, to be good, they must seek to do what is right. Hence, if contraception brings about more premoral evils than NFP, it is wrong, even if people cannot bring themselves to seek to use NFP or seek to use it but fail. A consistent analysis would hold that such people, lacking the requisite virtues, are not good people.

Even aside from the goodness/rightness distinction, if one were to take ability to easily do or avoid some act as reason to believe that act is good or evil, the morality of the tradition in question would have to be radically altered. How many of us love our neighbors as ourselves? How many of us love God with all our heart, mind, and strength? Hanigan's second argument against NFP proves much too much, for if it succeeds in showing NFP to be non-obligatory, it also succeeds in showing as non-obligatory the law of love spoken of by Christ.

Hence, proportionalism, though originally conceived as a way of justifying contraception, in the end excludes the use of contraception. The development of the theory to exclude cases of bombing civilians in war or framing innocent people led to the conditions of necessity and chronological simultaneity in proportionate reason. These conditions exclude the most common motives for using contraception, including financial stability, family harmony, and career advancement. The condition of avoiding superfluous evil led to the elimination of various means of contraception, including the pill. The principle that in conflict situations one should choose the lesser of two evils led to the conclusion that one should choose NFP over contraception. And finally, the goodness/rightness distinction undermined the argument given in favor of contraception that NFP is too difficult for most people to strive after or achieve because the common couple lacks the requisite virtues. Of course, I am not, in this entire discussion, taking any substantive views on the matters of proportionalism or contraception. Rather, I am only making the disquieting suggestion that either proportionalism or approval of contraception must be abandoned by the many who advocate both.

NOTES

[1] In fact, my own interest in these questions began with Janet Smith's reflections on Thomas and Proportionalism in *Humanae Vitae: A Generation Later*.

[2] I am indebted here to the summary of James Walter whose article "Proportionate Reason and its Three Levels of Inquiry: Structuring the Ongoing Debate" appears in this volume (see below 398-410) though I have changed his order of presentation and slightly altered the list itself.

[3] This conclusion needs to take into account the many species and varieties of consequentialism if it is to be firmly established.

[4] See, for instance, J. Billings study (0%) in the *Journal of the Irish Medical Association* 70 (April 1977): 6; H. Klaus's study (1.17%) in *Contraception* 19 (June 1979): 6; W.H.O. Study (2.8%) in *Fertility and Sterility* 36 (1981): 591; J.X. Xu and D.W. Zang (1.18%) in *Reproduction and Contraception* vol. 13, no.3 (June 1993): 194-200; and R.E.J. Ryder (0.4%) in the *British Medical Journal* vol. 307 (Sept. 1993): 723-26.

[5] The introduction of James F. Keenan's *Goodness and Rightness in Thomas Aquinas's Summa Theologiae* (Washington, D.C.: Georgetown University Press, 1992) provides a short history of the distinction beginning with G.E. Moore which is accurate save perhaps in suggesting that the first author who noted that goodness and badness can be said of an agent's motives and rightness and wrongness of an agent's actions (e.g., the agent is good but the action is wrong, and vice versa) is Bruno Schüller. One can find this coupling and mutual independence earlier in, for example, J.J.C. Smart's defense of utilitarianism printed in 1961 and

reprinted in 1973 as *Utilitarianism For and Against* with Bernard Williams, (Cambridge, Cambridge University Press, 1982), 48-49.

BIBLIOGRAPHY

Abbott, Walter, S.J., ed. 1966. *The Documents of Vatican II*. New York: American Press.
Allen, Joseph L. 1963. The Relation of Strategy and Morality. *Ethics* 72: 167-78.
Alonso, Vincente M. 1937. *El principio del doble effecto en los commentadores de Sancto Tomas de Aquino*. Diss. Rome.
Anscombe, Elizabeth.1958. Modern Moral Philosophy. *Philosophy* 33: 26-42.
———. 1963. *Intention*. New York: Cornell University Press.
———. 1982. Action, Intention, and Double Effect. *Proceedings of the American Catholic Philosophical Association* 56: 12-25.
Aquinas, Thomas. *Opera omnia*. Rome: Leonine edit. 1882- .
Ashley, Benedict. 1985. *Theologies of the Body: Humanist and Christian*. Braintree, MA: Pope John XXIII Center.
———. and Kevin O'Rourke. 1997. *Health Care Ethics*. Washington, D.C.: Georgetown University Press.
Aulisio, Mark P. 1996. On the Importance of the Intention/Foresight Distinction. *American Catholic Philosophical Quarterly* vol. LXX, no. 2: 189-205.
Ayer, A.J. 1959. *Philosophical Essays*. London: Macmillan & Co.
Beauchamp, Tom, ed. 1996. *Intending Death: The Ethics of Suicide and Euthanasia*. New Jersey: Prentice Hall.
———. and James Childress. 1979. *Principles of Biomedical Ethics*. New York Oxford.
Becker, E. 1973. *The Denial of Death*. New York: The Free Press; London: Collier Macmillan.
———. 1975. *Escape from Evil*. New York: The Free Press; London: Collier Macmillan.
Belmans, Theo G. 1980. *Le sens objectif de l'agir humain: Pour relire la moral conjugale de Saint Thomas*. Vatical Cituy: Libertia Editrice Vaticana.
Bennet, Jonathan Francis. 1995. *The Act Itself*. Oxford: Clarendon Press.
Bidney, David. 1968. Cultural Relativism. *International Encyclopedia of the Social Sciences*, edited by David Sills. Vol. III, col. 544.
Bockle, Franz. 1976. Glaube und Handeln. *Concilium* 120: 641-47.
Bok, Sissela. 1978. *Lying: Moral Choice in Public and Private Life*. New York: Pantheon Books.
Boyle, Joseph. 1977. Double Effect and a Certain Type of Embryotomy. *Irish Theological Quarterly* 44: 303-318.
———. 1978. *Praeter Intentionem* in Aquinas. *The Thomist* 42: 649-665.
———. 1980. Toward Understanding the Principle of Double Effect. *Ethics* 90: 527-538.
———. 1984. The Principle of Double Effect: Good Actions Entangled in Evil. *Moral Theology Today*. St. Louis, MO: The Pope John XXIII Center: 243-260.
Brandt, Richard B. 1979. *A Theory of the Good and the Right*. Oxford: Clarendon.
———. 1983. The Real and Alleged Problems of Utilitarianism. *Hastings Center Report* 13.2: 37-43.
Bratman, Michael.1987. *Intention, Plans, and Practical Reason*. Cambridge, MA: Harvard University Press.

Brock, Dan W. 1973. Recent Work in Utilitarianism. *American Philosophical Quarterly* 10: 241-276.

———. 1983. Can Pleasure Be Bad for You? *Hastings Center Report* 13: 30-34.

Bursten, B. 1972. The Manipulative Personality. *Archives of General Psychiatry* 26: 318-21.

Cahill, Lisa. 1984. Contemporary Challenge to Exceptionless Moral Norms. *Moral Theology Today*. St. Louis, MO: The Pope John XXIII Center: 121-135.

———. 1981. Teleology, Utilitarianism, and Christian Ethics. *Theological Studies* 42: 601-629.

Cavanaugh, Thomas Anthony. 1995. *Double Effect Reasoning: A Critique and Defense*. University of Notre Dame, Diss.

———. 1996. The Intended/Foreseen Distinction's Ethical Relevance. *Philosophical Papers* XXV, no. 3: 179-188.

———. 1997. Aquinas's Account of Double Effect. *The Thomist* 61: 107-121.

Cessario, Romanus. 1988. Casuistry and Revisionism: Structural Similarities in Method and Content" *Humanae Vitae: 20 Anni Dopo Atti del II Congresso Internazionale di Teologia Morale* Rome: citta Nuova Editrice.

———. and Augustine DiNoia, eds, 1999. *Veritatis Splendor and the Renewal of Moral Theology*. Chicago: Midwest Theological Forum.

Christie, Dolores, L. 1990. *Adequately Considered: An American Perspective on Louis Janssens' Personalist Morals*. Louvain: Peeters Press.

Clark, Stephen B. 1980. *Man and Woman in Christ: An Examination of the Roles of Men and Women in Light of Scripture and the Social Sciences*. Ann Arbor, Mich: Servant Books.

Connery, John. 1973. Morality of Consequences: A Critical Appraisal. *Theological Studies* 34: 396-414.

———. 1979. Morality of Consequences. *Readings in Moral Theology* No. 1. Edited by Charles Curran and Richard McCormick, S.J. New York: Paulist.

———. 1981. Catholic Ethics: Has the Norm for Rule-Making Changed? *Theological Studies* 42: 232-250.

———. 1983. The Teleology of Proportionate Reason. *Theological Studies* 44: 489-496.

Curran, Charles. 1969. *A New Look at Christian Morality*. Notre Dame, In: Fides.

———. 1970. *Contemporary Problems in Moral Theology*. Notre Dame, In: Fides.

———. 1979. Utilitarianism and Contemporary Moral Theology: Situating the Debates. *Readings in Moral Theology No. 1: Moral Norms and Catholic Tradition*. Edited by Charles E. Curran and Richard A. McCormick, S.J. New York: Paulist Press.

———. 1979. Moral Theology in Light of Reactions to *Humanae Vitae*. *Transition and Tradition*. Notre Dame: University of Notre Dame Press.

———. 1985. *Directions in Fundamental Moral Theology*. Notre Dame: University of Notre Dame Press.

———. ed. 1990. *Moral Theology Challenges for the Future: Essays in Honor of Richard McCormick*. New York: Paulist Press.

———. 995. The Manual and Casuistry of Aloysius Sabetti. *The Context of Casuistry*. Edited by James Keenan and Thomas Shannon. Washington, DC: Georgetown University Press.

De Broglie, J. 1969. Conflict de devoirs et contraception. *Doctor communis* 22: 154-175.

Dedek, John F. 1979. Intrinsically Evil Acts: An Historical Study of the Mind of St. Thomas. *The Thomist* 43: 385-413.

———. 1980. Premarital Sex: The Theological Argument from Peter Lombard to *Theological Studies* 41: 643-667.

———. 1983. Intrinsically Evil Acts: The Emergence of a Doctrine. *Recherches de Théologie Ancienne et Médiévale* 43: 191-226.

De Finance, J. 1967. *Éthique Générale*. Rome: Gregorian University Press.

Demmer, Klaus. 1974. *Die Lebensentscheidung: ihre moraltheologischen Grundlagen*. Munchen-Paderborn-Wien: Schöningh.

———. 1981. Deuten und Wählen: Vorbermerkungen zu einer moraltheologischen Handlungstheorie. *Gregorianum* 62: 231-275.

———. 1985. *Deuten und Handeln: Grundlagen und Grundfragen der Fundamentalmoral*. Frieburg: Universitätsverlag.

Dewan, Lawrence. 1982. 'Objectum': Notes on the Invention of a Word. *Archives D'Histoire Doctrinale et Littéraire du Moyen Age*: 37-96.

———. 1995. St. Thomas, James Keenan, and the Will. *Science et Esprit* vol. XLVII: 153-176.

Di Ianni, Albert. 1979. The Direct/Indirect Distinction in Morals. *Readings in Moral Theology No. 1: Moral Norms and Catholic Tradition*. Edited by Charles E. Curran and Richard A. McCormick, S.J. New York: Paulist Press.

Donagan, Alan. 1979. *The Theory of Morality*. Chicago: University of Chicago Press.

Duffey, Michael. 1985. The Moral-Nonmoral Distinction in Catholic Ethics. *The Thomist* 49: 343-366.

Evans, Donald. 1971. Paul Ramsey on Exceptionless Moral Rules. *The American Journal of Jurisprudence* 16: 184-214.

Fagothey, A. 1981. *Fagothey's Right and Reason: Ethics in Theory and Practice*. 7th edition. Revised by M. A. Gonsalves. St Louis: Mosby.

Finnis, John. 1980. *Natural Law and Natural Rights*. Oxford and New York: Oxford University Press.

———. 987. The Act of the Person. *Persona, Verita, e Morale*. Rome: Citta Nuova Editrice.

———. 1988. The Consistent Ethic-A Philosophical Critique. *Joseph Bernardin's Consistent Ethic of Life*. Edited by Thomas G. Fuechtmann. Kansas City: Sheed & Ward.

———. 1991a. Object and Intention in Moral Judgments According to Aquinas. *The Thomist* 55: 1-27.

———. 1991b. *Moral Absolutes: Tradition, Revision, and Truth*. Washington D.C: The Catholic University of America Press.

———. 1992. 'Historical Consciousness' and Theological Foundations. *Gilson Lecture*. Toronto: University of Toronto Press.

———. 1993. Reason, Relativism, and Christian Ethics. *Anthropotes* 8:10: 211-230.

Fischer, John Martin, Mark Ravizza, and David Copp. 1993. Quinn on Double Effect: The Problem of Closeness. *Ethics* 103: 707-725.

Flannery, Kevin. 1993. What is Included in a Means to an End? *Gregorianum* 74: 499-512.

Foot, Philippa. 1993. Utilitarianism and the Virtues. *Proceedings and Addresses of the American Philosophical Association* 57: 273-283.

Frankena, William K. 1963. *Ethics*. Englewood Cliffs, N.J.: Prentice-Hall.

———. 1978. McCormick and the Traditional Distinction. *Doing Evil to Achieve Good.* Edited by Ramsey and McCormick. Marquette: Marquette University Press: 145-64.

Freidman, C.M., et al. 1974. The Decision-Making Process and the Outcome of Therapeutic Abortion. *American Journal of Psychiatry* 131: 1332-1337.

Fuchs, Josef. 1970. *Human Values and Christian Morality.* Dublin: Gill and Macmillan.

———. 1971. The Absoluteness of Moral Terms. *Gregorianum* 52: 415-485.

———. 1983. *Personal Responsibility and Christian Morality.* Washington D.C.: Georgetown University Press.

———. 1984. *Christian Ethics in a Secular Arena.* Translated by Bernard Hoose and Brian McNeil. Washington D.C.: Georgetown University Press.

———. 1990. The Absolute in Morality and the Christian Conscience. *Gregorianum* 71: 697-711.

———. 1997. *Für eine menschliche Moral: Grundfragen der theologischen Ethik.* Freiburg, Schweiz: Univ.-Verl [with appendix of 400+ entry bibliography of Fuch's works].

Ghoos, J. 1951. L'Acte a Double Effet Étude de Théolgie Positive. *Ephemerides Theologicae Lovanienses* XXVII: 30-52.

Gleick, James. 1983. Exploring the Labyrinth of the Mind. *New York Times Magazine,* Aug. 21, 1983: 23-24.

Grisez, Germain G. 1970a. Toward a Consistent Natural-Law Ethics of Killing. *The American Journal of Jurisprudence* 15: 64-96.

———. 1970b. *Abortion: The Myths, the Realities, and the Arguments.* Washington: Corpus Books.

———. and Russell Shaw. 1974. *Beyond the New Morality: The Responsibilities of Freedom.* Notre Dame: University of Notre Dame Press.

———. 1978. Against Consequentialism. *American Journal of Jurisprudence* 23: 21-72.

———. and John C. Ford. 1978. Contraception and the Infallibility of the Ordinary Magisterium. *Theological Studies* 39: 263-277.

———. and Joseph Boyle, Jr. 1979. *Life and Death with Liberty and Justice.* Notre Dame: University of Notre Dame Press.

———. 1983. *The Way of the Lord Jesus, Volume I: Christian Moral Principles.* Chicago: Franciscan Herald Press.

———. 1985. Moral Absolutes: A Critique of the View of Josef Fuchs, S.J. *Anthropos* 1:2: 155-201.

Gula, Richard M., S.S. 1978. *What are They Saying About Moral Norms?* New York: Paulist Press.

Gustafson, James. 1966. Context Versus Principles: A Misplaced Debate in Christian Ethics. *New Theology No. 3.* Edited by M. E. Marty and D. G. Peerman. London.

———. 1970. A Protestant Ethical Approach. *The Morality of Abortion.* Edited by John Noonan, Jr. Cambridge: Harvard.

———. 1981. *Ethics from a Theocentric Perspective.* Chicago: University of Chicago Press.

Hallet, Garth. 1983. *Christian Moral Reasoning: An Analytic Guide.* Notre Dame: University of Notre Dame Press.

———. 1995. *Greater Good: The Case for Proportionalism.* Washington, D.C.: Georgetown University Press.

Bibliography 481

Hanigan, James. 1995. Veritatis Splendor and Sexual Ethics. *Veritatis Splendor American Responses*. Kansas City: Sheed & Ward.

Hamel, Edoudard, S.J. 1969. *Les dix paroles: Perspectives bibliques*. Brussels: Desclee de Brouwer.

Häring, B. 1967. *Das Gesetz Christi*, Bd. 3. Freiburg.

Hart, H.L.A. 1968. Intention and Punishment. *Punishment and Responsibility: Essays in the Philsophy of Law*. New York: Oxford University Press.

Hauerwas, Stanley. 1971. Abortion and Normative Ethics. *Cross Currents* Fall: 399-414.

Healy, Edwin, S.J. 1956. *Medical Ethics*. Chicago: Loyola University Press.

Hillers, Delbert R. 1969. *Covenant: The History of a Biblical Idea*. Baltimore: Johns Hopkins Press.

Hoose, Bernard. 1987. *Proportionalism: The American Debate and Its European Roots*. Washington: Georgetown University Press.

Hurley, Dennis E. 1966. A New Moral Principle: When Right and Duty Clash. *The Furrow* 17: 619-22.

———. 1981. *Ethics from a Theocentric Perspective* Chicago: Univ. of Chicago.

Janssens, Louis. 1947. Daden met meerdere gevolgen. *Collectanea Mechliniensia* 32: 621-33.

———. 1963. Morale conjungale et progestogenès. *Ephemerides Theologicae Lovanienses* 39: 787-826.

———. 1972. Ontic Evil and Moral Evil. *Louvain Studies* 4.2: 115-56.

———. 1976-77. Norms and Priorities in a Love Ethics. *Louvain Studies* 6: 207-238.

———. 1987. A Moral Understanding of Some Arguments of Saint Thomas. *Ephemerides Theologicae Lovanienses* 63: 354-360.

———. 1982. St. Thomas Aquinas and the Question of Proportionality. *Louvain Studies* 6.3: 26-46.

———. 1987. Ontic Good and Evil-Premoral Values and Disvalues. *Louvain Studies* 12.1: 62-82.

———. 1994. Teleology and Proportionality: Thoughts about the Encyclical *Veritatis Splendor*. *The Splendor of Accuracy: An Examination of The Assertions Made by Veritatis Splendor*. Edited by Joseph A. Selling and Jan Jans. Grand Rapids, Michigan: William B. Eerdmans Publishing Co. [A complete bibliography of Janssens' career may be found as an appendix in *Personalist Morals: Essays in Honor of Professor Louis Janssens*. Edited by Joseph Selling. Leuven: Leuven University Press, 1988.]

Jensen, Steven John. 1993. *Intrinsically Evil Actions According to St. Thomas Aquinas*. Diss. University of Notre Dame

Jensen, Steven John. 1997. A Defense of Physicalism. *The Thomist* 61: 377-404.

Johnson, Mark. 1992. Proportionalism and a Text of the Young Aquinas: Quodlibetum IX, Q. 7, A. 2. *Theological Studies* 53: 683-699.

Johnstone, Brain V. 1994. Erroneous Conscience in *Veritatis splendor* and the Theological Tradition. *The Splendor of Accuracy: An Examination of the Assertions Made by Veritatis Spendor* Joseph Selling and Jan Jans, eds., Grand Rapids, Michigan: WmB Eerdmans Publishing Co.

Jörgensen, J. 1955. *St Francis of Assisi*. Garden City, New York: Image Books.

Kaczor, Christopher. 1997. Exceptionless Norms in Aristotle? Thomas Aquinas and 20th Century Interpreters of the *Nicomachean Ethics*. *The Thomist* 61: 33-62.

———. 1997. Review of Garth Hallet, *Greater Good: The Case for Proportionalism. The Review of Metaphysics*. L.4: 898-899.

———. 1997. Review of *Veritatis Splendor: American Responses. Studies in Christian Ethics* vol. 10, no.2: 86-87.

———. 1998. Double Effect Reasoning: From Gury to Knauer. *Theological Studies* 59: 297-316.

———. forthcoming. *Proportionalism and the Natural Law Tradition.* Washington, D.C.: Catholic University Press.

———. forthcoming. Distinguishing Intention from Foresight. What is Included in a Means to an End. *International Philosophical Quarterly.*

Kant, Immanuel. 1959. *Foundations of the Metaphysics of Morals.* Translated by Lewis White Beck. Indianapolis: Bobbs Merrill Co.

Kanzian, Christian. 1997. Species Actus Dupliciter Considerari Potest: Thomas von Aquins These und ihre Relevanz für die moderne Handlungstheorie. *Zeitschrift für Katholische Theologie* vol. 119.1: 51-63.

Keane, Philip. 1982. The Objective Moral Order: Reflections on Recent Research. *Theological Studies* 43: 260-278.

Keenan, James. 1992. *Goodness and Rightness in Thomas Aquinas's Summa theologiae.* Washington, D.C.: Georgetown University Press.

———. 1993. Can a Wrong Action Be Good? The Development of Theological Opinion on Erroneous Conscience" *Église et Théologie* 24: 205-219;

Kelly, G. S.J. 1958. *Medico-Moral Problems.* St. Louis: Catholic Hospital Association.

Kennedy, E.C. and V. J. Heckler. 1972. *The Catholic Priest in the United States: Psychological Investigations.* Washington D.C.: United States Catholic Conference.

Kerber, Walter. ed. 1982. *Sittliche Normen.* Düsseldorf: Patmos.

Kiely, Bartholomew M.. 1980. *Psychology and Moral Theology: Lines of Convergence.* Rome: Gregorian University Press.

———. 1985. The Impracticality of Proportionalism. *Gregorianum* 66: 655-86.

Knauer, Peter, S.J. 1970. Überlegungen zur moraltheologischen Prinzipienlehre der Enzyklika '*Humanae vitae*'. *Theologie und Philosophie* 45: 321-60.

———. 1979. The Hermenutical Function of the Principle of Double Effect. *Readings in Moral Theology vol. 1: Moral Norms and Catholic Tradition.* Edited by Charles E. Curran and Richard A. McCormick, S.J. New York: Paulist Press.

———. 1980. Fundamentalethik: teleologische als deontologische Normenbegründung. *Theologie und Philosophie* 55: 60-74.

Kosnik, A., et al. 1977. *Human Sexuality: New Directions in American Catholic Thought.* New York: Paulist Press.

Kramer, H.G. 1935. *The Indirect Voluntary or Voluntarium in Causa*, STD Dissertation, Catholic University of America, Washington.

Lee, Patrick. 1981. Permanence of the Ten Commandments: St. Thomas and His Modern Commentators. *Theological Studies* 42: 422-443.

Levine, C. 1976. Role-Taking Standpoint and Adolescent Use of Kohlberg's Conventional Stages of Moral Judgment. *Journal of Personality and Social Psychology* 34: 41-46.

Liebhart, L. 1963. Sterilisierende Drogen. *Theologisch-Praktische Quartalschrift* 111: 192.

Lidz, T. 1968. *The Person: His Development Throughout the Life Cycle.* New York-London: Basic Books.

Bibliography

Lisska, Anthony J. 1996. *Aquinas's Theory of Natural Law: An Analytic Reconstruction.* Oxford: Clarendon Press.

Lonergan, Bernard. 1958. *Insight: A Study in Human Understanding.* London: Longmans Green.

———. 1973. *Method in Theology.* New York: Herder.

MacDonald, Sebastian. 1983. Can Moral Theology Be Appropriate? *Thomist* 47: 541-49.

Mahoney, 1990. *The Making of Moral Theology.* Oxford: Oxford University Press.

Mangan, Joseph. 1949. An Historical Analysis of the Principle of Double Effect. *Theological Studies* 10: 41-61.

Mansholt, M. 1972. Brief van N. Malsatti (February 9, 1972). *Sélection hebdomadaire du journal 'Le Monde'* from April 6 to 12, 1972; 6-7.

Marcel, Gabriel. 1965. *Being and Having. An Existentialist Diary.* New York: Harper and Row.

Marshner, William H. 1995. The Evaluation of Human Actions. *The Thomist* 59: 347-370.

Mausback-Ermecke. 1961. *Kath. Moraltheologie* Bd. 3. Munster.

May, William E. 1984. Aquinas and Janssens on the Moral Meaning of Human Acts. *The Thomist* 48: 566-606.

McArthur, Harney K. 1960. *Understanding the Sermon on the Mount.* London: Epworth.

McCormick, Richard A., S.J. Notes on Moral Theology. *Theological Studies.* 33: 68-119.

———. 1974. Proxy Consent in the Experimentation Situation. *Perspectives in Biology and Medicine* vol. 18, no.1: 1-20.

———. 1978. *Doing Evil to Achieve Good; Moral Choice in Conflict Situations.* Edited with Paul Ramsey. Chicago: Loyola University Press.

———. 1979a. Abortion: A Changing Morality and Policy? *Bioethics.* 2nd ed. Edited by Thomas Shannon. New York: Paulist.

———. 1979b. Does Religious Faith Add to Ethical Perception? *Introduction to Christian Ethics: A Reader.* Edited by Ronald P. Hamel and Kenneth R. Himes, OFM. New York: Paulist Press.

———. 1981a. *Notes on Moral Theology, 1965 through 1980.* Washington, D.C.: University Press of America.

———. 1981b. Bioethics and Method. *Theology Digest.* 29.4: 303-318.

———. 1982. Notes on Moral Theology: 1981. *Theological Studies.* 43: 69-124.

———. 1983. Notes on Moral Theology: 1982. *Theological Studies.* 44: 71-122.

———. 1984. *Notes on Moral Theology, 1981-1984.* Washington, D.C.: University Press of America.

———. 1985. Notes on Moral Theology: 1984. *Theological Studies* 46: 50-64.

———. 1987. *Health Care and Medicine in the Catholic Tradition.* New York: The Crossroad Publishing Company.

———. 1989a. Moral Theology 1940-1989: An Overview. *Theological Studies* 50: 3-24.

———. 1989b. *The Critical Calling: Reflections on Moral Dilemmas Since Vatican II.* Washington, D.C.: Georgetown University Press.

———. 1994. Some Early Reactions to *Veritatis splendor. Theological Studies* 55: 481-506.

———. . 1995. Birth Regulation, *Veritatis splendor,* and Other ways of Viewing Things. *Église et Théologie* 26: 31-42.

Milhanven, John G. 1968. Moral Absolutes in Thomas Aquinas. *Absolutes in Moral Theology?* Edited by Charles E. Curran. Washington: Corpus.

Mullady, Brian Thomas. 1986. *The Meaning of the Term 'Moral' in St. Thomas Aquinas.* Vatican City: Libreria Editrice Vaticana.

Nozick, Robert. *Anarchy, State, and Utopia.* New York: Basic Books.

O'Connell, Timothy. 1978a. *Changing Roman Catholic Moral Theology: A Study in Josef Fuchs.* Diss. Fordham University, New York.

———. 1978b. *Principles for a Catholic Morality.* New York: Seabury.

Odozor, Paulinus Ikechukwu. 1995. *Richard A. McCormick and the Renewal of Moral Theology.* Notre Dame: University of Notre Dame Press. [Lengthy bibliography of McCormick's work in appendix.]

Ogletree, Thomas. 1983. *The Use of the Bible in Christian Ethics.* Philadelphia: Fortress.

Pinckaers, Servais. 1982. La question des actes intrinsèquement mauvais et le 'proportionalisme.' *Revue Thomiste* 82: 181-212.

———. 1986. *Ce qu'on ne peut jamais faire.* Editions Universitaires, Fribourg.

Porter, Jean. 1989. Moral Rules and Moral Actions: A Comparison of Aquinas and Modern Moral Theology. *The Journal of Religious Ethics* 17: 123-149.

———. 1990. *The Recovery of Virtue: The Relevance of Aquinas for Christian Ethics.* Louisville, KY: John Knox Press.

———. 1995. The Moral Act in *Veritatis splendor* and in *Aquinas's Summa theologiae*: A Comparative Analysis. *Veritatis splendor: American Responses.* Edited by Michael E. Allsopp & John J. O'Keefe. Kansas City, MO: Sheed and Ward.

———. 1996. 'Direct' and 'Indirect' in Grisez's Moral Theory. *Theological Studies* 57: 611-632.

Quay, Paul. 1961. Contraception and Conjugal Love. *Theological Studies* 22: 18-40.

———. 1983. The Unity and Structure of the Human Act. *Listening* 18:3: 260-274.

———. 1985. The Disvalue of Ontic Evil. *Theological Studies* 46: 262-286.

Quinn, W.S. 1989. Actions, Intentions, and Consequences: The Doctrine of Double Effect. *Philosophy and Public Affairs* 18: 334-351.

Quirk, Michael. 1997. Why the Debate on Proportionalism is Misconceived. *Modern Theology* 13: 501-524.

Rachels, James. 1995. Active and Passive Euthanasia. *New England Journal of Medicine* vol. 292, no. 2: 78-80.

Rahner, Karl, SJ. 1972. The Problem of Genetic Manipulation. *Theological Investigations.* New York: Herder and Herder.

Ramsey, Paul. 1961 *War and the Christian Conscience: How Shall Modern War be Conducted Justly?* Durham, N.C.: Duke University Press.

———. 1968. The Case of Curious Exception. *Norm and Context in Christian Ethics.* Edited by Gene Outka and Paul Ramsey. Philadelphia: Fortress.

———. 1978. Incommensurability and Indeterminancy in Moral Choice. *Doing Evil to Achieve Good; Moral Choice in Conflict Situations.* Edited by Ramsey and McCormick. Chicago: Loyola University Press.

———. 1978. *Basic Christian Ethics.* Chicago: Univ., of Chicago.

Rawls, John. 1971. *A Theory of Justice.* Cambridge, Mass: Harvard University Press.

Rendu, C. 1965. La regulation des naissances dans le cadre familial et chretien. *Nouvelle revue théologique* 87: 606-31.

Rhonheimer, Martin. 1993. 'Ethics of Norms' and the Lost Virtues: Searching the Roots of the Crisis of Ethical Reasoning. *Anthropotes* IX, 2: 231-243.

———. 1994. Intrinsically Evil Acts and the Moral Viewpoint: Clarifying a Central Teaching of Veritatis Splendor. *The Thomist* 58: 1- 39.

———. 1995. Intentional Actions and the Meaning of Object: A Reply to Richard McCormick. *The Thomist* 59: 279-311.

Rigali, Nobert, S.J. 1983. The Moral Act. *Horizons* 10/2: 252-66.

Robinson, J.A.T. 1964. *Christian Moral Today*. London.

———. 1979. *Wrestling with Romans*. Philadelphia: Westminster Press.

Robbins, Lionel. 1957. *The Economic Problem in Peace and War: Some Reflections on Objectives and Mechanisms*. London: Macmillan.

Rowntree, Stephen, S.J. 1982. Ethical Issues of Life and Death. *Thought* 57: 449-64.

Ruf, A.K., and E. J. Cooper. 1982. *Grundkurs: Sexualmoral*. Freiburg: Herder.

Salzman, Todd. 1995. *Deontology and Teleology: An Investigation of the Normative Debate in Roman Catholic Moral Theology*. Leuven: Leuven University Press.

Scheffler, Samuel. 1982. *The Rejection of Consequentialism: A Philosophical Investigation of the Considerations Underlying Rival Moral Conceptions*. Oxford: Clarendon Press.

Scheler, Max. 1973. *Formalism in Ethics and Non-Formal Ethics of Value*. Evanston: Northwestern.

Schilling, O. 1957. *Handbuch der Moraltheologie* Bd. 3. Stuttgart.

Schillebeeckx, E., O.P. 1963. *Marriage: Human Reality and Saving Mystery*. Translated by N.D. Smith. New York: Sheed and Ward.

Schnackenburg, Rudolf. 1965. *The Moral Teaching of the New Testament*. New York: Herder and Herder.

Schockenhoff, Eberhard. 1996. *Naturrecht und Menschenwürde*. Mainz: Matthias-Grünewald-Verlag.

Scholz, Franz. 1975. Durch ethische Grenzsituation aufgewortene Normenproblem. *Theologische-praktische Quartalschrift* 123: 341-355.

———. 1979. Problems on Norms Raised by Ethical Borderline Situations: Beginnings of a Solution in Thomas Aquinas and Bonaventure. *Readings in Moral Theology vol. 1: Moral Norms and Catholic Tradition*. Edited by Charles E. Curran and Richard A. McCormick, S.J. New York: Paulist Press.

Schüller, Bruno. S.J. 1970a. Zur Problematik allgemein verbindlicher ethischer Grundsätze. *Theologie und Philosophie* 45: 1-23.

———. 1970b. Typen ethischer Argumentation in der katholischen Moraltheologie. *Theologie und Philosophie* 45: 526-550.

———. 1978. The Double Effect in Catholic Thought: A Reevaluation. *Doing Evil to Achieve Good: Moral Choice in Conflict Situations*. Edited by McCormick and Ramsey. Chicago: Loyola University Press.

———. 1979a. Direct Killing/Indirect Killing. *Readings in Moral Theology No. 1: Moral Norms and Catholic Tradition*. Edited by Charles E. Curran and Richard A. McCormick, S.J. New York: Paulist Press.

———. 1979b. Various Types of Grounding for Ethical Norms. *Readings in Moral Theology No. 1: Moral Norms and Catholic Tradition*. Edited by Charles E. Curran and Richard A. McCormick, S.J. New York: Paulist Press.

———. 1980. Christianity and the New Man: The Moral Dimension—Specificity of Christian Ethics. *Theology and Discovery: Essays in Honor of Karl Rahner S.J.* Milwaukee, WI: Marquette University Press.

———. 1986. *Wholly Human: Essays on the Theory and Language of Morality*. Translated by Peter Heinegg. Washington, D.C.: Georgetown University Press.

Selling, Joseph. 1980. The Problem of Reinterpreting the Principle of Double Effect. *Louvain Studies* 8: 47-62.

———. 1994. Louis Janssens' Interpretation of Aquinas: A Response to Recent Criticism. *Louvain Studies* 19: 66.

———. 1994. The Context and the Arguments of *Veritatis splendor*. *The Splendor of Accuracy: An Examination of the Assertions Made by Veritatis Splendor*. Edited by Joseph A. Selling and Jan Jans. Grand Rapids, Michigan: William B. Eerdmans Publishing Co.

Sen, Amartya. 1982. Rights and Agency. *Philosophy and Public Affairs* 11/1: 19-32.

———. 1983. Evaluator Relativity and Consequential Evaluation. *Philosophy and Public Affairs* 12/2: 113-132.

Smart, J.J.C. 1967. Utilitarianism. *Encyclopedia of Philosophy* ed. Paul Edwards, editor New York: Macmillan, vol. 8: 210.

Smith, Janet E. 1991. *Humanae Vitae: A Generation Later*. Washington, D.C.: The Catholic University of America Press.

———. 1999. Moral Terminology and Proportionalism. *Recovering Nature: Essays in Natural Philosophy, Ethics, and Metaphysics in Honor of Ralph McInerny*. Ed. John P. O'Callaghan and Thomas S. Hibbs. Notre Dame: University of Notre Dame Press.

Socarides, C.W. 1978. The Sexual Deviations and the Diagnostic Manual. *American Journal of Psychotherapy* 32: 414-426.

Spohn, William, S.J. 1983. The Reasoning Heart. *Theological Studies* 44: 30-52.

Stanke, Gerhard. 1984. *Die Lehre von den "Quellen der Moralität." Darstellung und Diskussion der neuscholastischen Aussagen und neuerer Ansätze*, Studien zur Geschichte der katholischen Moraltheologie, 26. Regensburg: Friedrich Pustet.

Stevens, Clifford. 1995. A Matter of Credibility. *Veritatis Splendor: American Responses*. Edited by Michael E. Allsopp & John J. O'Keefe. Kansas City, MO: Sheed and Ward.

Sunshine, Edward R. 1995. 'The Splendor of Truth' and the Rhetoric of Morality. *Veritatis Splendor: American Responses*. Edited by Michael E. Allsopp & John J. O'Keefe. Kansas City, MO: Sheed and Ward.

Talvacchia, Kathleen and Mary Elizabeth Walsh. 1995. *The Splendor of Truth*: A Feminist Critique. *Veritatis Splendor: American Responses*. Edited by Michael E. Allsopp & John J. O'Keefe. Kansas City, MO: Sheed and Ward.

Tooley, Michael. 1972. Abortion and Infanticide. *Philosophy and Public Affairs* 2: 37-65.

———. 1993. *Abortion and Infanticide*. Oxford: Clarendon Press.

Ugorji, L. I. 1993. *The Principle of Double Effect; A Critical Appraisal of its Traditional Understanding and its Modern Reinterpretation*. Frankfurt am Main: Peter Lang.

Vacek, Edward, S.J. 1982. Scheler's Phenomenology of Love. *Journal of Religion* 62: 156-177.

———. 1984. God's Action and Ours. *Emmanuel* 90: 370-76.

———. 1985. Proportionalism: One View of the Debate. *Theological Studies* 46: 287-314.

Van der Marck, William. 1964. De autonome menselijke samenleving als sakrament van de Godsgemeenschap. *Tijdschrift voor Theologie* IV: 151-176.

———. 1967. *Toward a Christian Ethic: A Renewal of Moral Theology*. Westminster: Newman Press.

Bibliography

Van der Poel, Cornelius. 1968. The Principle of Double Effect. *Absolutes in Moral Theology*. Edited by Charles Curran. Washington: Corpus Books.
Vandervelde, George. 1983. Creation and Cross in the Christology of Edward Schillebeeckx. *Journal of Ecumenical Studies* 20: 257-71.
Wallraff, H.J. 1968. Die katholische Soziallehre—ein Gefüge von offenen Sätzen. *Eigentumspolitik, Arbeit und Mitbestimmung*. Cologne.
Walter, James J. 1984. Proportionate Reason and its Three Levels of Inquiry: Structuring the Ongoing Debate. *Louvain Studies* 10: 30-40.
———. 1995. Proportionalism. *The Harper Collins Encyclopedia of Catholicism*. Edited by Richard McBrien. San Francisco: Harper San Francisco: 1058.
Weiß, A. M. 1996. *Sittlicher Wert und nichtsittliche Werte. Zur Relevanz der Unterscheidung in der moraltheologischen Diskussion um deontologische Normen*. Freiburg: Universitätsverlag Freiburg Schweiz.
Williams, Bernard and J.J.C. Smart. 1973. *Utilitarianism For and Against*. Cambridge: Cambridge University Press.
———. ed. 1982. *Utilitarianism and Beyond*. Cambridge: Cambridge University Press.
———. 1981. Utilitarianism and Moral Self-Indulgence. *Moral Luck: Philosophical Papers 1973-1980*. Cambridge: Cambridge University Press.
Wolbert, Werner. 1992. *Vom Nutzen der Gerechtigkeit. Zur Diskussion um Utilitarismus und Teleologische Theorie*. Freiburg: Universitätsverlag.
———. 1994. Die 'in sich schlechten' Handlungen und der Konsequentialismus. *Moraltheologie im Abseits?* Edited by Dietmar Mieth, Freiburg, Basel, Wien: Herder.
———. 1996. Konsistenzprobleme im Tötungsverbot. *Freiburger Zeitschrift für Philosophy und Theologie* 43: 199-240.
Zalba, M, S.J. 1957. *Theologiae Moralis Summa* vol. II. Madrid: La Editorial Catolica.

INDEX

Abelard, 100, 376
abortion, 9, 162, 166-168, 173, 178, 181-184, 188-189, 209-210, 213-215, 217, 277, 289, 292, 307-308, 338, 341, 368, 377, 390, 416, 418, 430, 432, 454, 469, 481-482, 484, 487
absolute, 9, 13, 32-33, 50, 53, 60-64, 66, 69-71, 74-75, 80, 82, 90, 95-96, 98, 103-105, 107-108, 126, 131, 142, 145, 151-152, 154-155, 158, 170, 179, 190-191, 204, 215-218, 233, 235-236, 257, 277, 309, 317, 320-321, 324-325, 338-339, 345, 353, 355, 357-360, 363, 368, 375, 377, 388, 399, 412-414, 435, 437, 439, 444-445, 464, 481
absoluteness, 3, 6, 60-63, 66-67, 75-76, 80-81, 85, 87, 92, 94, 130, 152, 191, 214, 317, 321-322, 326, 339, 355, 405, 481
adultery, 21, 24, 59, 110, 112, 171, 186, 215, 295, 302, 307-308, 311, 315-317, 320, 335, 342, 354, 357-359, 363, 366-368, 376, 439, 444-445, 450, 470
amputation, 38, 44-45, 52, 179, 385-386, 395, 401
Aquinas, 3, 10, 12, 18, 20, 26, 72, 89, 98, 270, 279, 292-293, 296, 309, 320, 360, 374, 377, 379, 382-385, 390-392, 406, 424, 429, 474, 476, 478-480, 482-487
Aristotle, 39, 108, 110, 125, 245, 249, 274, 278-279, 289-290, 383, 418, 421, 446, 453, 482
art, 102, 108, 113, 134, 145-146, 277, 390, 435
Augustine, 19-20, 23, 134, 361, 370, 373, 375-377, 389-390, 392, 431, 479

behavior, 16, 32, 39, 46, 49, 51, 54, 56, 61, 63-64, 66-68, 71-80, 83, 89, 92-93, 124, 131, 134, 140, 147, 206, 222, 242, 258, 265, 274, 278, 285, 290, 321-322, 325, 334-335, 337, 347, 353, 376-377, 381-382, 414, 445-446, 453, 457-458, 465, 468

Bentham, 240, 248, 250, 253-254, 261, 269, 289-290
Bonaventure, 486
bonum ex integra causa, 298
borderline situations, 486
Boyle, 14, 291, 294, 372, 389, 414-415, 417, 423-424, 426-432, 435-436, 478, 481

Caiaphas, 372
Cajetan, 391
capital punishment, 88, 186, 201-202, 251-252, 277, 316, 324, 385-387
Casti Connubii, 52, 59, 373
character, 16, 22, 27, 31, 54, 56-57, 62, 66-67, 78, 90, 95, 114, 137-138, 153, 159, 161, 185, 195, 207, 209, 213, 224, 247, 252, 258, 279, 322, 326, 348, 350, 367, 371, 379, 382, 389, 415-416, 421, 443, 448, 454, 464, 475
Church, 10-11, 16, 51, 62, 64-71, 75, 78, 95-97, 166, 168, 217, 290, 295-296, 306-309, 319, 325-326, 328, 330-331, 333-334, 340-341, 353-356, 359-370, 387, 405, 411, 460, 468
circumstances, 10-11, 28, 30-31, 44-47, 51, 56, 58, 78, 84-88, 114, 128, 132, 148, 151, 154-155, 162, 164, 170, 177, 181, 189-190, 194, 201, 204, 206, 208, 212, 216, 227, 233-235, 293, 298, 301-303, 307, 309, 315, 324, 397, 399, 402, 408-409, 413-415, 419, 439, 459, 467
Collins, 389-390, 464, 488
commensuration of goods, 270, 275, 347
commitments, 239, 241, 255, 275-277, 287-288, 358, 388, 424-425
conflict situations, 6, 9, 14, 18, 179, 184, 195, 197, 200-201, 208, 210, 244, 393, 403, 464, 471, 476, 484-486
Connery, 3, 6, 8, 15, 18, 295, 369, 395, 406, 410, 462, 479
conscience, 49, 56-57, 62, 74-75, 90, 92-93, 96, 98, 121, 163, 213-215, 228, 232, 239, 273-274, 293, 318-

Index

319, 327, 343-344, 349, 379, 419, 481-483, 485
consequence, 41, 43, 65, 72, 75, 82, 90, 119, 123, 150-152, 154-161, 163, 165, 230, 234, 249, 282, 315, 442, 445
consequentialism, 3, 6, 239-249, 257-261, 265-267, 271, 276, 279, 282, 284-292, 314, 369, 412, 417-418, 437, 456, 462, 464, 468-469, 476, 481, 486
contraception, 10-11, 51-56, 98, 148, 155, 161, 166, 190-193, 289, 317, 320, 335, 338, 349, 366-370, 460, 467-473, 475-476, 479, 481
craniotomy, 157
Curran, 6, 95-98, 165, 169, 195, 206, 237, 403, 405, 462-463, 479-480, 483, 485-486, 488

Decalogue, 356-358, 366, 370, 372
Dedek, 237, 480
deliberation, 101, 112, 139, 244, 258-262, 264, 279, 344, 346, 378-379, 381, 450, 454
desire, 35-36, 151, 153, 210, 219, 250-254, 265, 269, 279, 382, 387, 399, 406, 431, 446, 450, 452, 468, 470, 475
deterrence, 186, 294
disproportionate, 178, 182, 206, 208, 211, 269, 271, 400, 404
discernment, 65, 76, 93, 98, 209, 336, 361, 388, 431, 465
dissent, 326, 353, 369
doing evil, 6, 15, 18, 329, 392, 403-405, 435, 464, 471, 481, 484-486

efficiency, 241, 245, 249, 270, 344
effectiveness, 80, 137, 220, 234, 312, 347, 374
Enlightenment, 371, 385, 412
euthanasia, 9, 166, 289, 377, 478, 485
exceptionless moral norms, 10, 12, 15, 376, 462, 479
exceptions, 32, 43, 45, 51, 80-84, 97, 144, 235, 308-309, 323, 345, 357, 415, 419, 435, 444
exegesis, 63, 325, 353, 367, 369

fairness, 307, 345, 387-389
faith, 17, 57, 60-61, 63, 67-68, 70, 90, 93, 129, 131-133, 140-141, 143, 162, 208, 218, 226, 236-237, 257, 278, 289-290, 292, 319, 321, 327-331, 334, 348, 353, 355, 357-364, 366-367, 369-372, 374, 376, 384, 425, 463, 484
family, 8, 47, 78, 91, 152, 171, 191, 199, 216, 225, 268, 282, 289, 293, 338, 342, 368, 425, 429, 469-473, 476
feeling, 119-120, 141, 263, 293, 348, 382, 422, 456, 458
feelings, 109, 130, 239, 281, 371, 376, 382, 386, 388-389, 402
finis operantis, 28-29, 38, 42, 48, 58, 102-103
finis operis, 28-29, 34, 38, 42, 46, 48, 53, 57-58, 100, 102-103, 110, 139, 146-147, 169, 178
Finnis, 3, 7-8, 12-16, 289, 294, 369, 371-375, 377-378, 381, 384, 387-389, 391, 435, 467-468, 480
fontes moralitatis, 28, 84
Ford, 166, 213, 254, 294, 367-368, 370, 481
fornication, 21, 24, 309, 315, 368, 376
free choice, 20, 23, 58, 67, 216, 218, 226-227, 261, 291, 317, 321, 327-328, 346, 348, 359, 371-372, 378, 382-384, 389
Fuchs, 3, 6-8, 12-13, 18, 60, 86, 96-97, 178, 214, 237, 307, 310, 317-330, 332-339, 342-345, 347-357, 359, 364-366, 369, 392, 405-406, 411-414, 416, 419, 434-436, 474, 481, 485

genocide, 339, 377
God, 17, 40, 49, 61-63, 65, 67-68, 95, 98, 106, 125, 134, 139-140, 163-164, 167, 202, 211, 217, 223-225, 229, 235-237, 249, 256-257, 277-278, 289, 291-292, 295, 317, 319-321, 325, 327-332, 339-342, 350-353, 355-362, 365-367, 370-374, 378, 382-384, 390-392, 406-407, 409, 411-413, 422, 424, 429, 433-435, 442, 450, 453, 459, 463, 467, 475, 487

Golden Rule, 329, 345, 388
good faith, 57, 129, 133, 162
grace, 40, 60, 134, 210, 237, 250, 319-321, 327, 330-331, 341, 372
Grisez, 3, 6-8, 12, 14-16, 18, 170-171, 175, 184-190, 195, 198-199, 213-214, 239, 253, 271-272, 291, 317, 367-370, 372, 374, 388-391, 399, 406, 412, 414-415, 417, 423-432, 434-436, 449-450, 463-464, 481, 485
Gury, 305, 315, 483

hard cases, 410
Hallet, 17-18, 410, 481, 483
historicity, 72-73, 81, 88, 144, 321, 326, 334, 414
Hoose, 467, 481-482
Humanae Vitae, 82-83, 96-98, 167, 317, 368-369, 373, 412, 460, 464, 467-468, 476, 479, 483, 487
human nature, 72-73, 115, 142, 288, 296, 320, 330, 341, 355, 427, 433, 450
hysterectomy, 157

incommensurability, 252, 257, 275
infanticide, 487
injury, 26-27, 31-32, 36, 46, 98, 183-184, 301, 387
infallibility, 70, 359-360, 362-365, 367-368, 370, 481
intention, 13, 22-23, 26-29, 31, 33-34, 37, 44-45, 48-49, 52-54, 57, 83-88, 102, 110, 114-118, 126, 128-129, 132-133, 135, 137, 146, 151, 166, 169, 171, 173, 176-178, 182, 184, 190, 195-196, 198-199, 205, 210, 214, 217, 222-223, 230-234, 297-303, 305-306, 310, 313, 315-316, 323-324, 349-351, 368, 376-379, 381-386, 392, 395-396, 401, 415, 429-430, 432, 439, 446-447, 475, 478, 480, 482-483
integral human fulfillment, 332, 340, 357
intrinsece mala, 82, 392
intrinsically evil acts, 10, 14, 149, 246, 324, 439, 480, 486

Janssens, 3, 6, 8, 12-13, 18, 33, 96, 100, 300-301, 303, 402, 404-405, 407, 479, 482, 484, 487
Jew, 64, 277, 325, 366, 390
Jewish, 64-65, 71, 257, 291-292, 355-356, 366, 369, 389
John Paul II, 8, 16, 331, 367, 369, 464

Kingdom, 63, 65, 325, 330-333, 340-342, 353-354, 357-359, 366, 378, 382, 389
Knauer, 3, 6, 8, 11-12, 15-16, 18, 98, 130, 147, 169-171, 195, 207, 213, 296-297, 299, 303-305, 312-313, 394, 399, 404, 449, 451, 462, 464, 483

lesser evil, 15, 82-83, 158, 189, 194, 197, 200, 205, 212, 242, 244-245, 266, 292, 304, 353, 376, 440, 472
Lombard, 376-377, 380, 480
love, 18, 48, 55-56, 60-61, 63, 67, 70, 81, 90, 97-98, 107-108, 110, 118, 123, 130-131, 140, 169, 193, 198, 209-212, 219, 225, 245, 250, 257, 284, 287, 289, 319, 321, 328-330, 341-342, 350-351, 356, 365, 369, 371-372, 378, 385, 389-390, 404, 408, 414-416, 418, 430-431, 434-435, 452, 464, 474-476, 482, 487

McCormick, 3, 6, 8-9, 11, 13-19, 58-59, 95-97, 165-166, 192, 237, 244, 271-272, 284, 289, 292, 314, 316, 385, 390, 395, 397-400, 402-406, 409, 414-416, 418, 423, 427-430, 432, 434-436, 444, 462-464, 468-470, 472, 479-481, 483-486
MacIntyre, 406, 462, 464
Mahoney, 17, 484
Mangan, 57, 126, 213, 484
Martyr, 375
masturbation, 468
maximize, 13, 408, 418, 440
May, 2, 8, 10-16, 18, 28-29, 31, 33, 35-39, 41-45, 47, 49-53, 55-56, 58-59, 63, 66, 69-70, 72, 75-76, 79, 82-85, 87, 89, 91-93, 95, 109-110, 119-121, 123, 129-130, 132, 136, 150-164, 167, 169-170, 172-173, 176,

Index

179-180, 182, 185-195, 197-199, 201-204, 215-217, 219, 221, 223, 226-229, 231-232, 234, 236-237, 239, 242, 248, 251, 258, 266, 270-271, 273, 290, 294, 296-297, 299-300, 303-304, 307, 309-315, 321, 323-325, 341-342, 344, 350-351, 353, 365, 369-370, 372-376, 378, 380-388, 390, 396, 402, 405-407, 410, 412-415, 418-422, 424-427, 429, 431-435, 437, 439-441, 445-447, 449-453, 455-464, 467, 469-471, 473-474, 482, 484

Milhaven, 97, 237

Mill, 261, 290

means, 2, 10, 12-13, 27-29, 31, 33, 37-38, 41-43, 53-56, 59, 64, 66, 71, 74, 81, 85-86, 89, 95, 102, 104-108, 111-116, 118-119, 121-132, 134, 136-139, 141, 144-147, 149-150, 152-153, 155, 157-160, 162, 164-167, 170-173, 175-176, 178-180, 186-188, 191, 193, 195, 197-202, 204, 206-207, 209-212, 214, 217, 223, 225, 227, 230-231, 240, 244, 249, 251-252, 255-256, 260, 263, 268-272, 285-286, 288, 290-292, 294, 297-298, 301, 304, 306, 309-313, 315, 323, 326, 330-331, 333, 338-339, 341, 343, 345-347, 350, 352, 359, 373, 377-385, 387, 390-392, 394, 397-398, 401-402, 404, 407-408, 411-412, 415, 417, 420, 429-430, 435, 437-439, 458, 462-463, 467-468, 470-472, 474, 476, 480, 483

merit, 332, 439

moral absolutes, 3, 7, 317-318, 320, 324, 335-340, 342, 351-353, 356-357, 363, 366, 368-369, 372, 375-376, 378, 382, 389-390, 467-468, 480-481, 485

moral evil, 3, 6, 10, 13, 26, 30, 41, 48, 53, 55, 83, 100, 118, 120, 125, 128, 131, 147, 149, 151-153, 158-159, 164, 169-170, 190-192, 194-195, 197, 216, 235, 260, 297, 302, 306-308, 311, 374, 392, 404, 438, 482

moral norms, 6, 10, 12, 15-16, 60-63, 65-66, 71-73, 76, 80-81, 83, 85-87, 92, 160, 165, 196, 206, 215-216, 236-237, 244-245, 274-276, 279-280, 285, 292-293, 317, 319-320, 322-325, 327, 332, 336, 340, 342, 344-345, 355, 357, 365, 367-368, 370, 373, 376, 380, 382, 388, 392, 403-404, 435, 437, 455, 458, 462, 479-481, 483, 486

moral principles, 240, 249, 347-348, 369, 388, 390-391, 468, 481

murder, 31-32, 34, 43, 45-47, 49, 51, 88-89, 117, 127, 143, 154-155, 167, 172-173, 222, 286, 295, 324, 380, 390, 417, 465, 469

natural law, 6, 16, 18, 33, 70-72, 74-76, 80, 89, 95-96, 98, 240, 275, 289, 321, 326, 330, 337, 340, 364, 366-367, 407, 414, 433, 480, 484

negative norms, 83, 357, 444-445

New Testament, 63, 66, 95, 236-237, 325, 329, 354-356, 358, 369-370, 389, 486

noncombatants, 192-193, 206-207, 366, 378-379

O'Connell, 406-407, 418, 433, 485

Old Testament, 65, 295, 342, 356

pain, 119, 152-153, 191, 203-204, 211-212, 252-253, 268, 385-386, 392, 423, 450

St. Paul, 228, 304, 325, 331, 337, 352, 354, 356, 358, 373-374, 425

per se, 31, 57, 107, 117, 127-129, 132, 135, 147, 164, 376, 383-384, 391, 442

Paul VI, 167, 293, 367-369, 373, 464, 466

Pius XI, 51-54, 167, 367

Pius XII, 55, 59, 167, 331, 367

practical knowledge, 77

practical principles, 184

premoral evil, 13, 83, 179-180, 182, 203, 221, 297, 307, 310, 316, 324, 349, 351, 374, 394, 401, 470-472

proportionality, 18, 39, 196, 206-210, 352, 395, 403, 430, 482

Providence, 20, 353, 357, 374-375, 378, 384, 463

prudence, 39-40, 207, 347, 389, 435, 442
punishment, 47, 88, 186, 190, 201-202, 251-252, 277, 316, 318, 324, 385-387, 482

Quay, 3, 6, 8, 14, 18, 215, 232, 406, 463, 485

rape, 173, 176, 196, 202, 410
Rahner, 68, 86, 93, 95, 348-349, 485-486
rationalization, 15, 281-282, 284, 287, 318, 349
religion, 255, 277-278, 285, 292, 390, 453, 487
responsibility, 50-51, 56, 93-94, 99, 150-151, 156, 164, 272-273, 280, 286, 292, 294, 318, 335, 342, 353, 362, 374-375, 380, 387-388, 390, 417, 425, 434-436, 447, 453-454, 472, 481-482
revelation, 62, 66, 68, 132, 134, 218, 224, 295, 321, 355-362, 365-369
revenge, 118, 205, 329, 343, 350, 386-387

Scholz, 392, 486
Schüller, 3, 6, 8, 13, 15, 18, 95-98, 148, 156, 165, 187, 190-194, 196-198, 201, 214, 237, 292, 297, 315, 384, 392, 408, 473-474, 476, 486
self-defense, 21, 26, 31, 34, 42, 46-47, 83, 115-118, 126-127, 142, 144, 159, 164, 166, 169, 173, 179, 181-182, 184, 186, 201-202, 228, 270, 301, 303-305, 313, 315-316, 350, 385, 415, 443, 469-471
self-destruction, 341, 359
sex, 78, 217, 358, 368, 381-382, 466, 480
side effects, 16, 185, 244, 256, 273, 352, 375, 380-383, 385-387
situation ethics, 47-49, 86, 215, 415
slavery, 335, 341, 410, 412, 446
states of affairs, 287, 378, 380
sterilization, 148, 166-168, 203-204, 381
suicide, 89, 148-150, 155, 166, 289, 324, 350, 377-378, 389, 450, 464, 478

technical, 121, 209, 250, 270, 274, 279-280, 286, 330, 338, 344, 347, 465, 473
Ten Commandments, 295, 356, 370, 392, 483
theft, 28, 43, 46, 51, 59, 114, 129, 390
Thomas Aquinas, 3, 10, 12, 18, 20, 26, 98, 270, 279, 292, 296, 320, 360, 474, 476, 482-483, 485-486
transplantation, 178, 182, 386

utilitarianism, 9, 187-188, 245-249, 289, 293, 402, 405, 408, 417, 419, 421, 426, 434, 476-480, 487-488
Vacek, 3, 7-8, 406, 416, 433, 435, 467, 487
value, 26, 28, 33-38, 40, 42, 44, 46, 49, 51, 53, 55-56, 58-59, 62, 71, 76-77, 81, 83-87, 89, 93, 97, 123, 126, 129-130, 136-137, 144, 152, 158-159, 163, 169, 177, 179, 181, 185, 189, 191, 194, 197-198, 204, 207-208, 211, 216-221, 223-236, 238, 245, 249, 252-253, 263, 269-270, 285, 290, 292, 299, 315, 322-323, 343, 345, 348, 359, 387, 394-399, 401-402, 404, 407, 409, 411, 414, 416-426, 428, 430-431, 433-435, 440, 446, 448-449, 451, 458, 464, 469, 486
values, 3, 6, 13-14, 18, 34-36, 50, 54, 59, 63, 65, 77-79, 88-89, 91, 94, 96-97, 120, 122-123, 129, 140, 144, 164, 180, 188, 190, 195, 201, 203, 206, 208, 215-230, 232-238, 252, 256, 260, 265, 270, 272, 277, 280, 289-290, 292, 299, 305, 312-314, 319-320, 322-324, 343, 348-349, 397, 402-404, 408-409, 413-414, 416-424, 426, 428, 430-431, 435, 448-451, 456-458, 463-464, 466, 469, 472, 474, 481-482, 485
virtue, 40, 72, 82, 87, 91, 103, 107-108, 114, 117, 123, 127, 133, 212, 237, 248, 260, 328, 347, 411, 421, 462, 464, 475, 485
vocation, 40, 137, 330-332, 341, 353, 388, 464-465

Williams, 213, 287, 289, 294, 465, 477, 488

Marquette Studies in Philosophy
Andrew Tallon, Editor
Standing orders accepted
denotes available as eBook

Harry Klocker, S.J. *William of Ockham and the Divine Freedom.* ISBN 0-87462-001-5. 141 pages, pp., index. $15. Second edition, reviewed, corrected and with a new Introduction.*

Margaret Monahan Hogan. *Finality and Marriage.* ISBN 0-87462-600-5. 122 pp. Paper. $15.*

Gerald A. McCool, S.J. *The Neo-Thomists.* ISBN 0-87462-601-1. 175 pp. Paper. $20.*

Max Scheler. *Ressentiment.* ISBN 0-87462-602-1. 172 pp. Paper. $20. New Introduction by Manfred S. Frings.*

Knud Løgstrup. *Metaphysics.* Translated by Dr. Russell Dees ISBN 0-87462-603-X. Volume I, 342 pp. Paper. $35.* ISBN 0-67462-607-2. Volume II, 402 pp. Paper. $40. Two volume set priced at $70.*

Howard P. Kainz. *Democracy and the "Kingdom of God".* ISBN 0-87462-610-2. 250 pp. Paper. $25.

Manfred Frings. *Max Scheler. A Concise Introduction into the World of a Great Thinker* ISBN 0-87462-605-6. 200 pp. Paper. $20. Second ed., rev. New Foreword by the author.*

G. Heath King. *Existence Thought Style: Perspectives of a Primary Relation, portrayed through the work of Søren Kierkegaard.* English edition by Timothy Kircher. ISBN 0-87462-606-4. 187 pp., index. Paper. $20.*

Augustine Shutte. *Philosophy for Africa.* ISBN 0-87462-608-0. 184 pp. Paper. $20.

Paul Ricoeur. *Key to Husserl's Ideas I.* Translated by Bond Harris and Jacqueline Bouchard Spurlock. With a Foreword by Pol Vandevelde. ISBN 0-87462-609-9. 176 pp., index. Paper. $20.*

Karl Jaspers. *Reason and Existenz.* Afterword by Pol Vandevelde. ISBN 0-87462-611-0. 180 pp. Paper. $20.

Gregory R. Beabout. *Freedom and Its Misuses: Kierkegaard on Anxiety and Despair* ISBN 0-87462-612-9. 192 pp., index. Paper. $20.*

Manfred S. Frings. *The Mind of Max Scheler. The First Comprehensive Guide Based on the Complete Works* ISBN 0-87462-613-7. 328 pp. Paper. $35.*

Claude Pavur. *Nietzsche Humanist.* ISBN 0-87462-614-5. 214 pp., index. Paper. $25.*

Pierre Rousselot. *Intelligence: Sense of Being, Faculty of God.* Translation of *L'Intellectualisme de saint Thomas* with a Foreword and Notes by Andrew Tallon. ISBN 0-87462-615-3. 236 pp., index. Paper. $25.*

Immanuel Kant. *Critique of Practical Reason.* Translation by H.W. Cassirer. Edited by G. Heath King and Ronald Weitzman and with an Introduction by D.M. MacKinnon. ISBN 0-87462-616-1. Paper. 218 pp. $20.*

Gabriel Marcel's Perspectives on *The Broken World*. Translated by Katharine Rose Hanley. *The Broken World,* A Four-Act Play followed by "Concrete Approaches to Investigating the Ontological Mystery." Six orignal illustrations by Stephen Healy. Commentaries by Henri Gouhier and Marcel Belay. Eight Appendices. Introduction by Ralph McInerny. Bibliographies. ISBN 0-87462-617-X. paperbound. 242 pp. $25.*

Karl-Otto Apel. *Towards a Transformation of Philosophy.* New Foreword by Pol Vandevelde. ISBN 0-87462-619-6. Paper. 308 pp. $35.

Gene Fendt. *Is Hamlet a Religious Drama? As Essay on a Question in Kierkegaard.* ISBN 0-87462-620-X. Paper. 264 pp. $30.*

Marquette Studies in Theology
Andrew Tallon, Editor
Standing orders accepted
denotes available as eBook

Frederick M. Bliss. *Understanding Reception.* ISBN 0-87462-625-0. 180 pp., index, bibliography. Paper. $20.*

Martin Albl, Paul Eddy, Renée Mirkes, OSF, editors. *Directions in New Testament Methods* ISBN 0-87462-626-9. 129 pp. Annotated bibliography. Paper. $15. Foreword by William S. Kurz.*

Robert M. Doran. *Subject and Psyche.* ISBN 0-87462-627-7. 285 pp. Paper. $25. Second ed., rev. With a new Foreword by the author.*

Kenneth Hagen, editor. *The Bible in the Churches. How Various Christians Interpret the Scriptures* ISBN 0-87462-628-5. 218 pp. Paper. $25. Third, revised editon. New chapter on Reformed tradition. Index.*

Jamie T. Phelps, O.P., editor. *Black and Catholic: The Challenge and Gift of Black Folk. Contributions of African American Experience and Thought to Catholic Theology.* ISBN 0-87462-629-3. 182 pp. Index. Paper. $20. Foreword by Patrick Carey.*

Karl Rahner. *Spirit in the World.* New, Corrected Translation by William Dych. Foreword by Francis Fiorenza. ISBN 0-87462-630-7. COMPUTER DISK VERSION. $10. Available on 3.5 inch disk; specify Macintosh or Windows. By a special arrangement with Continuum Publishing Co.*

Karl Rahner. *Hearer of the Word.* New Translation of the First Edition by Joseph Donceel. Edited and with an Introduction by Andrew Tallon. COMPUTER DISK VERSION. Autumn, 1994. $10. Available on 3.5 inch disk; specify Macintosh or Windows. By a special arrangement with Continuum Publishing Co. ISBN 0-87462-631-5. *

Robert M. Doran. *Theological Foundations. Vol. 1 Intentionality and Psyche.* ISBN 0-87462-632-3. 484 pp. Paper. $50.*

Robert M. Doran. *Theological Foundations. Vol. 2 Theology and Culture.* ISBN 0-87462-633-1. 533 pp. Paper. $55.*

Patrick W. Carey. *Orestes A. Brownson: A Bibliography, 1826-1876.* ISBN 0-87462-634-X. 212 pp. Index. Paper. $25.*

John Martinetti, S.J. *Reason to Believe Today.* ISBN 0-87462-635-8. 216 pp. Paper. $25.*

George H. Tavard. *Trina Deitas: The Controversy between Hincmar and Gottschalk* ISBN 0-87462-636-6. 160 pp. Paper. $20.*

Jeanne Cover, IBVM. *Love–The Driving Force. Mary Ward's Spirituality. Its Significance for Moral Theology* ISBN 0-87462-637-4. 217 pp. Paper. $25.*

David A. Boileau, editor. *Principles of Catholic Social Teaching.* ISBN 0-87462-638-2. 204 pp. Paper. $25.*

Michael Purcell. *Mystery and Method: The Other in Rahner and Levinas.* With a Foreword by Andrew Tallon. ISBN 0-87462-639-0. Paper. 394 pp. $45.*

W.W. Meissner, S.J., M.D. *To the Greater Glory: A Psychological Study of Ignatian Spirituality.* ISBN 0-87462-640-4. Paper. 657 pp. $65.

Virginia M. Shaddy, editor. *Catholic Theology in the University: Source of Wholeness.* ISBN 0-87462-641-2. Paper. 120 pp. $15.*

Subscibe to *e-News from Marquette University Press*
Email universitypress@marquette.edu with the word "subscribe" as the subject.
Visit Marquette University Press online: **www.marquette.edu/mupress/**